An Illustrated Speculum Humanae Salvationis

An Illustrated Speculum Humanae Salvationis

Green Collection MS 000321

By

Melinda Nielsen

With iconographical notes by

David Lyle Jeffrey

BRILL

LEIDEN | BOSTON

Library of Congress Cataloging-in-Publication Data

Names: Nielsen, Melinda, translator.
Title: An illustrated Speculum humanae salvationis : Green Collection MS 000321 / by Melinda Nielsen.
Other titles: Speculum humanae salvationis.
Description: Leiden ; Boston : Brill, [2022] | Includes bibliographical references and indexes.
Identifiers: LCCN 2021045740 | ISBN 9789004416512 (hardback ; acid-free paper) | ISBN 9789004499072 (ebook)
Subjects: LCSH: Salvation–Early works to 1800. | Typology (Theology)–Early works to 1800. | Bible–History of Biblical events. | Latin poetry, Medieval and modern–Translations into English.
Classification: LCC BT750 .I45 2022 | DDC 220.6/8–dc23/eng/20211130
LC record available at https://lccn.loc.gov/2021045740

Typeface for the Latin, Greek, and Cyrillic scripts: "Brill". See and download: brill.com/brill-typeface.

ISBN 978-90-04-41651-2 (hardback)
ISBN 978-90-04-49907-2 (e-book)

This book is printed on acid-free paper and produced in a sustainable manner.

Contents

Acknowledgements

A number of outstanding students in Baylor University's Honors College contributed to this volume, aiding in transcription, translation, and research on source material. Particular recognition is due to Zerek Dodson, Jackson Perry, and Erin Russo, whose work won undergraduate research and scholarly achievement grants.

Other student researchers include: Rachel Butcher, Randolph Davidson, Amy Freeman, Cynthia Liu, Joseph Lloyd, Kara Kopchinski, Gabriel Pederson, Megan Renz, Erika Smith, Marcie Smith, Jesse Watters, and David Welch. It has been a joy to collaborate with such a talented group of young scholars–and more than scholars, friends: *ecce ego et tu, et spero quod tertius christus inter nos sit.*

Independent reader Nicole Eddy's eagle eye, generous spirit, and rapier wit were instrumental in the completion of the volume. All errors remaining are my own.

Melinda Nielsen
Baylor University

Speculum Provenance Summary

Provenance

1. **fol. 1**: "Istu(m) libr(um) dedit monast(er)io s(an)c(t)i Joh(ann)is in Stams. M(a)-g(iste)r chu(o)nrad(us) pictor ducis Leupoldi p(ro) signo sp(eci)al(is) a(m)icicie". (Master Konrad, painter to Duke Leopold dedicated this book to the monastery of St John at Stams as a token of his particular friendship). The Cistercian monastery of Stams had been founded in 1273 by Count Meinhard II of Tyrol-Görz and Elisabeth of Wittelsbach, the widow of the Stauffer Konrad IV. Stams became the burial place of the princes of Tyrol. In the right margin in a different hand and using a different ink is the date: "anno d(omi)n … / m ccc lxxx …", the last figure cut off. The death of Duke Leopold III in **1386** may serve as a 'terminus ante quem'.
2. In **1774** Count Nikolaus Páffy of Erdöd gave the codex to Count Franz Koháry of Csábrag, cf. an entry and a note of ownership of count Franz dated **1789** on **fol. 1**.[1]
3. Zürich, Switzerland, private collection of Caflisch family bought **1932** in private transaction, by descent to:
4. Zürich, Switzerland, private collection of Professor Dr. Lucius Caflisch (cited in 1962 exhibition catalog), sold in private transaction in 2007 to:
5. Stalden, Switzerland, Dr. Jörn Günther Rare Books AG;[2]
6. October 2010, sold to Hobby Lobby. (Jörn Günther had brought the volume to the United States with the books he was presenting at the International Fine Arts & Antiques Dealer Show held 22–28 October 2010 [NYC].)

Exhibitions

Europäische Kunst um 1400, Vienna 1962.

1 'I C' is written in the margin a bit lower down, in pencil. In the same box, at the lower part and at an angle, not formally laid out, is written in ink, 'Comitis Francisci Koháry de Csábrag et scritna, perpetui Comitis Hontensis et in Murany 1789', recording ownership by Count Franz Koháry of Csábrag, who was given the volume by Count Nikolaus Páffy of Erdöd in 1774.

Under the boxes, written larger by the same hand, is; 'Speculum Humanæ Salvationis cum Rythmis et Figuris', followed faintly in pencil by 'Fol. Scriptur', and below that, to the right, still by the same hand 'donum excellentissimi Domini Comitis Nicolai Palffy ab Erdöd, Aurei Velleris Equitis, et per Regum Hungariæ Judicis Curiæ regæ. 1774.' At the left foot is written, small and in black ink, probably by the same hand, 'fogli 53'.

2 According to a representative of the book dealer, "As the book remained inside of Switzerland, there was no need of an export license for us to purchase it, nor for us to sell it. As far as we know there are no claims against prior owners of the item."

Publications

Masterpieces. Catalogue 9. Dr. Jörn Günther—Antiquariat. Hamburg 2008, no. 11.
Exh. cat., Vienna 1962, no. 192: *Europäische Kunst um 1400*, Vienna 1962.
Trattner 1999, p. 298: Irma Trattner, “Die Marienkrönungstafel im Zisterzienserstift Stams in Tirol. Ihre Stellung zwischen Süd und Nord”, in *Das Münster* 52, 1999, pp. 298–310.

Introduction

The medieval Latin poem *Speculum humanae salvationis* (known in English as *The Mirror of Human Salvation*) was one of the most popular works of the fourteenth and fifteenth centuries with preachers and laity alike. Using a typological approach[1] to interpretation, the text of the *Speculum humanae salvationis* combines Old Testament and New Testament events and figures to depict an integrated narrative of redemption. As such, the *Speculum* is not only an influential model of medieval biblical interpretation, but also a fascinating case study in allegorical reading habits and the interplay between text and image. This Museum of the Bible *Speculum* manuscript contains hundreds of images which accompany the more than 5000 lines of verse. These images systematically complement the verbal teaching to illuminate in iconography how, from a Christian perspective, all of human history points to Jesus Christ.

Although the *Speculum humanae salvationis* survives in hundreds of manuscripts and early print books in every major European language, there is no full modern edition and translation. This dearth is particularly unfortunate as the *Speculum* was used a resource for medieval preaching, and thus its influence extended culturally far beyond the circulation of its actual texts. This Scholars Initiative project comprises the first modern transcription and English translation of the full Latin *Speculum*, accompanied by annotations tracing the biblical references and detailed notes explaining the visual iconography. The project thus makes this significant text of medieval exegesis newly accessible to readers in the university, pulpit, and pew today.

1 Introduction to and Description of the Manuscript (Michelle P. Brown)

The *Speculum humanae salvationis*, or 'Mirror of human salvation', is an anonymous composition, originally written in Latin, in rhyming verse, sometime between 1309 (as a reference to the Avignon papacy indicates) and 1324 (the date on two copies) as part of the genre of encyclopedic speculum literature. An early preface says that its author withheld his name through humility, but there are some signs that he was a cleric, perhaps a Dominican, and Ludolph of Saxony and Vincent of Beauvais have been proposed as

1 Typology is an interpretive approach that seeks to discern connections between Old and New Testament themes and passages by focusing on the study and interpretation of types and symbols. For example, the bronze serpent raised up by Moses in the wilderness is a "type" of Christ raised up on the Cross; similarly both King David and the lamb sacrificed at Passover are Old Testament "types" of Christ. Originally (and always primarily) focused on the Bible, typology could also be applied to other literature and narratives, human history, and even natural history (as the *Speculum* does) as medieval interpreters sought to interpret "all things" in reference to Christ, sometimes in conjunction with drawing out moral interpretations.

 | DOI:10.1163/9789004499072_002

authors. It was soon translated into German, French (in at least two versions), English, Dutch, and Czech, and the popularity of this theological work is demonstrated by the fact that it survives in some 420 manuscripts, many of them illustrated. There were also many fifteenth-century blockbook editions (printed with woodblocks) and sixteen incunabula editions of the text. It vied in popularity in the genre competing with the *Biblia pauperum* and the *Ars moriendi* and was made in versions suited to all purses. Fine fully painted and gilded Flemish editions were produced in the fifteenth century for Philip the Good and other aristocratic patrons, whilst line drawings and then wood engravings served the needs of other less wealthy people.

The images demonstrate the relationship between the Old and New Testaments through the work's central preoccupation with the doctrine of the Fall and Redemption. These connections are explored in an image cycle in which a scene from the New Testament is linked to three scenes showing its prefiguration in the Old Testament. This technique is known as typology. This didactic technique evidently suited the aim of convincing the late medieval world of peril of damnation and the urgent need for salvation.

The arrangement of the text is fairly standardized. After a short Prologue and Prohemium, the first two chapters deal with the Creation, the Fall of Satan, the story of Adam and Eve and the Flood. Then follow forty more double-page chapters where a New Testament event is compared with three from the Old Testament, with four pictures each above a column of text. Usually each chapter occupies one two-page opening. The last three chapters cover the Seven Stations of the Cross, and the Seven Joys and Sorrows of the Virgin. A complete standard version has fifty-two leaves, or 104 pages, and 192 illustrations (including a blank page at the beginning and end). The blockbook editions were much shorter, with 116 pictures, two to each woodblock.

The text layout follows a scheme of twenty-five lines per column, with two columns per page, one under each miniature, so a hundred lines per standard chapter. Sometimes there are captions over the pictures as well, the content of which vary. Many copies reduced the text by omitting the non-standard chapters at the beginning or end, whilst others expanded the content with calendars and commentaries, or extra illustrations.

The layout of the images was also quite stable, partly because most images had to retain their correspondence with their opposite number, although the style and expense of the books varied and the pictures also migrated to other media, including its serving as a model for the *Vision of Augustus* in Rogier van der Weyden's *Bladelin Altarpiece* and other Early Netherlandish artworks. It was also used as a pattern-book for stained glass, tapestries and sculpture.

With the advent of printing, the work appeared in four blockbook editions, two in Latin and two in Dutch, combining woodblock prints with movable type text, and then in sixteen incunable editions by 1500. Hind places the woodblock editions in Holland, from about 1470–1475, with the Netherlands as the focus of trade in this type of book. Incunable editions by Laurens Janszoon Coster and Günther Zainer of Augsburg also appeared in the early 1470s, making the speculum one of the first printed works. Further incunabulum editions include Latin, German, French, Spanish and Dutch versions It appears the *Prohemium* may have been sold separately as a pamphlet, as one version speaks of its usefulness for "poor preachers who cannot afford the entire book". Theological divisions and changes in approach during the Reformation finally led to the demise of what had been a popular theological teaching tool.

1.1 *The Manuscript*

GC. MS. 000321, Illustrated *Speculum humanae salvationis*

Manuscript on vellum with pen-and-ink drawings by Magister Konrad, painter to Duke Leopold III of Austria, who dedicated this book to the monastery of St John at Stams. An unusual manuscript from the Tyrol, Austria, before 1386, on a theme of biblical didactic typology.

1.2 *Text*

Fol. 1: unfinished drawing of Adam delving (either a sketch for, or modelled upon, that on fol. 6)—fol. 1^v: Preface—fol. 4: blank—fol. 4^v: Speculum humanae salvationis—fol. 46^v: Stations of Christ's Passion—fol. 48^v: Seven Sorrows of the Virgin—fol. 50^v: Seven Joys of the Virgin—fol. 52^v: Prayers to the Virgin; ending of text on fol. 53.

The author of the *Speculum humanae salvationis*, or "Mirror of Salvation," remains anonymous. The manuscripts whose texts come closest to the original variant were written in Bologna and the earliest surviving textual evidence dates around 1320. The *Speculum*, which deals with Man's Salvation through Christ and the Virgin, probably had its sources in the spirituality of the mendicant orders. The illustrations are deployed across openings, the verso showing an episode from the New Testament (the so-called anti-type) and the facing recto presenting three scenes from the Old Testament (type). In the pictorial sense, as well as in their content, the episodes of the Old correspond to those of the New Testament, in other words, they 'pre-figure' it. This use of typological didactic imagery was popularized by St Jerome and was adopted by Bede and Aquinas, inter alia. The Jewish system of Pardes also includes typology as an exegetical mode.

The text comprises 45 chapters beginning with the Fall of Lucifer, continuing to the Creation of Man and the Flood, while the main portion of the text gives an account of the Salvation of Man through Christ and culminates in the Last Judgement. Chapters 43 to 45 comprise seven scenes of Christ's Passion, the Seven Sorrows and Seven Joys of the Virgin.

1.3 *Codicology*

49 leaves. The text is complete. 292×226 mm, written space (including images) 240×174 mm. Pricked (slit marks) and ruled in ink, with single bounding lines, for double columns of 27 lines, of which 25 are text lines, with ruling for the column pictures above.

Quire numeration is contemporary.

1^8, 2^8 (wants 3, stub), 3^8, 4^8, 5^8, 6^8, 7^6.

Ferrous corrosion marks on first few vellum leaves at back and front from metal cornerpieces from a medieval binding. The volume is in very good condition, with only slight traces of former use. Late 18th-century brown morocco binding on five raised cords, with gold tooled lozenges on spine and red label tooled in gold 'Specul. Human. Salvat., with green leather label below gold tooled M.S. 1370. Pretty red and green hand-printed endpapers with stripes and flowers, resembling wallpaper design, but on a small scale. Followed by a linen paper flyleaf at both front and rear. Pink silk bookmark. Red fore-edges.

1.4 *Provenance*

1. fol. 1: "Istu(m) libr(um) dedit monast(er)io s(an)c(t)i Joh(ann)is in Stams. M(a)g(iste)r chu(o)nrad(us) pictor ducis Leupoldi p(ro) signo sp(eci)al(is) a(m)icicie". In the right margin in a different hand and using a different ink the date: "anno d(omi)n …/m ccc lxxx …". On the recto of the first vellum leaf (text begins on the verso) is a drawing by the main artist of Adam about to break ground with a spade and in the image box to the right is a cloud shape containing original inscription, in ink, Istu(m) libr(um) dedit monast(er)io s(an)(t)i johannis in Stams. Magister Chuonrad(us) Pictor ducis Leupoldi. Pro signo sp(eci)al(is) a(m)icicie' (Master Konrad, painter to Duke Leopold dedicated this book to the monastery of St John at Stams as a token of his particular friendship). The Cistercian monastery of Stams had been founded in 1273 by Count Meinhard II of Tyrol-Görz and Elisabeth of Wittelsbach, the widow of the Stauffer Konrad IV. Stams became the burial place of the princes of Tyrol. The same ink as the cloud is used to write in the adjacent margin, next to the box, 'anno dni m° ccc lxxx …'. the last figure cut off. The death of Duke Leopold III in 1386 may serve as a 'terminus ante quem'. Leopold III (1 November 1351–9 July 1386), known as the Just, a member of the House of Habsburg, was Duke of Austria from 1365. As head of the Leopoldian line, he ruled over the Inner Austrian duchies of Carinthia, Styria, and Carniola as well as the County of Tyrol and Further Austria from 1379 until his death.

'I C' is written in the margin a bit lower down, in pencil. In the same box, at the lower part and at an angle, not formally laid out, is written in ink, 'Comitis Francisci Koháry de Csábrag et scritna, perpetui Comitis Hontensis et in Murany 1789', recording ownership by Count Franz Koháry of Csábrag, who was given the volume by Count Nikolaus Páffy of Erdöd in 1774.

Under the boxes, written larger by the same hand, is 'Speculum Humanæ Salvationis cum Rythmis et Figuris', followed faintly in pencil by 'Fol. Scriptur', and below that, to the right, still by the same hand 'donum excellentissimi Domini Comitis Nicolai Palffy ab Erdöd, Aurei Velleris Equitis, et per Regum Hungariæ Judicis Curiæ regæ. 1774.' At the left foot is written, small and in black ink, probably by the same hand, 'fogli 53'.

Purchased for the Green Collection from a private collection in Europe. GC. MS. 000321 written in pencil at top left on the verso of the front endpaper, with NT in pencil below. At mid foot on the following paper flyleaf is '8' in pencil.

1.5 *Script and Decoration*

Script is a Gothic textualis semi-quadrata of medium quality, in black ink, with some scribal corrections between the lines.

Rubrics by the text hand, Lombardic capitals and chapter marks in red, with litterae notabiliores at the beginnings of verses touched in red. 192 column-wide pen-and-ink drawings in the upper third of the page, in the beginning coloured with washes. Paragraphus marks are also in red, added by the rubricator even though they had already been supplied in black ink by the scribe.

The text begins on the verso of the first vellum flyleaf with a prologue, introduced by a red and black puzzle initial with red flourishing. Minor initials in red, some with black flourishing. The final two folia, carrying the prologue to the Life of the Virgin and a prayer to the Virgin, have green initials with red flourishing.

A contemporary cursive hand has labelled some iconographic elements in the miniatures and has also added some marginal annotations relating text to the appropriate figures.

1.6 *Illumination*

The complete cycle of illustrations amounts to 192 images. Only the first 8 images are colored, in a dark red/brown which is also watered to give a pink wash, and green, 9,10 and 12 have a touch of red to cheeks and angels' wings. After that the only colour is red to castle and shields, and on some images there is an attempt to provide modelling in text ink wash. Christ with the doctors also has pink cheeks. On Adam and Eve with the tree, the same pale yellow/brown ink used to flourish the initial below is used as a modelling wash, probably indicating that the colourist was the same for both elements. This ink occurs occasionally as a wash, but otherwise the text and drawing ink is black. There are no signs of under-drawing and the images seem to have been drawn straight onto the vellum with pen and ink.

The front image of Adam delving is based on that of Adam and Eve working later in the book, and is either a trial or, more likely, a pictorial colophon by Magister Conrad equating his labour with that of Adam, the first man. The pale ink for wash and flourishing is that used for the cloud and date (and the wash on the legs of the adjacent pictorial colophon), implying that they are all by Master Conrad.

The illumination begins with the Fall of Lucifer, followed by 6 miniatures culminating in Noah's Ark. Scenes from the life of the Virgin precede the Incarnation of Christ. The cycle from the Annunciation, through the Passion to Christ's descent to the limbo is the most lavishly illustrated portion. Pictures from other sources praise the completion of Salvation in Christ and his mother. A wholly New Testament cycle of Christ's Passion follows, while the Seven Sorrows and the Seven Joys of the Virgin are inspired by various other sources.

Edgar Breitenbach, whose ground-breaking study of the illustration of the *Speculum* appeared in 1930, divided the 350 manuscripts accessible to him into several groups. Our manuscript belonged to the so-called German group, which he saw headed by a codex from St Mang in Füssen (Augsburg, Universitätsbibliothek, cod. I.2.20 23), while Fingernagel 1997 preferred one of the manuscripts in Munich (Bayerische Staatsbibliothek, clm 23433), of higher artistic quality, as the key representative of the group. Among others, M140 of the Pierpont Morgan Library in New York is one of the most important companion pieces. The German group shows a freer treatment of the original compositions that is particularly found in Italian *Speculum* manuscripts. It renounces symmetrical depictions, favouring a more conventional iconography instead. At the same time there are conspicuous inconsistencies within the group that seem to indicate alterations from a prototype.

Magister Chuonradus, who is named in the dedication note, is likely to be identifiable with the court painter Konrad von Tiergarten from Merano, who is also seen as the author of the central panel of an altarpiece from Stams which depicts the Coronation of the Virgin, and reveals a strong Italian influence (Stiftsammlung Stams, Tyrol, see Trattner 1999, p. 298). Konrad is documented between 1379 and 1406 and the Coronation panel is dated to the 1390's. However, a stylistic comparison of this work would be fruitless, as our *Speculum* and the panel follow different prototypes. The present codex would appear to be closely related to a manuscript from the group clustered around the codices in Munich and New York and this shows that Master Konrad must have had access to a work from this group. If Konrad donated his *Speculum* to the monastery, this investment would appear to have proved worthwhile, as it may have led to the important commission of the altarpiece. Interestingly, he chose to depart from the northern european codex sources in favour of Italian influences when working on the altarpiece. This change in taste may have owed something to the marriage of Duke Leopold in 1365, to Viridis Visconti (1352–1414), second daughter of Barnabò Visconti, Lord of Milan. A closer examination of the present codex may thus provide interesting new clues for the broader study of *Speculum* manuscripts as well as of painting in the Tyrol.

1.7 *Bibliography*

Exhn cat., Vienna 1962, no. 192; Trattner 1999, p. 298. Breitenbach 1930, pp. 70f.; Harrsen 1958, no. 38; Frankenberger/ Rupp (ed.) 1987, no. 14; exhn cat. Stams 1995; Fingernagel / Roland 1997, no. 123; Hernad 2000, no. 249.

Hind, Arthur M. (1935). *An Introduction to a History of Woodcut*, Houghton Mifflin Co., reprinted Dover Publications, (1963), pp. 245–247 and *passim*.

Mayor, A. Hyatt (1971). *Prints and People*, Metropolitan Museum of Art/Princeton. nos. 33,34.

Wilson, Adrian, and Joyce Lancaster Wilson (1984). *A Medieval Mirror*. Berkeley: University of California Press. online edition Includes many illustrations, including a full set of woodcut pictures with notes in Chapter 6.

The Miroure of Mans Salvacionne: A Fifteenth Century Translation into English of the Specu-

lum Humanae Salvationis and now for the first time printed from a ms. *in the Possession of A.H. Huth. With Preface and Glossary* London, 1888: Roxburghe 118;

The mirour of mans saluacioune: a Middle English translation of Speculum humanae salvationis: a critical edition of the fifteenth-century manuscript illustrated from Der Spiegel der menschen Behaltnis, Speyer, Drach, c.1475 [notes and introduction by] Avril Henry Aldershot, 1986: English qHM190 1986-H

Scholarly work about the text:

Adrian Wilson & Joyce Lancaster Wilson *A medieval mirror, Speculum humanae salvationis, 1324–1500* Hunterian Add. f. 52

For digital facsimiles of other *Speculum* manuscripts and early printed editions, see:

http://special.lib.gla.ac.uk/exhibns/month/sep2000.html
https://www.loc.gov/resource/rbc0001.2014rosen0048/

2 *Speculum* Images (David Lyle Jeffrey)

About one third of the 420 extant copies of the *Speculum humanae salvationis* are illustrated, in many cases with more color and refinement than our manuscript, of which only the first few are colored. As is typical of the late medieval speculum genre, this is a teaching manuscript designed to provide a typological guide to relations between the Old and New Testaments. It uses up to three Old Testament narratives to provide antitypes for a New Testament event, or, as is the case here, to assemble a Marian typology, especially prominent in the first and last third of the manuscript.

The illuminator is unlikely to have been responsible for the antitypes chosen. Many of these derive from non-biblical sources such as the *Historia scholastica* of Peter Comestor (ca. 1173), a required text at Paris until the mid-fourteenth century. In its pages canonical biblical narrative is expanded with Jewish and pagan legenda. The writings of Josephus are a means by which some (but not all) of the Jewish legends are transmitted. Similar legends from the Christian era were collected in the *Legenda aurea* or *Golden Legend* of Jacobus de Voragine, a mid-thirteenth-century collection of saints' lore and miracle stories; popular versions in medieval vernacular (e.g., *Cursor mundi*) of the thirteenth and fourteenth centuries tended to weave biblical narrative with pagan and Jewish material to create a form of Christian "universal history" to which the biblical story is central. Medieval fascination with exotic lands (e.g., "marvels of the East") and wondrous or miraculous romances did not by the fourteenth century always distinguish clearly between canonical biblical and other narratives as to religious authority. This is particularly evident in the Marian focus of salvation history in the *Speculum humanae salvationis*, which acts as a catechetical primer for Marian devotion. Nevertheless, most traditional iconography already established for biblical illustration applies generally here, with some Christological iconography transferred from Christ to the Virgin Mary.

Where the derivation of narrative is particularly oblique to the biblical text, and hence sometimes to the visual iconography, I have noted probable sources.

3 On This Edition (Melinda Nielsen)

3.1 *Methodology*

This diplomatic edition seeks to give a snapshot of the life and usage of one manuscript and emendation is accordingly at a minimum, except when necessary for sense or syntax. For instance, we have not sought to regularize u/v usage, which varies throughout. Unless otherwise noted, emendations and variants are drawn from the only existing but partial Latin critical edition by J. Lutz and Perdrizet, P. *Speculum humanæ salvationis*, 2 Vols. (Leipzig, 1907).

3.2 *Manuscripts, Early Printed Books, Editions Consulted*

A Paris, Bibliothèque nationale, lat. 9584.
B Paris, Bibliothèque nationale, lat. 9585.
b Brixen, Freskomalereien im Kreuzgang des Doms,
C Paris, Bibliothèque de l'Arsenal, lat. 593,
D Paris, Bibliothèque de l'Arsenal, lat. 39
F Freiburg im Breisgau, Universitätsbibliothek, 179
G Green Collection, Oklahoma City, MS. 000321
K Kremsmünster, Stiftsbibliothek, 243
L *Speculum*, critical ed. J. Lutz and P. Perdrizet (Leipzig, 1907).
M München, *Königliche* Bibliothek, *clm.* 9491
S München, *Königliche* Bibliothek, clm. 146
W Schlettstadt, Stadtbibliothek, 52
X Blockbook, reprint ed. by Berjeau (London, 1861).

3.3 *Transcription Conventions*

Based on *A Guide to Western Historical Scripts from Antiquity to 1600*, ed. Michelle Brown (Toronto, 1993), 6–7.

Textual omission by the scribe: angled brackets or half square brackets.

Empty where the omission is not made good, ⟨ ⟩.
Occupied where it is made good, ⟨est⟩.
Where another source has been used and the supplement is not conjectural, half brackets are used, ⸤est⸥.

Textual interpolation by the scribe: braces.

Where the transcriber wishes to cancel, {est}.

Problematical readings: obeli, alias daggers.

Used where the text is corrupt or obscure, or where the transcriber is unsure of the correct reading, †est†.

Scribal insertions: slashes.

On the writing line, ˊestˋ; between the lines, ˋestˊ; marginal, ˵est˶.

Cancellations: square brackets.

By washing, scraping or pouncing, cancelled letters illegible [ ], or legible [est].
By crossing out, illegible [–], legible [–est].
By expunctuation [ẹṣṭ].

Substitutions: square brackets and a slash.

Actually on letters cancelled by washing, scraping or pounding,
illegible cancellation, [/est],
legible cancellation, [et/est].
Above letters cancelled by crossing out,
illegible cancellation, [–\est],
legible cancellation, [–et\est].
Above letters cancelled by expunctuation, [ẹṭ\est].
By transformation (where the original letter is adapted to form another letter), [o>a].
By simple addition (where the new letter is simply written over or above the original letter), on a suppressed letter, [o+a], above a suppressed letter, [o+\a].

Accidental loss (*trimming, rodent activity, staining, etc*): double square brackets.

Number of lost letters unknown, ⟦ ⟧.
Number of lost letters estimated ⟦***⟧

Rubrics, titles, lemmata, etc: italicization.

Punctuation and capitalization: modern pauses of equivalent or near equivalent values are substituted for the numerous punctuation systems of the period. Capitalization follows that of the manuscript wherever possible.

Later corrections, etc.: these are indicated using the symbols outlined above, but dating and any other observations are commented upon in a footnote.

Line numbering: original line numbers have not been cited, other than when specified in the commentaries. Marginal numbers accompanying transcriptions are imposed to assist in reference during reading.

Speculum humanae salvationis: Transcription and Translation

∵

⌊Prohemium⌋[1]

1va *Incipit prohemium istius libri qui dicitur speculum humane saluacionis*
Incipit prohemium cuiusdam noue compilacionis.
Cuius nomen et tytulus est speculum humane saluacionis.
Expediens videtur et utile quod primo in hoc prohemio exponatur
De quibus materiis et hystoriis in quolibet capitulo dicatur.
Et qui diligenter hoc prohemium prestuduerit
De facili totum librum quasi intelligere poterit.
In capitulo primo[2] agitur de casu luciferi et suorum sociorum
Et de formacione ade et eue et dignitate ipsorum.
In secundo capitulo agitur de precepti transgressione
Et de hominis eiectione et exilii huius prolongacione.
In predictis duobus capitulis patet nostra dampanacio
In aliis capitulis sequentibus patet nostra reconciliacio.
Sed notandum quod in singulis capitulis modus iste seruatur
Quod de nouo testamento primo una ueritas recitatur.
Postea de ueteri testamento tres hystorie applicantur
Que ipsam ueritatem prefigurasse comprobantur.
¶In tercio capitulo incipit quasi inicium[3] nostre saluacionis
Ubi agitur de concepcione et sanctifacione beate uirginis.
Cum enim deus humanam naturam assumere decreuisset
Congruum fuit ut matrem de qua nasceretur premitteret.
Istud figuratum ˋeratˊ per regem astragem et eius filiam
Per fontem ⌊signatum⌋[4] in orto conclusum et per stellam balaam.
Astragi monstratum est quod filia sua regem cyrum generaret
Joachim dictum est quod filiam gigneret[5] que christum portaret.
Et per hanc conclusam in utero mulieris spiritus sanctus signaret[6]
Per quam homo tamquam per maris stellam repatriaret.
¶In quarto capitulo agitur de beate uirginis natiuiutate
Que figurata fuit per uirgam egressam de radice yesse.
Item per clausam portam quam dominus ezechieli demonstrauit
Et per templum salomonis quod salomon domino edificauit.
Maria enim ortum habuit de radice yesse

[1] There are no images for the prefactory material, but on the previous title page is the Frontispiece: Peasant preparing soil with a mattock as if digging a trench, closely modeled after an image of Adam in a mosaic of the early 13th century in San Marco, Venice. The artist, as suggested in Michelle Brown's introduction, may be likening his own labours to the fate of Adam. [2] For biblical and medieval source material, see specified chapter of main text [3] inicium] nuncium, x. For methodology and transcription conventions, see Introduction, 3 [4] signatum, X] figuratum, G [5] quod … gigneret] quod anna uxor sua generaret que, X [6] signaret] sanctificaret, X

Proem

Here begins the proem of that book which is called the Mirror of Human Salvation

Here begins the proem of a certain new compilation
whose name or title is the *Mirror of Human Salvation*.
It seems expedient and useful to first describe in this prologue
which subjects and stories are related in which chapter,
and he who diligently studies this proem
will be able to easily understand nearly the whole book.
The first chapter treats of the fall of Lucifer and his allies,
and the fashioning of Adam and Eve and their worth.
The second chapter treats of the breaking of God's command,
and the expulsion of man, and his long exile.
In the two aforementioned chapters our condemnation is revealed
and in the other following chapters our reconciliation is revealed.
But it must be noted that in each chapter the same method is used
in which one reality from the New Testament is first recapitulated,
and afterwards three stories from the Old Testament are added
which are acknowledged to have prefigured that reality.
The third chapter introduces, as it were, the beginning of our salvation
when it treats of the conception and sanctification of the Blessed Virgin.
For when God humbled himself to assume human nature
it was fitting that he should send ahead the mother from whom he would be born.
That event was symbolized through King Astrages and his daughter,
through the sealed fountain in the enclosed garden, and through Balaam's star.
Astrages was shown that his daughter would beget King Cyrus;
Joachim was told that he would have a daughter who would bear the Christ.
And the Holy Spirit would seal her, enclosed in the womb of a woman,
through whom man would be brought home, as if by the star of the sea.
The fourth chapter treats of the birth of the Blessed Virgin
which was symbolized by the sprout emerging from the root of Jesse;
likewise by the closed gate which the Lord showed to Ezekiel;
and by the temple of Solomon which he built for God.
For Mary held the one born from the root of Jesse,

Quam domin⸍us⸌[1] preordinauit portam suam et templum suum esse.
¶In quinto capitulo agitur quomodo maria fuit in templo domino oblata
Et hec oblacio fuit olim in tribus figuris premonstrata.
Per mensam solis in sabulo que fuit oblata in templo solis materialis.
Sic maria fuit oblata in templo solis ueri eternalis.
¶[2]Item per filiam yepte que fuit oblata domino licet indirecte.
Sed maria fuit oblata domino rite et perfecte.
Item per [h]ortum[3] suspensibilem de quo regina persarum patriam suam ui⸌⸌debat.⸍⸍
Ita maria oblata in templo domini semper contemplacioni insistebat.
¶In viº capitulo agitur quomodo maria fuit viro desponsata
Et hec desponsacio fuit etiam tribus figuris premonstrata.
Per virginem saram raguelis filiam que septem viris fuit tradita.
Et tamen mundam seruauit animam suam ab omni concupiencia.
Item per turrim illam fortissimam que dicebatur Baris
Quam duo custodes defendere poterant a manibus cunctis.
Item per turrim dauid in quo mille clipei dependebant

1vb ⌞Quia⌟[4] mille uirtutes et multo plures maria resplendebat.
¶In viiº capitulo agitur quomodo maria fuit impregnata
Et hec ⌞impregnacio⌟[5] fuit tribus figuris demonstrata.
Ipsa⸍m⸌[6] enim rubus ardens et vellus rore madens prefigurauit
Et uirgo rebecca que nuncium abrahe et camelos potauit.
¶In octauo capitulo agitur de natiuitate ihesu christi.
Et tres figure sunt que deseruiunt natiuitati isti.
Videlicet vitis pincerne pharaonis et uirga aaron que floruit
Et uirg[/o] cum puero quam sibilla in circulo iuxta solem vidit.
¶In nono capitulo agitur epyphania domini.
Et hanc prefigurauit stella quam viderunt in oriente magi.
Item tres fortes qui attulerunt aquam de bethleem regi dauid.
Idem etiam salomon cum throno suo eburneo premonstrauit.
¶In decimo capitulo agitur quomodo uenit ad templum uirgo maria
Et praesentauit ibi filium suum christum ihesum qui est vera sophia.
Hoc prefigurauit archa testamenti quam fecit beseleel.
Et candelabrum aureum et oblatus domino puer samuel.
¶In xiº capitulo agitur quomodo ydola egipti omnia corruerunt
Quomodo maria et ioseph cum puero ihesum in egiptum introiuerunt.
Hoc prefiguratum fuit per ymaginem virginis cum puero

---

[1] Added later by black-ink scribe [2] This paragraph marking may be in error [3] h intentionally erased or destroyed with the partial fading in the lines below it [4] Quia, X] quo, G [5] impregnacio, X] figuracio, G [6] Added later by black-ink scribe

she whom the Lord preordained to be his own gate and temple.
The fifth chapter sets forth how Mary was offered to the Lord in the temple
and this oblation was presaged in the past by three figures:
by the table of the sun in the sand, consecrated in the temple for the golden vessels,
so Mary was offered in the temple of the true eternal Sun;
also by the daughter of Jephte who was offered to the Lord by another,
but Mary was offered to the lord rightly and perfectly;
also by the hanging garden from which the queen of Persia viewed her country;
so Mary, set apart in the temple of the Lord, always persevered in contemplation.
The sixth chapter sets forth how Mary was betrothed to a man
and this espousal was presaged by three figures:
by the holy virgin, the daughter of Raguel, who was given to seven husbands
and who yet saved her own pure spirit from all from concupiscence;
also by that exceedingly strong tower called Baris
which two guards were able to defend from all attackers;
likewise by the tower of David upon which a thousand shields hung

because a thousand virtues and many more shone in Mary.
The seventh chapter sets forth how Mary became pregnant,
and this conception was demonstrated by three figures:
for the burning bush and the fleece wet with dew prefigured her,
as did the virgin Rebecca who gave water to the camels and the messenger of Abraham.
The eighth chapter treats of the birth of Jesus Christ
and there are three figures which anticipated that birth:
namely the vine of pharoah's cupbearer, and Aaron's rod which flowered,
and the virgin with the boy, whom the Sibyl beheld encircled by the sun.
The ninth chapter treats of the Epiphany of the Lord,
and the star which the magi saw in the east prefigured this event;
similarly, the three strong men who brought water to King David from Bethlehem;
and likewise Solomon presaged it with his ivory throne.
The tenth chapter sets forth how the Virgin Mary came to the temple
and there presented her own son Jesus Christ who is true wisdom.
The ark of the covenant which Bezelel wrought prefigured this reality,
as did the golden candelabra, and the boy Samuel who was offered to the Lord.
The eleventh chapter sets forth how all the idols of Egypt fell to the ground
just as Mary and Joseph entered Egypt with the boy Jesus.
This was prefigured by the image of the Virgin with a boy

Que propter vaticinium Jeremie facta fuit in egipto.
Item per coronam pharonis quam puer moyses confregit
Et per lapidem sine manibus qui statuam in puluerem redegit.
⸌¶⸍In xiiº capitulo agitur quomodo christus fuit baptizatus
Et iste baptismus fuit per mare eneum prefiguratus.
Item per neaman leporsum in iordane mundatum
Et per iordanem in transitu filorum israel siccatum.
¶In xiiiº decimo capitulo agitur quomodo dyabolus christum temptauit
Et quomodo ipsum christus in gula superbia et auaricia superauit.
Primam uictoriam olim prefigurauit daniel
Qui interfecit draconem et destruxit bel.
Secundam prefigurauit dauid qui Golyam interfecit
Terciam prefigurauit dauid quando leonem et ursum interfecit.
¶In xiiiiº decimo capitulo agitur quomodo christus recepit mariam penitentem
Et quoniam paratus est recipere quemlibet penitere uolentem.
Et hoc patet per manassen qui supra numerum arene maris peccauit.
Cuius poenitentiam dominus recipiens de captiuitate liberauit
Item in prodigo filio quem pater misericorditer recepit
Et in rege dauid qui post adulterium et homicidium poenitentiam egit
¶In xvº capitulo agitur quomodo christus in die palmarum fleuit.
Quomodo receptus fuit et quomodo mercantes de templo eiecit.
Primum figuratum fuit in lamentacione ieremie
Secundum in honore exhibito dauid post necem golye.
Tercium id est flagellacionem christi Elyodorus prefigurabat.
Qui propter spolium templi flagello ualde uapulabat.
¶In xviº capitulo agitur de cena domini sacrosancta
Cuius sacramentum olim prefiguratum erat per manna.
Et hoc etiam agnus pascale assus pretendebat

2ra ⸌Et⸍ ⸌Melchisedech⸍[1] qui abrahe panem et uinum offerebat.
¶In xviiº capitulo agitur quomodo christus hostes suos prostrauit
Quod figurauit sampson qui mille uiros cum mandibula necauit.
Item sangor qui cum fomere occidit sexcentos
Et dauid qui uno impetu interfecit octigentos.
¶In xviiiº capitulo agitur quomodo iudas dominum osculo tradebat.
Etiam quomodo sibi populus iudaicus malum pro bono reddebat.
Hec figurata sunt per joab qui amasam dolose osculabatur
Et per regem saul qui regem dauid pro bonis gestis persequebatur.
Istud etiam chaym malignus ille prefigurauit

[1] Added later by black-ink scribe

which was made in Eygpt on account of the prophesy of Jeremiah;
likewise by the crown of Pharaoh which the boy Moses shattered;
and by the stone which pounded the statue into dust without hands.
The twelfth chapter sets forth how Christ was baptized
and that the baptism was prefigured by the bronze vessel;
likewise by the leper Naaman, cleansed in the Jordan;
and by the Jordan, dried up during the passage of the children of Israel.
The thirteenth chapter sets forth how Satan tempted Christ,
and how Christ rose above the temptation of gluttony, pride, and avarice.
Daniel formerly prefigured the first victory
when he killed the dragon and destroyed Bel;
David prefigured the second victory when he killed Goliath;
David prefigured the third when he killed the lion and bear.
The fourteenth chapter sets forth how Christ received back the repentant Mary
and that he was ready to accept anyone willing to repent.
And this is shown through Manasseh whose sins outnumbered the sands of the sea,
yet the Lord, receiving his penance, freed him from captivity;
likewise by the prodigal son whom the merciful father received;
and by King David who did penance after adultery and murder.
The fifteenth sets forth how Christ wept on Palm Sunday,
how he was received, and how he threw the traders out of the temple.
First this was prefigured in the lamentation of Jeremiah;
secondly, in the honor paid to David after death of Goliath;
thirdly, Heliodorus prefigured the scourging of Christ
when he, because of the spoils of the temple, was severely flogged with the lash.
The sixteenth chapter treats of the most holy supper of the Lord,
of which the sacrament was previously prefigured through manna;
and also the roasted Pascal lamb anticipated this;

and Melchizidech who offered bread and wine to Abraham.
The seventeenth chapter sets forth how Christ prostrated his enemies,
which Sampson prefigured when he killed a thousand men with a jawbone;
likewise Sangar who killed six hundred men with a ploughshare;
and David who killed eight hundred men in one assault.
The eighteenth chapter sets forth how Judas betrayed the Lord with a kiss,
and how the Jewish people returned to him evil for good.
This itself was prefigured by Joab who duplicitously kissed Amasam;
and by King Saul who pursued King David on account of his good deeds.
The malicious Cain also prefigured that event

Qui fratrem suum sine causa fraudulenter necauit.
¶In xixº capitulo agitur quomodo christus fuit uelatus
Illusus consputus derisus colaphizatus.
Istud ydolatre uituli conflatilis prefigurauit
Quia hur ipsis contradicentem ⸌⸌sputis⸍⸍ suffocauit.[1]
Item kam qui patrem suum iniquum derisit
Et gens philistu⸌m⸍ quam sampsonem excecauit et illusit.
¶In xxº ⸤capitulo⸥ agitur quomodo christus fuit flagellatus
Et hoc prefigurauit achor ad arborem ligatus.
Item lamech quem due uxores sue afflixerunt
Ita due gentes christum flagellauerunt.
Gens paganorum cecidit eum uirgis et flagellis
Gens iudeorum percussit eum obprobriis et linguis pessimis.
Istud etiam prefigurauit iob quem sathan percussit ulceribus
Et uxor sua uerbis contumeliis et obprobriis.
¶In xxi capitulo agitur quomodo christus fuit spinis coronatus
Consputus derisus et multipliciter dehonestatus.
Et hec zerobabel per appemen concubinam proposuit
Que regi quondam contumeliam magnam exhibuit.
Item per ⸍s⸌emei[2] qui regi dauid maledixit
Et super eum puluerem lutum lapides proiecit.
Hoc etiam Amon rex amonitarum prefigurauit
Qui nuncios pro pace missos turpiter dehonestauit.
¶In xxºii capitulo agitur quomodo christus eductus est crucem baiulans.
Et hoc figurauit ysaac ligna sua portans.
Item heres vinee qui de uinea sua est eiectus
Et a colonis vinee perfidis iniquis interfectus.
⸌⸌hoc etiam per botrum illum mirabilem prefigurabatur
Qui a duobus uiris in terra promissionis in desertum portabatur.
Ita christus a duobus populis de ierusalem est eductus etiam eiectus
Et in monte caluarie pessima morte interfectus.⸍⸍[3]
¶In xxºiii capitulo agitur quomodo christus cruci affigebatur
Et quomodo ipse pro crucifixoribus deprecabatur.
Hoc Jubal musice artis inuentor prefigurauit
Quod fabricante Tubalkaym dulces tonos cantauit.
Ita christus in fabricacione sue crucifixionis
Cantauit patri suo canticum dulcissime oracionis.

---

[1] Cross mark indicates addition of *sputis* before *suffocauit* [2] Added later by black-ink scribe [3] These four lines ("hoc … interfectus") originally omitted, and added at the bottom of the column in a browner ink and smaller writing

when he deceitfully slew his own brother for no reason.
The nineteenth chapter sets forth how Christ was blindfolded,
mocked, spat upon, derided, and beaten.
The idol of the molten calf prefigured that,
because Hur, objecting to it, was choked in spittle;
likewise Ham who unjustly ridiculed his father;
and the Philistines who blinded and made sport of Sampson.
The twentieth chapter sets forth how Christ was scourged:
and Achior, bound to a tree, prefigured this;
likewise Lamech whom his own two wives injured
just as two peoples scourged Christ.
The race of pagans beat him with rods and whips,
and the Jewish race injured him with abusive and evil tongues.
And Job prefigured that event, for Satan afflicted him with sores
and his own wife afflicted him with insults and taunts.
The twenty-first chapter sets forth how Christ was crowned with thorns,
spit upon, derided, and many times dishonored;
and Zerubbabel represented this through the concubine Apama
who formerly expressed great scorn of the king;
likewise by Shemei who reviled King David
and cast rubble, mud, and stones at him;
and this also King Amon of the Ammonites prefigured
who foully dishonored envoys sent to make peace.
The twenty-second chapter sets forth how Christ was led out bearing the cross.
And Isaac prefigured this, carrying his own firewood;
likewise the heir of the vineyard who was driven away from his own vines
and was slain by the treacherous, wicked tennants of the vineyard.
⟨This was also prefigured by the miraculous cluster of grapes
which was carried by two men from the promised land into the desert.
Likewise Christ was led away and also cast out from Jerusalem by two peoples,
and on Mount Calvary was killed by the worst kind of death.⟩
The twenty-third chapter sets forth how Christ was nailed to the cross
and how he himself prayed for his crucifiers.
Tubal, the inventor of musical arts prefigured this
because Tubal-cain sang sweet tunes while working,
so Christ, during the shaping of his own cross,
sang to his father the sweetest canticle of prayer.

Tam dulcis et suauis erat domino illa melodia
Quod conuertit eadem hora de populo tria milia.
Crucifixionem christi etiam ysiaias prefigurauit
Quem rex manasses cum serra lignea secari mandauit.
Item rex moab qui immolauit proprium filium ob hanc causam.

2rb Ut deus liberaret ab obsidione ciuitatem suam.
¶In xxiiii° capitulo agitur ˋetˊ tres figure continentur
Que passionem et mortem christi prefigurasse uidentur.
Prima est arbor grandis quam nabuchodonosor vidit
Quam uigil id est angelus domini succidi iussit.
Germen radicum eius in terra dimittendum dicebat
Quia licet christus occideretur tamen a morte resurrecturus erat.
Secundo rex Codrus mortem christi pulchre prefigurauit
Qui se ipsum propter populum suum in mortem donauit.
Tercio Eleasar qui morte sua bestiam necauit.
Ita christus morte sua mortem nostram mortificauit.
¶In xxv capitulo agitur quomodo christus morte sua fuit derisus
Licet ante mortem fuerit multipliciter illusus.
Istud prefigurauit Michol qui regem dauid derisit
Illa hora quando ˵ante˶ archam domini in cythera lusit.
Et etiam post zitharizacionem deridere non cessauit
Quando eum subsannando nudatis scurtis comparauit.
Istud etiam patet in absolone qui tribus lanceis erat transfixus
Et super hoc ab armigeris Joab gladiis est consectus.
Ita christus tribus doloribus erat cruciatus.
Et super hoc gladiis turpium linguarum est mactatus.
Ita adhuc a multis christus rursus crucifigitur
Sicut in epistula pauli inuenitur.
Tales ˋenimˊ[1] rex Enilmˋrˊoˋdˊach[2] iniquus prefigurauit
Qui corpus patris sui defuncti exhumauit.
Et illud in trecentas partes secuit et diuisit
Et trecentis uulturibus deuoroandum distribuit.
¶In xxvi° capitulo agitur de luctu et dolore beate uirginis
Qui prefiguratus fuit olim in tribus figuris.
Figuratus fuit per iacob qui inconsolabiliter luxit
Quando tunicam filii sui lacertam et cruentam respexit.
Item dolorem marie prefigurauit adam et eua

[1] Added later by black-ink scribe [2] Added later by black-ink scribe

So sweet and so delightful was that melody by the Lord
that it converted three thousand people that same hour.
Isaiah also prefigured the crucifixion of Christ,
whom King Manasses ordered to be cut up with a wooden saw;
likewise King Moab when he sacrificed his son for the sake of the people

that God might free his people from the siege.
And in the twenty-fourth chapter three figures are contained
which are understood to prefigure the passion and death of Christ.
First is the great tree that Nebuchadnezzar saw
which a watchman, that is, the angel of the Lord, ordered to be cut down.
He declared that the shoot must send down its roots in the earth
because although Christ was slain he nevertheless rose from the dead;
secondly King Codrus who gave himself over to death for the sake of his people,
beautifully foreshadowed the death of Christ;
thirdly Eleasar who killed a beast by his death
just as Christ by his death destroyed our death.
The twenty-fifth chapter sets forth how Christ was mocked at his death
although before his death he had been ridiculed repeatedly.
Michol prefigured that when she mocked King David
the time when he played the harp before the ark of the Lord.
And even after the music, she did not stop mocking him
when she treated him like a naked clown by her scorn.
This also is shown in Absalom, who was pierced by three lances
and furthermore was dismembered by the swords of Joab's soldiers.
So too was Christ crucified in threefold anguish
and was lacerated by the blades of foul tongues.
So still now is Christ crucified again by many tongues
just as is found in the epistle of Paul.
The wicked King Evil-Merodach prefigured such behavior,
when he dug up the body of his own dead father.
And he severed it and divided it into three hundred parts
and distributed it to be devoured to three hundred vultures.
The twenty-sixth chapter treats of the grief and sorrow of the Blessed Virgin,
who was once prefigured in three figures.
She was symbolized through Jacob who mourned inconsolably
when he gazed upon the ripped and bloody tunic of his son;
likewise Adam and Eve prefigured the sorrow of Mary

Qui centum annis luxerunt pro nece filii sui seua.
Item Neomi que orbata filiis pulchra noluit uocari
Sed mara id est amaram se dixit uelle appellari.
¶In xxviiº capitulo agitur quomodo corpus domini est sepultum
Et de dolore marie uirginis et matris eius iuxta sepulchrum.
Et hoc per regem dauid olim prefigurabatur
Qui feretrum Abner cum luctu et fletu sequebatur.
Item per Joseph qui in cysternam in deserto est missus
Et per Jonam qui in mari a Ceto est [missus] deglutitus.
¶In xxviiiº capitulo agitur quod christus infernum intrauit
Et sanctos patres cum desiderio expectantes letificauit.
Et hoc per angelum qui tres pueros in fornace refrigerauit
Et abacuc qui danielem in lacu leonum cibauit
Idem patet per [cysternam] strucionem qui cum sanguine vermiculi
Liberauit pullum suum de inclusione uitr[e]i.
¶In xxixº capitulo agitur quomodo christus dyabolum superauit.

2va Et hoc olim ille robustus bananias prefigurauit.
Qui ad leonem in cysternam descendebat
Et eum baculo suo sternens interficiebat.
Istud etiam patet per sampsonem qui leonem delacerauit
Et per ayoch qui regem Eglon pinguissimum perforauit.
¶In xxxº capitulo agitur quomodo maria etiam dyabolum superauit.
Et nos tamquam mater nostra de aduersario nostro uindicauit.
Omnia enim que christus tolerauit per multiplicem passionem
Hec maria mater eius scilicet tolerauit per terrenam compassionem.
Sicut ergo christus superauit dyabolum per suam passionem
Ita maria superauit eum per maternam compassionem.
Istud prefiguratum fuit per Judith que holifernem decollauit
Et yael que sysaram per tympera clauo perforauit.
Item per reginam thamari que caput cyri abscidit
Et in urnam plenam sanguine humano misit.
Sacia inquit te sanuine humano quem sitisti
De quo inuita tua numquam saciari potuisti.
¶In xxxi capitulo agitur quomodo christus sanctos de inferno liberauit
Et hoc olim exitus filiorum israel de egipto prefigurauit
Item abraham quem dominus liberauit de hur caldeorum
\\Item loth quem dominus liberauit de subuersione sodomorum.//[1]

[1] Skipped line inserted at bottom of column by scribe, and insertion marks renewed by black-ink corrector

when they grieved one hundred years in Seva for the death of their son;
also Naomi who, having lost her sons, did not desire to be called 'Beautiful,'
but in bitterness she said that she wished to be called Mara, 'Bitter'.
The twenty-seventh chapter sets forth how the body of the Lord was buried
and the sorrow of Mary, virgin and mother, near the tomb:
and this was formerly prefigured by King David
who followed the bier of Abner with mourning and weeping;
and likewise by Joseph who was thrown in the cistern;
and by Jonah who was swallowed by a whale in the sea.
The twenty-eighth chapter relates that Christ entered into hell
and gladdened the holy fathers, waiting for him with longing.
And this was prefigured through the angel who kept three boys cool in the furnace;
and by Habakkuk, who fed Daniel in the den of lions.
This same thing is made manifest by the ostrich who with crimson blood
freed his young from captivity in a vase.
The twenty-ninth chapter sets forth how Christ conquered the devil.

And the valiant Bananias formerly prefigured this.
When he descended to the lion in the pit
and, striking him down with his club, slew him.
And such is shown by Sampson who tore the lion in pieces
and by Ehud who stabbed the obese king Eglon.
The thirtieth chapter set forth how Mary also overcame the devil
and our mother, at it were, delievered us from our adversary.
For all that Christ endured through his manifold passion,
these things Mary his mother endured through her earthly suffering.
Therefore just as Christ conquered the devil through his passion,
so Mary conquered him through her maternal compassion.
That was prefigured by Judith who decapitated Holofernes;
and by Jael who pierced Sisara through the temples with a spike;
likewise by Queen Tomyris who cut off the head of Cyrus
and thew it into an urn full of human blood.
The Sacian queen said, "you were thirsty for human blood
by which you will never be able to be satisfied in your life."
The thirty-first chapter sets forth how Christ freed the holy ones from hell
and the exodus of the children of Israel from Egypt previously prefigured this;
likewise Abraham whom the Lord rescued from Ur of the Chaldeans;
⟨likewise the Lord saved Lot from the destruction of Sodom.⟩

¶In xxxii capitulo agitur quomodo christus resurrexit
Et hoc patet per sampsonem qui port⸌a⸍s Gaze destruxit.
Item per ionam qui post triduum exiuit de uentre ceti
Et per lapidem reprobatum qui factus est in caput anguli
¶In xxxiii capitulo agitur quomodo christus celos ascendit
Et hoc scala illa quam uidit iacob preostendit.
Item ouis perdita que inuenta in domum repertabatur
Et helyas qui per currum in paradysum transferebatur.
¶In xxxiiii capitulo agitur de spiritus ⸌⸌sancti⸍⸍ missione
Et de omnium linguarum scientie collacione.
Istud figuratum fuit in turri ubi prima lingua fuit uariata
Et in monte syna ubi quinquagesima die lex est data.
Item per superhabundanciam olei quem excreuit
Et omnia uasa uacua paupercule uidue repleuit.
⌞¶⌟[1] In xxxv capitulo agitur de luctu marie post christi ascensum
Quem prefigurauit anna thobie post filii sui recessum.
Item patet per mulierem que dragmam perditam cum dolore quesiuit
Et per Michol que sponso suo sibi ablato semper luxit
¶In xxxvi capitulo agitur quomodo christus mariam in celum assumpsit.
Et hoc patet ⸌⸌per archam⸍⸍ quam dauid in domum suam introduxit
Item per signum magnum quod apperauit in celo
Et per matrem salomonis quam locauit ad dexteram suam in throno.
¶In xxxviiº capitulo agitur quomodo maria deum mundo offensum placab⸌at⸍[2]
Sicut dominus beato dominico in quamdam uisione monstrabat.
Quando dominus offensus contra mundum tres lanceas fibrabat.
Et beata uirgo se interponens iram eius mitigabat.
Istud patet per abygayl que iram dauid contra Nabal placabat
Et per mulierem tetiguitem que absolonem patri reconciliabat.

2vb Et per mulierem sapientem in urbe abela
Que inpugnacionem joab sapienter remouit ab ea.
¶In xxxviiiº capitulo agitur quomodo maria nostra protectrix existit
Que ab ira dei a laqueis dyaboli a dolo mundi nos protegit.
Primum patet per Tharbis. que urbem saba a moyse defensauit.
⸌Secundum per mulierem in Thebes que abymalech excerebrauit.⸍[3]
[–Tercium] patet per Michol que dauid per fenestram dimisit

[1] Customary paragraph marker is omitted at this point [2] Added later by black-ink scribe [3] This line is written above the column in a browner ink and slightly smaller size, with marks indicating that it should replace the line that appears in the text as this point, "Tercium patet per mulierem in Thebes que abymalech excerebrauit"

and rescued him from the ambush of his enemy Saul.
The thirty-ninth chapter sets forth how Christ shows the Father his wounds
and Mary shows her heart and breast to her son,
and how she prays for us poor sinners,
and who is there who is able to refuse such beseechings?
First this is shown by Antipater who showed his scars to Caesar;
secondly this is shown by Esther who interceded with King Ahasuerus for the Jews.
The fortieth chapter sets forth concerning the severity of the Last Judgement
which a certain nobleman prefigured in a parable,
he handed over his goods to his servants, went away into a far-off region,
and having accepted the crown, returned and required an account from them.
Likewise by the prudent virgins who denied oil to the foolish ones,
because then neither God nor the saints will give the oil of mercy to the damned.
Likewise it is shown through the writing, "Mane, Thechel, Phares,"
which means, "numbered, weighed, and divided."
⟨For that justice will be conducted through number and payments
and consummated through the perpetual division of the good and evil men.⟩
The forty-first chapter treats of the horrible pain of the damned
which David prefigured in the killing of his enemies.
Some he cut up with knives and some he sawed into pieces;
some he killed with sleighs and nail-studded carriages.
Gideon foreshadowed it in the city Sochot
when he tore the scoffers to pieces with thorns and thistles.
The Egyptians and Pharaoh also prefigured this,
whom the Lord buried together in the Red Sea.
So too at the last judgement everyone in hell
will be bound together with the demons and Lucifer by the Lord.
The forty-second chapter treats of the joy of the blessed and their glory
which they will have without end in the presence of almighty God.
The figure of this is shown in the glory of Solomon
because we read that no one has lived in such glory.
The second figure of eternal joy is shown to be the banquet of Ahasuerus
because we read that there was no feast so long and so ceremonial.
The third figure is reasonably found in the feasts of the sons of Job,
since we read no feasts were made so continuously or in such quantity.
The forty-third chapter sets forth how we may escape the punishments of the damned
and how we may become worthy of the glory of the blessed.
If we desire to obtain that joy and to avoid the punishments
we ought to help Christ to carry his heavy cross.

Quibus autem modis christus in portando crucem iuuatur
In eodem capitulo per exemplum lucide declaratur.
¶In xliiiiº capitulo agitur de vii tristiciis que habuit maria
Propter dilectum filium suum ihesum christum qui est vera sophia.

3ra ¶In xlv capitulo agitur de vii gaudiis eiusdem gloriose virginis.
Et terminantur capitula huius libelli et uoluminis.
Predictum librum de contentis huius libri compilaui
Et propter pauperes predicatores apponere curaui.
Quod si forte nequiuerint totum librum comparare
Si sciunt hystorias possunt ex ipso prohemio predicare.

⌊Prologus⌋

⌊qui⌋ *Ad*[1] iusticiam erudiunt multos
Fulgebunt iusti quasi stelle in perpetuas eternitates.[2]
Hinc est quod ad erudicionem multorum decreui librum compilare.
In quo legentes possunt erudicionem accipere et dare.
In presenti autem uita nichil estimo homini utilius esse
Quam deum creatorem suum et propriam condicionem nosce.[3]
Hanc condicionem[4] possunt litterati habere ex scripturis
Rudes autem erudiri debent in libris laycorum id est in picturis.
Quapropter ad gloriam dei et pro erudicione indoctorum
Cum dei adiutorio decreui compilare librum laycorum.
Ut autem tam clericis quam laycis possit doctrinam dare
Satago illum facili quodammodo dictamine elucidare.
Intendo autem primo monstrare casum luciferi et angelorum
Deinde lapsum primorum parentum et posterorum suorum.
Postea quomodo deus nos per incarnacionem suam liberauit
Et quibus figuris olim incarnacionem suam premonstrauit.
Notandum autem quod in hoc opusculo uarie hystorie traduntur[5]
Que non de uerbo ad uerbum per omnia exponuntur.
Quia doctor non aliud de hystoria exponere tenetur
Nisi quod ad suum propositum pertinere uidetur.
Ut autem istud melius et elucidius uideatur
Una similitudo siue parabola talis audiatur.

---

[1] The initial A is three-lines high and rubricated to mark the beginning of the prologue [2] Dn. 12.3, see Phlp. 2.15 [3] See Col. 3.10, Eph. 4.24 [4] condicionem] cognitionem, L [5] traduntur] tanguntur, L

And the way that Christ is helped to carry the cross
is clearly described with examples in this same chapter.
The forty-fourth chapter treats of the seven sorrows which Mary had
for the sake of her dear son Jesus Christ, who is true wisdom.

The forty-fifth chapter treats of the seven joys of the same glorious Virgin.
And the chapters of this little book and volume are concluded.
I compiled this proem about the contents of this book
and I took pains to place it here for the sake of poor preachers
so that, if by chance they should be unable to buy the whole book,
yet knowing the stories, they could still preach from this proem.

Prologue

Those just men who instruct many in justice
will shine like stars for all eternity.
On account of this, I decided to compile a book for the instruction of many,
through which readers can both get and give learning.
And in the present life I think nothing to be more profitable for man
than to know his creator and his own condition.
The literate can learn this condition from the written words,
but the illiterate should be taught by the books of the laity, that is, in pictures.
Therefore for the glory of God and for the instruction of the unlearned
I decided, with the help of God, to compile a book for the laity.
In order, however, that it can impart teaching to both clerics and laity,
I am taking pains to explain it in fairly simple language.
And I intend first to show the fall of Lucifer and the angels,
then the fall of the first parents and their descendants
afterwards how God freed us through his incarnation,
and by what figures he presaged his incarnation in former times.
Yet it must be noted that in this little work various stories are related
which are not explained word by word in their entirety;
for a teacher is not obligated to explain any other part of the story
except what seems to pertain to his purpose.
And in order that this might be seen better and more clearly
an illustration or parable should be heard:

¶Abbacia quedam quercum ualde magnum in se stantem habebat.
Quam propter artitudinem loci precidi ⌞et⌟ exstirpari oportebat.
Qua precisa officiales ad ipsam conuenerunt
Et singuli quod suo officio congruebat elegerunt.
Magister fabrorum inferiorem truncum abscidit
Quem sibi ad fabricandum aptum uidit.
Magister sutorum cortices sibi elegit
Quas pro corio suo preparando in puluerem redegit.
Magister porcorum glandes sibi adoptauit
Quibus porcellos suos saginare cogitauit
Magister edificatorum elegit sibi stipitem erectum
Ut inde carpentaret tigna et tectum.
Magister piscatorum elegit sibi curuaturas
Ut inde faceret nauium iuncturas.
Magister molendinorum radices effodiebat
Quas propter sui firmitatem molendinis competere uidebat.
Magister pistorum ramos in unum coniecit
De quibus postea fornacem suam calefecit.
Sacrista frondes uiridas deportauit
Et cum eis in festiuitate ecclesiam stipauit.

3rb
Scriptor librorum carpsit gallas siue pomas forte centum
De quibus sibi aptauit[1] attramentum.
Magister cellarii sibi quasdam particulas composuit.
De quibus amphoras et alia fieri uoluit.
Ad ultimum magister coquorum fragmenta colligebat
Et ad ignem coquine deferebat.
Ab uno quoque illud assumebatur
Quod suo officio competere uidebatur.
Illud quod uni pro officio suo ualebat
Hoc alteri pro suo non congruebat.
Idem modus in hystoria exponenda tenetur
Quilibet doctor colligit de ea quod pro suo proposito congruum uidetur.
Eundem modum in hoc opusculo[2] seruabo
Particulam hystorie mihi congrue[3] solummodo recitabo.
Totam hystoriam per omnia nolo recitare
Ne legentibus et audientibus tedium uidear generare.
Notandum etiam quod conuenienter et reuera

---

[1] aptauit] temperavit, L [2] There appears to be a crease or repair from here until line 28 [3] congrue] congruam, L

a certain abbey had standing within it a large strong oak,
which, because of the confinement of the place, it was fitting to cut down and root out.
When it was cut down, the masters gathered around it
and each one chose what suited his position.
The master-carpenter hewed off the lower trunk for himself
which he saw to be suitable for construction.
The master-cobbler chose for himself bits of bark
which he ground to dust for tanning his skins.
The master of the pigs selected acorns for himself
with which he thought to fatten his pigs.
The master-builder chose for himself a straight stake
so that from it he might make beams and roof.
The master of the fisherman chose curved branches for himself
so that from it he could make ships' joinings.
The master-miller dug out the roots,
which he saw to be fit for his mill on account of their strength.
The master-bakers heaped the branches together
and by them afterwards he heated his oven.
The sacristan carried off the green branches
and he filled the Church with these on feast days.

The writer of books plucked about a hundred gall apples for himself
from which he prepared writing ink for himself.
The master-steward compiled certain small pieces for himself
from which he wanted pitchers and other things to be made
finally the master-cook gathered scraps
and brought them to the kitchen fire.
Each one took that part
which seemed fit for his job.
What worked well for the role of one
was not fitting to that of another.
The same method is used to expound upon story:
every teacher collects from each story what seems apt to his purpose.
I will observe the same method in this little work;
I will relate only the little part of a story apt to my purpose.
I do not intend to relate the whole story in all its parts
lest I seem to weary my readers and hearers.
Also it should be noted that, suitably and in truth

Sacra scriptura est tamquam mollis cera.
Que iuxta sigilli impressionem
Capit in se forme dispositionem.
Ut si forte continet leonem in se sigillum
Cera mollis impressa statim in dispositionem capit illum.
Et si forte aliud sigillum aquilam continebit
Eadem cera illi impressa speciem aquile continebit habebit.
Sic una res aliquando significat dyabolum aliquando christum.
Nec mirari debemus scripture modum istum.
Quia secundum diuersas alicuius rei uel persone acciones
Diuerse possunt sibi attribui significaciones.
Cum enim rex dauid ⸤adulterium et⸥[1] homicidium perpetrauit.[2]
Non christum sed dyabolum significauit uel figurauit.
Cum autem inimicos suos amabat et ipsis bene faciebat
Non dyaboli sed christi figuram tenebat.
Nec etiam incusandum est quod per iniquum aliquando christus designetur
Quia tunc interpretacio nominis uel actus competens intuetur.
Quamuis enim absolon patrem suum inique persequebatur
Tamen per eum christus propter aliquas similitudines designatur.
Non ideo quia absolon inique contra patrem suum agebat
Sed quia pulcherrimus fuit et in arbore suspensus erat.[3]
Christus enim erat speciosus forma pre filiis hominum
Et in arbore crucis suspensus emisit spiritum.[4]
Sampson quadam uice urbem gazam introiuit
Et nocte illa ibidem cum merectrice dormiuit.[5]
Inimici eius portas urbis concluserunt
Et mane ipsum interficere intenderunt.
Sampson aut media nocte de sompno surgebat
Et portam urbis claudens tollens eam secum deferebat.
Quamuis sampson forsan cum illa meretrice peccabat
Tamen dominum nostrum Ihesum christum prefigurabat.

3va Non ideo quia cum meretrice illa concubebat.
Sed quia nocte surgebat et portas urbis confringebat.
Sic christus media nocte de sompno mortis resurrexit
et portas inferi destruens captiuos secum uexit.

[1] adulterium et, L] ad ultimum, G [2] 2 Kings 11.15–17, 12.9 [3] 2 Kings 14.25, 2 Kings 18.9 [4] See Dn. 7.13, Mk. 14.62, Mt. 27.50, Lk. 23.46 [5] Jdg. 16.1–3

sacred Scripture is like soft wax,
which, after it is stamped by a seal,
takes on the design of the stamp.
So that if the seal has on it, for instance, a lion,
the soft wax when stamped immediately takes on that design.
And if afterward another seal has, for instance, an eagle
that same wax (when stamped again) will have the appearance of an eagle.
So too, a thing at one time signifies the devil and at another, Christ.
Nor should we wonder at this aspect of Scripture.
Because different meanings are able to be attributed
to the different actions of things or person.
For when King David committed adultery and murder,
he signified (or symbolized) not Christ but rather the devil.
When, however, David loved his enemies and did good to them,
he contained the figure of Christ rather than the devil.
Nor should anyone complain that Christ is sometimes designated by an evildoer,
because in context this is a fitting interpretation of the person or act.
Indeed, although Absalom wrongly persecuted his father,
yet through him Christ is designated because of some likenesses;
not because Absalom wrongly marched against his father
but because he was exceedingly beautiful and hung on a tree.
For Christ was more handsome in appearance than the sons of men
and, hung on the tree of the cross, he breathed out his spirit.
Sampson entered a certain quarter in the city of Gaza
and that night slept there with a prostitute.
His enemies shut the gates of the city
and intended to kill him in the morning.
But Sampson woke up in the middle of the night
and limping, carrying the gate of the city, brought it with him.
Although perhaps Sampson sinned with that prostitute
nevertheless he prefigured our Lord Jesus Christ.

Not because he slept with that prostitute
but because in the middle of the night he arose and destroyed the gates of the city.
So Christ in the middle of the night arose from the sleep of death
and, destroying the gates of hell, he carried off the captives with him.

¶Hoc notabilia idcirco introduxi et annotaui
Quia studentibus in sacra scriptura utilia esse iudicaui.
Ut si forte studentes in hoc libello talia inueniant
Quod modus exponendi talis est mihi non inuertant.
O bone ihesu da ut hoc opusculum tibi complaceat
Proximos edificet ⌞et me⌟[1] gratum tibi faciat.

4va *primum Capitulum huius libri.*[2]

Incipit speculum humane saluacionis
In quo patet casus hominis et modus reparacionis.
In hoc speculo potest homo considerare
Quam ob causam creator omnium decreuit hominem creare.
†Primo etiam angelorum casum quo etiam per dya⌞boli⌟ fra⌞u⌟dem sit dampnatus[3]†
Et quomodo per misericordiam dei sit reformatus.
Lucifer igitur erexit se contra creatorem suum deum eternum
Et in ictu oculi de excelso celorum solio proiectus est in infernum
Et ob hanc causam decreuit deus hominem creare
Ut per ipsum posset casum luciferi et suorum sociorum restaurare.
Quapropter dyabolus homini inuidens sibi insidiabatur
Et ad precepti transgressionem ipsum inducere nitebatur.
Quoddam ergo genus serpentis sibi dyabolus eligebat
Qui serpens ibat erectus et uirgineum caput habebat[4]
Hunc serpentem fraudulentem decepcionis artifex intrabat.
Et per os eius loquens uerba deceptoria mulieri narrabat.[5]
Temptauit autem mulierem tamquam minus prouidam
Reputans prudentem et industrium uirum esse adam.
Accessit ad mulierem solam sine uiro existentem
Quia solam facilius decepit dyabolus quam socios habentem.
Decepit ita dyabolus matrem nostram euam
Inducens ergo totum genus humanum ad mortem ualde seueram.

[1] et me, L] ut, G [2] Left Panel: Fall of Lucifer. *Creator tocius creature*. The text illustrates Is. 14.12–15, a passage generally interpreted as referring to the expulsion of Lucifer from the court of heaven for his overweening pride. The main image shows God, "Creator of all creatures" (Creator omnium creaturarum) in a mandorla, surrounded by his faithful angels, decreeing banishment of Lucifer for his presumption to be "the most high" (Vg. *Similis ero Altissimo*). In the predella we see a de-feathered Lucifer, set upon by a toad and a dragon, forcing him into hell-mouth, here represented by a bear. [3] Primo … dampnatus] potest etiam homo videre quomodo per diaboli fraudem sit damnatus, L [4] *Historia Scholastica Genesis* 21. See also *Legenda Aurea* (51)
[5] See Gen. 3.1–7 ff.

Because of this, I introduced and noted the remarkable things
which I judged to be useful for those studying Sacred Scripture
so that if by chance students should discover such things in this little book
they should not turn away because this is my manner of explanation.
O good Jesus, grant that this little work may find favor with you,
may it edify my neighbors and make me pleasing to you.

The First Chapter of this Book.

Here begins the Mirror of Man's Salvation
in which the fall of mankind and the method of restoration is laid out.
In this mirror, man can consider
why the Creator of all things deigned to create man,
and, first, the fall of the angels, and also how he was damned through the devil's deception,
and how through the mercy of God mankind is remade.
Lucifer, therefore, raised himself against eternal God, his creator
and in a blink of an eye, from the highest throne of the heavens, he was cast into hell.
And for this reason, God decided to create man
so that, through him, he might be able to repair the fall of Lucifer and his allies.
Wherefore the devil, envying man, was laying traps for him
and was striving to lead him into transgressing against the commandment.
Therefore, the devil chose for himself a certain kind of serpent
who walked upright and had a virgin's head
the creator of deception entered this fraudulent serpent.
And, speaking through its mouth, he related deceitful words to the woman.
And he tempted the woman as if the less prudent one,
considering the man Adam to be prudent and diligent.
He drew near to the woman alone, without the man being present
because more easily does the devil deceive the one alone, than the one having companions.
Thus the devil deceived our mother, Eve
thereby leading the whole human race into a most cruel death.

Notandum autem hoc dictum ualde diligenter quia ab origine mundi hec fuerunt.
Quod omnia peccata in hunc mundum propter primum peccatum transierunt.[1]
Notandum etiam quod vir in agro damasco est formatus[2]
Et a domino in paradysum uoluptatis est translatus

4vb[3] Mulier autem in paradyso est formata
Et de costis uiri dormientis est parata.
Deus autem ipsam quodam modo super uirum honestauit[4]
Quam eam in loco uoluptatis plasmauit.
Non fecit eam sicut uirum de limo terre
Sed de osse nobilis uiri ade et de eius carne.
Non est facta de pede ne a uiro despiceretur
Nec de capite ne supra uirum dominaretur.
Sed est facta de latere maritali
Et data est uiro pro consorte et sociale collaterali.[5]
Que si sibi in honore collato humiliter perstitisset
Numquam molestiam a uiro aliquam sustinuisset.
Sed quia dyabolo credens deo uoluit assimilari
A uiro meruit affligi si delinquerit et molestari.
Mulier enim credidit dyabolo non maritus
Sed uir consentit mulieri licet inuitus.
Mulier institit uiro ut secum de fructu manducaret
Qui tantum dilexit eam ut comederet ne eam contristaret.
Salomon propter amorem mulierum ydola adorauit
Non tamen deos uel deum esse putauit.[6]
Sic adam propter amorem mulieris secum comedebat
Non tamen similem se deo posse fieri credebat.[7]
Mulier plus ergo quam uir peccauit[8]
Quia se fieri deo forte similem estimauit.
Aliud que ⸤peccatum⸥[9] super addebat
Eo quod uirum blande ad peccatum trahebat.

[1] Line is missing from L [2] *HS Genesis* 13 and 24, and *LA* (51.141) [3] Right Panel: Creation of Eve. *Creatio ade et eue.* The illustration shows the Creator pulling Eve from Adam's rib; the upward branching tree behind Adam's head suggests the lineage that will follow; iconographically, to show the roots in his head rather than his 'loins' may be intended to refer to the purity of procreation before the Fall. Illustrating Gen. 2.18–24. [4] honestauit] honorauit, L [5] See *Summa Theologiae* I.92.3 [6] 3 Kings 11.4 [7] 1 Tim. 2.14; *HS Genesis* 22; Augustine, *Genesi ad litteram*, 11.42, 59 [8] See *ST* II(2).163.4 [9] peccatum, L] peccet, G

This truth must be noted very diligently, as from the world's birth these things were so:
that all the sins on this earth happen on account of the first sin.
It must be noted also that the man was formed in the field of Damascus
and was carried from the Lord into a paradise of pleasure

however, the woman was formed in paradise
and was produced from the ribs of the sleeping man.
God, however, dignified her somewhat more than the man,
because he molded her in the place of pleasure.
He did not make her, as the man, from the dirt of the earth
but from the bone of the noble man Adam and from his flesh.
She was not made from his foot, lest she be looked down upon by man
nor from his head, lest she have dominion over the man.
But she was made from her husband's side
and was given to man as a partner and ally at his side.
If she had persisted humbly with him in parallel honor
she would never have suffered any harm from the man.
But since, believing the devil, she wanted to be made like God
she deserved to be beaten by the man (if she sinned), and to be harmed.
For the woman—not her husband—believed the devil
but the man agreed with the woman, although hesitantly.
The woman urged the man to eat from the fruit with her
he loved her so much that he ate, lest he make her unhappy.
Solomon worshipped idols on account of the love of women
yet he did not think that they were gods or God.
Thus Adam, on account of the love of woman, ate with her
yet he did not believe that they could become like God.
The woman, therefore, sinned more than the man
since she judged that she might perhaps become like God.
Over and above, she added another sin
in that she enticed the man to sin.

5a[1]
Licet enim in textu biblie aperte non inueniatur
Tamen certum est quod breuibus uerbis bla[n]dis ei adulabatur.
O uir aduerte qualis et quanta est fraus mulieris
Caue tibi a muliere blanda ne defrauderis.
Respice adam opus manuum dei et fortissimum sampsonem.
Respice dauid uirum secundum cor dei et sapientissimum salomonem.
Si tales et tantos decepit ars mulieris
Quomodo qui tu non talis es et tantus a muliere securus eris.
Virum adam quem dyabolus temptare non audebat
Hunc mulier audacior dyabolo defraudare presumebat.
Dyabolus itaque mulierem defraudabat
Mulier vero uirum et omnes posteros condempnabat.
Et si homo in mandato dei perseuerasset
Numquam penam numquam mortem aliquam gustasset.
Nullam sustineret debilitatem uel lassitudinem.
Nullam sentiret infirmitatem uel egritudinem.
Sine gemitu et dolore et tristicia matris portaretur
Sine fletu et merore et labore graui nasceretur.
Non nouisset luctum neque aliquam tribulacionem
Non sustineret uerecundiam neque aliquam confusionem.
Aures eius numquam obsurdescerent
Et dentes eius numquam obstupescerent
Oculi eius numquam caligarent
Et pedes eius numquam claudicarent.
Nec flumina nec fontes eum submergerent
Nec ignis nec estus solis eum combussissent.

5b[2]
Nulla bestia nulla auis ipsum infestaret
Nullus aer nulla aura eum molestaret.
Numquam homines inter se lites habuissent
Tamquam fratres mutuo se dilexissent.
Subiecta esset homini omnis creatura
Semper in gaudio uiueret sine cura.
Et cum deo creatori suo placuisset

[1] Left Panel: Marriage of Adam and Eve. Institution of marriage: Gen. 2.22–25. The artist represents Adam and Eve in a much smaller scale than he does their Creator, perhaps partly as a way of suggesting their infant-like innocence. [2] Right Panel: Temptation of Eve. Gen. 3.1–5. The biblical serpent here becomes a griffin-like monster, but smaller than human scale and with a pleasant, avuncular face. The Tree of the Knowledge of Good and Evil is made to resemble a palm. These features enhance the seductive allure.

For although it may not be found openly in the text of the Bible
yet it is certain that she flattered him with short, persuasive words.
O man, take heed of what kind and how great a woman's wiles are!
Guard yourself from a flattering woman, lest you be deceived.
Consider Adam, the work of the hands of God, and strongest Samson.
Consider David, a man after God's own heart, and wisest Solomon.
If woman's guile entrapped men so great and so many,
how will you, who are so great and such a kind, be safe from woman?
The devil did not dare to tempt the man, Adam
this woman, more reckless, presumed to deceive the devil.
And so the devil deceived the woman,
but the woman condemned the man and all her descendants.
And if man had persevered in the commandment of God
he would never have tasted any punishment, never any death
he would have suffered no weakness or weariness.
He would have felt no infirmity or sickness.
He would be carried in his mother's womb without groaning and sorrow and sadness.
Without weeping and grief and hard labor would he be born.
He would not have known grief, nor any tribulation
he would not have suffered shame nor any confusion.
His ears would never become deaf,
and his teeth would never grow dull,
his eyes would never cloud over with blindness,
and his feet would never be lame.
Neither rivers nor streams would drown him,
neither fire nor the heat of the sun could scald him.

No beast, no bird would disturb him
no wind, no breeze would molest him.
Men would have never had quarrels among themselves;
like brothers they would have loved each other.
Every creature would be subject to mankind
he would live always in joy, without a care.
And when it was pleasing to God, his creator,

Cum corpore et anima ipsum in celum assumpsisset.
Nullus autem homo presumat inuestigare
Cur deus hominem quem sciebat casurum uoluit creare.
Cur etiam ipsos angelos creare uolebat
Quorum casum certissime precognoscebat.
Et quare cor pharaonis uoluit indurare[1]
Cor autem marie magdalene ad penitentiam mollificare.
Quare petro ter se neganti contriciones immisit
Iudam autem in suo peccato desperare permisit.[2]
Quare uni latoni gratiam conuersionis immisit[3]
Et socio suo similem gratiam dare non curauit.[4]
Quare unum peccatorem turbat et alium non turbat
Nullus quicumque [presumens][5] prudens inuestigare presumat.
Hec enim dei opera et hiis similia
Humanis ingeniis sunt inscrutabilia.
Huiusmodi questiones paulus breuiter soluere uidetur
Quem inquit uult iudicat deus et cui uult miseretur.[6]
O bone ihesu da nobis tuum iudicium ita tenere
Ut possimus tecum in perpetuum commanere.[7]

5vb *Secundum capitulum*[8]

*I*n precedentibus audiuimus quomodo deus hominem honorauit
Consequenter audiamus quomodo homo se ipsum uilificauit.
Homo cum in honore esset non intellexit[9]
Eiectus est quia contra deum creatorem suum se erexit
Eiectus est de paradyso uoluptatis
In hanc vallem miserie et paupertatis.[10]
Paruipendit[11] sibi impensum honorem
Et inuenit tribulacionem et dolorem.
Exiuit paradysum locum gaudiosum et amenum.
Intrauit locum doloribus et aduersitatibus plenum.

---

[1] Ex 9.12 [2] Mt. 26.33–35, Mt. 27.3–5 [3] immisit] inspiravit, L [4] Lk. 23.39–43 [5] Deleted by scribal subpunctuation [6] See Rom. 9.18 [7] O … commanere] *O bone Jesu, fac nos in celis tecum regnare / Et cum sanctis angelis te sine fine laudare!* M. (Lines omitted entirely in L.) [8] Left Panel: The Moment of the Fall. Gen. 3.6. Eve finds Adam under a different tree, a fig, and offers him the fruit she has picked from the Tree of the Knowledge of Good and Evil. [9] See Ps. 48.21 [10] Gen. 3.23–24 [11] Paruipendit] parum pependit, L

he would take him up body and soul into heaven.
But let no man presume to search into
why God wanted to create man, whom he knew would fall,
and why he wanted to create the angels,
of whose fall he certainly knew beforehand,
and for what reason he wanted to harden the heart of Pharaoh
but to soften the heart of Mary Magdalene to repentance.
For what reason he admitted Peter, who was denying him three times
but permitted Judas to despair in his sin.
For what reason he allowed one thief the grace of conversion
and cared not to give his companion similar grace,
for what reason he disturbs one sinner and not another
no one however wise should presume to search into [this].
For these works of God and those like them
are inscrutable to human capacity.
Paul seems to solve questions of this sort in brief.
He says, "God judges whom he wishes and has mercy on whom he wishes."
O good Jesus, grant us to comprehend your judgment in such a way
that we might be able to dwell with you forever.

Chapter Two

In the last chapter we have heard how God honored mankind;
next let us hear how man debased himself.
Man, although he was in honor, did not understand.
He was cast out because he raised himself against God his Creator;
he was cast out from the paradise of delight
into this valley of misery and poverty.
He esteemed of little value for himself his considerable honor
and sought tribulation and sorrow.
He left paradise, a place joyful and delightful;
he entered a place filled with sorrows and adversities.
He entered the fraudulent and false world,

Intrauit mundum fraudulosum et fallacem
Multa bona promittentem et in omnibus mendacem.
Promittit enim mundus homini longam uitam dare
Sed ueniente morte non ualet ad punctum prolongare.[1]
Promittit corpori diuinam sanitatem
Et inducit anime et corpori perpetuam infirmitatem.
Promittit multas diuicias et magnum honorem.
Sed in fine dat homini putredinem et fetorem.
Et licet aliquando tribuat homini bona mundana
Tamen omnia indurabilia sunt et uana.[2]
Nam hominis uitam non possunt prolongare
Nec a mortis potestate sufficiunt defensare.[3]
In extrema pietate neccesitate nullum prestatur homini iuuamen
Sed uix tribuitur corpori uilissimum lintheamen.
Mundus ergo iste recte videtur esse tamquam sambucus

5vb[4] Cuius flos est pulcher sed amarus fructus.
Sic pulchra videtur mundi delectacio
Sed fructus eius est eterna dampnacio.
Mundus etiam iste traditori conuenienter comparatur
Per quem christus osculo doloso tradebatur.[5]
Tale signum mundus dat demonibus
Quale iudas dedit ihesu christi hostibus.
Quem osculatus fuero diuicias et honores dando
Ipse est tenete eum eternaliter cruciando.
Verumtamen diuicie non semper sunt ad dampnacionem
Sed multis prosunt ad eternam saluacionem.[6]
Dixit enim daniel nabuchodonosor regi
Peccata tua elemosinis redime viam salu⸌tis⸍ dans ei.[7]
Deus enim potentes non abicit cum sit ipse potens
Si utuntur temporalibus sic thobias dixit filium suum docens.
Si multum tibi fuerit habundanter tribue
Si modicum fuerit id ipsum libenter impartiri stude.[8]
Diuicie non dampnant sed amor ipsarum[9]

---

[1] prolongare] prorogare, L [2] See Ecl. 1.2, 12.8 [3] See Mt. 16.26, Mk. 8.36, Lk. 9.25 [4] Right Panel: Expulsion from Eden. Gen. 3.7–24. The artist depicts Adam and Eve holding fig leaves over their genitalia, a tradition well established since the catacombs, despite the provision of tunics crafted by God from animal skins, previously announced in Genesis 3.31. In a mosaic in San Marco, Venice (c. 1215–1225), Adam and Eve are shown wearing tunics, but this is very rare. The same mosaic seems to have been known to the artist; his Adam "delving" with a mattock in the frontispiece is drawn directly from the San Marco mosaic. [5] See Lk. 22.48 [6] See Tb. 4.7–8 [7] Dn. 4.27 [8] Tb. 4.7–9 [9] Cf. 1 Tim. 6.10

which promises many good things and is in all things deceitful.
For the world promises to give man long life,
but, as death comes, cannot prolong it for a moment.
It promises immortal health to the body,
and introduces perpetual sickness to the soul and the body.
It promises much wealth and great honor,
but in the end it gives corruption and stench to man.
And although at times that it grants worldly goods to man;
nevertheless, all are perishable and hollow.
For they are not able to prolong the life of man
nor do they suffice to defend from the power of death.
At the last need, no aid is provided to man;
and scarcely the vilest linen cloth is provided for the body.
Therefore, the world is seen rightly to be just like the elder-tree

whose flower is beautiful but [whose] fruit is bitter.
So the delights of the world seem beautiful,
but its fruit is eternal damnation.
The world also is fittingly compared to that traitor
through whom Christ was handed over by a false kiss.
The world gives such a sign to the demons
such as Judas gave to the enemies of Jesus Christ:
"The one whom I will have kissed (by giving him wealth and honors)—
it is he. Seize him to crucify eternally."
Yet however, wealth is not always for damnation
but for many it is profitable toward eternal salvation.
Indeed, Daniel said to King Nebuchadnezzar,
"Redeem your sins by alms," giving him the path of salvation.
For God does not abandon the powerful since He is Himself powerful,
if they use temporal things as Tobias said, teaching his son:
"If you have much, give abundantly;
if you have a little bit, be eager to freely share it."
Wealth damns not, but rather love of the same,

Nec esce coninquinant hominem sed indiscretus amor ipsarum.[1]
Nec etiam pulchra uestis peccat si cor est deo datum
Quia quilibet uestiri poterit sine peccato secundum suum statum.
Quem deus uult esse regem nec decet indui sacco
Et quem ordinauit esse rusticum non conuenit uti serico.
Quilibet ergo utatur rebus secundum statum sibi concessum[2]
Caueat aut diligentissime ne faciat excessum.[3]

6a[4] In omni enim re semper debitus modus est tenendus
Et excessus cum magna diligencia precauendus.[5]
Mundum ergo qui nos tradere nititur temporalia[6] ministrando
Vincere debemus debitum usum et modum seruando.
Has impugnaciones homo a mundo non sustinuisset
Si in paradyso uoluptatis permansisset.
In paradyso fuisset homo sine omni infestacione
Hic uix transit homo unam horam sine uexacione.[7]
Nunc insidiatur ei suus apertus inimicus
Nunc defraudate nititur suus fere[8] amicus.
Interdum uexat eum minima musca uel pulex
Ledit eum minimus vermiculus uel culex.
Et merito a creaturis et elementis impugnatur.
Qui[9] contra creatorem suum erigebatur.
Terra [–tribula]stimulat eum tribulis et sentibus
Bestie terre lacerant eum dentibus et cornibus.
Aqua inuoluit eum fluc[/u]tibus et procellis
Pirate aquarum inuadunt eum rapinis et bellis.
Aer inficit eum pestilencia et corrupcione
Aues aeris rumpunt eum rostrorum et unguium inuasione.
Ignis redigit {in} carnem et ossa eius in cinerem
Fumus ignis inducit oculis eius caliginem.
In paradyso nullus homo fuisset alterius inimicus
Hic inter multos nullus inuenitur uerus amicus.
Quam diu autem homo habet diuicias et honores

[1] See 1John 2.15–17 [2] Cf. 1Tim. 6.9 [3] See Prov. 30.8–9, Phlp. 4.5 [4] Left Panel: Adam and Eve at Work. Adam is again "delving" whilst Eve, shown with her two sons Cain and Abel, is spinning, a traditional figure for her own labors. Gen. 3.19, 4.1–2. [5] See 1Tim. 6.11–12 [6] temporalia] corporalia, L [7] See Job 5.6–7 [8] fere] familiaris, L [9] Qui] quia, L

nor does food defile men but indiscriminate love of the same.
Nor indeed does beautiful clothing transgress if the heart has been given to God
because everyone will be able to be clothed without sin according to his own position.
It is not appropriate that he be clothed with sackcloth whom God wishes to be a king,
and it is not fitting that he use silk whom God has ordained to be a farmer.
let everyone, therefore, use things according to the position granted to him
or rather let him take most diligent care lest he commit excess.

For in each thing, the proper manner must always be considered
and transgression must with great diligence be guarded against.
The world, therefore, which endeavors to betray us by providing temporal things,
we ought to conquer by maintaining proper use and measure.
Man would not have sustained these assaults from the world
if he had remained in the Paradise of delight.
In Paradise man would have been free from all attack;
here man scarcely passes one hour without harassment.
Now his open enemy lies in wait for him;
now his friend relies for the most part upon fraud.
Sometimes the smallest fly or flea harasses him;
the smallest worm or gnat hurts him.
And as he deserves he is assaulted by creatures and by the elements,
he who was raised up against his Creator.
The earth pricks him with thorns and briars;
the beasts of the field wound him with their teeth and horns.
Water covers him with floods and with storms;
the pirates of the sea assault him with plundering and battles.
The air infects him with pestilence and decay;
the birds of the air strike him with an attack from their beaks and claws.
Fire reduces his flesh and bones to ash,
the smoke of the fire blinds his eyes.
No man in Paradise would have been the enemy of another;
here among many men, no true friend is found.
As long as a man has wealth and honor, however,

6b2

Multos videtur habere amicos et fautores.[1]
Sed statim cum inceperit amicorum iuuamine indigere
Vix unum amicum experietur se habere.
Verus amicus comprobatur in articulo necessitatis
Quem non acced[a\i]t plaga ´neque`[3] occursio aduersitatis
Qui se et sua pro amico suo exponere non veretur[4]
Hic magnam caritatem habere non perhibetur.
Sed clementissimus deus maiorem caritatem habuit
Qui se et sua pro inimicis suis id est pro nobis exposuit.
Eramus enim inimi`ci´ dei et perpetuo carceri adiudicati.
Sed per suam misericordiam sumus misericorditer liberati.[5]
Oportebat enim nos omnes carcerem inferni ingredi
De quo non poteramus alicuius adiutorio [ ]eripi.
Tandem pater misericordiarum et deus tocius consolationis[6]
Clementer respexit statum nostre dampnacionis.
Et decreuit nos per semetipsum liberare
Super quo placuit sibi signum nobis per oliuam dare.
Quam columba inclusis in archa deferebat[7]
Que misericordiam dei futuram inclusis in ⌞lymbo⌟[8] pretendebat.
Sed non solum hiis qui erant in archa promittebatur
Sed et toti mundo signum salutis in oliua dabatur.
Sed hic idem premonstrauit deus in multis figuris
Sicut patet studiose lectori in diuinis scripturis.
O bone ihesu instrue nos ut sacras scripturas discamus
Et tuam in eis caritatem ad nos intelligere ualeamus.

6va

Capitulum tercium.[9]

Quoniam modum nostre redempcionis scire desideramus
Primo de annunciacione beate marie incipiamus.
Cum enim beata uentura erat christi incarnacio

---

[2] Right Panel: The Flood. Noah's ark is here depicted as a box-like floating castle, showing both the raven (*carnix*) which did not return and the dove (*columba*) with its olive branch, that did. Gen. 8.6–12. [1] See Prov. 14.20 [3] Added later by black ink scribe [4] Cf. John 15.13 [5] See Rom. 5.8–11 [6] 2 Cor. 1.3–4 [7] Gen. 8.8–9 [8] lymbo, L] archa, G [9] Left Panel: Annunciation to Anna. From the *Protoevangelion of James* 4.2; a non-canonical story popularized in the *Legenda Aurea* or *Golden Legend* of Jacobus de Voragine, there linked to the doctrine of the Immaculate Conception. The dove descends toward Anna's mouth; elsewhere it is shown kissing her, but with a clear analogy to the Annunciation to Mary intended, the dove is here still in flight. The announcement of the birth of Mary here parallels that of Cyrus, both of whom were chosen by God (Is. 44.28).

he seems to have many friends and patrons.
But as soon as he begins to need the help of his friends,
he will discover himself to have scarcely one friend.
A true friend is proved in the moment of need.
He whom neither plague nor an encounter with adversity approaches,
who does not fear to expose himself or his own on behalf of his friend
this man is not said to have great charity.
But the most merciful God had greater charity
who exposed Himself and His own on behalf of His enemies, that is, for us.
We were indeed enemies of God and had been sentenced to the eternal prison.
But through His mercy we have been mercifully set free.
For it was fitting that we all enter into the prison of hell
from which we would not have been able to be snatched by the help of anyone else.
At last, the Father of mercies and God of all consolations
mercifully regarded our condition of damnation.
And He decided to free us through Himself.
Concerning this it pleased him to give us a sign by means of the olive tree,
which the dove carried to those shut up in the Ark,
which presented the future compassion of God to those shut up in Limbo.
But not only was it sent to those who in the Ark were wandering,
but also the sign of salvation was given to the whole world in the olive tree.
But God has revealed this same thing in many figures
as is clear in the divine Scriptures to the zealous reader.
O good Jesus, instruct us that we may learn the sacred Scriptures
and in them we may be able to understand your charity to us.

Chapter Three

Because we desire to know the means of our redemption,
let us first begin with the annunciation [of the birth] of Blessed Mary.
For when the blessed Incarnation of Christ was to come

Necessarium fuit ut precederet matris sue generacio.
Quod ut facilius et lucidius intelligatur
Una parabola siue similitudo primo audiatur.
¶Homo quidam ab iericho in ierusalem[1] descendebat
Et in desertum ueniens in latrones incidebat.
Qui eum spoliauerunt et uulnerauerunt
Et semiuiuum reliquentes abierunt.
Uenientes autem sacerdotes et leuite ipsum pertransibant
Et[2] uulnera ipsius sanare nequebant.
Tandem samaritanus quidam illi appropinquabat
Et misericordia motus uulnera eius sanabat.
Et nisi samaritanus ille aduenisset
Nunquam sauciatus ille sanatus fuisset.
In hac parabola genus humanum siue homo designatur
Qui spoliatus est bonis et graciis sibi a deo datis
Et uulneratus est uulnere perpetue mortalitatis.
Qui multo tempore quasi semiuiuus iacebat
Quia in anima mortuus erat licet corpore uiuebat.
Quem nec sacer⸌dos⸍[3] nec leuita sanare potuerunt
Quia nec circumcisio nec pecunia hominem ad patriam reduxerunt.
Tandem samaritanus quidam appropinquabat

6vb[4] Et sauciati uulnera misericorditer sanabat.
Samaritanus custos interpretatur
Per quem christus custos noster designatur.
Et nisi custos [iste][5] in hunc mundum uenisset
Numquam homo in uitam eternam introisset.
Laudemus et benedicamus dominum ihesum christum
Qui uenit in hunc mundum sanare semiuiuum istum.
Cum autem filius dei in hunc mundum uenire satagebat
Uirginem de qua nasceretur premittere disponebat.
Misit ergo angelum qui concepcionem eius nunciauit
Et sanctificacionem eius in utero et nomen pariter intimauit.

---

[1] Lk. 10.30–35 [2] Et] quia L [3] Main text in lighter brown ink, and a small arrow points to "sacerdos" written out in full in margin in a later hand [4] Right Panel: King Astrages' Dream. Herodotus tells the story of this son of Cyaxares, who ascended to the throne of the Median Dynasty in the mid-6th century B.C. He had a dream in which his daughter gave birth to a son who would usurp him. The child turns out to be Cyrus, liberator of the Jewish exiles. Here the king sees a vine growing from his daughter's womb which then bore fruit and overshadowed his kingdom. Astrages is mentioned in deutrocanonical Dn. 13. [5] There is an erasure mark here

it was necessary that the birth of his mother should happen first,
so that it may be understood more easily and clearly,
a parable or illustration may first be heard.
A certain man went down from Jericho to Jerusalem
and, reaching a wilderness, he fell in with thieves
who robbed him and wounded him
and went away, leaving him half-dead.
But priests and Levites passed by him as they came
and they were not able to heal his wounds.
Finally, a certain Samaritan approached him
and, moved by mercy, healed his wounds.
And unless that Samaritan had come
the wounded man would never have been cured.
In this parable the human race or mankind is indicated,
who was robbed of the goods and graces given to him by God
and was wounded with the wound of everlasting death.
He lay for a long time as if half-dead,
since he was dead in spirit, although he was alive in body.
And neither the priest nor the Levite was able to heal him
since neither circumcision nor money brought man back to his homeland.
Finally, a certain Samaritan drew near

and mercifully healed the wounds of the injured man.
The Samaritan is interpreted as the Guardian
through whom Christ our Guardian is indicated.
And unless that Guardian had come into this world
man would never have entered into eternal life.
Let us praise and bless the Lord Jesus Christ
who came into this world to heal the one half-dead.
And when the Son of God made ready to come into the world
he arranged to send first the virgin through whom he would be born.
Therefore, he sent an angel who announced her conception
and made known her sanctification in the womb and her name likewise.

Hec est beatissima uirgo maria
Per quam uenit hinc sauciato[1] saucia pia.
Quam etiam deus in multis figuris premonstrauit
Et prophetarum oculis multipliciter insinuauit. *prima figura.*
¶Rex astrages uisionem mirabilem uidebat
Quod uidelicet de utero filie sue uitis pulcherrima crescebat
Que frondibus et foliis se amenissime dilatabat.
Et fructus proferens totum regnum suum subumbrabat.
Dictum est autem ei quam interpretacionem hec uisio gerat
Quod uidelicet de filia sua rex magnus nasciturus erat.
Hec filia post hoc cyrum regem genuerauit
Qui filios israel de captiuitate babilonica liberauit.[2]
Hec est litteralis huius uisionis significacio
Sed alia est mistica eius prefiguracio.

7a[3] Astragi monstratum est quod filia sua cyrum regem generaret
Joachim nunciatum est quod filia sua regem christum portaret.
Cyrus rex liberauit iudeos de captiuitate babylonica.
Et rex christus liberauit nos de captiuite dyabolica.
Filia ergo regis astragis figurauit mariam
Que protulit mundo uitem ueram et piam.
Benedicta sis tu o summi regis filia.
Flos candens super omnia lylia.
Benedicta sit tue concepcionis annunciacio
Per quam habuit ortum nostre captiuitatis liberacio
Benedictus sit deus pater qui te nobis destinauit
Benedictus sit dei filius qui te in matrem adoptauit.
Benedictus sit spiritus sanctus qui te in utero sanctificauit
Benedictus sit uterquam parens qui te mundo generauit.
¶De hac beatissima filia etiam salomon precinebat *secunda figura.*
Que in utero matris sue sanctificari debebat.
Nam ortum conclusum eam in canticis nominauit
Et fonti signato id est sigillato eam comparauit.[4]
Que[5] cum uirum[6] adhuc in utero conclusum ferebat
Spiritus sanctus ei sanctificaciom infundebat.
Et sigillo sancte trinitatis sic eam signabat.

---

[1] sauciato] sanatio, L [2] 1 Esdras 1.1–8, Dn. 13.65, 1 Esdras 5.13 [3] Left Panel: *Hortus Conclusus*. The enclosed garden, with a sealed fountain, is a figure for the virginity of Mary, drawing on the allegorizing of Canticle of Canticles 4.12 in the commentary by Bernard of Clairvaux and in St. Anthony of Padua's *In Domenica XV post Pentecosten*, 2.453. [4] Ct. 4.12 [5] Que] Quam, L [6] uirum] mater, L

This maiden is the most blessed Virgin Mary
through whom he next came, a pious remedy for the wounded
whom God revealed before in many figures
and announced to the eyes of the prophets in many ways. *Figure One*
King Astrages beheld a miraculous vision,
namely, that an exceedingly beautiful vine grew from the womb of his daughter
which spread out most pleasantly its fronds and leaves
and, producing fruit, was shading his whole kingdom.
And it was said to him what interpretation this vision bears:
namely, that a great king would be born from his daughter.
After this, this daughter gave birth to king Cyrus
who freed Israel from Babylonian captivity.
This is the literal significance of this vision
but its mystical prefiguration is something else.

It was shown to Astrages that his daughter would give birth to King Cyrus;
it was announced to Joachim that his daughter would bear Christ the King.
King Cyrus freed the Jews from Babylonian captivity;
and Christ the King freed us from diabolical captivity.
Therefore, the daughter of King Astrages symbolized Mary
who brought forth for the world a true and loving vine.
Blessed be you, O daughter of the highest King,
flower shining more than all lilies!
Blessed be the annunciation of your conception
through which liberation from our captivity arose!
Blessed be God the Father who designed you for us!
Blessed be the Son of God who chose you as his mother!
Blessed be the Holy Spirit who sanctified you in the womb!
Blessed be both parents who gave birth to you in the world!
Concerning this blessed daughter even Solomon predicted *Figure Two*
that she ought to be sanctified in the womb of her mother.
For in Canticles he called her an enclosed garden,
and compared her to a sealed-up spring (that is, a sealed spring).
And when she bore the man still enclosed in her womb,
the Holy Spirit poured his sanctification into her.
And thus sealed her with the seal of the Holy Trinity

Quod in eam numquam aliquid coinquinatum intrabat
O maria tu es uere ortus omnium deliciarum
Et fons indeficiens siciencium animarum.
¶Spiritus sanctus etiam nobis mariam necessarium ostendebat *tercia figura*.

7b[2] Quando per os balaam ortum eius promittebat[1]
Promisit enim quod de iacob oriretur stella
Per quam figurabatur maria futura dei cella.
Balaam populo israhelitico maledicere cogitabat
Sed spiritus sanctus maledicionem in benedicionem transmutabat.[3]
Per quod etiam spiritus sanctus figuraliter preostendebat.
Quod nostra maledictio in benedicionem conuerti debebat.
Et fieret mediante quadam puella
Cuius ortum prefigurabat in quadam stella.
Hec est beatissima maria uera stella maris
Fluctuancium ductrix adiutrix singularis.
Sine hac stella non poteramus hoc ⌊feruidum⌋[4] mare transire
Nec ad portum celestis patrie peruenire.
Quapropter deus ortum marie per stellam precinebat
Quia nos ad celestem patriam reducere disponebat.
Gratias agamus deo qui dedit nobis hanc maris stellam
Per quam effugere possumus huius maris periculosam procellam.
O peccator quantumcum que peccasti noli desperare
Hanc benedictam stellam oculis cordis contemplare.
In dubiis in periculis in neccessitatibus ipsam intuere.
Ipsa dirigit ipsa protegit ipsa perducit uere.
Hanc stellam theophilus respexit
Et ipsa eum pie ad portum salutis transuexit.
O bone Ihesu da nobis hanc stellam ita contemplari
Ut a cunctis periculis semper mereamur liberari.

[2] Right Panel: Balaam's Ass. In Nm. 22.21–35 the story is told of a miscreant prophet being barred from his journey by an angel of the Lord, visible to his donkey but not to himself. Admonished, Balaam prophesies that "a star shall come out of Jacob; a scepter shall rise out of Israel" (Nm. 24.17). Although traditionally seen as a messianic prophecy and applied to Christ (e.g., *Glossa Ordinaria*, PL 113, col. 426) the star is here adapted to the Virgin Mary, called *stella maris*, "star of the sea" through a scribal error in copying an etymology of Mary's Hebrew name. By the 8th-century hymn of Paschasius Radbertus, *Ave, Maris Stella*, it had become a Marian title, long divorced from the biblical prophecy. [1] Nm. 24.17–19 [3] Nm. 22.12, 38, Nm. 23.7–9, 18–24
[4] feruidum, L] feruide, G

because no defilement ever entered into her.
O Mary, you are truly the source of all delights
and an unfailing spring for our parched souls.
And the Holy Spirit revealed that Mary was necessary to us *Figure Three*

when through Balaam's mouth he promised her birth.
For he promised that a star would arise from Jacob
through which Mary was symbolized, the future sanctuary of God.
Balaam thought to curse the Israelite people
but the Holy Spirit transformed the curse into a blessing.
And through this the Holy Spirit figuratively revealed
that our curse ought to be turned into blessing.
And it would come about by the mediation of a certain girl
whose birth was prefigured in a certain star.
This is the most blessed Mary, true star of the sea
the solitary helper-guide of those tossed at sea.
Without this star, we would not be able to cross this raging sea
nor to come into the port of the heavenly fatherland.
Accordingly, God presaged the birth of Mary through a star
since he arranged to lead us back to our heavenly homeland.
Let us give thanks to God who gave to us this star of the sea
through whom we are able to escape the dangerous tempests of this sea.
O sinner, howsoever greatly you have sinned—do not despair.
With the eyes of the heart, contemplate this blessed Star
gaze upon her in doubts, in dangers, in times of need.
Truly she directs, she protects, she guides.
Theophilus observed this star
and she led him faithfully to the harbor of salvation.
O good Jesus, grant to us to contemplate this star in such a way
that we might always be worthy to be rescued from all dangers.

7va *Capitulum quartum.*[1]

*I*n precedenti capitulo audiuimus de beate uirginis annunciacione
Consequenter audiamus de ipsius ortu siue generacione.
Progenies Marie suuˋmˊ[2] processum habuit de stirpe yesse patris dauid.
De quo ysaias pulchre per spiritum vaticinauit.
//Prophecia ysaie legitur hec esse *prima figura*.
Egredietur uirga de radice yesse.
Et flos de radice eius descendet[3]
Super quem septiformis gratia spiritus sancti requiescebat.
Hec uirgo est maria fecundata per celestem rorem
Que produxit nobis christum amenissimum florem.
In hoc flore inueniuntur vii medicamenta bona
Per quem designatur sancti spiritus vii dona.
Inueniuntur in hoc flore tactus odor et fructus.
Color et folia succus et gustus.
Hec vii sunt egrotanti anime ualde medicinalia
Contra vii peccata mortalia.
Tactu huius floris homo tumore superbo exhonoratur
Hoc d⌊o⌋no timoris ad cognicionem sui humiliatur.
Qui enim cogitat quam tactus est lucifer propter superbie tumorem
Humiliat se et incipit habere dei timorem.
Si enim deus a luciferis angelis noluit superbiam sustinere
Multo minus vvlt hominem superbientem secum habere.
Ipsi habebant gratias unde quodammodo poterant gloriari
Quid habet putredinosus homo de quo poterit eleuari.
Odore huius floris duricia inuidi cordis mollificatur

7vb[4] Et dono pietatis ad compassionem afflictorum liberatur[5].
Inuidus enim ad nullius afflictionem conmouetur

[1] Left Panel: Nativity of the Virgin. Recounted briefly in the *Protoevangelion of James* (3.11), this image depicts Anna going into labor, supported by two women, a motif found in reference both to Mary and to Olympias, Alexander the Great's mother. See Grabar, *Christian Iconography: A Study of its Origins*, 129–130; figs. 306–310.
[2] Added later by a corrector with darker ink [3] descendet] ascendet, L; [4] Right Panel: Vines from the Root of Jesse. The text in Is. 11.1–2 refers to the Messiah as a rod or shoot (Vg. virga) out of the stem of Jesse, an image frequently found next to the Matthean genealogy of Christ (Mt. 1.1–18), where Joseph is identified as in the direct lineage. The idea here in the SHS text, namely that Mary was of the stock of Jesse, has no biblical warrant but a later association, indebted to the *Protoevangelion* which makes her to be "of the tribe of David" (9.4). Tertullian's *De carne Christi* 21.5 connects the term *virga* (shoot) to *virgo* (virgin) and applies it to Mary. The connection is supported by both St. Augustine and St. Jerome, who see Joseph as a kinsman redeemer. The flowering stem of Jesse is connected to the seven fruits of the Holy Spirit, though the text makes it clear that these derive from the "flower," which is Christ. [5] liberatur] dilatator, L

Chapter Four

In the last chapter, we heard about the annunciation of the Blessed Virgin
next let us hear about her origin or birth.
Mary's family came from the stock of Jesse, the father of David.
As Isaiah beautifully foretold through the Spirit.
This is the prophecy of Isaiah: *Figure One*
"A rod will come out of the root of Jesse.
And from his root a flower shall come forth"
upon which the sevenfold grace of the Holy Spirit was resting.
This is the virgin Mary, made fruitful by the celestial dew,
she who brought us Christ, the loveliest flower.
From this flower come seven good remedies
which indicate the seven gifts of the Holy Spirit.
In this flower are touch, scent, and fruit,
color and petals, juice and taste.
These seven are great balms for a sick soul,
against the seven deadly sins.
By the touch of this flower man is deprived of the swelling of pride;
by this gift of fear, a man is humbled to self-examination.
For he who considers how Lucifer was stricken because of the swelling of his pride
abases himself and begins to fear God.
For if God did not suffer pride from the angels of Lucifer
how much less does he want with him a proud man?
They themselves had grace by which they could be glorified in some way;
what does corrupt man have to lift him?
The scent of this flower softens the hardness of an envious heart

and by the gift of piety, it is freed to show compassion for the afflicted.
For the envious man is moved by the affliction of no one;

Pius autem omni afflicto compatitur et miseretur.
Qui ergo susceperit odorem id est exempla sui saluatoris
Pius et compassiuus est afflictis omnibus horis.
Exemplo enim domini nostri ihesu christi flet cum flentibus[1]
Et compatitur tam in anima quam in corpore pacientibus.
Fructu huius floris vesania ire remouetur
Et dono sciencie homo ⌊decenter⌋[2] conuersari cum hominibus edocetur.
Homo iracundus nullam habet mentis discrecionem
Et ideo nescit bonam et decentem conuersacionem.
Donum sciencie mansuetum est et suaue
Et docet bene conuersari in medio nacionis praue.[3]
Qui ergo huius floris fructum id est christi opera uoluerit imitari
Ex ipsis operibus discit cum hominibus debite conuersari.
Colore huius floris paralisis accidie propulsatur
Et dono fortitudinis ad sustinendum homo corroboratur.
Nullam enim sentit penam nec ⌊veretur⌋[4] laborem
Qui intuetur huius floris id est crucifixi colorem
Si enim elephas ⌊adspectu⌋[5] sanguinis uue ad pugnam animatur[6]
Multo magis homo ⌊adspectu⌋ sanguinis christi ad laborem fortificatur.
Qui ergo deuote respexerit roseum colorem huius floris
Hylariter [compara⌊t⌋ur] compatitur || et sustinet omnibus horis.||[7]
Foliis huius floris ydropias auaricie profugatur
Et per donum consilii sitis pecuniarum refrenatur.

8a[8]
Folia huius floris sunt uerba christi et eius doctrina
Qua consuluit contempnere temporalia propter diuina.[9]
Quicumque hanc doctrinam diligenter studet retinere
Hic spiritum in se perhibetur habere.
Et talis non curat temporalia sibi congregare
Sed ea que habet paratus est indignantibus ministrare.
Succu huius floris replecio gule expuitur
Et donum[10] intellectus sensus cognicionis acuitur.
Succus enim habet colorem uiridem qui visum clarificat
Et donum intellectus sensus[11] cognicionis purificat.

[1] See Rom. 12.15 [2] decenter, L] docetur, G [3] See Ja. 3.17 [4] veretur, L] feret, G [5] adspectu, L] asumptu, G. See also following line [6] 1 Mcc. 6.34 [7] compatitur} operatur (as G appears to have done before scribal correction) [8] Left Panel: The Closed Gate. The closed gate of Ez. 44.1–3 became by the 13th century one of the signs of Mary's perpetual virginity, largely through the Marian typology popularized by St. Anthony of Padua, *Purificatione Sancta Mariae* 3.722. [9] See Col. 3.2 [10] donum] dono, L [11] Possible eyeskip and duplicated line] Et dono intellectus Christus ad cognitionem cestestium invitat, L

the pious man, however, has compassion and shows mercy to everyone afflicted.
Therefore, he who will have drawn in the scent (that is, the example of his Savior)
is pious and compassionate to the afflicted at all times.
For according to the example of our Lord Jesus Christ, he weeps with those who weep
and has compassion as much for those who suffer in mind as in body.
By the fruit of this flower the madness of anger is removed,
and by the gift of knowledge man is taught to live decently among men.
The angry man has no discernment of mind
and for this reason is ignorant of good and fitting behavior.
The gift of knowledge is gentle and also sweet,
and it teaches to live well in the midst of a depraved people.
Thus he who wishes to imitate the fruit of this flower (that is, the works of Christ)
learns from Christ's works to live properly with mankind.
By the color of this flower the paralysis of sloth is repulsed
and by the gift of fortitude man is strengthened to endure.
For he feels no pain, nor fears work,
who considers the color of this flower (that is, of the crucified one).
For if an elephant is incited to battle by the sight of the blood of a grape
how much more is man strengthened for labor by the sight of the blood of Christ.
Therefore, he who looks devoutly upon the rosy color of this flower
suffers cheerfully and endures all hours.
By the petals of this flower the bloating of avarice is put to flight
and through the gift of counsel the thirst for wealth is restrained.

The petals of this flower are the words of Christ and his teaching,
which counseled [us] to think little of temporal things for the sake of divine things.
Whoever diligently strives to keep this teaching
he is reported to have Christ's spirit in himself,
and such a one does not take pains to gather together fleeting things for himself
but he is ready to give what he has to the poor.
By the juice of this flower fullness of gluttony is rejected
and the gift of the understanding, of sense, of knowledge is sharpened.
For the juice has a green color which clarifies the vision
and purifies the gift of the understanding, of sense, of knowledge.

Gulosus non cognoscit celestia sed terestia
Sed donum intellectus docet per terestia cognoscere celestia.
Ut si videmus clarum solem et delicabilem florem
Cognoscimus clarum et delicabilem esse illorum conditorem.
Gustu huius floris delicacio luxurie amarificatur
Et dono sapientie id est sapide sciencie anima delicatur.
Cum enim gustauerit homo spiritus sancti dulcedinem
Omnem delicacionem carnis reputat amaritudinem.
Sicut enim gustato melle non sapit palato cibus naturalis
Sic gustato spiritu sancto desipit omnis uoluptas carnalis.
O quam magna multitudo dulcedinis tue domine
Quam abscondisti timentibus te.[1] *secunda figura.*
¶Patet igitur in uirga yesse unde maria sit exorta
Sed quomodo florem produxit patet in clausa porta.
Clausam portam ezechiel in spiritu uidebat[2]

8b[3] Que numquam in eternum aperiri debebat.
Dominus solus per eam clausam uolebat transire
In quo patet modus parturicionis mire.
Intelligat hoc qui potest
Non ⌊sicut⌋[4] nos nascimur christus natus est.
Non esset mirum aperire portam et transire
Sed mirabile est ualde per clausam portam ire.
¶Salomon etiam domino templum edificauit *tercia figura.*
In quo mistice ortum marie prefigurauit.
Templum salomonis habuit pinnacula tria
Per que signatur triplex aureola in maria.
Prima est uirgin[e]um[5] quia uirginitatem primo uouit
Secunda est matyrum quia martyr in anima fuit.[6]
Habuit denique aureolam predicatorum et doctorum.
Quia erat evvangelistarum edoctrix et apostolorum.
Templum erat constructum de marmore candido
Et ornatus intrinsecus auro mundissimo.
Sic maria erat candida nitore mundissime castitatis.
Et ornata intrinsecus auro persanctissime caritatis.

---

[1] Ps. 30.20 [2] Ez. 44.1–3 [3] Right Panel: Temple of Solomon. This simple image is likewise traceable to Antonian typology for Mary (*In Domenica XV post Pentecosten* 2.453). As the Temple of Solomon was intended as a sanctuary for the divine presence, so Mary's womb (cf. Ez. 40–44; 3 Kings 6.11–14). The triple haloes (towers) signify her sovereignty over the three spiritual estates: virgins, martyrs, and teachers of the Church. [4] sicut, L] sufficit, G [5] The scribe appears to have written *uirgineum*, and then scrubbed out the "e", leaving a large gap [6] See Lk. 2.35

A gluttonous man does not understand heavenly things but earthly ones.
But the gift of understanding teaches how to perceive the heavenly through the earthly.
So that, if we see the bright sun or a lovely flower,
we recognize the Creator of those things to be bright and lovely.
By the taste of this flower the pleasure of lust is made bitter
and the soul takes pleasure in the gift of wisdom (that is, prudent knowledge).
For when a person has tasted the sweetness of the Holy Spirit,
every pleasure of the flesh he considers bitterness.
For just as after honey is tasted, natural food does not have savor to the palate,
so when the Holy Spirit is tasted, every carnal pleasure looses its relish.
"O how great is the multitude of your sweetness, Lord,
which you have prepared for those who fear you." *Figure Two*
Therefore, how Mary would come to be is revealed in the rod of Jesse,
but how she brought forth the flower is revealed in the closed gate.
Ezekiel beheld in a vision a closed gate

which never should be opened in eternity.
The Lord alone wished to pass through that closed gate,
by which the manner of his wonderful birth is revealed.
Let anyone understand this who can.
Christ was not born as we were born;
it would not be wonderful to open a gate and go through,
but it is exceedingly wonderful to go through a closed gate.
Also Solomon built a temple to the Lord *Figure Three*
by which the birth of Mary was mystically prefigured.
The temple of Solomon had three pinnacles
through which the triple halo on Mary is signified.
The first is the halo of virgins, because she vowed virginity from the beginning;
the second is of martyrs, because she was a martyr in spirit.
Finally, she had the halo of the teachers and doctors [of the Church],
because she was the teacher of the evangelists and apostles.
The temple was constructed from shining white marble
and decorated within with the purest gold.
In such a way was Mary shining white with the sheen of purest chastity
and decorated within with the gold of most holy charity.

O quam pulchra est casta generacio cum caritate
O quam pulchra est maria ornata caritate et castitate.
In templo erat coclea per quam sursum ascendebatur
In maria erat diuinitas per quam nobis ascensus in celum parabatur.
O bone ihesu da nobis meritis tue sanctissime matris
Sursum ascendentem[1] ad gloriam dei patris. amen.

8va *Capitulum quintum.*[2]

*I*n precedenti capitulo audiumus quomodo beata uirgo fuit nata
Consequenter audiamus quomodo fuit in templo domino oblata.[3]
Cumque minima[4] esset parentes eam ad templum attulerunt
Et ut domino seruiret et litteras disceret pontifici tradiderunt.
[5]Cuius oblacio per mensam solis in zabulo prefigurabatur
De qua particula ⌊historie⌋[6] breuiter audiatur.
Piscatores quidam rete suum in mare proiecerunt
Et causa mirabili mensam auream extraxerunt.
Mensa illa erat tota de auro puro et multum preciosa
Et videbatur omnium oculis mirabiliter speciosa.
Ibidem in littore maris templum quoddam erat edificatum
Et in honore solis quem gens illa coluit dedicatum.
Ad templum illud mensa illa est deportata
Et ipso soli tamquam deo quem colebant oblata.
Mensa illa per totum mundum usa est hoc uocabulo
Et communiter dicebatur mensa solis in sabulo.
Sabulum enim arenosa terra appellatur
Et ibi templum solis in arenoso loco habebatur.
Per mensam igitur solis maria est pulchre figurata
Que vero soli id est summo deo est oblata.

[1]ascendentem] ascendere, L [2]Left Panel: Mary Presented in the Temple. From *Protoevangelion* chs. 7, 8; *Pseudo Matthew.*, ch. 4. The image shows Mary as if she were a statue on a pedestal, crowned and being worshipped by her parents Joachim and Anna and a bishop. The Feast of the Presentation of Mary (Nov. 21) appeared in the Eastern Church sometime in the 6th century, but not until the 11th century in southern Italy and then officially in the papal chapel at Avignon in 1372 by a decree of Gregory IX. Inclusion in the SHS iconographic program indicates the influence of earlier depictions, such as that of Giotto (Scrovegni Chapel, 1305) and the dramatic office for the Presentation by Philippe de Mezières (1327–1405) indicates a vigorous campaign for this feast throughout the 14th century. [3]Protoevangelium of James 7 [4]minima] triennis, L [5]Another scribe has added "prima figura" in the margin to the left of this line and has renumbered the other figure on this page. There are two additional, faint markings in this margin area: 1. A note to rubricate a large initial "I" and a sign for a figure. The figure sign was missed during rubrication, hence the corrections. [6]historie, L] hostie, G

O how lovely is a chaste begetting with charity!
O how lovely is Mary, decorated with charity and chastity!
In the temple, there was a spiral stair through which one ascended upwards;
in Mary, there was the godhead through which the ascent to heaven was prepared for us.
O good Jesus, grant us, according to the merits of your most holy mother,
to ascend upwards to the glory of God the Father. Amen.

Chapter Five

In the last chapter, we heard how the Blessed Virgin was born,
next let us hear how she was offered to the Lord in the temple.
When she was very small, her parents brought her to the temple
and they gave her over to the priest so that she might serve the Lord and learn the letters.
Her dedication was prefigured through the Table of the Sun in the sand
concerning a little part of the story we shall briefly hear.
Certain fishermen cast forth their net into the sea
and miraculously drew out a golden table
That table was completely made from pure gold and was very precious
and seemed wonderously beautiful to the eyes of all.
In the same place on the shore of the sea, a certain temple was built
and was dedicated in honor of the sun, which that nation worshipped.
The table was conveyed to that temple
and presented to the Sun-God himself, as it were, whom they worshipped.
That table was used throughout the whole world by this designation
and was commonly spoken of as the "Table of the Sun in the sand".
For the ground of the beach is called "sand"
and the temple of the sun was established there in a sandy place.
Therefore, through the Table of the Sun, Mary is symbolized beautifully,
who was indeed was offered to the sun (that is, the highest God).

Mensa solis oblata est in templo solis materialis
Maria oblata est in templo solis eternalis.
Mensam solis multi et magni uidere affectabant
Marie ortum tam angeli quam homines desiderabant.
Mensa solis facta fuit de materia purissima

8vb[1] Et maria fuit mente et corpore mundissima
Pulchre maria est per mensam prefigurata.
Quia per eam celestis esca nobis est collata.
Nam ipsa filium dei ihesum christum nobis generauerit
Qui nos suo corpore et sanguine refocillauit.
Benedicta sit ista beatissima mensa
Per quam collata est nobis esca tam salubris et inmensa.
Benedicti sint parentes qui eam generauerunt
Et eam pro nostra salute domino deo obtulerunt. [–*Prima*]\secunda/ *figura*.
¶In ueteri testamento nullum legimus filiam suam domino obtulisse
Nisi yepte qui legitur eam immolasse et occidisse.[2]
Yepte obtulit filiam suam domino sed indiscrete et non recte.
Ioachim et anna obtulerunt filiam suam domino rite et perfecte.
Ipsi enim filiam suam non immolauerunt neque occiderunt
Sed viuam ut domino viua deseruiret obtulerunt.
Yepte fecit uotum quod a sanctis doctoribus uituperatur
Maria fecit uotum quod tam a deo quam ab angelis collaudatur.
Filia yepte defleuit quod uirgo mori debebat
Maria primo uotum uirginitatis innuebat.
Illa defleuit quod nullam prolem post se relinquebat
Dolens quod de sua posteritate christus nasciturus non erat.
Et quod illa infelicem se reputans defleuit
Hoc maria felix et felicissima feliciter inuenit.
Filia yepte oblata est post uictoriam pro gratiarum actione
Maria oblata est ante uictoriam pro uictorie collacione.

9a[3] Filia yepte oblata est pro uictoria hostium temporalium
Et per mariam facta est uictoria hostium infernalium.

---

[1] Right Panel: Golden Table of the Sun. This is the second of nine legends from pagan mythology employed in SHS typology. The story of the finding of a marvelous golden table while net-fishing in the sea near a temple to the Sun God was incorporated earlier in the *Bible Historiée* as a prefigurement of Mary in the Temple as the altar. [2] Jdg. 11.29–39 [3] Left Panel: Sacrifice of Jephte's Daughter. The story in Jdg. 11.30–39, conventionally used as an example of the potentially tragic consequences of a rash promise, is here a foil for the wise vow of Joachim and Anna. The young virgin daughter of Jephte is crowned, keeping the visual parallel with Mary, and kneels for her death on an altar.

The Table of the Sun was offered in the temple of the material sun
Mary was presented in the temple of the Eternal Sun.
The many and the great were desiring to see the Table of the Sun;
both angels and men were longing for the coming of Mary.
The Table of the Sun was made from the purest material

and Mary was in mind and body most pure.
Beautifully is Mary prefigured through the Table
since through her, heavenly food is conveyed to us.
For she herself bore for us Jesus Christ, the son of God,
who revived us with his own body and blood.
Blessed be that most blessed table
through which such health-giving and boundless food is conveyed to us.
Blessed be the parents who bore her
and presented her to the Lord God for our salvation. *Figure Two*
In the Old Testament, we read that no one offered his daughter to the Lord
except for Jephthah, who, it is read, sacrificed and killed her.
Jephthah offered his daughter to the Lord, but did so unwisely and not properly;
Joachim and Anna presented their daughter to the Lord appropriately and perfectly.
For they themselves neither sacrificed nor killed their own daughter,
but they offered her alive, so that living, she might serve the Lord.
Jephthah made a vow that is condemned by the holy teachers;
Mary made a vow that is praised as much by God as by the angels.
Jephthah's daughter lamented that she should die a virgin;
Mary signified from the first her vow of virginity.
The daughter of Jephthah lamented that no offspring remained behind her,
grieving because the Christ would not be born from her offspring.
And she lamented that, considering herself unfortunate;
this vow Mary, the happy and most happy one, accepted joyfully.
Jephthah's daughter was offered after a victory in thanksgiving;
Mary was offered before the victory as a donation for the victory.

Jephthah's daughter was offered for victory over temporal enemies
and through Mary the victory over infernal enemies was accomplished.

Illa indiscrete oblata est deo postea seruire nequiuit
Maria post oblacionem suam semper domino seruiuit.
Qualiter autem deo seruiuit et quam uitam amplexabatur *tercia figura.*
Hoc in orto illo qui suspensilia dictus erat prefigurabatur.
Quem rex persarum uxori sue in alta structura plantauit
De quo patriam suam delonge contemplari desiderauit.
Per quod contemplatiua uita marie designatur
Que patriam celestem semper contemplari nitebatur.
Nam omni tempore contemplationi et deuocioni erat intenta
Numquam ociosa numquam secularis est inuenta.
Semper contemplationi aut oracioni deuotissime se dabat
Aut lecione aut operacione se diligentissime occupabat.
Psalmodiam aut uersus ymnidicos iubilando psallebat.
Sepius in oracione et deuocione dulcissime flebat.
Pro salute generis humani sine intermissione dominum exorabat
Scripturas de aduentu christi freqenter legere non cessabat.
Quidquid in scripturis de incarnacione ⌊et⌋ aduentu dei inueniebat
Hoc osculando et amplexando dulciter relegebat.
Quando cetere uirgines ad propria remeabant
Ipsa semper in templo domini esse affectabat
Ipsa manebat ipsa [ipsa] studebat
Ipsa legendo et relegendo proficiebat.
Que in templo domini lauanda erant ipsa lauabat

9b[1] Et que mundanda erant ipsa mundabat.
Numquam dormitare numquam dormire consueuit
Nisi quando necessitas legittima ipsam coegit.
Et licet dormuit uel dormitaret eius corpus[2]
Et tamen semper eius iunior vigilaret animus.
Et hoc est quod salomon ex eius persona indicat
Ego dormio et cor meum uigilat[3]
Tam prudenter tam humiliter tam deuote se habebat.
Quod uita ipsius cunctis uiuentibus exemplum prebebat.
Sermo eius erat ualde discretus et perrarus[4]

[1] Right Panel: Queen of Persia's Garden. The fabulous hanging gardens, according to such ancient writers as Strabo, Diodorus Siculus, Quintus Curtius, and Josephus, were built by Nabuchodonosor for his Median wife. Garden imagery for Mary is more typically drawn from allegories of the Canticles of Canticles; here the author seeks to characterize the splendor of the contemplative life, with the Temple being figured as a spiritual garden of delight. [2] Stain damage for this and the next three lines (4–7) [3] Ct. 5.2 [4] perrarus] parcus, L

The former woman was unwisely offered to God; afterwards she was unable to serve.
Mary, after her dedication, served the Lord at all times.
And how she served God and what life she lived *Figure Three*
was prefigured in that garden which was called "the hanging gardens,"
which the king of the Persians planted for his wife in a tall building
from which she desired to gaze upon her homeland from afar.
Through the garden the contemplative life of Mary is indicated
who was always striving to contemplate the heavenly kingdom.
For she was intent at all times on contemplation and devotion.
Never was she found idle, never worldly.
She always gave herself to contemplation or prayer most devoutly
or she occupied herself most diligently with reading or working.
She sang psalms or hymnal verses with rejoicing.
Very often was she weeping most sweetly in prayer and devotion.
She entreated the Lord for the salvation of the human race without interruption
she did not cease to frequently read the scriptures concerning the coming of Christ.
Whatever she found in the scriptures concerning the Incarnation [and] coming of God
she re-read sweetly, with kissing and cherishing.
When the other virgins were returning to their own homes,
she desired to live always in the temple of the Lord.
She remained there; she studied;
she made progress by reading and reading over again.
She washed those things in the temple of the Lord which needed to be washed

and she cleansed those things that needed to be cleansed.
She never became accustomed to drowsing, never to sleeping,
except when real necessity forced her.
And although her body rested or slept,
yet always her inner soul would keep watch.
And this is what Solomon himself reveals:
"I sleep and my heart stands watch."
So prudently, so humbly, so devoutly was she comporting herself
that her life offered an example to all living.
Her speech was extremely discreet and very rare:

Semper dulcis semper suauis numquam amarus.
Nullum pauperem nullum debilem despiciebat
Dulciter omnes salutabat et dulciter reddebat.
Ultra quam dici {non} potest humilis erat misericors et deuota
Tamquam diuinis intenta et deo dedita tota.
Libros prophetarum et sanctas litteras optime intelligebat
Utpote quam spiritus sanctus doctor optimus instruebat.
Numquam in uirum proiecit oculum nec infixit aspectum
Numquam ceruicem numquam collum portabat erectum.
Oculos ad terram defixos inter homines semper habebat
Sed cor sursum in celum erectum gerebat.
Quidquid boni quidquid laudis potest dici scribi uel cantari
Hoc de beatissima uirgine secure potest predicari.
O bone ihesu da nobis eam in hoc seculo sic laudare
Ut tecum et secum in eternum mereamur habitare.

9va *Capitulum vi*[1]

*I*n precepti capitulo audiuimus quomodo maria est oblata
Consequenter audiamus quomodo et quare uiro fuit desponsata
Quare dominus uoluit matrem suam uiro desˊponsariˋ[2]
De hiis possunt viii raciones assignaˊriˋ
Primo ne per fornicacionem concepisse ˊputareturˋ
Et tamquam fornicatrix in iudicione condempnˊaˋreˊturˋ
Secundo ut uirgo uiri adiutorio et ministerio frˊuereturˋ
Et quocunque pergeret non soliuaga et uana putaretur.
Tercio ne dyabolus incarnacionem christi inuestigaret.
Et uirginem sine uiro concepisse considˋerˊaret.
Quarto ut maria testem sue castitatis habere probaretur
Quia plus marito suo quam cuiquam alteri crederetur.
Quinto ut series genealogi[ạ]e per uirum texeretur
Et genealogia christi a ioseph uirum marie produceretur.
Mos enim scripture ˋeratˊ genealogiam ducere non ad uxores
Sed tantummodo ad sponsos et ad mares.

---

[1] Left Panel: Betrothal of Joseph and Mary. Pseudo-Matthew 8.12 mentions the marriage; in canonical accounts in Mt. 2 and Lk. 2 Mary is referred to simply as Joseph's "betrothed," and an oath of betrothal rather than marriage per se is what our text has here (fol. 10, line 1). This makes Mary a paragon of virginity, in ecclesiology considered the highest state of the religious life. [2] There is an ink spill in the ms at this column down, but it has been soaked up and the letters re-inked in darker and thinner letters

always soft, always sweet, never bitter.
She looked down on no poor person, no cripple;
she greeted all sweetly and replied [to all] sweetly.
She was humble, merciful, and devout, beyond what can be described,
like one intent on divine things and wholly dedicated to God.
She understood excellently the books of the prophets and the holy writings
as is natural, as the Holy Spirit, the best teacher, was instructing her.
She never cast her eye nor fixed her gaze upon a man;
she never carried her head or her neck up high.
Among people she always kept her eyes fixed on the ground,
but she bore her heart upwards into lofty heaven.
Anything good, anything praise-worthy that can be said, written, or sung—
these things can be safely affirmed concerning the most Blessed Virgin.
O good Jesus, grant us to praise her in such a way in this world,
that we may worthily dwell with you and with her in eternity.

Chapter Six

In the last chapter we heard how Mary was offered up,
next let us hear how and in what way she was betrothed to a man.
Why the Lord wished his mother to be espoused to that man
eight reasons are able to be given.
First, lest she be thought to have conceived through fornication
and like a fornicator be condemned in judgment.
Second, that the virgin might benefit from the help and service of a man
and that wherever she would travel, she might not be thought alone and idle.
Third, lest the devil look closely into the incarnation of Christ
and observe that the virgin had conceived without a man.
Fourth, that Mary might have a witness to her chastity
because credence would be given to her husband more than any other.
Fifth, so that the line of genealogy might be wrought through the husband,
and the genealogy of Christ might be derived from Joseph, the husband of Mary.
Indeed, the habit of scripture was to derive genealogy not by the wives
but only by husbands and males.

Sexto ut matri⌊mo⌋nium[1] sanctum esset approbaret
Et a nullo spernendum et incusandum demonstraret.
UII° ut uirginitatem in matrimonio seruari licere deceret[2]
Si uterque coniux ratum et placitum teneret.
Octauo ne coniugati de salute sua desperarent
Et uirgines tantum electas et se despectas cogitarent.
Omnem enim statum et bene seruatum dominus approbare ueniebat
Et ideo mater sua uirgo et desponsata et uidua erat.
Quamuis autem hii tres status sancti esse approbarentur

9vb[3] Tamen inter se differenciam magnam habere uidentur.
Matrimonium sanctum et bonum esse approbatur
Si tamen tempus modus intencio debite teneatur.
Melior autem est matrimonio castitas uidualis
Sed optima est et superexcellit mundicia uirginalis.
Matrimonio debetur fructus tricesimus
Viduis sexagesimus virginibus centesimus.
Preciosum perhibetur ˋesseˊ auricalcum
Preciosuis argentum sed preciosissimum aurum.
Lucifer mane consurgens uidetur esse lucidus
Luna autem est lucidior sed sol lucidissimus.
Dulcis uidetur esse leticia et delectacio huius seculi
Dulcior vere est amenitas paradysi sed dulcissima celi.
Quamuis autem et superexcellat et optima ⌊sit uirginitas⌋
Tamen non ualet nisi seruetur simul mentis integritas.
Qui enim uirginitatem seruat carne et ˋnonˊ mente
Non habebit aureolam uirginum in eternitate.
Que autem mente uirgo est et si uiolenter corrumpatur
Non perdit aureolam sed dupliciter remuneratur.
Habebit enim aureolam pro mentis virginitate
In super premium pro passione violenter sibi illate.
Aureola autem perdita per mentis corrupcionem
Recuperari potest in hac uita per contricionem.
Que autem carne uoluntarie uiolatur
Illius aureola⌊m⌋[4] nulla contricione recuperatur.

---

[1] matrimonium, L] matri omnium, G [2] deceret] doceret, L [3] Right Panel: Marriage of Sara and Tobias. The account of this strange marriage in Tb. 6.10–7.14, a 3rd-century B.C. diaspora legend. is designed to stress the theme of kinsman-redeemer, a feature which connects it to the narratives about Joseph and Mary. Whereas in the previous image Joseph and Mary's hands are joined by "supreme pontifex," here the officiant is Sara's father, Raguel, not an unusual Jewish practice in the diaspora. [4] aureola, L] aureolam, G

Sixth, so that he might confirm that the marriage state is holy
and that he might show that it should be scorned or blamed by no one.
Seventh, that so it might be suitable to allow virginity to be preserved in marriage
if each spouse should have consented and be agreeable.
Eighth, lest the married should despair for their salvation
and think virgins so elect and themselves despicable.
For the Lord came to confirm every state and service when well served,
and therefore, his own mother was a virgin, and married, and widowed.
However, although these three states were confirmed as holy,

nevertheless, between them there seems to be a great difference.
Marriage is confirmed to be holy and good
if adhered to properly in time, manner, and intention.
Moreover, the chastity of the widow is better than marriage,
but the chastity of the virgin is best and surpasses purity.
Fruit thirtyfold is owed to marriage,
to widows, sixtyfold, and to virgins a hundredfold.
Brass is regarded as precious,
silver as more precious, but gold as most precious.
The morning star arising early seems to be bright,
the moon is yet brighter, but the sun is brightest.
The joys and pleasure of this life seem to be sweet;
sweeter truly is the delight of paradise, but the sweetest that is of heaven.
And although virginity both excels above and is best,
yet it does not avail unless at the same time integrity of mind be preserved.
For she who keeps virginity with flesh and not with the mind
will not have the halo of virgins in eternity.
But if she, who is a virgin in her mind, is violently raped,
she does not lose her halo but it is compensated twice over.
She will indeed have the halo for virginity of mind
in addition to a reward for the suffering brought violently against her.
Moreover, the halo lost through the corruption of the mind
can be restored through contrition in this life.
Yet she who is defiled willingly in the flesh
may not restore her halo by any amount of contrition.

10a[1] ¶Maria autem licet uiro in desponsacione iungeretur *prima figura*
Tamen mente et carne uirgo in eternum permansisse perhibetur.
Et tamen dicere potuit sicut sara raguelis filia
Munde seruaui animam meam ab omni concupiscentia.[2]
Sara uii uiris desponsata fuit
Et tamen uirgo intacta permansit.
Quanto magis potuit maria unum sponsum habere
Et tamen uirgo immaculata in eternum permanere.
Si saram a septem uiris custodiuit a⌊s⌋modeus
Quomodo ab uno uiro non custodiret matrem suam uerus deus.
Quocienscumque ioseph matrem dei aspiciebat
Splendorem quendam diuinum ab ipsa procedere uidebat.
Et ideo numquam faciem intueri audebat.
Nisi forte quando hoc aliquando casu aliquo accidebat.
Tobyas et sara tribus noctibus castitatem seruauerunt
Maria et ioseph toto tempore uite sue virgines permanserunt.
Joseph uirgo erat et de progenie dauid natus
Et diuino nutu marie tamquam custos associatus.
Non quod Maria ipsius custodia aliquatenus indigeret
Sed ut propter humanam suspicionem eum custodem haberet.
Ipsa enim custodem uerum et summum deum habebat
Qui eam ab omni hostili incursion custodiebat.
Habuit ergo unum custodem celestem
Et alium custodem terrestrem.

10b[3] ¶Qua propter hec uirgo tam sancta et tam singularis *secunda figura*
Comparatur turri cuius uocabulum erat ⌊b⌋aris[4].
Que defendi poterat ab omnibus uiuentibus
Duobus tantummodo custodibus ipsam custodientibus.
Tam fortissima et tam inuincibilis fuit maria.
Cuius precipuus custos erat deus uera sophia.
Qui etiam tam fortissime et inuincibiler communiuit
Et numquam aliqua hostilis impugnacio eam impediuit.

---

[1] Left Panel: Tower of Bari: This tower was a citadel north of Jerusalem's Temple Mount, built by the Hasmoneans, referred to in the *Letter of Aristeas* 100, possibly a successor to the tower mentioned by Nehemiah (2.8, 7.2) and mentioned also by Josephus, *Wars of the Jews* (1.149–151, 5.4). The two guards are an inflection; the normal resident was the high priest. [2] Cf. Tb. 3.17 [3] Right Panel: Tower of David. Adorned (as the caption says) with its legendary thousand shields (*turris david cum mille clippeis*), this is a much more common type for the Virgin, occurring not only in the table of Anthony of Padua, but also in the popular commentary by Bernard of Clairvaux (PL 183, col. 1074) on the 11th-century hymn *Salve Regina*. [4] baris, L] paris, G

And although Mary was joined to a man in a betrothal, *Figure One*
nevertheless, she is said to have remained a virgin in mind and flesh for eternity.
And still she was able to say, just as Sara, the daughter of Raguel,
"In purity I kept my spirit from all concupiscence."
Sara was betrothed to seven men
and still she remained an untouched virgin.
How much more was Mary able to have one spouse
and yet to remain an immaculate virgin for eternity.
If Asmodeus guarded Sara from seven men,
in what way might not the true God guard his mother from one man?
Whenever Joseph beheld the mother of God
he saw that a certain divine brilliance proceeded from her.
And for that reason, he never dared to gaze upon her face,
except perhaps when by some chance he sometimes happened to.
Tobias and Sara remained chaste for three nights;
Mary and Joseph for the time of their whole life remained virgins.
Joseph was a virgin and born from the family of David
and by divine will was joined as a guardian to Mary.
Not because Mary would require his protection in any way,
but so that, on account of human suspicion she might have a guardian.
Indeed, she had for her guardian the true and highest God,
who guarded her from the attack of every enemy.
Therefore, she had one heavenly guardian
and another earthly guardian.

Wherefore, this Virgin, so holy and so unique, *Figure Two*
is compared to the tower whose name was Baris,
which was able to be defended from all living things
with merely two guards guarding it.
So very strong and so invincible was Mary,
whose special guardian was God, true wisdom.
And He also so strongly and invincibly strengthened her
and never did any attack of the enemy hinder her.

¶Qua propter etiam turri dauid comparatura eius uita *tercia figura.*
Que mille clipeis erat communita.
Clipei secum uirtutes et opera uirtuosa
Quibus munita erat uirginis uita gloriosa.
In tantum erat communita et bene firmata
Quod superabat omnes temptaciones et omnia peccata.
Et non solum a se temptaciones et peccata repellebat
Sed etiam ab aliis quibus radios sue gratie infundebat.
Quamuis enim maria uirgo pulcherrima erat
Tamen numquam ab aliquo male concupisci poterat.
Sicut enim cypressus odore suo fugat serpentes
Sic maria gratia sua depulit ⸌male concupiscentes⸍[1] malas concupiscentias.
Et sicut in uinea florente nequeunt serpentes habitare
Sic marie nulla mala concupiscentia potuit appropinquare.
O bone ihesu concede nobis malas concupiscentias remoueri
Et corda nostra dono tue gratie repleri.

10va

Capitulum vii[2]

*I*n precedenti capitulo audiuimus marie desponsacionem
Consequenter audiamus ipsius mirabilem ⌊impregnacionem⌋[3].
Cumque maria in ierusalem esset ioseph desponsata
Ad domum parentum in nazareth est reuocata.
Interim autem quod ioseph neccesariis nuptiarum intendebat
Ipso nesciente maria per spiritum sanctum concipiebat.
Non est suspicandum quod angelus inuenerit eam sine clasura
Cui solus deus sapuit et sine deo uiluit omnis creatura.
Ipsa non tamquam dyna sola curiose diuagabatur[4]
Nec tamquam Thamar cum uiro familiariter conuersabatur.[5]
Ipsa enim tamquam sara filia raguelis[6] numquam uirum desiderauit
Et tamquam iudith solita ieiuniis et oracionibus uacauit.[7]
Ideo ioseph grauidam eam considerans stupebat

[1] Later hand has added ⟨# *male concupiscentes*⟩ [2] Left Panel: Annunciation. This narrative (Lk. 1.26–38) has acquired some of the richest iconographic detail of all biblical subjects. In this image Mary is shown seated on a throne, sometimes thought of as the throne of Solomon, in which case she can be regarded as Lady Wisdom (Prov. 8.22–30) and her throne as *sedes sapientia*, the seat of wisdom. The tri-foliate apex of her gothic seat suggests the Trinity, and her arms crossed on her breast signify her words of consent, *ecce ancilla domine*, "behold the handmaiden of the Lord" (Lk. 1.38). As is customary after Giotto and the Franciscan *Meditationes Vitae Christi*, the angel kneels, as would a courier before a regal lady. [3] impregnacionem, L] impugnacionem, G [4] Gen. 34.1–2 [5] Gen. 38 [6] Tb. 3.7–8 [7] Jdt. 8.4–6

Therefore, her life may be also compared to the tower of David, *Figure Three*
which was reinforced with a thousand shields.
The shields upon her were virtues and virtuous works
with which glorious life of the Virgin was fortified
in so great a way was she fortified and well strengthened
that she conquered all temptations and all sins.
And not only did she repel temptations and sins from herself
but also from others, on whom the rays of her grace poured out.
Although indeed the Virgin Mary was very beautiful,
nevertheless, she was never able to be desired wickedly by anyone.
For just as the cypress chases away serpents with its scent,
so Mary with her grace dispells inordinate desires;
and just as serpents cannot reside in a flowering vine,
so no evil desire was able to draw near to Mary.
O Good Jesus, grant to us that evil desires might be removed
and our hearts filled by the gift of your grace.

Chapter Seven

In the last chapter, we heard of Mary's betrothal,
now let us hear of her miraclous pregnancy.
When Mary had been betrothed to Joseph in Jerusalem
she was called back to the house of her parents in Nazareth.
But meanwhile, because Joseph was turning his attention to the necessities of marriage,
without him knowing, Mary conceived through the Holy Spirit.
It must not be suspected that an angel found her outside her cloister,
for whom God alone was wise and without God every creature became vile.
She herself was not wandering away curiously like Dinah,
nor like Tamar was she was conversing with a man on friendly terms.
For she herself was like Sarah, the daughter of Raguel; she never desired a man,
and like Judith [she was] accustomed to fasting and was at leisure for prayers.
For this reason Joseph, seeing her pregnant, was stunned

Et timens ac tremens hoc apud se mente reuoluebat.
Inpossibile est hanc per fornicacionem concepisse
Quam constat [quam] tam sancte tam caste tam abstinenter uixisse.
Non erat commessatrix. non potatrix. non deliciosa
Non curisatrix. non saltatrix non iocosa.
Publica loca semper uitabat et quantum potuit uitabat
Solitariam uitam et contemplatiuam semper habebat
Omnia mundana solacia et gaudia aspernabatur
Tantum in rebus diuinis et celestibus delectabatur.
A puericia sua in templo domini remanebat
Ut cum nullo virorum aliquid commune habebat.
Et nunc postquam ad domum parentum repatriauit

10vb1 Semper in cubiculo clausa in oracionibus perseuerauit.
Unde igitur potest hanc concepisse grauidacionem
Que numquam alicui peccato dedit occasionem.
Forsan in ea nunc impletum est istud ysaie vaticinium
Ecce uirgo concipiet et pariet filium.[2]
Hec est forte illa de semine iacob puella
Quam spiritus sanctus olim per os balaam pronunciauit in stella.[3]
In quo spiritus sanctus insinuare uolebat.
Quod filius dei de uirgine nasci debebat.
¶H⌊a⌋ec[4] uirgo potest forsan illa uirgo florifera esse. *prima figura*.
Que uaticinabatur egressura de radice yesse.
Forsan hec est forte illa uirgo de qua christum nascetur
Qui de semine dauid filii yesse nasciturus perhibetur.
Aliud autem nequaquam de hac sanctissima estimari potest
Idcirco certissimum ⌊est⌋ quod ipsa mater christi est.
Non sum ego dignus cum tali uirgine habitare
Quapropter expedit mihi a complecione nupciarum cessare.
Et ne forte aliqua sinistra suspicio in populo oriatur
Oportet ut occulte et ualde caute dimittatur.[5]

---

[1] Right Panel: Moses and The Burning Bush. This story from Ex. 3.1–6 is not mentioned in the text until fol. 11r. The image is opaque, not least because it is difficult to perceive the burning bush and impossible to know whether Moses really has taken off his shoes. However, the phrase *rubus ardens* and the labeling of the kneeling figure as *Moyses* is clear. The burning bush which is never consumed, and from which God speaks, is another common image in Marian typology, deriving not from typological exegesis before the 12th century (cf. *Glossa Ordinaria*, PL 113, col. 191) but from Byzantine sources. Representing Mary's perpetual virginity, it is another popular type found, e.g., in Anthony of Padua, *Sermo in Purificatione Santae Mariae* 3.722. [2] Is. 7.14 [3] Nm. 24.17 [4] This chapter contains two of the very rare places where "hec" is written out fully rather than abbreviated [5] Mt. 1.19

and fearing and trembling, he was brooding upon this to himself in his mind.
"It is impossible that this woman conceived through fornication,
who, it is certain, lived so virtuously, so chastely, so abstinently.
She was not a glutton, nor a drunkard, nor luxurious,
not a singer, nor a vigorous dancer, nor full of jest.
She always avoided public places and fled as much as she was able;
she always possessed a solitary and contemplative life.
All earthly comfort and joy she rejected,
as much as she was rejoicing in divine and heavenly things.
From her childhood she abided in the temple with God
with the result that she held nothing in common with any man.
And now, after she returned to the home of her parents,

she was persevering in prayer always in her secluded room,
where, then, afterward this woman became with child,
she who never gave occasion for any sin.
Perhaps in her is now fulfilled that prophesy of Isaiah:
'Behold, a virgin will conceive and bear a son.'
This is by chance that girl from the seed of Jacob,
whom the Holy Spirit once, through the mouth of Balaam, proclaimed in the star,
in whom the Holy Spirit wished to enter,
because the son of God ought to be born from a virgin.
This virgin can perhaps be that flowering virgin, *Figure One*
who was prophesied would come from the root of Jesse.
Perhaps this is, by chance, that virgin from whom the Christ will be born,
he who it is said will be born from the seed of David, son of Jesse.
Nothing else at all can be thought concerning this most holy woman—
on that account it is most certain that she is the mother of the Christ.
I am not worthy to live with such a virgin
accordingly, it is suitable for me to cease from fulfillment of the marriage.
And lest, by chance, some untoward suspicion arises among the people,
it is fitting that she be set aside secretly and with great caution."

Joseph indignum se reputans cum maria timuit habitare
Sicut iohannes qui non fuit ausus christum baptizare.[1]
Centurio rogauit christum ne sub tectum suum introuenieret[2]
Petrus rogauit eum ut de [m/n]a[n/u]i[3,4] sua exiret.
Mulier sunamitis timuit cohabitacionem helye[5]
Sic ioseph cohabitacionem matris dei marie.

11a[6] Cumque ioseph mariam accipere trepidaret
Missus est angelus dei qui mentem eius solidaret.
Qui dixit ei uirginem dimittendam non esse
Et non ab homine sed a spiritu sancto concepisse.[7]
¶Hec autem concepcio tam mirabilis et tam inmensa *secunda figura.*
Fuit moysi in rubo ardenti preostensa.[8]
Rubus sustinuit ignem et non perdidit [uirginitatem] uiriditatem
Maria concepit filium et non amisit uirginitatem.
Dominus ipse habitauit in illo rubo ardente
Et ipse deus habitauit in marie grauidando uentre.
Descendit in rubum per iudeorum liberacionem
Descendit in mariam propter nostram redempcionem.
Descendit in rubum ut educeret iudeos de egipto
Descendit in mariam ut eriperet nos de inferno.
Cum autem deus incarnari uolebat
Mariam solam pre omnibus mundi diligebat[9]
¶Et hoc fuit in uell⌊er⌋e gedeonis prefiguratum
Quod celesti rore legitur esse madidatum.[10]
Solum enim uellus celestem rorem capiebat
Et tota terra circumiacens sicca manebat.
Ita maria sola diuino rore reperiebatur[11]
Et in toto mundo nulla digna inueniebatur.
Multe filie congregauerunt diuicias
Maria autem sola supergressa est uniuersas.[12]
Orauit gedeon ut deus signum in uellere sibi daret

[1] Mt. 3.14 [2] Mt. 8.8, Lk. 7.6 [3] The scribe originally wrote *manu*; the extra minims have been erased by scraping to make *naui* [4] Lk. 5.8 [5] 3 Kings 17.7–16 or 4 Kings 4.8–10 [6] Left Panel: Gideon's Fleece. The biblical account (Jdg. 6.36–40) has Gideon seeking a sign from the Lord of his calling. He sets out a fleece; if it alone is free of dew but the ground is wet in the morning, he will believe. Nonetheless he asks for a second demonstration, reversing the wet and dry of the first. Like Ezekiel's "closed gate" and the burning bush of Moses, Gideon's fleece (*vellus gedeonis*) is regarded as a sign of Mary's preserved virginity. St. Anthony of Padua refers to it in his *Annunciatione Sanctae Mariae Virginis* 3.836. [7] Mt. 1.20, Prot. evg. of James 14 [8] Ex. 3.2 ff. [9] omnibus … diligebat, G] mulieribus mundi eligebat, L [10] Jdg. 6.36–40 [11] reperiebatur] replebatur, L [12] See Prov. 31.29

Joseph, considering himself unworthy, was afraid to live with Mary
just like John, who did not dare to baptize Christ.
The centurion asked Christ not to enter under his roof;
Peter asked him to go away from his boat.
The Shunammite woman was afraid of living together with Elijah;
in such a way was Joseph afraid of living together with Mary, the mother of God.

When Joseph wavered in receiving Mary,
an angel of God was sent to resolve his mind.
He told him that the virgin must not be sent away
and that she had conceived not by man but by the Holy Spirit.
This conception, moreover, so wonderful and so boundless, *Figure Two*
was foreshadowed to Moses in the burning bush.
The bush withstood the fire and its greenery did not perish;
Mary conceived a son and did not lose her virginity.
The Lord himself dwelt in that burning bush
and God himself dwelt in Mary's swelling belly.
He descended into the bush for the liberation of the Jews;
he descended into Mary for the sake of our redemption.
He descended into the bush in order to lead the Jews out of Egypt;
he descended into Mary in order to snatch us from hell.
And when God wished to be made flesh,
he preferred Mary alone before all the people of the world.
And this was prefigured in the fleece of Gideon,
which, it is read, was drenched by the celestial dew.
For the fleece alone received the celestial dew
and all the ground lying around it remained dry.
Thus Mary alone was discovered by the divine dew
and in the whole world no other worthy woman was found.
Many daughters gathered together riches,
but only Mary advanced above them all.
Gideon prayed that God would give him a sign in the fleece

11b2 S⌊i⌋[1] per eum filios israel ab omnibus liberaret.
Replecio ergo uelleris signum erat liberacionis
Concepcio ergo marie signum extitit nostre redempcionis.
Vellus igitur gedeonis est benedicta uirgo maria
De quo uellere fecit igitur tunicam ihesus christus uera sophia.
Qui uestiri uoluit tunica nostre humanitatis
Ut nos uestiret stola perpetue iocunditatis.
Vellus gedeonis suscepit rorem sine lane lesione
Maria concepit filium sine carnis corrupcione.
Gedeon expressit rorem et [/con]cam ex eo repleuit
Maria enixa est filium qui totum mundum rore gratie repleuit.
¶Hec autem concepcio marie facta est per annunciacionem angeli *tercia figura.*
Quod figuratum est in seruo abrahe et rebecca batuelis[3]
Abraham emisit elyeasar seruum suum de uirgine prouidere
Quam filius suus ysaac sponsam deberet habere.
Rebecca autem nuncio abrahe petenti potum tribuebat
Et ideo eam filio domini sui in sponsam eligebat.
Sic pater celestis misit mundo archangelum gabrielem
Qui filio dei quereret uirginem et matrem.[4]
Gabriel autem uirginem decentissimam scilicet mariam inuenit
Que sibi ⌊potum⌋[5] id est nunciacioni sue consensum dedit.
Rebecca non autem solum nuncium sed etiam camelos potauit
Maria autem tam angelis quam hominibus fontem uite propinauit.
O bone ihesu da nobis tuam incarnacionem ita uenerari
Ut poculo fontis uite in eternum mereamur saciari.

---

[2] Right Panel: Rebecca and Eleazar. This covenant narrative (Gen. 24.1–27) is very important in Jewish tradition, but unusual in Marian typology. The parallels are somewhat tendentious in our text, but both are stories about a proposal of marriage in which an emissary or ambassador brings the proposal. Rebecca in this image is crowned like the Virgin Mary in several others, probably to strengthen the analogy. It may be of pertinence that the famous Vienna Genesis, a manuscript of late antiquity (4th to 5th century) was in the royal library of Leopold III, having been acquired by Leopold I, and has an illumination illustrative of this feature on the pertinent page. [1] Si, L] Sed, G [3] Gen. 24, Gen. 15.2 [4] Lk. 1.26 [5] potum, L] potuit, G

if through him, the sons of Israel would be freed from every enemy.
Therefore, the saturation of the fleece was a sign of liberation;
therefore, Mary's conceiving exists as a sign of our redemption.
Therefore, the fleece of Gideon is the blessed Virgin Mary,
from which fleece true Wisdom, Jesus Christ, then made a robe.
He wished to be clothed with the robe of our humanity
so that we might be clothed with the stole of eternal joy.
The fleece of Gideon received the dew without injury to the wool;
Mary conceived a son without corruption of her flesh.
Gideon wrung out the dew and filled up a vessel from it;
Mary gave birth to a son who filled up the whole world with the dew of grace.
But Mary's conception was done through the annunciation of the angel, *Figure Three*
which was symbolized in Abraham's servant and Rebekah [daughter] of Bethuel
Abraham sent out Eliezer his servant to see about a maiden
that his son Isaac should have as a bride.
And Rebekah granted a drink to Abraham's messenger when he asked for it,
and for this reason he selected her to be betrothed to the son of his master.
So too the heavenly Father sent his archangel Gabriel to earth
to seek a virgin and mother for the son of God.
And Gabriel found the most fitting virgin, that is, Mary,
who gave a drink to him (that is, her consent to the annunciation).
Moreover, Rebekah gave water not only to the messenger but also to his camels,
and Mary gave the fountain of life as much to angels as to men.
O good Jesus, grant us to revere your Incarnation in such a way
that we may merit to be satisfied for all eternity by a draught from the fountain of life.

11va *Capitulum viii*[1].

*I*n precendenti capitulo audiuimus de christi concepcione
Consequenter audiamus de ipsius humana generacione.
Hanc generacionem non solum angeli desiderabant.
Sed et patres sancti desideranter expectabant et clamabant.
Emitte agnum tuum domine dominatorem terre[2]
Et mitte lucem tuam et ueritatem tuam deus eterne.[3]
Ostende nobis faciem tuam et salui erimus[4]
Ostende filium tuum quem exspectamus et querimus.[5]
Utinam disrumperet celos et descenderet[6]
Ut nos de captiuitate dyaboli liberaret.[7]
Domine inclina celos tuos et descende[8]
Ad liberandum nos dexteram tue maiestatis extende.[9]
Reminiscere miseracionum tuarum antiquarum
Veni et recipe[10] nos de potestate tenebrarum.[11]
Veni domine ut fideles prophete tui et veraces inueniantur
Et promissiones tue et figure tue compleantur.
Veni domine cito festina et noli tardare
Relaxa facinora plebis tue et incarnare.
Nullus angelus nullus homo sufficit nos liberare.[12]
Libera nos tu pie domine qui dignatus es nos creare.
Misertus igitur pius deus assumpsit humanitatem[13]
Vt destrueret diutinam captiuitatem.
Qui olim dixit penitet me fecisse hominem.[14] *prima figura.*
Et hoc figuratum fuit quondam in pincerna pharaonis

11vb[16] Qui in carcere positus vidit sompnum sue liberacionis.[15]
Videbatur siquidem sibi quod coram se uitis de terra excrescebat
Que in se tres propagines siue tres ramos habebat.

---

[1] Left Panel: Christ's Nativity. In Lk. 2.7 we learn that, deprived or room in an inn, Mary has given birth elsewhere—inferentially a stable—since after she has wrapped him in the usual swaddling cloths she lays him in a manger and in this image worships him along with the ox and ass of Is. 1.3, who recognize him even when God's people do not. Joseph, here represented as a frail old man, ponders at a distance. He leans on a staff, in the fashion sometimes used to represent a shepherd. [2] Is. 16.1 [3] Ps. 42.3 [4] Ps. 30.17, Ps. 79.4 [5] See Mt. 11.3, Tit. 2.13 [6] Is. 64.1 [7] See Rom. 8.2 [8] Ps. 143.5 [9] See Ex. 15.6, Act. 7.55, Hbr. 1.3, Hbr. 8.1 [10] recipe] eripe, L [11] Col. 1.13 [12] See 2 Cor. 3.5 [13] Phlp. 2.7 [14] Gen. 6.6–7 [16] Right Panel: The Dream of Pharaoh's Cupbearer. In Gen. 40.9–14 Pharaoh's imprisoned butler has a dream in which he sees a lush grape vine from which he picks grapes and makes wine for his alienated master. Here we are dependent on the text for the story, since all we have in the image is the sleeping prisoner and the vine. The typology is drawn from the butler's release after three days, connected to the period of Christ's entombment; the royal wine prefigures the Eucharist. The typology is rare. [15] Gen. 40.1–13

Chapter Eight

In the last chapter we heard about the conception of Christ,
now let us hear about his human birth.
Not only were the angels longing for this birth,
but also the holy patriarchs in longing were awaiting it and crying out:
"Send your lamb, Lord, as a ruler of the earth
and send forth your light and your truth, eternal God.
Show us your face and we shall be saved!
Reveal your Son for whom we hope and search.
If only he would shatter the heavens and descend,
so that he might free us from the captivity of the devil.
Lord, bow your heavens and descend;
stretch forth the right hand of your majesty to free us.
Remember the misery of your former people;
come and snatch us from the power of darkness.
Come, Lord, that your prophets might be found faithful and true
and that your promises and figures may be fulfilled.
Come quickly, Lord, make haste and do not tarry.
Forgive the crimes of your people and become flesh.
No angel or man is able to free us.
Free us, merciful Lord, you who have deigned to create us."
Showing pity, then, the merciful God took on human nature,
so that He might destroy a long captivity,
He who formerly said, "I am sorry that I made man." *Figure One*
And this was symbolized formerly by the cupbearer of Pharoah,

who, when imprisoned, dreamed of his own freedom.
It seemed to him that a vine grew up before him from the earth,
which in itself had three shoots or three branches.

Vitis exorta vuas non protulit in momento statim
Sed incepit florere et vuas producere paulatim.
Captiuus ciphum pharaonis manu tenebat
Et uuas in eum exprimens poculum pharaoni offerebat.
Post hec audiuit huius sompnii interpretacionem
⸤Quod⸥ post tres dies obtineret liberacionem.
Illa fuit huius sompnii litteralis interpretacio
Sed ista et ipsius mistica prefiguracio.
Ante saluatoris nostri humanam natiuitatem
Sustinuit humanum genus mirabilem captiuitatem.
Tandem uitis id est christus de terra id est de maria excrescebat
Que in se tres propagines id est tres res mirabiles in se habebat.
Habuit enim in se christus carnem animam et diuinitatem[1]
Que tria destruxerunt nostram captiuitatem.
Uel tres propagines sunt tres persone sancte trinitatis.
Que liberauerunt nos de carcere dyabolice captiuitatis
Non tamen statim post christi ortum humanum genus est liberatum[2]
Sed quando vinum sanguinis sui in cruce regi celesti est oblatum.
Tercio die postquam hoc vinum in passione est expressum.
Genus humanum de captiuitate est egressum
Hoc vinum celestem regem ita inebriauit
Quod omnem offensam humano generi liberaliter relaxauit

12a[3] Hoc etiam uinum deus nobis misericorditer reliquit
Et per cottidianam oblacionem sub sacramento instituit.
Ut omni die regi celesti pro mundi offensa offeratur
Quia non est dies in qua Deus a mundo non offendatur[4]
Benedicta sit saluatoris nostri diuina clemencia
A quo data est nobis tam salubris medicina.
Benedicta sit beatissima uirgo maria
Ex qua processit tam saluberrima uitis et tam pia.[5]
Cumque christus nasceretur vinee Engadi floruerunt[6]

---

[1] See 1 Cor. 12.12, 2 Cor. 13.4 [2] Cf. Rom. 4.25, 1 Pt. 1.3 [3] Left Panel: Aaron's Budding Rod. When God chose a high priest for service under Moses a leader from each of the twelve tribes of Israel came with a rod in hand, signed with his name, to indicate the tribe. Placed before the tabernacle, the rods were examined the next day and Aaron's was found to have produced blossoms and ripe almonds (Nm. 17.1–8). This story also was adapted to Marian typology by connecting this passage with the "rod out of the root of Jesse" (Is. 11.1) which, like Aaron's, blooms miraculously; see, e.g., in St. Anthony of Padua, *In Annunciatione Sanctae Mariae Virginis* 3.836. This connection was well enough known that Konrad could represent the typology simply with a verdant tree standing among eleven staves with the rubric *virga Aaron*. [4] Cf. 2 Cor. 5.19 [5] See John 15 [6] Cf. Ct. 1.14; see also *LA*

The vine having grown up did not bear grapes immediately in the moment,
but began to bloom and produce grapes gradually.
The captive held Pharoah's goblet in his hand
and squeezing grapes into it, offered the cup to Pharoah.
After this he heard the interpretation of his dream,
that after three days he would obtain freedom.
That interpretation of this dream was literal,
but the following is the mystical prefiguration of it.
Before the human birth of our savior
the human race endured an extraordinary captivity.
Finally, the vine—which is Christ—grew up from the earth—which is Mary;
the vine had in itself three shoots, which is to say he had in himself three wonderful parts.
For Christ had in himself flesh, spirit, and divinity,
which three destroyed our captivity.
Alternatively, the three shoots are the three persons of the holy Trinity
who freed us from the prison of diabolic captivity.
Yet after the birth of Christ, the human race was not immediately freed,
but only when the wine of his blood was offered in on the cross to the heavenly king,
on the third day after this vine was squeezed out in the passion,
did the human race go out from captivity.
This wine so intoxicated the heavenly king
that he freely released every offense from the human race.

God also graciously left this wine for us
and instituted it as a daily offering under the form of a sacrament
that it be offered every day to the king of heaven for the offenses of the world
because there is not a day on which God is not offended by the world.
Blessed be the divine mercy of our savior,
from whom such a health-giving medicine is given to us.
Blessed be the most blessed virgin Mary,
from whom proceeded such a health-giving and merciful vine.
When Christ was born the vines of Engadi blossomed,

Et christum per uitem signatum venisse ostenderunt.
Benedicta sit Ihesu christi saluatoris nostri natiuitas
De qua orta est angelis et hominibus ⌊tanta⌋[1] utilitas.
Per ipsam enim homo de captiuitate dyaboli est liberatus[2]
Et per ipsam est lapsus angelorum destauratus.[3]
¶Ecce audiuimus natiuitatis christi ⌊utilitatem⌋[4] *secunda figura*
Audiamus etiam natiuitatis christi modum et qualitatem.
Modus signatus est in uirga Aaron amigdola
Que floruit et fructificauit uirtute diuina.[5]
Sic ergo illa uirgo mirabiliter contra naturam germinauit.
Ita Maria supra ordinem nature mirabiliter filium generauit.
Virga Aaron protulit fructum sine plantacione.
Maria genuit filium sine virili commixtione.[6]
Vir⌊ga⌋ florens Aaron dignum sacerdocio ⌊monstrauit⌋[7,8]
Maria pariens magnum sacerdotem portauit[9]
In teste amigdolina dulcis nucleus latebat.

12rb[10] In testa carnis christi dulcissima deitas abscondita erat.
In uirga Aaron inuenimus frondium viriditatem
Florum suauitatem et fructuum ubertatem.
Sic Maria habuit uiriditatem virginitatis
Suauitatem pietatis et ubertatem perpetue societatis.[11]
¶Non solum autem christus Iudeis ortum suum premonstrauit *tercia figura.*
Sed etiam paganis patefacere non recusauit.[12]
Non enim propter Iudeos tantum in mundum ueniebat
Sed omnes homines saluos facere intendebat.[13]
Circa idem tempus Octauianus toto orbi dominabatur[14]
Et ideo a Romanis tamquam deus reputabatur.
Ipse a sibillam prophetissam consulebat
Si in mundo aliquis eo maior futurus erat.
Eadem die quando christus in Iudea nascebatur
Sibilla Rome circulum aureum iuxta solem contemplabatur.

---

[1] tanta, L] facta est, G [2] Cf. Gal. 1.4, 1John. 3.8, Hbr. 2.14–15 [3] See Rom. 16.20, Apc. 20.1–3 [4] utilitatem, L] nativitatem G [5] Nm. 17.8 [6] Is. 7.14, Mt. 1.18 [7] monstrauit, L] intrauit, G [8] Nm. 17 [9] Lk. 2 and the presentation of Jesus to Simeon and Hannah [10] Right Panel: Sibyl and Augustus. A Christian tradition appealing to the Roman sibyl, dating back to Lactantius, eventually morphed into a supposed meeting between the Roman prophetess and the emperor Augustus in which Augustus is said to have asked her whether he should call himself a god. She advised against it, directing his attention to a solar aura in which the Virgin and Child appeared. This story is found in the *Golden Legend* 4 and appears widely in humble works such as the *Biblia Pauperum* as well as in more exalted art, e.g. the Ghent altarpiece of the Van Eyck brothers. [11] societatis] *satietats, L* [12] Cf. Mt. 16.21, Mt. 17.9, 23, Mt. 20.19, Mt. 26.2, 32, Mk. 8.31, Mk. 9.31, Mk. 10.34, Mk. 14.28, Lk. 9.22, Lk. 18.33, Lk. 24.7 [13] See Mt. 18.11, Lk. 19.10 [14] Lk. 2.1

and they showed that Christ, signified by the vine, had come.
Blessed be the birth of Jesus Christ our Savior,
from which gain accrued to angels and men.
For through it man was freed from the captivity of the devil.
And through it the destroyer of angels fell.
Behold we have heard of the good effects of birth of Christ; *Figure Two*
let us also hear the method and nature of the birth of Christ.
The method was signified in the almond branch of Aaron
which has bloomed and has borne fruit with divine virtue.
In this way, therefore, that virgin has miraculously given birth contrary to nature.
So Mary miraculously bore a son above the order of nature.
The branch of Aaron brought forth fruit without planting.
Mary begot a son without a man's embrace.
The flowering rod showed Aaron worthy of the priesthood.
Mary being with child carried a great priest.
The sweenut was concealed in the almond shell.

In the shell of Christ's flesh his most sweet godhead was hidden.
In the rod of Aaron we find the greenness of fronds,
a sweetness of flowers, and the abundance of fruits.
Thus Mary had the verdure of virginity
the sweetness of piety and the richness of everlasting communion.
And not only did Christ predict his birth to the Jews, *Figure Three*
but he also did not refuse to reveal it to the pagans.
For he came into the world not because of the Jews alone,
but he intended to save all men.
About the same time Octavian was ruling over all the earth
and therefore he was thought of as a god by the Romans.
He himself consulted a sibyl, a prophetess, [to see]
if there would be another greater than him in the world.
On the same day when Christ was born in Judea,
the Sibyl of Rome beheld a gold circle around the sun.

In circulo illo uirgo pulcherrima residebat
Que puerum speciosissimum in gremio gerebat.
Quod illa Cesari Octauiano narrauit[1]
Et regem potenciorem ipso natum esse intimauit.
O quam potens est rex regum et dominus dominorum[2]
Qui humanum genus liberauit de captiuitate demonorum.
Potenciam huius regis Cesar Augustus formidauit
Et ab omnibus deus uocari et reputari recusauit.
O bone Ihesu ⌊da⌋[3] pro nobis ita tuam honorare natiuitatem
Ut non incidamus iterato in dyabolicam captiuitatem.

12va *Capitulum ix*[4]

*I*n precedenti capitulo audiuimus de christi generacione
Consequenter audiamus de magorum oblacione.[5]
Eadem die cum christus in iudea esset natus *prima figura.*
Ortus eius tribus magis in oriente est nunciatus.
Viderunt namque stellam nouam in qua puer apparebat
Supra cuius caput crux aurea splendebat.
Audieruntque uocem magnam dicentem sibi
Ite in iudeam et nouum regem natum inuenietis ibi.
Tres isti festinantes in iudeam pergebant
Et regi celi nato sua munera offerebant. *secunda figura.*
¶Hii tres magi per tres robustos prefigurati fuerunt
Qui regi dauid aquam in cysterna bethleem attulerunt.[6]
Istorum robustorum uirtus et audacia multum commendatur
Sic magorum aduentus et oblacio ualde approbatur.
Tres robusti exercitum inimicorum non timuerunt
Sed uiriliter castra eorum transeuntes aquam hausuerunt
Sic tres magi potenciam herodis non formidauerunt.
Sed audacter iudeam intrantes de nouo rege interrogauerunt.

---

[1] narrauit] monstravit, L [2] 1 Tim. 6.15, Apc. 19.16 [3] da] L, and usually part of the concluding formula in G [4] Left Panel: Adoration of the Magi. The story in Matthew's gospel (2.1–11) affords one of the most popular and widely disseminated subjects in Christian art, beginning as early as mid-4th-century sarcophagus art and continuing in popularity through the 17th century. Here it appears earlier than we would expect to see it in other contexts, where the adoration of the shepherds, presentation in the Temple, and circumcision precede it. The artist follows a 12th-century composition found, among other places, on the west front of the cathedral in Verona, but here, as is usual for this period, the oldest of the Magi kneels, uncrowned, proffering his gift, while the second draws attention to the star, visible through the window over Mary's head. [5] Mt. 2 [6] 2 Kings. 23.16

In that circle an exceedingly beautiful virgin resided
who carried the most splendid child in her lap.
The woman described that to Caesar Octavian
and announced that a king more powerful than him would be born.
O how powerful is the King of Kings and Lord of Lords,
who liberated the human race from the captivity of demons.
Caesar Augustus dreaded the power of this King,
and he refused to be thought of and called god by all.
O good Jesus grant us to honor your birth in such a way
that we do not fall again into diabolic captivity.

Chapter Nine

In the last chapter we heard about the birth of Christ,
now let us hear about the offering of the Magi.
On the same day as Christ was born in Judea, *Figure One*
his coming was announced to the three Magi in the East.
For they saw a new star in which a boy appeared,
above whose head, a golden cross shone.
And they heard a great voice saying to them:
"Go into Judea and there you will find the newborn king."
Hurrying, those three traveled to Judea,
and they offered their own gifts to the one born King of Heaven. *Figure Two*
These three Magi were prefigured through the three strong men,
who brought water in the cistern of Bethlehem to the King David.
The power and boldness of those strong men is often commended,
in the same way the arrival and offering of the Magi was greatly approved.
As the three strong men did not fear the host of the enemy,
but drew the water, courageously passing through their camp,
thus the three Magi were not afraid of the power of Herod,
but, boldly entering Judea, they questioned concerning the new king.

Caspar. balthasar. melchior. nomina sunt magorum
abysai. solochai. batlias nomina robustorum.
Tres robusti perrexerunt bethleem pro aqua cysterne
Tres magi uenerunt bethleem pro aqua gratie eterne.
Tres robusti hausuerunt aquam de cysterna terresti
Tres magi susceperunt aquam gratie de patria celesti.
Figurabat ergo illa bethlehemita cysterna

12vbl Quod bethleem nasciturus esset celestis pincerna.
Qui propinaret aquam gratie omni sicienti
Et daret aquam uite gratis precium[2] non habenti.[3]
Dauid rex aquam ablatam deo pro gratiarum accione offerebat
Gaudens et exultans quod tam robustos uiros habebat.
Christus autem rex celi et terre gaudebat et exultabat
Quia aduentus magorum conuersacionem gencium prefigurabat.
Dauid rex uidetur sitisse non aquam sed suorum uirtutem
Christus uidetur sitisse nostram conuersacionem et salutem.
Tres robusti bethleem breui tempore et hora perrexerunt
Tres magi de oriente breui tempore bethleem peruenerunt.
Si queratur quomodo tam spacium tam cito potuerunt transmeare
Dicendum est quod christo nato non inpossibile hoc dare.
Qui enim duxit abacuc subito de iudea in babylonem[4]
Cito perducere potuit de oriente in iudeorum regionem.
Venientes igitur magi bethleem coram puero procidebant
Aurum thus et mirram ei offerebant.
¶Figura huius regis noui et huius oblacionis *tercia figura.*
Premonstrata fuit olim in regno regis salomonis.
Salomon rex licet puer esset tamen sapientissimus fuit[5]
Deus puer factus non minus sapiens quam antea extitit.
Salomon rex residebat in throno de ebore mundissimo.[6]
Qui uestitus erat auro optimo et mundissimo
Vniuersi reges terre regem salomonem uidere desiderabant
Et ei munera preciosissima et carissima portabant.

[1] Right Panel: The Magi see the Star. The biblical source in Mt. 2.2 is adumbrated by such texts as the 13th-century *Meditationes Vitae Christi*, a widely disseminated Franciscan gospel paraphrase, also sometimes illustrated. The Magi are said to have seen the star appear on the day of Christ's birth; their journey is important to Christian theology in that they are gentiles and prefigure the Church (ed. Ragusa and Green, 46–53).
[2] precium] potum, L [3] See John 4.10–14 [4] Dn. 14.32–38 [5] 3 Kings 2.1–9 [6] 3 Kings 10.18–20

Caspar, Balthasar, and Melchior are the names of the Magi;
Abishai, Sobochai, and Benaiah are the names of the strong men.
The three strong men hastened to Bethlehem for the water from the cistern;
three Magi went to Bethlehem for the water of eternal grace.
The three strong men drew water from the earthly cistern;
the three Magi took up the water of grace from the heavenly country.
Therefore, that cistern of Bethlehem symbolized

that a heavenly cupbearer would be born in Bethlehem,
who would give the water of grace to all the thirsty,
and would give the water of life freely to the one not having its price.
King David offered the fetched water to God in thanksgiving,
rejoicing and exulting that he had such strong men.
And Christ, king of the heavens and the earth, was rejoicing and exulting
because the arrival of the Magi prefigured the conversion of the nations.
David the king seems to have thirsted not for water but the excellence of his own men,
Christ seems to have thirsted for our conversion and salvation.
The three strong men proceeded quickly to Bethlehem;
the Three Magi from the East reached Bethlehem in a short time.
If it is asked how they were able to go so far so quickly,
it should be said that with Christ born, this was not impossible to do.
For he who led Habakkuk suddenly from Judea into Babylon,
was able to quickly bring them from the East into the region of Judea.
Coming to Bethlehem, then, the Magi, fell down in the presence of the boy,
and offered to him gold, incense, and myrrh.
A symbol of this new king and this offering *Figure Three*
was foreshadowed once in the kingdom of King Solomon.
King Solomon, although he was a boy, was yet exceedingly wise.
God, having become a boy, was not less wise than he was before.
King Solomon sat on a throne made of finest ivory;
he was clothed with the best and purest gold.
All the kings of the earth were desiring to see King Solomon
and bore very costly and precious gifts to him.

13a[1]
Sed regina saba tanta et talia munera ei offereba{n}t
Quanta et qualia in ierusalem prius uisa non fuerant.[2]
Thronus veri salomonis est beatissima uirgo maria
In quo residebat christus Ihesus vera sophia.
Thronus iste factus erat de nobilissimo thesauro
De ebore uidelicet candido et fusus[3] nimis auro.
Ebur propter sui candoris[4] frigiditatem
Designat virginalis munditie castitatem.
Ebur antiquum capit colorem rubeum
Sic antiqua et longa castitas reputatur martyrium.
Aurum quia in ualore suo precellit omne metallum
Significat caritatem que mater est omnium uirtutem.
Maria ergo dicitur eburnea propter uirginalem castitatem
Et auro uestita propter perfectissimam caritatem.
Et pulchre uirginitati coniungitur caritas
Quia sine caritate coram deo nichil reputatur uirginitas.
Et sicut fur non timet lampadem non ardentem
Sic dyabolus non timet uirginem caritatem non habentem.[5]
Thronus salomonis super sex gradus erat exaltatus
Et maria superexcellit beatorum sex status
Superexcellit omnem statum patriarcharum prophetarum et apostolorum.
Statum quoque martyrum confessorum atque uirginum.
Vel sex gradus thronus salomonis habebat
Quia post VI etates mundi maria nata erat.
XII leunculi super thronum sex gradus exornabant

13b[6]
Quia XII apostoli marie tanquam regine ministrabant
Vel XII leunculi thronum decorauerunt
Quia XII patriarche [progenies] progenitores marie extiterunt.
Duos leones magnos thronus habebat

[1] Left Panel: Three Soldiers Bring Water to David. In this ingenious adaptation of the Old Testament story recorded in 2 Kings 23.15–16, the *Glossa Ordinaria* (PL 113.578) provides the Marian typology, namely that the mystical sense signifies the "true water in Bethlehem provided by the Son of David, born of the Virgin." The three young men are here paralleled to the Magi, traditionally represented as three in number. [2] 3 Kings 10.1–10 [3] fusus] fulvus, L [4] candoris] candorem, L [5] See Mt. 25.1–13 [6] Right Panel: Solomon Visited by the Queen of Saba. Another parallel visit of royalty to a throne of wisdom. The text says that "all the kings of the world" desired to see Solomon, but the Queen of Saba's visit is featured, in that she brought rich gifts. Mary's typological association with the throne of Solomon or *sedes sapientia* strengthens the connection (3 Kings 10.1–10). Shown are the twelve lions carved on the steps of Solomon's throne, made analogous to the twelve disciples in the SHS text, but instead of the Queen of Saba approaching Solomon we see on the throne Mary herself as Queen, with two arms extending toward her from the margins, presumably figuring divine revelation and support.

But the Queen of Sheba was offering gifts, so many and so excellent,
of such greatness and of such a nature as had not before been seen in Jerusalem.
The throne of the true Solomon is the most Blessed Virgin Mary
in whom Christ Jesus, True Wisdom, was residing.
That throne had been made from most noble treasure,
namely, from shining ivory and cast from much gold.
Ivory, on account of the coolness of its whiteness,
indicates the purity of virginal cleaness.
Ancient ivory holds the color red;
in the same way long-standing and ongoing chastity is considered a martyrdom.
Because gold in its own value excels all metal,
it signifies charity, which is the mother of all virtue.
Mary therefore is described as ivory on account of her chaste virginity
and clad in gold on account of her most holy charity.
And charity is joined with beautiful virginity
for without charity virginity is considered worthless in the presence of God.
And just as the thief does not fear the lamp that is not burning,
so the devil does not fear the virgin who does not have charity.
The throne of Solomon rose above six steps
and Mary surpasses the six states of the blessed.
She surpasses each state of the patriarchs, of the prophets, and of the apostles,
also the state of the martyrs, confessors, and virgins.
And the throne of Solomon had six steps,
because after the six ages of the earth, Mary was born.
Twelve lion carvings adorned the six steps above the throne,

because the twelve apostles were serving Mary as if a queen,
or the twelve lion carvings decorated the throne,
because the twelve patriarchs were the forefathers of Mary.
The throne had two great lions,

⌊Quia⌋[1] duas tabulas preceptorum maria corde et opere tenebat.[2]
Summitas ipsius throni erat rotunda
Quia maria erat sine angulo sordium et tota munda.
Due manus sedile hinc inde tenebant
Quia pater et spiritus sanctus a matre filii nunquam recedebant.
Hic est thronus quem verus rex salomon sibi ipsi fecerat
Et in uniuersis regnis mundi opus tale non erat.
Magi igitur uenientes assumpserunt munera talia
Quia talia uiderentur congrua et non alia.
Aurum enim propter sui nobilitatem munus est regale
Per quod ostendebant puerum esse regem et se decere tale.
Thus autem oblacio erat sacerdotalis
Et puer ille erat talis sacerdos cui nunquam fuit equalis.
Cum mirra solebant antiqua corpora mortuorum condire
Et christus rex et sacerdos uoluit pro salute nostra mortem subire.
Nos ergo debemus offerre cum christo aurum dilectionis
Eo quod pura dilectione subiit penam humane passionis.
Thus deuote laudis per gratiarum actionem
Et ⌊mirram⌋[3] compassionis per mortis eius recordacionem.
O bone ihesu da nobis ita te diligere et tibi condolere
Ut te in celis perhenniter mereamur uidere.

13va

Capitulum x[4]

*I*n precedenti capitulo audiuimus quomodo christus fuit a magis adoratus
Consequenter audiamus quomodo sit in templo domino presentatus.[5]
Quadragesima die post christi natiuitatem
Perrexit beata uirgo ad purificacionis sue sollempnitatem.
Sed ipsa non habuit necesse de purificacione
Quia conceperat filium sine uirili conmixtione.
Voluit tamen purificacionem peragere ut ritum legis exequeretur

[1] Quia L] Per, G, Et, X [2] See Lk. 10.27 [3] mirram L] mirra, G [4] Left Panel: Presentation at the Temple. In the account in Luke (Lk. 2.22–35), Jesus is brought to the Temple again, not as in his first visit eight days after his birth as the Law required for circumcision (Lk. 2.21) but this time with Mary after forty days for her ritual of purification (Lv. 12.2–8). The image shown here seems to refer to the circumcision, though it shows the infant Jesus sitting upon an altar, perhaps reflecting Simeon's prediction of Christ's death and Mary's sorrow (Lk. 2.34–35). An altar is likewise present in the *Meditationes Vitae Christi* illustrations (Ragusa and Green, figs. 48–52 and text, 59–62). Here, instead of the blessing by Simeon, there is a blessing by Jesus with two fingers and thumb extended, as he gazes up toward an altar lamp such as in a medieval church might burn over the altar and tabernacle. [5] Lk. 2.22ff.

because Mary kept the two tablets of the commandments in heart and deed.
The top of his throne was round,
for Mary was without defilement in any corner and wholly clean.
Two hands were holding the seat on either side,
because the Father and the Holy Spirit never withdrew from the Mother of the Son.
This is the throne which the true King Solomon had made for himself
and there was no work similar in the all the kingdoms of the earth.
Coming, then, the Magi took such gifts
because such gifts and not others seemed suitable.
For gold is a royal gift on account of its own nobility,
through which they were showing that the boy was a king and such a thing was fitting for him.
Incense, however, was the priestly offering,
and that boy was a priest like whom there has never been an equal.
The ancients used to embalm the bodies of the dead with myrrh,
and Christ, king and priest, wished to undergo death for our salvation.
We therefore ought to offer, along with Christ, the gold of love
because he underwent with pure love the punishment of human suffering;
we ought to offer the incense of devout praise by giving thanks;
and the myrrh of compassion in remembrance of his death.
O good Jesus, grant to us so to love you and to suffer with you,
that we might be worthy to see You eternally in heaven.

Chapter Ten

In the last chapter, we heard how Christ was adored by the Magi;
next let us hear how he was presented to the Lord in the temple.
On the fortieth day after Christ's birth
the Blessed Virgin made haste to the solemnity of her purification.
But she herself did not have need of purification
because she had conceived her son without a man's embrace.
Yet she wished to complete the purification so that the rite of Law might be fulfilled

Ne preuaricatrix legis esse iudicaretur.[1]
Preuaricatrix enim legis nequaquam erat
Quia omnia que legis erant diligentissime tenebat.
¶Quapropter ipsa est per archam testamenti prefigurata *prima figura*.
In qua inclusa erant omnia legis mandata.
In archa enim erant due lapidee tabule moysi.
In quibus scripta erant decem precepta dei.[2]
Que propter audiencium et legencium ⸜delecacionem⸝[3] hic annotabo.
Et breui quadam glosula hic elucidabo.
//Primum[4] est deos alienos non adorabis
Id est deum verum coles et super eum nichil amabis.
//Secundum est non assumes nomen in uanum dei tui
Id est non blasphemes nec iurabis indebite nomine sui.
//Tercium est ⌊memento⌋[5] ut diem sabbati sanctifices
Ut scilicet in eo mortaliter non pecces et opera illicita uites.
//Quartum est honora patres tuos ipsis debite obediendo
Necessaria ministrando et animabus eorum miserendo.
//Quintum est non occides opere uerbo negligencia cogitacione

13vb[7,8] Auxilio consensu malo exemplo nec aliqua cogitacione.[6]
//Sextum est non mechaberis videlicet ⌊operando⌋[9] cogitando loquendo.
Nec iuridicione tua fornicacionem aliquam sustinendo.
//Septimum est non furaberis aliena tibi aliquomodo attrahando.
Nec ⌊re⌋[10] aliena inuito suo domino ex industria utendo.
//Octauum est non falsum testimonium contra proximum tuum dices
Id est omne mendacium et dolum et detractionem deuites.
//Nonum est domum uel agrum proximi tui non debes desiderare
Tali uidelicet mente quod uelles sibi[11] cum suo dampno adoptare.
//Decimum est uxorem seruum ancillam proximi non concupisces
Precedens de re immobili istud de mobili intelliges.

---

[1] See Lv. 12.2–8 [2] Ex. 20.3–17 [3] delecacionem] utilitatem L [4] Each commandment is flagged by double slash marks resembling // [5] memento] supplied in L [7] Right Panel: Ark of the Covenant. The image shows the carrying poles (Ex. 25.10–22) and tablets of the law of Moses which the *archa testamenti* contained, but it does not show the surmounted cherubim (Ex. 25.17–22). While the *Glossa Ordinaria* (PL 113.267) says, with Bede, that it is possible to see the ark as antitype of the Church, here it is described as an antitype of Mary, a connection first made in the East by St. Gregory the Thaumaturgus in the 3rd century as well as by St. Dionysius around the same time. As the original ark marked the presence of the *shikenah kavod*, or divine glory, so Mary is seen as the container for the incarnate deity. St. Ambrose adopted and extended the typology (*Serm.* 42.6) in the 4th century, ensuring acceptance in the Western church. [8] MS: A simple drawing of the Ark of the Covenant, captioned "archa testamenti" [6] G, X] occasione, L [9] operando, L, X] comparando, G [10] re, L] te, G, X [11] sibi] tibi, L

lest she be judged a transgressor of the Law.
For she was by no means a transgressor of the Law
because she was most attentively keeping all things that were of the Law.
Wherefore she herself was prefigured through the Ark of the Covenant, *Figure One*
in which all the commands of the Law were enclosed.
For in the Ark were the two stone tablets of Moses,
on which were written the Ten Commandments of God.
Which, for the sake of the delight to those hearing and reading, I will write down here
and briefly explain here with a short gloss.
The first is, you shall not worship foreign gods;
that is, you shall worship the true God and love nothing above him.
The second is, you shall not take the name of your God in vain;
that is, you shall not blaspheme nor take an oath in his name without cause.
The third is, remember that you should keep the day of the Sabbath holy;
namely, so that on it you should not sin mortally, and avoid forbidden deeds.
The fourth is, honor your parents by duly obeying them,
attending to their needs and showing mercy on their souls.
The fifth is, you shall not kill by deed, word, negligence, thought,

aid, agreement, evil example, nor any thought.
The sixth is, you shall not commit adultery; that is, by doing, thinking, speaking,
nor by tolerating any fornication in your jurisdiction.
The seventh is, you shall not steal things not belonging to you by bearing them away somehow,
nor by using another's possessions out of diligence with its master unwilling.
The eighth is, you shall not speak false testimony against your neighbor;
that is, you shall shun all lying, and deceit, and slander.
The ninth is, you ought not to desire the house or field of your neighbor
with such a mind that what you are really desiring is to bring about his ruin for him.
The tenth is, you shall not covet your neighbor's wife, slave, [or] handmaiden;
you shall understand that the former is about immovable things, the latter portable property.

Hec duo ultima in nullo videretur discrepare
Nisi quod {tr}es immobiles et mobiles uolunt designare.
Omnia ista dei mandata maria diligenter obseruabat
Et ideo archa testamenti ipsam figuraliter prefigurabat.
Archa etiam testamenti librum legis continebat.
Et maria libros sacre scripture libenter habebat.[1]
In archa etiam erat virga aaron que quondam floruit[2]
Et maria floruit et benedictum fructum uentris sui protulit.
Archa etiam urnam auream cum manna continebat[3]
Et maria nobis verum manna celi offerebat.
Archa testamenti de lignis sechim imputribili erat facta[4]
Et maria in putredine uel puluere nequaquam est redacta.
Archa quatuor circulos aureos in ⌊lateribus⌋[5] habebat
Et maria quatuor uirtutes originales[6] in se gerebat.

14a[7] Que sunt temperancia · prudentia · fortitudo et iusticia
Hec sunt omnium uirtutum radices et inicia.
Archa habebat duos uectes aureos quibus portabatur
Per quos duplex caritas scilicet dei et proximi in maria designatur.
Archa tam intrinsecus quam extrinsecus deaurata erat
Maria intus et foris virtutibus resplendebat. *secunda figura.*
¶Quapropter etiam ipsa pulchre prefigurata est candelabro aureo
Quod lucebat ierosolimis et in domini templo.
Super quod vii lampades ardentes stabant[8]
Que vii opera misericordie in marie prefigurabant.
Que sunt ista cibare esurientem et potare sicientem
Vestire nudum et colligere hospicium non habentem.
Infirmos uisitare et vinctis compati et liberare
Mortuos sepelire et necessaria funeralia ministrare.
Nullus dubitet opera misericordie in maria plenarie fuisse.
Quam constat matrem pietatis et reginam misericordie extitisse.
Quomodo mater tocius misericordie opera misericordie non impleret
Quomodo candelabrum diuino igne accensum non luceret.

[1] habebat] legebat, L [2] Nm. 17.8 [3] Ex. 16.33, Hbr. 9.4 [4] Ex. 25.10 ff. [5] lateribus, L] latentibus, G [6] originales] cardinales, L [7] Left Panel: Seven-branched Candlestick. The original seven-branched menorah was part of the furniture of the tabernacle (Ex. 25.31–40) as the source of light in the Holy of Holies. Here the *aureum candelabrum* signifies Mary's "resplendent virtues," especially the seven works of Mercy, though in the *Glossa* they are the seven gifts of the Holy Spirit (PL 113.269) "exemplified in Christ and his faithful following him" (The Jewish Hanukkah menorah is symbolic of the eight-day feast of lights and therefore has eight branches with a central, ninth "servant" branch). [8] Ex. 25.31–40, Ex. 27.21

These last two commandments, it seems, differ in no way
except that they wish to denote immovable and movable properties.
Mary was observing attentively all those commandments of God,
and for this reason the Ark of the Covenant prefigured her allegorically.
Also, the Ark of the Covenant contained the Book of the Law
and Mary eagerly held the books of sacred Scripture.
In the Ark also there was the staff of Aaron, which once blossomed,
and Mary blossomed and brought forth the blessed fruit of her womb.
Also the Ark contained a golden urn with manna,
and Mary offered us the true manna of heaven.
The Ark of the Covenant was made from incorruptible shittim wood,
and Mary was by no means reduced to decay or dust.
The Ark had four golden rings on its sides
and Mary bore four original virtues in herself,

which are temperance, prudence, fortitude, and justice.
These are the roots and beginnings of all virtues.
The Ark had two golden poles by which it was carried,
through which the twofold love in Mary is indicated, namely, of God and neighbor.
The Ark was gilded as much inwardly as outwardly;
Mary was resplendent with virtues inside and out. *Figure Two*
Wherefore, she herself was also beautifully prefigured by the golden candelabrum,
which was shining in Jerusalem in the Temple of the Lord,
upon which seven burning lamps were standing,
which prefigured the seven works of mercy in Mary.
These are to feed him who hungers and give drink to him who thirsts;
to clothe the naked and welcome him who does not have lodging;
to visit the sick and have compassion for the fettered and free them;
to bury the dead and administer the necessary funeral rites.
Let no one doubt that the works of mercy were complete in Mary,
who, it is certain, was the mother of piety and the queen of mercy.
How could the mother of all mercy not fill up the works of mercy?
How could a candlestick kindled with divine fire, not shine?

Ipsa enim est candelabrum et ipsa est lucerna
Ipsa est lampas ardens accensa luce superna.
Ipsa tota splendens est et tota luminosa
Ipsa aurora rutilans et tamquam sol radiosa.
Ipsa lucet et splendet super omnia astra celorum
Ipsa est luna huius noctis mundi et lux angelorum.
Hoc candelabrum et eius candelam honoramus

14b[2] Quando in festo purifica⸌cionis accensas⸍[1] candelas baiulamus.
Maria enim domino ⸌candela⌊m⌋ sua⸍[3] purificacione offerebat
Quando symeon lumen ad reuelacionem gencium concinebat.[4]
Christus marie filius est accensa candela
Propter triplicem materiam que inuenitur in ea.
Sunt enim in candela ⸌ignis lichnus⸍ et cera.
Sic in christo erant caro anima ⸌christi diuinitas⸍ uera.
Hec candela pro humano genere est domino oblata
Per quam nox tenebrarum nostrarum est illuminata.
¶Oblacio huius beatissime et gloriosissime candele *tercia figura.*
Quondam prefigurata fuit in puero samuele.[5]
Anna uxor Elkane sterilis prolem non habebat
Et pro puero deum exorans lacrimas uberrime fundebat.
Anne igitur sterili[s] deus contra morem nature filium donauit
Marie uirgini supra cursum nature filium inspirauit.
Anna filium suum samuelem uocans obtulit eum deo
Maria filium suum sanctum ihesum appellans obtulit eum patri vero.
Anna obtulit filium qui iudeos erat propugnaturus
Maria obtulit filium qui mundum erat protecturus.
Filius anne postea a iudeis est refutatus
Filius marie ab eis est morte turpissima condempnatus.
Hoc est quod symeon marie prophetando predicebat
Quod gladius filii sui ipsius animam pertransire debebat.[6]

---

[2] Right Panel: Samuel Dedicated at the Temple. The books associated with Samuel begin with his mother Anna (1Kings 1–2), hitherto barren like Rachel, praying to God in the Temple for the gift of a son. The *sacerdos* is Eli, who hears her prayer. The *Glossa* makes Anna a figure for the Church (PL 113.539), but makes no connection between the dedication of Samuel and the dedication of Jesus. Bernard of Clairvaux sees her as a figure for the Virgin Mary, partly on account of the analogy between her song (1Kings 2.1–10) and Mary's Magnificat (Lk. 1.46–55). [1] Two small holes in the parchment have created lacunae in ll. 1–2 and 6–7, probably from later damage. A later scribe has attempted to repair the damage by scribbling the missing words in the margin in a lighter brown and more angular hand. [3] candelam] candela L, *pace* the corrector [4] Lk. 2.32 [5] 1Kings 1.5 [6] Lk. 2.35

For she is a candlestick and she herself is a lamp;
she is a burning lamp, kindled with heavenly light.
She is wholly glittering and wholly luminous;
she is the reddening dawn and radiant like the sun.
She shines and glitters beyond all the stars of the sky;
she is the moon of this world's night and the light of angels.
We honor this candlestick and its light

when we carry lighted candles in the Feast of Purification.
For Mary offered a candle to the Lord during her own purification
when Simeon sang, "a light for revelation to the Gentiles."
Christ, Mary's son, is the lighted candle
on account of the threefold material which is found in it.
For in a candle there is fire, wick, and wax.
Likewise, in Christ there were flesh, soul, and Christ's true divinity.
This candle was offered to the Lord on behalf of the human race:
through it the night of our darkness was illuminated.
The offering of this most blessed and most glorious candle *Figure Three*
had once been prefigured in the boy Samuel.
Anna, the barren wife of Elkanah, did not have offspring
and, entreating God for a boy, she wept most copiously.
So to barren Anna, God—against the custom of nature—granted a son.
Into Mary, a virgin, he—beyond the course of nature—breathed a son.
Anna, calling her son Samuel, offered him to God.
Mary, naming her holy son Jesus, offered him to his true Father.
Anna offered a son who would contend for the Jews.
Mary offered a son who was going to protect the world.
The son of Anna was afterward rejected by the Jews.
the son of Mary was condemned by them to the basest death.
This is what Simeon foretold to Mary by prophesying
that her son's sword should pierce her own soul.

O bone ihesu da nobis tuam presentacionem ita uenerari
Ut tibi in templo celesti mereamur manibus angelorum presentari.

14va *Capitulum xi*[1]

*I*n precedenti capitulo audiuimus quomodo christus ⸌est obla⸍[2]us
Consequenter audiamus quomodo in egip⟦tum est fu⟧gatus.
Cumque rex herodes quereret occidere christum
Ioseph premonitus ab angelo fugit cum eo in egiptum.[3]
Statim quando christus et mater eius cum ioseph in egiptum intrauerunt
[4]Omnia ydola egipti et statu⟦e co⟧rruerunt.
[5,6]Et hoc quondam Jeremias egipci⟦is pro⟧phetauerat
Quando in egiptum per captiuitatem ductus fuerat.[7]
[8]Quem cum egipcii sanctam prophetam cognouerunt[9]
Scissitabant ab eo si aliqua mirabilia in egipto futura erat.
Qui dixit quod in futuro quedam uirgo esset paritura
Et tunc omnes dii et omnia ydola egipti essent ruitura.
Egipcii ergo illum puerum potenciorem diis suis iudicauerunt.
Et qualem sibi reuerenciam exhiberent inter se tractauerunt.
Ymaginem igitur uirginis cum puero pulcherrimo sculpebant
Et sibi diuinos honores iuxta suum modum exhibebant.
Interrogati postea a tholomeo cur hoc facerent.
Dixerunt quod talem propheciam adhuc implendam expectarent.
Hec autem prophecia quam predixerat sanctus ille propheta
Christo intrante egyptum cum matre est impleta.
[10]Nam omnia ydola egipti et statue corruerunt
Et uirginem sicut predictum fuerat peperisse iudicauerunt.

---

[1] Left Panel: Flight into Egypt and Falling Idols. Here we venture again into apocryphal texts, especially the First Infancy Gospel (4.21–5.12). Mt. 2.14–15 connects the sojourn of the holy family in Egypt with the prophecy (Is. 19.1; Hos. 11.1), "out of Egypt have I called my son," verses in which the presence of the Lord in judgment includes the phrase, "the idols of Egypt will totter in his presence." Here the narrative is conflated on the pattern of the *Glossa* (PL 113.1260) and popular elaborations such as the *Meditationes Vitae Christi* (Ragusa and Green, 68), which themselves draw on the account in Pseudo Matthew. The caption summarizes the synthetic exegesis. [2] Due to a hole in the parchment, this line was later corrected in brown ink in the right margin. The subsequent holes in the membrane in ll. 2, 6, and 7 have not been repaired or emended. [3] Mt. 2.13 [4] *Historia Scholastica* Evangelium 10 [5] The *HS* Evang. attributes the prophesy to Is. 19.1 [6] "prima" is written faintly in the left margin. Only one figure mark in this chapter has been rubricated (ln. 23), and is misnumbered. [7] Jer. 43.5–13 [8] *HS* Tobias 3. See also *The Lives of the Prophets*, an apocryphal narrative of the OT prophets generally attributed (by Comestor as well as modern scholars) to the fourth-century Epiphanius of Salamis [9] G, K] audiuissent, L [10] See the Gospel of Pseudo-Matthew 22–24

O good Jesus, grant us to adore your presentation in such a way
that we should be worthy to be presented to you in the heavenly temple by the hands of angels.

Chapter Eleven

In the last chapter, we heard about the presentation of Christ,
now let us hear how he fled into Egypt.
When King Herod was seeking to kill Christ,
Joseph, having been forewarned by an angel, fled with him into Egypt.
Immediately when Christ and his mother entered into Egypt with Joseph
all the idols and statues of Egypt toppled over.
And this Jeremiah once had prophesied to the Egyptians
when he had been led into Egypt through captivity.
When the Egyptians recognized him as a holy prophet,
they inquired from him if there would be any miracles in Egypt.
He said that in the future, a certain virgin would give birth
and then all gods and all idols of Egypt would collapse.
Therefore the Egyptians deemed the boy more powerful than their own gods
and they discussed among themselves what kind of reverance they would show him.
Therefore they carved an image of a virgin with a most beautiful boy
and were offering it divine honors according to their own custom.
Questioned afterwards by Ptolemy why they were doing this,
they said that they were still waiting for such a prophecy to be fulfilled.
But this prophecy which that holy prophet had foretold
was fulfilled by Christ entering Egypt with his mother.
For all the idols and statues of Egypt toppled over
and they concluded that the virgin, just as it had been foretold, had given birth.

¶Hoc idem etiam erat figuratum in moyse et pharaone *prima figura*[1].
In fractione dei sui hammonis et corone.
Pharao enim rex egipti coronam regalem habebat

14[vb2] In qua ymago dei sui hammonis artificialiter sculpta erat.
Vaticinatum est egipciis quod de iudeis quidam puer nasceretur
Per quem populus iudaicus liberaretur et eigptus destrueretur.
Precepit igitur pharao ut iudei pueros suos in flumen proicerent
Ut sic illum quem timebant pariter interimerent.
Amram autem et iochabet decreuerunt se ab inuicem separare
Quia mallent carere liberis quam ad necem procreare.
Receperunt autem rursum[3] a deo ut simul habitarent
Quia puerum quem egipcii timebant ipsi generarent.
Concepit ergo Jochabet et peperit pulcherrimum filium.
Et abscondit eum tribus mensibus intra suum domicilium.[4]
Cumque diucius eum occultare non ualebat
In viscellam eum recludens in flumen exponebat.
Eadem hora filia pharaonis secus flumen deambulauit
Et puerum inueniens sibi in filium adoptauit.
Quem illa moysen uocat fecit educari
Et postea decreuit eum regi pharaoni u⌊i⌋dendum[5] presentari
[6]Cui pharao alludens coronam suam sibi imponebat
Quam ille proiciens ad terram penitus confringebat.
Quod uidens quidam pontifex ydolorum exclamauit
Hic puer est quem nobis occidendum deus monstrauit.
Cumque euaginato gladio ipsum occidere uoluisset
Dixerunt quidam quod puer hoc ex insipiencia fecisset.
In cuius rei argumentum carbones uiuos quidam sibi offerebat
De quibus puer nutu dei in os suum proiciebat.

---

[1] in the margins is written "iia"—"secunda", but not rubricated. See above note for confusion about the numbering of figures in this chapter. [2] Right Panel: Egyptian Madonna. Under the caption *ymago virginis cum puero* is not, as we might expect, given the mention of Ptolemy, a statue of Isis and Horus, always seated in the manner of a Christian maiestas, but rather a crowned and standing Virgin with a young Jesus, apparently floating in mid-air, holding two scepters topped with sycamore leaves. A source here is the *Historia Scholastica* on Tobit. [3] rursum] responsum, *L* [4] Ex. 1.22–2.10 [5] uidendum, L] vadendum, G [6] *HS* Exodus 4

This same thing was also symbolized in Moses and Pharaoh *Figure One*
in the shattering of his god Amun and the crown.
For Pharaoh, king of Egypt, had a regal crown

on which the image of his god Amun was artfully carved.
It was prophesied to the Egyptians that a certain boy would be born of the Jews
through whom the Jewish people would be freed and Egypt destroyed.
Therefore Pharaoh commanded the Jews to cast their sons into the river
so that, in this way, they should also do away with that boy whom they feared.
But Amram and Jochebed mutually decided to separate from one another
since they would rather lack children than beget children for slaughter.
However, they received in return [a response] from God that they should live together
because they themselves would beget the boy whom the Egyptians feared.
Thus Jochebed conceived and gave birth to a most beautiful son.
And she concealed him inside her own house for three months.
And when she could not hide him any longer,
Enclosing him in a small wicker basket, she put him out in the river.
That very hour, Pharaoh's daughter was going for a stroll along the river
and finding the boy, she adopted him as her son.
She called him Moses, had him drawn out,
and afterwards decided that he should be presented to the King Pharaoh to be seen.
And playing with him, Pharaoh placed his own crown on him
which Moses, tossing on the ground, shattered thoroughly.
Seeing this, a certain priest of idols exclaimed:
"This boy is he whom the god taught us must be killed!"
And when he wished to kill him with unsheathed sword,
some people said that the boy had done it out of foolishness.
In proof of which fact someone offered him live coals
which the boy, by the will of God, tossed into his mouth.

15a[1]
Saluatus ˋestˊ ergo moyses nutu dei et uixit
Et procedente tempore iudeos de egipciaca seruitute eduxit.
Et que ⌊hic⌋[2] narrata sunt de puero isto
Figuraliter partim conueniunt puero ihesu christo.
Rex pharao iudeos pueros suos submergere coegit.
Et ut puerum moysen pariter submergerent satagit.
Ita rex herodes omnes pueros bethleem occidi mandauit.
Quia puerum ihesum pariter cum eis occidere affectauit.[3]
Moysen nutu dei saluatus est [de gladio herodis] de nece pharaonis.
Sic christus nutu dei saluatus est de gladio herodis.
Moysen natus est ut filios israel educeret de egypto
Christus homo factus est ut nos eriperet de inferno.
Moyses deum egipti cum corona confregit
Christus omnia ydola egipti et deos eorum in nichilum redegit.
[4]¶Hanc ruinam ydolorum etiam illa statua pretendebat
Quam rex nabuchodonosor in sompnis uidebat.[5]
Huius statue caput et collum erant ex auro
Brachia vero ipsius et pectus erant ex argento.
Venter autem ymaginis et femora erant ex ere
Tybie autem ipsius uidebantur materiam ferri habere.
Pedum pars quedam erat fictilis id est terrea
Quedam vero pars eorum uidebatur ferrea.
De monte autem sine manibus quidam lapis est abscisus
Et in pedes eius ymaginis siue ydoli est illisus.
Contriuitque eam et in puluerem omnino redegit

[1] Left Panel: Moses Shatters Pharoah's Crown. There is a caption within the image, *moyses puer*. The story told in our text derives ultimately from a Jewish midrash on Ex. 4.10, where it is used to explain how Moses came to have a speech defect (Shemot Rabba 1.3.1). Reiterated in Josephus' *Antiquities of the Jews* (2.234) and the *Historia Scholastica* (19), it became a popular inclusion in late medieval art. Shown here is the boy Moses on pain of death for childishly tipping the crown off Pharaoh's head, being offered a choice between a bowl of jewels and a chafer of hot coals to test whether he had precocious intentions of usurpation. Guided by Gabriel (not shown here), he chooses a hot coal and puts it in his mouth, thus permanently damaging his lips but saving his life. This event is connected to the paranoia of Pharaoh in ordering the death of all male children of the Jews (Ex. 1.8–22). [2] hic, L] a quo G [3] Mt. 2.16 [4] "tertia" is noted in the left margin [5] Dn. 2.31–35

Therefore Moses was saved by the will of God, and he lived,
and in the coming time he led the Jews out of Egyptian servitude.
And things that have been told about that boy
in part correspond symbolically with the boy Jesus Christ.
King Pharaoh forced the Jews to drown their boys
and he took pains that they should drown the boy Moses as well.
So too King Herod ordered that all the boys of Bethlehem be killed,
since he strove to kill the boy Jesus along with them.
Moses, by the will of God, was saved from the slaughter of Pharaoh.
Likewise Christ, by the will of God, was saved from the sword of Herod.
Moses was born in order to lead the sons of Israel from Egypt;
Christ became man in order to snatch us up from hell.
Moses shattered Egypt's god along with the crown;
Christ reduced all the idols of Egypt and their gods to nothing.
The collapse of the idols was also anticipated by that statue
which King Nebuchadnezzar saw in his dreams.
The head and neck of this statue were made of gold,
but its arms and chest were of silver,
while the stomach and thighs of the image were of bronze,
and its legs seemed to consist of iron material.
One part of the feet was clay (that is, earthen)
but the other part of them seemed iron.
However, from the mountain, a stone was hewed off without hands
and was beat against the feet of the image or idol
and crushed it and reduced it utterly to dust

15b[1] Et postea idem lapis in montem maximum excreuit.
Lapis iste significat filium dei ihesum christum
Qui pro salute generis humani uenit in mundum istum.
Lapis abscisus est de monte sine manibus
Christus natus est de maria sine tactibus maritalibus.
Lapis iste scilicet christus contriuit in egipto omnia ydola
Siue aurea erant siue argentea.
Erea pariter contriuit et etiam ferrea.
Confregit quoque fictilia id est terrea.
Omnes iste materie erant in predicta ymagine siue statua
Et omnia ydola corruerunt de quacumque materia.
Lapis ille contrita statua in montem magnum excreuit
Quia destructa ydolatria fides christi iam per totem mundum inoleuit.
Vel lapis iste crescebat et mons magnus factus est
Quia hostis christi herodes quasi ad nichilum redactus est.
Christus autem rediens in iudeam crescebat
Etate et sapientia coram deo et hominibus proficiebat.[2]
Et tandem creuit in montem talem et tantum
Quod sua immensitate repleuit tam mundum quam celum.[3]
Et quis ascendet in montem domini istum
Nisi innocens manibus et mundo corde hic uidebit christum.[4]
Hic accipiet benedicionem a domino
Et misericordiam a deo salutari suo.
O bone ihesu da nobis ut mundo corde tibi seruiamus
Et in montem tuum ascendentes te sine fine uideamus.

---

[1] Right Panel: Nebuchadnezzar and the Shattered Statue. It is titled with the caption *rex nabuchondonosor*, and has the caption *statua eius sompni* in the image. Dn. 2.31–45 gives the interpretation of the king's dream, which may be said to symbolize a history of tyrannies or empires, to follow from the Babylonian empire, greatest of worldly powers. At the end of this history, symbolized by the statue's feet being admixture of iron and clay, a stone "hewn out of the mountain without hands" falls on the feet, causing the statue to fall to the ground in pieces. All we see in the image is Nebuchadnezzar sleeping with the ambiguous *statua eius sompni* above him, a typical pictorial locus for the subject of a dream vision. Usually interpreted eschatologically with reference to the second advent of Christ, here it becomes also another sign of Mary's virginity.

[2] Lk. 2.52

[3] See Jer. 23.24

[4] Ps. 23.3, See Mt. 5.8

and then that same stone grew up into the highest mountain.
That stone signifies the son of God, Jesus Christ
who, for the salvation of the human race, came into the world.
The stone was hewed off from the mountain without hands
Christ was born from Mary without marital embrace;
That stone—namely Christ—crushed all the idols in Egypt
whether they were gold or silver.
Bronze idols it smashed equally, and also iron.
It also shattered clay (that is, earthen) idols.
All those materials were in the aforementioned image (or statue)
and all the idols, of whatever material, toppled over.
That stone—once the statue was crushed—grew up into a great mountain
since after idolatry was destroyed the faith of Christ now grew throughout the whole world.
Or, that stone grew and became a great mountain
since the enemy of Christ, Herod, was (so to speak) reduced to nothing.
Moreover, Christ, returning to Judea, grew up;
he advanced in age and in wisdom in the sight of God and men.
And finally, he grew into a mountain of such a kind and of such size
that he filled up the earth, as well as heaven, with his own infinity.
And who shall ascend that mountain of the Lord
except the one innocent in hands and clean of heart, he will see Christ.
He shall receive a blessing from the Lord
and the mercy from his saving God.
O good Jesus, grant us that we may serve you with a pure heart
and that, ascending your mountain, we may see you without end.

15va

Capitulum xii[1]

*I*n precedenti capitulo audiuimus quomodo christus in egiptum est fugatus
Consequenter audiamus quomodo a iohanne in iordane sit baptizatus.[2]
Cumque tricesimum etatis sue annum inchoaret
Venit ad iordanem ut eum iohannes baptizaret
Christus autem filius dei uiui[3] baptismo non indigebat
Sed pro salute generis humani baptizari uolebat.
Et ⌊ut⌋[4] tactu sui sacri corporis aquis hanc uirtutem daret.
Ut homo in eis baptizatus et mundatus regnum celorum intraret.
¶Et istud in mari eneo id est in lauatorio erat prefiguratum *prima figura*.
Quod ante introitum templi irosolimis fuit collocatum.[5]
Sacerdotes enim qui templum domini ingressuri erant
In hoc lauatorio se lauari neccesse habebant.
Ita omnes qui uoluerint ⌊intrare⌋[6] in celeste domini templum
Necesse habent ut prius lauentur per baptismum.
[7]Notandum autem quod triplex est baptismus
Videlicet fluminis sanguinis et flaminis.
Baptismo fluminis baptizamur per aque immersionem
Baptsimo sanguinis per martyrii passionem.
Baptismo flaminis id est spiritus sancti homo baptizatur
Si non habet baptistam et cum proposito baptismi moriatur.
Si autem superuixerit non sufficit ei solum propositum.
Nisi susceperit ab aliquo si potest aque baptismum.
Nec ualet alicui baptismus sanguinis siue martyrium
Si potest et non uult suscipere aque baptismum.[8]
Baptismus ergo aque siue fluminis est summe necessarius

---

[1] Left Panel: Baptism of Christ. The baptism is attended by two angels who do not appear in the biblical text (John 1.29–34; Mt. 3.13–17) or in the text of the SHS. Nor does our text mention the dove which descends on Christ or the voice of God from heaven, saying, "This is my beloved son in whom I am well pleased" (Mt. 3.16–17). This probably owes to the focus of our text on the types of sacramental baptism more than the narrative itself. [2] Lk. 3.21–23, Mt. 3.13–15 [3] Mt. 16.16 [4] ut, L] neque, G [5] 3 Kings 7.23–26, 2 Par. 4.2–5. See also *HS*. 3 Kings 9.9, Ex. 30.17–21, *HS*. Ex. 67 [6] intrare] L, X [7] See Peter Lombard, *Sententiae* (Book 4, ch. 29 [Distinction IV, ch. 4]). Lombard cites Augustine for the authority of both: *De Civitate Dei* 13 for baptism through blood, and *De baptismo* V.24.34, for baptism through contrition. See also *ST* III.66.11, in which Aquinas cites the *glossa ordinaria* on Hbr. 6:1–2: "pluraliter dicit, quia est baptismus aquae, poenitentiae, et sanguinis". [8] See Augustine, *De baptisma* IV.25.32

Chapter Twelve

In the last chapter, we heard how Christ fled into Egypt,
next let us hear how he was baptized by John in the Jordan.
When he began the thirtieth year of his life
he came to the Jordan, so that John could baptize him.
Christ, the son of the living God, did not require baptism
but was wanting to be baptized for the sake of the salvation of the human race.
And to give this virtue to the waters by the touch of his sacred body
that man, baptized and cleansed in them, should enter the Kingdom of Heaven.
And that was prefigured in the Bronze Sea (that is, in the wash basin) *Figure One*
which had been placed before the entrance to the Temple in Jerusalem.
For the priests who were about to enter the Temple of the Lord
were required to wash themselves in this basin.
So too everyone who purposes [to enter] into the Heavenly Temple of the Lord
is required to be washed beforehand through baptism.
It must be noted, moreover, that baptism is threefold:
namely, of the river, of blood, and of the priest.
By the baptism of the river, we are baptized through the immersion of water;
by the baptism of blood, through the passion of martyrdom;
by the baptism of the priest (that is, of the Holy Spirit) is a man baptized
if he does not have anyone to baptize him and dies with an intention of baptism.
But if he survives, the intention alone does not suffice for him
unless he undertakes—from anyone, so long as he is able—the baptism of water.
Nor can the baptism of blood (or martyrdom) have worth for anyone
if he is able to undertake the baptism of water, and yet does not want to do so.
Thus the baptism of water (or the river) is the most necessary

15vb[1] Templum domini celeste ingredi uolentibus
Baptismus autem fluminis debet fieri in pura aqua
Non in uino non in lacte nec in quacumque materia alia.
Mare eneum siue lauatorium factum erat ex ere
In quo consueuerunt artifices quelibet metalla commiscere.[2]
Ita in qualibet lingua possunt uerba baptismi pronunciari.
Sed tamen approbata forma uerborum debet seruari.
Quilibet etiam homo potest conferre baptismum
Si intendit facere quod ecclesia instituit faciendum.
Duodecim boues enei mare portauerunt
Quia xii apostoli baptismum christi per totum mundum dilatauerunt.
Nec pretereundum est quod hoc lauatorium siue mare eneum
Circumtectum et ornatum erat speculis mulierum.[3]
Ut ingressi in templum se specularentur et uiderent
Si aliquam maculam uel aliquam indecenciam haberent.
Per quod figurabatur quod baptismus requirit conscientie perfectionem
Peccati displicenciam et cordis contricionem.
Quapropter iohannes baptista quibusdam phariseis dicebat
Quos ad baptismum sine contricione accedere uidebat.
Ge⌊ni⌋mina uiperarum quomodo iram futuri iudicis effugietis[4]
Qui uidelicet baptismum suscipitis et contricionem non habetis.
Qui autem susceperit baptismum cum cordis contricione
Mundatur ab omni peccatorum suorum sordidacione.
¶Istud etiam quondam figuratum fuit in naaman syro *secunda figura.*
Qui leprosus erat et mundatus est in iordane modo miro.[5]

---

[1] Right Panel: Brazen Laver of the Temple. This is titled with the caption *mare eneum in lauatorio*. Purification before sacred functions was an important stipulation in Jewish law, and in Solomon's Temple (3 Kings 7.23–24; 2 Par. 4.2–6) was constructed a massive basin, nearly eight feet tall, with a circumference of forty-five feet, heavily decorated with bronze oxen and supported on the backs of twelve oxen, of which only half are pictured here. That priests had to be purified before making a sacrifice is here paralleled to the reasons given for Christ as an eternal high priest to identify with the requirement for the sake of human salvation, but also to indicate by means of the twelve oxen the twelve disciples and the apostolic obligation to baptize those who would be saved. Cf. *Historia Scholastica*, Ex. 70. [2] 1 Par. 18.8 [3] Cf. Ex. 3.8, *HS*. Ex. 67 [4] Mt. 3.7, Lk. 3.7 [5] 4 Kings 5.1–14

For those wishing to enter the Heavenly Temple of the Lord
the baptism of river, moreover, ought to be done in pure water
not in wine, nor in milk, nor in any other material whatsoever.
The Sea of Bronze (or wash basin) was made from a bronze
in which the craftsmen were wont to mingle all sorts of metals.
Thus the words of baptism can be pronounced in whatever language
but nevertheless, the established form of the words should be preserved.
Also, any person at all can confer baptism
if he aims to do what the Church has established should be done.
Twelve oxen supported the Sea of Bronze [in the Temple]
because the twelve apostles have spread the baptism of Christ throughout the whole world.
Nor should it be overlooked that this wash basin (or Bronze Sea)
was covered all around and decorated with women's mirrors
so that those entering into the Temple might examine themselves and see
if they had any blemish or any indecency.
Through which it was prefigured that baptism requires perfection of conscience,
disapproval of sin, and contrition of heart.
On account of which John the Baptist said to certain Pharisees
whom he saw approaching baptism without contrition:
"You brood of vipers, how shall you flee the wrath of the judge to come?
You obviously are undertaking baptism and do not have contrition!"
But he who has received baptism with contrition of heart
is cleansed from all the foulness of his sins.
That also had once been prefigured in Naaman, the Syrian *Figure Two*
who was leprous and was cleansed in the Jordan in a wonderous way.

16a[1]

Naaman erat gentilis et ignorabat deum
Et tamen uenit pro cura ad prophetam dei helyseum.
Ad ⸍i⸌[n]ussum[2] autem helyse⸍i⸌[um][3] sepcies in iordane lauabatur
Et sic ab omni lepra sua mundabatur.
Helyseus per septenam aque iordanis locionem
Prefigurauit vii mortalium peccatorum in baptismo ablucionem.
Caro naaman per iordanem facta est ut caro paruuli
Ita peccatores per baptismum efficiuntur mundi et puri[4].
Et statim antequam iterum peccarent morerientur.
Sine omni impedimento regnum celorum ingrederentur.
Et hoc innuitur in eo quod celum apertum est super christum
Quando suscepit in aqua iordanis a iohanne baptismum.[5]
Quicumque ergo regnum celorum intrare uoluerit
Non intrabit nisi prius ut predictum est baptizatus fuerit.
¶Istud etiam prefiguratum fuit olim in transitu iordanis *tercia figura*.
Quando filii israel intrauerunt terram promissionis.[6]
Quando enim filii israel terram promissionis intrauerunt
Prius iordanem figuram baptismatis transiuerunt.
Sic oportet omnes per lauacrum baptismi transire
Qui desiderant ad ueram terram promissionis peruenire.
⌊Archa⌋[7] domini in medio iordanis portabatur et ibi stabat
Omnis autem populus cum pecoribus suis transmeabant.
Aqua autem que erat in superiori parte arche non processit
Sed instar montis sese super se congessit.
Aqua autem a parte inferiori in mare defluebat

[1] Left Panel. The Cleansing of Naaman the Leper. The image is titled with the caption *naaman leprosus mundatur in iordane*. In 4 Kings 5.1–14 the story of Naaman's astonishment at being cleansed of his distress by obeying Eliseus's direction is a vindication of the prophet's authentic delegation; to immerse himself seven times in the Jordan is taken by him as at first an insult but he humbles himself and obeys, with complete healing as a result. The connection is here made between the seven-times immersion of Naaman and removal of the stain of all seven deadly sins in baptism; this antitype is a late addition to the traditional association with baptism, e.g., in St. Ambrose (*De mysteriis 3.17*) and Tertullian (Adv. Marcion *9.10*) and is not mentioned in the *Glossa* (PL 113. 613–614). The image here shows Naaman, identified clearly in the rubric, with an attendant on each side and arms crossed in the *ancilla domine* posture, linking his humility with that of Mary. [2] Added later by black ink scribe [3] Added later by black ink scribe [4] puri] pueri, L [5] Mt. 3.16, Lk. 3.21, Mk. 1.10 [6] Jos. 3–4 [7] Archa, L] Aqua, G

Naaman was a gentile and was ignorant of God
yet nevertheless he came to Elisha, a prophet of God, for healing.
And at the order of Elisha, he was bathed seven times in the Jordan
and in this way he was cleansed from all his leprosy.
Elisha, through the seven-fold washing of the water of the Jordan,
prefigured the washing away of the seven deadly sins in baptism.
Naaman's skin became, through the Jordan, like the skin of a young boy
in this way sinners, through baptism, are made clean and pure.
And were they to die immediately, before they sin again,
they would enter the Kingdom of Heaven without any barrier.
And this is indicated in the fact that Heaven opened above Christ
when he received baptism from John in the water of the Jordan.
Thus, whosoever may wish to enter the Kingdom of Heaven
shall not enter unless he has been baptized beforehand, as said before.
That also had been once prefigured in the crossing of the Jordan *Figure Three*
when the sons of Israel entered the Promised Land.
For when the sons of Israel entered the Promised Land
they first passed over the Jordan—a symbol of baptism.
Thus to pass through the cleansing of baptism is proper for everyone
who desires to reach the true Promised Land.
The Ark of the Lord was carried into the middle of the Jordan and stood there,
and all the people were passing through with their herds.
Moreover, the water that was upstream from the Ark did not continue flowing
but piled up on top of itself in the likeness of a mountain.
However, the water downstream drained away into the sea

16b1 Et inferior alueus iordanis siccus remanebat.
Tulit autem populus xii lapides de iordanis alueo
Et fecerunt ⸤cumulum⸥[2] in littore pro memoriali perpetuo.
Xii lapides de littore in alueum reportauerunt
Et in loco ubi archa steterat cumulum composuerunt.
Sicque omnis populus alueum iordanis sicco pede transibat
Et postea fluuius iordanis ad pristinum statum redibat.
Archa testimenti que in medio iordanis stabat.
Christum qui in iordane baptizandus erat figurabat.
In archa erat uirga aaron que quondam floruerat.[3]
Et christus per florem huius uirge figuratus fuerat.
In archa etiam manna panis celi erat[4]
Et christus est panis viuus qui de celo descendebat.[5]
In archa etiam erat deuteronomius liber legis
Et idem deus homo factus est qui dedit legem iudeis.
In archa etiam erant x domini precepta
Quia idem deus qui dedit precepta instituit baptisma.
Archa de ligno ⸤sethym⸥[6] imputribili facta fuit
Et caro christi licet moreretur et sepeliretur non tamen computriuit.
Archa erat lignea et tam ⸤intra⸥[7] quam extra auro polita
Et christus erat deitas tam in morte ⸤quam⸥[8] in uita semper unita.
Duodecim lapides testimoniales xii sunt apostoli
Qui ⸌per⸍ orbem terrarum testificati sunt baptismum christi.
O bone ihesu da nobis baptismum tuum ita uenerari
Vt tecum in perpetua gloria mereamur coronari[9].

[1] Right Panel: The Ark Borne Over the Jordan. This is titled with the caption *archa in qua erat uirga aaron et manna celi et testamento*. Here again the Jordan River occasions a typological connection. The biblical narrative (Jos. 3.1–17) recounts how the ark of the Covenant preceded the people of Israel across the Jordan, and how the waters miraculously diminished and piled up in a heap upstream at a place called Adam (13–16), a reiteration of their exodus experience at the Red Sea. This passage into the Promised Land through the Jordan, following the Ark, was traditionally seen, as the *Glossa* puts it, "to prefigure the mysteries of baptism" (PL 113.608) in which the believer follows Christ. The hump under the Ark in this image may be intended to represent the walled-up water. [2] cumulum] L [3] Nm. 17.8, cf. *SHS*. ch. 10 [4] Ex. 16.33 [5] John 6.51 [6] sethym, L] tectum, G. The scribe appears to have struggled with the unusual Hebrew name. [7] intra] L [8] quam, L] tam, G [9] coronari] commorari L

and the lower channel of the Jordan remained dry.
The people also took twelve stones from the riverbed of the Jordan
and made a mound on the shore for an everlasting memorial.
They carried the twelve stones from the shore back into the riverbed
and, in the place where the Ark had stood, they constructed a mound.
And thus all the people passed through the riverbed of the Jordan with dry feet
and after that the river of the Jordan returned to its original state.
The Ark of the Covenant, which stood in the middle of the Jordan,
symbolized Christ, who would be baptized in the Jordan.
In the Ark was Aaron's staff, which had once flowered.
And Christ was symbolized through the flower of this staff.
In the Ark was also manna, the bread of heaven
and Christ is the living bread, which descended from heaven.
In the Ark was also Deuteronomy, the book of the Law
and the same God who gave the Jews the Law became a man.
In the Ark were also the Ten Commandments of the Lord
since the same God who gave the Commandments established baptism.
The Ark had been made from incorruptible shittim wood
and although flesh of Christ died and was buried, nevertheless it did not decay.
The Ark was wooden and polished with gold as much within as without
and Christ was as divine in death as in life, always unified.
The twelve stones are testimonies of the twelve apostles
who were witnesses to the baptism of Christ throughout the whole world.
O good Jesus, grant us to revere your baptism in such a way
that we may worthily be crowned with you in everlasting glory.

16va [1]⸌*Capitulum xiii*⸍[2]

*I*n[3] precedenti capitulo audiuimus quomodo christus a iohanne fuit baptizatus
Consequenter audiamus quomodo a dyabolo fuit tripliciter temptatus.[4]
Post baptismum ductus est ihesus in desertum a spiritu
Id est ihesus intrauit in desertum ex spiritus sancti instinctu.
Non est sic intelligendum quod duxerit eum per aerem
Sicut angelus abacuc prophetam in babylonem.[5]
Sic etiam nec dyabolus eum duxit supra templum
Quod ut facilius intelligatur uideamus per e⌞xe⌟mplum.
Hoc uerbum duxit non omni loco ponitur pro ambulare
Aliquando enim solet inductionem uel ducatum significare.
Moyses duxit filios israel de egipto
Non ergo sequitur quod baiolauerit eos in dorso.
Sic dyabolus christum non per aera ducendo baiulauit
Sed in forma hominis ei apparens verbis laudis secum ire persuauit.[6]
Christus autem propter nos temptaciones sustinere uolebat
Sibi consensit et secum templum et montem ascendebat.
[7]Voluit autem christus temptari pro nostra instructione
Vt ostenderet neminem in hoc mundo sine temptacione.
Si enim christus filius dei a dyabolo temptari uoluit
Nullus putet quod sine temptacione [liberat][8] uiuere possit.
Et si forsan homo ab una temptacione liberatur
Statim alia sibi a demonibus preparatur.
Quapropter christus non est temptatus ab uno tantum uicio sed a tribus
Quia demones temptant nos uiciis multipliciis.
Et si hominibus deus etiam suam et angelorum custodiam non dedisset

---

[1] The chapter number was added by a correcting scribe, likely the same one who labeled the figures, and was not rubricated [2] Left Panel: Temptation of Christ in the Wilderness. The image has three internal captions, all reading *dyabolus*. There are two parallel accounts of this event in the gospels (Mt. 4.1–11; Lk. 4.1–13), each recounting three temptations of Jesus in the wilderness during his forty-day fast. The three temptations—of the flesh, the world, and the devil—rejected by Christ, are often represented (as here) by gluttony, pride, and avarice, though vainglory sometimes substitutes for pride e.g., *Meditationes Vitae Christi*, (Ragusa and Green, 120–123). Though the devil is frequently depicted with horns, he appears here dressed like a religious teacher and has a pleasant demeanor. [3] The scribe working on the main text had already written an "I" (partially rubber out now) at the beginning of this line, before the rubricator added the large, red initial "I". [4] Mt. 4.1–11, Lk. 4.1–13. *Duxit* is used in Luke, *assumpsit* in Matthew [5] Dn. 14.32–38 [6] See Aquinas, *Sup. Evang. Matthaei*, ch. 4 [7] See *ST* III.41.1 [8] Scribal deletion, after eye-skip to the next line

Chapter Thirteen

In the last chapter, we heard how Christ was baptized by John,
next let us hear how he was tempted three times by the devil.
After the baptism, Jesus was led into the wilderness by the Spirit
that is, Jesus entered into the wilderness by the prompting of the Holy Spirit.
It must therefore not be thought that it took him through the air
as an angel [had led] the prophet Habakkuk into Babylon.
The devil did not also in this way lead him atop the Temple,
which, that it may be more easily understood, let us perceive by means of an example:
this word "led" cannot be substituted in every place for "to walk"
for sometimes it is accustomed to denote "leading along" or "guiding."
Moses led the sons of Israel from Egypt
it does not therefore follow that he physically carried them on his back.
Thus, the Devil did not physically carry Christ through the air "by leading [him]"
but, appearing to him in human form he persuaded him with praise to go with him.
Moreover, Christ was desiring to undergo temptations on our account
he consented and climbed the Temple and the mountain with him.
But Christ desired to be tempted for our instruction
in order to show that no one in this world is without temptation.
For if Christ, the son of God, wished to be tempted by the Devil
none should think it possible to live without temptation.
And if, perhaps, man were freed from one temptation,
others would immediately be prepared for him by demons.
On account of which Christ was not tempted by only one vice, but by three,
since demons tempt us with multiple vices.
And if God had not also given people his protection and the protection of angels,

16vb[1] Nullus homo temptaciones euadere posset.
Nam ˋsicutˊ radius solis plenus videtur esse pulueribus
Ita mundus iste plenus est demonibus.[2]
Et ideo si aliquem per temptaciones cecidisse uidemus
Ex intimo cordis sibi compati debemus.
Non statim debemus eum temptare[3] uel publicare
Sed proposse peccatum eius occultare et excusare.
Si autem non poterimus excusare facti perpetracionem
Excusemus prout poterimus ipsius intencionem.
Si autem tale fuerit quod neutrum possimus excusare
Debet quilibet in se gemiscere et sic cogitare.
O quantum deterius tibi[4] miseri pluries accidisset
Si deus per misericordiam suam te[5] non custodisset.
¶Notandum tamen quod temptator proposuit christo tria uicia
Que sunt gula superbia et auaricia.
Cumque ihesus xl diebus et xl noctibus ieiunasset
Suspicatus est sathanas quod famelicus esset.
Solet autem dyabolus temptare hominem per tale peccatum
Ad quod uiderit eum magis inclinatum.
Cum autem ihesum famelicum esse autumaret
Cogitabat apud se ut de gula eum temptaret.
Temptator primo hominem per gulam inuadit
Quia incrassatus cicius quam abstinens in peccatum cadit.
Quapropter primos parentes de gula primo temptabat
Et ad comedendum fructum prohibitum in{ue}stigabat.[6]

17a[7] Frustra igitur contra alia uicia nititur aliquis repugnare
Nisi prius discat gulam et immoderanciam refrenare.

[1] Right Panel: Daniel Destroys Bel and Kills the Dragon. The image contains three captions: *ydolum belis*, *daniel*, and *et draco*. This late deutero-canonical addition to Daniel (Dn. 14) adds more tests of power involving the idol (Bel) and a dragon the people were also said to worship. Daniel exposes the deceit of Bel's priests and the fiction of their god, killing the dragon by feeding it hairballs, exemplifying the motif of the "destroyer destroyed." The story is taken as a prefigurement of Christ's victory over Satan in the wilderness. The image shows a man with a Bel mask (horned) eating some of the food and drink sacrificed to the idol, while Daniel tosses one of his hairballs into the dragon's mouth. [2] See *LA*, ch. 145 [3] temptare] condemnare, L [4] tibi] mihi, L [5] te] me, L [6] inuestigabat] instigauit, C [7] Left Panel: David about to behead Goliath. The image is titled with two captions: *dauid and Golias*. The first of two stories about David's prowess in the biblical source actually follows this one in SHS, largely for typological reasons: the victory over Goliath figures forth a triumph over vainglory through true humility. No attempt is made to show Goliath to scale, and the sling by which David kills him is missing in action; it appears here that the boy David kills him with the sword. The biblical narrative (1 Kings 17.48–51) alone does not provide the typological connection; in the *Glossa* Goliath "signifies truly the pride of the Devil," whilst David, "*id est Christus*," defeats him in single combat, even as Christ conquers Satan, on behalf of the people of God in both cases (PL 113.556).

no man would be able to escape temptation.
For just as a ray of the sun appears to be full of dust
so this world is full of demons.
And for this reason, if we see someone has fallen into temptation
we ought to commiserate with him from the depths of our heart.
We ought not to immediately test or shame him,
but, to the extent of our power, to conceal and excuse his sin.
Moreover, should we not be able to excuse the perpetration of the deed,
we may excuse, as much as we are able, its intention.
But if there should be such a [sin] for which we can excuse neither,
anyone ought to groan within himself and think thus:
"O how much worse would likely have happened to a wretch like you
if God in his mercy had not been guarding you."
It must be noted, moreover, that the tempter put before Christ three vices,
which are gluttony, pride, and avarice.
And when Jesus had fasted for forty days and forty nights,
Satan supposed that he would be hungry.
And the Devil is used to tempting a man with the sort of sin
to which he sees him to be more inclined.
And when he reckoned that Jesus was hungry,
he thought to himself how he might tempt him through gluttony.
The tempter first enters into a man by means of gluttony,
since he falls more swiftly into sin fattened than abstinent.
Accordingly, he tempted the first parents by gluttony in the beginning
and he sought out the fruit forbidden to be eaten.

Therefore one struggles in vain to fight back against the other vices
unless he first learns to curb gluttony and immoderation.

Christus ergo dyabolum in temptacione gule superauit *prima figura*.
¶Et hoc quondam daniel in ydolo belis et dracone prefigurauit.[1]
In babylone ydolum belis pro deo colebatur
Quod multum comedere et multum bibere dicebatur.
Cottidie enim offerebantur ei panes xii mensurarum.
Sex amphore uini et carnes xl ouium coctarum.
Sacerdotes autem ydoli per uiam subterraneam noctibus intrauerunt
Et uxores et liberos [secum] secum adducentess hec omnia consumpsuerunt.
Quorum uestigia pedum daniel per cineres inuenit
Et de licencia regis bel destruens illos interemit.
Ibidem etiam quidam draco in spelunca latitabat[2]
Qu⸤e⸥m[3] tota gens illa tamquam deum estimabat.
Quem statutis horis sacerdos suus cibum suum sibi offerebat
Quem ille gratanter accipiens semper ibi permanebat
Daniel autem massam de pice et adipe et pilis confecit.
Et de licencia regis eam in os draconis proiecit
Quam cum comedisset statim est ruptus
Et sic uterque deuorator per danielem est destructus.
Daniel ergo qui istos deuoratores et gulosos ⸤adnichilauit⸥[4]
Christum qui temptacionem gule uicit prefigurauit. *secunda figura*.
¶Christus etiam superauit dyabolum in temptacione superbie
Et hoc prefiguratum est olim in dauid et nece golye[5]
Golyas superbissime de fortitudine sua se iactabat.

17b[6] Et nullum sibi similem inter omnes filios israel estimabat
Dauid autem ipsum cum funda ad terram deiecit
Et proprio gladio cum dei adiutorio ipsum interfecit.
Golyas iste gygas superbus figuram tene⸤t⸥[7] luciferi
Qui in regno celorum affectauit similis deo fieri.[8]
Dauid autem pastor qui hunc superbum gigantem prostrauit
Christus est qui te⸤m⸥ptacionem superbie humiliter superauit.
Temptaciones superbie diuerse sunt et ubique generales
Quia regnant non tantum inter seculares[9] ⸍sed⸌ etiam inter claustrales.
Sepe enim quem nulla uicia uincere possunt
Vana gloria et appetitus humanae[10] laudis corrumpunt.

[1] Dn. 14.2–21 [2] Dn. 14.22–26 [3] quem, L] quam, G [4] adnichilauit, L] adhumauit, G [5] 1 Kings 17. Cf. *Glossa ordinaria* [6] Right Panel: David Fights a Bear, Having Previously Killed a Lion. There is a caption in the image, *dauid*. This account of David's bravery (1 Kings 17.34–36) is minimalist, but the lion and bear are here taken to represent avarice, also defeated by Christ in his resistance to the devil. [7] tenet, L] tenens [8] See Is. 14.12–14 [9] Corrected from "et" [10] A rare occurrence of the genitive "ae" ending written out fully

Thus Christ overcame the Devil in the temptation of gluttony *Figure One*
and this Daniel once prefigured in the idol of Bel and the dragon.
In Babylon, an idol of Bel was worshipped as a god
which was said to eat much and drink much.
Indeed, every day twelve measures of bread were offered to it,
six measures of wine, and the meat of forty cooked sheep.
However, the priests of the idol entered through an underground passage during the nights
and bringing their wives and children with them, they consumed all these things.
Daniel discovered their footprints by means of ashes
and destroying Bel (with the permission of the king), he killed them [the priests].
In the same place, a certain dragon was lurking in a cave
which that whole nation considered to be like a god.
Its priest, at decreed hours, used to offer it food
which it joyfully accepted, always remaining there.
But Daniel made a lump from tar, and fat, and hair.
And, with the permission of the king, he threw it into the dragon's mouth.
When it had eaten the lump, it immediately burst,
and thus each "devourer" was destroyed, thanks to Daniel.
Thus Daniel, who destroyed those devourers and gluttons,
prefigured Christ, who conquered the temptation of gluttony. *Figure Two*
Christ also overcame the Devil in the temptation of pride
and this was once prefigured in David and the slaying of Goliath.
Goliath was boasting very arrogantly of his own strength

and considered no one among all the sons of Israel to be a match for himself
but David cast him to the ground with his sling
and killed him with his own sword, by God's assistance.
Goliath, that prideful giant, contains a figure of Lucifer
who desired to become like God in the Kingdom of Heaven.
But David, a shepherd, who laid low this haughty giant
is Christ, who humbly overcame the temptation of pride.
The temptations of pride are diverse and are common everywhere
since they hold sway not only among laypeople but also among the cloistered.
For often he whom no vice can conquer
vainglory and an appetite for human praise do corrupt.

Sepe enim sub ueste uilissima latitat mens tam elata
Sicut sub purpura imperatoris deaurata.
¶Tercio christus dyabolum in temptacione auarice superauit *tercia figura*.
Hoc et dauid in nece leonis et ursi prefigurauit.[1]
Leo et ursus conuenienter auariciam prefigurabant
Quia auferendo sibi ouem rapinam perpetrabant.
Dauid autem ouem suam eripiens raptores interfecit
Et christus superata temptacione auarice sathanam a se reiecit.[2]
Abiecto autem sathan accesserunt angeli
Et tamquam uictori et triumphatori ministrabant ei.[3]
Sic qui uiriliter pugnando contra dyabolum triumphauerit
Ministerio et consorcio sanctorum angelorum dignus erit
O bone ihesu da nobis in cunctis temptacionibus ita [superare] triumphare.
Ut tecum mereamur in eterna gloria inhabitare.

17va

Capitulum xiiii[4]

*I*n precedenti capitulo audiuimus quomodo dyablus christum temptauit
Consequenter audiamus quomodo christus mariam magdalenam curauit.[5]
Cumque ihesu christus xxx^{m} annum inciperet a iohanne est baptizatus
Et statim post baptismum a dyablo est temptatus
Postea cepit populo predicare et baptizare
Exemplo et doctrina viam salutis monstrare.
In principio sue predicacionis emisit hanc dulcem sonum
Penitentiam agite apropinquabit enim regnum celorum.[6]
Per penitentiam predicauit regni celestis apercionem
Ante aduentum suum numquam audiuit homo talem sermonem.
Fidelis sermo et omni accepcione dignus.
Per penitentiam meretur regnum celorum peccator malignus.
Istud apparet in peccatrice magdalena
Que fuit vii demoniis id est uiciis mortalibus plena.

---

[1] 1 Kings 17.34–37 [2] reiecit] deiecit, L [3] Mt. 4.11 [4] Left Panel: The Penitence of Mary Magdalene. The image is titled with the caption *quomodo christus curauit mariam magdalenam*, and a caption inside the image reads *magdala*. While the penitent woman who washes the feet of Jesus in the house of Simon the Pharisee is not named in that passage (Lk. 7.36–8.1), the immediately following story about Mary Magdalene has served to make the biblical connection. In this image the table is not a triniculum but a European-style rectangular table, and while Jesus asks Simon about the measure of love, a prostrate Magdalene (though with no visible alabaster jar, her usual sign) kisses his feet. Mary Magdalene, thought to be a woman of ill repute before her conversion (Mk. 16.9) was one of the most popular subjects from the gospels; she is illustrated in much this way in the *Meditationes Vitae Christi* (Ragusa and Green, fig. 155), but there with her conventional alabaster jar. [5] Lk. 8.2, Mk. 16.9 [6] Mt. 4.17

For often beneath the meanest garment lurks a mind as haughty
as that beneath the gilded purple of an emperor.
Thirdly, Christ overcame the Devil in the temptation of avarice. *Figure Three*
And David prefigured this by slaying the lion and the bear.
The lion and the bear suitably prefigured avarice
since, by carrying away a sheep for themselves, they committed theft.
But David, rescuing his sheep, killed the thieves,
and Christ, having overcome the temptation of avarice, repelled Satan from himself.
After Satan was overthrown, the angels approached
and they ministered to him just as a victor and conqueror.
In this way he who will have triumphed over the Devil by staunch fighting
shall be worthy of the care and company of heavenly angels.
O good Jesus, grant us to triumph amid all temptations in such a way
that we may be worthy to abide with you in eternal glory.

Chapter Fourteen

In the last chapter we heard how the devil tempted Christ;
next let us hear how Christ healed Mary Magdalene.
When Christ Jesus was thirty years old, he was baptized by John,
and immediately after his baptism, he was tempted by the devil.
Afterwards, he began to preach to the people and to baptize,
to show them by his example and teaching the way of salvation.
In the beginning of his preaching, he sent forth this sweet sound:
"Repent, for the kingdom of heaven will draw near."
He preached the opening of the kingdom of heaven through penitence,
before his coming, never had man heard such a message,
a true message and worthy of acceptance by all.
Through penitence the evil sinner is made worthy of the kingdom of heaven.
This is made clear in the sinner Mary Magdalene,
who was filled with seven demons, that is, by the seven deadly sins,

Que eiecta sunt ab ea per contricionem et penitentiam
Et ipsa misericorditer consecuta est dei clemenciam.
Nullus ergo peccator debet de misericordia dei desperare
Quia deus presto est cunctis penitentibus debita relaxare.[1]
Insuper penitentes ad regnum celorum reuocat
¶Quod ante aduentum christi nulli penitentia fieri poterat *prima figura*.
Istud deus per regem manassen olim prefigurabat[2]
Quem propter penitentias in regem reuocabat.
Manasses infinitis peccatis offenderat deum
Prophetas suos occidens et nichil reputans eum.
Tot prophetas eum arguentes cruciauit

17vb[4]
Quot[3] plateas ierusalem sanguine prophetarum purpurauit
Sanctum prophetam ysaiam qui ipsum de sceleribus suis redarguit.
Cum serra lignea per medium dissecari fecit[5]
Tandem post multa scelera ab hostibus suis est captiuatus
Et in exilium deductus carceri deputatus.
Cumque esset in carcere cepit penitentiam habere
Ex toto corde perpetrata scelera deflere.
Orauitque dominum profusis lacrimis amaris
Peccaui inquit donec super numerum arene maris.
Et iam non sum dignus uidere celi altitudinem
Propter iniquitatum mearum [altitudinem] multitudinem.
Iram tuam deus clementissime irritaui
Et malum coram te feci et illicita perpetraui.
Misertus dominus ostendit ei suam clemenciam
Et misericorditer acceptauit eius penitentiam.
Nam de carcere et de captiuitate eum liberauit
Et in regnum suum et ierusalem ipsum reuocauit.
Per hunc manassen peccator malignus designatur
Qui cum sine timore peccat deum non curare comprobatur.
Prophetas domini ipsum arguentes cruciat
Quando predicatores et doctores audire recusat.

---

[1] See 1John 1.9, 2Pt. 3.9, Ps. 86.5, Ps. 102.8, 17, Prov. 28.13, Is. 55.7, 2 Par. 7.14 [2] 4Kings 21.9–16, 2 Par. 33.1–13 [4] Right Panel: The Penitence of Manasses in Captivity. The image is titled with the caption *rex mannasen poenitentie eius depictus*. Even as Magdalene suggests that a person deep in sin can repent and be saved, so does King Manasses (4Kings 21.1–18), infamous slaughterer of God's prophets, including Isaiah. Deposed and led away by the Assyrians with a hook through his nose, he found leisure to repent in captivity (2 Par. 33.11–18) and was eventually restored to his throne. We see his constraining chain; anachronistically, he wears a Crusader's cross on his tunic, suggesting his 'return' in Christian fashion. [3] MS. read *Quot* [5] Cf. *Ascension of Isaiah* 5.1, 11 (first century Apocryphal Jewish Text), See Hbr. 11.37

which were cast out from her by contrition and penitence,
and this same woman mercifully obtained the clemency of God.
Therefore, no sinner should despair of the mercy of God,
because God is ready to forgive the debts of all who are penitent.
Furthermore, he calls back penitents to the kingdom of heaven
which, before the coming of Christ, was possible through no amount of penitence. *Figure One*
God at one time prefigured that through King Manasses,
whom he called back to the kingdom on account of his penitence.
Manasses had offended God with innumerable sins,
killing his prophets and esteeming him [God] not at all.
He tortured so many prophets who accused him

that he turned the streets of Jerusalem crimson with the blood of the prophets.
He caused the holy prophet Isaiah, who admonished him for his sins,
to be cut in half with a wooden saw.
Finally, after many crimes, he was captured by his enemies,
and, led into exile, he was condemned to a prison.
And when he was in prison, he began to be penitent,
and with his whole heart to bewail the crimes he had committed.
And he prayed to the Lord, pouring forth bitter tears:
"I have sinned," he said, "until my sins are more than the number of the sand of the sea,
and now I am not worthy to look on the height of heaven
on account of the multitude of my iniquities.
I have aroused your wrath, most merciful God,
and I have done evil in your presence and committed unlawful deeds."
God, having pitied him, showed his mercy to him
and compassionately accepted his repentance,
for he freed him from prison and captivity
and called him back to his kingdom and to Jerusalem.
Through this Manasses is the evil sinner signified,
who, when he sins without fear, is proven not to care about God.
The sinner tortures the prophets of the Lord who accuse him
when he refuses to hear the preachers and teachers.

Et quam[/diu][1] talis peccator perseuerat in peccato mortali
Tamdiu probatur esse in captiuitate dyaboli.
Si autem ex toto corde suo egerit penitentiam
Dominus paratus est sibi succurere per suam clemencia⌊m⌋.

18a[2] ¶Hoc idem dominus innuit per quandam parabolam *secunda figura*.
Quam predicauit de filio prodigo secundum lucam.[3]
Qui recedens a patre suo in regionem longinquam
Et in luxuriose consumpsit omnem suam substantiam.
Et tunc incipiens egere ad quandam uillam ueniebat
Et uni ciuium adherens porcos suos pascebat.
Prodigus ille filius peccatorem significat.
Qui a patre suo celesti recedit quando mortaliter peccat.
Et tunc in regione illa longinqua est filius iste malus
⌊Quia⌋[4] secundum prophetam longe est a peccatoribus sa[u/.]lus.[5]
Et talis luxuriose consumit suam substantiam
Quando sensus suos et uires conuertit in maliciam.
Et tunc adheret uni ciuium id est lucifero et pascere⌊t⌋ porcos.
Qui sceleribus suis criminosis cibat dyabolos.
Post hoc filius prodigus peruenit ad tantam neccesitatem famis.
Quod cupiebat replere uentrem suum cum siliquis.
Tunc ad se reuersus penitentiam agere incipiebat
Quia penuria et neccesitas ipsum compellebat.
Et in hic possumus notare saluatoris clemenciam
Qui etiam peccatores compellit agere penitentiam.
In tantum enim salutem nostram querit et diligit
Quod omnibus modis quibus potest nos sibi attrahit.
Quosdam enim sibi attrahit per internam inspiracionem
Aliquos aut attrahit per salutiferam predicacionem.
Quos etiam allicit per beneficiorum largicionem.

[1] Added later by black ink scribe [2] Left Panel: The Father Welcomes his Prodigal Son. The image is titled with the caption *prodigus filius reuersus ad patrem*. In this third story in the penitence sequence (Lk. 15.11–32) we have the most celebrated of repentance stories in the New Testament, in part because of its multi-layered richness and allegorical character. Illustrations of this parable only begin to appear in the 11th century, though it had featured in the theology of penitence and reconciliation since St. Ambrose highlighted the story in his *De poenitentia*. The boy on the right, holding a cup, may be the servant who brings a ring at the father's command, indicating the wayward son's restoration into full communion with the father. [3] Lk. 15.11–32 [4] Quia, L] Qui, G [5] Ps. 118.155

And as long as such a sinner perseveres in mortal sin,
so long is he judged to be in the captivity of the devil.
If, however, with his whole heart he repents,
the Lord is prepared to help him by his mercy.

This same thing the Lord hinted through a certain parable *Figure Two*
which he preached about a prodigal son, according to Luke.
Going away from his father into a far-off land,
he wantonly consumed all his substance,
and then, beginning to be in need, he came to a certain town
and, attaching himself to one of the citizens, fed his pigs.
That prodigal son signifies the sinner,
who departs from his heavenly Father when he commits mortal sin,
and then he is that wicked son in that far-off land
since, according to the prophet, "Salvation is far from the wicked."
And such a man wantonly consumes his substance
when he turns his senses and strength to evil.
And then he devotes himself to one of the citizens—that is, to Lucifer—and fed pigs,
he who by his wicked crimes feeds the devils.
After this the prodigal son arrived at such dire need from hunger
that he desired to fill his own stomach with the husks.
Then, having returned to himself, he began to repent
because destitution and need compelled him.
And in this we can mark the mercy of the Savior,
who also compels sinners to repent—
for so much does He seek and love our salvation
that He draws us to Himself by every method he can.
For he draws certain men to him through internal inspiration,
but others he draws through salvation-bearing preaching.
He also draws some through the generosity of his blessings.

18b[1] Quosdam uero compellit per flagellacionem.
Isto modo filius prodigus compellabatur
Quapropter penitenciam ductus ad patrem suum reuertebatur.
Videns autem pater eum a longe sibi occurrebat
Et in amplexus eius et in oscula eius ruebat.
Sic deus occurrit penitenti per graciam preuenientem
Et recipit eum per clemenciam omnia scelera dimittentem.
¶Istud etiam prefiguratum fuit olim in rege dauid *tercia figura.*
Qui adulterium et homicidium in uria perpetuauit
Cumque redargutus a nathan peccaui diceret[2]
Paratus erat pius deus ut sibi statim dimitteret.
Nam cum diceret peccaui statim natham respondit
Dominus transtulit peccatum tuum id est dimisit.
O quam magna est pietas tua domine et quam ineffabilis[3]
Qui nullum penitentem cuiuscumque condicionis despicis.
Non respuisti petrum paulum thomam et matheum.
Dauid achab[4] manassen latronem[5] achior[6] zacheum.
Niniuitas[7] samaritanam raab ruth et adulteram[8]
Theophilum gilpertum taydem et mariam egipciacam.
Eunuchum[9] symonem[10] cornelium[11] ezechiam
Magdalenam longinum et moysi mariam.
Non ergo propter immanitatem peccorum nostrorum desperemus
Quia diuersos testes diuine misericordie habemus.
O bone ihesu concede nobis ueram et perfectam penitentiam
Per quam peruenire mereamur ad tuam mellifluam presenciam.

[1] Right Panel: David Repents before Nathan. The image is titled with the caption *penituit peccatum in uria*, and contains the captions *natan qui dauid redarguit* and *dauid trystis*. This story is about how a parable brings about conviction of sin, contrition, confession, and repentance (2 Kings 12.1–15). It is commonly cited in penitential manuals written after the Fourth Lateran Council (1215), a widely diffused example of which was by Raymond de Pennaforte. It occurs there and elsewhere with a series of notorious sinners who repent and are forgiven. In this image the hand gestures of Nathan indicate that he is making his declaration, "Thou art the man!" The hands of King David indicate both that he is hearing and taking the point. [2] 2 Kings 12.13 [3] See Ps. 70.15, 19 [4] 3 Kings 21.25–29 [5] Lk. 23.39–43 [6] Jdt. 5.5, 14.26 [7] Jon. 3.6–10, Mt. 12.41 [8] John 8.2–11 [9] Act. 8.26–39 [10] Act. 8.9–14 [11] Act. 10

Certain men, however, he compels through scourging.
In this way was the prodigal son compelled;
on account of this, having been brought to penitence, he returned to his father.
Seeing him from far off, moreover, his father ran to meet him
and rushed to embrace and kiss him.
So too does God run to meet the penitent through his prevenient grace,
and in his mercy he receives the one who leaves behind all his sins.
That also was once prefigured by King David *Figure Three*
who committed adultery and homicide against Uriah.
And when he was admonished by Nathan, he said, "I have sinned."
The righteous God was prepared to forgive him immediately;
for when he said, "I have sinned," immediately Nathan responded,
"The Lord has taken away your sin"—that is, he forgave him.
O how great and how inexpressible is your righteousness, Lord—
you, who despise no penitent of any condition whatever.
You did not reject Peter, Paul, Thomas, or Matthew;
David, Ahab, Manasses, the thief, Achior, Zaccheus,
the Ninevites, the Samaritan woman, Rahab, Ruth, or the adulterous woman;
Theophilus, Gilbert, Thaidum, or Mary of Egypt;
the eunuch, Simon, Cornelius, Ezechial,
the Magdalene, Longinus, and Miriam [the sister] of Moses.
Let us therefore not despair on account of the enormity of our sins,
for we have many witnesses to divine mercy.
O good Jesus, grant us true and perfect penitence,
through which we may worthily attain to your sweet presence.

18va

Capitulum xv[1]

*I*n precedenti capitulo audiuimus quomodo conuersio magdalene est facta
Consequenter audiamus que circa christum in die palmarum sunt peracta.
In illa enim die tria principaliter notabilia contigerunt
Que olim per tres figuras premonstrata fuerunt.
Videns enim iesus ciutatem ierusalem fleuit
Cum laudibus susceptus fuit mercantes de templo eiecit.
Primo notandum est quod iesus uidens ciuitatem flebat
Compaciens ciuitati de miseria que ille iminebat.
¶Iste fletus domini nostri {nostri} saluatoris iam pretaxatus
Fuit olim in lamentationibus Jeremie prefiguratus.
Qui deflebat desolacionem ierusalem factam per babylonios[2]
Ita iesus deflebat desolacionem eius futuram per romanos.
Sic et nos exemplo christi ex compassione flere debemus
Quando proximos nostros afflictos uel affligendos videmus.[3]
Plus est compati afflicto quam bon⌊a⌋[4] temporalia erogare
Quia compaciens afflicto videtur aliquid de se ipso sibi dare.
Compati debemus tam malefactoribus nostris quam inimicis[5]
Exemplo christi qui compassus est suis inimicis.
Inpossibile est illum misericordiam dei et gratiam non mereri
Qui scit afflictis compati ex corde et misereri.
¶Secundo notandum est quod populus christo ⸌cum⸍[6] laudibus obuiauit *secunda figura.*
Et hoc olim prefiguratum fuit per regem dauid.
Cui populus post mortem golye cum laudibus obuiabat
Et canticum laudis in honore ipsius decantabat.[7]
In quo cantico ipsum dauid regi Sauli preferebant

---

[1] Left Panel: Triumphal Entry. The narrative of Christ's entry into Jerusalem on "the foal of an ass" is, from the 4th century on, one of the most frequently depicted of biblical stories. Recounted in all four gospels (Mt. 21.1–11; Mk. 11.1–10; Lk. 19.28–40; John 12.12–19), the accounts in Matthew and John see it as a fulfillment of the prophecy of Zechariah (Zech. 9.9). Here the palm branches, symbols both of victory and peace, and garments spread in honor of a king, coupled with the crowd chanting Ps. 117.26, make it clear that Jesus is seen as the Messiah. The palm tree here is fruited (possibly with dates), an unusual feature probably intended to suggest the "fullness of time" had come—i.e., that the time was ripe for Jesus to fulfill his destiny at Passover. Otherwise the image is closely modeled after that in a 13th-century French Gospel, Add. MS 17868. [2] See Lam. in its entirety [3] See Mt. 5.4, Rom. 12.15–16 [4] bona] bono, G [5] inimicis] amicis, L. See Prov. 24.17, Ob. 1.12, Mt. 5.44, Lk. 6.27–28, Rom. 12.21–22 [6] Added contemporarily by scribe [7] 1 Kings 17.50–51, 18.6–7

Chapter Fifteen

In the last chapter we heard how the conversion of the Magdalene happened,
next let us hear what occurred around Christ on Palm Sunday.
For on that day three notable things happened,
which had been presaged formerly by three figures:
Jesus, seeing the city of Jerusalem, wept;
he was received with praise; he threw out the merchants from the temple.
First it ought to be observed that Jesus, seeing the city, wept.
Pitying the city for the misery that hung over it.
That weeping of our Lord Savior mentioned already
was previously prefigured in the lamentations of Jeremiah,
who was lamenting the desolation of Jerusalem caused by the Babylonians;
so Jesus was lamenting its future destruction by the Romans.
And so we ought to mourn in pity according to the example of Christ
when we see our neighbors suffering or about to suffer.
It is better to have pity on a suffering person than to expend material goods,
because the one who shows pity on one suffering give part of himself to him.
So we ought to pity both evildoers and our enemies
according to the example of Christ who felt compassion for his own enemies.
It is impossible for him to forfeit the mercy and grace of God,
who knows to have pity on the afflicted and to show mercy from the heart.
Secondly it must be observed that the people met Christ with praises *Figure Two*
and this had formerly been prefigured by King David
whom the people meet with praise after the death of Goliath
and sang a hymn of praise in his honor;
in which song they were exalting David over King Saul

18vb[1]
Et sauli mille. et dauid x milia attribuebant.
Dauid dominum nostrum iesum christum prefigurauit
Qui golyam id est dyabolum aduersarium nostrum superauit.[2]
Iste verus dauid id est christus in die palmarum
Honoratus fuit multipliciter in occursu turbarum.
Quidam osanna filio dauid acclamabant
Quidam benedictus qui uenit in nomine domini personabant.[3]
Quidam regem israel eum asserebant
Quidam eum saluatorem mundi concinebant.
Quidam cum floribus quidam cum palmis occurrerunt
Quidam uestimenta sua in uia prostrauerunt.
Mistice ierusalem uisio pacis interpretatur
Per quam fidelis anima spiritual⌊iter⌋[4] designatur.
Ad hanc saluator noster omni hora paratus est uenire
Et nos ei in occursum per contricionem debemus ire.
Laudes domino clamosis uocibus decantamus
Quando in confessione peccata nostra cum gemitibus recitamus.
Ramos palmarum ad laudem dei manibus portamus
Quando corpora nostra in satisfactione discipline castigamus.
Vestimenta nostra in uia ad honorem dei prosternimus
Quando temporalia nostra erogamus christi pauperibus.
Cum floribus domino occurrimus et honoramus
Quando misericordie operibus et diuersis uirtutibus nos ornamus
Christum Iesum qui uenit in nomine domini benedicimus.
Quando pro beneficiis nobis ˋimpensisˊ[5] deuote sibi grates dicimus.

19a[6]
Regem eum et dominum nostrum esse protestamur
Si omnia opera nostra cum timore dei et reuerencia operamur.
¶Tercio notandum est quod ihesus flagellum de funiculis fecit *tercia figura.*
Et ementes et uendentes flagellando de templo eiecit.[7]
Mensas peruertit nummulariorum et effudit es eorum

[1] Right Panel: Jeremiah Weeping over Jerusalem. The image is titled with the caption *lamentationes jeremie*. The Lamentations of Jeremiah (1.1), "*O vos omnes*," are words put in the mouth of Jesus in the liturgy for Palm Sunday, given that as he approached the city Jesus wept over it (Lk. 19.41), a feature explicitly mentioned in the SHS text, here as an exhortation to pity those who are afflicted. The hand under the chin is figurative of lamentation despite the expression on Jeremiah's face. [2] See 1 Pt. 5.8 [3] Mt. 21.8–9, Mk. 11.8–9, Lk. 19.36–38, John 12.13 [4] spiritualiter, L] spiritualis, G [5] Inserted above line contemporarily by scribe [6] Left Panel: The Triumph of David. When David entered Jerusalem in victorious procession following his victory over Goliath and the rout of the Philistine army (1 Kings 18.6–7) he received a joyous acclamation from the women of Jerusalem, typologically pre-figuring Christ's triumphal entry a week before his Passion. In this image David is greeted by crowned daughters of Jerusalem, one of whom bears a palm branch and two of whom carry flasks of oil, suggesting his anointing. [7] John 2.15

and they were alloting thousands to Saul and ten thousands to David.
David prefigured our Lord Jesus Christ,
who overcame Goliath, that is the devil, our adversary.
The true David—that is Christ—on Palm Sunday
was honored in many different ways in the gathering of the crowds.
Some shouted, "Hosanna to the son of David";
some chanted, "Blessed is he who comes in the name of the Lord."
Some proclaimed him as the king of Israel;
some cheered him as the savior of the world.
Some ran to meet him with flowers and with palms;
some laid their own garments in the road.
Jerusalem is interpreted mystically as a vision of peace
through which the faithful soul is indicated spiritually.
Our Savior is prepared to come to it at every hour
and we ought to go to meet him through contrition.
We chant praise to the Lord with loud voices
when we recite our sins in confession with groans.
We carry palm branches in our hands to praise God
when we chasten our bodies in atoning discipline.
We lay down our garments in the road to honor God
when we expend our material goods for Christ's poor.
We run to meet the Lord and we honor him with flowers
when we adorn ourselves with works of mercy and with manifold virtues.
We bless Christ Jesus who comes in the name of the Lord
when we graciously give thanks to him for the kindnesses shown us.

We affirm that he is our king and Lord
if we perform all our deeds with fear of God and reverence.
Thirdly it must be observed that Jesus made a whip from cords *Figure Two*
and he drove out from the temple those buying and selling by flogging them.
He overturned the tables of the bankers and poured out their money

Nam et erant ipsi usurarii et columbiste[1] phariseorum.[2]
Hec autem flagellacio domini iam recitata
Olim fuit in eliodoro prefigurata.
⸍R⸌ex[3] enim Se⸌u⸍leucius misit principem suum eliodorum.
Ut iret in ierusalem et spoliaret ibi domini templum.[4]
Cumque audacter intrasset in templum manu armata
⸤Statim contra eum uindicta dei est prouocata⸥[5]
Ex improuiso enim affuit quidam equus horribilis
Et qui sedebat super eum armatus erat et terribilis
Equus autem elyodoro priores calces immisit
Et ipsum deiciens fremebundus ad terram collisit.
Affuerunt insuper alii duo robustissimi adolescentes
Elyodorum flagellis usque ad mortem percucientes.
Quo facto predictus eques[6] et duo adolescentes disparuerunt
Et elyodorum tamquam mortuum flagella relinquerunt.
Sed orante per eo summo pontifice ouans reuixit
Et rediens ad dominum ⸌suum⸍ Se⸌u⸍lentium dixit.
Si habet rex aliquando hostem cuius mortem affectat
Illum ad spoliandum templum ierosolymis mittat.
Elyodorus flagellatus fuit propter templum dei spoliacionem

19b[7] Judei spoliati fuerunt propter usure palliacionem
Pharisei enim posuerunt in templo colibistas et nummularios.
Qui uolentibus offerre mutuo dabant denarios.
Et quia iuxta legem usuras accipere non debebant[8]
Collibia tamen id est munuscula parua recipiebant.
Ficus vuas nuces poma uocabant collibia
Amigdola pullos anseres columbas et similia.
Sicque usuram fraudulenter sub pallio tegebant
Hec uerba domini in ezechiele scripta non attendebant.
Usuram et omnem superhabundanciam non accipiatis[9]

---

[1] There are slight indications of erasure or other damage, but it has not affected the legibility of this word [2] Mt. 21.12, Mk. 11.15–16, Lk. 19.45, John 2.14–16 [3] The capital letter *R* was added later to this manuscript, as indicated by its darker color. It was written over the preexisting letter, although it is unclear what that letter was. [4] See 2 Mcc. 3.23–38 [5] L] Olim fuit in eliodoro prefigurata, G, duplication of line 8 [6] eques] equus, L [7] Right Panel: Heliodorus is Scourged. The image is titled with the caption *elyodorus vapulsus est propter spolium templi*. This story from Jewish deutero-canonical literature (2 Mcc. 3.4–35) tells how a Seleucid general, while attempting a raid on the Temple treasure, was miraculously struck down by a mounted heavenly warrior and two assistants, preventing him from absconding with funds intended for the support of widows and orphans. This story is seen as prefiguring that of Jesus cleansing the Temple by driving out the money-changers (Mt. 21.12–16; Mk. 11.15–19; Lk. 19.45–46; John 2.13–17), not shown here. Representations of this New Testament story are uncommon before the 15th century. [8] Ex. 22.25, Lv. 25.36–37, Dt. 23.20 [9] Ez. 18.8, 22.12

for they themselves were the interest-collectors and money-changers of the Pharisees.
But the Lord's flogging of them has already been recounted:
formerly these things had been prefigured in Heliodorus.
For the king Seuleucus sent his own prince Heliodorus.
So that he might go into Jerusalem and plunder the temple of the Lord there.
And when he had boldly entered armed into the temple,
at once the vengeance of God was roused against him.
For a dreadful horse appeared unexpectedly
and the one riding him was armed and terrible.
And the horse struck Heliodorus with his front hooves
and snorting and knocking him down, he dashed him to the ground.
In addition, two other very strong young men approached,
beating Heliodorus with whips to the point of death.
After which deed the beforementioned rider and the two young men disappeared
and they abandoned Heliodorus, as if dead from the whipping.
But when high priest prayed on his behalf, he revived, rejoicing
and returning to his own lord Seuleucus, he said:
"If a king ever has an enemy and desires his death,
let the king send him to destroy the temple of Jerusalem."
Heliodorus was beaten on account of plundering the temple of God;

the Jews were despoiled because of secret usury.
For the Pharisees placed money-changers and bankers in the temple
who would give denarii in exchange to those who wished to offer sacrifice.
And since according to the law they were not supposed to receive interest,
they were accepting, nonetheless, small presents like tidbits.
They called them "little presents": figs, grapes, nuts, and fruits,
almonds, hens, geese, pigeons, and such things.
And so they were hiding usury fraudulently under a cloak.
They did not listen to the words of the Lord, written in Ezekiel.
"You should reject interest and everything beyond measure."

O fratres karissimi uerbum hoc diligenti [animo] memoria recommendatis.
Sed prohdolor multi christiani hodie in ecclesia sunt
Qui fraudulenter similem usure palliacionem faciunt.
Qui mutuum non dant pure propter dei dilicionem
Sed propter munera uel seruicia fauorem uel promocionem.
Hii peccant grauiter uerbum illud domini non ponderantes
Mutuum date nichil inde sperantes.[1]
Tales dominus de templo suo celesti expellet[2]
Et radicem eorum de terra uiuencium euellet.
Studeamus ergo templum dei et diuinum cultum uenerari.
Si nolumus a domino flagello perpetuo flagellari.
Relinquamus etiam usuram et omnem speciem usure
Ne[3] expellamur a domino de templo glorie future.
O bone ihesu doce nos hec omnia taliter custodire
Ut mereamur in templo glorie tue eternaliter introire.[4]

19[va]

Capitulum xvi[5]

*I*n precedenti capitulo audiuimus de palmarum die.[6]
Consequenter audiamus de cena et sacramento eucharistie.
Appropinquante tempore quo christus uoluit subire passionem
Decreuit pro memoriali perpetuo instituere sacram communionem.[7]
Et ut nobis suam dilectissimam[8] dilectionem demonstraret[9]
Placuit sibi ut se ipsum nobis in cibum daret[10].
¶Istud olim in manna celi fuit prefiguratum *prima figura*.
Quod filiis israel in deserto de celo donatum.[11]
Magnam dilectionem dominus iudeis videtur exhibuisse

---

[1] Lk. 6.35 [2] See 1 Cor. 6.9–10, Apc. 22.15 [3] There is a slight erasure mark over the "e," as well as possible remnants of a c, suggesting that the word could be *nec* or that the scribe accidentally tried to add the letter c [4] See Hag. 2.10, Apc. 21.22–26 [5] Left Panel: The Lord's Supper and Sacrament. The initiation of the Eucharist is narrated in all four gospels (Mt. 26.20–30; Mk. 14.17–25; Lk. 22.14–23; John 13.18–30) but iconographic elements derive also from the bread of life discourse (John 6.30–40) and the account of Paul, employed liturgically (as found in 1 Cor. 10.16–17; 11.23–34). The passage in John 6 connects to the account of the manna in the wilderness (Ex. 16.4–15), which follows here. The representation is conventional, except that only eight disciples are shown, including John, "the beloved disciple," leaning again Jesus; the foreground figure without a nimbus, drinking from a cup, may represent Judas. The small figure in the hooded garb of an itinerant friar, pointing to the cup, may function to identify the doctrine of the sacrament. The paschal lamb on the table is an antitype of the "lamb of God who takes away the sins of the world" (John 1.29). [6] de … die] de Christi in Ierusalem equtatione, C [7] Mt. 26.18–30, Mk. 14.13–25, Lk. 22.15, 19, John 13.1, 1 Cor. 11.23–26 [8] Other mss. read *dulce* [9] See John 13.1, 34–35 [10] See Mt. 26.26–28, Mk. 14.22–24, Lk. 22.19–20 [11] Ex. 16.14–36

O dearest brothers, may you store up this saying in an attentive memory!
But alas, today there are many Christians in the church
who fraudulently conduct a similarly concealed usury,
who do not lend purely for the love of God,
But for the sake of gifts or services, favor or promotion.
These people sin gravely, not considering that word of God:
"Lend, hoping for nothing thereby."
Such ones the Lord will expel from his own heavenly temple
and he will pull up their root from the land of the living.
Let us therefore learn to honor the temple of God and his holy worship.
If we do not wish to be scourged perpetually with a whip by the Lord.
Let us also abandon usury and every kind of interest
lest we be expelled by the Lord from the temple of future glory.
O good Jesus, teach us to keep all these things in such a way
that we may be worthy to enter the temple of your glory eternally.

Chapter Sixteen

In the last chapter, we heard about Palm Sunday;
now let us hear about the supper and sacrament of the Eucharist.
When the time was drawing near in which Christ was about to undergo the passion,
he decided to institute holy communion as a perpetual remembrance.
And so that he might demonstrate to us his dearest love.
It was pleasing to him that he should give himself to us in the meal.
It was once prefigured in the manna of heaven *Figure One*
which was given from heaven to the sons of Israel in the desert.
The Lord seems to have shown great love to the Jews

Sed infinicies [nobis] magis perhibetur nobis contulisse.[1]
Dedit enim iudeis panem manna licet materialem et temporalem.
Nobis autem contulit panem supersubstantialem et eternalem.
Manna dicebatur panis celi numquam tamen fuit in celo vero[2]
Sed creatum erat a deo in aere siue in celo aereo.
Christus autem saluator noster est panis verus et uiuus[3]
Qui de celo vero descendens factus est noster cibus.
Judeis vero solummodo figuram veri panis tribuit
Nobis autem non figuram sed ueritatem dei[4] panis contulit.
//Notandum autem quod multa fuerunt in manna figuraliter premonstrata
Que in sacra eucharistia sunt veraciter consumata.
Manna celi ualde mirabilis nature esse uidebatur
Quia in radio solis liquifiebat et ad ignem indu⌊r⌋ebatur.
Ita eucharistia in cordibus uanis liquefit et euanescit
In cordibus ignitis perdurat et recedere nescit.
Mali enim sumunt eucharistiam ad suam damnacionem[5]

19vb[6] Boni autem ad diuinam et perpetuam consolacionem.
Cumque descendebat manna descend⌊ebat⌋[7] similis et ros celi[8]
Per quod innuitur quod dignis cum eucharistia confertur gratia dei.
Manna erat album et ad modum niuis candidum
Per quod innuitur quod communicans debet habere cor purum et mundum.
Manna habebat in se omne delectamentum cibi terrestris
Sed eucharistia habet in se delectamentum cibi celestis.
Hoc autem delectamentum non sumitur in sacramenti masticatione
Sed in sanctis meditacionibus celestium contemplacione.
Gustus manne in omnem saporem prout quilibet desiderabat conuertebatur
Sed dulcedini christi nullus sapor huius mundi assimilatur.[9]
Qui de hac dulcedine perfect⌊a⌋[10] semel gustaret
Omne delecamentum habemus seculi absinthium reputaret.
Petrus de ista dulcedine in monte thabor gustauerat[11]
Statim tabernacula facere et semper ibi manere affectabat.
Precepit autem Moyses populo ut mane ante ortus solis exirent
Et singuli pro illo die sibi unum gomor colligerent.[12]

---

[1] See 1John 3.1 [2] See Ps. 77.24, Ps. 104.40 [3] John 6.31–59 [4] sed … dei] sed veritatem veri panis, L [5] See 1Cor. 11.27–30, Hbr. 10.29 [6] Right Panel: Manna in the Wilderness. Moses is shown signifying the miraculous blessing while the four figures around him gather manna in baskets (Ex. 16.14–17). Traditional exegesis summarized in the *Glossa* (PL 113.235–240) connected this miracle with the bread of life discourse in John 6 and the Eucharist. [7] descendebat, L] descenderebat G [8] Ex. 16.13–22 [9] See Ps. 118.103, Wis. 16.20, John 1.1, 1Pt. 2.3 [10] L] perfecte, G [11] See Mt. 17.1–9, Mk. 9.2–9, 2Pt. 1.17–18 [12] See Ex. 16.16–18. A omer a unit of measurement for dry volume, equaling about two quarts.

but he is understood to have bestowed infinitely more love on us.
For he gave the Jews bread—manna—although only material and temporal.
But on us he conferred bread supersubstantial and eternal.
Manna was called "the bread of heaven." However, it was never truly in heaven
but it was made by God in the sky or in the physical heavens.
But Christ our savior is our true and living bread
who, descending from the true heaven, became our food.
Indeed, he granted to the Jews only the figure of the true bread
but on us he bestowed not the figure but the reality of the bread of God.
Yet it should be noted that many things were presaged figurally in the manna
which are truly consummated in the holy Eucharist.
The manna from heaven appeared to be certainly of a miraculous nature
since in the ray of the sun it evaporated and in fire it hardened.
In this manner the Eucharist evaporates in empty hearts and vanishes.
In flaming hearts it endures and does not depart.
For the wicked consume the Eucharist to their own damnation,

but the good for their divine and perpetual consolation.
And when the manna descended, the dew of heaven also descended at the same time,
through which it is shown that the grace of God is conferred on the worthy together with the Eucharist.
Manna was white and pure like the snow,
through which it is shown that the communicant ought to have a heart pure and clean.
Manna contained in itself all the delights of earthly food
but the Eucharist holds in itself the delights of heavenly food.
Yet this delight is not received in chewing the sacrament
but in holy meditation and contemplation of heavenly things.
The taste of manna was changed to whatever flavor each person desired,
but no taste in this world is comparable to the sweetness of Christ.
He who once tasted this perfect sweetness
would consider all the delights of the world we have as mere wormwood.
Peter had tasted that sweetness on Mt. Tabor
and at once he desired to build tabernacles and remain there always.
Moses, moreover, taught the people that in the morning before sunrise they should go out

Contigit autem miraculose quod uoraces qui plus collegerunt
Quando ad propria redibant non plus quam gomor habuerunt.
Similiter et illi qui plenam mensuram colligere non potuerunt
Cum ad propria redirent plenam mensuram inuenerunt.
S⸤ic⸥[1] communicans qui plures hostias receperit
Non plus habet ille ˋquamˊ[2] qui tantum unam acceperit.
Similiter et ille qui particulam hostie sumpserit
Non habet minus quam ille qui integrum uel plures sumpserit.

20a[3] ¶Cena domini fuit prefigurata in agno pascali *secunda figura.*
Quia feria quinta ante parasceuen. a iudeis solebant manducari.
Hunc dominus primo precepit filiis Israel manducare
Quando decreuit eos de egypciaca servutute liberare.[4]
Ita christi sacramentum eucharistie tunc primum instituit
Quando nos de dyabolica potestate eripere uoluit.
Quando filii Israel agnum pascalem manducabant
Succincti erant baculos in manibus tenebant et stabant.
Ita communicantes debent esse succinti per mentis et corporis castitatem[5]
Et tenere baculos per recte fidei firmitatem.
Debent etiam erecti stare in bona uita quam inchoauerunt
Et se non iterum reponere in lutum de quo surrexerunt.
Agnus edebatur lactucis agrestibus que sunt amare
Et nos debemus corpus domini cum amara contricione manducare
Qui comedebant agnum tenebant⸤ur⸥ pedes suos calciare.[6]
Et per pedes s⸤o⸥let[7] sacra scriptura desideria designare.
Communicantes ergo pedes suos calciare tenentur
Cauendo ne desidˊerˋia ˊipˋsorum[8] sorde aliqua maculentur.
Agnus pascalis non fuit coctus aqua sed assus igne
Et communicans debet esse ignitus caritate ut manducet digne.
¶Christus eucharistiam sub specie panis et uini donauit *tercia figura.*
Hoc olim melchisidech rex et sacerdos prefigurauit.[9]

---

[1] Sic, L] Sed, G [2] squeezed in very faintly in ink at unknown point [3] Left Panel: Preparing the Passover Lamb. The image shows the instruction of God through Moses on the eve of the Jews departure from Egypt (Ex. 12.1–11)—the lamb to be prepared and eaten with everyone girded, shod, and staff in hand for the journey. One of the figures wears what was thought to be a Jewish hat, while the others look like 14th-century people. The Passover directions were extensively allegorized according to the pattern in the SHS text. See, e.g., the *Glossa* (PL 113.218–219) and Gregory of Nyssa's *De vita Moisis*. [4] Ex. 12.1–51 [5] See Ps. 65.18, 1 Cor. 11.28–30 [6] Ex. 12.11 [7] solet L] scilicet, G. The Hebrew word *regel* (feet) is regularly used as a euphemism for genitalia, and the double entendre carries on into the fathers. [8] The MS. shows signs of correction by the "black-ink corrector" at this point, with the *er* being inserted in *desideria* and the first two letters and macron of *ipsorum* being written over [9] See Gen. 14.1–24

and that each for that day might collect for himself one omor.
But it happened miraculously that greedy men who would collect more
had, when they returned home, no more than one omor.
And similarly those who could not obtain the full measure
discovered a full measure when they returned home.
So the communicant who received many hosts
has no more than he who received just one.
And similarly he who consumes a fragment of a host
has no less than that man who consumes a whole host or several hosts.

The Lord's supper was prefigured in the Paschal lamb, *Figure Two*
because they were eaten according to custom by the Jews on the Thursday before the Day of Preparation.
The Lord first instructed the sons of Israel to eat it
when he deigned to free them from Egyptian servitude.
So Christ first instituted then the Eucharistic sacrament
when he wanted to snatch us away from the power of the devil.
When the sons of Israel were eating the Paschal lamb
they were belted, holding staffs in their hands, and standing upright.
So too those receiving communion ought to be girt by purity of mind and body
and hold staffs by means of the firmness of upright faith.
They should also stand upright in the good life which they began
and not return again to the mud from which they have arisen.
The lamb was eaten with wild herbs which are bitter,
and we ought to eat the body of the Lord with bitter contrition.
Those who consumed the lamb had their feet sandaled.
And through 'feet' Holy Scripture was accustomed to indicate the desires.
Communicants, therefore are understood to have their feet shod,
by taking care that their desires not be corrupted by any filth.
The paschal lamb was not cooked by water but roasted by fire.
And the communicant must be aflame with charity so that he may eat worthily.
Christ gave the Eucharist under the appearance of bread and wine; *Figure Three*
formerly Melchizedek, king and priest, prefigured this.

Quattuor reges ⸢terram⸣[1] in quo Abraham habitabat uastauerunt.
Et multa spolia et loth cum multis captiuis adduxerunt.
Abraham autem cum suis ipsos insequebatur

20b[2] Et percutiens cum captiuis ad propria reuertebatur
Occurrit autem ei melchisedech offerens panem et uinum.
In quo figurabatur hoc sacramentum diuinum.
Melchisedech erat rex et sacerdos dei altissimi
Et gerebat figuram domini nostri Ihesu christi.
Christus enim est rex qui omnia regna creauit[3]
Ipse enim est sacerdos qui primam missam celebrauit.
Melchisedech rex et sacerdos panem et uinum obtulit.
Christus sub species panis et vini hoc sacramentum instituit.
Quapropter sacerdos secundum ordinem melchisedech appellatur.[4]
Quia hoc sacramentum in oblacione Melchisedech prefigurabatur.[5]
Melchisedech erat sacerdos et etiam princeps regalis
In quo pulchre prefigurabatur dignitas sacerdotalis.
Sacerdotes enim possunt dici principes regales[6]
Quia in dignitate precellunt omnes principes imperiales.
Excellunt etiam in potestate patriarchas et prophetas
Et etiam quodammodo ipsas uirtutes angelicas.[7]
Sacerdotes enim sacramenta conficiunt quod angeli facere nequeunt
Nec patriarche nec prophete olim facere potuerunt.
Per Mariam filius dei olim semel incarnabatur.
Per sacerdotem autem sepius panis in carnem substantiatur.
Sacerdotes igitur propter sacramentum debemus honorare
Quos christus confectores sui sacramenti dignatus est ordinare.
O bone Iesu da nobis sacramentum tuum ita uenerari
Ut a te numquam mereamur in perpetuum separari.

[1] *terram* inserted at end of line and properly place marked by main scribe [2] Right Panel: Melchisedech gives Abraham Bread and Wine. This early Old Testament story provides another antitype for the Eucharist (Gen. 14.18–29), all the more because Ps. 109.4 characterizes Melchisedech (lit. "king and priest"), of mysterious origin and without human parents, even as the Messiah to come. Hbr. 5.6–10 quotes this messianic psalm in explicit reference to Christ as the eternal great high priest. Melchisedech, here crowned as a king, presents a medieval altar tabernacle (containing the consecrated host), offering to Abraham the bread and wine eucharistically. His title (*rex Salem*), "King of Salem" (king of peace, but also of Jeru-salem), makes this typology easy to follow. [3] See Mt. 28.18, Apc. 17.14, 19.16 [4] Ps. 109.4, Hbr. 6.19–20 [5] See Hbr. 7.1–17 [6] See 1 Pt. 2.9–10 [7] See 1 Pt. 1.10–12, 1 Pt. 2.5, Rom. 12.1

Four kings laid waste to the land in which Abraham was living,
and they carried off many spoils and Lot, together with many captives.
However, Abraham was following them with his own men.

He attacked them and he turned back home with the captives.
And Melchizedek met him, offering bread and wine
in which this sacrament of God was symbolized.
Melchizedek was the king and priest of God Most High
and he was a figure of our Lord Jesus Christ.
For Christ is the king who created all kingly authorities.
He himself is the priest who celebrated the first mass.
Melchizedek, king and priest, offered bread and wine;
Christ instituted this sacrament beneath the appearance of bread and wine.
Accordingly, he is called a priest in the order of Melchizedek
because this sacrament was prefigured by the offering of Melchizedek.
Melchizedek was a priest and also a royal prince
in whom the dignity of the priestly order was beautifully prefigured.
For priests can be called royal princes
because they excel all imperial princes in honor.
They surpass in power even the patriarchs and prophets.
And also in a certain way in the angelic powers themselves.
For priests perform the sacraments which the angels are unable to make
and which neither patriarch nor prophet could make formerly.
Through Mary the Son of God was once incarnated;
through the priest, however, bread is regularly transubstantiated into flesh.
Accordingly, on account of the sacrament, we should honor priests
whom Christ deemed worthy to ordain as preparers of his sacrament.
O good Jesus grant us so to venerate your sacrament
that we may never deserve to be separated from you forever.

20va

Capitulum xvii[1]

*I*n precendenti capitulo audiuimus quomodo christus eucharistiam instaurauit
Consequenter audiamus quomodo hostibus suis occurens ipse prostrauit.
Cumque iudas cum aliis percepisset sacram communionem
Abiit ut faceret hostium christi congregacionem.
O quanta erat christi benignitas et clemencia
O quanta erat iude malignitas et demencia.[2]
Christus eum sacramento corporis et sanguinis sui cibauit[3]
Et ipse de tradicione illius in corde suo tractauit.[4]
Christus sciens omnia noluit eum perdere neque sacramentum sibi negare
In quo uoluit sacerdotibus formam communicandi dare.
Sacerdos sciens aliquem cum mortali ad communionem accedere
Non debet sibi negare ne uideatur eum prodere.
Abiit igitur iudas ut inimicos christi congregaret[5]
Christus autem iuit ad locum quem sciebat iudas ut eum ibi expectaret.[6]
Venerunt ergo armati gladiis et fustibus[7]
Querentes eum in tenebris cum lucernis et facibus.
Ihesus autem absque armis in occursum eorum iuit
Et quem quererent cum omni mansuetudine quesiuit.
Illi autem tamquam gygantes contra eum steterunt
Et ut iesum nazarenum quererent responderunt.
Jesus autem mitissimum et dulcissimum dabat eis responsum
Dicens humili uoce et benigno animo ego sum.
Quo audito omnes retrorsum abierunt
Et tanquam mortui coram eo in terram corruerunt.[8]
O dementissimi iudei quid prodest uobis tanta multitudo

20vb[10]

Qui uiliter iacetis prostrati mitissimo uerbo uno.[9]
Quid prosunt uobis multa et diuersa uestra consilia
Quorum prostrata uno uerbo tanta milia.
Quid prodest uobis armatura uestra tam terribilis
Que uno uerbo perterrita perhibetur esse inutilis.

[1] Left Panel: Roman Soldiers Fall Back Before Christ. The mild acknowledgment by Jesus that he is the one the solders are seeking (John 18.6) causes them to jump back in fear and stumble over each other. In this image Jesus carries a codex book like a Bible, signifying that he is the Logos of God made flesh. This "one little word" which fells the enemy seems to have established a theme. [2] See Act. 1.16–20 [3] John 13.18, 26–30, Mt. 26.21–25, Mk. 14.18–21, Ps. 41.9 [4] Mt. 26.14–16 [5] See John 13.26–31 [6] Lk. 22.39 [7] Mt. 26.47, Mk. 14.43, John 18.3 [8] John 18.4–7 [10] Right Panel: Samson Slays a Thousand Philistines. The antitype here is found in Jdg. 15.11–17, one of the prodigious feats of strength and ferocity attributed to Samson; here it instances an extensive list of displays of power by which Jesus could have saved himself if he wished. [9] See Prov. 15.1

Chapter Seventeen

In the last chapter we heard how Christ instituted the Eucharist.
Now let us hear how, closing with his enemies, he cast down them down.
And when Judas had taken the sacrament of communion with the others
he left in order to assemble the enemies of Christ.
O how great was the kindness and mercy of Christ!
O how great was the malice and folly of Judas!
Christ fed him with the sacrament of his own body and blood
and Judas mulled over the betrayal of Christ in his heart.
Christ, knowing all, refused to condemn him and also did not wish to refuse him the sacrament
in which he wanted to give the pattern for communion to the priests.
A priest, knowing that anyone in mortal sin has come forward for communion,
should not refuse communion to him lest he appear to condemn him.
Then Judas left in order that he might assemble the enemies of Christ,
but Christ went to a place which Judas knew so that he could wait there for them.
Therefore the men came, armed with swords and clubs,
seeking him in the darkness with oil-lamps and torches.
But Jesus went without weapons to meet them
and with all gentleness questioned them, "whom were they seeking?"
But they, like giants, stood firm against him
and they responded that they were seeking Jesus of Nazareth.
Jesus, however, gave them a most calm and sweet reply,
saying, with humble voice and kind spirit, "I am He."
Having heard this, all stepped backward
and fell to the ground before him, as if dead.
O most senseless Jews, what good is such a crowd to you,

you who basely lie flat, having been overthrown by one very gentle word?
What advantage are your many and varied counsels to you
whose great thousand were overthrown by one word?
What advantage are your dreadful arms to you,
which, when frightened by one word, are rendered useless?

Nonne ⌊uidetis⌋[1] christum solum potenciorem omnibus vobis esse[2]
Et si uellet omnes uos interficere posse.
Immo posset precipere terram sub pedibus uestris aperiri.
Et uos omnes ⌊uiuos⌋[3] tanquam dathan et abyrom deglutiri.[4]
Vel posset ignem et sulphur super uos pluere
Et tanquam sodomam et gomorram consumere.[5]
Vel posset per aquas celi uos omnes delere
Sicut olim deleuit totum mundum fere.[6]
Vel posset uos tamquam uxorem loth in lapides mutare[7]
Vel tamquam egipcios diuersis plagis molestare.[8]
Vel posset uos omnes conuertere in puluerem et cinerem
Sicut exercitum Sennacherip CLXXX milia hominum[9]
Vel posset uos interficere per mortem subitaneam
Sicut olim interfecit filios iude her et onam.[10]
Vel posset uos omnes interficere per gladium angelicum
Sicut sub dauid interfecit maximum populum.
Vel posset omnes uos in potestate dyaboli dare
Sicut temporibus thobie dedit septem uiros sare.[11]
Vel posset ignem mittere qui consumeret uos
Sicut Thore cum suis et duos quinquagenarios[12]

21a[14] Vel posset mittere in uos ignitos serpentes[13]
Sicut olim in predecessores uestros sibi contradicentes.
Vel posset uos discerpere per immissos leones
Sicut olim in samaria regis salmasar colones.[15]
Vel posset uos dilacerare per rapidorum ursorum dentes
Sicut olim quadraginta[16] pueros elyseum deridentes.[17]
Vel posset uos tamquam elyodorum flagellare et conculcare[18]
Vel tamquam ethyocum putrefacione et uermibus necare.[19]
Vel posset uos percutere per subitam lepram
Sicut olim percussit Gesi et sororem moysi mariam.[20]
Vel posset uos percutere cecitate et acrisia
Sicut sub elyseo percussus fuit ⌊exercitus⌋[21] de Syria.[22]

---

[1] videtis, L] videns G [2] See Mt. 26.53 [3] vivos, L] binos, G [4] Nm. 16.27–35, 2.9, Dt. 11.6, Ps. 105.17–18 [5] Gen. 19.24–25, Dt. 29.23 [6] Gen. 7.17–24 [7] Gen. 19.26, Lk. 17.32 [8] Ex. 9.12–51 [9] 4 Kings 19.35–37, 2 Mcc. 8.19, 15.22 [10] Gen. 38.7–10 [11] Tb. 3.7–8 [12] Nm. 16.1–35, 26.9 [14] Left Panel: Shamgar Kills Six Hundred with a Ploughshare. In the briefest of references (Jdg. 3.31) we learn of one Samgar who killed six hundred Philistines with an ox-goad (here *fomere*: ploughshare) and becomes one of the deliverers of Israel. [13] Nm. 21.6, Wis. 16.5, 10.7, 1 Cor. 10.9 [15] 4 Kings 17.24–26 [16] Forty-two youths is the number attested to L, as well as in 2 Kings 2.33–34 [17] 4 Kings 2.23–24 [18] 2 Mcc. 3.24–29 [19] Act. 12.21–23 [20] Nm. 12.10–15 [21] Ms. reads *extentus* [22] 4 Kings 6.14–18

Do you not see that Christ alone is more powerful than all of you?
And that if he wanted to, he could kill you all?
Nay rather, he could instruct the earth beneath your feet open,
and you all to be swallowed alive just like Dathan and Abiram.
Or he could have rained fire and sulfur over you
and consume you just like Sodom and Gomorra.
Or he could have blotted you out with all waters of the sky
as he once obliterated nearly the whole world.
Or he could have changed you into stones like Lot's wife
or afflicted you with different plagues like the Egyptians.
Or he could have turned you all into dust and ashes,
as the army of Sennacherib, of one hundred eighty thousand men,
or he could have slain you through sudden death
as once he slew Er and Onan, the sons of Judah.
Or he could have slain you all with an angelic sword
just as under David he slew a great number of people.
Or he could have given you all into the power of a demon
as in the time of Tobit, he gave the seven husbands of Sara.
Or he could have sent fire which would have consumed you
like Korah with his men and two hundred and fifty (soldiers).

Or he could have sent among you serpents that had been set on fire,
as once were sent against your predecessors who were murmuring against him.
Or he could have torn you to pieces by lions set upon you,
as once he did in Samaria to the citizens of King Shalmaneser.
On the other hand, he could have torn you apart by means of the teeth of fierce bears
like once he did to the forty boys mocking Elisha.
Or he could scourge and trample upon you just like Heliodorus;
or kill you with putrefaction and worms like Herod of Antioch;
or he could have struck you with sudden leprosy
as once he struck Jesse and Miriam the sister of Moses.
Or he could strike you down with blindness and confusion
just as, in the time of Elisha, the army of Syria was struck.

Vel posset omnium uestrum brachia arida facere et indurare
Sicut olim fecit Jeroboam in Bethol iuxta altare.[1]
Vel posset omnia arma uestra consumere dentibus vermium
Sicut consumpsit in exercitu Syrorum omnes cordas arcuum.
Omnia hec et similia si uellet posset se defendere
Sed non uult nisi ad modicum uos prosternere.
Hoc autem fecit ut ostendat se uoluntarie mortem sustinere.
Et si uellet reniti non possetis eum capere nec tenere.
Cum igitur christus ostendisset suam uictoriam et potenciam
Dedit eis resurgendi et se capiendi licenciam.
¶Hec uictoria hostium christi iam recitata *prima figura.*
Fuit olim in sampsone et Sangar et dauid prefigurata.
Sampson cum mandibula asini strauit mille uiros[2]

21b[4] ¶Et Sangar cum fomere interfecit sexcentos.[3] *secunda figura.*
Sed[5] isti dei adiutorio tot hostes prostrauerunt
Non est mirum quod coram christo omnes hostes eius corruerunt.
¶Scriptura regem Dauid tenerrimum ligni vermiculum dicit.[6] *tercia figura.*
Qui octigentos uiros uno impetu occidit.
Vermiculus ligni dum tangitur mollissimus videtur
Sed cum tangit durissimum lignum perforare perhibetur.
Sic Dauid cum esset inter domesticos nullus eo micior
Sed in iudicio et contra hostes in prelio nullus eo durior.
Sic christus in hoc mundo erat mitissimus et pacientissimus[7]
In iudicio autem contra hostes erat districtissimus.
Conuersabatur enim mansuete et incessit inermis
Et sustinuit ut uiliter tractaretur ut vermis.
Et videtur querulose deplangere in psalmo
Vt de se dicit. ego sum vermis et non homo.[8]
Videtur autem non tantum vermis sed uermiculus ligni
Quia in ligno crucis occiderunt e⌊um⌋[9] maligni.
Conuenienter etiam tenerrimus appellatur
Quia caro sua tenerrima et nobilissima esse comprobatur.
Et quanto caro sua erat mollior et tenerior
Tanto passio sua erat grauior et asperior.

---

[1] 3 Kings 13.1–4 [2] Jdg. 15.14–16 [4] Right Panel: David Slays Eight Hundred. The reference to eight hundred killed at one time is actually accorded not to David but to one of his "mighty men" eulogized at the time of his death. This deed is attributed to Jasheb-Basshebeth the Tachmonite (2 Kings 23.8). [3] Jdg. 3.31 [5] MS. reads *Sed* [6] 2 Kings 23.8 [7] See Mt. 11.29, Apc. 19.11–16 [8] Ps. 21.7 [9] eum, L] ei, G

Alternately he could have made all of your arms wither and stiffen,
just as once he did to Jeroboam in Bethol near the altar.
Or he could have consumed all of your weapons with the gnawing of worms
just as he consumed all the bows-strings in the army of the Syrians.
He could have done all these and similar things if he had wanted to defend himself
But he wanted only to cast you down a little bit.
And he did this that he might show that he endured his death voluntarily.
And if he had wanted to resist, you would not have been able to capture nor hold him.
When, therefore, Christ had displayed his victory and power,
he gave to them permission to arise up and take him.
This victory of Christ over his enemies which was now described, *Figure One*
was once prefigured in Sampson, Shamgar, and David.
Sampson laid low a thousand men with the jawbone of an ass,

and Shamgar killed six hundred with a plowshare. *Figure Two*
But they slew all their enemies with the help of God.
It is not surprising that all Christ's enemies fell before him.
Scripture calls King David "the most tender little woodworm," *Figure Three*
who struck down eight hundred men in one attack.
The little woodworm seems exceedingly soft when it is touched—
but when it touches the hardest wood, it is said to pierce it.
So when David was among his household, no one was milder than he.
But in judgment and against the enemies in battle, no one was harder than he.
So Christ on this earth was most mild and most patient
but in judgment against his enemies, he was most severe.
For he lived gently and went forth unarmed,
and he endured being dragged as vilely as a worm.
And he seems to lament mournfully in a psalm
as he says about himself, "I am a worm and not a man."
He seems, though, not only a worm but a little woodworm.
Because on the wood of the cross the evil ones killed him.
And he is called 'most tender' very aptly,
because his flesh was proven to be the most tender and most noble.
And however much his flesh was milder and more tender,
so much more was his passion heavier and more bitter.

Et ideo clamat in trenis ad omnes transeuntes per uiam
Et attendant et uideant si umquam viderint similem penam.[1]
O bone Iesu da nobis ita tuam amare penam et uidere
Vt tecum mereamur in patria uidere et gaudere.

21va *Capitulum xviii*[2]

*I*n precedenti capitulo audiuimus quomodo christus hostes suos prostrauit
Consequenter audiamus quomodo iudas eum in dolo salutauit.
Iudas traditor saluatoris nostri dedit iudeis osculi signum[3]
Quod iniquum supra modum [et malignum] nimis erat et malignum.
Osculum enim semper consueuit esse signum dilectionis
Hoc iniquus iudas permutauit in signum tradicionis.[4]
¶Ista iniqua salutacio que in christo tam dolose fuit perpetrata *prima figura.*
Olim fuit in Joab et in amasan prefigurata.
Joab amasan salutans dolosa mente fratrem uocabat[5]
Et iudas christum salutans iniqua intencione christum magistrum appellabat.[6]
Joab dextra mentum amase quasi osculum tenebat
Et sinistra gladium educens ipsum perimebat.
Sic iudas quasi dextra uidetur mentum christi tenuisse
Quia legitur sibi aue rabi blande dixisse.
Sinistra uero uidetur gladium eduxisse et ipsum perforasse.
Quia legitur sibi insidias sub blandis uerbis occultasse.
O iuda que ⸤causa⸥[7] est quod saluatorem tuum tradidisti
Quid enim tibi mali fecit quod sic aduersus eum agere uoluisti.[8]
Ipse tibi appendebat apostolicum honorem et dignitatem
Et quare exercuisti contra eum tantam malignitatem.
Ipse te super LXXII discipulos elegit in apostolum[9]
Et tu exhibuisti te sibi pre omnibus falsissimum.
Ipse te connumerauit inter suos specialissimos XII apostolos[10,11]

[1] Lam. 1.12. See also Hbr. 2.9–10, 14–15, 17–18, 4.15 [2] Left Panel: Betrayal of Christ. This portion of the gospel narrative (Mt. 26.47–56; Mk. 14.10–46; Lk. 22.47–53; John 18.1–11) was one of the first given visual representation in Christian art, appearing frequently after the 6th century. While in representation from the early 6th-century mosaic in S. Apollinaire Nuovo, Ravenna through to a painting of the mid-15th century at S.S. Annunziata, Florence, Judas approaches from the viewer's left, it is customary when including the incident of Peter slicing off the ear of Malchus to have Judas, as here, approach on the right. [3] Mt. 26.48–49, Mk. 14.44–45, Lk. 2.47–48 [4] Lk. 22.48 [5] 2 Kings 20.8–10 [6] Mt. 26.49, Mk. 14.45 [7] MS. reads *cura* [8] Mt. 26.14–16, Mk. 14.10–11, Lk. 22.3–6, John 18.2–5 [9] Lk. 10.1 [10] Other mss. read *amicos* [11] Mt. 10.1–2, Mk. 3.14, Lk. 6.13–16

And therefore he cries out in lamentations to all those passing by along the road
and let them take notice and see if at any time they may have seen a similar pain.
O good Jesus, grant us to love your pain and see it, so
that we may worthily see and rejoice with you in our father's country.

Chapter Eighteen

In the last chapter we heard how Christ cast down his own enemies.
Now let us hear how Judas greeted him deceitfully.
Judas, the betrayer of our savior, gave the sign of a kiss to the Jews,
a sign that was wicked beyond measure and was very evil.
For a kiss was always wont to be a sign of affection.
Wicked Judas changed it into a sign of betrayal.
That wicked greeting, which was performed on Christ so deceitfully, *Figure One*
was once prefigured in Joab and in Amasa.
Greeting Amasa, Joab called him 'brother' with a deceitful mind,
and Judas, in greeting Christ, called Christ 'Teacher' with a wicked intention.
Joab took the Amasa's chin in is right hand as if to kiss him,
and, drawing the sword with left hand, he killed him.
So too Judas seems to have held the chin of Christ in his right hand
since he is said to have spoken "hail, Rabbi" fawningly.
Truly it appears that he drew the sword with his left hand and pierced Christ,
since it is read about him that he hid treacheries beneath smooth words.
O Judas, what is the reason that you handed over your savior?
What evil did he do to you that you wished to turn against him?
He weighed out apostolic honor and dignity for you,
and why did you perform so much malice against him?
He chose you above the seventy-two disciples to be an apostle,
and you showed yourself to him as the most false of all.
He counted you among his very own most special twelve apostles,

Et tu dereliquisti eum et accessisti ad suos inimicos.
Ipse te assumpsit ad secreta sua cum aliis apostolis

21vb2 Et tu misisti[1] secreta consilia contra eum cum hostibus suis.
Ipse te sine sacculo et sine pera misit
Et quocunque ueniebas ipso prouidente nichil tibi defuit.[3]
Tu autem nunc hev immemor es talis et tante prouidencie
Venis eum tradere pro modica quantitate pecunie.[4]
Ipse tibi contulit auctoritatem ut infirmos curares[5]
Et tu cogitasti ut eum infirmum faceres et ligares.
Ipse tibi dedit potestatem super eiectionem demoniorum
Et tu tradidisti ⌊eum⌋[6] in potestatem inimicorum.
Ipse te fecit suum bursiferum et procuratorem
Et tu fecisti te suum aduersarium et traditorem.[7]
Ipse te constituit super suam et suorum pecuniam
Sibi et suis per modum elemosine collatam.[8]
Tu ad libitum tuum ea uti potuisti
Cur ergo dominum tuum pro modica pecunia uendidisti.
Tu furabaris ex loculo domini tui quantum uolebas
Cur ergo eum pro XXX denariis uendebas.[9]
Ipse te dignatus est suo sanctissimo corpore cibare
Et [−non] tu non es uerecundus cor[10] suum iudeis in mortem dare.[11]
Ipse te potauit sui sanctissimi sanguinis nectare
Et tu non timuisti sanguinem eius fundendum tradere.[12]
Ipse non uerecundabatur tibi ministrare et pedes lauare[13]
Et tu non uerecundabaris eum tam fraudulentur salutare.[14]
Ipse tibi suum mellifluum os ad osculum non negauit
Et tamen cor tuum in sua malicia perseuerauerit.

2 Right Panel: Joab Slays Amasa. In the rebellion of Absalom against his father David he made Amasa captain of the army instead of Joab, who served under David (2 Kings 17.25). After David's victory, he ordered Amasa to assemble the army of Judah, but Amasa delayed. Joab, feigning to gave a Amasa a kiss of peace, ran him through with the sword in his right hand (2 Kings 20.8–12); though the SHS text says "left hand" the image is accurate. The typological connection, however, is tendentious, and not representative of mainstream exegesis. 1 misisti] iniisti, L 3 Lk. 9.3, 22.35–36 4 Mt. 26.15 5 Mt. 10.1, Mk. 3.15 6 L] 7 Mt. 26.14–16, Mk. 14.10, Lk. 6.16, 22.3–6, John 13.2, 26 8 John 12.6, 13.29 9 Mt. 26.15 10 uerecundus cor] *veritum corpus*, L 11 John 13.26–27 12 Mt. 26.27–29, Mk. 14.24–25, Lk. 22.20–22 13 John 13.4–5 14 Mt. 26.48–49, Mk. 14.44–45, Lk. 22.47–48

and you abandoned him and approached his enemies.
He took you into his secrets along with the other apostles

and you dispatched secret plots against him with his enemies.
He sent you out without a purse and without a bag
and whenever you went, you lacked nothing due to his care.
Now, however, alas! you are forgetful of such a man and of such care:
you go to hand him over for a small amount of money.
He conferred on you authority to care for the weak
and you pondered how you would make him weak and bind him.
He gave you power to cast out emons,
and you yourself handed him over to the power of his enemies.
He made you his purse-holder and overseer,
and you made yourself his adversary and betrayer.
He set you over his and his companion's money,
collected for him and for his companions by alms.
You were able to use these as you pleased;
why, then, did you sell your lord for a small amount of money?
You stole from the money-box of your Lord as much as you wanted,
why, then, were you selling him for thirty denarii?
He deemed you worthy to eat from his own most holy body,
and you are not ashamed to give his heart to the Jews for death.
He gave you to drink of his own most sacred blood for nourishment,
and you did not fear to hand over his blood to be poured out.
He was not ashamed to minister to you and to wash your feet,
and you were not ashamed to greet him so fraudulently.
He did not refuse you his sweet mouth for a kiss,
and nevertheless your heart persevered in its malice.

22a[2]
Cum autem eum dolose salutares ipse te uocauit amicum[1]
Et tamen non et mutatum ab incepto cor tuum iniquum.
Ipse tradicionem tuam petro et aliis apostolis prodere noluit
Quia sciuit quod te odissent hoc precauere uoluit.
In ueteri lege scriptum erat dentem pro dente oculum pro oculo[3]
Nunquam tamen licitum fuerat reddere malum pro bono.
Sed tu iniquissime iuda malum pro bono reddidisti
Quia talem. et tamen beneficiorem tuum tradidisti.
Similiter et complices tui iudei malum pro ⌞bono⌟[4] reddiderunt
Qui saluatorem suum in ligno suspenderunt. *secunda figura.*
¶Te igitur iuda et o uos iudei olim saul prefigurauit
Qui genero suo dauid malum pro bono reddere non cessauit.
Dauid factus est gener saul ducens filiam suam in uxorem
Et tamen saul machinabatur eius internecacionem.[5]
Sic filius dei sumpsit ex uestro genere humanam naturam.
Et uos congregastis ad interficiendum eum armaturam.
Dauid hostem saulis uidelicet golyam superauit
Et saul sibi tamquam hosti suo insidias mortis intentauit.[6]
Sic deus pharaonem et omnes inimicos uestros sepius deuicit
Et nunc insana mens uestra sibi tamquam inimico contradicit
Dauid spiritum malignum a saule pluries fugauit.
Et ad confodiendum eum ipse lanceam suam uibrauit.[7]
Sic saluator uester a multis ydolatriis uos sepius reuocauit.
Nunc autem uesania uestra in mortem eius arma parauit.
Dauid erat egrediens et progrediens ad imperium regis

22b[8]
Et ipse tamen rex semper aspirauit ad necem eius.
Sic christus perambulauit regionem uestram et ueritatem uero[9] docuit
Et uos queritis eum occidere qui uobis semper profuit et numquam nocuit.
Dauid dolorem saulis cytharizando mitigauit[10]
Et tamen ille ipsi dolorem et mortem inferre affectauit.
Sic et christus languidos uestros sanauit et mortuos suscitauit.
Et congregacio uestra ad occidendum ipsum se armauit.

---

[2] Left Panel: Saul Repay's David's Kindness with Evil. Saul, jealous of David's popularity (see Left Panel, 19R) and brooding with what the *Glossa* calls a *spiritus malum*, seeks twice to spear David, even while the boy is playing his harp to sooth the jealous king (1 Kings 18.8–12). Saul is here an antitype of Judas in "repaying good with evil." [1] Mt. 26.50 [3] Lv. 29.20 [4] bono L] malo, G [5] 1 Kings 18.20–29 [6] 1 Kings 17 [7] 1 Kings 18.10–11, 19.9–10 [8] Right Panel: Cain Slays Abel. In another antitype, likewise attributing to Judas the motive of jealousy, we are reminded that Cain killed his brother in a fit of jealous rage that Abel's sacrifice proved more acceptable than his own. The two figures in the background represent the brothers after they have worshiped, Cain making his invidious comparison (Gen. 4.3–8). [9] veritatem uero] viam veritas vos, L [10] 1 Kings 16.23

Yet when you were greeting him deceifully, the same man called you "friend,"
and still your wicked heart was not changed from its intention.
Christ did not wish to reveal your betrayal to Peter and the rest of the apostles,
since he knew that they would hate you: he wanted to avert this.
In the old law there was written, "A tooth for a tooth, an eye for an eye"
but it never was permissible to return evil for good.
But you, most wicked Judas, returned evil for good,
since you handed over such a person, and on top of that, your beneficiary.
And similarly your allies among the Jews returned evil for good
who hung their own savior on a tree. *Figure Two*
Accordingly Saul formerly prefigured you, Judas, and you Jews,
for he did not stop returning evil for good to his own son-in-law David.
David became the son-in-law of Saul, wedding his daughter,
and yet Saul was planning his murder.
So the son of God took on human nature from your race.
And you assembled weapons for destroying him.
David overcame Goliath, the enemy of Saul,
and Saul laid a deadly trap for him, as if for an enemy.
So God defeated Pharaoh and all your enemies repeatedly,
and now your senseless mind murmurs against him as if against an enemy.
David fled the evil spirit of Saul often,
and Saul threw his lance at him to pin him.
So too your savior called you back often from many idolatries.
Now, however, your madness has prepared the weapons for his death.
David was setting out and advancing on behalf of the king's power

and yet the king himself desired his death.
So too Christ walked around your region and taught the truth most truly,
and you seek to kill him who always did good for you and never harm.
David assuaged Saul's sorrow by playing the harp,
and yet Saul tried to bring sorrow and death on him.
And so Christ healed your ailing and revived your dead
and your assemblage armed itself to kill him.

¶Vos igitur estis similes chaym. qui fratri suo sine causa inuidit
Qui nichil mali sibi fecererat et tamen ipsum occidit.[1]
Munera que obtulit abel grata sunt apud deum
⸌⸌Et hoc erat causa si tamen causa dici potest quod occidit eum[2]
Sic christum gratus erat turbis. et acceptus erat apud deum.⸍⸍
Et ideo dicitis si dimittimus eum sic omnes credent in eum.[3]
Et si omnes crederent in eum quid obesset
Nonne omnia sunt uera et salutaria que docet.
kaym eduxit foras fratrem suum uerbis blandis
Et eductum interfecit uerberibus nephandis.
Sic et iudas verbis blandis christum salutauit
Et hostibus suis interficiendum dolose presentauit.
kaym interfecit uterinum suum fratrem
Judas et iudei occiderunt christum fratrem suum et patrem.
Pater omnium est quia nos omnes creauit
Frater noster est quia humanam naturam sibi adoptauit.
O bone ihesu qui dignatus es fieri frater noster
Miserere nostri et protege nos sicut clementissimus pater.

22va[5]

Capitulum ⸍xviiii⸌[4]

*I*n precendenti capitulo audimus quomodo christus fuit traditus et osculatus
Consequenter audiamus quomodo fuit derisus consputus et uelatus.[6]
Cumque cohoors christum comprehenderet et ligaret
Contigit ut Petrus cuidam seruo auriculam amputaret.
Statim Iesus ibidem benignitatem suam demonstrabat
Et auriculam illius tangens statim sanabat.
Duxerunt autem eum primo ad domum anne
Qui erat socer summi pontificis videlicet cayphe.
Cumque annas christum de sua doctrina interrogaret
Respondit quod ab hiis qui audierant eam inuestigaret.
Ipse enim in angulis ⸍docere⸌ non sedebat.[7]
Sed in templo et in synagoga vbi totus populus conueniebat.
Statim unus seruorum manum suam leuabat

[1] Gen. 4.3–15 [2] This line and the following were originally omitted, and added contemporaneously by the scribe at the bottom of the column [3] John 11.48 [5] Left Panel: Christ Blindfolded and Abused. In his trial before the Sanhedrin and high priests Annas and Caiphas, following his sentence of death (Mt. 26.67 ff.; Mk. 14.65; Lk. 22.63–65) Jesus is blindfolded, abused, and mocked. This image is rare before the 14th century. [4] Added later [6] Mt. 26.51–58, John 18.10–24 [7] Word order corrected contemporaneously by scribe

And so you are like Cain, who hated his own brother without reason:
he had done no harm to Cain and yet Cain killed him.
The gifts which Abel offered were pleasing to God,
and this was the reason—if it can be called a reason—that Cain killed him.
So Christ was pleasing to the crowds and was acceptable before God
and then you said, "If we let him go on like this, everyone will believe in him."
And if everyone were to believe in him, what harm would it do?
Isn't everything that he teaches true and life-giving?
Cain led his own brother forth with suave words,
and after leading him out, killed him with deadly strokes.
So also Judas greeted Christ with suave words.
And craftily gave him to his enemies to be killed.
Cain killed his own brother, born of the same mother;
Judas and the Jews killed Christ, their own brother and father.
He is the father of all since he created us all;
he is our brother since he took human nature upon himself.
O good Jesus, who deigned to be made our brother
have mercy on us and shelter us just as a most clement father.

Chapter Nineteen

In the last chapter we heard how Christ was handed over and kissed;
next let us hear how he was mocked, spat on, and blindfolded.
When the soldiers had arrested and bound Christ,
it came about that Peter cut off the ear of a certain slave.
At once Jesus demonstrated his mercy in that place,
and, touching his ear, healed it directly.
But they led him away at the first to the house of Annas
who was the father-in-law of the high priest, that is, Caiphas.
When Annas questioned Christ about his teaching,
he responded that he should question those who had listened to him.
For he had not been sitting in the corner to teach
but in the temple and the synagogue where all the people assembled.
At once one of the slaves raised his hand

Et igitur alapam maximam in maxillam suam dabat.
Iste creditur fuisse ille seruus videlicet malchus
Cuius auriculam modicum antea sanauerat christus.
Christus autem se non uindicabat nec repercuciebat
Sed cum omni mansuetudine humiliter sustinebat.
O fratres si aliquis ex uobis talem alapam suscepisset
Et si posset quod christus potuit quid fecisset.
Forsan cum petro euaginato gladio repercussisset.
Vel cum iacobo et iohane ignem de celo super eum misisset.[1]
Non sic faciendum est fratres sed attendite christi doctrinam
Qui te percussit in unam maxillam prebe ei et reliquam.[2]
Duxerunt igitur iudei ihesum ligatum de domo anne.

22vb[3] Et perduxerunt eum multis contumeliis ad domum cayphe.
Ibi congregati sunt seniores populi ut consilium inirent
Quomodo contra ihesum causam mortis et occasiones inuenirent.
Omnia autem que aduersus eum confingere potuerunt
Insufficiencia et omnimoda mendosa fuerunt.
Tandem adiurauit eum cayphas per deum ut `quis´[4] esset diceret
Si ipse christus fili⌊us⌋[5] dei uiui esset.
Cumque adiuratus se filium dei esse fateretur
Responderunt omnes quod merito propter hoc morti adiudicaretur.
Velauerunt ergo oculos eius quodam uelamine
Et maculauerunt faciem eius multo sputamine.
Dederuntque ei alapas dicentes quod prophetizaret
Et quis esset qui eum percuteret enarraret.
Omnem contumeliam quam sibi irrogare potuerunt
Hoc illi iniquissimi iudei sine misericordia fecerunt.
Hec contumelia tante derisionis et tam prophane
Durauit in domo cayphe tota nocte usque ad mane.
O quanta erat saluatoris mansuetudo et paciencia
O quanta erat iudeorum seuicia et insipiencia.
Oculos qui cuncta perspiciunt uelauerunt
Eum qui omnia scit percucientem se nescire putauerunt.
Faciem illam delectabilem in quam angeli prospicere desiderant

[1] Lk. 9.54 [2] Lk. 6.29, Mt. 5.39 [3] Right Panel: Christ on his Throne of Judgment. In this image, though somewhat obscure, Christ seems to be seated with former interrogators on one side and perhaps disciples on the other. The lack of rubric makes a positive identification difficult, but the relative tranquility of the scene, in contrast to the previous one, would seem to be connected to the last ten lines of ch. 19 in the SHS text.
[4] Added above the text line contemporaneously by scribe [5] L] filii, G

and then gave Jesus a great blow on his cheek.
That man is believed to have been that slave (that is, Malchus)
whose ear Christ had healed a little while before.
Yet Christ did not defend himself, nor strike back
but bore it humbly with all gentleness.
Oh brothers, if anyone of you had received such a blow
and if he was able to do what Christ was able to do—what he would have done!
Perhaps with Peter, he would have struck with a drawn sword;
or with James and John, he would have sent down fire from heaven upon him.
But, brothers, do not act in this way; but heed rather the teaching of Christ:
to him who strikes you on one cheek, offer also the other.
The Jews led Jesus bound from the house of Annas.

And they led him with much abuse to the house of Caiphas.
There the elders of the people were gathered for a council
on how they might find against Jesus a cause and occasion for death.
However, everything which they were able to devise against him
was insufficient and false in every way.
Finally, Caiphas urged him by God to say who he was:
if he was the Christ, the son of the living God.
And when, having been urged, he confessed that he was the son of God,
they all answered that because of this, he deserved to be condemned to death.
Therefore they covered his eyes with a blindfold,
and they splattered his face with much spittle.
And they slapped him, saying that he should prophesize
and say who it was who was striking him.
Every abuse which they were able to inflict on him
those most wicked Jews did without mercy.
This abuse, so mocking and so profane,
continued in the house of Caiphas for the whole night until the morning.
Oh, how great was the gentleness and patience of the Savior;
oh, how great was the savagery and the folly of the Jews,
they veiled those eyes which see everything;
they thought that he who knows all things did not know who was striking him.
That beloved face which the angels were longing to see

Sputis suis immundissimis maculare non timebant.
Manus illius ligare presumpserunt
Cuius manus in principio celum et terram plasmauerunt.

23a[1] Illum prophetare subsannatorie dicebant
†In quem prophete olim uirtute†[2] prophetandi habebant.
Illum satagebant per uelamen oculorum excecare
Qui olim dignatus est eos per columpnam ignis illuminare.[3]
Faciem suam non sunt ueriti sputis suis operire.
Qui olim operuit eos per columpnam nubis satis mire.
¶Judei isti qui faciem christi sputis suis maculauerunt *prima figura.*
Per ydolatras uituli conflatilis prefigurati fuerunt.[4]
Cumque filii israel deos alienos sibi facere uolebant
Aaron et hur maritus marie ipsis resistebant.
Et tunc illi indignati in hur irruerunt
Et in eum expuentes ipsum sputis suffocauerunt.
Illi indigabantur hur. quia eorum ydolatrie resistebat
Pharisei indignabantur christo quia eorum tradiciones reprehendebat.
¶Isti enim iudei qui christum subsannando deriserunt
Olim per cham filium noe prefigurati fuerunt.[5]
Cham qui merito debuisset patrem suum honorasse
Legitur eum nequiter derisisse et subsannasse.
Sic iudei debuissent merito christo reuerentiam exhibuisse.
Sed probantur prochdolor eum inhonorasse et derisisse.
Et quamuis noe perhibetur inhoneste derisus a proprio filio
Tamen inhonestior multum videtur fuisse christi derisio.
Noe fuit derisus in tabernaculo vbi nullus uidebat
Christus derisus fuit in domo pontificis vbi multitudo erat.
Noe derisus est dormiens et nesciens.

[1] Left Panel: Ham Mocks Noah. Ham (Canaan), one of the three sons of Noe, found his father drunk on wine from his new vineyard and uncovered. The text suggests that he called his two brothers to look. Unlike his brothers, who walked backward with a blanket to "cover the nakedness of their father" (Gen. 9.20–27), Ham appears to have been an irreverent voyeur. The *Glossa* compares this event to the willingness of the Jews to mock and to gaze on the naked Jesus on the cross and calls Ham "the father of sinners" (PL 113.112). [2] In quem prophete olim uirtute] A quo prophete olim uirtutem, L [3] Ex. 13.21, 40.38 [4] Ex. 32.1–8 [5] Gen. 9.22–25

they did not fear to stain with their own most foul spit.
They dared to bind the hands of him
whose hands in the beginning gave form to heaven and earth.

They mockingly said that he prophesied,
through whom the prophets formerly received the power to prophesy.
They attempted to confuse him by blindfolding his eyes,
who once deigned to bring them light by a column of fire.
They did not fear to cover his face with their spittle
who once miraculously concealed them by a column of cloud.
Those Jews who stained the face of Christ with their spit
were prefigured through the idolatrous worshippers of the molten calf.
And when the sons of Israel were wanting to make foreign gods for themselves,
Aaron and Hur (the husband of Miriam) were resisting against them.
And then, angered, they attacked Hur
and spitting on him, they suffocated him with their spittle.
They were angry with Hur, because he resisted their idolatry;
the Pharisees were angry with Christ, because he rebuked their traditions.
Indeed, those Jews who mocked Christ with insults
once were prefigured through Ham, the son of Noah.
Ham, who by rights ought to have honored his father most,
is read to have meanly laughed and mocked at him.
So too the Jews by rights ought to have shown to Christ reverence.
But they are known, alas!, to have dishonored and mocked him.
And however much Noah was treated dishonorably, mocked by his own son
yet much more dishononable did the mockery of Christ appear!
Noah was mocked in his tent, where no one saw;
Christ was mocked in the high priest's house, where there was a crowd.
Noah was mocked while he was sleeping and unaware;

23[b2] Christus derisus fuit[1] uigilans omnia uidens et audiens.
Noe derisus est solummodo ab uno filio
Christus derisus est ab omnibus et a toto conscilio.
Noe habuit duos filios sibi condolentes
Christus nullos habuit sibi in aliquo compacientes.
Predicti etiam iudei ⸌qui⸍[3] christum sic deluserunt *tercia figura*.
Olim philistiim hostibus[4] sampsonis prefigurati fuerunt.
Philistiim enim captiuauerunt et excecauerunt sampsonem
Et illudentes ei habuerunt e⌊um⌋[5] in derisionem.[6]
Sampson propter suam maximam fortitudinem
Gerit figuram christi per quandam similitudines.
Sampson quadam uice uoluntarie se ligari faciebat
Sic christus sponte a iudeis ligari et derideri uolebat.
Quadam autem uice alia quando sampsoni placuit
Tunc se de inimicis horribiliter uindicauit.
Ita in fine seculorum de inimicis christi futurum erit
Cum ipse in potestate et maiestate ad iudicandum uenerit.
Qualem vindictam tunc contra inimicos suos facturus est
Nulla scriptura nulla lingua explicare possunt.
Tunc mallent inimici eius omnem penam sustinere
Quam faciem ⸍tam⸌[7] irati iudicis et uindicis videre.
Tunc enim dicet eis ite uos maledicti in ignem eternum
Amicis autem uenite possidite premium sempiternum.[8]
O bone Ihesu da nobis tibi tam placite deseruire
Vt hanc benedictam uocacionem a te mereamur audire.

23[va] *Capitulum xx*[9]

*I*n precedenti capitulo audiuimus quomodo christus fuit illusus et uelatus
Consequenter audiamus quomodo fuit ad columpnam ligatus.[10]

---

[2] Right Panel: Achior Tied to a Pillar. Though at first glance this might appear to be another Samson story, the SHS text refers to a story in the deutero-canonical book of Judith, in which the Ammonite general Achior tries to warn Holofernes, commander of the Assyrian army, against attacking Israel. Enraged, Holofernes has Achior bound and brought to Bethulia to die with the Israelites (Jdt. 5.5–6, 13). In the text Achior is bound, but not, as in this illustration, to pillars. There is no reference to Samson in Gaza in this part of the SHS text. Achior occasionally occurs as an antitype in stained glass (Schiller, *Iconography of Christ in Art*, 1. 268). [1] fuit] est, L [3] Corrected subsequently by the black-ink scribe [4] Added contemporaneously by the scribe by means of a hair-line superscription [5] L] ei, G [6] Jdg. 16.20–31 [7] added at unknown point above the line by a carrot [8] Mt. 25.41, Mt. 25.34 [9] Left Panel: Flagellation of Christ. The scourging of Jesus before his crucifixion (Mt. 27.26; Mk. 15.15; John 19.1) is a common image after the 9th century. Usually the victim was bound to a pillar with his bare back exposed. [10] John 19.1

Christ was mocked, awake and seeing and hearing everything.
Noah was mocked only by one son;
Christ was mocked by everyone and by the whole council.
Noah had two sons consoling him;
Christ had no one showing compassion for him in anything.
And the aforementioned Jews who mocked Christ in this way
were once prefigured by the Philistine enemies of Samson.
For the Philistines captured and blinded Samson
and sporting with him, they held him in mockery.
Samson, because of his exceedingly great courage,
bore a certain likeness to the figure of Christ.
On one occasion, Samson voluntarily caused himself to be bound;
so too Christ of his own accord willed to be bound and mocked by the Jews.
Yet on another occasion, when it pleased Sampson,
then he revenged himself very horribly on his enemies.
So too at the end of the world, it will be for the enemies of Christ
when he will have come in power and majesty to render judgment.
What kind of vengeance will be made against his enemies then,
no written words, no tongues are able to explain.
Then would his enemies prefer to undergo every punishment
than see the face of so angry a judge and avenger.
For then he will say to them, "Go you cursed ones into the eternal fire,"
but to his friends, "Come, possess your eternal reward."
O good Jesus, grant to us to serve you so agreeably
that we may worthily hear from you this blessed call.

Chapter Twenty

In the last chapter we heard how Christ was mocked and blindfolded;
next we will hear how he was bound to a pillar.

Cumque tota nocte habuissent eum derisum
Mane facto duxerunt ipsum ad pylati presidis iudicium.
Cumque pylatus de accusacione ipsum quereret
Dixerunt quod malefactor et seductor populi esset.
Et quod seduxisset omnem populum non solum in iudea
Sed etiam in patria sua hoc est in galylea.
Audiens autem pylatus quod homo galyleus erat
Misit eum ad herodem quia ad iudicium eius pertinebat.
In illa die herodes et pylatus facti sunt amici
Sed antea fuerant adinuicem inimici.
Herodes christum non uiderat sed multa de eo audierat
Et ideo de aduentu ipsius multum gauisus erat.
Magn[u]m enim eum ⟦uel⟧[1] nigromanticum[2] estimabat
Et aliqua miraculosa signa ab eo uidere affectabat.
Cumque herodes eum de multis interrogaret
Ipse subticuit ita quod nullum responsum daret.
Quod uidens herodes estimabat eum non sanum esse
Et illudens ei induit eum pro derisu alba ueste.
Et sic remisit eum ad iudicium pylati presidis
Dicens se non inuenisse in eo aliquam causam mortis.[3]
Herodes nesciens quid pretenderet ueste alba eum induebat
Quia spiritus sanctus occulte hoc agens innocenciam christi ostendebat.
Sicut enim per caypham insinuat mortis christi experienciam

23vb[4] Ita etiam per herodem demonstrauit ipsius innocenciam.
Pylatus igitur interrogauit iudeos si aliquam causam haberent.
Propter quam ipsum ad mortem condempnare ualerent.
Tunc illi tres causas contra ihesum composuerunt.
Et eas in medio proferentes coram omnibus dixerunt.
Hic dixit se templum dei hoc manu factum posse dissipare
Et post triduum aliud non manu factum reedificare.[5]
Dixit etiam quod tributum non esset dandum cesari romanorum
Et gloriabatur se esse regem iudeorum.
Primas duas causas friuolas esse reputauit
De tercia autem diligenter interrogauit.

[1] Erasures [2] This line has several damaged words. *Magnum* appears to be erased at the end due to a scribal error (a macron over the n and u). *Nigromanticum*, although damaged at the beginning, is clear enough to deduce. The third word looks like the abbreviation for *uel*, but doesn't fit well in context. [3] Lk. 23.11
[4] Right Panel: The Blinding of Achior. While the text in Judith does not mention a tree, this image may have been intended to provide more symmetry with the previous one. [5] Mk. 14.58

When they had mocked him for the whole night,
when the morning came, they led him to the court of Pilate, the governor.
And when Pilate questioned him concerning the accusation,
they said that he was an evildoer and deceiver of the people.
And because he had led astray all people not only in Judea
but also in his own homeland, that is, in Galilee.
And, Pilate, hearing that he was a Galilean man,
sent him to Herod because he was under his courts' jurisdiction.
On that day Herod and Pilate became friends,
although previously they were mutually enemies.
Herod had not seen Christ but had heard many things about him,
and for that reason he rejoiced greatly about his coming.
For he supposed that Christ was a great magician,
and he was wanting to see some miraculous signs from him.
And when Herod interrogated him concerning many things,
Christ kept silent, so that he gave no response.
Herod, seeing this, supposed that he was not sane,
and sporting with him, he clothed him with a white garment for mockery.
And thus he sent him back to the court of the governor Pilate,
saying that he had not found any reason to put him to death.
Herod, not knowing what he was doing, clothed him with a white garment,
for the Holy Spirit was secretly doing this to show the innocence of Christ.
For just as he proclaimed through Caiaphas the expediendency of Christ's death

so the Holy Spirit also demonstrated his innocence through Herod.
Then Pilate asked the Jews whether they had any accusation
for which they could condemn him to death.
Then they put forward three accusations against Jesus.
And presenting them in the middle [of the assembly] said them before all:
he said that he could destroy the temple of God that he had made with his hand,
and after three days that he could rebuild something not made by hand.
Also he said that taxes shouldn't be given to the Caesar of Rome,
and he was boasting that he was the king of the Jews.
He thought that the first two reasons were trivial.
Concerning the third accusation, however, he questioned them diligently.

Cesar enim regnum iudeorum romano imperio subiacerat
Et gens iudea illo tempore nullum regem quam cesarem habebat
Pylatus autem a cesare super iudeos constitutus erat.
Quapropter quod aliquis se regem iudeorum diceret audire non petat.[1]
Ihesus autem regnum suum de hoc mundo non esse narrauit
Quo audito pylatus de hac accusacione nichil curauit.
Pylatus ergo cogitauit quomodo furor iudeorum posset mitigari
Et uidebatur sibi expediens quod faceret eum flagellari.
Vt sic ⌊opprobio⌋[2] saciati a morte cessarent
Ne etiam ipsum de insufficienti iudicio accusarent.
Milites igitur pylati ihesum flagellabant
Et pecunia phariseorum corrupti eum plus uerberabant.
¶Hec flagellacio prefigurata fuit per achyor principem *prima figura*.
Quem serui holiferne ligauerunt ad arborem.[3]

24a[4] Achior ligatus est per holofernis satellites
Christus ligatus fuit ad columpnam per pylati milites.
Achior propter ueritatem quam dixerat fuit ligatus
Ihesus propter ueritatem quam predicauerat fuit flagellatus.
Achyor ligabatur quia noluit holoferni loqui placencia
Christus ligatus est quia reprehendit iudeos cum disciplina.
Achyor ligatus est quia gloriam dei magnificabat
Christus flagellatus est quia nomen sui patris manifestabat.
¶Notandum est autem quod due gentes christum flagellauerunt. *secunda figura*.
Et ille per duas uxores lamech prefigurate fuerunt.
Due uxores lamech appellabantur Sella et ada[5]
Due gentes fuerunt gentilitas et synagoga.
Sella et ada maritum suum uerbis et uerberibus afflixerunt
Gentilitas et synagoga saluatorem suum flagellauerunt.
Gentilitas uerberauit eum flagellis et uirgis

---

[1] petat] poterat, L [2] L] [3] Jdt. 6.1–16 [4] Left Panel: Lamech Berated by his Wives. In the canonical text (Gen. 4.19–24) we learn that Lamech's two wives, Ada and Sella, were the mothers of shepherds, musicians, and metal workers, but beyond that only that Lamech sang to his wives a boasting song about his having killed a man for revenge. The *Glossa* (PL 113.101–102) regards him as representative of *voluptas carnis*—the archetypal bigamist. An apocryphal Jewish text Asher 2.32–36 says that his wives berated him for killing Cain, and would no longer sleep with him (cf. Rashi, super Gen. 4.23–24; Bereshit Rabbah 4.23–24; 23.2). There are reasons to believe that these Jewish legendary *midrashim* entered into Christian lore sometime between the 11th and 14th centuries, but the SHS inclusion is tendentious, the alleged analogy being that Ada and Sella are said to be of two races, even as were the Jewish and Roman tormentors of Christ, and that Lamech's victim was Cain, identified with sinful rebellion against God (PL 113.102). The *Historia Scholastica* on Gen. 28 is likely an immediate source. [5] Gen. 4.19–23

For Caesar had placed the kingdom of the Jews beneath Roman rule,
and the Jewish people in that time had no other king but Caesar,
moreover, Pilate had been set over the Jews by Caesar.
Accordingly he would not desire to hear someone say he is the king of the Jews.
But Jesus explained that his kingdom is not of this world.
Having heard this, Pilate cared nothing about this accusation.
Therefore Pilate considered how he could calm the fury of the Jews.
And so it seemed to him expedient to have Jesus flogged
so that, with their hatred thus satisfied, they would draw back from putting him to death,
and lest they accuse him of an insufficient trial,
the soldiers of Pilate then flogged Jesus,
and those soldiers who were bribed by the Pharisees beat him even more.
This scourging had been prefigured through the general Achior, *Figure One*
whom the slaves of Holefernes tied to a tree.

Achior was bound by the guards of Holofernes;
Christ was bound to a pillar by the soldiers of Pilate.
Achior, on account of the truth which he had spoken, was bound;
Jesus, on account of the truth which he had proclaimed, was flogged.
Achior was bound because he refused to speak suavely to Holofernes;
Christ was bound because he upbraided the Jews with his teaching.
Achior was bound because he was magnifying the glory of God;
Christ was flogged because he declared the name of his father.
It ought to be noted, moreover, that two races flogged Christ, *Figure Two*
and that they had been prefigured by the two wives of Lamech.
The two wives of Lamech were called Zillah and Adah,
the two peoples were Paganism and Synagogue.
Zillah and Adah beat their husband with words and blows;
the pagans and the Jews flogged their own Savior.
The pagans beat him with whips and rods;

Synagoga flagellauit eum uerbis et linguis.
¶Hec etiam flagellacio in christo duobus modis perpetrata *tercia figura.*
Olim fuit in beati Job flagellacione prefigurata.
Beatus Job fuit flagellatus duobus modis
Quia sathan [uerberauit] eum uerberibus flagellauit. Et uxor uerbis.[1]
De flagello sathane sustinuit dolorem in carne
De flagello lingue habuit turbacionem in corde.
Non suffecit dyabolo quod flagellauit carnem exterius
Nisi etiam instigaret uxorem qu⌊e⌋[2] irritaret cor interius.
Sic non sufficit iudeis quod christus cedebatur flagellis

24b[3] Nisi eciam ipsi affligerent eum acutissimis uerbis.
A planta usque ad uerticem in beato sanitas non erat
Sic in carne christi nichil inconcussum remanebat.
Et quanto christi caro erat nobilior et tenerior
Tanto fuit dolor ipsius amarior et asperior.
O homo recogita quantam sustinuit christus pro te passionem
Et ne tradas iterato animam tuam in perdicionem.
Attende si umquam talem penam audiuisti uel uidisti[4]
Qualis fuit passio domini nostri ihesu christi.
Aduerte quam habuit ad te christus dilectionem
Qui tantam pro tua salute sustinuit passionem.
Considera simul quantum tu versa uice propter christum sustinuisti
Quantum gratitudinis et quantum seruicii sibi reddidisti.
Omne bonum quod facis diebus uite tue
Non correspondet minime sanguinis sui gutte.
Noli ergo murmurare si contingerit[5] te modicum sustinere.
Sed sanguinem ihesu christi oculis moralibus[6] intuere.
Amaritudinem tuam cum sanguine christi commiscere
Et uideretur tibi quecumque sustinueris esse dulce.
Sustine in hac uita modicam flagellacionem
Vt in futuro effugias perpetuam dampnacionem.
Postula a domino ut in hoc seculo ita corripiaris
Vt post mortem regnum dei sine pena ingredi merearis

[1] Job 2.9 [2] quae, L] quod, G [3] Right Panel: Job Tormented by his Wife and Satan. Satan been permitted to strike Job's body with boils, but his wife adds insult to his injuries by mocking his trust in God, telling him to "curse God and die" (Job 2.7–9). The point of analogy here seems to be that just as righteous Job was abused both physically and spiritually, though innocent, so too was Christ. The image shows beleaguered Job sitting on his dung heap, meekly accepting blows (the whip of his wife is figurative for her sharp words). This typology is not found in standard commentaries, e.g., those of Gregory, Aquinas or the *Glossa*. [4] See Lam. 1.12
[5] contingerit] contigerit, L [6] moralibus] mentalibus, L

the Jews beat him with words and tongues.
Also this scourging was performed on Christ in two ways. *Figure Three*
Formerly it had been prefigured in the scourging of blessed Job.
Blessed Job had been flogged in two ways,
because Satan flogged him with blows and his wife with words.
Job endured pain in his flesh from the whip of Satan;
he had turmoil in his heart from the whip of the tongue.
It was not sufficient for the devil that he flog his flesh externally,
unless he also incites Job's wife to trouble his heart on the inside.
Thus it is not enough for the Jews that Christ be slashed by whips,

unless they also afflict him with the sharpest words.
From his sole all the way to the crown, health was not in that holy man.
So too nothing in the flesh of Christ remained unbruised.
And in proportion as the flesh of Christ was more noble and tender,
so much was his sorrow more bitter and more severe.
O man, consider how great the suffering was which Christ endured for you,
and don't hand over your soul into damnation once again.
Consider if ever you heard or beheld such pain
as the passion of our Lord Jesus Christ.
Observe the love that Christ had for you,
he who endured such great suffering for your salvation.
Consider at the same time how much you, in turn, have endured for the sake of Christ,
how much gratitude and service you give back to him,
every good thing that you do in the days of your life—
it does not equal the smallest drop of his blood.
And so don't complain if it happens that you endure a moderate amount,
but contemplate the blood of Jesus Christ with the eyes of the moral sense.
Mix your bitterness with the blood of Christ,
and it may seem to you that whatever you endure is sweet.
Endure in this life a little bit of scourging,
so that in the future you may escape eternal damnation.
Beg the Lord that you may be so punished in this world,
that after death you may be worthy to enter the kingdom of God without penalty.

O bone ihesu in hac uita percute nos flagella
Vt post mortem gustemus celica mella.

24va *Capitulum xxi*[1]

In precedenti capitulo audiuimus quomodo christus fuit flagellatus
Consequenter audiamus quomodo fuit spinis coronatus.[2]
Pylatus precepit militibus ut ihesum flagellarent
Sed iudei dederunt ipsis munera ut eum plus solito verberarent.
Consuetudo legis erat ad maius xl uerbera dari[3]
Sed iudei procurauerunt supra ihesum verbera multiplicari.
Et non suffecit eis ut ultra debitum flagellarent
Sed excogitauerunt nouam penam ut eum spinis coronarent.
Et ut ipsum subsannatorie tamquam regem adorarent
Et insignia regalia scilicet sceptrum purpuram sibi darent.
Consuetudo fuit maleficos aliquando uerberari
Sed non erat ius legis hominem debere spinis coronari.
O iniqui iudei inuentores nouarum maliciarum
Quanta sustinebitis genera nouarum penarum.
Qui enim excogitant nouorum malorum machinamenta
Recipient noua et inaudita tormenta.
Mensura qua mensi fueritis uobis remecietur[4]
Et multum addetur quia p⌊o⌋ena numquam finietur.
Cum igitur ihesum flagellarent non eum uestierunt
Sed clamide coccinea siue purpura eum circumdederunt.[5]
Purpura consueuit esse unum insigne regale
Et ideo pro derisione dederunt sibi pallium tale.
Secundum regale insigne est aureum dyadema
Loco cuius imponebatur christo spinea corona.
Tercium regale insigne est aureum sceptrum.

[1] Left Panel: The Crown of Thorns. This image refers to the second mocking of Christ. Unlike many earlier, Byzantine-influenced images, which show Christ crowned with the thorns while standing, and taunted by Roman soldiers as in the biblical text (Mt. 27.27–30; Mk. 15.16–19; John 19.2–3), this image has Jesus seated and mocked by Jewish figures, much as in the image of Giotto at Padua earlier in the century. Christ here is shown as impassive. [2] Mt. 27.28–29, Mk. 15.17, John 19.1 [3] Dt. 25.3 [4] Mt. 7.2, Mk. 4.24, Lk. 6.38 [5] Mt. 27.28–29

O good Jesus, scourge us with a whip in this life
so that after death we may taste heavenly sweetness.

Chapter Twenty-One

In the last chapter we heard how Christ was scourged,
next let us hear how he was crowned with thorns.
Pilate ordered soldiers to scourge Jesus
but the Jews gave them gifts so that they would whip him more than was customary.
The custom of the law was to give forty lashes at the most,
but the Jews took care to multiply the lashes upon Jesus.
And it was not enough for them that they should scourge him beyond what was owed
but they contrived a new punishment: to crown him with thorns,
and to mockingly worship him like a king,
and give him regal emblems, namely, a scepter and a purple robe.
It was the custom to sometimes beat evildoers
but it was not the custom of the law that a man should be crowned with thorns.
O unjust Jews, devisors of new malice,
how many kinds of new punishments you yourselves will undergo!
For they who invent the instruments of new evils
shall receive new and unheard of torments.
The measure by which you have measured shall be measured out to you again:
and more will be added, since the punishments will never cease.
Therefore, when they scourged Jesus they did not clothe him
but they tied around him a robe dyed scarlet or purple.
Purple was by custom a sign of royalty,
and therefore for the sake of mockery they gave him such a cloak.
The second regal symbol is a golden diadem,
in place of which, a thorny crown was placed upon Christ.
The third regal symbol is a golden scepter,

24vb Loco cuius dederunt in dextram eius arundinem.
Honor regis requirit ut fle⸍x⸌is[1] genibus udeneretur
Et christus flexis genibus tamquam rex salutetur.
Consuetum est offerri regi munera ⌊r⌋egalia[2]
⸍Pro⸌[3] Quibus dederunt alapas christo et sputamina.
Percuciebant etiam caput suum harundine
Inprimentes ei acutissimos aculeos corone spinee.
O impiissimi iudei cur regem uestrum tam crudeliter tractastis
Vt[4] sua beneficia uobis exhibita non recogitastis.
Ipse enim acutos scopulos sub pedibus uestris complanauit
Et crudelitas uestra caput eius acutis spinis perforauit.
Ipse pietatem exhibuit calceis uestris et pedibus
Et uos impietatem exhibuistis capiti eius.
Ipse conseruauit uestes uestras xl annis sine corrupcione[5]
Et uos spoliastis eum uestibus eius pro derisione.
Ipse flagellauit propter uos pharaonem et egiptum.[6]
Et uos sine culpa flagellastis ipsum.
Ipse per moysem confregit propter uos coronam regis egipti
Et uos coronam de spinis imposuistis ipsi.
Ipse inter omnes reges terrarum co{no}ram uobis humiliauit
Et ingratitudo uestra ipsum tamquam regem derisorie adorauit.
Ipse uos honorauit super omnium gencium naciones
Et uos inhonorastis eum per multiplices illusiones.
Ipse mirabiliter uicit hostes uestros uno mille persequendo
Et per duos decem milia fugando.[7]

25^{a} Et uos contra christum solummodo multa milia congregastis
Et duos populos contra unum hominem coadunastis.
Quomodo persequebatur vnus mille . et duo fugarunt x. milia
Nisi quia deus uoluit idcirco factum est ita.
Et quomodo omnis congregacio vestra solum christum cepisset
Nisi deus ipsum in potestatem uestram tradidisset.
¶Hec autem illusio que christo in coronacione est illata *prima figura*.[8]
Olim fuit in appemen concubina regis prefigurata.[9]

---

[1] Corrected contemporarily by scribe [2] regalia, L] legalia, G [3] The word is squeezed in at the beginning of the line [4] Ut] et, L [5] Dt. 8.4, Dt. 29.5 [6] Ex. 7–14 [7] Cf. Is. 30.17, Lv. 26.8, Dt. 32.30 [8] Right Panel: The Concubine Apamea Taking the Crown. This story essentially repeats that of the child Moses tipping off the crown of Pharaoh (Left Panel, 15R), but here the shaming of a besotted king by his concubine (1Esdras 4.29–32) is apparently an antitype of the mocking of Christ—though the apropos is hard to grasp. In the deutero-canonical text the story is part of a demonstrative argument about the superiority of women to men. [9] 3Esdras 4.29–31. Cf. Josephus, *Ant. Jud.* XI.3

in place of which they put a reed into his right hand.
The honor of a king requires that he be revered on bended knee
and Christ was hailed as king on bended knee.
It is the custom to offer regal gifts to a king
instead of which they gave him slaps and spittle.
They also struck his head with a switch,
pressing in the very sharp spines of the thorny crown.
O most wicked Jews, why did you treat your king so cruelly
that you did not consider the kindnesses he showed to you?
For he himself smoothed the sharp stones beneath your feet
and your cruelty pierced his head with sharp thorns.
He himself showed merciful care for your shoes and feet,
and you showed disregard for his head.
He himself preserved your garments for forty years without corruption
and you stripped him of his clothes for mockery.
He himself scourged Pharaoh and Egypt for your sake,
and you scourged him without guilt.
He himself through Moses shattered the crown of the king of Egypt on your behalf,
and you placed a crown of thorns on him.
He himself humbled all the kings of the earth in your presence,
and your ingratitude worshipped him like a king mockingly.
He himself honored you above all nations of peoples
and you dishonored him with many insults.
He himself wonderously conquered your enemies, with one chasing a thousand
and through two putting to flight ten thousand.

And you brought together many thousands against Christ alone
and united two peoples against one man.
How did one chase a thousand, and two put ten thousand to flight
if not because God desired that it happen in such a way?
And how could all of your assembly take Christ alone,
if God had not handed him over to your power?
Moreover, this jeering, which was offered to Christ in that coronation (Figure One)
once was prefigured in Apame, the concubine of the king.

Appemen coronam regalem de capite eius accepit
Et capiti suo in presencia ipsius regis imposuit.
Ita synagoga christum corona sua id est honore debito spoli\\auit.//
Et ipsum corona spinea in suam contumeliam coronauit.
Appemen regi alapas palmis suis dedit in maxillam
Quod rex libenter sustinens non indignabatur contra illam
I[ ]ta[1] rex celi sustinuit a iudeis alapas et colaphos.
Et tamen non ostendit indignacionem aliquam contra eos.
Rex ille concubinam appemen in tantum amauit
Quod omnia ab ipsa sibi pro ludo illata pacienter portauit.
Christus synagogam multo plus amare comprobatur
A qua tam immania cum tanta pacientia paciebatur.
¶Talem pacientiam christi olim rex dauid prefigurauit *secunda figura*.[2]
Qui ab iniquo semey tanta mala tam pacienter tolerauit.[3]
Semey proiecit super dauid lapides ligna et lutum
Sic synanoga in iecit in christum palmas et spinas et sputum.
Semey dauid uirum sanguineum et uirum belial uocauit

25b Synagoga christum seductorem et maleficum appellauit.
Abysai uoluisset semey occidisse sed dauid prohibuit
Angeli occidissent derisores christi sed ipse non permisit.[4]
Christus enim uenit in mundum pro peccatis nostris pati
Vt nos reconciliaret per suum sanguinem deo patri.
Non ideo uenit in mundum ut aliquos interficeret
Sed ut pacem et concordiam inter deum et homines conficeret.
Ipse autem a iudeis non est pacifice tractatus
Qui tantis derisionibus ab eis est inhonoratus.
¶Quapropter ipsum olim prefigurauerunt nuncii dauid *tertia figura*[5,6]
Quos annon rex amenitarum tam turpiter dehonestauit.[7]
Dauid misit nuncios regi annon ad pacem restaurandam
Quorum uestes ipse precidit usque ad nates et mediam barbam.
Sic deus filium suum ad pacem faciendam in mundum destinauit
Quem synagoga nudans uestibus barbam ipsius sputis maculauit.

---

[1] A mistake was scrubbed out between the capital 'I' and the 't' [2] Left Panel: Semei mocks David. The narrative tells how Semei, a kinsman of Saul, cursed David in public and threw stones at him (2 Kings 16.5–13); the SHS text adds sticks (*lignum* in the illustration) and dirt (*lutum*); David receives the abuse in patience, forbidding Abisai (figure on the left) to kill Semei. [3] 2 Kings 16.5–14 [4] See Mt. 26.53 [5] Right Panel: Hanon Insults the Messengers of David. Hanon was an Ammonite king: the SHS closely follows the cryptic biblical account (2 Kings 10.4), except that the artist modestly underrepresents it (the Hebrew implies that the messengers were sent away naked from the waist down, and with half their beards cut off). [6] A light "tertia" is visible in the right margin, placed as a guide for the figure mark [7] 2 Kings 10.3–4

Apame took the royal crown from his head
and placed it on her own head in the presence of the king himself.
In such a way did the synagogue strip Christ of his crown, that is, the honor owed to him.
And it crowned him with a thorny crown in his humiliation.
Apame slapped the king on the cheek with her hands.
Willingly enduring the slap, the king did not grow angry with her.
In such a way, the king of heaven endured slaps and blows from the Jews
and yet he did not display any indignation against them.
The king loved his concubine Apame so much
that he bore patiently everything offered to him by her as a game.
Christ proved that he loved the synagogue much more:
he suffered such immense things at its hands with such great patience.
Such patience of Christ's was once prefigured in King David (Figure Two)
who tolerated such great evils so patiently from unjust Semei.
Semei threw stones, branches, and mud upon David;
so too the synagogue cast slaps and thorns and spittle onto Christ.
Semei called Daniel a man of blood and a man of Belial.

The synagogue named Christ a seducer and an evildoer.
Abishai had wanted to slay Semei, but David held [him] back;
angels would have slain the mockers of Christ, but he did not permit [it].
For Christ came into the world to suffer for our sins,
so that we might be reconciled to God the Father through his blood.
For that reason, he did not come into the world to kill anyone,
but to bring about peace and harmony between God and men.
Yet he was not treated peaceably by the Jews,
he who was dishonored by them with such great mockeries.
On account of which the messengers of David once prefigured him (Figure Three)
whom Hanun, king of the Ammonites, so basely dishonored.
David sent messengers to King Hanun to restore the peace
he cut off their garments all the way to the buttocks and cut off half of the beard.
In such a way, God appointed his son to make peace on earth
and the synagogue, stripping him of his clothes, stained his beard with their spittle.

Christus uenit pacem inter deum et hominem restaurare
Quam infra vque milia annorum nullus potuit reformare.
Gentiles in reformacione pacis effundunt sanguinem
Iudei autem consueuerunt effundere aquam[1]
Christus autem effudit tamquam aquam et sanguinem
Vt eo firmius seruemus illam quam ipse fecit pacem.
Gentiles fundunt sanguinem animalis. iudei ⌞aquam⌟[2] fluminis
Sed christus effudit sanguinem et aquam proprii lateris.[3]
O bone ihesu doce nos hanc pacem seruare
Vt tecum mereamur in eterna ˊpaceˋ semper habitare.

25va *Capitulum xxii*

In precedenti capitulo audiuimus de christi coronacione
Consequentur audiamus de crucis ipsius baiulacione.[4]
Cumque ihesus esset flagellatus illusus et coronatus
Eduxit eum pylatus ostendens populo qualiter esset tractatus.
Hoc ideo fecit ut ipsi tali contumelia et afflictione
Essent contenti et cessarent ab eius interfectione.[5]
Illi autem tamquam rabidi canes in eum frenduerunt
Et crucifige eum crucifige eum omnes exclamauerunt.[6]
Cupiens autem pylatus eum de manibus eorum liberare
Dixit se uelle ipsius unum captiuum liberum dare.
Tunc illi pecierunt sibi dari barrabam latronem
Ihesum autem postulauerunt tradi ad patibuli suspendionem.
O impiissimi iudei cur non petiuistis ihesum liberum dimitti.
Qui liberauit nos[7] de captiuitate babylonis et egipti.
Videns autem pylatus quod non proficeret sed magis tumultus fieret
Lauit manus ut per hoc innocentem se a sanguine ihesu ostenderet
Hoc agebat per pylatum occulte spiritus sanctus
Innuens ˊquodˋ [autem] ihesus [et] moriturus esset innocens et iustus.
Vxor autem pylati dixit quod multum de ihesu per sompnia uidisset
Et ipsum dimittendum eo quod homo iustus esset.[8]
Hoc fecerat dyabolus cupiens impedire christi passionem
Et sic impediret humani generis redempcionem.
Et quod pylatus tantum videtur pro christi liberacione institisse

[1] 1 Kings 7.6 [2] aquam, L] autem, G [3] John 19.34 [4] John 19.17 [5] Cf. Mt. 27.15–26, Mk. 15.6–15, Lk 23.17–24
[6] John 19.5, 19.16 [7] nos] *vos, L* [8] Mt. 27.19

Christ came to restore peace between God and men
which no one could restore within five thousand years.
The heathens pour out blood in the restoration of peace;
the Jews, however, were accustomed to pouring out offerings of water.
Yet Christ poured out both water and blood
so that we might more faithfully preserve that peace, which he himself made.
The heathens pour animal blood, and the Jews a river of water,
but Christ poured out water and blood from his own side.
O good Jesus, teach us to preserve this peace
that we might be worthy to abide with you in eternal peace forever.

Chapter Twenty-two

In the last chapter we heard of the crowning of Christ,
next we will hear of the carrying of his cross
and when Jesus was scourged and mocked and crowned,
Pilate led him out, showing the people how he had been treated.
He did this so that with that same great abuse and affliction
they would be content, and would hold back from killing him.
However, they gnashed their teeth against him like rabid dogs,
and they all shouted "Crucify him! Crucify him!"
But Pilate, desiring to free him from their hands,
said that he wished to give them one freed captive.
Then they asked that the thief Barabbas be given to them,
but they demanded that Jesus be handed over for hanging on a gibbet.
O most wicked Jews, why did you not ask that Jesus be sent away free,
who freed us from the captivity of Babylon and Egypt?
And Pilate, seeing that he could not proceed, but that the uproar was growing greater,
washed his hands so that by this he could show himself to be innocent of the blood of Jesus.
The Holy Spirit was acting secretly through Pilate,
showing that Jesus would die as one innocent and righteous.
Moreover, the wife of Pilate said that she had seen much concerning Jesus in dreams,
and that he ought to be let go for this reason, namely that he was a righteous man.
The devil had done this, wanting to hinder the Passion of Christ,
and so to hinder the redemption of the human race.
And because Pilate appeared to have insisted so much on freeing Christ,

Putatur totum ex instinctu dyaboli sicut uxor sua fecisse.
Dyabolus enim per eos nitebatur impedire nostram redempcionem

25[vb1] Sicut olim per adam et euam fecit nostram dampnacionem.
Dyabolus enim uidens sanctos patres in lymbo exultare
Conniciebat quod christus per suam passionem uellet eos liberare.
Quo propter per presidem passionem christi impedire instabat
Et ipsum per stimulum suum id est per feminam magis instigabat.
O quam deceptorius stimulus dyaboli est femina blanda
Per quam tam blande stimulat uiros ad mala perpetranda.
Milites igitur pylati ihesum ueste purpurea exuerunt
Et uestibus suis quibus spoliatus fuerat reinduerunt.
Inposuerunt autem humeris suis crucem portandam
Et hoc fecerunt ad maiorem ipsius contumeliam.
Lignum enim patibuli tunc temporis maledictum esse dicebant
Et idcirco nec milites pylati nec iudei illud portare uolebant.
Crux ergo ⌊que⌋[2] tunc reputabatur maledicta et ignominosa
Per passionem christi facta est benedicta et gloriosa.
Et que tunc erat patibulum furum et supplicium latronum
Modo depingitur in frontibus principum regum et imperatorum.
Et in qua tunc malefici socii dyaboli suspendebantur
Per eam nunc demones puniuntur et effugantur.
¶Hec autem baiulacio crucis christi ihesu iam narrata *prima figura*.[3]
Olim fuit in ysaac filio abrahe prefigurata.[4]
Ysaac enim ligna propriis humeris afferebat
In quibus eum pater suus ymmolare domino intendebat.
Sic christus humeris crucis patibulum baiulabat
In quo gens iudeorum ⸌eum⸍ suspendere affectabat.

26[a] Ysaac autem per adiutorium angeli a morte est liberatus
Et aries in dumis[5] pendens loco ipsius est immolatus.

[1] Right Panel: Isaac Carries Wood for the Sacrifice. Perhaps the most well-established of all antitypes for the previous image in Christian art is the last stage of the journey of Abraham and his son Isaac up Mount Moriah to obey the command of God that Isaac should be sacrificed (Gen. 22.6–8). Isaac carries a bundle of wood, Abraham his bowl of fire and an ominous sword; the latter is reminiscent of the more detailed image in the *Biblia Pauperum*. [2] que, L] qui, G [3] Left Panel: Christ Carries his Cross. The torturous walk to Golgotha was normally made more brutal by the condemned being forced to carry their own cross (John 19.16). When Jesus proved too weak from his scourging, the soldiers compelled Simon of Cyrene to shoulder it instead (Mt. 27.31 ff.; Mk. 15.20–21; Lk. 23.26). The figure shows Simon on the right taking over; the other figure is not identified. The image is unusually cryptic for this period, probably in order to provide symmetry with the antitype to follow. [4] Gen. 22.1–13 [5] in dumis, G] in cornibus, L

he is deemed to have done the whole thing by the impulsion of the devil, just like his wife.
For the devil was striving to hinder our redemption through them,

just as formerly he accomplished our damnation through Adam and Eve.
For the devil, seeing the holy fathers rejoice in Limbo,
was guessing that Christ wished to free them through his Passion.
For which reason he was trying to hinder the Passion of Christ through the governor,
and he was urging him more with his own goad, that is, through the woman.
Oh how deceitful a goad of the devil is an alluring woman,
through whom he so alluringly incites men to commit evils!
Therefore, the soldiers of Pilate stripped Jesus of his purple garment,
and they returned his own garments, of which he had been stripped.
And they placed a cross on his shoulders to be carried,
and they did this to insult him more greatly.
For they then maintained that the wood of the cross was cursed
and therefore neither the soldiers of Pilate nor the Jews wanted to carry it.
But the cross, which then was thought cursed and disgraceful,
through the Passion of Christ was made blessed and glorious.
And what in the past was the thieves' gibbet and punishment of thieves,
now is depicted on the foreheads of princes, kings, and emperors.
On it then the criminal associates of the devil were hung;
through it now the demons are punished and are driven away.
Moreover, the carrying of the cross of Christ by Jesus, which just now was described, (Figure One)
was formerly prefigured in Isaac, the son of Abraham.
For Isaac was bearing on his own shoulders the wood
on which his own father was intending to sacrifice him to the Lord.
So too Christ was bearing the gibbet of the cross on his shoulders,
on which the Jewish people desired to hang him.

Moreover, Isaac was freed from death through the help of an angel,
and a ram, hanging in the thorn bushes, was sacrificed in his place.

Pro christo nec aries nec aliqua creatura paciebatur
Sed ipse solus omnia sustinuit et pro nobis immolabatur
Ysaac audiens quod pater eum domino immolare uolebat
Voluntarium se ad immolandum[1] esse dicebat.
Sic filius dei precepta patris usque ad mortem tenuit
Et se ad omnia patris imperia uoluntarium exhibuit.
Nam pater et filius et spiritus sanctus misterium consilii habebant
Nam ex se unum pro salute generis humani \\mittere//[2]disponebant.
Cumque pater diceret quem mittam et quis ibit ex uobis
Respondit filius ecce ego mitt⌞e⌟[3] me quia sum paratus.[4]
Vade inquit pater in mundum et cum hominibus conuersare ibi
Et pacienter sustine quidquid ad paciendum fuerit tibi.
Missus igitur filius dei uiui conuersatus est in iudea
Et non peperc⌞erunt⌟[5] ei sed uiliter interfectus est ab ea.
¶Istud insinuauit christus in quadam parabola *secunda figura.*[6]
Quam predicando iudeis tamquam figuram proposuit de uinea[7]
Homo quidam uineam plantauit et eam circumsepiuit
Et construxit in ea turrim et torcular colonis commisit.
Tempore fructuum misit seruos qui fructus exigebant
Quos illi apprehendentes cedebant et interficiebant.
Quod audiens dominus misit alios seruos plures prioribus
Quibus illi fecerunt sicut fecerunt primis.
Ad ultimum misit eis vnicum filium

26b Si forte uererentur occidere illum.
Quem coloni apprehendentes de vinea eiecerunt
Et attrocius eum quasi seruos interfecerunt.
Per uineam istam significatur iudea siue plebs iudaica
Per vii muros ierusalem angelorum custodia.
Per turrim autem significatur templum salomonis
Per torcular altare holocausti et oblacionis.

---

[1] immolandum] obediendum, L [2] The scribe indicated that he should have placed *mittere* before *disponebant* by using two little vertical lines before each word, although on the manuscript *mittere* is written in the right margin [3] mittte, L] mitto, G [4] Is. 6.8 [5] pepercerunt, L] peperciens, G [6] Left Panel: Wicked Husbandmen Kill the Vineyard Owner's Son. This parable of Jesus (Mt. 21.33–41; Mk. 12. 1–9; Lk. 20.9–16) was a response to a question put by the Pharisees concerning ultimate authority. In effect it is a miniature for the story of Israel's rebelliousness, rejection of the prophets, and imminent murder of God's son—God having been represented as absent owner of a vineyard usurped by delinquent tenants wishing to seize ownership for themselves. The patristic exegesis assembled by Thomas Aquinas in his *Catena Aurea* (1.727–731) allegorizes the winepress as the altar, the tower as the Temple, shown here as the backdrop for the murder of the vineyard owner's son, universally taken to figure forth Christ himself. [7] Mk. 12, Lk. 20.9–16

Neither the ram nor another creature suffered on behalf of Christ,
but he himself alone suffered everything and was sacrificed on our behalf.
Isaac, hearing that his father wanted to sacrifice him to the Lord,
said that he was willing to be sacrificed.
So the son of God kept the commands of the father to death,
and he showed himself willing [to obey] all the commands of his father.
For the Father and Son and Holy Spirit had in mind secret knowledge of a plan,
for they were arranging to send one of themselves for the salvation of the human race.
And when the father said, "Whom will I send, and which of us will go?",
the son responded, "Here I am! Send me, for I am ready."
"Go," the father said, "into the world, and dwell there with men,
and patiently bear whatever will be there for you to suffer."
Therefore, the son of the living God dwelled in Judea,
and not sparing him, rather he was killed contemptuously by it.
Christ conveyed that in a certain parable, (Figure Two)
which in his preaching to the Jews he set forth just like a figure, concerning a vineyard:
a certain man planted a vineyard and hedged it in,
and he built a tower in it and attached a press for the tenants.
In the time of harvest, he sent servants, who were demanding the crops.
Seizing them, the tenants struck down and killed them.
Hearing that, the master sent other servants, more than before;
the tenants did to them just as they did to first ones.
Finally, he sent to them his only son—

perhaps they would fear to kill him.
Seizing him, the tenants cast him out from the vineyard,
and they killed him quite cruelly, just as they did the servants.
Through the vineyard is signified Judea or the Jewish people.
Through the seven walls the Jerusalem and the guardianship of the angels is signified.
And through the tower, however, the temple of Solomon is signified;
through the press, the altar of sacrifice and offering.

Serui missi prophete domini fuerunt
Quos illi diuersis modis afflixerunt et interfecerunt.[1]
Ysaiah serrabant Jeremiam lapidabant
⌊Eze⌋lchielem excerebrabant amos clauo perforabant.
Tandem misit unicum filium suum ihesum christum.
Et attrocius quam aliquem alium interfecerunt istum.
Patibulum suum humeris ipsius imposuerunt.
Et eicientes eum de uinea id est de ierusalem occiderunt.
Duo populi erant qui ihesum ad interficiendum eduxerunt
Videlicet iudei qui corde et gentiles qui opere hoc fecerunt. *tertia figura.*[2]
¶Isti olim per duos exploratores prefigurati erant
Qui botrum de terra promissionis ad desertum deferebant
Per botrum figurabatur filius dei ihesus christus[3]
Qui per hos duos populos de ierusalem locum caluarie est eductus.
Per ⌊b⌋otrum[4] illum probantur filii israel terre promisse bonitatem
Per doctrinam christi possumus nos considerare celi suauitatem.
O bone ihesu doce nos dulcedinem uite eterne considerare
Vt tecum mereamur in ea in perpetuum habitare.

26va

Capitulum xxiii

In precedenti capitulo audiuimus quomodo christus crucem baiulauit
Consequenter audiamus quomodo pro suis crucifixoribus exorauit.[5]
Tota nocte et die illusionibus in tantum fatigatus erat
Quod illam grauem ˋcrucemˊ per se portare non ualebat.
Tunc angariauerunt quendam videlicet symonem syrenensem[6]
Vt adiuuaret ihesum baiulare suam crucem
Cumque uenissent ad montem caluarie et uiderent eum fatigatum.
Dederunt ei acetum felle mixtum et vinum mirratum.[7]
Hunc potum malicia iudeorum commiscuerat
Sicut olim per prophetam de ipsis prophetatum fuerat.
Accipientes autem milites crucem posuerunt super terram
Et nudantes ihesum extenderunt eum super ipsam.
Primam autem manum clauo cruci affixerunt

[1] Cf. Mt. 23.26–37 [2] Right Panel: The Grapes of Eschol. The huge cluster (Heb. *eschol*) of grapes brought back by the spies to Moses from their foray into Canaan was so prodigious that it took two men to carry it between them on a pole (Nm. 13.23–25). The grapes are taken by the *Glossa* to be an antitype of Christ, the fruit redeemed from the alien country, which is made to stand for the Jewish law (*PL* 113.402–403). [3] Nm. 13.24–25. [4] botrum, L] potrum, G [5] Lk. 23.34 [6] Mt. 27.32 [7] Ps. 68.22, Mt. 27.34

The servants sent were the prophets of God,
whom they afflicted and killed in various ways.
They sawed up Isaiah, stoned Jeremiah,
knocked out the brains of Ezechiel, stabbed Amos with a spike.
Finally, he sent his only son, Jesus Christ.
And they killed that him more cruelly than any other.
They placed their own cross on his shoulders
and casting him out of the vineyard, that is, out of Jerusalem, they killed him.
There were two peoples who led forth Jesus to be killed
namely, the Jews, who did it in their heart, and the Gentiles who did it in deed (Figure Two).
Formerly they had been prefigured through the two explorers,
who brought back a cluster of grapes from the promised land to the desert.
Through the cluster of grapes is symbolized Jesus Christ the son of God
who through these two peoples was led forth from Jerusalem to the place of Calvary.
Through the grape cluster it was demonstrated that the children of Israel had been promised the land's bounty;
through the teaching of Christ we are able to contemplate the sweetness of heaven.
O good Jesus, teach us to contemplate the sweetness of eternal life
so that with you we may become worthy to dwell in it forever.

Chapter Twenty-three

In the last chapter, we heard how Christ carried the cross
now let us hear how he prayed for his crucifiers.
He had been so exhausted by the mockery through the whole night and day
that he was not strong enough to carry that heavy cross himself.
Then they compelled someone—that is, Simon of Cyrene—
to help Jesus bear his cross.
When they had come to Mount Calvary and they saw that he was tired,
they gave him vinegar mixed with gall, and wine mixed with myrrh.
The malice of the Jews had compounded this drink
just as the Prophet once had foretold about them,
and taking the cross, the soldiers put it on the ground
and stripping Jesus, they stretched him out on it.
And they nailed the first hand to the cross,

Et aliam funibus trahentes ad aliud foramen extenderunt.
Quam cum affixissent pedes similiter funibus extendebant
Et cum clauo cruci ambos affigebant.
Hanc extensionem dicit dominus in psalmos et tangit de ea
Foderunt manus meas et pedes dinumerauerunt omnia ossa mea.[1]
Cum autem ihesus pateretur hanc crudelissimam acerbitatem
Ostendit eis suam clemenciam et caritatem.
Et nobis exemplum diligendi inimicos donauit
Nam pro ipsis patrem suum celestem exorauit.[2]
Quando enim inimicos diligimus et pro eis oramus
Filios dei et fratres christi nos esse demonstramus.
Christus enim docuit ut inimicos nostros amemus.[3]

26vb[4] Vt filii patris sui qui in celis est esse possimus
Non est magnum diligere benefactores et amicos.
Sed maximum est amare persecutores et inimicos.[5]
Milites igitur christum super terram cruci affixerunt
Et post hec ipsum uiuum cum cruce in altum leuauerunt.
Hec autem oratio que a christo in crucifixione est prolata *prima figura*.[6]
Fuit in jubal fratre Tubalkayin prefigurata.[7]
Jubal et tubalkaim filii lamech fuerunt
Qui inuentores artis ferrarie et musice extiterunt.
Quando enim tubalkaim cum malleis sonos faciebat
Jubal ex sonitu malleorum melodiam inueniebat.
Ad talem ergo melodiam et malleorum fabricacionem
Comparamus christi oracionem et crucifixorum malleacionem.
Quando enim crucifixores Ihesum ad crucem fabricabant
Christus dulcissimam melodiam patri decantabat.
Pater dimitte illis quia nesciunt quid faciunt[8]
Ignorant enim quod filius tuus sit quem crucifigunt.
Si enim iudei et gentiles filium dei agnouissent

[1] Ps. 21.17–18 [2] Lk. 23.34 [3] Mt. 5.44, Lk. 6.27–36 [4] Right Panel: Tubalcain at his Anvil. The genealogy of human arts given in Genesis 4 is cryptic, but the *Glossa* (PL 113.101) cites Josephus as transmitting the Jewish lore than made Tubalcain the inventor of weapons of war (Gen. Rabbah 23.2.2; Yashar Bereshit 10b). The notion that Jubal got the idea of making music from the clanging of his brother's anvil can be found in the commentaries of Pierre Bersuire, Vincent de Beauvais, and Albericus, the Third Vatican Mythographer. [5] Mt. 5.44–47 [6] Left Panel: Elevation of the Cross. Before the 15th century illustrations show little in the way of an historically accurate depiction of the process of crucifixion; this image, with the nailing completed only after the cross has been elevated, is an example. Sparse detail in the biblical text itself (none of the four gospels includes it), and the fact that crucifixion ceased to be a method of execution after the rule of Constantine account for a wide variety of representations. [7] Gen. 4.21–22 [8] Lk. 23.34

and pulling the other with ropes, they stretched it to the other side.
When they had nailed it, they stretched out his feet with ropes
and nailed both to the cross.
The Lord spoke of this outstretching in the Psalms and said about it:
"They have pierced my hands and feet, they have numbered all my bones."
But when Jesus suffered this most cruel bitterness
he showed them his mercy and love
and gave us an example of loving our enemies.
For he prayed to his heavenly father on their behalf.
For when we love our enemies and pray for them,
we show ourselves to be sons of God and brothers of Christ,
for Christ taught that we should love our enemies

so that we might be children of his father who is in heaven.
It is not much to love our friends and benefactors,
but it is the greatest thing to love our enemies and persecutors.
Then the soldiers nailed Christ to the cross on the ground
and then lifted him on high, alive on the cross.
This prayer, which Christ lifted up at the crucifixion, (Figure One)
was prefigured in Jubal, the brother of Tubalcain:
Jubal and Tubalcain were sons of Lamech,
who are known as the inventors of ironworking and music,
for while Tubalcain's mallets were hammering,
Jubal heard a melody in the sound of the mallets.
To this melody and hammer's pounding
we compare Christ's prayer and the hammer-strokes of the crucifiers.
For while the crucifiers were putting Jesus on the cross,
Christ was singing the sweetest melody to the Father.
"Father forgive them, for they know not what they do.
For they do not know that it is your son whom they crucify."
For if the Jews and Gentiles had recognized the Son of God

Numquam regem glorie crucifixissent.[1]
Tante enim dulcedinis erat hec dulcissima melodia
Quod eadem hora conuersi sunt hominum tria milia.[2]
Congrue iudei per inuentore⌊m⌋[3] artis fabrice figurati fuerunt
Qui ipsi hunc modum crucifigendi primo inuenerunt.
Non enim erat iuris quod homo cruci cum clauis annectaretur
Sed ut funibus suspenderetur donec moreretur.

27a[4] Bene et inuentor melodie ihesum christum prefigurabat
Quia ipse primus erat qui talem melodiam deo decantabat.
Christus non solum pro crucifixoribus suis exorauit
Sed pro salute tocius mundi patrem suum efflagitauit.
Et quamuis multi olim pro peccatis hominum orauerunt.
Tamen nec per oraciones nec per sacrificia exauditi fuerunt.
Christus autem orauit cum lacrimis et clamore ualido
Et exauditus est pro sua reuerencia illud quod peciit inpetrando.[5]
¶Hanc etiam crucifixionem christi ysaias prefigurauit
Quem gens iudaica nimis inhumaniter mactauit.
Judei enim ipsum cum lignea serra per medium sectabant
Et per hoc mortem christi satis conuenienter prefigurabant.
Judei enim christum cum serra lignea per medium diuiserunt
Quia animam eius et corpus per crucem ab inuicem separauerunt.
Quamuis autem animam et carnem ab inuicem diuidebant
Numquam tamen deitatem a neutra earum diuidere ualebant.
Deitas enim a carne mortua non fuit separata
Nec ab anima similiter fuit aliquatenus segregata.
Deus enim filium suum in morte derelinquere noluit
Sed eum pro nobis in mortem tradere uoluit.
O quam inmensa dilectione nos pater celestis diligebat
Qui tam dilectum filium pro nobis in mortem tradebat.[6]
O inestimabilis dilectio diuine caritatis
Vt dilectum filium daret pro filiis iniquitatis.
Quis umquam uidit simile uel quis audiuit tale

[1] See Ps. 23.7–10 [2] Act. 2.41 [3] inuentorem, L] inuetores, G [4] Left Panel: Isaiah Sawn in Half. The image departs from the tradition that Isaiah was executed by King Manasseh during his general purge of prophets by being bound in the trunk of a hollow tree and sawn in two (Ta'an 26b; Yerushalmi 4.68d; Tosepta Targ. Is. 66.1; Sanhedrin 10.28c). The tradition of Isaiah's martyrdom entered into Christian literature, via Hbr. 11.37, through Justin Martyr's *Dialogue with Trypho* among other sources, and is adumbrated in Comestor's *Historia Scholastica*. [5] See Hbr. 5.7 [6] John 3.16, 1John 4.9

they would never have crucified the King of Glory.
And this melody was so sweet
that three thousand people were converted in one hour.
The inventor of ironworking fittingly symbolized the Jews,
who first devised this means of crucifixion for him,
for it was not lawful for a man to be fixed on the cross with nails,
but to be suspended by ropes until he died.

And the inventor of melody excellently prefigured Jesus Christ
because he was the first to sing such a song to God.
Not only did Christ pray for his crucifiers
but he entreated his father on behalf of the whole world.
And though many people before him had prayed for the sins of men,
nevertheless their prayers and sacrifices were not heard.
But Christ prayed with tears and great weeping
and his request was granted on account of his piety.
The crucifixion of Christ was prefigured by Isaiah,
whom the Jewish people most cruelly slaughtered.
For the Jews sawed him in half with a wooden saw
and through this they fittingly prefigured the death of Christ.
For the Jews cut Christ in half with a wooden saw
because they separated his body and soul from each other on the cross.
Although they separated his soul and body from each other,
they were not able to separate his divinity from either one.
For his divinity was not separated from the dead flesh
nor likewise was it separated in any way from his soul.
For God did not wish to forsake his son in death
but willed to give him over to death on our behalf.
O how great is the love with which the heavenly Father loves us
who for our sake gave over so beloved a son to death!
O the unfathomable love of God's charity,
that he should give his beloved son for the children of sin!
Who ever saw the like or heard such a thing?

27b Et quis sufficit hanc dilectionem ad plenum enarrare[1]
¶Hec autem dilectio dei patris tam inmensa *tercia figura.*
Olim fuit in rege ⸍m⸌oab[2] per figuram preostensa.[3]
Ciuitas huius regis fuit ab hostibus circumuallata
Et gens inhabitans defecit fame et siti atenuata.
Rex autem ciues suos tantum amabat
Quod proprium filium supra murum pro eis immolabat.[4]
Per ciuitatem illam mundus iste prefigurabatur
Et per ciues humanum genus designabatur.
Ciuitas ista obsessa erat ab exercitu demoniorum
Ante aduentum christi plus quam quinque milibus annorum.
Et omnes ciues in tantum delicati erant
Quod per se hanc obsidionem dissoluere non ualebant.
Tandem pater misericordiarum et deus tocius consolacionis[5]
Pie respexit angustie nostre obsidionis.
Et in tantum dilexit nos ut filium suum in mortem daret
Vt sic ab obsidione dyabolica nos liberaret.
Rex moab immolabat filium suum in mortem pro amicis
Sed deus dedit filium suum in mortem pro inimicis.
Et quid est quod possimus ei pro tanta dilectione retribuere
Nisi hoc quod studeamus ipsum ex corde uiceuersa diligere.
Diligamus eum quomodo ipse prior nos dilexit[6]
Et angustias nostre obsidionis tam pie respexit.
O bone ihesu concede nobis ut in hoc seculo te ita diligamus
Vt tecum in futuro seculo in perpetuum maneamus.

27va[7] *xxiiii Capitulum*

In precendenti capitulo audiuimus quomodo christus in cruce orauit
Consequenter audiamus quibus figuris mortem suam premonstrauit.
¶Rex nabuchodonosor per sompnium arborem magnam videbat[8]

---

[1] Right Panel: Moab Sacrifices his Firstborn. In the wake of his defeat in battle, the Moabite king sacrificed his son and successor on the wall as a burnt offering (4Kings 3.27). The SHS interpretation is eisegesis: the connection is opaque at best, at worst, contradictory. [2] Added by scribe in superscript to replace an initial i [3] 4Kings 3 [4] 4Kings 3.27 [5] 2Cor. 1.3 [6] 1John 4.19 [7] Left Panel: Crucifixion. The earliest surviving images of Christ nailed to the cross are 5th century. The degree of detail varies widely from the gospel descriptions (Mt. 27.33–50; Mk. 15.22–41; Lk. 23.33–49; John 19.17–37); illustrative images may or may not contain the two thieves and representation of the disciplines and holy women; the more attenuated versions reduce the attendant figures to the Virgin Mary and beloved disciple John, as is apparently the case here. [8] Dn. 4.1–34

And who can tell of this love in full?
But this great love of God the Father
was once foreshown in the king of Moab through a figure.
The city of this king was besieged by enemies
and the people inside were broken, weakened by hunger and thirst.
But the king loved his people so much
that he sacrificed his own son for them on the wall.
That city prefigured the world
and the citizens signify the human race.
That city was besieged by an army of demons
more than five thousand years before Christ's coming.
And the citizens were all so weak
that they could not break the siege by themselves.
At last the Father of mercies and God of all comfort
mercifully considered the difficulty of our siege.
And he loved us so much that he gave his own son unto death
so that by this he might liberate us from the siege of the devil.
The king of Moab offered up his own son unto death for his friends,
but God gave his own son unto death for his enemies.
And what is there that we can give back to him in return for such love,
except to strive to love him back from the heart?
Let us love him in the way he first loved us
and so mercifully observed the difficulties of our siege.
O good Jesus, grant us so to love you in this age
that we may abide with you forever in the age to come.

Chapter Twenty-four

In the last chapter, we heard how Christ prayed on the cross;
next we shall hear with what figures he foreshadowed his own death.
King Nebuchadnezzer saw a great tree in a dream.

Que in celum se extendens ramos per mundum extendebat.[1]
Hec arbor ipsum regem nabuchodonosor designabat.
Sed mystice christum regem in mundo futurum prefigurabat.
Cuius potestas super omnes celos exaltatur
Et per totum orbem super omnes potestates mundi dilatatur.[2]
Omnes bestie subter eam et uolucres in ea morabantur
Et omnes de fructibus suis uescebantur et nutriebantur.[3]
Per quod satis conuenienter innuebatur
Quod omnis creatura per gratiam christi sustentatur.[4]
Et ecce angelus adueniens iussit arborem succidi[5]
Per quod figurabatur quod christus debebat crucifigi.
Dixit quod omnes rami eius essent amputandi
Innuens quod omnes discipuli eius essent a christo separandi.[6]
Addidit etiam omnia folia arboris esse excucienda
Innuens omnia christi documenta a iudeis contempnenda.
Adiecit etiam quod omnes fructus arboris deberent dispergi
Innuens quod omnia opera christi a iudeis deberent uilipendi.
Item dixit quod omnes bestie et uolucres ab ea fugere deberent
Quia nec homines nec angeli christo auxilium preberent.[7]
Addiditque quod licet arbor illa esset succidenda
Tamen radix eius ad germinandum esset in terra dimittenda.[8]
Per quod innuebatur quod licet christus esset moriturus

27vb[10] Tamen non esset in morte moriturus[9] sed resurrecturus.
Adiecitque quod nabuchodonosor quem arbor ad litteram pretendebat
Vinculo ferreo et eneo ligari debebat.[11]
Per hoc innuebatur quod christus ad columpnam esset ligandus
Et clauis ferreis patibulo crucis affigendus.[12]
Addiditque quod idem rex deberet rore celi madidari
Innuens ad litteram eum nudum extra homines debere morari.[13]
Per hoc figurabatur quod christus extra urbem deberet crucifigi[14]
Et rore celi tingi id est proprio cruore perfundi
Adiecitque quod idem rex tamquam bestia esset cibandus[15]

---

[1] Dn. 4.9, 18 [2] See Ps. 61.12, 65.7, Jer. 10.12, Dn. 4.31 [3] Dn. 4.9, 18 [4] 2 Cor. 12.9–10. See John 1.16–17 [5] Dn. 4.11, 20 [6] Dn. 4.20, Mt. 26.56, Mk. 14.50 [7] Cf. Mt. 27.46, Mk. 15.34, Rom. 5.12, 1 Cor. 15.21 [8] Dn. 4.12, 20 [10] Right Panel: Dream of Nabuchodonosor. The book of Daniel returns here with the story of the dream of Nabuchodonosor in which his imperial greatness is figured as a great, leafy tree in which all manner of birds and animals find shelter. A heavenly messenger then comes and the tree is cut down—a prophecy of Nabuchodonosor's imminent fall (Dn. 4.4–27). The pelican in the tree is a symbol for Christ, since it was thought to feed its chicks with its own blood. [9] moriturus] permansurus, L [11] Dn. 4.12, 20 [12] Mt. 27.31, Mk. 15.20, Lk. 23.33, John 19.16 [13] Dn. 4.12–20, 22, 30 [14] John 19.20 [15] Dn. 4.12.20, 22, 29–30

Reaching to heaven, it stretched its branches through the world.
This tree indicated King Nebuchadnezzer himself,
but mystically it prefigured that Christ was going to be king in the world,
his power lifted up over all the heavens
and extended above all the world's powers across the whole globe.
All the beasts lingered underneath it and the birds on it,
and all ate and were nourished by its fruits.
Through this it is shown fittingly enough
that every creature is sustained through the grace of Christ.
And behold, an angel arrived and ordered that the tree be cut down.
Through this it was shown that Christ ought to be crucified.
He said that all its branches should be cut off,
showing that all his disciples were to be dispersed from Christ.
And also he added that all the leaves of the tree should be shaken off
showing that all the proofs of Christ were to be despised by the Jews.
And he also added that all the fruit of the tree ought to be scattered
showing that the works of Christ should be despised by the Jews.
Likewise, he said that all beasts and birds would flee from it
because neither men nor angels offered aid to Christ.
And he added that it is fitting for this tree to be cut down
but for its root to be left in the earth in order to sprout again.
Through this it was shown that although Christ would die,

Nevertheless, he would not in his death truly die but would be resurrected.
And he added that Nebuchadnezzar, whom the tree signified on the literal level,
would be bound with shackles of iron and brass.
Through this it was shown that Christ would be bound to a post
and would be fixed with iron nails to the gibbet of the cross.
And he added that this same king would be wet with the dew of heaven,
showing literally that he would dwell naked, away from men.
This symbolized that Christ would be crucified outside the city
and would be wet with the dew of heaven, that is, drenched with his own blood
And he said furthermore that this same king would be fed like a beast,

Innuens quod christus felle et aceto ⸌esset⸍ potandus.[1]
Addiditque quod cor eius deberet ab humano commutari
Et cor bestie pro corde hominis deberet sibi dari.[2]
Per hoc innuebatur quod iudei ihesum non tamquam homine tractarent
Sed tamquam feram uel vermem conspuerent et cruciarent.[3]
Vel quod ipsi non tamquam homines se christo exhiberent.
Sed tamquam bestie contra ipsum dentibus striderent.
Adiecit quod per ipsum predictum regem vii tempora essent mutanda
Quia passio christi per vii horas esset prolonganda.[4]
Addiditque quod hoc esset decretum in sententia vigilum id est angelorum
Et hoc etiam sermo et peticio sanctorum.[5]
Per quod innuebatur quod mors christi tam angelis quam sanctis necessaria erat
Quia per ipsam angelorum restauracio et sanctorum liberacio fieri debebat.
Adiecitque quod per eundem regem deueniret ad noticiam omnium[6]
Quod deus excelsus regnat super omnia regna hominum.[7]

28[a] In quo innuebatur quod predicacio christi et suorum
Ostenderet se mundo deum verum omnium seculorum.[8]
Addiditque quod deus posset dare regnum homini cui uellet
Et quod super hoc hominem humillimum constitueret.[9]
Per hoc innuebatur quod christus esset humillimus hominum
Et ideo deus constitueret eum regem omnium.[10]
Sic ergo [prefigurabatur] patet quomodo per arborem istam prefigurabatur christus.
Qui ex pre ordinacione patris est per nobis crucifixus.[11]
Et quamuis passio christi fuit a patre celesti preordinata
Tamen non inuite sed uoluntarie est ab ipso acceptata.[12] *secunda figura.*[13]
¶Et illud codrus rex grecorum olim per figuram premonstrauit[14]
Qui pro ciuibus suis liberandis sponte mortem acceptauit.
Ciuitas enim atheniensis obsessa erat
Et per nullius subuencionem liberari poterat.
Tunc predictus rex consuluit deum appolinem

[1] Mt. 27.34, Mk. 15.23, Lk. 23.36, John 19.29 [2] Dn. 4.13 [3] Mt. 26.67, 27.30, Mk. 15.19 [4] Dn. 4.13, 20, 22, 29 [5] Dn. 4.14 [6] See Mt. 24.27, 30, Mk. 13.26, Lk. 17.24, 27, Act. 1.11, 1 Th. 4.15–17, Apc. 1.7 [7] See Is. 6.3, Apc. 4.8–11, 20.4–6, 22.5 [8] Cf. John 1.14, Rom. 1.19–20, Hbr. 1.1–14 [9] See Dn. 4.14, 32, 5.21 [10] Phlp. 2.7–9 [11] Mt. 20.28, Mk. 2.17, Lk. 19.10, John 3.16–17, 6.38, 12.27, Gal. 4.4–5, 1 John 4.10 [12] Mt. 26.39, Mk. 14.36, Lk. 22.42, John 4.34, 5.30, 6.38 [13] Left Panel: King Codrus Gives his Life for the People. Codrus was last of the semi-mythical kings of Athens (ca. 1089–1068 B.C.). His reputation for personal self-sacrifice for his people is recounted in Lycurgus, *Against Leocrates* (84–87), an oration of the 4th century, and mentioned also by Aristotle (*Athenian Constitution* 3). In the upper half of the image Codrus is shown to be recognized by the Dorian enemy, who refuses to kill him; in the lower half the king dresses as a common soldier and goes out to meet his death, thus saving the city. [14] Cf. Lycurgus, *Against Leocrates*, 84–87

showing that Christ would be given gall and vinegar to drink
and he added that his heart would be changed from human,
and a beast's heart would be given to him instead of a human's.
Through this it was shown that the Jews would not treat Jesus as they do men
but like a beast or serpent they spat on and tortured him;
or that the Jews did not act toward Christ as men would,
but like beasts they gnashed their teeth at him.
He added that seven seasons would pass for this aforementioned king
because the suffering of Christ would last seven hours.
And he added that this would be the decree in the sentence of the watchmen, that is, the angels,
and this would also be the word and will of the saints.
Through this it was shown that the death of Christ was necessary for both the angels and the saints
because through it the restoration of angels and the liberation of saints would occur.
And he added that through this same king, it would come to the notice of all
that God reigns on high over all the kingdoms of men.

In this way it was shown that the preaching of Christ and his followers
would reveal him to the world as the true God of all ages.
And he added that God could give the kingdom to whom he wished
and that he would set a very humble man to rule over it.
Through this, it was shown that Christ was the most humble of all men
and therefore God established him as king of all.
So therefore it is shown how that tree prefigured Christ,
who was crucified for us according to his father's plan.
And although the suffering of Christ was predetermined by the heavenly father
yet he did not accept it grudgingly, but of his free will. (Figure Two)
And Codrus, king of the Greeks, once prefigured this,
he who willingly died to free his citizens.
Indeed, the city of Athens was besieged
and no one's assistance was able to free it.
Then this king asked the god Apollo

Si per aliquem modum posset liberare ciuitatem.
Et quamuis paganus esset et non cognosceret deum
Tamen nutu ˋdeiˊ recepit per appollinem responsum uerum.
Dictum est ei quod ciuitas nullo modo posset liberari
Nisi oporteret ipsum ab hostibus occidi et mactari.
Qui in tantum dilexit suos qui erant in urbem
Quod exiuit de urbe uolens subire propter eos mortem.
Hostes autem scientes nolebant ei in aliquo nocere
Cupientes pocius ciuitatem quam ipsius mortem habere.
Quo audito et experto rex ad ciuitatem rediit

28b[1] Et uestes regias exuens et seruiles induens iterum exiuit
Statim hostes in eum irruentes interfecerunt
Quia ipsum regem esse in seruili habitu non cognouerunt.
Cum autem uiderent regem mortuum de capcione urbis desperauerunt
Et ab impugnancione cessantes ad propria redierunt.
Sic christus nos dilexit ut se in mortem sponte daret
Vt nos a demonum obsidione liberaret.[2]
Induit autem se carne humana quasi ueste seruili[3]
Quia in ueste regali id est in deitate non posset occidi.
Sed etiam ipsum regem glorie esse cognouissent
Numquam eum sic delusissent nec occidissent.
Et ˊnonˋ solum christus obsidionem nostre captiuitatis dissipauit
¶Sed etiam morte sua mortem nostram destruxit et necauit.[4]
Et hoc fuit olim per eleasar machabeum prefiguratum
Qui se morti exposuit ut perimeret elephantem loricatum.[5]
Quondam enim exercitus gentilium contra filios Israelis bellauit
Eleasar occurrens elephantem eorum lancea perforauit.
Qui sauciatus vvlnere mortifero cecidit
Et super occisorem suum cadens ipsum oppressit.
Fortis impegit in fortem et ambo corruerunt
Sic eleazar in elephantem et ambo mortui fuerunt.[6]
Ita christus fortis mortem inuasit fortem
Et per mortem suam nostram mortificauit mortem.[7]

[1] Right Panel: Eleazar Maccabeus Kills the Elephant. A complimentary Jewish story of personal heroism and sacrifice is the attack by Eleazar, son of Saura, on the armored elephant of the enemy (1 Mcc. 6.32–47). The elephants had castle-like fortified saddles sufficient to hold four bowmen, and they cleared a path for horses and infantry to follow. Eleazar fought his way through to the largest elephant and killed it with a spear-thrust from below, but it then fell and crushed him, though the image here shows him being trampled. [2] John 3.16, Phlp. 2.7–8 [3] Phlp. 2.7–8 [4] 1 Cor. 15.54–57, Hbr. 2.14, Apc. 1.18 [5] 1 Mcc. 6.43–46 [6] 1 Mcc. 6.43–46 [7] 1 Cor. 15.54–57, Hbr. 2.14, Apc. 1.18

if there was any way he could free the city.
And although he was a pagan and did not know God
nevertheless, with God's approval, he received a true answer from Apollo.
He was told that the city could in no way be freed
unless it should happen that he be cut down and slaughtered by his enemies.
He so greatly loved his people who were in the city
that he went out of the city, wanting to undergo death on their behalf.
And his enemies, knowing this, did not want to harm him in any way
for they wanted to have the city more than his death.
Having heard and learned this, the king returned to the city

and changing his royal garb for that of a slave, he went out again
his enemies at once attacked and killed him
because they did not know he was the king in his slave's clothes.
However, when they saw the king dead, they despaired of capturing the city
and they gave up the fight and returned to their country.
In the same way Christ loved us so that he willingly gave himself up unto death
that he might free us from the siege of demons.
Moreover, he clothed himself in human flesh, as though in servile garb,
because in royal dress, that is in his divinity, he could not be killed.
But had they known that he was the king of glory
they would never have mocked him as they did, nor killed him.
And not only Christ did end the siege of our captivity
but also destroyed and killed our death with his own.
And this was once prefigured through Eleazar Machabeus
who exposed himself to death so that he might kill the armored elephant.
For when the Gentile army fought against the sons of Israel
Eleazar came against their elephant and pierced it with his lance.
It fell with a deadly wound
and, falling on top of his killer, crushed him.
The strong rushed against the strong and both fell together:
so Eleazar rushed against the elephant and both died.
So also did strong Christ assault strong death
and through his own death he put to death our death.

O bone ihesu qui per mortem tuam dignatus es nos liberare
Fac nos post hanc uitam tecum semper habitare.[1]

28va *Capitulum xxv*[2]

In precedenti capitulo audiuimus quomodo christus fuit occisus
Consequenter audiamus quomodo etiam post mortem fuit derisus
Non enim suffecit iudeis quod eum interfecerunt
Sed etiam post mortem diuersimode deriserunt.
Istud etiam michol filia saulis prefigurauit *prima figura*.[3]
Que regem dauid uirum suum derisit et subsannauit.[4]
Dauid ad laudem dei cytharizando subsiliebat
Quem michol per fenestram prospiciens deridebat
Non suffecit ei quod infra citharizacionem derisat.
Nisi etiam derideret postquam eam dimiserat.
Tamquam minus gloriosum ipsum appellauit
Et nudatis scurris eum contumeliose comparuauit.
Sic synagoga christum plus quam scurrum dehonestauit.
Quando barrabam soluens christum inter latrones ⌞condempnauit⌟.[5]
Dauid zitharizando prefigurauit christum
Quia sicut chordas in cithara sic in cruce extenderunt ipsum.
O quam dulcem melodiam hec cithara decantauit
Quando cum lacrimis et clamore ualido pro nobis orauit.[6]
Quando latroni sero penitenti paradysum promisit[7]
Quando matrem discipulo et discipulum matri commisit.[8]
Quando dixit se pro nostra salute sitire[9]
Et consumatum esse quidquid pro nobis debuit subire.[10]
Quando hely hely lamasabathani exclamabat[11]
Et spiritum suum patri suo commendabat[12]
Infra hanc citharizacionem synagoga ipsum subsannauit.

[1] See Apc. 21.3 [2] Left Panel: Christ Mocked on the Cross. The four figures labeled *derisores* in the image are identified with *synagoga* in the text. [3] Right Panel: David Mocked by Michol. Michol, daughter of Saul and wife to David, disapproved intensely of David's dance before the ark (2 Kings 6.16–23). She is identified as *Michol quae regem david derisit*, fortunately, since there is no visual reference to the dance in this image (14). The typological analogy to the mocking of Christ, consolidated in the *Glossa* (PL 113.568) had become conventional by the 11th century. [4] 2 Kings 6.16–23 [5] condempnauit, L] commendauit, G. Cf. John 18.40 [6] Lk. 23.34, 46 [7] Lk. 23.43 [8] John 19.27 [9] John 19.28 [10] John 19.30 [11] Mt. 27.46, Mk. 15.34 [12] Lk. 23.46

O good Jesus, who through your death deigned to free us
cause us to dwell forever with you after this life.

Chapter Twenty-five

In the last chapter, we heard how Christ was killed.
Next let us hear how he was mocked, even after his death.
For it was not enough for the Jews to kill him,
but even after his death they mocked him in various ways.
This thing Michal, the daughter of Saul, also prefigured (Figure One)
who mocked and sneered at her husband, King David.
David was dancing to the music of the lyre in praise of God.
Michal, espying him through her window, mocked him.
It was not enough for her to mock him during his lyre-playing
unless she also made fun after he had stopped.
So she called him less glorious
and compared him insolently to naked fools.
In such a way the synagogue humiliated Christ more than a fool,
when, releasing Barabbas, it condemned Christ among the robbers.
David, by playing the lyre, prefigured Christ,
because they stretched him out on the cross just like the strings on a lyre.
O how sweet the melody this lyre sang
when he prayed for us with tears and a mighty cry,
when he promised paradise to the thief who repented at the last,
when he entrusted his mother to the disciple and the disciple to his mother,
when he said that he thirsted for our salvation
and that whatever he had to undergo was accomplished on our behalf,
when he exclaimed “Eli, Eli, lama sabachthani”
and commended his spirit to his Father!
The synagogue sneered at him during this lyre-playing

28vb Et postquam emisit spiritum subsannare non cessauit.
¶Istud etiam fuit olim in absolone preostensum[1] *secunda figura*.[2]
Quem legimus pulcherrimum fuisse et in arbore suspensum.
Quem uidens quidam cucurrit ad ioab et sibi hoc dixit.[3]
Qui ueniens tres lanceas in corde ipsius fixit.
In hoc non sunt contenti armigeri ioab qui affuerunt
Sed etiam gladiis ipsum crudelissime inuaserunt.
Per absolon significatur speciosus pre filiis hominum christus.[4]
Qui in cruce tribus lanceis id est tribus doloribus est confixus.
Primum habuit ex propriarum penarum magnitudine
Secundum ex dulce[5] matris sue amaritudine.
Tercium dolorem propter peccatores dampnandos sustinuit
Quibus suam amaram vitam[6] non prodesse presciuit.
Et quamuis christus [/co]nfixus[7] fuit tantis doloribus
Tamen iudei super hec inuaserunt eum linguarum suarum gladiis.
Hoc modo omnes uoluntarii peccatores inuadunt christum.
Qui sponte peccando iterato crucifigunt ipsum. *tertia figura*.[8]
¶Isti olim prefigurati fuerunt per enilmerodach regem[9]
Qui deseui⌊era⌋t in suum mortuum et sepultum patrem.
Corpus patris de sepulchro effossum in trecentas partes diuisit
Et trecentis vvlturibus ad deuorandum distribuit.
Ita mali christiani in patrem suum christum pro eis mortuum deseuiunt
Quando uoluntarie peccando ipsum iterato crucifigunt.
Plus peccant qui offendunt christum regnantem in diuinitate
Quam qui crucifixerunt eum conuersantem in humanitate.

29a Christum semel crucifixum conatur inuadere et rursus vvlnerare
Qui sine timore peccat uel qui presumat de peccato se iactare.

---

[1] 2 Kings 18.9–15 [2] Left Panel: Death of Absalom. After his unsuccessful rebellion against his father David, Absalom was riding his mule away when under an oak tree his famous long hair caught in low branches, leaving him dangling. Although David had ordered that his son not be harmed, Joab slew him with three lances through the heart. The SHS text is cryptic, but nonetheless elaborates a further mutilation recorded in the biblical account (2 Kings 18.8–17), which has his head rather than hair caught in the oak, the detail about his hair having been added by Josephus. [3] 2 Kings 18.10 [4] Ps. 44.3 [5] dulce] dilecte, L [6] uitam] passionem, L [7] confixus] crucifixus, L (In G, the first two letters *co* are a correction and the previous letter(s) have been scratched out) [8] Right Panel: Evilmerodach Mutilates the Dead Body of his Father. Amel-Marduk is said to have been made king of Babylon after the death of his father Nabuchodonosor (Lev. Rabbah 18.2); in order to convince the people his father really was dead (Targ. Sheni), he exhumed and mutilated the body. This story is mentioned by Jerome in his commentary on Isaiah 14.19, as also by Josephus and the *Historia Scholastica* on Dn. 3, from which this account is likely borrowed. Our image depicts the ravens carrying off pieces of the rotting body to devour. [9] Cf. *HS* Dn. 4

And after he sent out his spirit, it did not cease sneering.
This thing was once foreshown in Absalom. (Figure Two)
We read that he was most comely and hung in a tree.
Seeing him, a certain person ran to Joab and told him this.
Approaching, Joab thrust three lances in his heart.
Joab's armor-bearers who were present were not content with this,
but they too fell upon him with their swords most cruelly.
Through Absalom, handsome beyond the sons of man, is signified Christ,
who was nailed on the cross with three lances, that is, with three sorrows:
The first sorrow he had from the greatness of his own punishment;
the second from the sweet suffering of his mother;
the third sorrow he underwent on account of sinners about to be damned—
he foresaw that his own bitter life would not benefit them.
And although Christ was nailed with such great sorrows
nevertheless, on top of these, the Jews attacked him with the swords of their tongues.
In this way, all willing sinners attack Christ
who willingly crucify him again by sinning. (Figure Three)
They were once prefigured through King Evilmerodach
who raged against his dead and buried father.
He sliced up the body of his father—dug up from his tomb—into three hundred pieces
and distributed [them] to three hundred vultures to be devoured.
In such a way bad Christians rage against their father, Christ—dead for them—
when they crucify him again by willingly sinning.
Those who offend against Christ while he is reigning in divinity sin more
than those who crucified him while he was dwelling among humanity.

Although Christ has already been crucified once, he attempts to attack and wound him again
who sins without fear or who presumes to boast of his sin.

Crucem christi ad crucifigendum eum [vi]detur perhibetur[1] carpentare.
Qui ad perpetrandum mala conatur consilia et auxilia prestare.
Dorso christi crucem ⌊ad⌋ bauilandam imponere perhibetur[2]
Qui peccatum suum diuine ordinacioni attribuere uidetur.
In faciem christi perhibetur despectiue conspuere
Qui non agit grates deo de ⌊quolibet⌋[3] quibus sibi dato munere.
A tergo christum perhibetur colaphis verberare
Qui proximum post tergum suum nititur infamare.
Faciem autem christi perhibetur alapis contondere
Qui proximum in presencia sua presumit confundere.
Caput christi videtur uulnerare spinis
Qui ecclesias nititur inuadere iniuriis et rapinis.
Oculos domini omnia conspicientes conatur uelare
Qui malum pro bono nituntur uendere dare uel mutuare.
Vestimenta christi sibi perhibentur diuidere[4]
Qui res proximorum suorum presumunt distribuere.
Dominum ihesum christum cum iuda doloso corde osculatur[5]
Qui proximo suo fraudulenter adulatur.
Dominum cum iuda dolose perhibetur salutare[6]
Qui proximo suo promittit quod non intendit seruare.
Dominum cum iudeis videtur deridere et subsannare
Qui pro laude humana nititur orare uel eleemosinas dare.[7]
Et ⟨l⟩oculos christi cum iuda fure portare comprobatur[8]

29b Qui de rebus sibi commissis aliquid subtrahit et furatur.
Pedes christi perhibentur clauis ferreis perforare
Qui magis theatra et tabernas quam templa solent uisitare.
Crucem cum symone syreneo portare comprobatur[9]
Qui non uoluntarie sed quasi coactus bonum operatur.
Clauos christi perhibetur crucis fabricare
Qui inter proximos nititur discordia seminare.
Dominum perhibentur subsannare cum sinistro latrone[10]
Qui ficte confitentur et qui menciuntur in confessione.
Cum iuda comprobantur semet ipsos suspendere
Qui nolunt ueniam petere et satisfaccionem intendere.[11]
Manus christi videtur cum funibus colligare

[1] Throughout the rest of the chapter, the MS. reads "perhibe(n)tur" consistently in place of where L reads "vide(n)tur" [2] Cf. Lk. 23.26 [3] Quolibet, L] quibus, G [4] Mt. 27.35 [5] Mt. 26.49 [6] Mt. 26.49 [7] Cf. Mt. 6.5 [8] John 13.29 [9] Lk. 23.26 [10] Lk. 23.39 [11] Cf. Mt. 27.3–5

He is said to build the cross of Christ to crucify him
who tries to offer advice and aid for the perpetration of evil.
He is said to lay the cross on Christ's back to be carried
who is seen to attribute his sin to God's plan.
He is said to spit contemptuously in the face of Christ
who does not give thanks to God for the gifts given him.
He is said to scourge Christ with blows on his back
who strives to discredit his neighbor behind his back.
And he is said to bruise the face of Christ with slaps
who presumes to put his neighbor to shame in his own presence.
He is seen to wound the head of Christ with thorns
who strives to attack churches with injustices and pillaging.
He tries to blindfold the Lord's eyes, which see all things,
who strives to sell, give, or borrow evil for good.
They are said to divide the garments of Christ for themselves
who presume to distribute the property of their neighbors.
In company with Judas, he kisses the Lord Jesus Christ with a malicious heart
who flatters his neighbor fraudulently.
In company with Judas, he is said to greet the Lord deceitfully,
who promises his neighbor that which he does not intend to carry out.
He is seen to deride and mock the Lord in company with the Jews
who strives—for human praise—to pray or to give alms.
And he is acknowledged to carry the purse of Christ in company with Judas the thief

who removes and steals anything from the things entrusted to him.
They are said to pierce the feet of Christ with iron nails,
who are more accustomed to visit the theater and tavern than the temple.
He is acknowledged to carry the cross with Simon of Cyrene,
who does good not voluntarily, but as if coerced.
He is said to fashion the nails of Christ's cross,
who strives to sow discord between his neighbors.
He is said to mock the Lord with the thief on the left
who falsely confesses and who lies in his confession.
They are acknowledged to hang themselves with Judas
who do not wish to seek mercy and make amends.
He is seen to bind the hands of Christ with ropes

Quando[1] non credit deo quod possit sibi neccessaria sua dare.
Manus domini videtur clauis configere et uulnerare
Qui de bonis a deo sibi datis non uult eleemosinas erogare.
Dominum cum iuda pro temporali pecunia comprobatur uendere[2]
Qui bona sua pro uana gloria studet expendere
Vinum mirratum comprobantur domino bibendum exhibere[3]
Qui hereses sub pallio ueritatis student docere.
Acetum felle mixtum perhibentur domino propinare[4]
Qui de male acquisitis presumunt domino sacrificare.
Domino cum iuda osculo tradicione[5] tradere perhibentur
Qui cum mortalibus accedere ad corpus domini non uerentur.
O bone ihesu da nobis tuo sacratissimo sacramento ita cibari[6]
Vt a te numquam in perpetuum mereamur separari.

29va *Capitulum xxvi*[7]

In precedentibus audiuimus saluatoris nostri passionem
Consequenter audiamus dulcissime eius matris dolorem.
Quando saluator passionem suam tolerauit
Affuit maria et secum omnia per compassionem portauit.
Tunc impletum est quod predixerat ei symeon iustus[8]
Tuam ipsius animam pertransibit gladius.[9] *prima figura.*[10]
¶Dolorem quem maria ex compassione filii sui tolerauit
Jacob deploracione filii sui ioseph figurauit.[11]
Jacob filium suum ioseph super omnes diligebat

[1] Quando] Qui, L [2] Mt. 26.15 [3] Mk. 15.23 [4] Mt. 27.34 [5] tradicione] traditore, L [6] Cf. Aquinas, *ST* III.80.4–6 [7] Left Panel: Deposition from the Cross. The image shows Christ's body being taken from the cross by two men and a woman who receives the body, presumably the Virgin Mary, as frequently elsewhere depicted. Though the biblical account does not describe the scene in this way (Mt. 27.57–66; Mk. 15.42–47; Lk. 23.50–56; John 19.38–43), the deposition or descent from the cross is widely depicted in medieval art, especially after the 11th century. Representing Mary as receiving the body is unusual; more commonly it is Joseph of Arimathea (here removing nails from Jesus' feet), Nicodemus, or a disciple. The Pietà begins to appear in sculpture in 14th century Germany, but does not occur in painting until much later than the SHS. While the ladder appears in the 12th century, it is much more common from the 14th century on. [8] Lk. 2.25 [9] Lk. 2.35 [10] Right Panel: Jacob Mourns over Joseph's Coat. The story of Jacob being deceived by his sons into thinking the torn and bloody coat of Joseph indicates his death (Gen. 37) is here construed as an antitype for the sorrow Mary feels at the actual death of her son; the many-colored coat is depicted as essentially whole. The biblical exegesis of the *Glossa* (PL 113.166) contrasts the tattered coat of Joseph with the undivided garment of Christ at the foot of the cross. The visual symmetry in this image is obtained by having *Jacob patriarcha* looking at the coat while supported on each side by one of his sons; the verbal connection is effected by the equation in the text of Christ's flesh with his "garment". [11] Gen. 37.3–35

when he does not trust that God is able to give him the things he needs.
He is seen to fasten together and wound the hands of the Lord with nails
who is unwilling to disburse alms out of the goods given to him by God.
He is acknowledged to sell the Lord for the money of the world with Judas
who strives to expend his goods for the sake of vainglory.
They are acknowledged to offer wine mixed with myrrh to the Lord to drink
who strive to teach heresies under the cloak of truth.
They are said to give the Lord vinegar mixed with gall to drink
who from wrongfully acquired things presume to sacrifice to the Lord.
They are said to betray the Lord with a kiss of betrayal with Judas
who, in mortal [sin], do not tremble to approach the body of the Lord.
O good Jesus, grant us to be nourished with your most holy sacrament in such a way
that we may never become worthy to be separated from you in perpetuity.

Chapter Twenty-six

In the last [chapters], we heard about the Passion of our savior,
next let us hear of the sorrow of his most sweet mother.
When the savior endured his Passion
Mary was present and suffered everything with him through compassion.
Thus what Simeon the just man had foretold to her was fulfilled:
"A sword will pierce your own soul." (Figure One)
The pain which Mary endured out of compassion for her son,
Jacob prefigured by lamentation for his son Joseph.
Jacob loved his son Joseph more than anyone

Et ideo inuidia fratrum suorum ipsum interficere intendebat.
Fecit autem iacob filio suo ioseph tunicam polimitam
Variis coloribus et figuris artificialiter politam.
Quem cum misisset pater ad fratres vbi gregem pascebant
Illi apprehendentes eum interficere uolebant.
Sed nutu dei ipsum ismahelitis uendiderunt
Et tunicam eius lacerantes sanguine edi asperserunt.
Et mittentes qui portarent ostenderunt eam patri.
Vt uideret si esset tunica ioseph filii sui.
Quam uidens pater scidit uestimenta sua et cepit flere.
Dicens filium suum deuoratum dentibus pessime fere.
Quod audientes filii eius ad ipsum conueniebant
Et ipsum in luctu suo consolari satagebant.
Ipse autem ad consolacionem eorum minime attendit
Et nullam uolen[te]s recipere consolacionem sic respondit.
Descendam lugens ad filium meum in infernum.[1]

29vb Quia noluit consolari in hac uita in eternum.
Ita maria filium suum lugens in infernum descendisset
Et secum semper mansisset si possibile fuisset.
Quantum putatis fratres karissimi maria planxit et luxit
Quando filii sui tunicam id est carnem laceratam conspexit.
Tunica ioseph fuit sanguine edi cruentata
Sed tunica christi fuit proprio cruore madidata.
Et vere christum deuorauit fera pessima
Hoc est iudeorum inuidia iniquissima.
Iacob ex dolore suo scidit uestes suas sed exteriores
Maria autem scidit uestimenta sua scilicet vires interiores.
Omnes filii iacob ad ipsum congregati fuerunt
Et tamen dolorem eius dilinire non potuerunt.
Et si totus mundus ad mariam congregatus fuisset
Ipsa tamen numquam sine filio aliquam consolacionem suscepisset.
Jacob xii filios habuit de amissione unius ita doluit
Quanto magis maria dolere potuit que unum filium habens eundem amisit.
¶Iste etiam dolor marie inmensus fuit prefiguratus *secunda figura*.[2]

---

[1] Gen. 37.35 [2] Left Panel: Adam and Eve Mourn Abel. This narrative derives from ch. 25 of the *Historica Scholastica*, the late 12th-century biblical paraphrase and universal history that was required reading at Paris until the mid-14th century. This story of Adam and Eve mourning Abel for a full century serves here not as a true antitype but as a minor comparison with the Virgin's lament. Abel in this image seems large and lively, despite the text.

and for that reason, the envy of his brothers was bent upon killing him.
Moreover, Jacob made for his son Joseph a many-colored robe,
artfully adorned with various colors and shapes.
When his father had sent him to his brothers where they were pasturing the flock,
they, seizing him, wanted to kill him.
But, by the will of God, they sold him to the Ishmaelites
and tearing his robe, they spattered it with the blood of a young goat
and sending ones to carry it, they showed it to their father
so that he might see if the robe was Joseph's, his son's.
Seeing it, their father tore his garments and began to weep,
saying that his son had been devoured by the teeth of the worst wild beast.
Hearing this, his sons assembled near him
and were busy comforting him in his grief.
He himself, however, paid very little attention to their comforting
and wishing to receive no comfort, he responded thus:
"Grieving shall I descend to my son in hell,"

because he did not wish to be comforted in this life forever.
In such a way Mary, weeping for her son, would have descended into hell
and would have remained with him always, if that had been possible.
Dearest brothers, how much do you think Mary wailed and lamented
when she saw the robe of her son—that is, his flesh—torn?
The robe of Joseph was stained with the blood of a young goat,
but the robe of Christ was moistened with his own gore.
And truly the worst wild beast devoured Christ—
that is, the most wicked envy of the Jews.
Jacob tore his clothes from his sorrow, but [only] the outer ones;
Mary, however, tore her garments, namely, her inner nature.
All the sons of Jacob assembled near him
and yet they could not soothe his sorrow.
And if the whole world had gathered about Mary
nevertheless, she would never have received any comfort without her son.
Jacob had twelve sons; from the loss of one he suffered so;
how much more could Mary suffer, who, having one son, lost that one.
That immense sorrow of Mary had also been prefigured (Figure Two)

Quando abel ab iniquo chaym fuit occisus et mactatus.[1]
De ipsius interfectione adam et eua in tantum doluerunt
Quod eius necem centum annis deplanxerunt.[2]
Et quamuis dolor eorum videtur magnus fuisse
Tamen dolor marie comprobatur maior fuisse[3]
Quanto enim res que diligitur est carior
Tanto dolor de amissione ipsius erit grauior.

30a
Numquam erat amor maior quam inter mariam et eius natum
Quod nullum dolorem inuenimus dolori marie equipparatum.
Dolor ade et eue legitur multum durasse
Quia leguntur centum annis in luctu perseuerasse.
Sed si christus per centum milia annorum in morte perseuerasset
Maria numquam medio tempore a luctu et merore cessasset.
Cum igitur ioseph corpus christi de cruce deponeret
Affuit maria ut ipsum inter brachia sua attolleret.
Tunc ⸤fasciculus mirre⸥[4], inter ubera eius commemorabatur
Sicut in canticis canticorum de ipsa cantatur.
O quam amarus mirre ⸤fasciculus⸥[5] fuit in cordis marie
Toleracio penarum quas sustinuit christus tota nocte et die.
Quanto vinum dulcius et nobilius esse comprobatur
Tanto fit acrius et amarius quando transmutatur.
Sic quanto amor marie ad filium erat dulcior
Tanto dolor eius in compassione christi factus est amarior.
[6]¶Quapropter ⸤maria⸥[7] fuit olim per Noemy prefigurata[8]
Que propter mortem filiorum suorum multum fuit amaricata.
Vnde dixit nolite me uocare noemy quod est pulchra
Sed uocate me mara quod est amara.
Valde enim omnipotens me amaritudine repleuit[9]
Hoc dixit quando orbacionem duorum filiorum defleuit.
Conuenienter autem maria per noemy est designata

---

[1] Gen. 4 [2] *HS*. Gen. 25 [3] fuisse] exstitisse, L [4] fasciculus mirre] uasciculus marie, G (Emended to be consistent with Ct. 1.13. See also *SHS* chap. 30, ll. 2–9). Ct. 1.12–13 [5] fasciculus] uasculus, G [6] Right Panel: Noemi Mourns her Dead Son and Husband. In the book of Ruth, Noemi suffers the death of her husband first, then subsequently of both her sons. Her mourning is not mentioned in the canonical text, but when she and her two daughters-in-law arrive as refugees back in Bethlehem, she rejects her name ("Pleasant") and says she should be called Mara ("bitter"), because "the Almighty has afflicted me" (Rt. 1.20–21). The *Glossa* (PL 113.534) connects her sorrowful self-declaration in Bethlehem with the mystery of the Passion. In this image Noemi is identified, with her daughters Ruth and Orpha likewise, one on each side, without head covering to suggest their youth. [7] L] malia, G [8] Rt. 1 [9] Rt. 1.20

when Abel was killed and slaughtered by the unjust Cain.
Adam and Eve suffered so greatly on account of the killing of that one
that they bewailed his death for a hundred years.
And although their sorrow seemed to have been great,
nevertheless, Mary's sorrow is acknowledged to have been greater.
For the dearer a beloved thing is
the graver the sorrow from its loss will be.

There was never a love greater than that between Mary and her son
with the result that we find no sorrow comparable to Mary's sorrow.
It is read that the pain of Adam and Eve was greatly hardened
since they are read to have persevered in grief for a hundred years.
But if Christ had persevered in death for a hundred thousand years,
Mary would never have ceased from grief and sorrow.
When, therefore, Joseph took down the body of Christ from the cross,
Mary was present in order to lift him between her arms.
Then the little bundle of myrrh between her breasts was remembered
just as was sung concerning her in the canticle of canticles.
O how bitter was the little bundle of myrrh in the heart of Mary,
the endurance of the punishments which Christ underwent a whole night and a day.
It is agreed that the more sweet and noble a wine is,
the sharper and more bitter it becomes when it is turned sour.
Thus, the sweeter Mary's love for her son was,
the more bitter her sorrow became in fellow-suffering with Christ.
On account of which, evil things [Mary] was once prefigured through Naomi
who, on account of the death of her sons, was greatly embittered.
Therefore she said: "Don't call me Naomi, that is, 'beautiful one,'
but call me Mara, that is, 'bitter one.'
For the Almighty has filled me exceedingly with bitterness."
She said this when she mourned the deprivation of her two sons.
Moreover, Mary is appropriately indicated through Naomi

Quia non erat solum uno sed duobus filiis orbata.
Vnum filium habuit per carnalem progenituram

30b Alium autem ⸌mater⸍[1] ⸤misericordie⸥[2] adoptauerat sibi per curam
Verus et carnalis filius marie erat ihesus
Adoptiuus autem humanum uniuersum genus.
Carnalis filius mortuus erat morte corporali
Adoptiuus autem mortuus erat morte spirituali.
In[3] passione enim domini totum genus humanum fidere reliquerat
Et ideo omnis homo mortuus in anima erat
Pro utroque magnam amaritudinem sustinebat.
Quia utrumque ex magno affectu cordis diligebat.
Et quamuis filium suum plusquam se ipsam amaret
Tamen sibi placuit ut per mortem suam nos liberaret.
Maluit enim dulcissima mater nostra illum cruciari.
Quam nos morte perpetua eternaliter condempnari.
Ex hoc possumus perpendere quantum maria nos amabat
Que dilectum filium suum pro nostra salute mori affectabat.
Quando enim una res pro alia datur uel commutatur
Res que accipitur plus amari videtur quam illa que datur.
Videtur ergo quod maria nos quodammodo plusquam filium diligebat
Que pocius ipsum crucifigi quam nos condempnari uolebat.
Ex hoc etiam perpendere possumus quam pater celestis nos amabat
Qui vnigenitum filium suum pro nobis in mortem dabat.[4]
Ambo igitur tam pater quam mater nos multum amauerunt
Et ut eo⸌s⸍[5] toto corde reamemus bene meruerunt.
O bone ihesu da nobis hanc dulcedinem ita recogitare
Vt tecum mereamur in celis eternaliter habitare.

30va *Capitulum xxvii*

In precedenti capitulo audiuimus quomodo christus de cruce est depositus
Consequenter audiamus quomodo fuit sepultus.[6]
Ioseph et nychodemus corpus in syndone inuoluerunt
Et co⸤n⸥dientes aromatibus in monumentum posuerunt.
Maria affuit cum miserabili planctu et lamentacione

---

[1] Inserted superscript with caret by the same hand as the main text [2] L] marie, G [3] In] Ante, L [4] John 3.16 [5] Squeezed in by a correcting scribe [6] Mt. 27.57–60, Mk. 15.43–47, Lk. 23.50–56, John 19.40–42

since she was not bereaved of just one son, but of two sons:
one son she had through physical birth,

but the other, the mother of mercy had adopted for herself through her care.
The true and corporeal son of Mary was Jesus;
her adoptive son, however, is the whole human race.
The fleshly son was dead from a physical death;
the adopted one, however, was dead from a spiritual death.
For in the Passion of the Lord, the whole human race had abandoned faith
and for that reason, every human being was dead in spirit.
Because of both [sons] she was undergoing great anguish
since she loved both out of the great devotion of her heart.
And although she loved her son more than her own self,
nevertheless it pleased her that he should free us through his death.
For our sweetest mother preferred him to be crucified
rather than for us to be condemned eternally to a perpetual death.
From this we can judge how much Mary loved us,
who desired her own beloved son to die for our salvation.
For when one thing is given or exchanged for another,
the thing that is received seems to be loved more than that which is given.
Therefore, it is seen that Mary loved us in some ways more than her son:
she wished for him to be crucified rather than for us to be condemned.
From this also we can judge how the heavenly Father loved us
who gave his only begotten son over to death for us.
Therefore, both the Father and the mother loved us greatly
and they well deserve that we should love them in return with our whole heart.
O good Jesus, grant us to reflect on this sweetness in such a way
that we may worthily dwell with you in the heavens eternally.

Chapter Twenty-seven

In the last chapter we heard how Christ was taken down from the cross;
next let us hear how he was buried.
Joseph and Nicodemus wrapped his body in fine linen
and, embalming him with spices, they placed him into the tomb.
Mary was nearby, with miserable wailing and lamentation,

Cum luctu et multarum lacrimarum effusione.
Nulla lingua sufficit eius dolorem enarrare.
Nec aliqua mens sufficit eius tristiciam cogitare.
In tantum tota nocte et die planctu fatigata erat
Quod uix exequias filii sui ad sepulchrum sequi poterat.
Tot osculis et amplexibus filii corpus constringebat
Quod omnis populus sibi compaciens querulando dicebat.
O qualem crudelitatem impiissimi hodie exercuere
In hac tam pulcherrima et delectabili muliere.
In tantum planxit luxit ingemuit et plorauit.
Quod alios ad compaciendum et complorandum prouocauit.
Quis uni tam turbatissime mater non compateretur
Quis ad tantarum lacrimarum effusiones non emolliretur.
Nunc manus filii nunc pedes eius deosculabatur
Nunc collum eius nunc latus stringendo amplexabatur.
Nunc pectus proprium pugnis percuciebat et tundebat.
Nunc manus cum effusione lacrimarum constringebat
Nunc intuebatur vvlnera filii sui nunc oculos
Nunc o⌊s⌋culis corruit super pectus eius nunc super os.
Nimis bestiale cor habere uideretur

30vb1 Qui tantis lacrimis et lamentacionibus non compateretur
Bestialis porcus porco clamanti commouetur
Et quis tam turbatissime matri non [comp][2] miseretur.
Ihesus compassus est et fleuit cum maria magdalena.[3]
Et quis non fleret cum uirgine tam amena.
Delfini dicuntur mortuis suis compati et eos sepelire
Et quomodo potest homo planctum marie sine dolore audire.
¶Dolorem quem maria in sepultura filii sui tolerauit *prima figura*.[4]

[1] Right Panel: David Mourns Abner. Abner had switched loyalties to David during consolidation of his rule, but was killed by Joab, David's general, in revenge for the death of Asael his brother in an earlier battle. The state funeral for Abner is described (2 Kings 3.30–34) in some detail, with David in procession with others following Abner's coffin. *David rex* is here shown much larger in scale than the four pallbearers. The story is not normative in typology but here seems to be included merely as a part of a mourning theme linked to the Passion. [2] The scribe appears to have accidentally skipped his eyes two lines above, which mistake he caught on the third letter [3] John 11.31–36 [4] Left Panel: Entombment of Christ. This image, as is typical for the period, shows Christ's body being laid in a sarcophagus, unlike early Eastern depictions which follow the biblical account by having the body carried into a sepulcher. Present at the scene are the Virgin, arms raised in anguish, and three of the other women, including Mary Magdalene and Mary Salome. The kneeling figure in front of the tomb, touching Jesus' hand, may be Nicodemus. While the biblical accounts (see 29V Left Panel) are cryptic, depictions are frequent, with our image showing in the highly expressive Virgin Mary some eastern influence.

with grief and the shedding of many tears.
No tongue suffices to describe her sorrow
nor is any mind sufficient to imagine her sadness.
She was worn out so greatly with wailing all night and day,
that scarcely she was able to follow the funeral processions of her son to his grave.
She was holding her son's body tight with so many kisses and embraces
that all the people, feeling compassion for her lamenting, were saying:
"O what sort of cruelty did those most wicked ones practice today
against so beautiful and delightful a woman!"
So greatly did she wail, mourn, groan, and weep
that she stirred up some others to suffering and lamenting with her.
What mother would not have pity on one so so distraught?
Who would not be softened at the shedding of such great tears?
She was kissing now the hands, now the feet of her son;
now she was embracing his neck, now holding his sides.
Now she was beating and bruising her own chest with her fists.
Now she was squeezing his hands while shedding tears,
now she was gazing at the wounds of her son, now his eyes;
now she heaped kisses on his chest, now on his mouth.
He would have seemed to have a heart savage beyond measure

who would not pity such tears and lamentations.
A savage pig is moved by a pig's cries
and who would not pity a mother so distressed?
Jesus had compassion and wept with Mary Magdalene.
And who would not weep with a virgin so beautiful?
Dolphins are said to pity the deaths of their own and to bury them.
And how can a person hear the lament of Mary without sorrow?
The sorrow which Mary bore in the burial of her son (Figure One)

Olim dauid in exequiis abner prefigurauit.[1]
Abner a ioab fraudulenter interfectus erat[2]
Cuius interfectionem rex dauid sequens feretrum deflebat[3]
Et non solum ipse super exequias eius deplorabat.
Sed et alios ad plorandum incitabat.
Scindite inquit uestimenta et plangite
Vnde ignoratis quando[4] princeps maximus cecidit in israel hodie.
Non est occisus sicut ignaui et malefici qui meruerunt
Sed sicut iusti coram filiis iniquitatis cadere consueuerunt.[5]
Ita beata uirgo in die parasceue dicere potuit
Quando filius eius ab iniquis iudeis occisus fuit.
Scindite uestimenta uestra videlicet interiora et plangite
Num ignoratis quod princeps maximus in israel occisus est hodie.[6]
O quam maximus princeps in israel occisus erat
Cui omnis creatura compassionem exhibebat.
Sol subtraxit radios suos ne estu ipsius moreretur[7]
Aer obscuratus fuit ut nuditas eius non uideretur.[8]

31ª Terra tremuit ut crucifixores terrerentur
Templum et uelum scissum est ut pharisei compaterentur.
Petre scindebantur et sonum magnum dabant[9]
Quia enim discipuli tacuerunt lapides clamabant.[10]
Monumenta aperta ut mortui resurgerent
Et potenciam huius principis timendo[11] innotescerent.
Multi enim surguntes homin⌊ibus⌋ apparuerunt[12]
Qui potenciam huius princepis manifestauerunt.
Dyabolus in sinistro brachio crucis sedens mirabatur
Quis ille esset quem omnis creatura reuerebatur.
Philosophi anteniensi videntes solem obscurari[13]
Dixerunt deum nature in angustiis esse et pati.
Edificauerunt altare ignoto deo
Qui manifestandus erat futuro seculo.[14]
Huius igitur principis exequias deplang⌊a⌋mus[15]
Et corda nostra intima compassione scindamus.

[1] 4 Kings 3.38 [2] 2 Kings 3.27 [3] 2 Kings 3.31–34 [4] Unde … quando, G] Num … quod, L. (See lines below where Mary repeats the exclamation.) [5] 2 Kings. 3.33–34 [6] Cf. Mt. 27.37, 42, John 18.37 [7] moreretur] ureretur, L [8] Mk. 15.33–38, Lk. 23.44–49 [9] Mt. 27.51, Mk. 15.38, Lk. 23.44–45 [10] See Lk. 19.40 [11] timendo] mundo, L [12] Mt. 27.52–53 [13] Lk. 23.45 [14] Cf. Act. 17.23 [15] deplangamus, L] deplangimus, G

David formerly prefigured in funeral rites of Abner.
Abner was deceitfully killed by Joab.
And King David bemoaned his slaughter, following the bier.
And not only was he himself mourning at the Abner's funeral rites
but he also prompted others to weep.
"Tear your clothing," he said, "and mourn.
Therefore you are unknowing, when the greatest ruler died today in Israel."
He was not killed like the ignorant and wicked, who deserve it,
but like the just who are accustomed to fall before the children of sin.
In this way too the Blessed Virgin was able to speak on the Friday,
when her son had been killed by the unjust Jews:
"Tear your clothes," that is, your interior [clothes], "and mourn.
Don't you know that the greatest ruler was killed in Israel today?"
O how great was the ruler killed in Israel,
for whom all creation was showing compassion.
The sun withdrew its rays, lest he wither from its heat;
the air was darkened so that his nakedness would not be seen.

The earth trembled so that those who crucified him were terrified,
and the temple curtain was torn so that the Pharisees would suffer with him.
Rocks were rent and groaned,
for since the disciples kept silent, the stones were shouting.
Tombs were opened so that the dead could arise,
and they could make known the power of this prince to the fearful.
For many, rising up, appeared to the people
and demonstrated the power of the prince.
The devil, sitting on the left arm of the cross, wondered
who he might be, whom all creation revered.
The Athenian philosophers, seeing that the sun was darkened,
said that the god of nature was in diffculties and that he suffered.
They built altars to an unknown god
who would be made manifest in a future age.
Therefore let us bewail the passing of this prince,
and let us tear our innermost hearts with compassion.

¶Sepulturam christi etiam filii iacob prefigurauerunt *secunda figura*.[1]
\\ioseph// Qui fratrem /suum ioseph\[2] in cysternam miserunt.[3]
Filii iacob fratrem suum sine causa usque ad mortem oderunt
Ita iudei fratrem suum christum odio gratis habuerunt.
Filii iacob fratrem suum pro xxx denariis uendidebant
Iudei ipsum christum pro xxx denariis a iuda emebant.[4]
Filii iacob tunicam fratris sui dilacerauerunt
Iudei carnem christi virgis flagellis spinis clauis vvlnerauerunt.[5]
Tunica ioseph non sensit aliquam penam uel dolorem

31b[6] Sed caro christi in omnibus membris sustinuit passionem
Tunica ioseph thalaris usque ad talos descendebat[7]
Et in christo a uertice usque ad thalos sanitas nulla erat.
Filii iacob tunicam ioseph sanguine edi aspergebant
Sed tunica christi iudei proprio sanguine perfundebant.[8]
Filii iacob patrem suum nimis perturbauerunt
Sed iudei marie tristiciam maximam intulerunt.
Joseph fratribus suis quod in eo deliquerant relaxauit[9]
Et christus pro crucifixoribus suis patrem suum exorauit.[10]
Ioseph a fratribus suis uenditus factus est dominus egipti[11]
Christus a iudeis crucifixus factus est dominus celi et mundi.[12]
Filii iacob fratrem suum postea adorauerunt[13]
Et multi iudeorum post resurrectionem in christum crediderunt.[14]
Jacob audiens filium suum viuere multum gaudebat[15]
Maria uidens christum surrexisse magnum gaudium habebat.[16]
Joseph filius accrescens[17] uel incrementum interpretatur
Et fides christi de die in diem excreuit et iam ubique dilatatur.
¶Sepulturam christi olim etiam ionas prefigurauit[18]
Quem proiectum de naui in mare cethus deuorauit.[19]
Jonas fuit per tres dies et noctes in cetho[20]

[1] Left Panel: Joseph in the Cistern. Waiting in the well until his brothers should sell him in slavery to the traders headed to Egypt, Joseph appear here as if in a hot tub rather than a well, with his brothers Simeon and Judah pushing him down. See Gen. 37.24. [2] Heavily corrected by the black-ink scribe to reiterate the name Joseph midline, with insertion marks to show proper placement [3] Gen. 37.12–36 [4] Mt. 26.15 [5] Mt. 27.26–31, Mk. 15.17–20, John 19.1–3 [6] Right Panel: Jonah and the Great Fish. One of the oldest antitypes for Christ, referring specially to the days he was entombed, is the story of Jonah's undersea journey in the belly of a fish (Jon. 1.15–17). Jesus himself invoked the connection (Mt. 12.40) and variants of this image occur from the catacombs on to indicate the Christ's victory over the grave. [7] Gen. 37.3 [8] Mt. 27.28–30, Mk. 15.19–20, John 19.2, 5, Apc. 19.13 [9] Gen. 45.4–15, 50.17–20 [10] Lk. 23.34 [11] Gen. 45.8, 26 [12] Mt. 28.18 [13] Gen. 45.15, 50.17–18 [14] Act. 2.41, 4.4, 5.14, 9.42, 11.21, 24, 14.1, 15.5, 17.4, 12, 34, 18.8, 19.18, 21.20, 28.24 [15] Gen. 45.27–28 [16] Mt. 28.8 [17] Gen. 49.22 [18] Mt. 12.40 [19] Jon. 1.3–17 [20] John 2.1

The sons of Jacob also prefigured the burial of Christ (Figure Two)
when they hurled their own brother Joseph into a cistern.
The sons of Jacob hated their own brother without cause enough to kill him;
so too the Jews held their own brother in hatred for no reason.
The sons of Jacob sold their own brother for thirty denarii;
the Jews bought Christ himself from Judas for thirty denarii.
The sons of Jacob tore to pieces the tunic belonging to their own brother;
the Jews wounded the body of Christ with rods, whips, thorns, and nails.
The tunic of Joseph did not feel any pain or sadness,

but the flesh of Christ endured the Passion in every limb.
The long tunic of Joseph went down all the way to his ankles
and in Christ there was no health from head to toe.
The sons of Jacob splattered the tunic of Joseph with the blood of a young goat,
but the Jews drenched the tunic of Christ with his own blood.
The sons of Jacob grieved their own father exceedingly,
but the Jews inflicted the greatest sadness on Mary.
Joseph forgave his brothers that they had wronged him,
and Christ prayed to his father on behalf of his crucifiers.
Joseph, sold by his own brothers, became the lord of Egypt;
Christ, crucified by the Jews, became lord of heaven and earth.
The sons of Jacob adored their brother afterward,
and many of the Jews believed in Christ after the resurrection.
Jacob, hearing that his son was alive, rejoiced greatly;
Mary, seeing that Christ had resurrected, had much joy.
Joseph was interpreted the "growing son", or the increase
and the faith of Christ grew from day to day and now is extended everywhere.
Formerly Jonah also prefigured the burial of Christ:
a whale swallowed him, when he was thrown out of the ship into the sea.
Jonah was in the whale for three days and nights;

Ita christus erat per triduum in monumento.[1]
Quomodo autem hystoria Jone christo appropriatur
In capitulo de resurrectione manifestatur
O bone ihesu da nobis ita tuam sepulturam uenerari
Vt a te numquam in perpetuum mereamur separari.

31va *Capitulum xxviii*[2]

In precedenti capitulo audiuimus quomodo ioseph christum sepeliuit[3]
Consequenter audiamus quomodo christus infernum introiuit.[4]
Hora nona quando christus animam emittebat
Statim anima unita deitati ad inferna descendebat.
Est autem quadruplex infernus siue quatuor loca infernorum
Videlicet dampnatorum puerorum purgandorum et sanctorum.
¶[5] In inferno dampnatorum est fumus et ignis inextinguibilis
Aspectus terribilis et horror horribilis.[6]
Vermes conscientiarum et tenebre palpabiles
Frigus inenarrabile fetores intolerabiles.
Mutua inuidia et frequens imprecacio maledictionis
Fuga mortis et desperacio redempcionis.[7]
Semper sunt in moriendo et numquam moriuntur
Semper pene renouantur et numquam finiuntur.
Ad istud infernum christus numquam descendebat
Nec aliquas animas de ipso redimebat.
¶Super istum infernum est locus qui dicitur infernus puerorum
Incircumcisorum videlicet et non baptizatorum.
Ibi non est pena sensus sed tantum pena dampni
Et gaudium habent magnum de bonitate dei magni.
Magnitudo gaudii istorum puerorum
Excellit magnitudinem gaudiorum omnium mundanorum.

[1] Mk. 14.58, Lk. 2.19, 24.21, 46, 1 Cor. 15.3–4 [2] Left Panel: Christ in the Four Regions of Hell. According to St. Thomas Aquinas there are four levels in hell: Gehenna, Purgatory, the Limbo of the Children, and the Limbo of the Fathers (ST Supp. Q. 69, aa. 1–7). The pattern, without canonical warrant, may be derived from the apocryphal text 1 Enoch. Here, Gehenna appears to be the fiery bottom level, the next level the Limbo of the Children, the next highest the Limbo of the Fathers, with Purgatory at the top. These are the regions thought to have been visited by Christ in his Harrowing of Hell. [3] Lk. 23.50–53 [4] Mt. 12.40, Act. 2.29–31, 1 Pt. 3.18–20 [5] Paragraph markers for *figurae* written in faint black ink at two places in the first column but not rubricated. It appears as though a later reader mistook the image of the young men in the fire for the children in Limbo. [6] Cf. Mt. 5.22, Mk. 9.43–45 [7] Cf. Dt. 32.22; 2 Kings 22.6, Job 17.13, 16, Ps. 9.17, Prov. 27.20, Is. 5.14, Mt. 13.42, 50, 25.41, 46, Mk. 9.48, Act. 2.27, 2 Pt. 2.4, Apc. 14.10, 21.8, etc.

so Christ was in the tomb for three days.
And in what manner the story of Jonah pertains to Christ
is made clear in the chapter concerning Resurrection.
O good Jesus, grant us to revere your burial so
that we may never deserve to be separated from you forever.

Chapter Twenty-eight

In the last chapter we heard how Joseph buried Christ;
now let us hear how Christ entered Hell.
When Christ gave up his spirit at the ninth hour,
immediately his spirit, united with the divine nature, was descending into hell.
Yet Hell is fourfold or rather, there are four levels of hells,
that is, the place of the damned, that of the children, that of those to be cleansed, and that of the saints.
In the hell of the damned there is smoke and unquenchable fire;
a terrible vision and awful horror;
the worms of conscience and palpable shadows;
cold, indescribable, and unbearable stenches;
mutual hatred and continual imprecation of curses;
flight from death and despair of redemption;
they are always dying and they never perish;
the pains are always fresh and are never finished.
Christ never descended to that hell
and did not redeem any souls from it.
Above that hell is a place which is called the hell of the children:
that is, the uncircumcised and the unbaptized.
There it is not a pain of sensation, but only a pain of condemnation
and they have great joy from the kindness of great God.
The scope of those children's joy
excels the scope of all the world's joys.

Gaudent de hoc quod creatorem suum peccando non offenderunt
Et quod de inferno dampnatorum semper securi erunt.[1]
Quid autem de hiis deus facturus sit nullus potest scire

31vb Nec aliquis doctor sufficit diffinire.
Super hunc locum est infernus purgandorum
In illo est diuersitas penarum et dolorum multorum.
Nam secundum peccatorum quantitatem et qualitatem
Recipit quilibet ⌊purgationem⌋[2] et penalitatem.
Pena istorum potest mitigari per celebracionem missarum
Per oraciones et ieiunia et collacionem elemosinarum.
Per indulgencias et crucis accepcionem[3]
⸌Et⸍ per aliene penitentie assumpcionem.
Pena purgatorii non potest verbis explanari
Quia nulla pena in mundo potest illi comparari.
Sicut differt ignis uerus ab illo qui solet depingi
Sic differt ignis purgatorii ab igne materiali.
Super hunc locum infernus sanctorum esse comprobatur
Qui alio nomine synus abrahe[4] uel lymbus appellatur.
Hunc infernum olim omnes sancti intrauerunt
Qui ante resurrectionem christi mortui fuerunt.
Ad istud infernum christus descendit et intrauit
Et omnes qui in christo erant potenter liberauit.
In isto inferno fuit anima christi ab hora sue expiracionis
Vsque ad horam sue gloriose resurrectionis.
Sciendum autem quod licet anima fuerit a corpore separata
Tamen deitas neque ab anima neque a corpore fuit segregata.
In lymbo fuit deitas vnita anime corpore separata.
In sepulchro erat deitas vnita carne mortificata

32a[5] Quando christus lymbum intrauit sancti diuinitatem uiderunt
Et omne gaudium celi statim ibidem habuerunt.
Dicitur enim vbi est papa ibi est romana curia
Sic vbi erat deitas ibi erant celi gaudia.
Dixerat christus latroni cum adhuc penderet patibulo

[1] See 2 Kings 12.22–23, Apc. 7.9 [2] purgationem, L] peccator, G (with signs of erasures) [3] See Mt. 16.24, Lk. 9.23 [4] Lk. 16.19–31, 4 Mcc. 13.17 [5] Left Panel: Daniel in the Lion's Den. As Daniel in the midst of the lions' den (Dn. 6) was sustained until his deliverance, so, this analogy suggests, the Fathers in Limbo, namely the patriarchs and faithful who looked forward to Christ's coming were preserved from the ravages of hell by angelic ministrations until Christ came to deliver them.

They rejoice because of this—that they did not offend their Creator by sinning
and because always they were safe from the hell of the damned.
But no one is able to know what God may be going to do about these ones,

nor is any doctor [of the Church] able to define anything.
Above this place is the hell of those being cleansed.
In that place there is diversity of sufferings and of many sorrows.
For according to the number and character of his sins,
each one receives purgation and penalty.
Their pain can be relieved through the celebration of masses,
through prayers and fasting and the granting of alms,
through indulgences and taking up the cross
and through taking on another's penance.
The suffering of purgatory cannot be described with words
because no suffering on the earth can be compared to it.
Just as real flames differ from the way flames are wont to be painted,
so too does the fire of purgatory differ from physical fire.
Above this place the hell of the saints is established,
which by another name is called the bosom of Abraham or Limbo.
Formerly all the saints entered this hell
who had died before the resurrection of Christ.
It was to that hell Christ descended and entered,
and all who were in Christ he powerfully freed.
The soul of Christ was in that Hell from the hour of his death
until the hour of his glorious resurrection.
And it ought to be known that although the soul had been separated from the body,
still the divine nature was not removed from either his soul or body.
In Limbo the divine nature was united with the soul, having been separated from the body.
In the tomb the divine nature was united with the dead body.

When Christ entered Limbo, the saints beheld his divinity
and immediately they possessed every joy of heaven.
For it is said that where the pope is, there is the Roman court;
so too where the divinity was, there were the joys of heaven.
Christ had said to the thief when still he was hanging from the gibbet,

Amen dico tibi hodie mecum eris in paradyso.[1]
Hoc de paradyso terrestri non est exponendum
Sed de contemplatione deitatis est intelligendum.
Anima enim latronis cum anima christi lymbum ingrediebatur
Et ipsam deitatem cum aliis sanctis contemplabatur.
Et cum uiderunt sancti christum pre gaudio simul omnes exclamabant
Aduenisti desiderabilis quem nostra suspiria uocabant. *prima figura*.[2]
¶Istud figuratum erat in pueris in fornace babylonis[3]
Vbi ad ingressum angeli ignis versus est in suauitatem roris.
Si presencia angeli potuit pueros in medio ignis refrigerare
Multo magis christus in inferno potuit sanctos letificare.
Quod enim dominus angelum ad consolacionem puerorum in fornacem mittebat.
Prefigurauit quod ipse ad consolandum patres in infernum intrare uolebat.
Qui in fornace babylonis erant fuerunt pueri
Sic in lymbo non erant nisi innocentes et puri.
Qui enim ante plenariam satisfactionem decedebant
In purgatorio purgabantur et tamen in lymbum [dece] ascendebant.
¶Istud etiam prefiguratum fuit per danielem in lacum leonum[4]
Cui dominus misit per abacuch prandium.[5]
Daniel missus erat in lacum leonum a babylonis

32b Vt consumeretur a vii leonibus famelicis
D⌊ominus⌋[6] autem illum illesum a leonibus custodiuit
Et per angelum suum sibi refectionem sibi misit.
Sic deus patres in lymbo div a demonibus defensauit
Et tandem ipse ueniens diuina refectione ipsos pauit.
Lacus babylonis designat infernum
Vii autem leones numerum uniuersorum demonum.
Numerus demonum solet describi per vii demonia
Quia demones impugnant homines per peccata mortalia.
Horum peccatorum mortalium nomina sunt superbia et inuidia
Ira et accidia auaricia gula et luxuria.

[1] Lk. 23.32–33, 43 [2] Right Panel: Sidrach, Misach, and Abdenego in the Fiery Furnace. See Dn. 3.20–27. When Nabuchodonosor looks into the raging furnace he sees the three young men walking about, and a fourth with them "like unto the Son of God." Here the fourth is named simply "angel of God," while the furnace resembles an abbey. The coolness miraculously present in the midst of the fire is sometimes, as here, compared to the *refrigerium* afforded to those in hell by Christ's descent and harrowing. [3] Dn. 3.49–50 [4] Dn. 6.16–22 [5] Dn. 14.33–36 [6] Dominus, L] David, G

"Amen, I say to you, today you will be with me in Paradise."
This should not be explained as about the earthly paradise,
but should be understood to concern the vision of God.
For the soul of the robber entered Limbo in company with the soul of Christ
and he was contemplating the very divinity along with other saints.
And when the saints saw Christ they all exclaimed with joy at the same time,
"You have come, Beloved, whom our sighs were calling." (Figure One)
That event had been symbolized by the young men in the furnace of Babylon
when, at the angel's entrance, the fire was changed into the sweetness of dew.
If the presence of the angel was able to cool the young men in the middle of the fire,
so much more was Christ able much to gladden the saints in hell.
For because the Lord was sending an angel into the furnace to console the young men,
he prefigured that he himself willed to enter into hell for the consolation of the fathers.
Those who were in the furnace of Babylon were young men
just as none were in Limbo, unless they were innocent and pure.
For they who departed [this life] before their full penance
were cleansed in purgatory and ascended into Limbo.
And that had been prefigured through Daniel in the lions' den
to whom the Lord sent a meal by means of Habakkuk.
Daniel had been sent into the den of lions by the Babylonians

so that he would be consumed by seven hungry lions,
yet the Lord guarded him, uninjured by the lions
and he sent refreshment to him by his angel.
So too God defended the fathers in Limbo from demons for a long time
and at length coming himself he fed them with divine refreshment.
The pit of Babylon signifies hell,
and the seven lions signify the number of all the demons.
The number of the demons is customarily described as seven evil spirits,
since the demons fight against men through the deadly sins.
Of these deadly sins the names are pride and envy,
anger and sloth, avarice, gluttony, and lust.

Ista sunt tela demonum et arma dyabolica.[1] *tercia figura*.[2]
Quibus insidiantur hominibus et muniu´n`tur castra infernalia.
¶Quamuis autem infernus multis annis a demonibus munitus erat
Tamen christus sanguine suo faciliter eum confringebat.
Illud olim in strucione salomonis prefiguratum fuerat.
Cuius pullum rex salomon in uase uitreo incluserat.
Strucio cupiens liberare de inclusione suum pullum
Abiit in desertum et attulit inde quendam vermiculum.
Quem comprimens super vitrum sanguinem exprimebat
Et ad tactum illius vitrum per medium se scindebat.
Sic sanguis christi in patibulo crucis est expressus[3]
Infernus tamquam vitrum est confractus et homo liber egressus.
O bone ihesu dignare nos ab inferno custodire
Et fac nos ad tuam presenciam feliciter peruenire.

32va *Capitulum xxix*[4]

In precedenti capitulo audiuimus quomodo christus patres letificauit
Consequenter audiamus quomodo principem infernalem superauit.
Christus idcirco homo factus est ut dyabolum superare uolebat
Et hoc quadam vice per quandam similitudinem turbis proponebat.[5]
Dum fortis armatus id est dyabolus atrium suum custodit id est lymbum
In pace sunt omnia que possidet quod de patribus est intelligendum.
Si autem forcior id est christus superuenerit
Vniuersa arma sua sibi auferet et eum alligabit.
Dyabolus ad incarnacionem christi tam fortiter armatus erat
Quod in toto orbe nullus homo atrium suum confringere poterat.
Christus autem qui non tantum homo sed deus et homo extitit
Atrium suum intrauit [/et][6] ipsum per crucem suam deuicit.

---

[1] Cf. Eph. 6.10–17 [2] Right Panel: Ostrich Delivering its Young. To those familiar with the reference in Job 39.13 to the ostrich as a careless bird that leaves its eggs vulnerably out on the ground in the sun, this legend seems counterintuitive (*Historia Scholastica* on 3 Kings 8). It seems to be particular to several manuscripts of the SHS (ONB 2612, fol. 31^{r}; BNF Arsenal 593, fol. 22^{v}; BNF Latin 511, fol. 29; BNF Latin 512, fol. 30^{r}; PML M. 140, fol. 31^{r}; and PML M 766, fol. 50^{r}) from the 14th century. Our SHS text narrates the unusual legend. [3] Cf. John 19.34 [4] Left Panel: Christ Crushes Satan. The image seems to follow the pattern of images representing St. George defeating the dragon, except that here, instead of a spear or lance, Christ strikes Satan in the mouth with the foot of the cross. The banner resembles the standard of St. George, but the emblem on the crossbeams is apparently an image of the sun (cf. Mal. 4.2), though it may also allude to the crown of thorns. [5] Mt. 12.29, Mk. 3.27, Lk. 11.21–22 [6] Correction by scratching out. The scribe appears to have originally written an "x" here for "xpm"—"christum".

These are the arrows of the demons and the diabolical weapons (Figure Two)
with which they lie in ambush for men and fortify the infernal fortresses.
But although hell had been protected for many years by the demons,
nevertheless Christ easily destroyed it with his own blood.
Formerly that event had been prefigured in the ostrich of Solomon,
whose chick King Solomon had enclosed in a glass vase.
The ostrich, wanting to free its chick from the enclosure,
went out into the desert and thence brought back a certain worm.
Holding it above the glass, it squeezed out the blood
and at the touch of that blood, the glass split itself through the middle.
So too the blood of Christ was squeezed out on the gibbet of the cross,
hell was broken like glass, and man freely went out.
O good Jesus, deign to guard us from hell,
and make us happily arrive in your presence.

Chapter Twenty-nine

In the last chapter we heard how Christ gladdened the patriarchs;
next let us hear how he overcame the prince of hell.
Christ became man for this reason, that he wished to overcome the Devil.
And he made this known to the crowd on one occasion through a certain parable:
while the strong, armed man—that is, the Devil—guards his hall—that is, Limbo—
all the things which he owns are in peace: which must be understood about the patriarchs.
If however a stronger one—that is, Christ—should overcome [him]
he will take all his weapons from him and bind him up.
The Devil was armed so strongly against the incarnation of Christ
that in the whole world no man could destroy his hall.
Christ however, who existed not merely as man but as God and man,
entered his hall and conquered him by his cross.

¶Istud olim bananyas per figuram premonstrauit *prima figura*.[1]
Qui ad leonem[2] cysternam intrans cum uirga sua ipsum prostrauit.[3]
Sic christus intrauit ad dyabolum ad cysternam id est [/in inf]ernum[4]
Et per uirgam et baculum id est per crucem prostrauit ipsum.
Et hoc est quod verba prophete olim in psalmo pretenderunt
Virga tua et baculus tuus ipsa me consolata sunt.[5]
Virga hoc loco sumitur pro baculo quem homo ambulans manu portat
Vt per eum sustentetur et a canibus se defendat.
Crux ergo christi est baculus per quem[6] sustentamur ne cadamus
Per quem etiam canes infernales a nobis depellamus.
Per hunc baculum christus leonem infernalem prostrauit
Et eundem baculum nobis ad resistendum dyabolo donauit.
Attendite fratres quantum tenemur sanctam crucem honorare

32vb Per quam possimus hostes nostros scilicet demones superare.
Sicut per lignum paradysi dyabolus cepit hominem et carcerauit
Ita per lignum crucis christus contra dyabolum triumphauit.
Sanctam crucem tenemur multum honorare
Quam deus proprio sanguine dignatus est consecrare.
In cruce enim socii dyaboli id est malefici suspendebantur
Et per eam nunc demones puniuntur et fugantur.
Per crucem olim cumulus dampnatorum augebatur.
Et per eam nunc numerus[7] beatorum augmentatur.
Per crucem olim homines mortificabantur.
Et per eam nunc egri curantur et mortui suscitantur.
Per crucem olim augebatur quodamodo gaudium demoniorum
Et per eam nunc multiplicatur leticia angelorum.
Per crucem olim ⸤maligni⸥[8] propter crimina sua dampnabantur
Et per eam crimina nunc misericorditer relaxantur.
Crucem olim propter suam vilitatem statuebant in montem caluariarum
Sed modo propter sanctitatem suam constituitur in altaribus ecclesiarum.
Crucem olim quilibet propter suam igno⸤miniam⸥[9] tangere uerecundabatur.

[1] Right Panel: Banaias Slays the Lion. An Old Testament story (1 Par. 11.22), for which there is little canonical detail, except that it was a snowy day when Banaias, one of King David's "mighty men," descended into a pit and killed a lion there. The image assumes his weapon was a club, though the text says *virga*, rod. As in the following story, the heroic killing of a lion is typologically linked the defeat of Satan by Christ (cf. 1 Pt. 5.8). [2] 1 Pt. 5.8 [3] 2 Kings 23.20–21, 1 Par. 11.22–23, *HS* II Regum 22 [4] Corrected by scribe. The scribe probably skipped the "in" originally, proceeding directly to spell the beginning of "infernum." However, the scribe caught the mistake early enough to turn the "f" into the first "i" of the word. [5] Ps. 22.4 [6] quem] quod, L [7] L reverses "cumulus" and "numerus" between the two lines [8] maligni, L] magni, G [9] ignominu, L] ignominiam, G

This was once presaged through the figure of Banaias (Figure One)
who, entering a cistern [to fight] against a lion, laid it low with his rod.
In such a way Christ entered a cistern—that is, into hell—against the Devil
and through his rod and staff—that is, through the cross—he laid him low.
And this is what the words of the prophet asserted in the Psalm:
"Your rod and your staff, they have comforted me."
(The rod is used in this place instead of the staff, which a man, walking, carries in his hand
so that by it he may be supported and defend himself from dogs.)
Therefore, the cross of Christ is the staff by which we are supported, lest we fall,
and through which we may drive away even the hounds of hell from us.
Through this staff, Christ laid low the lion of hell,
and he gave this very staff to us to resist the Devil.
Pay heed, brothers, how much we should to honor the holy cross

through which we are able to overcome our enemies—namely, the demons.
Just as through the wood of paradise the Devil seized man and imprisoned [him],
so through the wood of the cross Christ triumphed against the Devil.
We should honor the holy cross greatly,
which God has deigned to hallow with his own blood.
For on the cross, the Devil's associates—that is, criminals—were hung
and now, through it, the demons are punished and put to flight.
Through the cross, the heap of the damned was at one time increased.
And now, through it, the number of the blessed is increased.
Through the cross, men were at one time destroyed.
And now, through it, the sick are cured and the dead revived.
Through the cross, the demons' joy was at one time increased to a certain degree
and now, through it, the happiness of angels is multiplied.
On the cross, great men were at one time condemned for of their crimes;
and now, through it, crimes are mercifully eased.
On account of its baseness, they set up the cross at one time on the mount of Calvary;
but now, on account of its holiness, it is arranged on the altars of churches.
Anyone was formerly ashamed to touch the cross on account of its dishonor;

Modo propter gloriam suam a principibus et regibus adoratur.
Fortem dyabolum quem totus mundus non potuit superare
Modo vnus puer per signum crucis potest [ef]fugare.
Hanc potestatem contulit sibi ille bellator fortis
Qui per eam uicit dyabolum et destruxit portas mortis.
¶Victoria christi olim prefigurata fuit per sampsonem *secunda figura*.[1]
Qui in vineis engadi dilacerauit leonem.[2]

33a Per fortissimum sampsonem fortissimus christus designatur
A quo infernalis leo id est dyabolus[3] potencia sua priuabatur.
Sampson perrexit ut desponsaret sibi uxorem
Et in itinere interfecit occurrentem sibi leonem[4]
Sic filius dei descendit de celo in hunc mundum
Vt cum humana natura contraheret matrimonium.
Sampson duxit in ⸌uxorem⸍ mulierem[5] thamnatheam
Filius dei post omnes naciones elegit sibi iudeam.
Vxor thamnathea sampsonem dolose defraudauit[6]
Sic et iudas[7] christum fraudulenter tractauit.
Sampson segetes et uineas hostium suorum succendit
Et contra eos pugnans et ab omnibus se defendit.
Sic christus de iudeis se postremum uindicauit.
Quando per exercitum romanorum iudeam uastauit.[8]
Sampson igitur figurauit christum fortissimum.
Qui superauit leonem infernalem nostrum inimicum.
¶Similiter Ayoch ambidexter olim christum prefigurauit[9] *tertia figura*.[10]
Qui eglon impiissimum hostem filiorum israel gladio perforauit.
Eglon rex crassus nimis et pinguissimus erat
Et impugnando iudeam filios israel opprimebat.
Ayoch autem cogitauit quomodo ipsum trucidaret
Et filios israel ab impugnacione eius liberaret.
Accessit ergo ad eum in atrium suum vbi residebat

---

[1] Left Panel: Samson Slays a Lion. This more familiar story (Jdg. 14.5–9) is regularly taken as a prefigurement of the victory of Christ over sin and death on behalf of the Church (e.g., *Glossa*, PL 113.531). [2] Jdg. 14.1–9, Ct. 1.13 [3] 1 Pt. 5.8 [4] Jdg. 14.5–6 [5] The scribe indicated that he should have placed "uxorem" before "mulierem" by using two little vertical lines before each word [6] Jdg. 14.1–20 [7] *iudea* has been corrected in a later hand to *iudas* by scraping the e and inserting an s [8] Jdg. 15.4–5, cf. Lk. 19.42–44 [9] Jdg. 3.15–30 [10] Right Panel: Aod Kills Eglon. This story of an assassination by stealth (Jdg. 3.15–26) describes how left-handed Aod made a dagger of about 18 inches in length, hid it under his clothes, and used it to stab the "exceedingly fat" King Eglon of Moab so deeply that he buried even the hilt of his dagger in the king's belly. The *Glossa* (PL 113.523) see this as prefiguring the "holy ambidextrousness" to be deployed against the devil, but does not, as here, see Ehud as prefiguring Christ.

now on account of its glory it is adored by princes and kings.
The strong devil, whom the whole world could not overcome,
now a lone boy can put to flight through the sign of the cross.
That strong warrior bestowed on it this power,
He who, through [the cross], conquered the Devil and destroyed the gates of death.
Christ's victory was once prefigured through Samson (Figure Two)
who, in the vineyards of En Gedi, tore a lion to pieces.

Through the very strong Samson is Christ signified, himself exceedingly strong,
by whom the hellish lion—that is, the Devil—was stripped of his power.
Samson made haste so that he might wed a woman
and on the way, he killed a lion who was rushing toward him.
In such a way did the Son of God descend from heaven onto this earth
so that he might contract a marriage with human nature.
Samson married a woman of Timnah;
the Son of God chose Judea for himself above all nations.
The woman of Timnah deceived Samson craftily,
and in such a way did the Jews treat Christ deceitfully.
Samson set aflame the fields and vineyards of his enemies
and fighting against them, he defended himself from all.
So Christ finally avenged himself on the Jews
when he laid waste to Judea through the Roman army.
Samson therefore prefigured Christ, exceedingly strong,
Who overcame the lion of hell, our enemy.
Similarly, the left-handed Ehud once prefigured Christ (Figure Three)
who pierced Eglon, that most wicked enemy of the sons of Israel, with the sword.
King Eglon was exceedingly fat and very plump
and was oppressing the sons of Israel by attacking Judea.
Ehud, however, reflected how he might slaughter Eglon
and free the sons of Israel from his attacks.
Therefore, he drew near to him in his hall where he resided

Et gladium sinistra manu in uentrem eius mittebat.
Misit autem tam ualide ut capulus ferrum sequeretur \\nota//

33b Et in pinguissimo ipsius adipe con⌊stringeretur⌋.[1]
Et relinquens gladium in eius uentre fugit et euasit
Et sic filios israel a tali inimico liberauit.
Eglon propter suum pinguissimum et amplum uentrem
Significat dyabolum amplissimum uentrem habentem.
Qui pinguissimus dicitur eo quod omnes homines deglutiuit
Quia totum genus humanum in uentrem eius introiuit.
Tandem dominus ihesus christus uentrem eius perforauit
Quando portas inferni gladio sue passionis penetrauit.
Dyabolus superauit hominem per dulcem pomi gustacionem
Et ideo superauit christus dyabolum per amarissimam passionem.
Et in hoc dedit nobis dominus exemplum quid[2] sit pugnandum
Quia contra dyabolum et uicia virtutibus est certandum.
Sicut enim in egritudinibus contraria contrariis curantur
Sic in pugna dyaboli vicia per uirtutes superantur.
Nemo coronatur nisi qui legittime certauerit[3]
Et nemo certare poterit nisi hostes habuerit.
Vvlt autem deus ut homines sustineant impungnaciones
Vt ex hoc in celo augeantur eorum retribuciones.[4]
Permittit etiam dominus ut eciam boni in sompnis temptentur
Vt etiam [–dominus][5] dormiendo eorum premia augmententur.
Quanto autem maiora et plura habuerit certamina
Tanto maiora et plura recipiet premia
O bone ihesu da nobis contra dyabolum et uicia taliter preliari
Vt a te mereamur corona perpetua coronari.

[1] constringeretur, L] confringeretur, G [2] quid] quomodo, L [3] 2 Tim. 2.5 [4] See *ST* 1.95.4. Aquinas quotes both Peter Lombard (*Sent.* ii., D, xxiv) and 2 Tim. 2.5, and on the issue of gaining merit through resisting temptation. [5] This word is both deleted through scribal subpunction and crossed through in red

and with his left hand thrust his sword into his [Eglon's] belly.
He thrust so powerfully, moreover, that the handle followed the blade

and was engulfed by his most greasy fat.
And leaving the sword in his belly, Ehud fled and escaped,
and thus he liberated sons of Israel from such a great enemy.
Eglon, on account of his very fat and large belly
represents the devil, who had the largest belly.
He is very fat, it is said, because he swallowed up all mankind
since the whole human race entered into his belly.
At last the Lord Jesus Christ pierced his belly
when he broke through the infernal gates with the sword of his Passion.
The Devil overcame man with the sweet taste of fruit
and for that reason, Christ overcame the Devil through the bitterest Passion.
And in this the Lord gave us an example [of] what should be fought
since one must use the virtues to wrestle against the Devil and vices.
For just as in diseases, contraries are cured by contraries,
so too in battle with the Devil, the vices are overcome through the virtues.
No one is crowned [in athletic contests] unless he has competed lawfully
and no one can compete unless he has opponents.
Moreover, God desires that men withstand attacks
so that by this, their rewards in heaven may be increased.
The Lord also permits that even the good may be tempted in dreams
so that, even while sleeping, their rewards may be increased.
And the greater and more numerous the trials one has,
the greater and more numerous the rewards one shall receive.
O good Jesus, grant us to battle against the devil and vices in such a manner
that we may become worthy to be crowned by you with an eternal crown.

33va *Capitulum xxx*[1]

In precendenti capitulo adiuimus quomodo christus uicit dyabolum per passionem
Consequenter audiamus quomodo maria uicit eundem per compassionem.
Omnia que christus in sua passione tolerabat
Hec maria per maternam compassionem secum portabat.[2]
Claui qui transierunt pedes filii sui et manus
Per compassionem transierunt[3] sanctissimi matris pectus.
Lancea que \\latus//[4] filii sui mortui perforauit
Per compassionem cor matris viuentis penetrauit.[5]
Aculei spinarum qui caput christi pupugerunt
Per compassionem cor genitricis eius uulnerauerunt.
Gladius acutissimarum linguarum quas christus audiuit
Per compassionem intimam marie animam pertransiuit.
Et sic christus superauit dyabolum per suam passionem
Ita etiam superauit eum maria per maternam compassionem.
Armis passionis christi maria se armauit
Quando contra dyabolum ad pugnam se preparauit. *prima figura.*[6]
¶Ipsa enim prefiguratur per Judith que restitit holoferni[7]
Quia ipsa se opposuit dyabolo principi inferni.
Judith induit se uestibus iocunditatis
Et ornauit caput suum mitra et pedes sandalis.[8]
Maria uestiuit se tunica filii sui inconsutili[9]
Et super induit se pallio derisionis eius duplici.
Vnum erat album in quo christus ab herode deridebatur
Aliud coccineum id est rubicundum in quo a militibus illudebatur.[10]
Et bene maria pallio albo et rubicundo induebatur

[1] Left Panel: Mary Crushes Satan with the Instruments of the Passion. The instruments of the Passion—nails, pincers, flail, hammer, tongs—were established as a focus for contemplation of Christ's sacrifice by the 13th century (e.g., *Meditationes Vitae Christi*, 74–84; ch. 78 adds the component developed here, that Mary's "great compassion adds to the Passion of her son, and conversely"; Ragusa and Green, 335). The *arma Christi*, or instruments of crucifixion used by Christ to defeat Satan, figure variously from the 11th to the 15th century in the iconography of contemplation. Transference from Christ to Mary is clearly influenced by the "Sorrows of Mary" devotion, which takes its cue from the prophecy of Simeon that "a sword shall pierce your soul, that the thoughts of many hearts may be revealed" (Lk. 1.35). In this image, the reed, scourge, bucket (sometimes associated with the vinegar), nails and pole of the flagellation are featured, with the later topped by a chalice symbolizing the Eucharist. Satan, prostrate at Mary's feat, appears dead. [2] Cf. Lk. 2.19 [3] transierunt] *penetrauerunt, L* (with parallel below) [4] Scribal emendation using the || indicator in the left margin [5] Cf. Lk. 2.35 [6] Right Panel: Judith Slays Holofernes. One of the most popular of medieval stories of valorous women originates in Judith 13. Here Judith is shown with the general's pilfered sword aloft, poised to behead the besotted Holofernes, drunk in her bed. The SHS author offers the image as an antitype to his extensive elaboration of the *arma Christi* in reference to the Sorrows of Mary. [7] Jdt. 13 [8] Jdt. 10.3 [9] Cf. John 19.23 [10] Mt. 27.28, Lk. 23.11

Chapter Thirty

In the last chapter, we heard how Christ conquered the devil through his Passion.
Next let us hear how Mary conquered him through compassion.
All the things that Christ endured in his Passion,
these Mary bore with him through her maternal compassion.
The nails that pierced the feet and hands of her son
pierced the breast of the most holy mother through compassion.
The lance which stabbed the side of her dead son
penetrated the heart of the living mother through compassion.
The spines of the thorns which punctured the head of Christ
wounded the heart of his mother through compassion.
The sword of the sharpest tongues that Christ heard
pierced through the inmost soul of Mary through compassion.
And just as Christ overcame the devil through his Passion,
so also did Mary overcome him with her maternal compassion.
Mary armed herself with the weapons of Christ's Passion
when she prepared herself for battle against the devil. (Figure One)
For she was prefigured through Judith, who withstood Holofernes,
since she opposed herself against the devil, the prince of hell.
Judith clothed herself with pleasing garments
and adorned her head with a headdress and her feet with sandals.
Mary clothed herself with the seamless tunic of her son
and on top [of this] she donned herself with the twofold cloak of his derision:
one cloak, in which Christ was mocked by Herod, was white;
the other, in which he was made sport of by the soldiers, was carmine (that is, red).
And Mary was elegantly clothed with the white cloak and with the red one

33vb Quia dilectus eius filius candidus et rubicundus[1] decantatur.
Tota eius passio comparatur †fasciculio[2] mirre[3]
Qui ⌊commorari⌋ debet inter ⌊ubera⌋[4]† diligentis anime.
Omnes autem penalitates christi maria diligenter collegit
Et ⌊per⌋ compassionem fasciculum mirre ex ipsis compegit.
Hunc fasciculum pro clipeo inter ubera sua collocauit
Et cum tali armatura contra hostem nostrum dimicauit.
In hoc fasci⌊c⌋ulo mirre erant simul omnia colligata
Que dilectissimo filio suo in passione fuerunt illata.
Gladii fuste lancee et arma quibus capiebatur
Lucerne ardentes et facule quibus in orto querebatur.
Tristicie pauor tremor et trina oratio[5,6]
Sudor sanguineus et angeli confortacio.
Quomodo turbis occurrit et uno uerbo omnes prostrauit
Et restituens eis uires se capiendum presentauit.
Cognicionis signum et osculum malignum
Dolosa salutacio et responsum christi [ma] benignum.
Crudelis christi captiuacio et vinculorum ligacio
Auricule reformacio[7] et discipulorum fugacio.
S[/in]don[i/e] reli[/cto][8] a dilecto suo iohanne[9]
Exultacio iudeorum et interrogacio anne.
Alapa serui pontificis et mansueta christi responsio
Trina negacio petri et eiusdem conuersio.
Nomina iudicum coram quibus ductus et accusatus
Annas cayphas herodes poncius pylatus

34a Columpna virge flagella sputa harundo et funiculi
Crux claui lancea mallei corona et tabula tytuli.[10]
Alape colaphi obprobria blasphemie et derisio[11]
Velamen oculorum propheti⌊z⌋a christ⌊e⌋[12] et uestimentorum diuisio.
Sors super tunicam et herodis album indumentum[13]
Tribuna iudicis. locio manuum et purpurum uestimentum.[14]
Sompnium uxoris pylati[15] et liberacio barrabe homicide[16]
Tumultus et clamor iudeorum et geminatum crucifige.[17]

---

[1] Ct. 5.10 [2] The scribe had difficulties with this word: the first *i* was originally a long *s*, corrected by scratching out, and an extraneous *i* was deleted by subpunction [3] Ct. 1.12 [4] commorari, L] comparari, G; ubera, L] uerbera, G [5] Mt. 27.46, Mk. 15.34, Lk. 23.24, 46 [6] See *ST* III.83.5 [7] Lk. 23.51 [8] These words have been heavily erased and corrected [9] Cf. Mk. 14.50–51, John 18.4–8, 20.2, *HS* Evangelorum 157 [10] John 19.19 [11] Mk. 15.29–32 [12] prophetiza christe, L] prophetia Christi, G [13] Lk. 22.64, 23.11 [14] John 19.2 [15] Mt. 27.19 [16] Mt. 27.26 [17] Mk. 15.13, Lk. 23.21, John 19.6

since her beloved son is described in song as white and red.
His whole Passion is compared with a little bundle of myrrh
which ought to remain between the breasts of her careful heart.
Moreover, Mary was carefuly gathering together all the punishments of Christ
and constructing the little bundle of myrrh from them through compassion.
This bundle she put between her breasts, as a shield
and with such great armor she battled against our enemy.
In this bundle of myrrh were at once gathered together everything
that she had borne from her most beloved son during the Passion:
the swords, clubs, lances, and weapons by which he was captured;
the burning lamps and torches with which he was sought in the garden;
the sadness, the dread, the shaking and the threefold prayer;
the bloody sweat and the angel's consolation;
how he came to meet the crowd, and with one word prostrated them all;
and restoring their powers, presented himself to be captured;
the sign of knowledge and the malicious kiss;
the deceitful greeting and Christ's friendly response;
the cruel captivity of Christ and the bondage of chains;
the restoration of the ear and the flight of the disciples
after the linen cloth was left behind by his beloved one, John;
the exultation of the Jews and the interrogation of Annas;
the slaps of the high priest's slave and the gentle response of Christ;
the threefold denial of Peter and his conversion;
the names of the judges, before whom he was led and accused
(Annas, Caiaphas, Herod, Pontius Pilate);

the pillar, the switches, the scourges, the spit, the rod, and the cords;
the cross, the nails, the lance, the hammers, the crown, and the placard with the title;
the slaps, the blows, the reproaches, the blasphemies, and the derision;
the veiling of his eyes, the "Prophesy, Christ!", and the division of [his] garments;
the lot [cast] about his tunic and the white robe given him by Herod;
the tribunal court, the washing of hands, and the purple garment;
the dream of Pilate's wife and the freeing of Barabbas the murderer;
the commotion and cries of the Jews and the repeated "Crucify [him]!";

Sitis christi acetabulum et acetum felle amaritatum
Arundo cum spongea[1] ysopus[2] et uinum mirratum.[3]
Oratio christi. clamor lacrime et latronis acceptacio[4]
Omnia verba christi uidete et discipuli iohannis commendacio.[5]
Expiracio christi.[6] lancea longini[7] cum ipsius illuminacione
Effluxio sanguinis et aque.[8] centurio cum sua protestacione.[9]
Obscuracio solis[10] terre motus scissio ueli et petrarum.[11]
\\Ruina partis templi apercio sepulchrorum[12] fetor et mons caluariarum//[13]
Triginta argentei[14] quibus christus erat uenditus et emptus
Desperacio iude[15] qui non est sanguine christi redemptus.
Hiis et aliis christi penalitatibus maria se armauit
Et tamquam propugnatrix nostra hostem nostrum deiecit et conculcauit.
Tunc implete sunt in ipsa premonstrate olim figure
Et quedam prophetica dicta sacre scripture
Super aspidem et basiliscum tu maria ambulabis
Leonem et draconem id est sathanam conculcabis.[16]
Et tu sathana insidiaberis calcaneo eius homines impugnando[17]

34b Ipsa conteret caput tuum per passionem te superando.[18,19]
¶Istud olim Jahel uxor abner Cynei[20] prefigurauit *secunda figura*.[21]
Que ⌊s⌋ysaram per tympora clauo ferreo perforauit.
[C/S][22]ysara erat princeps milicie Jabin regis
Et uastauit filios israel violenciam inferens eis.
Tandem a Jahel clauo per tympora est perforatus
Et populus israeliticus ab eius infestacionibus est liberatus.
Sic maria clauo sancte crucis hostem nostrum perforauit
Et eum potestate quam super nos habuit liberauit.

[1] Mt. 27.48 [2] John 19.29 [3] Mk. 15.33 [4] Lk. 23.42 [5] John 19.26–27, *HS* Evangelorum 157 [6] Mk. 15.37 [7] John 19.34, *LA* 47 [8] John 19.34 [9] Mk. 15.39 [10] Mk. 15.23 [11] Mt. 27.51 [12] Mt. 27.52 [13] See *HS Evangelorum* 170, *LA* 53. This line was originally skipped by the scribe, who realized the mistake at the end of the column, supplying it there. Cross-like glyphs, labeled 'a' and 'b', mark the position of the omission. [14] Mt. 26.15 [15] Mt. 27.3–5 [16] Ps. 90.13 [17] Due to the correction of the missing line above, this line does not appear in the MS as the last line of the column. A maniculum at the end of the line points upward to the next column. [18] Gen. 3.15 [19] Another maniculum at the beginning of this line assures the reader that this is next in the sequence [20] Jdg. 4.17–22 [21] Left Panel: Jahel Nails Sisara to the Floor. In this canonical narrative another *mulier fortis*, Haber's wife Jahel, friend of Debbora, pretends to offer refuge to the defeated general Sisara. After giving him some warm milk, she covers him with a blanket, and then, when he has fallen asleep, drives a tent-peg through his temple, pinning him to the ground (Jdg. 4.17–22). In this image she needs a better aim and a longer peg; Sisara's shield is the probable reason. Despite the erroneous rubric *rahel exor Abner* (rather than *Eber*), Jahel is here clearly identified, as in the *Glossa* (PL 113.525), with the Church. Since Mary is also a figure for the Church, the SHS author makes the extension to her as well. [22] Very noticeable later correction of the initial letter, from what looks to be originally a *c*

the thirst of Christ, the vinegar cup, and the vinegar made bitter with gall
the rod with the sponge, the hyssop, and the wine mixed with myrrh;
the prayer of Christ, the cry, the tears, and the acceptance of the thief;
all the words of Christ, the "Behold!", and the commendation of the disciple John;
the exhalation of Christ; the lance of Longinus with his enlightenment;
the outflow of blood and water; the centurion with his declaration;
the darkening of the sun, the movement of the earth, the rending of the curtain and the rocks;
the collapse of part of the temple, the opening of tombs, the stench, and the Mount of Calvary;
the thirty pieces of silver with which Christ was sold and purchased;
the despair of Judas, who was not redeemed by the blood of Christ—
with these and other hardships of Christ Mary armed herself
and as our champion, she cast down and trampled our enemy.
Then the figures previously foreshown were fulfilled in her
and a certain prophetic saying of Holy Scripture:
"Upon the viper and the basilisk shall you (Mary) walk.
The lion and the dragon"—that is, Satan—"shall you crush."
And you, Satan, "shall lie in wait for her heel" by attacking men.

"She will bruise your head" by overcoming you through the Passion.
Jahel, wife of Aber of the Cinites, once prefigured this, (Figure Two)
who pierced Sisara through the temples with an iron nail.
Sisara was general of King Jabin's army
and he ravaged the children of Israel, bringing violence against them.
At last, he was pierced through the temples with a nail by Jahel
and the Israelite people were delivered from his harassments.
Thus Mary pierced our enemy with a nail of the holy cross
and delivered him of the power that he had over us.

¶Regina thamari etiam mariam prefigurauit *tertia figura*.[1]
Que ⌞c⌟yrum[2] crudelissimum homicidam decollauit.
Qui tantum aspirabat ad homini interfectionem
Quod non potuit saciari humani sanguinis effusionem.
Omnibus contradicebat et omnia regna inuadebat
Nulli parcebat omnem quem potuit sanguinem fundebat.
Tandem regina Thamari ipsum capiens decollauit
Et caput in urnam plenam sanguine humano proiciens ait.
Sacia te nunc sanguine humano quem in tantum sitisti
Quod in uita tua numquam saciari potuisti.
Sic dyabolus qui ab inicio homicida erat
Numquam hominum dampnacione saciari poterat.
Sed regina celi ipsum per passionem filii superauit
Et eterna dampnacione quam nobis parauerat ipsum saciauit
O bone ihesu fac nos tuo adiutorio ita dyabolum superare
Vt in eternum mereamur tecum in tua gloria habitare.

34va *Capitulum xxxi*[3]

*I*n precedenti capitulo audiuimus quomodo dyabolus est superatus.
Consequenter audiamus quomodo homo de carcere est liberatus.
In die parasceue quando christus in cruce expirauit
Anima eius statim unita deitati infernum intrauit.
Non enim ut quidam putant usque ad noctem dominicam expectabat.
Sed statim ad consolandum incarceratos festinabat.
Si enim posset aliquis hodie amicum suum liberare
Iniquum esset usque ad diem tertium expectare.
Christus ergo fidelissimus amicus noster non expectauit

[1] Right Panel: Tomyris Beheads Cyrus. This story from the *Historia Scholastica* (on Dn. 19) draws on Heroditus (*Histories* 1.205–214) to recount the exploits of another *mulier fortis*. The beheading of Cyrus the Great followed a losing battle with Queen Tomiri in which he was killed; according to Heroditus she then had his headless body crucified. Eustace Deschamp wrote a poem about nine female worthies, including Tomyris, about the same time as the SHS appeared. [2] cyrum, L] tyrum, G [3] Left Panel: Christ Liberates Souls from Hell. Although there are no direct canonical biblical narratives to support it, the apocryphal Gospel of Nicodemus (5th century) consolidated the exegesis of numerous early Christian writers that between his death and resurrection Christ "descended into hell" (Apostles' Creed) and led forth the souls of those considered righteous, beginning with Adam and Eve, as in this figure. The gates of hell are imagined in the context of Ps. 23: "Lift up ye gates, ye everlasting doors, and the king of glory shall come in." Called in medieval English the "harrowing of hell" (from OE *herigan*, "to harry or despoil") this narrative became widely distributed in northern Europe after the 11th century. The demons jeering from the parapet are conventional, as is Christ's triumphant banner.

Queen Tomyris also prefigured Mary[1] (Figure Three)
who beheaded Cyrus, that most cruel murderer.
He strove so much to kill men
because he could not be satisfied by the pouring out of human blood.
He opposed everyone and attacked every kingdom.
He spared no one; he shed all the blood he could.
Finally, Queen Tomyris, capturing him, beheaded him
and throwing his head into an urn full of human blood, she said:
"Glut yourself now on human blood, for which you thirsted so greatly,
because in your life you could never be satisfied."
Thus the devil, who was a murderer from the start,
could never be satisfied with the damnation of mankind.
But the queen of heaven overcame him through the Passion of her son
and she sated him on the eternal damnation that he had prepared for us.
O good Jesus, cause us with your aid to overcome the devil in such a way
that we might worthily dwell with you in your glory forever.

Chapter Thirty-one

In the last chapter we heard how the devil was conquered.
Next we will hear how man was freed from prison.
On Friday, the day of preparation, when Christ breathed his last on the cross.
His spirit, united with God, at once entered hell.
For he did not, as some people suppose, wait until Sunday night
but immediately hurried to console the imprisoned.
For if someone were able to free his friend today
it would be unjust to wait until the third day.
Therefore, Christ, our most faithful friend, did not wait,

[1] See Herodotus, *Histories* 1.205–214

Sed statim peracta passione sanctos in carcere inferni uisitauit.
Et in hoc datur nobis exemplum quod si uolumus animabus subuenire
Si protrahimus suffragia non videtur eis expedire.
Grauissime enim et cum tedio expectare [expectare] comprobantur
Qui in[ ]tam[1] inenarrabilibus penis cruciantur.
Quidam faciunt caris suis per XXX ⌊dies⌋[2] XXX missas celebrari.
Hic bonum est sed utilius animabus illas primo die consumari.
Quia per XXX ⌊dies⌋ ibi expectare ualde est amarum
Et illud intelligatur de aliis suffragiis animarum.
Festinemus igitur quantocitius animabus in purgatorio subuenire
Quia hic per festinacionem christi probatur ipsis expedire.
Christus autem non statim patres eodem die liberauit
Sed ibi cum eis manens ipsos sui dilecti presentia letificauit.
Media autem nocte dominica quando a morte resurrexit
Tunc eos de captiuitate dyaboli eduxit et euexit.
¶Hoc autem captiuitas dyabolica iam pretaxata *prima figura.*

34vb[3] Olim fuit in captiuitate egypciaca prefigurata.
Filii israel in egipto a pharone grauiter opprimebantur
Et ad dominum pro liberacione sua lacrimabiliter uociferabantur.[4]
Misertus est dominus apparuit moysi in rubo ardente
Igne pleno et tamen integro et uiridi permanente.[5]
Misit autem dominus moysen ad pharonem
Et fecit per eum filiis israel captiuitatis sue liberacionem.
Ita genus humanum a principe tenebrarum detinebatur
Et ad dominum pro sua liberacione multipliter lamentabatur.
Deus in adiutorium meum intende[6]
Domine inclina celos tuos et descende.[7]
Libera me quia egenus et pauper ego sum[8]
Et nichil habeo quo me liberare possim.
Emitte manum tuam per quam liberer[9]
Emitte agnum tuum[10] cuius uictima reconcilier.
Emitte lucem tuam[11] ut tenebre a me repellantur[12]
Emitte veritatem tuam[13] ut prophete tui fideles inueniantur.[14]

[1] Erasure [2] dies, L] denariis, G. See ln. 17 [3] Right Panel: Moses Leads the Israelites out of Egypt. The Exodus narrative of liberation is a treasury of antitypes for both events and teachings in the gospels. The caption on this image, *exitus filiorum Israel de egypto* recalls Ps. 113.1. "When Israel went out of Egypt," one of the supplication psalms, was in the liturgy for Vespers, and well-known. The usual typology, as here, is Christological: as Moses led the people of God out of captivity, so Christ. [4] Ex. 2.23 [5] Ex. 3.2 [6] Ps. 69.2 [7] Ps. 143.5 [8] Ps. 108.21–22 [9] Ps. 143.7 [10] Is. 16.1 [11] Ps. 42.3 [12] John 1.5 [13] Ps. 42.3 [14] Sir. 36.18

but immediately, when the passion was completed, he visited the saints in the prison of hell.
And in this an example is given to us that, if we wish to relieve souls,
Prolonging their suffering does not seem to aid them;
for they are known to wait with great heaviness and weariness
who are being tortured by such indescribable punishments.
Some people have thirty masses celebrated for their dear ones over the course of thirty days:
this is good, but it is more beneficial for the souls that these be completed on the first day.
Because it is very bitter to wait for thirty days,
and that is understood from other intercessions for souls.
Therefore, let us make haste as quickly as possible to help the souls in purgatory
because, through Christ's haste, it is shown to be praiseworthy to deliver them.
Yet Christ did not immediately free the fathers on the same day
but, remaining there with them, gladdened them with the presence of his love.
And in the middle of the Sunday night when he rose from dead,
he then led them out and raised them up from the devil's captivity.
And this diabolical captivity had already been presaged. *Figure One*

It was formerly prefigured in the Egyptian captivity.
The Children of Israel were being harshly oppressed in Egypt by Pharaoh
and were tearfully crying out to the Lord for their deliverance.
The Lord had pity; he appeared to Moses in a burning bush,
which was full of flames, and yet remained whole and green.
And the Lord sent Moses to Pharaoh
and through him brought about deliverance for the sons of Israel from their captivity.
So too the human race was imprisoned by the Prince of Darkness
and was crying out to the Lord for its deliverance many times:
"God, come to my assistance;
Lord, bow your heavens and descend.
Free me, for I am needy and poor
and I have no means to free myself.
Stretch forth your hand, by which I may be freed!
Send forth your lamb, by whose sacrifice I may be reconciled!
Send forth your light, so that the darkness may be driven away from me!
Send forth your truth, so that your prophets may be found faithful!"

Hiis et aliis multis modis homo ad deum clamabat
Et dominus misertus est ei ipsum hoc modo liberabat.
Descendit in rubum ardentem sine rubi lesione
Hoc est in uirginem mariam sine uirginitatis amissione.
Dominus plagauit pharonem et omnem suam gentem
Et eduxit filios in terram lacte et melle fluentem.[1]
Ita christus plagauit dyabolum et omnem suam congregacionem
Et eduxit sanctos de inferno ad eternam refectionem.

35ra[2] Ibi pascuntur lacte hoc est dulci aspectu humanitatis
Et melle hoc est melliflua contemplacione diuinitatis.
Dominus uolens iudeos liberare precepit agnum immolari[3]
Sed quando uoluit nos liberare fecit semetipsum cruciari.
¶Hanc etiam liberacionem hominis deus prefigurauit *secunda figura.*
Quando patriarcham abraham de hur caldeorum liberauit.[4]
Caldei hur hoc est ignem pro deo coluerunt
Quod cum abraham ⌊renueret⌋[5] ipsum in ignem proiecerunt.
Deus autem uerus quem ipse coluit et adorauit
De igne caldeorum ipsum misericorditer liberauit.
Sicut ergo deus abraham conseruauit in igne sine combustione
Ita sanctos conseruauit in inferno sine omni lesione.
Et sicut dominus abraham eripuit et patrem multarum gencium fecit.[6]
Ita patres de inferno redemit et cetibus angelorum coniunxit.
¶Hanc etiam redempcionem hominis deus prefigurauit *tertia figura.*
Quando loth cum suis de sub⌊v⌋ersione[7] sodome liberauit.[8]
De sodomis tantum boni liberati fuerunt
Mali autem omnes igne et sulphure interierunt.
Sic christus bonos de lymbo solummodo redemit
De inferno{rum} autem dampnatorum nullum eripuit.[9]
Nullus ergo dicat deus confregit infernum
Et quis est qui recuperare potuit ipsum.
Non est confractus sed qui a principio mundi intrauerunt

---

[1] Ex. 3.8 [2] Left Panel: God Saves Abraham from Chaldean Fire. This story is not found in the canonical Genesis, but is a legend occurring in Gen. Rabbah 38.13 (and subsequently in the Qur'an). The illustration here is from the redaction of the *Historia Scholastica* for Gen. 40. The connection of Abraham's natal town Ur with "fire" is fanciful, but serves as an antitype for the harrowing of hell, in that God is said in the legend to have delivered Abraham from the fire. The arms of God reach down from an arc suggesting heaven, with arms on both sides of the arc. [3] Ex. 12.3–10 [4] Cf *HS* Genesis 40. The story also appears in the Genesis Midrash Rabbah 38:13 and also figures prominently in the Qur'an's account of Ibrahim. [5] renueret, L] memineret, G [6] Gen. 17.4 [7] L] submersione, G [8] Gen. 19.15–25 [9] See *ST* III.5, a. 2, 5

With these and many other expressions, man was crying out to God
and the Lord took pity on him. He freed him in this way:
he descended into the burning bush without damaging the bush—
that is, into the Virgin Mary without the loss of her virginity.
The Lord plagued Pharaoh and all his people
and led out his children into a land flowing with milk and honey.
In such a way, Christ struck at the devil and all his company
and led out the saints from hell to eternal refreshment.

There they are nourished with milk—that is, with the sweet face of his humanity
and with honey—that is, with the honey-sweet contemplation of his divinity.
The Lord, wanting to deliver the Jews, ordered a lamb to be sacrificed as an offering,
but when he wanted to deliver us, he gave himself to be crucified.
God also prefigured this deliverance of mankind *Figure Two*
when he delivered Abraham the patriarch from Ur of the Chaldeans.
The Chaldeans worshiped Ur (that is, fire) in place of God.
When Abraham refused to do that, they threw him into the fire.
But the true God, whom he worshiped and adored,
delivered him mercifully from the fire of the Chaldeans.
Thus, just as God preserved Abraham in the fire without him burning up,
so did he preserve the saints in hell without damage to any of them.
And just as the Lord rescued Abraham and made him the father of many nations.
So did he redeem the fathers from hell and unite them with the assemblage of angels.
God also prefigured this redemption for mankind *Figure Three*
when he delivered Lot with his household from the overthrow of Sodom.
Only the good had been delivered out of Sodom
but everyone evil perished by fire and brimstone.
Thus Christ set free the good only from Limbo,
but from hell he rescued none of the damned.
Therefore, let no one say "God has broken open hell
and who is there who could restore it?"
It was not breached, but rather those who entered, starting from the beginning of the world,

Numquam fuerunt erepti sed semper sine fine ibi erunt.[1]
O pie deus dignare nos ab illo inferno custodire

35rb[2] Et in hac uita purgare misericorditer et punire.
Hic cruciamina hic flagella hic plagas nobis inferas
Vt nos a perpetuis flagellacionibus eripias.
Quos enim amas dicis te uelle hic castigare[3]
Rogamus ergo piissime domine ut digneris nos sic amare.
Melius est nobis cum aduersitatibus ad te uenire
Quam per temporalem prosperitatem eternaliter interire.[4]
Si inter flagella pacientes sumus non attendas
S⌊ed⌋[5] uelimus nolimus semper nos per flagella saluare intendas.
Fragiles sumus et sine murmure non possimus sustinere
Sed tu piissime domine nobis pacientiam indulgere.
Notandum autem quod dominus precepit loth et suis montem ascendere
Non respicere retro sed ad ascendendum intendere.[6]
Sic homo quem deus per penitentiam eripuit
Non debet respicere per delectacionem ad peccata que derelinquit.
Sed debet de uirtute in uirtutem sursum ascendere
Et satisfactioni et operibus virtuosis uiriliter intendere.
Vxor loth respiciens retro versa est in lapidem
Et fere deserti et bestie lambunt eam.
Sic homo per recidiuacionem tamquam lapis induratur
Et a bestiis infernalibus lambitur et temptatur.
Quapropter montem uirtutum ascendamus ut saluemur
Et non respiciamus retro per recidiuacionem ne dampnemur.
O bone ihesu doce nos sic ascendere et celestia amare
Vt tecum in monte sancto tuo mereamur in perpetuum habitare.

---

[1] See Aquinas *ST* III.52.6 [2] Right Panel: Lot's Wife Turned to a Pillar of Salt. One of the messages in all the "deliverance from fire" narratives is that one ought not to look back or second-guess the escape (Gen. 19.15–26). The angel with a stalk of grain points the way, while Lot and his daughters (only one shown) climb into the hills. But Lot's wife looks back and is turned into a pillar (*Ionian*) of salt. [3] See Hbr. 12.6 [4] Mt. 18.8–9, Mk. 9.41–47 [5] Sed, L] Si, G [6] Gen. 19.15–26

were never rescued, but will be there forever, without end.
O pious God, deign to keep us from hell

and to purge and punish us mercifully in this life.
May you inflict on us torments here, scourges here, plagues here,
so that you may rescue us from eternal scourging.
For you say that those whom you love, you wish to chastise here.
Therefore, we ask, most merciful Lord, that you might deign to love us in such a way.
It is better for us to come to you with suffering
than to perish eternally through temporal prosperity.
If we suffer under the lashes, take no heed;
but, whether we are willing or unwilling, yet always endeavor to save us by affliction.
We are frail, and cannot endure without grumbling
but, most merciful Lord, grant us patience.
It should be noted, moreover, that the Lord ordered Lot and his household to climb the mountain,
not to look behind, but to pay attention to climbing.
So too the man whom God has saved through penance
should not look back by [indulging in] pleasure at the sins which he has left behind.
But ought to climb upwards from virtue to virtue
and to strive courageously with reparation and virtuous deeds.
Lot's wife, looking back, was turned into stone
and the wild animals and beasts of the wilderness licked her.
Thus a man is hardened like stone through a relapse into sin
and is licked and worried at by hellish beasts.
Accordingly let us climb the mountain of virtues and be saved
and not look back by a relapse into sin, lest we be damned.
O good Jesus, teach us to ascend in this way and to love heavenly things,
so that we may become worthy to dwell with you on your holy mountain forever.

35[va] *Capitulum xxxii*[1]

*I*n precedenti capitulo audiuimus de hominis redempcione
Consequenter audiamus de gloriosa christi resurrectione.
Sciendum autem quod sepulchrum domini est cauatum in petra[2]
Et uidetur esse tamquam duplex camera parua.[3]
Quando homo primo intrat inuenit cameram paruulam
Que excauata est in petra iacente non in terra sed super terram.
Et habet circa septem uel octo pedes tam in longum quam in latum
Et in altum quantum homo potest extendere manum.
Ex ista camera intratur per paruam hostiam in aliam
Que habet fere eundem longitudinem et altitudinem.
Et quando homo ingreditur per hostium paruulum iam prefatum
A dextris videt locum vbi corpus fuit collocatum.
Et est tamquam scampnum latitudinis circiter trium pedum.
Et longitudo extendit se de uno pariete ad alterum.
Altitudo predicti scampni habet fere pedem et dimidium
Et non est concauum ergo corpus non erat intra sed supra ipsum positum
Quidam peregrini hoc scampnum sepulchrum appellant
Sed iudei totam petram cum ambabus cameris sepulchrum uocant.
Hostium monumenti graui lapide erat obfirmatum
Sed sigillis iudeorum communitum et sigillatum.
Sepulto ˋenimˊ domino iudei signa sua lapidi apposuerunt
Et per talem modum ne furaretur corpus lapidem signauerunt.
Insuper paganos milites mercede et precio conducebant
Et eos ad custodiendum sepulchrum ibi ponebant.
Christus autem clauso hostio et saluis sigillis exiuit

35[vb4] Quia corpus glorificatum ipsum lapidem pertransiuit
Post hoc angelus domini in forma hominis de celo descendit.
Et uidentibus custodibus lapidem de hostio reuoluit
Cuius facies sicut fulgur et uestes albe erant
Terra tremuit et custodes territi uelut mortui iacebant.

---

[1] Left Panel: The Resurrection. Christ with his banner of victory rises from the tomb over the sleeping soldiers (Mt. 27.60–66, 28.1–15; Mk. 16; Lk. 24.1–7; John 20.1–9). The soldiers set to guard the tomb, here sleeping, are an interpolation derived from the command that the tomb should be guarded (Mt. 27.62–66). [2] Mt. 27.60–66, 28.1–15, Mk. 16, Lk. 24, John 20 [3] Cf. Mk. 16.5 [4] Right Panel: Samson Carries Away the Gates of Gaza. When the Philistines knew that Samson was asleep in their city they barred the gates so that he could not escape. Samson woke and carried off both gates and their anchor posts (Jdg. 16.1–3). Gregory the Great in his *Moralia in Iob* (19.7) established this feat as an antitype for Christ's bursting forth from the prison of his tomb. The illustration here closely parallels that in the *Biblia Pauperum*, plate 29.

Chapter Thirty-two

In the last chapter we heard about the redemption of mankind;
next we shall hear about the glorious resurrection of Christ.
Moreover, it should be known that the tomb of the Lord was carved in rock,
and it seems as if the small chamber were divided.
When a man first enters he finds a very small chamber,
which was hollowed into a rock lying not in the ground but above the ground,
and it is around seven or eight feet, both in length and width,
and in height as high as a man is able to raise his hand.
From that room, one enters through a small doorway into another
which has about the same measurement in length and depth.
And when a man enters through the small, aforementioned doorway,
to the right he sees the place that the body was laid
and there is a sort of bench nearly three feet wide,
and it stretchs itself from one wall to the other.
The height of the aforementioned bench is almost a foot and a half,
and it was not hollow. Therefore, the body was not placed within it but was placed upon it.
Some pilgrims call this bench his tomb,
but the Jews call the whole rock with both rooms the tomb.
The doorway of the sepulcher was fastened with a heavy stone,
but it was secured and sealed with the seals of the Jews.
For, when the lord was buried, the Jews set their own stamps on the stone,
and they sealed the stone in this way so that the body would not be stolen.
On top of that, they hired pagan soldiers with money and bribes,
and they placed them there to guard the tomb.
Yet Christ went out with the door closed and the seals intact,

since his glorified body passed through the rock itself.
Afterwards an angel of the Lord descended from heaven in the form of a man.
And he rolled back the stone from the doorway with the guards watching,
his appearance was like lightning and his clothes were white,
the earth trembled and the guards lay terrified, as if dead.

Cum autem uires recepissent ad iudeos redierunt
Et omnia que facta fuerant eis per ordinem narrauerunt.
Illi autem inito consilio dederunt ipsis pecuniam copiosam
Vt diuulgarent ubique de christo famam mendosam.
Vt dicerent ipsis dormientibus corpus esse furatum
Et hoc tam a iudeis quam a custodibus vbique diuulgatum.
¶Notandum est autem quod christus suam gloriosam resurrectionem *prima figura.*
Olim prefigurauerat per fortissimum sampsonem.
Sampson ciuitatem inimicorum suorum introiuit[1]
Et in ea nocte manens ibidem dormiuit.
Inimici autem eius portas ciuitatis concluserunt
Et ipsum mane interficere disposuerunt.
Sampson autem media nocte a sompno surgebat
Et portam cum postibus et ianuis secum ferebat.
Sic christus vrbem hostium suorum id est infernum potenter intrauit
Et ibi usque ad mediam noctem dominice diei habitauit.
Media autem nocte destructo inferno anima ad corpus rediit
Et sic christus qui mortuus fuerat resurrexit.
Multa corpora sanctorum cum ipso resurrexerunt.[2]
Et intrantes ciuitatem ierusalem multis apparuerunt.

36ra[3]
Et non est putandum quod in parasceue corpora surrexerunt
Sed illa die sepulchra solummodo aperta fuerunt.
Christus primogenitus mortuorum[4] surrexit primo
Et nunc[5] corpora sanctorum surrexerunt cum eo.
Et ita christo ascendente cum eo simul ascenderunt
⸤Non⸥[6] est credendum hiis qui dicunt quod iterum obierunt[7]
¶Christus etiam resurrectionem suam per jonam prefigurauit *secunda figura.*
Quem in uentrem ceti per triduum conseruauit.[8]
Jonas erat in naui que tempestatibus iactabatur
Et interitum omnium qui in ipsa erant minabatur.
Tunc dixit jonas nautis ut ipsum in mare iactarent
Et sic tempestas maris et pericula cessarent
Quem cum iactassent statim cetus eum deglutiuit
Et post triduum ipsum de ore uiuum in terram emisit.

---

[1] Jdg. 16.1–3 [2] Mt. 27.51–53 [3] Left Panel: The Fish Spits out Jonah. As the prophet went in to the maw of the great fish (31R Right Panel), now he comes out (Jon. 2.1–10), escaping his "three-day prison." Unusually, this image does not show the land. [4] Col. 1.18, Apc. 1.5 [5] nunc] tunc, L [6] Non, L] Hoc, G [7] Cf. Mt. 28.9–10, 16, Mk. 16.9, 12, 14, Lk. 24.14–16, 29–30, 36, John 20.16, 19, 26, 21.1–3, Act. 1.2–3, 1 Cor. 15.5–8 [8] Jon. 1.4–2.10

But when they had revived, they returned to the Jews,
and they told them all the things which had happened to them from first to last,
and, having hatched a plan, the Jews gave them a large amount of money
so that they might spread everywhere a false rumor about Christ:
that they should say that while they were sleeping, his body was stolen.
And this was spread everywhere by both the Jews and the guards.
And it must be noted that Christ formerly prefigured *Figure One*
his own glorious resurrection through Samson the mighty.
Samson entered his enemies' city,
and remaining there that night, he went to sleep.
However, his enemies closed the gates of the city
and they arranged to kill him in the morning.
However, Samson woke up in the middle of the night
and carried away with him the gate, along with the posts and the doors.
So too Christ powerfully entered the city of his own enemies, that is hell,
and there he stayed until the middle of that night on that Sunday.
And in the middle of the night when hell was destroyed, his soul returned to the body,
and so Christ, who had died, arose to life.
Many bodies of saints arose again with him.
And entering the city of Jerusalem, they appeared to many.

And it should not be thought that the bodies arose on Good Friday,
but rather on that day the tombs were merely opened.
Christ, the firstborn of the dead, arose first,
and now the bodies of the saints rose up with him.
And so when Christ rose, they rose with him at the same time.
They ought not be believed who say that they will die again.
Christ also prefigured his own resurrection through Jonah, *Figure Two*
whom he preserved for three days in the belly of a whale.
Jonah was on a ship which was tossed about by storms,
and endangered all the people who were on it.
Then Jonah told the sailors that they should throw him in the sea,
and that then the storm and dangers of the sea would cease;
when they had thrown him over, immediately a whale swallowed him.
And after three days it cast him alive out of its mouth onto the land.

Periculosum mare mundus iste designatur
In quo olim homo periculum mortis eterne paciebatur.
Christus autem sponte fecit se in cruce mortificari
Vt posset homo periculo eterne mortis liberari.
Deus autem incorruptum eum conseruauit
Et tercia die ipsum a mortuis resuscitauit.[1] *tercia figura.*
¶Hec resurrectio saluatoris nostri iam pretaxata
Fuit per lapidem quem reprobauerunt edificantes prefigurata.[2]
Temporibus salomonis cum templum domini edificaretur[3]
Contigit ut quidam lapis mirabilis ibi inueniretur.
Edificatores nullum locum sibi aptum inuenire potuerunt

36rb[4]
Et hoc pluries cum magno labore temptauerunt
Aut fuit nimis longus aut nimis spissus
Aut nimis breuis aut nimis dimissus.
Qua propter indignati edificantes ipsum eiciebant
Et omnes eum lapidem reprobatum proprio nomine dicebant.
Consumato autem templo lapis angularis ponendus erat
Qui in se duos parietes concludere et totum complere debebat.
Sed non est inuentus lapis qui posset illi aptari
Super quo non sufficiebant edificatores admirari.
Ad ultimum autem lapidem quem reprobauerunt adduxerunt
Et ipsum aptissimum pro angulari lapide inuenerunt.
Ad tam grande miraculum omnes stupebant
Et aliquid magnum futurum per hoc designari dicebant.
Christus erat lapis designatus[5] in sua passione
Sed factus ecclesie lapis angularis in sua resurrectione.
Tunc impleta est illa prophetia prophete magni
Lapidem quem reprobauerunt edificantes. hic factus est in caput a⌊n⌋guli.
A domino factum est istud et est mirabile in oculis nostris[6]
Qua propter cantatur prophetia hec in festo resurrectionis.
Lapis iste duos parietes in templo dei coadunauit
Quia christus de populo gentili et iudaico I ecclesiam edificauit.[7]

---

[1] 1 Cor. 15.3–4 [2] Ps. 117.22, Mt. 21.42, Mk. 12.10, Lk. 20.17–18. Cf. Is. 28.16 [3] 3 Kings 5 [4] Right Panel: Stone Rejected becomes the Keystone. Although sometimes represented as the cornerstone at the base of a building, here the "stone that the builders rejected" is a capstone on top of a tower. The phrase draws on a Messianic psalm quoted in Isaiah and in three gospels (Ps. 117.22; Is. 8.13–15; Mt. 21.42; Mk. 12.10; Lk. 20.17–18), among other sources. The narrative which relates this saying (sung in the Easter liturgy) to the building of Solomon's Temple does not derive from the biblical account in 3 Kings 6, but from a rabbinic tale of uncertain origin. [5] designatus] reprobatus, *L* [6] Ps. 117.22–23 [7] Cf. Mt. 16.18, 26.61, Mk. 14.58, John 2.19, Eph. 2.20

This world is symbolized by the dangerous sea,
in which man formerly was suffering from the danger of eternal death.
But Christ willingly gave himself to be killed on a cross,
so that man could be freed from the danger of eternal death.
Yet God preserved him, uncorrupted,
and on the third day he raised him from the dead. *Figure Three*
This aforementioned resurrection of our savior
was prefigured through the stone that the builders rejected.
In the times of Solomon when the temple of the Lord was built,
it happened that a certain marvelous stone was discovered there.
The builders were able to discover no fitting place for it,

and oftentimes they attempted it with great toil.
It was either too long or too wide
or too short or too low.
Accordingly, the angry builders threw it away,
and all were calling it "the rejected stone," as its own name.
However, when the temple was completed, a corner stone had to be placed,
which in itself ought to bring together the two walls and complete the whole thing.
But a stone was not found which could be made to fit it,
about which the builders could not marvel enough.
Finally, however, they brought forth the stone which they had rejected,
and they found that it was exceedingly suitable for the corner stone.
They were all confounded at such a great miracle,
and they said that some great future event was symbolized through this.
Christ was the stone, marked out in his passion,
but became the cornerstone of the church in his resurrection.
Then the prophecy of the great prophet was fulfilled,
"The stone which the builders rejected, it has become the cornerstone.
This was done by the Lord and is marvelous in our eyes."
Accordingly, this prophecy is sung on Easter.
That stone joined two walls of the temple of God
because Christ built one church from both the Gentiles and Jews.

In hoc edificio pro cemento usus est suo sanguine
Pro lapidibus autem usus est suo sanctissimo corpore.[1]
O bone ihesu presta nobis ut in tua ecclesia ita uiuamus
Vt in templo tuo celesti super tecum maneamus.

36va *Capitulum xxxiii*[2]

*I*n precedenti capitulo audiuimus de gloriosa christi resurrectione
Consequenter audiamus de admirabili eius ascensione.
Christus resurgens ex mortuis non statim ascendit
Sed xl diebus manens pluries se onstendit.[3]
XI die bis se discipulis suis demonstrauit
Et ipsis videntibus per nubem candidam celos penetrauit.
Discipuli autem stabant et post ipsum in celos aspexerunt.
Et ecce duo angeli in uestibus albis iuxta eos steterunt
Qui dixerunt ihesum sic ad iudicium debere uenire
Quemadmodum uidebant eum in celum ire.[4]
¶Hec ascensio olim in scala fuit prefigurata *prima figura*.
Que patriarche iacob in sompnis fuit demonstrata.[5]
Que una extremitate terram et alia in celum tangebat
Et milicia angelorum per eam descendebat et ascendebat.
Sic [/ch]ristus[6] de celo descendit et reascendit
Quando celestia et terrestria uisitare uoluit.
Oportebat enim quod mediator ⌊deus⌋[7] et homo esset[8]
Quia aliter pacem inter deum et hominem reformare non posset.
Deus enim altissimus est et homo infimus erat
Et ideo christus inter celum et terram scalam faciebat.
Nunc ⌊de⌋scendunt[9] angeli per illam gratiam nobis aportando
Et reascendunt animas nostras in celum reportando.
Numquam prius talis scala in mundo facta fuit
Et ideo numquam aliqua anima in celum ascendere potuit
Benedicta sit hec beatissima et utilissima scala

[1] See 1 Pt. 2.5 [2] Left Panel: Ascension of Christ. The gospel accounts represented (Mk. 16.12–19; Lk. 24.50–52) describe how, after his final commission to his disciples, Jesus rose into the clouds. Following this the disciples were comforted by two angels (Act. 1.9–11). The image here attempts a literal depiction, except for the kneeling female figure on the left who probably represents Mary, but of whom there is no mention in the text. [3] Cf. Mk. 16.12–19, Lk. 24.50–52, John 21.1 [4] Act. 1.9–11 [5] Gen. 28.10–18 [6] Here the letter chi appears to be added by a later scribe [7] *deus*, L] *dei*, G [8] Cf. 1. Tim. 2.5 [9] *descendunt*, L] *ascendant*, G

In this building he used his own blood instead of cement,
and he used his most holy body in place of stones.
O good Jesus, grant to us that we may so live in your church
that we may abide in your celestial temple above with you.

Chapter Thirty-Three

In the last chapter we heard about the glorious resurrection of Christ,
next we shall hear about his wonderful ascension.
Christ, rising from the dead, did not ascend immediately,
but stayed for forty days and showed himself several times.
On the fortieth day he showed himself twice to his disciples,
and with them watching, he entered the heavens in a bright cloud.
And the disciples were standing and looked into the heavens after him.
And lo, two angels in white garments stood near them
who said Jesus would come thus in judgment
in the way they were seeing him go into the sky.
This ascension formerly had been prefigured in the ladder *Figure One*
which had been shown in dreams to the patriarch Jacob.
One end of it was touching the earth and the other heaven,
and a host of angels were descending and ascending on it.
So Christ descended from heaven and ascended again,
when he wanted to visit heavenly and earthly places.
For it was fitting that he be God's mediator and a man,
since otherwise he would not be able to renew the peace between God and man.
For God is highest and man was lowest,
and therefore Christ made a ladder between heaven and earth.
Now the angels descend by it to carry grace to us,
and they ascend it again to carry our souls into heaven.
Never before was such a ladder made in the world,
and therefore no soul was ever able to ascend into heaven.
May this most blessed and most useful ladder be praised,

36vb[2]
Per quam parata est ascensio tam longa et tam mala[1].
¶Hanc etiam ascensionem christus in celum prenotauit *secunda figura*.
Quando parabolam de oue perdita et reinuenta predicauit.[3]
Dixit enim de quodam qui de centum ouibus unam [perdidit][4] amisit
Et dimittens lxxxx nouem in deserto ad querendum illam iuit.
Quam cum inuenisset multum exultabat
Et in humeris suis ipsam ponens in domum suam reportabat.
Conuocansque amicis suis gaudium suum illis indicauit
Et eos ad congaudendum sibi sollicite incitauit.
Per istum hominem deus est designatus
Quia pro nostra salute homo fieri est dignatus.
Centum oues faciunt unam et nonaginta nouem
Per hoc debemus intelligere nouem choros angelorum et hominem.[5]
Ex hiis una ouis perdita est et periit
Quando homo mandata dei transgressus eterna morte interiit.
Deus autem nouem choros angelorum in celo dimisit
Et ueniens in hunc mundum hominem perditum quesiuit.
Per xxxiii annos quesiuit et intantum se fatigauit.
Quod de toto corpore sudor sanguineus emanauit.[6]
Vide homo quantum te inuenire cupiebat
Qui cum tanto labore et tam longo tempore te querebat.
Inuenta⌊m⌋ autem ouem super humeros suos posuit et portauit
Quando crucem pro peccatis nostris propriis humeris bauilauit.
Attende homo quod nullam habuit fatigacionem inquirendo
Sed etiam usque ad mortem[7] te in celum referendo.

37ra[8]
Amicos suos ad congratulandum sibi inuitauit
Quando cum homine ascendit et omnem celi curiam letificauit.
O homo si cupis deum et omnem celi miliciam letificare
Studeas uitam tuam et etiam aliorum emendare.

---

[2] Right Panel: Jacob's Ladder. In Jacob's dream at Bethel (Gen. 28.12–17) he had been sleeping on a stone pillow; here he reclines on his elbow while two angels ascend a ladder into heaven. The ladder is taken to be an antitype for Christ's descent to the earth and his ascent from it (Augustine, *Contra Faustum* 12.25; cf. Serm. 89.5; 122.2), descent referring to the Incarnation and ascent to the Ascension. [1] mala] lata, L [3] Lk. 15.3–7, Mt. 18.12–14. The extended version of the parable in the Gospel of Luke is referenced verbatim in the following lines. [4] Deletion by scribal subpunction [5] Cf. Isidore of Seville, *Allegoriae quaedam sacrae scripturae* (Col. 121A, no. 173) [6] Lk. 22.44 [7] See Phlp. 2.8 [8] Left Panel. Good Shepherd and Lost Sheep. Less intuitive in its connection with the Ascension is the parable of the 99 sheep left behind for the sake of recovering one lost sheep depicted here (Lk. 15.3–7). The rejoicing of the good neighbors after the Good Shepherd (i.e., Christ) brings home the sheep (not "on his shoulders," as in our image) has been visually characterized since the biblical text (Lk. 15.7) as referring to the rejoicing of the angels over a single sinner who repents. Here the rejoicing in heaven seems to be linked to the completion of Jesus' ministry on earth.

through which has been prepared an ascension was prepared, so long and so grievous,
Christ also foretold this ascension into heaven *Figure Two*
when he told the parable of the lost sheep that was found again.
For he spoke about a certain shepherd, who, out of a hundred sheep, lost one
and leaving the ninety-nine in the desert, he went to search for that one.
When he had found it, he rejoiced greatly
and placing it on his shoulders, he carried it back into his house.
And calling together his friends, he showed them his joy
and eagerly encouraged them to rejoice with him.
Through that man God is indicated,
since, for the sake of our salvation, he deigned to become man.
The one hundred sheep make one and ninety-nine.
Through this, we should understand the nine choirs of angels and mankind.
Out of these, one sheep was lost and vanished
when mankind, having transgressed God's commands, perished in eternal death.
But God left the nine choirs of angels in heaven
and coming to this earth, searched for lost mankind.
For thirty-three years he searched, and he wearied himself to such a degree
that bloody sweat was flowing from his whole body.
Behold, man, how much he wished to find you,
he who was seeking you with such great labor and for so long a time!
Moreover, he placed the found sheep upon his shoulders and carried it
when he bore the cross on his own shoulders for the sake of our sin.
Consider, man, that he did not grow weary in searching,
nor in carrying you back to heaven, even to the point of death.

He invited his friends to rejoice with him
when he ascended with mankind and gladdened the entire court of heaven.
O man, if you desire to gladden God and all the host of heaven
you should strive to amend your life and the lives of others.

Lacrime enim peccatorum veraciter contritorum
Vinum et sicera[1] sunt omnipotentis dei et sanctorum.
Pura confessio peccatorum et deuota oratio
Sunt deo et sanctis zymbala bene sonancia et zytharizacio.
Panem desiderabilem[2] deo et sanctis exhibemus
Quando uoluntatem dei facimus et mandata eius implemus.
Tot genera ferculorum deo et sanctis ministramus.
In quot generibus bonorum operum vires nostras exercitamus.
Fercula de[i] et sanctorum aromatibus condiuntur
Quando bona opera nostra omnia cum discrecione perficiuntur. *tercia figura*.
¶Hec est ascensio saluatoris iam pretaxata
Olim fuit in translacione helye prefigurata.[3]
Helyas propheta legem dei in iudea predicauit
Et transgressores legis et ydolatras audacter increpauit.
Propter quod sustinuit a iudeis magnam persecucionem
Sed apud deum meruit in paradysum translacionem.
Ita ihesus christus in iudea viam ueritatis docuit
Et propter hoc a iudeis multas persecuciones sustinuit.
Sed deus illum super omnes celos exaltauit
Et nomen super omne nomen illi donauit.
Vt in nomine ihesu omne genu flectatur.

37rb[5] Et eum in gloria dei patris esse omnis lingua confiteatur.[4]
Vide homo quantas christus sustinuit persecuciones et quantam passionem
Priusquam ueniret ad supernam celestem exultacionem.
Si oportebat christum pati et ita in gloriam suam intrare
Multo magis oportet nos propter regnum tribulaciones tolerare.
Christus qui numquam peccatum fecit magnam sustinuit passionem
Et nos propter regnum dei nolumus sufferre modicam tribulacionem.
Et vere modicum et nichil est quod hic sustinemus
Respectv eterni premii quod in futuro recipiemus.[6]
Sicut minutissima gutta est respectv omnium fluuiorum
Ita est omnis tribulacio huius vite respectv eternorum premiorum.
Si totum gaudium mundi tamquam stelle et puluis terre multiplicaretur[7]

[1] Cf. Lk. 1.15 [2] Cf. Dn. 10.3 [3] 4 Kings 2 [5] Right Panel: Elijah Taken up in a Fiery Chariot. In this story of delegation of ministry and spirit followed by a miraculous ascent into heaven (4 Kings 2.9–12) the commentators have seen a compelling antitype for Christ's ascension following his Great Commission to the disciples to continue his ministry in the world. Elijah's translation is seen in general commentary (eg. *PL* 113.611) as prefiguring Christ in his ascension, while his disciple Elisha (*Elyseus* in the image) prefigures the Church.
[4] Phlp. 2.9–11 [6] See Rom. 8.18 [7] Cf. Gen. 22.17

For the tears of truly contrite sinners
are the wine and strong drink of the all-powerful God and of the saints.
An honest confession of sins and devout prayer
are pleasant sounding cymbals and harp-playing for God and the saints.
We presented longed-for bread to God and the saints
when we do the will of God and fulfill his commandments.
We serve up as many kinds of courses of food to God and the saints
as we employ our powers in good works.
The dishes of God and the saints are seasoned with spices
when we accomplish all our good works with discretion. *Figure Three*
This Ascension of our Savior was already predicted;
it was formerly prefigured in the translation of Elijah.
The prophet Elijah preached the law of God in Judea
and boldly rebuked transgressors of the law and idolaters.
On account of which he underwent great persecution from the Jews,
but before God he became worthy to be removed into paradise.
Thus Jesus Christ taught the way of truth in Judea
and on account of this, he underwent many persecutions by the Jews.
But God exalted him above all heavens
and granted him a name above every name.
So that in the name of Jesus, every knee should bow.

And let every tongue confess him to be in the glory of God the Father.
Behold, man, how great the persecutions and how great the Passion Christ withstood
before he came to his heavenly, celestial exultation.
If it was fitting for Christ to suffer and thus enter into his glory
how much more fitting should it be for us to endure tribulations for the kingdom's sake?
Christ, who never committed sin, endured a great Passion
yet for the sake of the kingdom of God, we are not willing to suffer moderate tribulation.
And indeed, what we withstand in this life is moderate and nothing
compared to the eternal reward, which we will receive in the future.
Just as the smallest drop is in comparison to all rivers
so is all the tribulation of this life in comparison to eternal rewards.
If all the joy in the world were multiplied like the stars and the dust of the earth

Absinthium[1] respectv minimi gaudii celi reputaretur.
Si latitudo orbis et firmamenti esset unum pergamentum
Magnitudo minimi gaudii non posset in eo describi ad plenum.
Si omnes aque incaustum essent totum illud consumeretur
Antequam minus gaudium celi ad plenum describeretur.
Si omnia ligna gramina et herbe essent calami scriptorum
Non sufficerent describere numerum gaudi⌊or⌋um eternorum.
Si omnes homines et omnes creature doctores[2] essent
Pulchritudinem dei et celi enarrare non possent.[3]
Si quilibet puluis terre esset millesies clarior sole
Tenebre essent in diuine claritatis comparacione.
O bone ihesu doce nos illuc taliter aspirare
Vt mereamur ibi in perpetuum tecum habitare.

37va *Capitulum xxxiiii*[4]

*I*n precedenti capitulo audiuimus de christi ascensione
Consequenter audiamus de sancti spiritus emissione.
Quando tempore passionis christi apropinquauit
Ipse discipulos suos multis sermonibus confortauit.
Predixit eis suam passionem et resurrectionem
Ascensionem et spiritus sancti missionem.
Modicum inquit uobiscum sum et ad patrem ibo
Non turbetur cor uestrum quia ad uos redibo.[5]
Vado in celum parare uobis locum
Et tunc ueniam et accipiam uos ad me ipsum.[6]
Vos estis qui mecum in temptacionibus meis permansistis
Et ideo in regno meo mecum edere et bibere meruistis.[7]
Mane`te´[8] in dilecione mea[9] et ego in uobis manebo

[1] Cf. Lam. 3.15 [2] doctores] predictores, L [3] The earliest attestation of the phrase appears to be by the first-century Rabbi jachanan ben Zakkai, who said "If all the skies were parchment, and if all the oceans ink, and the wood of all the trees were filed down to pens, it would hardly suffice to imprint ... the wisdom of my teachers." [4] Left Panel: Pentecost. Immediately following the longer account of the Ascension (Act. 1.6–11) comes the story of the descent of the Holy Spirit on the disciples, Mary, and other women and brethren of Jesus (Act. 1.14). The narrative of the miraculous tongues of fire and gift of languages on the Feast of Pentecost established a major liturgical feast in Christendom also, and while our image simply has rays emanating from the dove (symbolizing the Holy Spirit), the mighty wind and tongues of fire over each head are mentioned in the text at fol. 38R. [5] John 13.33 [6] John 14.2–3 [7] Lk. 22.28–30 [8] Scribal addition above the line, with a caret [9] John 15.9

it would be considered as wormwood in comparison to the smallest joy of heaven.
If the breadth of the earth and the firmament were one sheet of parchment
the greatness of the smallest joy could not be described on it in full.
If all the water were ink, all of it would be used up
before a slight joy of heaven was described in full.
If all the trees, grasses, and plants were pens for writing
they would not be enough to describe the number of eternal joys.
If all people and all created things were theologians,
they would not be able to recount the beauty of God and of heaven.
If all the dust of the earth were a thousand times brighter than the sun
there would be darkness in comparison to divine brightness.
O good Jesus, teach us to desire to reach to that place,
so that we may worthily dwell there with you eternally.

Chapter Thirty-four

In the last chapter, we heard about the ascension of Christ
next let us hear about the sending forth of the Holy Spirit.
When the time of Christ's Passion drew near
he encouraged his disciples with many speeches.
He foretold to them his Passion and resurrection,
the ascension and the sending of the Holy Spirit.
"For a little while," he said, "I am with you, and then I shall go to the Father
let not your heart be troubled, since I shall return to you.
I go to heaven to prepare a place for you
and then I shall come and take you to be with me.
You are those who have stayed with me in my trials
and for that reason, you are worthy to eat and drink with me in my kingdom.
Remain in my love and I shall remain in you

Et si per humanitatem abiero per deitatem semper uobiscum ero.
Sicut palmes non potest facere fructum nisi manserit in uite
Sic nec uos poteritis facere nisi manseritis in me.
Ego sum uitis uos autem palmites estis
Si in me manseritis multum fructum facere potestis.[1]
Vos estis palmites et ego sum uitis uera
Pater meus celestis est vinitor et agricola.
Omnem palmitem non auferentem fructum amputabit[2]
Et in ignem inferni eternaliter cremandum iactabit.[3]
Palmitem autem facientem fructum purgabit
Et sic maiorem fructum portabit[4]
Mundus quidem gaudebit uos autem contristabimini.

37vb[5] Sed tristicia uestra vertetur in gaudium quo non priuabimini
Mulier ˋcum´[6] parit tristiciam habet
Cum autem peperit filium omnem tristiciam obliuioni tradet.[7]
Sic et uos quidem in hac uita tristiciam paciemini[8]
Sed in futuro omnem tristiciam obliuiscimini.
Sed quia hec de recessu meo uobis locutus sum
Tristicia implebit et conturbabit cor uestrum.
Sˋc´itote quod expedit uobis ut ego ad patrem uadam[9]
Et alium paraclytum[10] id est spiritum sanctum uobis mittam.
Si enim non abiero paraclytus non ueniet ad uos
Si autem abiero mittam eum ad uos.[11]
Cum autem uenerit ille omnem ueritatem uos docebit
Et nunc cor uestrum de ipsius consolacione gaudebit.
Ipse uos de omnibus informabit
Et que uentura sunt ipse uobis annunciabit.[12]
Hiis et aliis multis uerbis discipulos consolabatur
Et spiritum sanctum se ipsis missurum pollicebatur.
Cum autem ascenderet dixit eis quod in ierusalem residerent
Quousque spiritum sanctum paraclitum acciperent.
Omnes ergo de monte oliueti ciuitatem intrauerunt[13]

---

[1] John 15.4–5 [2] John 15.1–2 [3] John 15.6 [4] John 15.2 [5] Right Panel: Tower of Babel. The gift of tongues at Pentecost, so that foreign people heard the disciples speak in their own mother tongue, is an obvious reversal of Babel (Gen. 11.1–9), in which, because their arrogant assertion that they would get to heaven on their own terms and by the ingenuity of their tall tower, God confounded people's speech, in effect creating a diversity of languages. In our image (titled *mutacio linguarum*), the *turis babel* is being constructed in the manner of a citadel; the workers are observed by Christ, here represented only by head and nimbus. [6] Scribal addition above the line, with a caret [7] John 16.20–22 [8] John 16.33 [9] John 16.6–7, 10 [10] John 14.16 [11] John 16.7b [12] John 16.13 [13] Act. 1.4–2.15

and if I go away as a man, I shall be with you always as God.
Just as the branch cannot produce fruit unless it remains on the vine
so you are not fruitful unless you remain in me.
I am the vine and you are the branches.
If you remain in me, you can produce much fruit.
You are the branches and I am the true vine.
My heavenly Father is the vine-dresser and gardener.
Every branch not bearing fruit he shall cut off
and shall throw into the fire of hell to burn everlastingly.
But the branch producing fruit he shall prune,
and thus it shall bear even more fruit.
The world indeed shall rejoice, yet you shall be saddened.

But your sadness shall turn into joy, of which you shall not be deprived.
A woman has grief when she gives birth,
but when she has borne a child, she forgets all her grief.
And so in this life you shall indeed suffer sadness
but in the time to come, you shall forget all your sadness
but since I have spoken to you these things concerning my departure,
sadness will fill up and disturb your heart.
Know that it is for your good that I go to the Father
and I shall send you another comforter, that is, the Holy Spirit.
For if I do not go away, the comforter will not come to you.
However, if I go I shall send him to you.
But when he comes, he will teach you the whole truth
and then he shall gladden your heart with his comfort.
He will instruct you in all things
and he will announce to you what is to come."
With these and many other words, he consoled his disciples
and promised he would send them the Holy Spirit.
However, when he rose, he said to them that they should remain in Jerusalem
until they receive the Holy Spirit, the paraclete.
Therefore, they all entered the city from the Mount of Olives

Et in quodam cenaculo simul in oratione perseuerauerunt.
In die autem pentecostes tercia die hora
Audita est supra cenaculum uox uenti ualde sonora.
In tantum sonora quod per totam ciuitatem audiebatur
Et totus populus illuc pro nimio stupore congregabatur.

38ra[2] Viderunt autem super [/cuiusque][1] caput quasi linguam igneam
H⌊o⌋c est flammam ignis ad modum lingue longam.
Iudei illo tempore in diuersis regionibus dispersi erant
Et tunc ordinante deo de qualibet regione aliqui conuenerant.
Et isti audierunt eos loquentes uariis linguis
Prout spiritus sanctus dabat eloqui illis.
Singuli lingua in quibus nati erant audiebant
Et nimis mirabantur super hoc et stupebant
Quidam tamen de euidenti miraculo doluerunt[3]
Et ipsos musto plenos et ebrios esse dixerunt.
Petrus autem respondens dixit eos adhuc ieiunare
Quia erat hora tercia et ad bibendum nimis mane.
Adiecit quoque quod illa prophetia n⌊unc⌋ esset impleta
Quam per spiritum sanctum dixerat Iohel propheta.
Quod scilicet serui et ancille domini spiritum sanctum essent acceptur[n/i][4]
Et tamquam prophete diuersas linguas locuturi.[5]
Et hec verba Iohelis illa die implebantur *prima figura*.
Quia tam mulieres quam uiri diuersis linguis loquebantur.
¶Mirabilis deus mirabiliter potenciam suam ostendit.
Sicut considerar⌊e⌋ potest qui diligenter opera sua attendit.
In turri babel vnam linguam in diuersas mutauit[6]
Modo unicuique intelligenciam omnium illarum donauit.
Et quomodo nunc istud miraculum facere potuisset
Si ⌊t⌋unc[7] diuisionem diuersarum linguarum non fecisset.
In eo igitur quod ⌊t⌋unc diuersas linguas creauit

[2] Left Panel: Moses Receives the Ten Commandments. The Jewish Feast of Pentecost celebrated the reception of the law fifty days after the exodus from Egypt. In the canonical account (Ex. 31.18) Moses is alone on the mountain, since any other person or even animal would have been struck dead for approaching it (Ex. 19.21–23). The image here depicts rather a scene from the *Historia Scholastica*, deriving from Jewish legend, which has the people joining Moses in supplication for the gift of the Decalogue. The one who hears the prayer from the clouded nimbus is Christ. [1] The original words here have been scratched out and replaced, likely by a later hand [3] doluerunt] dubitaverunt, L [4] This letter has been corrected from an "n" [5] Joel 2.28–29, Act. 2.17–18 [6] Gen. 11.1–9 [7] Tunc, L] nunc, G; and in following line

and they remained in prayer together in a certain upper room.
However, on the day of Pentecost, at the third hour
the resounding voice of the wind was heard strongly above the room.
It resounded to such an extent that it was heard through the whole city
and all the people congregated there in extreme perplexity.

Moreover, they saw above the head of each one a fiery tongue, as it were,
that is, a long flame of fire like a tongue.
The Jews at that time were dispersed in separate regions
and, as ordained by God, some had then come together from all sorts of regions.
And the Jews heard the disciples speaking in various languages
just as the Holy Spirit was granting them to speak plainly.
Each one heard the language in which he had been born
and they marveled greatly over this and were bewildered.
Certain ones nevertheless deplored the obvious miracle
and they said that the disciples were full of wine and intoxicated.
But Peter, responding, said that they had not yet broken their fast
since it was the third hour and too early for drinking.
He also pointed out that the prophecy had now been fulfilled
which Joel the prophet had spoken through the Holy Spirit,
namely, that the servants and handmaids of the Lord would receive the Holy Spirit
nd, like prophets, would speak various languages.
And these words of Joel were fulfilled that day *Figure One*
since the women as well as the men were speaking various languages.
The wonderful God remarkably demonstrated his power,
as he who attends to God's works diligently can contemplate.
In the tower of Babel he changed one language into many
and now he granted each person an understanding of all of them.
And how could he make that miracle now
if he had not made the division of the various languages then?
In this therefore, because he then created the various languages,

38rb[1]
Miraculum istud quasi per figuram demonstrauit.
Et sicut ⌊t⌋unc per linguas confudit edificantes turrim babel
Ita modo per linguas confudit inimicos suos israel.
Iudei enim multum confusi fuerunt
Quando tam grande miraculum audierunt.
¶Festum pentecosten quod modo agitur ab ecclesia *secunda figura.*
Olim quasi figuraliter peragebatur in synagoga.
Quinquagesima die postquam iudei de egipto exierunt
Decem precepta in monte syna a domino receperunt.[2]
Ita quinquagesima die postquam [n'/nos][3] fuimus de inferno liberati
Receperunt discipuli gratiam spiritus sancti.
Omnia ergo que circa iudeos facta sunt figurata fuerunt
Christiani autem omnia in ueritate receperunt. *tercia figura.*
¶Istud etiam prefiguratum fuit in sup⌊er⌋habundancia olei
Quod datum est paupercule uidue per preces helysei.[4]
Helyseus misericordia motus super pauperculam uiduam.
Impetrauit ei a domino maximam [ei] habundanciam.
Vidua nichil illa nisi modicum olei habebat
Et hoc in tantum augebatur quod omnia uasa que habuit implebat.
Per uiduam istam designatur sancta ecclesia
Que ablata suo sponso christo[5] uidebatur tamquam uidua.
Sed dominus misericordia motus dedit ei olei habundanciam
Hoc est spiritus sancti gratiam et linguarum intelligenciam.
O bone ihesu dignare nobis hoc oleum elargiri
Vt in extremo mereamur in tua gratia inueniri.

[1] Right Panel: Elisha Fills the Widow's Jars. Eliseus heard the plea of an impoverished widow and in order to save her sons from being taken into slavery to pay her debts, he told her to gather many vessels and pour her one vessel into all of them until full. The jars were then sold to pay her debt (4 Kings 4.1–7). There is no account of Elisha praying in the passage; the interpolation may derive from Varaita, 32 Middot via the *Acta Sanctorum* of Peter Damian. [2] *HS* Ex. 36. Cf. Ex. 20 [3] This has been added by a later hand with a caret. The original word was scratched out, but it appears to have been *n'*. Apparently a later scribe felt that the abbreviation wasn't clear enough. [4] 4 Kings 4.1–7 [5] Cf. Eph. 5.22–33

he demonstrated that miracle as if through a figure.
And just as he confused those building the tower of Babel then through languages,
so he confused now through languages his enemies in Israel.
For the Jews were greatly confused
when they heard so powerful a miracle.
The Feast of Pentecost, which is now performed by the church, *Figure Two*
was once, as it were, figuratively carried out in the synagogue.
On the fiftieth day after the Jews went out from Egypt
they received the ten commandments on the mountain of Sinai from the Lord.
So on the fiftieth day after we were freed from hell
the disciples received the grace of the Holy Spirit.
Thus, all the things that were done among the Jews had been prefigured.
The Christians, however, received everything in the fullness of truth. *Figure Three*
That thing was also prefigured in the overabundance of oil
which was given to the poor widow through the prayers of Elisha.
Elisha, moved by compassion over the poor widow,
obtained for her from the Lord the greatest abundance [of oil].
That widow had nothing except a little bit of oil
and this was increased to such an extent that she filled up all the vessels she had.
The Holy Church is indicated through that widow
who, having been snatched away from her husband Christ, seemed like a widow.
But the Lord, moved by compassion, gave her an abundance of oil,
that is, the grace of the Holy Spirit and the understanding of languages.
O good Jesus, deign to increase this oil for us,
so that at the moment of death we may worthily be found in your grace.

38va *Capitulum xxxv*[1]

*I*n precedenti capitulo audiuimus de spiritus sancti missione
Consequenter audiamus de beate uirginis sancta conuersacione.
Post ascensionem domini beata uirgo in ierusalem habitauit
Omnia loca filii sui que attingere potuit deuote uisitauit.
Et pre dulcedine amoris singula loca osculabatur
Cum genu flexionibus et oracionibus uenerabatur.
Multa lacrimarum effusione ipsa loca irrigabat
Quando mellifluam presenciam filii sui recogitabat.[2]
Visitauit in nazareth locum concepcionis
In bethleem locum generacionis et adoracionis.
In monte thabor locum transfiguracionis
In ierusalem singula loca contumelie et passionis.
Item visitauit montem syon vbi pedes discipulorum lauit
Et sacramentum eucharistie primitus instaurauit.
Villam Getzamany vbi in ort⌊o⌋[3] sanguinem sudauit
Vbi eum iudas tradidit et turba captiuauit
Domum anne cui primo fuit [ca]presentatus
Vbi alapam serui suscepit et in multis est accusatus.
Domum cayphe vbi fuit consputus et uelatus.
Illusus alapis cesus et colaphizatus.
Domum herodis vbi fuit pro derisu ueste alba indutus.
Ab herode et exercitu suo desputus et illusus.[4]
Pretorium pylati vbi fuit falso accusatus
Flagellis cesus corona spinea coronatus.
Locum gabatha qui etiam lycostratos consueuit appellari

38vb[6] Vbi pylatus condempnans ihesum sedit pro tribunali.[5]
Vi{ll}am etiam illam sepius cum luctu insequebatur
Per quam christus baiulans crucem ad mortem ducebatur

[1] Left Panel. The Virgin Revisits Holy Places. The Golden Legend (*LA*, 119) tells how after the Pentecost miracle Mary decided to visit notable scenes from Jesus' life, at each point in her pilgrimage kissing the ground. The image is arranged like a complex altarpiece, with Mary at the center. On the left, from the bottom up, are shown the Annunciation, Nativity, and foot-washing, on the right, from the top down, the Last Supper, Entombment, and Ascension. Surmounting all is a head of Christ, flanked by instruments of the Passion. [2] See *LA* (119) [3] L] ortu, G [4] Lk. 23.11 [6] Right Panel: Tobias Mourned by his Mother. When Tobias sends out Tobias to recover owed money, his mother weeps at the prospect of his not returning, but is reassured by her husband that he will have a guardian angel to see him home again (Tb. 5.17–22). The image shows the angel Raphael assisting Tobias up the hill as he begins his journey. The dog in the illustration is a reference to Tob. 5:16. Eventually *uxor Tobit* goes looking for her son (Tb. 11.5–6). [5] John 19.13

Chapter Thirty-Five

In the last chapter we heard about the sending of the Holy Spirit,
next let us hear about the holy conduct of the blessed Virgin.
After the ascension of the Lord, the blessed Virgin lived in Jerusalem.
All the shrines of her son that she could reach she visited devotedly
and she kissed each place out of the sweetness of love
when she adored with bent knee and prayers.
She watered the shrines with many shed tears
when she recalled the honey-sweet presence of her son.
In Nazareth, she visited the place of his conception;
in Bethlehem, the place of his birth and adoration;
on Mount Tabor, the place of his transfiguration;
in Jerusalem, each place of his humiliation and Passion.
Likewise, she visited Mount Zion, where he washed the feet of the disciples
and first celebrated the sacrament of the Eucharist;
the estate of Gethsemane, where he sweated blood in the garden,
where Judas betrayed him and the mob captured him;
the home of Annas, at which he was first presented,
where he bore the slaps of a slave and was accused of many things;
the home of Caiaphas, where he was spit upon and blindfolded,
Ridiculed, struck with blows, and cuffed about the ears;
the house of Herod, where he was clothed with a white garment in mockery,
spit on and ridiculed by Herod and his army;
the palace of Pilate, where he was falsely accused,
beaten with whips, crowned with a thorny crown;
the place of Gabbatha, which is also commonly called Lithostrotos

where Pilate, condemning Jesus, sat in the judgment seat.
Grieving, she also often followed that road
by which Christ, bearing the cross, was led to his death.

Item locum caluarie qui golgata dicebatur.
Vbi crucifixus aceto et felle potabatur.[1]
Ortum ioseph ab aromathia vbi erat sepultus
Et montem oliueti vbi tandem est assumptus
Item templum et alia loca vbi predicauerat et docuerat
Et loca vbi post resurrectionem suam apparuerat.
Omnia hec loca et plurima alia cum lacrimis uisitauit
Et absenciam sui filii lamentabiliter deplorauit
Lugere ⌊et⌋ dolere quam gaudere ipsa maluit.
Quamdiu melliflua presencia filii sui caruit.
¶Iste dolor et luctus gloriose uirginis marie[2]
Olim prefiguratus fuit in anna uxore thobie.
Que post abscessum filii sui semper luxit et fleuit
Nec consolari uoluit donec filius suus rediit
Omnes uias vbi erat spes redeundi circumspexit.
Et montes ascendens in ipsius occursum respexit.[3]
Presenciam filii sui esse diuicias putauit
Et eo presente paupertatem suam sibi sufficere affirmauit.
Sic maria semper in luctu perseuerauit.
Et omnes uias filii sui prout potuit ambulauit.
Presenciam filii sui super omnes diuicias computasset
Et eo presente paupertatem suam regnum estimasset.

39ra[4] ¶[5]Precedensque dolor etiam in evvangelio notatur
Vbi parabola de muliere querente dragmam recitatur.[6]
Que habens x dragmas vnam amisit
Et accendens lucernam eam diligenter quesiuit.
Et cum inuenisset eam gauisa est et exultabat
Et uicinas suas ad congratulandum sibi inuitabat.
Per hanc mulierem uirgo maria designatur
Que in hoc mundo x dragmas habuisse comprobatur.
De quibus unam videtur aliqualiter amisisse
Et alios ix semper ibi retinuisse.

---

[1] Mt. 27.48 [2] The figure indictor is missing, but should be around this line [3] Tb. 11.5–6 [4] Left Panel: Lost Silver Coin Found. The image here depicts the second parable about rejoicing when that which was lost is found (Lk. 15.8–10). A woman searching for a missing coin holds a lamp; she is surrounded by images of the ten coins, each worth about a day's wage. Like the story of the lost sheep which precedes it, it occasions focus on the joy of recovery (e.g., Augustine, *On the Merits and Remission of Sins* 1.40). [5] The cue for the mark (an arabic 2) is just barely visible to the left, but the rubricated figure indication is also missing here [6] Lk. 15.8–10

Likewise, the place of Calvary, which is called Golgotha
where, crucified, he was given vinegar and gall to drink;
the garden of Joseph of Arimathea, where he was buried;
and the Mount of Olives, where he was at last raised;
likewise, the temple and other places, where he preached and taught,
and the places where he appeared after his resurrection:
all these places and many others she visited with tears
and grieved over the absence of her son, full of sorrow.
She herself preferred to grieve and to suffer rather than to rejoice
while she lacked the honey-sweet presence of her son.
That sorrow and mourning of the glorious Virgin Mary
was once prefigured in Anna, the wife of Tobias,
who, after the departure of her son, was always mourning and weeping.
She did not wish to be comforted until her son returned.
She watched all the roads on which there was hope of him returning
and, climbing a mountain, she looked for a meeting with him.
She thought that the presence of her son was riches
and, with him present, she declared that her poverty was good enough for her.
So Mary always remained constant in grief
and she walked all the ways of her son that she could.
She would have esteemed the presence of her son above all riches
and with him present, she would have judged her poverty a kingdom.

And her surpassing sorrow was also noted in the Gospel
where the parable of the woman seeking the drachma is related.
She, having ten drachmas, lost one
and lighting a lamp, she searched for it diligently.
And when she had found it, she was glad and rejoiced
and invited her neighbors to rejoice with her.
Through this woman the Virgin Mary is indicated,
who on this earth is said to have had ten drachmas.
Of which, it seems she lost one somehow
and the other nine she always kept there.

Nouem dragma sunt presencia spirituum beatorum
Qui semper ueniebant ad eam de choris angelorum.
Decima fuit presencia humanitatis saluatoris
Quam amisit quodammodo in die ascensionis.
Hanc ualde diligenter multis annis quesiuit
Quando omnia loca filii sui cum luctu circumiuit.
Tandem inuenit eam in sua assumpcione
Quando dotata est eterna christi fruicione.
Lucernam quando eam quesiuit accendit
Per quam designatur bonum exemplum quod ostendit.
Nam conuersacio eius sancta tamquam lucerna ardebat
Et cunctis exemplum bonum et uiam uite ostendebat.
Predicta ergo loca debemus exemplo eius perambulare
Et compassionem[1] christi recolendo feruenter deplorare.
Quod si nequimus ea perambulare corporaliter

39rb[2] Perambulemus saltem ea deuoto corde spiritualiter.
¶Dolor beate marie uirginis iam pretaxatus *tercia figura*.
Etiam fuit olim in Mychol sponsa dauid prefiguratus.
Quam saul pater eius abstulit sponso suo dauid
Et alteri uiro cui nomen phaltyel desponsauit.[3]
Phaltyel autem vir iustus et bonus eam non cognoscebat
Quia legittimam uxorem esse eam sciebat.
Ipsa autem semper in luctu et merore preseuerauit
Donec reducta est ad sponsum suum uirum dauid.
Istud exponi potest de beata uirgine maria
Cuius sponsus erat filius dei vera sophia.
De cuius absencia ipsa in tantum dolebat
Quod semper in luctu semper in merore manebat.
Tanto ardore maria sponsum istum diligebat
Quod pre nimio amoris feruore languescebat.
Et hoc est quod ipsa dicit in cantic[u/is][4] canticorum
Insinuans suorum ardorem desideriorum.
Filie ierusalem nunciate dilec⌊t⌋o meo

[1] compassionem] passione, L [2] Right Panel: Saul Makes Michal Marry Phaltiel. In his anger at David, King Saul marries Michal, David's wife, to Phaltiel (1 Kings 25.44). When David takes her back (2 Kings 3.13–16), Phaltiel is said to follow behind, weeping. The canonical text does not suggest, as our text does, that Phaltiel had no sexual knowledge of Michal; that detail comes from the *Historia Scholastica* on 2 Kings 5, which seeks an analogy for Joseph. In the image Phaltiel also wears a crown, is protesting by his hand gestures, and Michal has her hand in the posture of lamentation. [3] 1 Kings 26.44, *HS II Regum* 5 [4] Corrected from an original *u*

The nine drachmas are the presence of the spirits of the blessed
who always came to her from the choirs of angels.
The tenth was the presence of the savior's humanity
which she lost, in a certain measure, on the day of Ascension.
This presence she sought very diligently for many years
when she traveled around all the shrines of her son with grief.
Finally, she found it in her own Assumption
when she was endowed with the eternal enjoyment of Christ.
She lit a lamp when she sought for it,
by which is indicated the good example that she showed.
For her holy manner of living burned like a lamp
and in all things, she showed a good example and the pathway of life.
Therefore, we ought to make circuit of the aforementioned shrines by her example
and fervently grieve by recalling the fellow suffering of Christ.
Because, if we cannot tread them physically

we should at least tread them spiritually, with a dedicated heart.
The pain of the blessed Virgin Mary [had been] already predicted *Figure Three*
and had even once been prefigured in Michal, the bride of David,
whom Saul, her father, took away from her husband David
and betrothed to another man, whose name was Phaltiel.
Phaltiel, however, a good and just man, did not know her [sexually]
because he realized that she was a lawfully married woman.
And she persisted always in grief and sorrow
until she was restored to her wedded husband, David.
That can be expounded concerning the blessed Virgin Mary,
whose spouse was the Son of God, true wisdom,
whose absence she suffered so greatly
that she remained always in grief, always in sorrow.
Mary loved that spouse [of hers] with such great ardor
that she grew faint from the very great heat of love.
And this is what she herself said in the Song of Songs,
making known the ardor of her desires:
"Daughters of Jerusalem, announce to my beloved

Quia amore langueo quem scilicet ad ipsum gero.[1]
Magnus dolor est matri in absencia filii
Sed maior dolor est sponse in absencia sponsi.
Marie autem dolor videtur fuisse maximus
Propter absenciam christi. qui erat ei sponsus et filius.
O bone ihesu fac nos hoc ita recogitare
Vt tecum et secum meramur perpetuo habitare.

39va *Capitulum xxxvi*[2]

In precedenti capitulo audiuimus de beate uirginis conuersacione
Consequenter audiamus de ipsius felici assumpcione.[3]
Quantum temporis superuixerit post christi ascensionem
De hoc non habemus certam determinacionem.
Quidam dicunt xii annos quidam vero plus.
Sed viginti quatuor annos dicit sanctus epyphanius.[4]
Et quamuis illud tempus determinatum habemus
Tamen hoc procerto dicere uel credere non audemus.
Quod si tantummodo per vnam horam superuixisset
Pre nimio desiderio lustrum uisum sibi fuisset.
Iacob xiiii annos graue seruitutis et laboris
Reputauit paucos dies propter magnitudinem amoris.[5]
Sic maria absenciam filii sui sibi per unam horam
Pre magnitudinem amoris reputauit lustriam moram.
Anime enim desideranti breuis hora longa videtur
Et pro illo quod desiderat labores graues non ueretur.
Tanta amore maria presenciam filii desiderauit

---

[1] Cf. Ct. 5.8 [2] Left Panel: Coronation of the Virgin. Mentioned by the *Legenda Aurea*, the assumption and coronation of the Virgin are not found in canonical New Testament texts but originate in the late 2nd-century "Discourse of St. John the Divine Concerning the Dormition of the Holy Mother of God." The apocryphal *Transitus Mariae* of the late 5th century contains the germ of much Marian typology. Even though it was condemned by Pope Gelasius it continued to inspire late Marian typology, including that of St. Anthony. First accepted in the East, the iconography of the coronation became popular in Italy from the 13th to the 15th centuries. The title *Regina coeli* appears in the 12th century. Our image is of the type represented by Paola Veneziano (1324). See also St. Anthony of Padua, *Sermo Demonica in Quadragesima* (1.91) and his *Assumptione Sanctae Mariae Virginis* (3.372). [3] See *LA* 119 [4] *LA* 119. Epiphanius Monachus, an eighth or ninth-century monk and priest in Constantinople, wrote a life of the Virgin Mary, *Ystoria gloriose semper virginis Marie.* [5] Gen. 29.20

That I grow faint with the love that I bear for him."
Great is the sorrow of a mother in the absence of her son
but greater is the sorrow of a bride in the absence of the bridegroom.
Yet Mary's sorrow seems to have been the greatest
on account of the absence of Christ, who was to her both spouse and son.
O good Jesus, cause us to consider this in such a way,
that we may merit to dwell with you and with her forever.

Chapter Thirty-Six

In the last chapter we heard of the Blessed Virgin's manner of life
next we shall hear of her happy Assumption.
How much time she lived on after Christ's Ascension:
concerning this we do not have a fixed conclusion.
Some say twelve years, others more.
But St. Epiphanius says twenty-four years
and although we hold that time not firmly established
yet we dare to assert or believe for certain
that if she had lived on only one hour longer
it would have seemed to her a period of purification due to her very great longing.
Jacob considered the fourteen years of hard slavery and labor
but a few days on account of the greatness of his love.
So too Mary considered the absence of her son for one hour
to be a purifying delay due to the greatness of her love.
For a short hour seems long to a desiring heart
and for the sake of that which it desires, it does not fear heavy labors.
With such love did Mary desire the presence of her son

Quod omnes huius uite labores nichil penitus reputauit.
Quod autem dominus eam in mundo tam div relinquebat
Quod pro consolacione discipulorum suorum faciebat.
Et ut quilibet homo per hoc factum consideret
Quod per multas tribulaciones regnum celorum intrare oportet.
Respice mariam et eius filium.
Aduerte christi passionem et matris eius exilium.
Respice apostolos et omnes amicos christi.

39vb[1] Aduerte quantas tribulaciones sustinuerunt isti.
Respice iohannem ⌊qui⌋[2] inter natos mulierum maiorem[3]
Et hoc recogitando leuius feres tuam tribulacionem.
Non te putes sine tribulacione coronari
Ex quo deus permisit matrem suam tam div exulari.
Peracto igitur hac miseria longo exilio
Assumpta est maria cum suo dilectissimo filio.
¶Hec assumpcio beate uirginis fuit olim prefigurata *prima figura*.
Quando archa domini in domum regis dauid est translata.
Rex dauid coram archa domini gaudens zitharizauit[4]
Et eam cum magno iubilo in domum suam deportauit.
In archa illa manna celi continebatur[5]
Et conuenienter per eam beata uirgo designatur.
Nam panem celi ipsa mundo generauit
Id est christum qui nos suo sacramento cibauit.
Archa de ligno cethim imputribili erat facta
Figurans quod maria in putredinem non est redacta.[6]
Licet scriptura non dicat tamen secure credi potest
Quod maria cum corpore et anima [quae][7] assumpta est.
Non est credendum quod maria mortua non fuerit
Sed mortua est verumtamen caro eius non computruit.
Anima coniuncta est corpori mortuo iterato
Et ita assumpta est in celum corpore glorificato.

[1] Right Panel: Ark of the Covenant Returned to the Temple. The ostensible text for this antitype is 2 Kings 6.1–5 but, as the SHS acknowledges, there is no biblical source, canonical or apocryphal, for this Marian exegesis and extrapolation. Because the Ark contained some manna from heaven, and because it was made from extremely perdurable wood, analogies led to further analogies. Canticle of Canticles allegories are also in the background, as noted. David plays his harp in celebration. [2] Erased by scratching out. This probably occurred after the entire line was written, given the large space remaining. [3] Mt. 11.11 [4] 2 Kings 6.14–15 [5] Ex. 16.32–34, Hbr. 9.4. See also *SHS* chapter 10 (fol. 13^{v}, col. B) and chapter 12 (fol. 16^{r}, col. B) [6] Ex. 25.10 ff. [7] Scratched out

that she inwardly considered all the labors of this life nothing,
but that the Lord left her in the world for a very long time.
He did that for the consolation of his disciples
and so that any person may, by this act, consider
that it is fitting to enter into the kingdom of heaven through many tribulations.
Consider Mary and her son;
be mindful of the Passion of Christ and the exile of his mother;
consider the apostles and all the friends of Christ;

Be mindful of how many tribulations they withstood
Consider John, greatest among those born of women
and by thinking of this, you will bear your tribulation more easily.
You should not suppose that you will be crowned without tribulation,
because of which God permitted his mother to be exiled for so long.
Therefore, once this long miserable exile was completed,
Mary was lifted up to her most beloved son.
This Assumption of the Blessed Virgin had once been prefigured *Figure One*
when the Ark of the Lord was transported into the house of King David.
King David, rejoicing, played the lyre before the Ark
and carried it with great joy into his house.
The manna of heaven was contained in the Ark
and the Blessed Virgin is suitably indicated through it.
For she begot the bread of heaven for the world,
that is, Christ, who fed us with his sacrament.
The Ark was made from incorruptible shittim wood,
figuring the fact that Mary was not reduced into rottenness.
Although Scripture may not say [so]; nevertheless it can be believed safely
that Mary was assumed with her body and her soul.
It ought not be believed that Mary was not dead:
but notwithstanding that she was dead, she did not decay in her flesh.
Her soul was united to her dead body again
and thus, with a glorified body, she was assumed into heaven.

Rex dauid qui coram domini archa subsiliendo citharizauit
⌞Regem⌟[1] celi et terre scilicet christum prefigurauit.

40a[3] Creden[/dum est][2] quod christus matri sue personaliter occurrebat
Et cum magno iubilo in domum suam introducebat.
Diuinis o⌞s⌟culis matrem dulcissimam est osculatus
Et mellifluis amplexibus ineffabiliter amplexatus.
Quod uidentes angeli admirantes stupebant
Et pre admiracione querentes inuicem dicebant.
Que est quae ascendit[4] de deserto deliciis affluens
Innixa super dilectum suum et tamquam sponsa blandiens.
Ad hec respondit maria sponsa dei vera
Inueni inquit quem quesiui et \quem/ diligit anima mea.
Tene⌞b⌟o eum et numquam dimittam eum[5]
Tamquam sponsum tamquam filium tamquam patrem meum.
Osculetur me osculo oris sui[6]
Vt perpetuo eius dulcedine debeam frui.
Leua eius sub capite meo
Vt possim semper uiuere et letari cum eo.
Et dextra illius amplexabitur me[7]
Quia secura sum quod numquam repellat[8] a se.
¶Notandum est quod assumpcio marie iam prefata *secunda figura*.
Etiam fuit iohanni in pathmos insula demonstrata.[9]
Signum enim magnum in celo apparebat
Nam mulierem quandam admirabilem in celo uidebat.
Mulier illa sole circumdata erat
Quia maria circumdata diuinitate in celum ascendebat.
Luna sub pedibus eius uidebatur.

[1] Regem, L] Rex, G [3] Left Panel: Woman Clothed with the Sun. A vision of the apostle John on Patmos of the "great sign" appearing in heaven—a woman with the sun for her garment, moon under her feet, and garlanded with twelve stars, who then gives birth to a child—became by the late 15th century a symbol of the Immaculate Conception. St. Epiphanius in the 4th century was among the first to identify the woman with the Virgin Mary. St. Bernard of Clairvaux followed suit (*De Beata Virgine* 2), but another tradition, represented by Pope Gregory the Great, makes the woman a symbol of the Church (*Moralia in Iob* 34.12). Our image and text follow the Marian interpretation, though the woman's garment is not sun-like. She stands on a moon both full and crescent, representing all its phases, while the SHS text makes the twelve stars refer to the apostles. This configuration comes to be basic to the iconography of the Immaculate Conception of Mary. [2] These words have been corrected by the black-ink scribe due to damage from a stain [4] L] descendit, G [5] Ct. 3.4 [6] Ct. 1.1 [7] Ct. 2.6 [8] repellat] repellet, L [9] See Apc. 12. See also *Glossa Ordinaria* on the passage.

King David, who played the lyre, leaping before the Ark of the Lord,
prefigured the King of heaven and earth: namely, Christ.

It ought to be believed that Christ went to meet his mother personally
and with a great cry of joy led her into his house.
With divine kisses he kissed the sweetest mother
and embraced her, with embraces dripping unutterably with sweetness.
Seeing this, the wondering angels were astonished
and were asking one another on account of their wonder, saying:
"Who is she, flowing with delights, who comes up from the desert
supported by her beloved and just like a charming bride?"
To this, Mary, the true bride of God, responded:
"I found," she said "the one whom I sought and whom my soul loved.
I shall hold him and shall never send him away
like my husband, like my son, like my father.
Let him kiss me with the kiss of his mouth
so that I might enjoy his perpetual sweetness.
His left hand beneath my head
so that I may be able to live forever and rejoice with him.
And his right hand shall embrace me
since I am sure that he would never drive me away."
It must be noted that the Assumption of Mary [had been] already foretold. *Figure Two*
It was shown also to John on the island of Patmos.
Truly a great sign appeared in the sky
for he saw a certain wondrous woman in the sky.
This woman was girded with the sun
because Mary, girded with divinity, ascended into heaven.
The moon appeared beneath her feet,

40b[1] Per quod perpetua stabilitas marie designatur.
Luna instabilis est et non div persistit plena
Et designat mundum istum et omnia terrena.
Hec instabilia comtempnens maria omnia sub pedibus concalcauit
Et ad celum vbi omnia stabilia sunt anhelauit.
Coronam etiam mulier in capite suo habebat
Que in se stellas xii continebat.
Corona consueuit esse honoris signum.
Et significat honorem gloriose uirgini condignum.
Per xii stellas apostoli omnes intelliguntur
Qui in decessu marie omnes affuisse creduntur.[2]
Mulieri sunt date due ale ad uolandum
Quia corpus et anim[e/a] marie in celum est assumptum.[3]
¶Item notandum est quod festiuitas huius assumpcionis *tercia figura*.
Etiam figurata fuit in matre regis salomonis.[4]
Salomon enim rex in throno gloriose sue residebat
Et matris sue thronum ad dextram suam poni faciebat.
In quem ipsam iuxta se honorifice collocauit
Fas non est ut tibi aliquid denegem ait.[5]
Sic et christus matrem suam a dextris suis locauit.
Et quodcumque ab eo pecierit sibi non negabit
O maria exora pro nobis tuum dulcissimum filium.
Vt nos sumat ad se post huius calamitatis exilium.
O bone ihesu exaudi matrem tuam orantem pro nobis
Et presta ut in eternum commaneamus uobis.

[1] Right Panel: Solomon Sets his Mother at his Right Hand. On the biblical account (3 Kings 2.13–25) this would seem an unpromising antitype for Mary, since Bethsabee's relayed request of a bride for her firstborn, while she was temporarily seated at Solomon's right hand, is met by angry rejection and the execution of her son. The story is radically attenuated here in order to make the case for Mary in heaven as intercessor. The hand iconography indicates Bethsabee's "one little request" and Solomon's singular refusal. [2] According to the *LA* 119 (itself drawing on earlier material), Mary summoned all the surviving disciples to her when the angel informed her of her coming assumption, which they witnessed [3] Quia … assumptum, G, K] *Per quas intelligitur assumptio tam corporis quam animae, L* [4] 3 Kings 2.19–20 [5] Cf. 3 Kings 2.17

through which the perpetual constancy of Mary is indicated.
The moon is inconstant, and does not remain full for a long time
and it indicates the earth and all earthly things.
Disdaining this inconstancy, Mary trod all these things under her feet
and longed for heaven, where all things are constant.
The woman also had a crown on her head
which contained in it twelve stars.
The crown is used as a sign of honor
and it signifies the honor befitting the Glorious Virgin.
All the apostles are understood through the twelve stars
who are believed to have all been present for the departure of Mary.
Two wings were given to the woman for flying
because the body and soul of Mary was taken up into heaven.
Likewise it must be noted that the feast of this Assumption *Figure Three*
had also been figured in the mother of King Solomon.
For King Solomon was seated on his glorious throne
and a throne for his mother was caused to be placed at his right-hand,
on which she situated [herself] honorably next to him.
"It is not lawful that I should deny you anything," he said.
And thus Christ placed his mother at his right hand.
And he shall not deny her whatsoever she should ask from him
O Mary, plead with your sweetest son for us,
that we might rise to him after the exile of the fall.
O good Jesus, hearken to your mother, who prays for us,
and grant that we might abide with both of you for eternity.

40va

Capitulum xxxvii[1]

*I*n precendenti capitulo adiuimus quomodo beata uirgo assumpta fuit
Consequenter audiamus quomodo ipsa mediatrix nostra extitit.
Quomodo iram dei contra mundum placare non cessat
Et peccatores suis piis interuencionibus deo reconciliat.
Mundus enim iste totus positus est in maligno
Creatorem suum non uenerans ore[2] condigno.
Vbique enim ueritas et caritas implicantur[3]
Superbia auaricia et luxuria dominantur.
Hiis tribus uiciis mundus repletus iam videtur
Et rarus est qui de hiis innoxius et immunis habetur.
Quidam enim fugiunt luxuriam tenentes castitatem
Qui tamen sordidantur per auaricie cupiditatem.
Quidam fugiunt auariciam tenentes paupertatem
Qui tame[m/n][4] maculantur per superbie uanitatem.
Quidam fugiunt superbiam tenentes humilitatem.
Qui tamen peccant per luxuriam uel per cupiditatem.
Quidam licet non luxurientur facto uel operacione
Tamen luxuriantur cogitacione et locucione.
Casti uolunt esse et tamen de carnalibus fabulantur
In auditu et in uisu [de] carnalium delectantur.
Quidam licet non superbiant per apparatum exterius
Habent tamen appetitum humanae[5] laudis interius.
Quidam detestantur auariciam eligentes paupertatem
Qui tamen multa appetunt et habunt semper suam neccesitatem.
Quidam uolunt esse pauperes sed sine defectu.

[1] Left Panel: Virgin Mary, St. Dominic, and St. Francis. The image shows all three interceding for the supplicants, whom Christ, holding three javelins, is show to be recognizing. The rubric over Mary reads "*maria placans iram dei*," indicating that without her intercession divine judgment would have fallen on the supplicants. The three lances of divine judgment are drawn from a vision of St. Dominic recounted in the *Legenda Aurea* 118. [2] ore] honore, L [3] implicantur] periclitantur, L [4] The letter was originally *m*, but subsequently corrected by erasure [5] One of the rare instances of the classical *–ae* orthography being spelled out

Chapter Thirty-Seven

In the previous chapter, we heard how the Blessed Virgin was assumed;
next let us hear how she became our intercessor:
how she does not cease to soften the wrath of God against the world
and reconciles sinners to God with her pious intercessions.
For the whole world was cast into evil,
not revering its creator with worthy speech.
For wherever truth and love are confounded,
pride, avarice, and dissipation have dominion.
The world appears already filled with these three vices
and rare is the one who is considered unharmed by these and immune.
For some flee dissipation, holding fast to chastity—
who nevertheless are dirtied through the desire of avarice.
Others flee avarice, holding fast to poverty—
who nevertheless are stained through the emptiness of pride.
Others flee pride, holding fast to humility—
who nevertheless sin through dissipation or through desire.
Others, although they are not riotous in deed or action,
nevertheless are wanton in thought and speech.
They wish to be unspotted, but nevertheless they tell tales of carnal matters;
they are delighted at the report and the sight of carnal things.
Others, although they are not prideful externally through splendor,
nevertheless, possess an appetite inwardly for human praise.
Others detest avarice, choosing poverty,
who nevertheless desire many things and always have their needs.
Others wish to be paupers, but without going short;

40vb[1] Quidam uolunt esse humiles sed sine despectu.
Superbia igitur luxuria et auaricia
Omnium peccatorum et malorum sunt inicia.
Superbia eiecit angelum de summo celo
Hominem de paradyso nabuchodonosor de regno.
Auaricia achior[2] et naboth[3] lapidauit
Ananiam et saphiram subitanea morte necauit.[4]
Luxuria totum mundum fere per aqua submersit
Sodomam et Gomorram per ignem subuertit.
Cottidie irritatur deus contra mundum propter hec tria
Sed placat iram eius [/mediatrix nostra virgo maria.][5]
Istud patet in quadam uisione et sompnio autentico[6]
Quod diuinitus ostensum est sanctissimo patri beato dominico.
Vidit siquidem ⸌christi⸍[7] dexteram manum eleuasse
Et tres lanceas contra mundum irato vvltu vibrasse.
Statim beatissima maria mediatrix astabat
Et mellifluis interuencionibus iram eius mitigabat.
Duos pugiles strennuissimos sibi offerebat
Quos ad conuersionem peccatorum in mundum mittere uolebat.
Vnus erat beatus dominicus pater fratrum [minorum][8] predicatorum
Alter vero beatus franciscus pater fratrum minorum.
Per hanc beatissimam visionem dominus mundo innocuit
Quod maria mediatrix inter deum et mundum extitit.
¶Quod autem beata uirgo mediatrix nostra futura erat *prima figura.*
Hoc olim per tres figuras prefiguratum fuerat.

---

[1] Right Panel: Abigail Intercedes with David. In 1 Kings 25.1–35 David is being heckled by a manic protester, Nabal (lit. "fool"), who, though wealthy, was corrupt in his dealings. When he refuses the servants of David basic hospitality, David determines to slay him, but his shepherds intercede with his wife Abigail to intercede in turn with David. Abigal prepares food and wine, meets David's party on the way, and intercedes on her husband's behalf. David spares Nabal in deference to Abigail's wishes but the Lord later strikes Nabal down, upon which David takes Abigail for his own wife. Jewish commentary (Megillah 15a; S.'Olam Rabbah 21) makes her the most important of David's wives, and the most beautiful. The *Glossa* praises her for her wisdom, but there is little mainstream commentary. Here, as in the *Cursor Mundi*, she is seen as an antitype of the Virgin Mary. The figure shows Abigail kneeling before Nabal (rubric) rather than David and two warriors, which one assumes is an error, since it would invalidate the antitype. [2] Jos. 7 [3] 3 Kings 21 [4] Act. 5.1–11 [5] These words have been written over an earlier, scratched out portion [6] *LA* 118. In the dream, St. Dominic sees Christ about to destroy the world with three spears on account of rampant pride, luxury, and avarice. However, Mary calms his wrath and produces St. Dominic as a "fidelem servum et pugilem strenuum, qui ubique discurrens mundum expugnabit et tuo dominio subjugabit", followed by a similar presentation of St. Francis. [7] Added by a later hand at the end of the line with the '||' indicator. The scribe had originally tried to squeeze in x^i with a caret, but erased this. [8] Eyeskip deleted by scribal subpunction

others wish to be humble, but without being looked down upon.
Thus, pride, dissipation, and avarice
are the beginnings of all sins and evils.
Pride cast down the angel from highest heaven,
man from paradise, Nebuchadnezzar from his kingdom.
Avarice stoned Achan and Naboth;
it destroyed Ananias and Sapphira with a sudden death.
Dissipation submerged almost the whole world under water;
it overthrew Sodom and Gomorrah through fire.
Every day, God is incited against the world on account of these three [vices]
but our intermediary, the Virgin Mary, softens his wrath.
This [intercession] is revealed in a certain vision and a true dream
which was shown by God to the most holy father, St. Dominic.
For he saw the right hand of Christ raised
and with a wrathful countenance, shake three lances trembled against the world.
At once the most blessed Mary stood by as intercessor
and softened his wrath with her honey-dripping intercessions.
She offered him two most vigorous fighters,
whom she wished to send into the world for the conversion of sinners.
One was the blessed Dominic, the founder of a brotherhood of preachers,
the other was in truth the blessed Francis, the founder of the Friars Minor.
In this blessed vision the Lord spared the earth
because Mary stood forth as an intermediary between God and the world.
And because the blessed Virgin would be our intermediary, *Figure One*
this had once been prefigured through three figures.

41a[2] Primo per abygayl uxorem stulti Nabal de camelo[1]
Que placauit regem dauid sauciatum furoris telo.
Stultus enim iste nabal per suam stulticiam
Prouocauit contra se regis dauid inimiciciam.
Stultorum infinitus est numerus.[3]
Hoc uerbum dicit sapiens de huius mundi peccatoribus.
Que enim inueniri poterit maior stulticia
Quam quod pro uilissimo peccato uenditur sempiterna leticia.
Hoc faciunt huius mundi peccatores stulti
De quorum numero heu hodie inueniuntur multi.
Nonne omnes stulti et stultissimi sunt
Qui plasmatori et factori suo contradicunt.
Ve iuxta prophetiam qui contradicunt {qui contradicunt} factori suo
Testa de samiis terre id est de vilissimo luto.
Stultum esset si testa luti contradiceret suo figulo.
Et stultissimi sunt qui contradicunt factori suo.
Tales stultos verus Dauid in furore suo sepe necaret
Si nostra abygail id est maria iram eius non placaret. *secunda figura.*
¶Istud etiam sapiens mulier illa theutuites[4] prefigurauit
Que absolonem fratricidam patri suo reconciliauit.
Per istum fratricidam scilicet absolonem
Intelligimus hoc loco uoluntarium peccatorem.
Qui enim uoluntarie contra domini peccat fratricida dicitur
Qui fratrem suum id est christum rursus crucifigere nititur.
Postquam ausus est fratrem suum necare

41b[5] Nusquam potuit in terra promissionis habitare.
In yessur[6] autem id est in terra gentilium est commoratus
Quousque per mulieres theutuitem est patri reconciliatus.
Sic peccator post peccati mortalis perpetracionem
Nullas habet in terra eterne promissionis habitaciones.

[2] Left Panel: Woman of Tekoa Intercedes. The woman intercedes on behalf of David's banished son Absalom, but, at the bidding of Joab, deceptively. When David discerns the plot, he agrees to let Absalom return, but it is the beginning of the demise of Absalom (2 Kings 14.1–24). Our image, however, has the *sapiens mulier* speaking not with David but *Absalon fratricida*, here crowned in the place of David. The rubric is clearly in error.
[1] 1 Kings 25 [3] Ecl. 1.15 [4] 2 Kings 14.1–24 [5] Right Panel: Wise Woman of Abel. During the rebellion of Seba the Benjaminite (2 Kings 20.1–22) Joab was sent to kill Seba and his clan. A "wise woman" of Abel interceded, and promised to throw Seba's head over the city wall of Abel, so satisfying Joab without further loss of life. Joab, "head of David's army," looks on the gesture favorably in the image, while "the wise woman of the city of Abel" dangles Seba's head, about to drop it. [6] 2 Kings 13

First, through Abigail, the wife of the foolish Nabal of Carmel
who soothed King David, wounded by the spear of madness.
For that fool Nabal through his folly
provoked the enmity of King David against himself.
"The number of fools is infinite":
The wise man said this word concerning the sinners of this earth.
For what greater foolishness could be found
than that eternal joy is sold for the sake of the basest sin.
This the foolish sinners of this earth do
among whose number—alas!—many are found today.
Are they not all fools and utter dunces
who speak against their creator and maker?
Woe to him, according to the prophecy, who speaks against his maker.
A shard of Samian earth, that is, from the basest clay,
would be foolish if the shard of clay were to contradict its potter.
And they are most foolish who contradict their maker.
Such foolish men would the just David often kill in his rage
if our Abigail—that is, Mary—did not soften his wrath. *Figure Two*
The wise woman of Thecua also prefigured that,
she who reconciled Absalom, killer of his own brother, to his father.
Through that fratricide—namely, Absalom—
we understand in this stead a voluntary sinner.
For the one who sins willingly against the Lord is said [to be] a fratricide:
he strives to crucify his brother (that is, Christ) again.
After Absalom had dared to kill his own brother

he could not live anywhere in the Promised Land.
However, in Geshur—that is, in the land of the Gentiles—he tarried,
until he was reconciled to his father through the Thecuite woman.
So too a sinner, after committing a mortal sin,
has no abode in the eternal Promised Land.

Quousque reconcilietur deo per mulierem theutuitem
Id est per mariam mediatricem piam et mitem.
¶Hec mediatrix beatissima iam prefata *tercia figura*.
Etiam fuit per mulierem prudentem in abela prefigurata.
Syba filius Bokri. erexit se contra dominum suum dauid
Et contradicens ei vrbem abelam intrauit.[1]
Quapropter Ioab princeps milicie dauid urbem obsedit
Et propter Sybam ipsum urbem euertere satagit.
Fuitque in ea mulier sapiens que per suam sapientiam
Furorem predicti principis conuertit in clemenciam.
De cuius consilio ciues caput Sybe amputauerunt
Et extra murum proicientes ciuitatem liberauerunt.
Syba contra regem se erigens superbiam designat
Que in abelam urbem id est in animam peccatoris intrat.
Et princeps celestis milicie contra eam dedignatur
Donec per mulieres sapientem id est per mariam reconciliatur.
De cuius consilio debet homo caput sybe id est superbie amputare
Vt sic possit principis superni id est gratiam christi recuperare.
O bone ihesu doce nos omnia uicia taliter vitare
Vt tecum in perhenni gloria mereamur habitare.

41va *Capitulum xxxviii*[2]

*I*n precedenti capitulo audiuimus quomodo maria est nostra mediatrix
Consequenter etiam audiamus quomodo est nostra defensatrix.
Defendit enim nos a dei vindicta et ab eius indignacione
A dyaboli infestacione et a mundi temptacione
¶Per mariam enim protecti sumus a dei indignacione.
Quod figuratum est ˊin tharbisˋ filia regis saba et moyse.[3]
Moyses enim cum exercitu egypciorum urbem saba obsedit
Nec erat aliquis qui hanc obsidionem dissoluere suffecit.
Tharbis autem filia regis in eadem urbe habitauit
Que urbem ab obsidione hoc modo liberauit.
Moyses enim erat amabilis valde et pulcher aspectu

---

[1] 2 Kings 20 [2] Left Panel: Mother of Mercy. This motif appears in fraternal iconography, especially Carthusians, Cistercians, and Dominicans, with Mary gathering monks under her robe. [3] See Josephus, *Antiquities of the Jews*, II.X.2

Until he is reconciled to God through the Thecuite woman—
that is, through Mary, our pious and mild intermediary.
This aforementioned most blessed intermediary *Figure Three*
was once prefigured through the prudent woman in Abel.
Sheba, the son of Bikri, set himself against his master, David,
and opposing him, entered the city of Abel.
On account of this, Joab, commander of David's army, besieged the city,
and because of Sheba, he endeavored to destroy the city itself.
And there was in [the city] a wise woman who, through her wisdom,
turned the rage of the aforementioned commander into mercy.
Because of her counsel, the citizens cut off Sheba's head
and throwing it outside the walls, they freed the city.
Sheba setting himself against the king indicates the pride
that entered into the city of Abel—that is, into the heart of the sinner.
And the commander of the heavenly army scorns it
until he is reconciled through the woman's wisdom—that is, through Mary.
Because of her counsel, a person ought to cut off the head of Sheba—that is, of pride—
so that in this way he may be able to regain the grace of the celestial general—that is, of Christ.
O good Jesus, teach us to shun all vices in such a manner
that we might merit to dwell with you in everlasting glory.

Chapter Thirty-eight

In the last chapter we heard how Mary is our mediator;
next let us hear also how she is our defender:
for she defends us from God's vengeance and anger,
from the attack of the devil, and from the temptation of the world.
Through Mary we are protected from the anger of God, *Figure One*
which is prefigured in Tharbis, the daughter of the king of Saba, and in Moses.
For Moses encircled the city of Saba with the Egyptian army,
and there was no one who was able to lift the siege.
However, Tharbis, the king's daughter, dwelt in that city,
and she delievered the city from the siege in this way:
Moses was very attractive and handsome in appearance,

Quem filia regis de muro contemplabatur crebro respectu.
Et in tantum pulchritudo moysi ei complacebat
Quod eum sponsum habere desideranter affectabat.
Tandem patri suo desiderium suum aperuit
Et se moysen principem exercitus diligere asseruit.
Placuit hoc regi et compleuit filie uoluptatem
Dans moysi filiam et cum ea ipsam ciuitatem.
Et sic cum adiutorio tharbis et eius consilio
Liberati sunt inclusi et dissoluta est obsidio.
Per pulchrum moysen et amabilem deus designator
Qui in psalmo speciosus forma pre filiis hominum predicatur.[1]
Iste prouocatus fuit ad iracundiam contra mundum
Propter transgressionem ade et eue primorum parentum.
Qua propter cum exercitu egypciorum id est demonum mundus bellauit.

41vb2 Et hec obsidio plus quam quinque milibus annorum durauit.
Et nullus inuentus ⌊est⌋ in mundo qui ad hoc sufficeret
Vt iram dei placaret et obsidionem dissolueret.
Tandem adamauit e⌊um⌋[3] filia regis id est maria
Et mitigauit iram eius sua interuencione pia.
¶Maria etiam defendit nos contra demonum temptaciones *secunda figura*.
Vniuersasque dyabolicas impugnaciones.
Hec defensetrix benedicta ualde est nobis necessaria
Quia prelia dyaboli multa sunt et uaria.
Quosdam enim inpugnat per tumorem superbie
Sicut patet in iesabel balthasar et oliferne.[4]
Quosdam temptat per odium et liuorem inuidie
Sicut patet in chaym saul et filiis iacob patriarche.[5]
Quosdam temptat de uindicta sicut patet in samey[6]
In absolone in iacob in iohane filiis zebedey.[7]
Quosdam temptat per incrudelitatem et diffidenciam

[1] Ps. 44.3 [2] Right Panel: Tharbus Defends the City Against Moses. This curious legend is found in Petrus Comestor's *Historia Scholastica* on Exodus 6, but originates in Jewish legend, based on an oblique reference in Nm. 12.1 to Moses having taken a Cushite wife. Tharbis was an Ethiopian princess whose city is being assailed by Moses, while he was still an Egyptian prince (Yashar Shemot 133b–136b; 138a; also Yalkut 1.168; cf. Josephus, *Antiquities of the Jews* 2.10.2). The image shows Tharbis suggesting to her father the king that she be given in marriage to Moses in order that he will lift the siege. Moses, his helmet thrown back, awaits the decision. [3] L] eam, G [4] Jezebel: 3 Kings 21.5–16; Balthasar: Dn. 5; Holifernes: Jdt. 5–6 [5] Cain: Gen. 4.5; Saul: 1 Kings 18; Sons of Jacob: Gen. 37 [6] 2 Kings 16.5–14 [7] Absalom: 2 Kings 13.23–28; James and John: Lk. 9.54

and the daughter of the king gazed at him from the wall, often looking at him.
And the beauty of Moses pleased her so much
that she ardently desired to have him as her husband.
At last she revealed her desire to her father
and declared that she loved Moses, the commander of the army.
This pleased the king and he fulfilled the desire of his daughter,
giving his daughter to Moses and with her the city itself
and so with the help of Tharbis and her counsel,
the besieged people were delievered and the siege was lifted.
Through the beauty and desirableness of Moses, God is signified,
whom a psalm foretold was lovely in form beyond the sons of men.
He had been stirred to anger against the world
because of the transgression of Adam and Eve our first parents.
On account of this, the world waged war with the Egyptian army, that is, evil spirits,

and the siege endured more than five thousand years
and no one was found in the world who would suffice
to placate the wrath of God and lift the siege.
Finally, the daughter of the king, that is, Mary, fell in love with him
and soothed his wrath with her gentle intercession.
Mary also defends us against the temptations of demons *Figure Two*
and against all diabolical attacks.
This blessed defender is very necessary to us
because the demonic battles are many and varied.
[Satan] attacks some people through the swelling of pride,
as is shown in Jezebel, Balthasar, and Holifernes.
He tempts some through hatred and the spite of envy
as is shown in Cain, Saul, and the sons of Jacob the Patriarch.
He tempts others to revenge as is shown in Semei,
in Absalom, and in James and John, the sons of Zebedee.
He tempts some through disbelief and despair,

Sicut patet in akab. et achas. moyse. et jeroboam.[1]
Quosdam temptat per irreuerenciam rebellionem et inobedinam
Sicut patet in dathan. abyron. chore et cham.[2]
Quosdam ad dandum praua consilia instigat
Sicut patet in achydophel. balaam et ionadap.[3]
Quosdam temptat de infidelitate et perfidia
Sicut patet in chaym. et ioab. in triphone et juda.[4]
Quosdam temptat de humani sanguinis effusione
Sicut patet in Cyro. manasse. anthyocho. et herode.[5]

42a[6] Quosdam temptat de proprie uite internicione
Sicut patet in achythophel abymalech iuda et saule.[7]
Hiis et aliis uiciis multis dyabolus nos inpugnat
Sed defensatrix nostra maria nos protegit et propugnat
Qua propter ipsam laudabilis illa mulier prefigurauit
Que turrim thebes ab inpugnacione abymelech defensauit.[8]
Populus timens abymelech super turrim se receperat
Abymelech autem eos cum turri succendere uolebat
Mulier autem fragmen mole desursum iactabat.
Et caput abymelech tangens ipsum excerebrabat.
Abymelech dolens a muliere se confusum
Et desperans de uita dixit ad armigerum suum
Euagina gladium tuum et interfice me
Ne uidear interfectus a muliere.
Abymelech iste superbus dyabolos designat
Qui institutos in turri id est in ecclesia continue inpugnat.
Sed defensatrix nostra mater dei maria
Protegit nos ab insidiis dyaboli protecione pia.
Et non solum defendit ab insidiis dyaboli
Set etiam protegit a temptacione huius mundi.
Et hec protectio est nobis ualde necessaria
Quia temptamenta mundi sunt multa et uaria.

[1] Ahab: 3 Kings 18; Ahaz: 4 Kings 16; Moses: Nm. 20.11; Jeroboam: 3 Kings 12.26–33 [2] Dathan, Abiram, Core: Nm. 16; Ham: Gen. 9.22–25 [3] Achitophel: 2 Kings 17.1–3; Balaam: Nm. 22; Jonadab: 2 Kings 13.3–5 [4] Cain: Gen. 4; Job: Job 1; Triphon: 1 Mcc. 12.39–13.32; Judas: Lk. 22.3–6 [5] Cyrus: Is. 41.2–25, 42.6, 45.1; Mannassa: 2 Par. 33.1–20; Antioch: Dn. 11.13–19; Herod: Act. 12, Mt. 2.16–18 [6] Left Panel: Theban Woman Kills Abimelech. Thebez the Canaanite city is here conflated with Thebes in Egypt. The story (Jdg. 9.50–58) is largely passed over in mainstream commentary; here it serves to extend the *mulier fortis* theme, with the woman of Thebes strong enough to hoist a millstone and drop it on Abimelech. He is shown asking one of his soldiers to administer the *coup de grace* so he may avoid the shame of being killed by a woman. [7] Ahithophel: 2 Kings 17.23; Abimelech: Jdg. 9.53–54; Judas: Mt. 27.5; Saul: 1 Kings 31.3–4 [8] Jdg. 9.50–55

as is shown in Ahab and Ahaz, Moses, and Jeroboam.
He tempts some men through irreverence, rebellion, and disobedience,
as is evident in Dathan, Abiram, Core, and Ham.
He instigates some to giving crooked counsel,
as is shown in Achitophel, Balaam, and Jonadab.
He tempts others with regard to broken faith and treachery
as is well-known in Cain and Job, in Triphone and Judas.
Some men he tempts with regard to the shedding of human blood.
As is shown in Cyrus, Mannassa, Antioch, and Herod.

He tempts some with regard to self-slaughter,
as is shown in Ahithophel, Abimelech, Judas, and Saul.
With these and many other vices the devil attacks us,
but our defender Mary shields us and counter-attacks.
Accordingly that praiseworthy woman prefigured her
who defended the tower of Thebes from the attack of Abimelech.
The people, fearing Abimelech, had retreated into a tower.
But Abimelech wanted to burn them along with the tower
However, a woman hurled a piece of a millstone from above
and, striking the head of Abimelech, smashed his skull.
Abimelech, grieving at having been undone by a woman
and despairing of life, said to his armor-bearer,
"Draw your sword and kill me
lest I appear to have been killed by a woman."
Abimelech, that proud man, signifies the demons
who continually battle against those drawn up in the tower, that is, in the church.
But our defender, the mother of God, Mary
shields us from snares of the devil with gentle protection.
And not only does she defend us from the snares of the devil
but she also shields us from the temptation of this world.
And this protection is truly necessary for us
because the temptations of the world are many and varied.

Maxime autem temptat mundus per appetitum dominandi
Per superbiam et desiderium diuicias congregandi.
Et hoc patet in Nemroch alexandro nabuchodonosor[1]

42b3 In natalia absolone adombesoch et codorlaomor.[2]
Quosdam temptat per uanam gloriam et laudem humanam
Sicut patet per aman. et ezechiam. et herodem agrippam.[4]
Quosdam temptat per auariciam furtum et spolium
Sicut patet per Iezy.[5] achor. et elyodorum.[6]
Quidam temptantur mundo per luxuriam et fornicacionem
Sicut patet per zambri. et amon. dauid. et salomonem.[7]
Quidam temptantur per stultiloquium et plasphemiam
Sicut patet per nabal. et senazerip. et roboam.[8]
Quidam per detractiones contumelias et errores
Sicut patet per mariam moysi. per thobie et iob vxores.[9]
Omnes temptaciones mundi vincere et euadere poterimus
Si propugnatricem nostram toto corde dilexerimus.
¶Istud olim prefiguratum fuit in dauid. *tercia figura*.
Qui filiam regis saul michol toto corde adamauit.[10]
Qua propter ipsa eum ab insidiis apparitorum eripuit.
Et per fenestram dimissum liberum abire permisit
Sic fecit maria suis amatoribus
Succurrens eis in omnibus suis temptacionibus.
Amemus igitur et honoremus dei genitricem mariam
Mediatricem et piam propugnationem nostram
Vt ipsa nos defendat a malis in hoc seculo.
Et interpellat pro nobis filium suum in celo.
O domine ihesu exaudi mariam pro nobis orantem
Et adiuua eam pro nostra salute pugnantem.

[1] Nimrod: 1 Par. 1.10; Gen. 10.8–9; Alexander: Dn. 8.5–8, 21–22; 1 Mcc. 1.1–9; Nebuchadnezzar: 2 Prm. 36.7 [3] Right Panel: Michal Helps David Escape. The biblical narrative in 1 Kings 19.11–17 illustrates a highlight in Michal's life when to protect David from the wrath of Saul she let him down from a window and put an effigy in his bed. Our image shows David escaping while, to buy time, Michal tells the soldiers that he is sick and cannot come out. While normative typology focuses on David and is Christological (e.g., *Glossa*, PL 113.558), the focus here is on Michal as an antitype of Mary. [2] Athalia: 4 Kings 11.1–16; Absalom: 2 Kings 15; Adoni-bezek: Jdg. 1.5–7; Chedorlaomer: Gen. 14.1–16 [4] Haman: Est. 3.1–7; Hezekiah: 4 Kings 20.13–16; Herod Agrippa: Act. 12.20–23; Josephus *Antiquities* 19.8.2, 343–361 [5] The 'y' is missing its tail [6] Jesse; Achan: Jos. 7; Heliodorus: 2 Mcc. 3, Dn. 11:20 [7] Zimri: Nm. 25.6–15; Amnon: 2 Kings 13.1–15; David: 2 Kings 11.1–5; Solomon: 3 Kings 11.1–6 [8] Nabal: 1 Kings 25.1–11; Sennacherib: Is. 36–37; Rehoboam: 3 Kings 12.1–15 [9] Miriam: Nm. 12; Tobias' Wife: Tb. 2.14, 10.1–7; Job's Wife: Job 2.9–10 [10] 1 Kings 19.8–17

Moreoever, the world tempts most greatly through the hunger for power,
through pride and the desire of accumulating riches.
And this is shown in Nimrod, Alexander, and Nebuchadnezzar,

and in Athaliah, Absalom, Adoni-bezek, and Chedor-laomer.
Some he tempts through vainglory and the praise of men
as it is shown by Haman, and Hezekiah, and Herod Agrippa.
Some he tempts through greed, theft, and plunder,
as it is shown by Jesse, Achan, and Heliodorus.
Certain men are tempted in the world through lust and fornication
just as is shown through Zimri and Amnon, David and Solomon.
Some are tempted through foolish speech and blasphemy
just as is shown through Nabal, Sennacherib, and Rehoboam.
Some through gossip, insults, and deceit,
as is shown by Miriam the sister of Moses, by the wives of Tobias and Job.
We will be able to conquer and escape from all the temptations of the world
if we love the one who fights for us with our whole heart.
This once was prefigured in David *Figure Three*
who, with his whole heart, fell in love with Michal the daughter of King Saul.
Accordingly, she rescued him from the snares of the officers
and let him go free, lowered down through the window.
So too has Mary done for her lovers
running to their aid in all their temptations.
In this way Mary treats her lovers, aiding them in all their temptations.
Let us therefore love and honor Mary, the mother of God,
our mediator and gentle champion,
so that she may defend us from evil in this world
and importune her son in heaven on our behalf.
O Lord Jesus, graciously hear Mary praying for us,
and uphold her as she fights for our salvation.

42va *Capitulum xxxix*[1]

*I*n precendenti capitulo audiuimus quomodo maria est nostra mediatrix
Consequenter audiamus quomodo in omnibus angustiis est nostra defensatrix.
Item audiamus quomodo christus pro nobis patri suo ostendit uulnera
Et maria ostendit filio pectus et ubera.
Sicut enim christus descendit propter nos de celo ad infernum
Ita reascendit in celum ut oraret pro nobis usque in sempiternum.[2]
Et ideo si peccauimus desperare non debemus
⸌a:⸍[3] ⸌Quia fidelem aduocatum apud deum habemus.⸍
⸌b:⸍ Quod autem christus uulnerum cycatrices patri monstrare uolebat
¶Hoc etiam olim per quandam figuram perostensum erat. *prima figura*
Antipater miles strenuus delatus fuit imperatori Julio
Quod infidelis fuisset et inutilis romano imperio.
Quapropter ille se exuens nudus coram imperatore stabat
Et ei cycatrices uulnerum coram omnibus ostendebat
Dixitque non esse opus verbis se expurgare
Cum cycatrices uiderentur eius fidelitatem acclamare.
Quod uidens cesar eius fidelitatem[4] approbabat
Et eum fidelem militem et strennuum affirmabat.
Pulchre christus prefiguratus fuit per istum antipatrem
Quia ipse semper pro nobis stat ante suum patrem.
Et cycatricibus suis ostendit se militem strennuum fuisse
Et mandatum patris eius tamquam fidelis miles impleuisse.
Qua propter tam fidelem militem non cessat honorare
Et quodcumque pecierit paratus est sibi dare.
Quam fidelis strennuus miles christus erat

42vb[5] Hoc in cycatricibus suis et cruentatis uestibus apparebat.
Omnia eius indumenta erant sanguinolenta
Sicut sunt uuas calcancium uestimenta.[6]
Ideo querebant angeli quare indumentum eius esset rubrum
Sicut in torculari vuas calcancium.[7]

[1] Left Panel: Christ Shows his Wounds to the Father. Here Christ, with the wounds of his crucifixion, is shown a mirror image of himself seated within a mandorla. [2] See Hbr. 7.25 [3] This line was originally skipped, but added by scribe and rubricated at the bottom of the column, with a: and b: to indicate proper position [4] fidelitatem] excusacionem, L [5] Right Panel: Antipater and Julius Caesar. When Antipater was challenged regarding his loyalty as a soldier he stripped, as here, to reveal his wounds suffered in battle. Julius Caesar is crowned like a medieval king. [6] Is. 63.3, Apc. 14.19–20 [7] Is. 63.1–6

Chapter Thirty-nine

In the last chapter we heard how Mary is our mediator;
now let us hear how she is our defender in all difficulties.
Likewise let us hear how Christ shows his wounds to his Father on our behalf,
and Mary shows her son her heart and bosom.
For just as Christ descended from heaven into hell for our sake,
so too he went back into heaven that he might pray for us continuously forever
and therefore, if we have sinned, we should not despair.
Because we have a faithful advocate before God.
And the fact that Christ desired to show the scars of his wounds to the Father,
was also shown formerly through a certain figure. *Figure One*
Antipater, a valiant soldier, was brought before the emperor Julius
because he had been disloyal and useless to the Roman imperial power.
Accordingly, stripping himself, he stood naked in front of the emperor
and he showed him the scars of his wounds before everyone.
And he said there was no need to justify himself with words
since his scars could be seen to proclaim his loyalty.
Seeing that, Caesar commended his loyalty,
and affirmed that he was a faithful and valiant soldier.
Christ was beautifully prefigured by this Antipater,
because he himself always stands before his Father on our behalf,
and proves by his scars that he had been a valiant soldier
and had fulfilled the command of his father like a faithful soldier.
Accordingly, God is not remiss to honor so faithful a soldier
and is ready to give him whatever he should ask for.
Just how faithful and valiant a soldier Christ was

was apparent in his wounds and bloodstained clothing.
All of his garments were blood-drenched,
just like the clothes of those who crush grapes with their feet.
Therefore, the angels were asking how his clothing was red
as that of those trampling grapes in a wine press.

Qui respondit quod torcular passionis ipse solus calcasset
Et de omnibus gentibus vir secum non fuisset.
Et notabiliter dixit quod de omnibus gentibus vir secum non fuerat
Quia tantum unica uirgo, id est maria, secum permanserat
Miles iste scilicet christus factus ⌊fuit⌋ more alamannico
Vbi in creacione militis solet dari colaphus in collo.
Set miles iste non recepit tantum colaphum unum
Sed colaphorum et alaparum quasi infinitum numerum.[1]
Dextrarius eius erat asinus cui insedit in die palmarum[2]
Campus prelii in quo pugnabat erat mons caluarariarum.[3]
Hasta eius fuit longini militis lancea[4]
Corona de acutissimis spinis erat sibi pro galea.[5]
Signum siue ornamentum galee fuit tabula tytuli[6]
Baltheus eius ⌊erant⌋ ligamenta et funiculi.
Patibulum crucis habebat pro clipeo et scuto
Pro calcaribus vsus est clauo ferreo uno.
Lorica sua qua totum corpus tegebatur
Erat cutis propria que in flagellacione totaliter concuciebatur
Gladius suus erat doctrina ⸌sancta⸍ quam docebat.[7]
Et pro cyrothecis manuum duos clauos ferreos habebat.

43a[8] ¶Armiger eius erat beatissima uirgo maria *secunda figura*
Que omnia arma eius gerebat compassione pia.
Sicut enim armiger ionathe in necessitate astitit[9]
Ita armigera christi in passione sibi fideliter affuit.
Vexillum predicti militis scilicet christi. duorum erat colorum
Quia in parte erat candidum et in parte rubicundum.
Erat enim factum ex alba ueste qua illusus fuit ab herode
Et coccinea qua illusus fuit in coronacione.[10]
Cum predictis armis miles iste tam fideliter laborauit[11]
Quod per mortem suam omnes inimicos suos superauit.

[1] Cf. Mt. 27.26, John 19.1 [2] Zech. 9.9, Mt. 21.1–10, John 12.14–15 [3] Mt. 27.33, Mk. 15.33, Lk. 23.33, John 19.17 [4] Cf. John 19.24 [5] Mt. 27.29, Mk. 15.17, John 19.2 [6] Mt. 27.37, Mk. 15.26, Lk. 23.38, John 19.19 [7] Cf. Hbr. 4.12
[8] Left Panel: The Virgin Shows her Breasts to Christ. Since she thus proves her maternal and nurturing care for her infant son Jesus, she now has the basis to request favors of him. There seems to be a tradition of pairing Jesus showing his wounds to the Father and Mary showing her breasts: e.g. Arnold of Bonneval. Bernardino of Siena (1380–1444): "Only the blessed Virgin Mary has done more for God, or just as much, as God has done for all humankind … God nourished us with the fruits of paradise, but she nourished him with her most holy milk, so that I may say this for the blessed virgin, who, however, God made himself, God is in some way under a greater obligation to us through her than we to God. (trans. in Hilda Graef, *Mary: A History of Doctrine and Devotion*, 1963.316–317)." [9] 1 Kings 14.1–15 [10] Lk. 23.11 [11] laborauit] pugnauit, L

He responded that he alone had tamped underfoot the winepress of the Passion,
and out of all the nations there had not been a man with him.
And he said notably that not one of all the men was with him
because only a single woman, that is, Mary, had remained with him.
That soldier—Christ—was made in German fashion:
where in the making of a soldier, it is usual to be given a stroke on the neck;
but this soldier did not undergo one such stroke
but a practically endless amount of blows and hits.
His warhorse was a donkey, on which he sat on Palm Sunday;
the field of battle on which he was fighting was the mount of Calvary;
his spear was the lance of the soldier, Longinus;
a crown of the sharpest thorns was like a helmet for him;
his standard, or the trappings of his helmet, was the tablet of wood with its inscription;
his belt was strips of cloth and cords;
he had the crossbeam of the cross for a shield and buckler;
for his boots, he used a single iron nail;
his cloak, with which all his body was covered,
was his own skin, which was wholly lacerated by scourging;
his sword was the sacred teaching that he taught;
and for his hands' gauntlets, he had two iron nails.

His armor-bearer was the most Blessed Virgin Mary *Figure Two*
who was holding all his weapons by her devout compassion.
For just as the armor-bearer of Jonathan stood nearby in the time of need,
so the armor-bearer of Christ was loyally with him in his passion.
The banner of the aforementioned soldier, that is, Christ, was of two colors
because it was partly white and partly red.
For it was made from a white garment with which he was taunted by Herod,
and a crimson one with which he was robed as a king in mockery.
With the aforementioned weapons, that soldier labored so faithfully
that through his death he conquered all of his enemies.

Post hec cum triumpho victoriosus in celum ascendit
Et patri suo cycatrices vvlnerum pro nobis orans ostendit.
Si quis ergo peccauerit licet innumerabiliter tamen non diffidat
Sed in hunc fidelissimum intercessorem confidat.[1]
Si enim in patrem uel in spiritum sanctum peccamus
Christus potest nos reconciliare et in hoc non diffidamus.
Et si peccauerimus in filium hoc est in ihesum christum
Habemus aduocatam fidelem que intercedit pro nobis apud ipsum.
Christus ostendit patri ˋsuoˊ cycatrices vvlnerum que tolerauit
Maria ostendit filio ubera quibus eum lactauit.
Sicut ergo christus conuenienter potest antipater appellari
Ita maria antifilia conuenienter potest nuncupari.
O fidelissime antipater et o fidelissima antifilia
Quam summe necessaria sunt nobis miseris uestra auxilia.
Quomodo posset ibi esse aliqua abnegacio

43b[2] Vbi tam dulcissima est supplicacio.
Quomodo enim posset clemens pater talis filii preces remouere
Quem uidet propter mandatum suum tales cycatrices habere.
Quomodo enim posset talis filius tali matri aliquid negare
Quos constat se mutuo tamquam se ipsos amare.
Nulli dubium quin deus semper exaudiat mariam
Quam pre omnibus mortalibus constituit celi reginam.[3]
¶Istud per figuram olim preostensum fuit in rege asuero *tercia figura*.
Qui dixit ad reginam hester postquam incaluisset mero.[4]
Pete a me quodcumque uolueris
Et si dimiduim regni mei pecieris impetrabis.
Tunc illa peciit populum suum ab iniquo aman defendi
Quem rex stans[5] precepit in patibulo suspendi.
Hester de gente iudeorum paupercula puella fuerat
Et rex eam pre omnibus elegerat et reginam constituerat.
Ita deus pre omnibus uirginibus mariam elegit
Et reginam celi ipsam constituit et fecit.
Et per eius interuencionem hostem nostrum condempnauit.
Et ipsi marie dimidium regni sui donauit.
Deus enim regnum suum in duas partes diuisit

---

[1] See Rom. 8.34, Hbr. 7.25 [2] Right Panel: Esther Intercedes with King Ahasuerus. The story (Est. 5, 7) focuses on Esther's intercession on behalf of her people to save their lives. Our image shows the Queen making her petition, while the king's hand gestures indicate "even so as you have asked." [3] See Apc. 12.1–6 [4] Est. 5–7
[5] stans] statim, L

After this the victor ascended in triumphal procession to heaven
and, entreating on our behalf, he shows the scars from his wounds to his father.
If anyone therefore should have sinned, however countlessly, yet let him not despair
but let him trust in this most faithful intercessor.
For if we sin against the Father or against the Holy Spirit
Christ is able to reconcile us and we should not despair about it.
And if we should sin against the son, that is, against Jesus Christ,
we have a faithful advocate who intercedes for us with him.
Christ shows his Father the scars of his wounds which he bore;
Mary showed her son the bosom with which she nursed him.
And just as Christ can aptly be called "Antipater";
so too Mary can aptly be named "Antifilia."
O most faithful Antipater and most faithful Antifilia!
How very necessary is your help to us wretched ones!
How could there possibly be any refusal there

where there is such very sweet supplication?
For how could the clement father set aside the prayers of such a son,
whom he sees bears wounds on account of his command?
For how could such a son deny anyone to such a mother
for whom it is right that they love each other just as they love themselves?
Let there be no doubt that God always hears Mary
whom he set above all mortal people as Queen of Heaven.
This thing was once shown through the figure of King Ahasuerus. *Figure Three*
He said to Queen Esther after he had grown heated with wine,
"Ask of me whatever you wish,
and if you should ask for half of my kingdom, you will obtain it."
Then she asked that her people be defended from evil Haman,
and, standing, the king ordered him to be hung on the gallows.
Esther had been a poor girl of the Jewish people
and the king had chosen her above all and had made her the queen.
And so God chose Mary above all maidens,
and established and made her the Queen of Heaven;
and through her intervention he condemned our enemy,
and to Mary herself, he gave half of his kingdom.
For God divided his kingdom into two parts:

Vnam partem sibi retinuit et aliam marie conmisit.
Due partes regni celestis sunt iusticia et misericordia
Per iusticiam minatur nobis deus per misericordiam succurrit maria.
O bone ihesu exora clementer pro nobis tuum patrem
Et exaudi libenter supplicantem pro nobis tuam matrem.

43va *Capitulum xl*[1]

*I*n precendenti capitulo audimus quomodo christus non cessat per nobis orare
Consequenter audiamus quomodo districte in iudicio uult iudicare.
¶Et hoc christus in quadam parabola proponebat *prima figura*.
Quando in hoc mundo predicando turbas docebat.
Dixit enim de homine uolente in regionem longinquam ire
Accipere sibi regnum et iterato redire.[2]
Qui tradidit seruis suis x minas ut cum eis luctarentur
Et quando redire{n}t cum lucro sibi redderentur.
Abiit igitur illuc et accepto regno rediit
Et ab uno quoque minam suam cum lucro repeciit
Qui multum acquisierat illum multum remunerauit
Qui autem minus illi mercedem minorem donauit.
Illum vero qui minam sine lucro restituit—
Non contentus in hoc pro lucro neglecto puniuit.
Hoc modo christus in die iudicii iudicabit
Quia secundum quantitatem lucri vnumquemque remunerabit.
Qui autem nichil fecerit non solum nichil recipiet
Sed etiam suam negligenciam in inferno perpetuo luget.
Non enim satis est hoc quod homo peccata dimittat
Sed oportet etiam quod bona opera faciat.
Austerus iudex metet vbi non seminauit[3]
Sed etiam a paganis queret bona opera quibus nullus predicauit.
Quanto magis christianis vvlt bona opera extorquere
Quibus tot salutaria documenta dignatus est exhibere.
Christus ostendet peccatoribus uulnera et passionis arma

[1] Left Panel: Last Judgment. The parable referred to is in Mt. 25.14–30, but the image, with the dead rising from their graves while Christ sits in judgment (in a mandorla) between redeemer saints on the left and martyrs on the right seems to draw on a variety of sources, including Mt. 25.31–46 and 1 Th. 4.16–17. [2] Mt. 25.14–30, Lk. 19.11–26 [3] See Mt. 7.15–20, 12.33–37, Lk. 3.9, Gal. 5.22

one part he retained and another part he entrusted to Mary.
The two halves of the heavenly kingdom are justice and mercy:
in justice, God warns us; in mercy, Mary runs to our aid.
O good Jesus, plead gently for us to your Father,
and generously hear your mother when she makes her entreaties for us.

Chapter Forty

In the last chapter we heard how Christ does not cease to pray for us,
now let us hear how severe his judgment will be.
Christ explained this in a certain parable *Figure One*
when, by preaching on this earth, he was teaching the masses.
For he spoke of a man who desired to go to a far-off region
to receive a kingdom for himself and to return again.
This man handed over ten talents to his servants so that they would be enriched by them
and that when he returned, the money might be given back to him with profit.
Then he left for that place, when he had received his kingdom, he returned again,
and from each one he asked for his talent back along with the profit.
The one who had gained much, the master rewarded him greatly;
but he who gained less received a smaller reward.
But as for the one who returned the talent without increase,
his master, dissatisfied with this, punished him for neglecting the profit.
In the same way Christ will judge on the day of judgment,
because he will reward each one in proportion to his profit.
And he who has done nothing will not merely receive nothing,
but will also mourn his omission in eternal fire.
For it is not enough to abandon sin
but it is fitting also to do good works.
The stern judge reaps where he has not sown,
but even seeks good works from the pagans to whom no one has preached.
How much more does he want to obtain good works from Christians
to whom he deigned to show so many salvific signs?
Christ will show sinners the wounds and weapons of his passion

43vb[1] Vt uideant quanta propter eos sustinuit tormenta,
Omnia enim arma ˋchristiˊ contra peccatorem stabunt
Et omnia uulnera eius super eum vindictam clamabunt.
Omnes creature ad impugnandum eum armabuntur
Et omnia elementa contra ipsum querulabuntur.
Terra querulabitur quod ipsum portauit et fructibus pauit
Et ipse sterilus arbor eam inutiliter occupauit.[2]
Ignis querulabitur quod calorem et lumen sibi prebebat
Et ipse verum lumen creatorem suum agnoscere nolebat.
Aer querulabitur quod ad spiramen eius fuit paratus
Et ipse de tanto beneficio domino suo fuit ingratus.
Aqua querulabitur quod ipsum potauit et piscibus saciauit
Et ipse creatori suo seruire non curauit.
Angelus suus querulabitur quod ipsum semper custodiuit
Et ipse propter dei et sui presenciam turpiter peccare non timuit.
Mater misericordie que nunc omnibus peccatoribus est parata
Tunc nullius erit adiutrix neque aduocata.
Piissimus filius qui mortem per peccatoribus suscepit.
Tunc de interitu et damnacione eorum ridebit.
Demones omnia peccata quantumcumque occulta denudabunt
Et angeli omnia bona neglecta ibi recitabunt.
Christus qui nunc piissimus est tam districte iudicabit
Quod nec propter preces nec propter aliquorum lacrimas senias mutabit.
Si enim maria et omnes sancti sanguinem flerent
Vnam animam dampnatam liberare non valerent.

44a[3] ¶Seueritas districti iudicii in x uirginibus demonstratur *secunda figura.*
De quibus in evvangelio parabola quedam recitatur.[4]
Prudentes uirgines fatuis oleum dare noluerunt
Quo innuitur quod sancti dampnatis in nullo condolebunt.
Oleum misericordie ipsis omnino dare negabunt.
Et de uindicata in eis facta letabuntur et exultabunt
Prudentes etiam uirgines fatuis subsannabant et deludebant
Quando eas ad uenditores olei ire iubˋeˊbant.

[1] Right Panel: Parable of the Talents. The image shows the happy lot of those who invested their talent wisely, one on each side of the lord, represented here as Christ enthroned in majesty, while the unprofitable servant lies bound at the feet of Christ, awaiting hiss grim fate (Lk. 19.12–27; Mt. 25.14–30). [2] Cf. Lk. 13.6–9 [3] Left Panel: Wise and Foolish Virgins. Jesus tells this parable in Matthew's gospel (Mt. 25.1–13) just before the parable of the talents and his discourse on the Last Judgment. The five virgins with oil for their lamps are crowned, signifying their eternal destination, while the five foolish virgins, having run out of oil, hold their hands to their chin in the gesture signifying weeping or lamentation. [4] Mt. 25.1–13

so that they might see what great torments he endured for them,
for all the weapons of Christ will stand up against the sinner
and all his wounds will cry out veangeance against him.
All creatures will be armed to fight against him
and all the elements will cry out against him.
The earth will cry out that it bore him and fed him on its fruits,
and he dwelt upon it in vain, like a fruitless tree.
The fire will cry out that it provided heat and light for him,
and he would not acknowledge his maker, the true light.
The air will cry out that it was made ready for him to breathe,
and he gave his master no thanks for such a great favor.
The water will cry out that he drank it and ate its fish
but he did not care to serve his creator.
His angel will cry out that he always guarded him
And he did not fear to sin shamefully before God or the angel.
The mother of mercy who now is ready to aid all sinners
will not be then a helper or advocate of any;
her most merciful son who died for sinners,
will then laugh at their death and damnation.
The demons will lay bare all the hidden sins, whatever they may be,
and the angels will read out there all the good works that were omitted.
Christ who is now most merciful will judge so severely
that he will commute the sentence neither for the sake of prayers nor anyone's tears.
For even if Mary and all the saints were to cry blood,
they would not be able to free one damned soul.

The severity of the eventual judgement is shown in the ten virgins *Figure Two*
about whom a certain parable is told in the Gospel.
The wise virgins would not give oil to the foolish ones
from which it is clear that the saints will not succor the damned at all.
They will altogether deny them the oil of mercy.
And they will rejoice and exult in the vengeance taken on them.
As the prudent virgins mocked and derided the foolish ones
When they were sending them to the sellers of oil,

Ita sancti dampnatos tunc uidebuntur illudere
Et eos ad uenditores olei mittere quasi uelint dicere.
Vos uendidistis eterna gaudia per uoluptate vana
Ite modo ad uenditores et emite uobis alia.
Omnes elemosinas et bona que aliquando fecistis
Pro laude humana et gloria uana uendidistis.
Quid prodest uobis nunc superbia uestra et gloria uana
Vbi est nunc omnis placencia et laus humana.
Videte nunc quantum ualent bona que uendidistis
Et quantum prosint uobis omnia transitoria que recepistis.
Quando autem fatue misericordiam in prudentibus non inueniebant
Apud sponsum misercordiam querebant et sibi apperiri petebant
Nullam vero misericordiam apud ipsum inuenerunt.
Sed amen dico uobis nescio uos ab ipso audierunt.[1]
Ita continget in die iudicii ipsis peccatoribus
Non inuenient misericordiam apud deum nec apud sanctos eius. *tercia figura.*
¶Modus etiam iudicandi in illa scriptura prefiguratus erat

44b[2] Quando manus domini contra regem balthasar scribebat.
Mane techel phares in periete scribebatur
Quod numerus appensio diuisio interpretabatur.[3]
Iudicium enim domini tractabitur per numerum et appensionem
Et consumabitur per malorum et bonorum perpetuam diuisionem.
Dominus enim secundum numerum meritorum secunda quemlibet iudicabit
Quia ipse omnia opera nostra et uerba numerauit.
Omnes etiam cogitaciones conatus et gressus ipse dicauit[4]
Omne tempus nobis impensum quomodo expensum ipse considerauit
Ipse etiam numerauit omnia dona que recepimus
Qualiter expendimus et quomodo et quamdiv poss~~i~~⟨e⟩dimus.
Omnia autem hec predicta que nunc numerat in statera pendet
Et cuius ualoris sint coram omnibus ostendet.
Tunc tanti ponderis erit obolus pauperculi hominis
Sicut mille talenta auri pape uel imperatoris.
Plus ponderabit ouum sine mortalibus largitum
Quam cum mortalibus aurum infinitum.
Plus ponderabit unum pater noster dictum ex deuocione.
Quam integrum psalterium cum tedio et sine attencione.

---

[1] Mt. 25.12, Lk. 13.27 [2] Right Panel: Balthasar's Feast. The story in Dn. 5 is a warning of the judgment of God against blasphemy. The giant hand entering from the left is not shown writing the dread words; rather, Balthasar is shown asking Daniel to translate and interpret them. [3] Dn. 5 [4] dicauit] notauit, L. Job 14:16

So also will the saints then seem to deride the damned
and to send them to the sellers of oil as if to say:
"You sold eternal joy for empty pleasure!
Go now to the merchants and buy your own.
All your alms and all the good deeds you have ever done,
you traded for human praise and empty glory.
What do pride and vainglory profit you now
where now is all that approval and human praise?
See now how much the good things which you traded away are worth
and what good are all those transitory things are that you received!"
And when the foolish virgins did not find mercy in the wise ones,
they sought mercy from the bridegroom and were begging him to open up to them
but indeed they found no mercy with him.
But they heard from him, "Amen, I say to you that I do not know you."
So it will happen to these sinners on the day of judgment:
they will not find mercy from God or his saints. *Figure Three*
The manner of judgment was prefigured in that scripture

when the hand of the Lord made an inscription against king Balthasar.
"Mane, Thecel, Phares" was written on the wall,
which was interpreted, "numbered, weighed, divided."
For the judgment of the Lord will be carried out through counting and weighing,
and will be completed by the enduring division of the wicked from the good.
For the Lord will judge according to the number of our merits, whatever they are,
because he himself has numbered all our deeds and words.
He has tested all our thoughts and has himself named our steps.
He has considered how expensive it was, every time he paid a price for us.
And he also numbered all the gifts that we have received,
how we spend them and the length of time and way in which we possess them.
All these aforementioned things that he now numbers he will weigh on the scale.
And he will reveal their worth before everyone.
Then will a poor man's small coin weigh as much
as a thousand gold talents of the pope or emperor.
An egg, given without mortal sin, will weigh more
than endless gold [given] with mortal sin;
one Our Father said out of devotion will weigh more
than the entire psalter said with sloth and without heed.

Ad ultimum autem phares hoc est diuisio sequetur.
Quia numerus dampnatorum a [/c]onsorcio dei et sanctorum diuidetur.
Tunc ibunt dampnati cum demonibus in perpetuum infernum
Boni autem intrabunt ad gaudios domini sui sempiternum.
Ad quod nos perducere dignetur ihesus christus rex celorum
Qui cum patre et spiritu sancto sint benedictus in secula seculorum. Amen.

44va[1] *Capitulum xli*

*I*n precendenti capitulo audiuimus de extrema examinacione
Consequenter audiamus de malorum et bonorum remuneracione.
Deus nunc clementissimus est in collacione beneficionorum
Sed in futuro iustissimus erit in retribucione stipendiorum.
Quia igitur homo meruit uel demeruit anima simul et corpore
Ideo in futuro punietur uel remunerabitur simul in utroque.
Corpora enim animabus suis ⌊reunientur⌋[2]
Et simul remunerabuntur uel simul punientur.
Corpora dampnatorum resurgent deformia et passibilia
Corpora vero bonorum resurgent pulchra etiam impassibilia.
Cum tanta deformitate corpus damnati resurget
Quod propriam manum uel pedem videre abhorrescet.
Quanto fuerint[3] crimina malorum abhomiabiliora
Tanto erunt corpora eorum deformia.
Et quanto fuerint[4] merita iustorum plura et maiora
Tanto erunt corpora eorum pulchriora et clariora.
Corpus minimi pueri qui in celo fuerit
Septemplicitur clarior sole erit.
Si alius fuerit in decuplo sanctior eo
Illius corpus erit in decuplo clarior illo.
Si alius cencies sanctior illo fuerit
Illius corpus cencies clarior eo erit.
Et si alius fuerit millesies sanctior

[1] Left Panel: The Punishments of Hell. There is no specific textual source for this image, but the principle employed, namely that the punishment of the damned for eternity should mirror the torments inflicted on the martyrs, is widespread in the 14th century and still visibly operative to the 16th century, e.g., in the hell panels of Hieronymous Bosch, similar to the following image. Here the torments wrought by the gleeful devils consist mainly of roasting. The gaping mouth at the lower right, swallowing sinners, is Hell Mouth. [2] reunientur, L] remunerentur, G [3] fuerint] *fuerunt, L* [4] fuerint] *fuerunt, L*

And finally, "Phares": this is the dividing that follows,
because the number of the damned will be divided from the communion of God and the saints.
Then the damned will go with the demons into eternal fire
but the good will enter into the joys of the Lord forever.
May Jesus Christ, king of heaven, deign to lead us there.
May he, with the Father and the Holy Spirit be blessed forever and ever. Amen.

Chapter Forty-one

In the last chapter we heard about the final judgement;
next let us hear about the recompense for the wicked and the good.
God is now most loving in the bounty of his kindnesses
but in the future he will be most just in paying back what we have earned.
Because, then, a man did good or did ill in his soul and body together;
for that reason, in the future he will be punished or rewarded at the same time in both.
Bodies, indeed, will be brought together with their souls
and together they will be rewarded or together punished.
The bodies of the damned will rise deformed and susceptible to pain,
but the bodies of the good will rise beautiful and also incapable of feeling pain.
With such deformity will the body of a damned man arise
that he will dread to see his own hand or foot.
However great were the abominable crimes of the evil ones,
so deformed will be their bodies.
And however much greater and the more numerous will have the rewards earned by the just,
so beautiful and shining will be their bodies.
The body of the least boy in heaven
will be seven times brighter than the sun.
If another will have been ten times more holy than he,
his body will be ten times brighter than that one.
If another will be a hundred times holier than he,
his body will be one hundred times brighter.
And if another will have been a thousand times holier,

Illius corpus millesies erit clarior.
Et sicut christus infinicies est omnibus sanctis sanctior

44vb[1]
Ita est infinicies corpus eius omnibus sanctis clarior
Corpora sanctorum in futura uita glorificabuntur
Et quattuor dotibus a domino dotabuntur.
Prima dos est claritas . secunda impassibilitas
Tercia subtilitas . quarenta agilitas.
Hee quattuor dotes iam pretaxate
Fuerunt olim in corpore christi quodammodo prefigurate.
Claritatem enim ostendit in sua transfiguracione
Quando facies eius resplenduit clarior sole.[2]
Subtilitatem ostendit in sua natiuitate
Quando natus fuit de matre salua uirginali integritate.
Agilitatem etiam tunc demonstrauit
Quando super undas maris siccis pedibus ambulauit[3]
Inpassibilitatem quodammodo in cena ostendit.
Quando corpus suum ad manducandos discipulis dedit.[4]
Anime etiam beatorum dotantur triplici dote
Videlicet cogitacione delectacione et comprehensione.
Anime autem et corpora malorum non dotabuntur
Sed sine intermissione eternaliter cruciabuntur.
Sicut enim predicauerunt[5] contra deum suum eternum
Ita punientur a deo in infernum sempiternum.
Dampnati numquam habebunt de peccato suo penitenciam
Et ideo deus numquam mutabit punicionis illius sentienciam.
Tam magna et inenarrabilis est pena inferni.
Quod nulla pena huius mundi potest ei comparari.

45a[6]
Omnia tormenta que martiribus sunt illata
Quasi nichil sunt penis infernalibus comparata.
Ysaias fuit serratus.[7] semias lapidatus
Amos per tympora transfixus ezechiel excerebratus.
Paulus ter virgis cesus semel lapidatur

[1] Right Panel: David's Revenge on Rabbath. The story in 2 Kings 12.27–31 does not involve any torture, only hard labor. The text here thus conforms more to the previous image. [2] Mt. 17.1–9, Mk. 9.2–8. Lk. 9.28–36 [3] Mt. 14.22–23 [4] Mt. 26.26, Mk. 14.22, Lk. 22.19, John 19.36, 1 Cor. 11.24 [5] predicauerunt] peccaverunt, L [6] Left Panel: Gideon's Revenge. The text (Jdg. 8.7–16) says only that Gideon "fought" the inhospitable rulers of Succoth with thorns and briars, but that he killed the men of Phanuel. Our image has the former hung upside down, naked ad beaten, while the men in the tower await their fate. [7] *Ascenscion of Isaiah* 1.1–3.12, 5.1–16

his body will be a thousand times brighter.
And just as Christ is infinitely holier than all the saints,

therefore, his body is infinitely brighter than all the saints.
The bodies of the saints in the future life will be glorified.
And they will be endowed with four gifts by the Lord.
The first gift is brightness; the second, insusceptibility to pain.
The third is delicacy; the fourth, agility.
These four gifts already spoken about
were formerly prefigured in Christ's body in a certain way.
For he showed clarity in his transfiguration
when his face shone brighter than the sun.
He displayed delicacy in his birth
when he was born from a mother sound and whole in her virginity.
Agility also was then shown
when he walked on top of the sea's waves with dry feet.
He showed a certain insensitivity to pain in the Supper
when he gave his body to his disciples to be eaten.
The souls of the blessed also will be given a threefold gift,
that is, thought, delight, and comprehension.
But the souls and the bodies of the evil will not receive these,
but without respite will be tortured eternally.
For just as they preached against their eternal God,
so they will be punished by God in eternal flame.
And surely the damned will never have repentance for their sin.
And therefore God will surely never change the sentence of their punishment.
So great and indescribable is the punishment of hell,
that no punishment of this world can be compared to it.

All the torments which have been have been brought against the martyrs
are like nothing compared to the pains of hell.
Isaiah was sawn up into pieces; Semias was stoned;
Amos was pierced through his temples; Ezekiel had his head bashed in.
Paul, having been beaten three times with rods, was stoned once:

Quinquies quadragenas vna minus accipiens decollabatur;[1]
Sanctus iacobus martyr qui dicitur intercisus
Menbrati fuit cultris et nouaculis diuisus.[2]
Bartholomeus fuit excoriatus petrus apostolis crucifixus.
Laurencius assatus petrus martyr gladio confixus.
Et si possent hoc modo singula tormenta martyrum enarrari
Tunc omnia non possent mimime pene inferni comparari.
Omnia enim ista tormenta sunt transitoria et breuia
Sed tormenta dampnatorum sunt infinita et perpetua.
Utuntur enim igne qui numquam extinguetur
Et roduntur verme qui numquam morietur.[3]
Vermis iste non est putandus materialis
Quia ibi non erit uita alicuius animalis.
Vermis ergo est remorsus consciencie
Qui mordebit animas dampnatorum sine fine.
Ibi erit aspectus demonum terribilis
Frigor et stridor dencium fames ⟨et⟩ sitis.[4]
Clamor et horror timor et tremor.
Vincula et carcer sulphur et feror.
Inuidia et maledicio fumus et tenebre.

45b[5] Pudor et confusio lamentacione et lacrime.
Desperacio liberacionis et omnis consolacionis.
Nulla intermissio continue punicionis.
¶Vindicta dei contra dampnatos iam narrata *figura prima.*
Fuit olim in dauid et urbe rabach prefigurata.[6]
Populum huius vrbis dauid terribiliter puniuit
Quosdam serrauit quosdam cultris membratim diuisit.
Super quosdam fecit carpenta ferrata transire
Quosdam per trahas discerpens fecit interire.
¶Istud etiam figuratum est in uiris sochot et gedeone.
In quos se ferociter uindicauit pro sua derisione.[7] *secunda figura.*
Populus vrbis sochot quadam uice gedeonem deridebat
Et ipse statim non se vindicans ad tempus expectabat.[8]
Post hoc rediens derisores suos horrenissime puniuit

---

[1] Act. 14.19, 16.22, 2 Cor. 11.25 [2] Act. 12.2 [3] Mk. 9.47 [4] Ps. 111.10, Mt. 8.12, 13.42–50, 22.13, 24.51, 25.30, Lk. 13.28 [5] Right Panel: Pharaoh's Army in the Red Sea. Ex. 14.27–28 describes how the wall of water is released and buries Pharaoh's troops and chariots. The image seems to show Moses and the Israelites passing over to safety (top) while the chariots and men of Pharaoh go down in the mud. [6] 2 Kings 12.17 [7] Jdg. 6 [8] expectabat] differebat

after enduring 199 stones, he was beheaded.
Saint James the martyr, who, it is said, was mutilated,
had his limbs cut off with knives and razors;
Bartholomew was flayed, and the apostle Peter crucified.
Lawrence was roasted, Peter the martyr was pierced through with a sword.
And if each of the torments of the martyrs might be described in this way,
then all of of them might not be able to be compared to the smallest pain of hell.
For all those torments are transitory and brief,
but the torments of the damned are infinite and eternal.
For they enjoy the fire which is never put out
and are gnawed at by the worm which will never die.
That worm should not be thought to be material
because there, the life of any animal will not exist.
The worm is, therefore, the gnawing of conscience
which will consume the souls of the damned without end.
In that place, there will be the terrible sight of demons;
cold and the gnashing of teeth; hunger and thirst;
wailing and horror, fear and trembling;
chains and also a prison; sulphur and wrath;
envy and slander, smoke and darkness;

shame and confusion, lamentation and tears;
hopelessness of release and of all consolation;
no respite from continuous punishment.
The vengeance of God against the damned that has now been told *Figure One*
was once prefigured in David and the city Rabbath.
David punished the people of this city terribly:
some he sawed into pieces, and some he dismembered with knives.
He caused an iron carriage to run over some of them,
and mangling certain others through dragging, he killed them.
That punishment is also prefigured in Gideon and the men of Sochot,
against whom he avenged himself fiercely on account of their mockery. *Figure Two*
The people of the city of Sochot, were mocking Gideon on one occasion
and he, not immediately avenging himself, awaited the right time.
After this, returning, he punished his mockers most horribly,

Nam spinis et tribulis ipsos discerpit et contriuit.
Sic christus suis derisoribus id est peccatoribus faciet
Modo non statim se vindicat sed in posterum se vindicet.[1]
Dicit enim sapiens quod parata est tormenta derisoribus
Et mallei percucientes stultorum corporibus.[2]
¶Istud etiam prefigurauerunt egipcii et pharaoh. *tercia figura*
Quos dominus simul omnes conclusit in mari rubo.[3]
Sic dampnati cum demonibus et lucifero.
Ad ultimum omnes simul concludentur in inferno.
O bone ihesu propter tuam amarissimam passionem
Longe fac a nobis illam miserabilem conclusionem.

45va[4]

Capitulum xlii

*I*n precendenti capitulo audiuimus de pena dampnatorum
Consequenter audiamus de [-penis] gaudiis benedictorum
Gaudia beatorum tam multa sunt quod nequeunt numerari
Tam inmensa et tam magna sunt quod nequeunt menserari.
Tam ineffebilia sunt quod nequeunt enarrari.
Tam durabilia sunt quod nequeunt terminari.
Gaudia que deus diligentibus preparauit
Oculus non uidit auris non audiuit nec cor cogitauit.[5]
Ibi est omnis pulchritudo et amenitas ob[iecta/lata][6] visui.
Ibi est omnis armonia et melodia resonans auditui.
Ibi est omne delecamentum sufficiens olfactui
Ibi est omnis suauitas delicias prebens tactui.
Ibi est omnis dulcedo influens gustui.
Ibi est perfectissimum uinculum amoris mutui.
Ibi cognoscemus dei patris potenciam
Filii sapienciam. sancti spiritus benignissimam clemenciam.
Ibi erit omnium bonorum affluencia
Ibi erit omnium malorum omnimoda absencia.
Ibi erit requies eterna sine labore
Ibi erit pax et securitas sine terrore.
Ibi demonum nulle erunt insidie neque impugnacio.

[1] se vindicet] eos puniet, L [2] Prov. 19.29 [3] Ex. 14.27–28 [4] Left Panel: Kingdom of Heaven. Envisioned here, without a textual source, are Mary, Queen of Heaven, and Jesus, surrounded by angels and worshiped by nuns and monks. [5] Dt. 29.4, Mt. 13.13 [6] obiectalata] obiecta, L

for with thorns and spiny plants he mutilated and bruised them.
Christ will do this to his mockers, that is, to sinners;
only he will not take his vengeance immediately but will avenge himself in the future.
For the wise man says that torment is prepared for the mockers
and the striking of a hammer for the bodies of the foolish.
The Egyptians and Pharoah also prefigured this, *Figure Three*
all of those whom the Lord completely buried together in the Red Sea.
So too the damned with the demons and Lucifer
finally, all will likewise be buried in hell.
O good Jesus, for the sake your most bitter passion,
remove far from us that miserable prison.

Chapter Forty-two

In the last chapter we heard about the punishment of the damned
next we will hear about the joys of the blessed.
The joys of the blessed are so many and great that they are unable to be counted;
so immense and so great are they that they cannot be measured.
So inexpressible are they are that they are unable to be described.
They are so lasting that they are unable to be brought to an end.
The joys which God has prepared for the diligent,
the eye does not see, nor does the ear hear, nor does the heart understand.
There every beauty and pleasantness is offered to the sight.
All harmony and melody exist there, resounding to the hearing.
There is every delight available to the sense of smell;
Every softness exists there, offering delights to the touch.
All sweetness exists there, flowing into the sense of taste.
The most perfect bond of mutual love is there.
There we will know the power of God the Father,
the wisdom of the Son, and the kindest mercy of the Holy Spirit.
An abundance of all good things will be there;
an absence of all bad things of every sort will be there.
There will be eternal rest without labor in that place;
peace and security without fear will be there.
No wiles nor attacks of demons will be there.

Ibi neque mundi neque carnis erit temptacio.
Ibi erit sapiencia sciencia sine ignorancia
Ibi erit amicitia et caritas sine inuidencia.
Ibi erit sanitas perpetua sine egretudine.

45vb[1] Ibi erit fortitudo stabilis sine lassitudine.
Ibi erit lux perpetua et claritas sine nubilo.
Ibi erit leticia sempiterna iugiter in iubilo.
Ibi erit pulchritudo et decor sine deformitate
Ibi erit agilitas et uelocitas sine tarditate.
Ibi erunt diuicie et potencia sine defectu.
Ibi erit gloria et honorificincia sine despectu
Ibi est flos iuuentutis qui numquam marcessit
Ibi est uita semper uirens que in euum[2] terminum nescit.
Ibi longeuitas mathusale[3] vix nuncius[4] uiderertur
Ibi fortitudo sampsonis paralisis reputaretur.[5]
Ibi uelocitas azahelis esset morosa tarditas[6]
Ibi sanitas caliph esset mortalis infirmitas.[7]
Ibi deformitas uideretur pulchritudo absolonis[8]
Ibi stulticia reputaretur sapiencia salomonis.[9]
Ibi consilium jethro et antythophel esset uanitas[10]
Ibi sciencia aristotilis et philosophorum rusticitas.
Ibi artifices optimi iram tubalchaim et neoma
Besechel et colyab arguerentur de impericia.[11]
Ibi cythera dauid. et musica jubal esset absurditas[12]
Ibi manna et uinum factum in chana esset acerbitas.[13]
Ibi paradysus ade et terra promissionis esset desertum
Ibi delicie ecclesiastes et tocius mundi essent absinthium.
Ibi regnum octuiani carcer et exilium uideretur
Ibi thesauri cresi et antichristi paupertas iudicarentur

[1]Right Panel: Solomon and Saba. The biblical story (3 Kings 10.1–13) returns, simply as a reminder that the Queen of Saba's worship of Solomon in his glory is an antitype for the Church adoring Christ in his eternal glory (*Glossa*, PL 113.601–602). [2]in euum] in eternum, L [3]Gen. 5.27 [4]nuncius] punctus, L [5]Jdg. 16.6 [6]2 Kings 2.18 [7]Jos. 14.11 [8]2 Kings 14.25 [9]3 Kings 3.9–12 [10]Jethro: Ex. 18.13–27; Ahithophel: 2 Kings 17 [11]Hiram: 3 Kings 5.1–12; Tubal-cain and Naamah: Gen. 4.22; Bezalel and Oholiab: Ex. 31.1–11 [12]David: 1 Kings 16.23; Jubal: Gen. 4.1 [13]Manna: Ex. 16.14–35; Wine in Cana: John 2

There will be temptation neither of the flesh nor of the world there.
Wisdom and knowledge without ignorance will be there;
there, friendship and charity will be without envy.
There, health will without illness.

There, steadfast strength will be without weariness.
Perpetual light and clarity without cloud will be there.
Everlasting happiness unendingly in joyful melody will be there.
Beauty and adornment will be there without deformity;
Agility and speed will be there without slowing.
Riches and power will be there without scarcity.
Glory and honour will be there without contempt;
there exists the flower of youth that never withers;
there exists a life, always flourishing, which never knows an end.
There the long life of Methuselah would be seen as a mere foreshadowing;
there the strength of Samson would be regarded as paralysis.
There the swiftness of Asahel would be lingering slowness;
there the health of Caleb would be mortal illness.
There the beauty of Absalom would appear to be deformity;
there the wisdom of Solomon would be regarded as foolishness.
There the counsel of Jethro and Ahithophel would be vanity;
there the knowledge of Aristotle and the philosophers would be simplicity.
There the best craftsmen, Hiram, Tubal-cain, and Naamah,
Bezelel and Oholiab, would betray a lack of skill.
There the harp of David and the music of Jubal would be absurdity;
there manna and the wine made in Cana would be bitterness.
There the paradise of Adam and the Promised Land would be a desert;
there the delights of Ecclesiastes and the whole world would be as wormwood.
There the kingdom of Octavian would seem to be prison and exile;
there the treasures of Croesus and of Antichrist would be judged poverty.

46a2 [/Ibi eris o homo dicior et potencior Creso et Augusto][1]
Cyro et nabuchodonosor et alexandro.[3]
Ibi eris fortior sampsone sangar et abysai.
Dauid et seminaa. bananya. et sobochay.[4]
Ibi eris pulchrior absolone. ioseph. Et moyse.
Judith. sussana. rebecca. sara. et Rachalie.[5]
Ibi longeuior enoch. helya. et mathusale.[6]
Et uelocior asahele. cusy. hercule. et etiam sole.[7]
Ibi sapiencior salomone et augustino.
Gregorio. jeronimo. abroso et thoma[s] de aquino.[8,9]
Ibi clarius contemplaberis dominum quam petrus iohannes etiam jacobus.
Ezechiel. ysaias. moyses. et stephanus.[10]
¶Figura huius eterne glorie potest gloria salomonis esse *prima figura*.
Quia nullum legimus in tanta gloria uixisse.[11]
Nullum inuenimus tantum fretum deliciis
Nullum legimus tantis hundasse diuiciis.
Regina saba audita eius fama ierusalem perrexit
Et uisa eius incredibili gloria prestupore dixit.
Maior est gloria tua quam rumor quem audiui
Et probaui quod media pars non est nunciata mihi.
Ita fatebitur anima cum ad celestem gloriam perueniret
Quod media pars uel millesima sibi nunciata non sit.
Vniuersa terra desiderabat uidere faciem salomonis
Et hoc leue[12] uidetur prefigurasse faciem saluatoris.
Omnis enim iocunditas et omne gaudium celi.

---

[2] Left Panel: Feast of Ahasuerus. The great banquet of Ahasuerus (Est. 1.3–8) lasted seven days. Here it becomes a medieval feast, with merry music, enjoyed by the king as well as his subjects. The *Glossa* compares this great historical feast with the still greater heavenly banquet which Christ is preparing for the Church (PL 113.739–740). [1] Much of this line has been scraped and rewritten in a ligher ink [3] Croesus (and Cyrus): cf. Pliny, *Nat. His.* 33.15; Nebuchadnezzar: 4 Kings 24.13. Alexander's riches are well-attested, e.g. Plutarch, *Life of Alexander* 20. [4] Sampson: Jdg. 16.6; Sangar: Jdg. 3.31; Abishai: 1 Par. 18.12, 2 Kings 21.17; David: cf. 1 Kings 17.48–49, 1 Kings 18.7; Shemiah: 1 Par. 15.8; Benaiah: 2 Kings 23.20; Sibbecai: 2 Kings 21.18 [5] Absalom: 2 Kings 14.25; Joseph: Gen. 39.6; Moses: Hbr. 11.23, Ex. 2.2; Judith: Jdt. 10.4; Susanna: Dn. 13.2; Rebecca: Gen. 24.16; Sarah: Gen. 12.11,14; Rachel: Gen. 29.17 [6] Enoch: Hbr. 11.5, cf. Gen. 5.24; Elijah: Mt. 17.3, Mk. 9.4, Lk. 9.30, cf. 4 Kings 2.11; Methuselah: Gen. 5.27 [7] Asahel: 2 Kings 2.18–23; Cushite: 2 Kings 18.21–32; Hercules; The Sun: cf. Ps. 18.6–7 [8] Solomon: 3 Kings 3.6–28 [9] MS. originally wrote *thomas* but the ultimate *s* was erased [10] Peter, John, James: see Mt. 17.1–8, Mk. 9.2–8, Lk. 9.28–36; Ezekiel: see Ez. 1; Isaiah: see Is. 6.1–3; Moses: see Ex. 33.21–23; Stephen: see Act. 7.55–60 [11] cf. 3 Kings 10.6–9 [12] leue] bene, L

There you will be, O man, richer and more powerful than Croesus and Augustus,
Cyrus, Nebuchadnezzar, and Alexander.
There you will be stronger than Sampson, Sangar, and Abishai,
David and Shemaiah, Benaiah, and Sobochai.
There you will be more beautiful than Absalom, Joseph, and Moses,
Judith, Susanna, Rebecca, Sarah, and Rachel.
There [you will be] longer living than Enoch, Elijah, and Methuselah
and faster than Asahel, the Cushite, Hercules, and even the sun.
There (you will be) wiser than Solomon and Augustine,
Gregory, Jerome, Ambrose, and Thomas Aquinas.
There you will contemplate the Lord more clearly than Peter, John and also James,
Ezekiel, Isaiah, Moses, and Stephen.
The glory of Solomon can be a figure of this eternal glory *Figure One*
because we read that no one resided in such glory.
We find none so supported by delights,
we read of none abounding in so many riches.
The queen of Sheba, having heard about his fame, went to Jerusalem
and when she had seen his unbelievable glory, she spoke with great amazement.
"Greater is your glory than that rumour which I heard,
and I declare that not a fraction was announced to me."
Thus, it shall be confessed, when the soul arrives in celestial glory
that not half or a one-thousandth part of this glory will have been foretold to it.
The entire earth was longing to see the face of Solomon,
and it seems that this trifling thing has prefigured the face of the saviour.
For all pleasantness and all the joy of heaven.

46b[1] Consistit in conspectu illius iocundissimi faciei.
Melius esset anime in inferno esse et eam uidere
Quam in celo et eius melliflua visione carere.
[Omnia/Anima][2] existenti in inferno nullam sentiret penam
Si uideret illam faciem delectabilem et amenam. *secunda figura*
¶Secunda figura illius potest conuiuium regni Assueri esse.
Quia nullum legimus tam sollempne conuiuium habuisse.[3]
Ad hoc conuiuium non solum magnates uocabantur.
Sed omnis populus tam viri quam femine inuitabantur.
Sic deus fecit grande conuiuium et omnes uocat ad se
Transite inquit omnes ad me qui concupiscitis me.[4]
Conuiuium assueri centum octoginta dies durauit
Sed istud perpetuo durabit que nobis christus preparauit.
¶Tercia figura potest accipi in conuiuiis filiorum iob[5] *tercia figura.*
Quia nullos legimus tam continua conuiuia fecisse et tot.
Septem erant filii et singuli suo die conuiuium preparabant
Et uocantes tres sorores suas continue conuiuabant.
Per ista tempora conuiuia intelligamus celestem iocunditatem
Per circuitum vii dierum perpetuam eternitatem.
vii filii possunt esse sancti vii etatum.
Tres filie uirtutes angelice trium ieraracharum.
Omnes habent sine intermissione semper conuiuia
Omnes erunt semper in sempiterna leticia.
O bone ihesu propter tuam benignissimam bonitatem
Perduc nos ad illam perpetuam iocunditatem.

46va[6] *Capitulum xliii*

*I*n precedenti capitulo audiuiumus de intolerabili pena dampnatorum
Et de ineffabili gaudio et premio beatorum.
Consequenter audiamus quomodo penam euadamus.
⸌Et ad gloriam beatorum feliciter peruenire ualeamus.⸍[7]

[1] Right Panel: Job's Children Feasting. This might seem a less promising antitype, for while they were feasting they were carried to excess, provoking Job to intercede for their forgiveness (Job 1.4–5). Indeed, at one such feast they all, save for a single servant, perished when a great wind blew down the house (Job 1.19). [2] Corrected in a later hand [3] Est. 1.1–4 [4] Cf. Mt. 11.28, 22.1–14, Lk. 14.15–24 [5] Job 1.4 [6] Left Panel: A Vision of Christ Bearing his Cross. In this story a hermit in his cell is granted a vision in which he is asked to bear the cross of Jesus. The image shows the recluse enclosed in his cell, while Jesus, bearing his cross, speaks to him. [7] This line was originally skipped and added at the bottom of the column. Maniculi indicate the proper placement.

Consist in gazing upon his most delightful face.
It would be better for a soul to be in hell and to see it
than to be in heaven and lack the very honey-sweet sight of his face.
The soul of someone existing in hell would feel no pain
if it should see that delightful and beautiful face. *Figure Two*
The banquet of the king Ahasuerus can be the second figure of this,
because we read of no one having had so august a banquet.
To this banquet not only great men were called
but all people, both men and women, were invited.
Indeed, God made a grand feast and calls all to it.
"Come," he says, "to me, all you who desire me."
The banquet of Ahasuerus lasted one hundred and eighty days,
but this, which Christ prepared for us, will endure forever.
The third prefiguration can be understood in the banquets of Job's sons, *Figure Three*
because we read of no one having had banquets which were so prolonged and so many.
Seven were the sons and they prepared banquets, each one on his own day
and calling their three sisters, they feasted continually.
By these temporal banquets let us understand the delight of heaven;
through the cycle of seven days, perpetual eternity.
The seven sons can be the spirits of the seven ages;
three daughters, the angelic virtues of the three hierarchies.
All hold their feasts always without intermission;
all men will always be in everlasting joy.
O good Jesus, for the sake of your kindest benevolence,
lead us to that unending delight.

Chapter Forty-three

In the last chapter, we heard about the intolerable pain of the damned
and about the ineffable joy and reward of the blessed.
Next let us hear how we may avoid punishment
and be able to come joyfully to the glory of the blessed.

Qui ad gloriam beatorum desiderat peruenire
Debet deum ex toto corde diligere et sibi fideliter seruire.
Et quodcumque seruicium nouerit deo esse accepcius.
In eo debet sibi seruire libencius et diligencius.
¶Quidam homo deo deuotus in cellula sua residebat
Qui domino deo ex toto corde seruire satagebat.
Hic exorabat dominum continuis et deuotis precibus
Vt sibi reuelaret quod seruicium esset sibi accepcius.
Quadam uice videt dominum ihesum christum ad se uenientem
Et magnam crucem dorso baiulantem et sibi dicentem.
Non poteris mihi gracius et accepcius seruicium ⸌prestare⸍[1]
Quam quod iuues me grauem crucem meam [baiulare][2]
Qui respondens oro inquit domine dulcissime doce me.
Quibus modis debeam tecum crucem tuam baiulare.
In corde inquit dominus per recordacionem et compassionem
Et in ore per crebram et deuotam gratiarum accionem.
In auribus per penarum mearum feruentem audicionem.
In dorso per proprie carnis tue assiduam castigacionem.
Vt igitur eternam penam dampnatorum euadere ualeamus
Et ad perpetuam gloriam beatorum peruenire valeamus.
Saluatori nostro corde ore opere gratias agamus.
Et ad honorem passionis eius has oraciones dicamus.

46vb[3] *Ad vesperas dic hanc oracionem.*
Gratias tibi ago benedicte domine mi ihesu christe.
Quia tu es deus meus et saluator meus vere.
Qui hora diei uespertina dilecionem tuam mihi ostendisti
Quando mihi exemplum perfectissime humilitatis exhibuisti.
Tu dulcissime domine pedes seruorum tuorum lauisti
Et pedes traditoris tui abluere et tergere non spreuisti.[4]
Rogo te domine per hanc humilatatem superhanbudantissimam
Vt repellas a me omnem superbiam et arroganciam.
Infunde cordi meo veram et perfectam humilitatem.
Per quam ascendere possim sursum ad celeste sublimitatem.
O dulcissime domine etiam tibi libenter gratias dicerem
Si scirem si dignus essem et sufficerem.

[1] Added subsequently by the black-ink corrector [2] baiulare] portare, L (Deleted erroneously by scribal subpunction) [3] Right Panel: Last Supper (Vespers). Classic depiction, with John leaning on Jesus (curiously, here without a cross in his nimbus), and showing nine disciples, with three lacking a nimbus. The first of a series of meditations on the Passion, arranged for the canonical hours. [4] John 13.1–17

He who desires to come to the glory of the blessed
ought to love God with his whole heart and faithfully serve him.
And whatever service he knows to be pleasing to God,
in that, he should serve him freely and diligently.
One man, devoted to God, was settled in his own cell.
He busied himself in serving the Lord God with all his heart.
This man cried out to the Lord with continual and devout prayers
that God should reveal to him what service was welcome to him.
On one occasion, he saw the Lord Jesus Christ coming toward him,
bearing a great cross on his back and saying to him:
"You will not be able to offer me a service more gracious and acceptable
than to help me to bear my heavy cross."
That man, responding, said, "I pray, most sweet Lord, teach me
in what way I should bear your cross with you."
The Lord said, "in your heart through recollection and compassion;
and in your mouth through frequent and fervent thanksgiving;
in your ears through fervently listening to my punishments;
on the back through the constant discipline of your own flesh."
In order that, therefore, we might be able to avoid the eternal punishment of the damned
and to come to the perpetual glory of the blessed,
let us give thanks in our heart, word, and deed to our Savior,
and let us say these prayers for the honor of his passion.

At Vespers, say this prayer
I give thanks to you, my blessed Lord Jesus Christ,
because you are my God and my savior in truth.
At the close of the day you showed your love for me
when you gave to me the example of perfect humility.
You, most sweet lord, washed the feet of your servants
and you did not disdain to wash and dry clean the feet of your betrayer.
I ask you, Lord, through this most overflowing humility
that you drive from me all pride and arrogance.
Pour true and perfect humility into my heart,
through which I might be able to ascend up to the heavenly peak.
O most sweet lord, I would give thanks to you cheerfully
if I knew if I was worthy and adequate

Pro tam inestimabili et in effabili dilecione
Quam mihi exhibuisti in tua sacra{men}tissima communione.
Corpus tuum sacrosanctum mihi misero in cibum dedisti
Et sangiunem tuum preciosum mihi indigno in potum [/prebuisti.][1,2]
⸌Quis sufficit tam inmensissimam dilecionem enarrare.⸍[3]
Quis sufficit pro tantis beneficiis aliquid digne redonare
Si cencies millesies corpus meum morti traderem
Pro tam mirificis beneficiis tuis quasi nichil facerem.
Per hanc mirabilem dilecionem te piissime domine rogo
Per hec stupenda beneficia te dulcissime ihesu exoro.
Vt in hora mortis mee mihi tuum sacramentum subueniat
Et ad tuam mellifluam presenciam feliciter perducat.[4]
Quod nobis omnibus prestare dignetur dominus ihesus christus.
Qui cum patre et spiritu sancto est in perpetuum benedictus. amen.

47ra[5] *Ad Compline.*
*G*ratias tibi ago domine mi ihesu christe.
Quia tu es deus meus et saluator meus vere.
Qui hora completorii dilecionem tuam mihi ostendisti
Quando propter me contremuisti et sudorem sanguineum fudisti[6]
Ad locum illum accessisti sponte et uoluntarie
Vbi inimici tui uolebant te capere et ligare.[7]
Benignissimam mansuetudinem ibidem demonstrasti.
Quando traditori tuo os tuum ad osculandum non negasti.[8]
Judei quibus ostendisti sepissime magnam dilecionem
Ceperunt te et ligauerunt te tamquam furem et latronem.
Discipuli tui qui dixerant se uelle tecum ire in mortem
Omnes fugebant a te quando uidebant hostium cohortem.
Tu dulcissime domine solus inter hostes tuos remansisti
Nullum adiutorem nullum defensorem habuisti.
Cum gladiis et fustibus cum lucernis et facibus es captiuatus.
Cum multis contumeliis anne primo es presentatus.[9]
Ille te de doctrina tua et de discipulis tuis interrogauit
Qui[a] doctrinam tuam et discipulorum tuorum reprehendere affectauit.

---

[1] John 6.51, 1 Cor. 10.16 [2] prebuisti] contulisti, L (Original word thoroughly erased and now written in very black ink) [3] This line was inserted at the bottom of the paragraph, with maniculum at the bottom of the column to show placement, as well as a a "b," a rubricated "+", and a "II", courtesy of the black-ink corrector [4] See Ex. 16.31 [5] Left Panel: Jesus in the Garden of Gethsemane (Prayer for Compline). The image shows Jesus praying that, if possible, he be spared the cup of suffering, here held out to him by an angel. [6] Lk. 22.44 [7] Mt. 26.36–56, Mk. 14.32–52, Lk. 22.39–53, John 18.1–11 [8] See *SHS* Ch. 18 [9] See *SHS* Ch. 19

before so unmeasureable and unspeakable a love
which you showed me in your most holy communion.
You gave to me, wretch that I am, your most holy body as food
and you offered your precious blood to me, unworthy, as drink.
Who can tell so immense a love,
who can give back anything worthy in return for such kindnesses?
If I were to hand over my body to death a hundredfold, a thousandfold
[it would be] as if I did nothing in return for your too-wonderful kindnesses.
I ask you, most righteous Lord, through this marvelous love,
I beseech you, most sweet Jesus, through this astounding kindness
that in the hour of my death you rescue me by means of your sacrament
and lead me joyfully to your honey-sweet presence.
May the Lord Jesus Christ deign to grant this to us all,
who is blessed with the Father and the Holy Spirit forever. Amen.

At Compline
I give thanks to you, my Lord Jesus Christ,
because you are truly my God and my savior.
For at the hour of compline, you showed your love to me
when for my sake you trembled and poured out bloody sweat.
You approached that place freely of your own accord
where your enemies wanted to capture and bind you.
In that very place, you showed your kind gentleness
when you did not turn away your face from the kiss of your betrayer.
The Jews, to whom you again and again showed great love,
seized you and bound you just as they would a thief and robber.
Your disciples (who had said that they wished themselves to die with you)
all fled from you when they saw the enemy cohort.
You, sweetest Lord, remained alone among your enemies
you had not a single ally or defender.
You were taken captive with swords and clubs, with lamps and torches.
You were first presented to Ananias with much abuse;
he questioned you about your teaching and your followers
because he desired to censure both your teaching and that of your disciples.

Sed tu domine pie cum omni mansuetudine respondisti
Et a seruo eius alapam tibi datam humiliter sustinuisti.[1]
O dulcissime domine per sudorem tuum sanguineum te rogo
Per captiuitatem tuam et vincula tua te exoro.
Quatenus absoluas me a vinculis omnium modorum delictorum
Et perducas me post hoc exilium ad gaudium beatorum.
Quod nobis omnibus prestare dignetur dominus noster ihesus christus.
Qui cum patre et spiritu sancto est in perpetuum benedictus. amen.

47rb[2] *Ad Matutinas.*

*G*ratias ago tibi domine benedicte mi ihesu christe.
Quia tu es deus meus et saluator meus vere
Qui hora matutina dilecionem tuam mihi ostendisti
Quando propter me in domo cayphe illudi uoluisti.[3]
Ibi principes et seniores populi congregati fuerunt
Et contra te causas et testimonia quesierunt.
Sed nullam causam mortis iustam inuenire poterant
Quia omnia testimonia eorum insufficiencia erant.
Cumque cayphas quesisset si filius dei uiui esses
Et tu filium dei viui confessus te esse fuisses.
Hoc iustam causam mortis esse iudicauerunt
Et reus est mortis omnes contra se[4] exclamauerunt.
Faciem tuam amabilem et gloriosam uelauerunt[5]
Colaphis et alapis multimodis certatim te verberauerunt
Dixeruntque te ipsis debere prophetizare
Et quis esset qui te percussisset deberes enarrare.
Faciem tuam delectabilem in qu[/am] desiderant angeli prospicere[6]
Non sunt veriti maculare suo nephando sputamine.
Oculos tuos lucidiores sole qui c⌊uncta⌋[7] conspiciunt
Obumbrare uelamine et execare [/nisi sunt][8]
O dulcissime domine rogo te per uelamen oculorum tuoum
Per contumeliam colaphorum alaparum et sputorum.
Vt dimittas mihi contumeliam omnium criminum meorum.
Qua ego miserrimus perpetraui in conspectu oculorum tuorum
Quod nobis omnibus prestare dignetur dominus noster ihesus christus.
Qui cum patre et spiritu sancto est in perpetuum benedictus. Amen.

[1] See Mt. 20.19, Lk. 23.16, John 19.1 [2] Right Panel: Betrayal (Prayer for Matins). The kiss of Judas, who here approaches from the left of Jesus. [3] See *SHS* Ch. 19 [4] se] te, L [5] See *SHS* Ch. 19 [6] 1 Pt. 1.12 [7] cuncta, L] contra, G [8] Added in a very dark ink in a later hand

But you, merciful Lord, responded with all gentleness
and humbly you bore the blow his servant gave you.
O sweetest Lord, I ask you by your bloody sweat,
I beseech you by your captivity and your chains,
that you free me from the bonds of all manner of sin
and may you lead me through this exile to the joy of the blessed.
May the Lord Jesus Christ deign to grant this to us all,
who with the Father and the Holy Spirit is blessed forever. Amen.

At Matins
I give thanks to you, my blessed Lord Jesus Christ,
because you are truly my God and my savior.
At the hour of matins you showed to me your love,
when for my sake you willed to be mocked in the house of Caiaphas
where the chief people and elders had gathered together,
and sought charges and witnesses against you.
But they were able to discover no just cause for death
because all of their witnesses were inadequate.
However, when Caiaphas had asked if you were the son of the living God
and you had confessed that you were the son of the living God,
they judged that this was a just cause for death,
and "He is sentenced to death," they all cried out against him.
They blindfolded your loveable and glorious face;
they beat you zealously with various buffets and blows
and told you that you should prophesy to them,
and that you should to say who it was who had struck you.
Your beloved countenance on which angels longed to gaze
they were not afraid to dishonor with their own wicked spit.
Your eyes, brighter than the sun, which see all things
they strove to hide with a veil and to blind.
O sweetest Lord, I beg you by the veil over your eyes,
by the abuse of the buffets, blows, and spit,
that you might forgive the insult of all my sins,
which I, most wretched, committed in your sight.
May the Lord Jesus Christ deign to grant this to us all,
he who with the Father and the Holy Spirit is blessed forever. Amen.

47va[1] *Ad primam.*

Gratias tibi ago domine benedicte mi ihesu christe.
Quia tu es deus meus et saluator meus vere.
Qui hora diei prima dilecionem tuam mihi ostendisti
Quando propter me ab herode et exercitu suo illudi uoluisti.[2]
Cum enim per totam noctem in domo cayphe esses illusus
Mane facto ad presidem pylatum es perductus.
Qui audiens te esse hominem galyleum
Misit te herodi quia iudicium talium pertinebat ad eum.
Herodes gauisus est spera⌊ns⌋[3] a te uidere aliquod signum.
Quia putabat te esse nigromanticum et malignum.
Plebs iudaica astans coram herode te accusabat
Et rex herodes multis sermonibus te interrogabat.
Tu vero unicum uerbum ei respondere noluisti
Quia tu eius maliciosam intencionem cordis cognouisti.
At ille induit te ueste alba pro derisu et contumelia.
Et tamquam non sane mentis homini illusit tibi cum sua familia.
Post illusionem remisit te ad iudicium pylati
Et ita fuerunt inimici simul reconciliati.
Hec omnia sustinuisti pie domine cum paciencia nimia
Non propter tuas culpas sed propter mea scelerosa crimina.
Per has contumelias rogo domine tuam benignam clemenciam
Quatenus mihi conferas in omnibus tribulationibus veram pacienciam.
Vt in hac uita aduersitates ita ualeam tolerare
Vt tecum in regno tuo in perpetuum merear habitare.
Quod nobis omnibus prestare dignetur dominus ihesus christus.
Qui cum patre et spiritu sancto est in perpetuum benedictus. amen.

47vb[4] *Ad Tertiam.*

Gratias ago tibi benedicte domine mi ihesu christe.
Quia tu es deus meus et saluator meus vere.
Qui hora diei tercia dilecionem tuam mihi ostendisti
Quando propter me flagellari[5] et spinis coronari uoluisti[6].
Tamquam maleficum ad colupnam te ligauerunt

[1] Left Panel: Pilate Washes his Hands (Prayer for Prime). Pilate, crowned like a medieval king, washes his hands in a gesture by which he hopes to remain guiltless of the crucifixion of Jesus. [2] See SHS Ch. 20 [3] sperans, L] sperat⟨*a⟩, G [4] Right Panel: Flagellation (Prayer for Terce). Two figures, small in scale to emphasize the centrality of Christ, scourge him with whips. [5] See SHS Ch. 20 [6] See SHS Ch. 21

At Prime
I give thanks to you, my blessed Lord Jesus Christ,
because you are truly my God and my savior.
At the first hour of the day you showed me your love
when for my sake you willed to be mocked by Herod and his soldiers.
For after you had been mocked in the house of Caiaphas all night
and day began, you were led to the governor Pilate.
He, hearing that you were a man of Galilee,
sent you to Herod because the judgement of such men belonged to him.
Herod was glad, hoping to see some marvel from you.
For he thought that you were a necromancer and wicked man.
The Jewish people accused you, standing before Herod.
And King Herod put many questions to you.
Truly you did not wish to answer a single word to him
for you knew the wicked intention of his heart.
But he dressed you in a white robe for derision and insult,
and he, as well as his household, ridiculed you as if you were not in your right mind.
After the mockery, he sent you back to the court of Pilate
and so his enemies were reconciled together.
All this you endured, merciful Lord, with exceeding patience
not on account your faults, but because of the wickedness of my sins.
By these insults, Lord, I beg your gentle clemency,
that you give me true patience in all trials,
so that in this life I may be willing to endure adversities in this way
so that I may become worthy to live eternally with you in your kingdom.
May the Lord Jesus Christ deign to grant this to us all,
who with the Father and the Holy Spirit is blessed forever. Amen.

At Terce
I give thanks to you, my blessed Lord Jesus Christ,
because you are truly my God and my savior.
At the third hour of the day you showed me your love
when for my sake you willed to be scourged and crowned with thorns.
They bound you like a criminal to the column;

Virgis et flagellis tam inhumaniter te percusserunt.
Quod in toto corpore tuo nulla sanitas erat
Et sanguis tuus preciosus ex ipso riuulatim effluebat.
Coronam de acutissimis spinis plectebant
Et eam capiti tuo loco dyadematis imponebant.
Veste coccinea pro pallio regali te induebant.
Arundinem pro ceptro regio in dextera tua dabant.
Et coram te genua flectentes te salutabant
Et subsannatorie te regem iudeorum uocabant.
Caput tuum uenerandum arundine percuciebant
Colaphis et alapis te percuciebant et conspuebant
Sputis eorum tuo sanguine admixtis maculabaris
Et tamquam leprosus aspectu horribile videbaris.
O dulcissime ihesu rogo te per tuam crudelissimam flagellacionem
Et exoro per tuam amarissimam coronacionem.
Quatenus velim nolim me ita digneris hic flagellare
Vt in futuro flagellis iracundie tue non merear uapulare
Vt etiam flagello acerbi purgatorii non senciam
Sed sine omni flagella ad eternam perueniam gloriam.
Quod nobis omnibus prestare dignetur dominus ihesus christus.
Qui cum patre et spiritu sancto est benedictus. amen.

48ra[1] *Ad Sextam.*
Gratias tibi ago benedicte domine ihesu christe.
Quia tu es deus meus et saluator meus vere.
Qui hora diei sexta dilecionem mihi ostendisti
Quando propter me morti adiudicari et crucifigi uoluisti.[2]
Post multas accusaciones pilatus manus suas lauit
Et te in patibulum crucis suspendedum sentenciauit.
Crucem tuam tuis humeris baiulandam imponebant
Et hoc ad maiorem tuam contumeliam faciebant.
Super crucem te extendentes funibus traxerunt
Et manus et pedes ⌞tuos⌟[3] clauis ferreis affixerunt.
Post hoc in altum cum cruce te erexerunt.
Et diuersis subsannacionibus et chachinnis te deriserunt.
Ibidem pie domine dilecionem tuam maximam demonstrasti
Quando pro ipsis precem tuum suppliciter exorasti.

---

[1] Left Panel: Christ Carries Out his Cross (Prayer for Sext). In a compression of scenes, Pilate looks on from a dais as Jesus is led out by Roman soldiers, carrying his cross. [2] See *SHS* Ch. 22 [3] tuos, L] tuis, G

they struck you so viciously with rods and whips,
that in the whole of your body there was no health
and your precious blood flowed out of it in a stream.
They wove a crown from the sharpest thorns
and placed it on your head in place of a diadem.
For a royal cloak they clothed you in a scarlet robe.
For a royal scepter in your right hand, they gave you a reed.
And bending their knees before you, they saluted you
and they deridingly called you the King of the Jews.
With the reed they struck your head, worthy of veneration;
they spat on you and beat you with cuffs and slaps.
You were dirtied by their spit mixed with your blood
and you seemed like a leper with a horrible appearance.
O sweetest Jesus, I beg you by your cruellest flagellation
and I beseech you by your most bitter coronation
that, whether I am willing or unwilling, you might deign to scourge me here in that way,
so that in the future I might not deserve to be beaten with the scourges of your wrath,
and also that I might not feel the scourges of harsh Purgatory,
but arrive at eternal glory without any scourge.
May our Lord Jesus Christ deign to grant this to us all,
who is blessed with the Father and the Holy Spirit forever. Amen.

At Sext
I give thanks to you, blessed Lord Jesus Christ,
because you are truly my God and my savior.
At the sixth hour of the day you showed me your love
when for my sake you willed to be condemned to death and crucified.
After many accusations Pilate washed his hands
and decreed that you be hung on the gallows of the cross.
They placed your cross on your shoulders for you to carry
and they did this for your greater humiliation.
Stretching you out, they pulled you upon the cross with ropes
and staked your hands and feet with iron nails.
After this, they raised you into the sky with the cross
and they derided you with various insults and jeering.
Then, merciful Lord, you proved your greatest love
when as a suppliant you breathed out your prayer for them.

Preter hoc dilectissime ihesu aliam contumeliam sustinuisti
Quando matrem tuam iuxta crucem amarissime[1] respexisti.
Ad ampliandam tuam contumeliam duos latrones adducebant
Et te in medio ipsorum tamquam consortem suspendebant.
Quorum vni inmensissimam misericordiam tuam ostendisti
Cui in extremis contricionem immisisti et paradysum promisisti.[2]
O dulcissime domine rogo te per sentenciam supra datam
Et exoro te per omnem penam tibi innocenter illatam.
Vt me ab horribili sentencia sinistrorum eripias
Vt cum collegio dextorum in regnum tuum intromittas.[3]
Quod nobis omnibus prestare dignetur dominus ihesus christus.
Qui cum patre et spiritu sancto est in perpetuum benedictus. amen.

48rb[4,5] *Ad Nonam.*
*G*ratias ago tibi benedicte mi domine ihesu christe.
Quia tu es deus meus et saluator meus vere.
Qui hora diei nona dilectionem tuam mihi ostendisti
Quando propter me in crucis patibulo mortuus fuisti.[6]
Lamentacionem nimis [magnam] miserandam planxisti.
Quando hely hely lamasabathani dixisti.
Deus meus deus meus ut quid dereliquisti me.
Cum tamen deus tuus numquam fuerit seperatus a te.
Deinde dulcissime domine mi dixisti sicio
Et dabant tibi vinum mirratum cum aceto felle mixto.[7]
Diuersimodis derisionibus contra te ⌊blasph⌋emauerunt[8]
Omnes quas potuerunt contumelias tibi intulerunt.
Post hec amantissime ihesu consumatum est dixisti
Et spiritum tuum patri commendans mortuus fuisti.
Tunc latus tuum lancea perforauerunt
De quo sanguis et aqua in medicamentum meum effluxerunt.
Omnes creature tibi compati et condolere uidebantur
Sol obscuratus est et petre scindebantur.
Terre motus factus est et monumenta aperta fuerunt.
Et multi sanctorum post resurrecionem tuam resurrexerunt.

---

[1] amarissime] turbatissimam, L [2] Lk. 23.40–43 [3] See Mt. 25.31–46 [4] Right Panel: Crucifixion (Prayer for Nones). This is a classic "*stabat mater iuxtra cruces*" image, with supplicant Mary on the left and John the beloved disciple carrying a codex gospel and holding his hand under his chin in a gesture of lamentation. [5] This series of prayed meditations on the Passion of Christ, arranged for the canonical hours of the religious life, resemble but do not precisely parallel those found toward the end of the *Meditationes Vitae Christi* (74–83). [6] See *SHS* Ch. 25 [7] Mt. 27.34, Mk. 15.23; See also Ps. 68.22 [8] BLASPHEMAUERUNT: L] plasmauerunt, G

O merciful Lord, I beg you by your most bitter death,
while you pour out for me your most favorable grace,
that I may thus wish to love you and so serve you
that after this exile I might be worthy to come to the glory of the blessed.
May Lord Jesus Christ deign to grant this to us all,
who with the Father and the Holy Spirit is blessed forever. Amen.

Chapter Forty-Four, Concerning the Seven Sorrows of the Blessed Virgin

In the last chapter we heard about the sevenfold thanksgiving
which we should to say to our Lord Jesus Christ for his passion.
Now let us hear of the seven greetings and honey-sweet prayers
which we should to recite to the Blessed Virgin on account of her seven sorrows.
For just as it is pleasing to the Lord to call to mind His passion and punishments
so it is also pleasing to the Blessed Virgin to meditate on her sorrows.
There was a certain brother in the Order of Preachers
who greatly loved the Lord Jesus Christ and his mother.
His meditations often revolved around the punishments of Christ
and the sorrows and sadnesses of his most sweet Mother.
This man constantly beseeched the Lord in his prayers
that he might to some extent allow him to understand his own sufferings.
At last the Lord granted his pious petitions
and revealed to him a small portion of his Passion.
Accordingly, it seemed to him that his hands and feet were stretched out
and with the greatest anguish he was pierced with iron nails.
Afterwards he humbly entreated the Blessed Virgin from his inmost heart
that she would reveal something to him of her various sorrows.
And it seemed to him that the sharpest sword approached
and pierced his heart with the greatest sorrow.
That brother, because of his meditation and thanksgiving,
gained divine revelation and eternal consolation.
On account of which we gladly entrust to the Lord the aforementioned thanksgivings
and the following 'Aves' to his most glorious mother Mary,
so that in this life we may obtain freedom from all sadness
and in the future life we may obtain the enjoyment of eternal happiness.

48vb[1] *prima tristicia beate virginis.*

¶*A*ve maria mater christi pia celestis imperatrix.
Tv es uirgo dya tristium in hac uia clemens consolatrix.
Obsecro te piissima domina per cunctas tuas tristicias
Quas in hac uita perpessa es multas et uarias.
Vt mihi misero subuenire digneris in quacumque tribulacione
Et consolari non abnuas cum tua melliflua consolacione.
Quamuis diuerse et multe fuerint tue tristicie et dolores
Tamen precipue vii fuerunt principales et maiores.
Primam tristiciam mater piissima tunc habuisti
Quando prophetiam symeonis in templo domini audiuisti.[2]
Cum magno gaudio et leticia ad templum veniebas
Cum [-de][3] magno dolore et tristicia de templo recedebas.
In offerendo filium tuum tanto patri magnam habebas leticiam
Sed illa ibidem subito \con/uersa[4] est in magnam tristiciam.
Antiquus enim ille symeon tristes rumores tibi nunciauit
Quando tibi de gladio dilectissimi filii tui prophetizauit.
Quem transiturum dicebat tuam dilectissimam animam
De quibus uerbis concepisti in corde tuo non modicam tristiciam.
Intencionem huius prophecie per optime intelligebas
Et de ipsa [super] deinceps tristiciam in corde gerebas.
Per hanc tristiciam tuam mater clementissima rogo te
Ora dilectum filium tuum dominum nostrum ihesum christum pro me.
Quatenus me per suam amarissimam passionem
Perducat post hoc exilium ad eternam consolacionem.
Quod nobis prestare dignetur dominus noster ihesus christus.
Qui cum patre et spiritu sanco est in perpetuum benedictus. amen.

49ra[5] *Secunda tristicia*

*A*ve maria mater christi pia celestis imperatrix
Tu es uirgo dya tristium in hac uia clemens consolatrix.
Secundam tristiciam mater dulcissima tunc habuisti
Quando cum filio tuo dilecto in egipto fugisti.[6]
Rex herodes filium querere et interficere cogitabat

---

[1] Right Panel: First Sorrow: Simeon's Prophecy. Technically the First Sorrow of the Virgin was to hear that as a result of her son's coming a sword would pierce her heart. Originating with the Servite order in 1233, this devotional cycle was popularized by St. Bridgit of Sweden. The iconography also features in some instances seven swords. [2] Lk. 2.25–35 [3] Deleted by scribal subpunction and struck through by rubricator [4] Inserted by a carrot [5] Left Panel: Second Sorrow: The Angel's Warning to Joseph to Flee to Egypt. The Second Sorrow sometimes called for showing the slaughter of the innocents by Herod, an image omitted here. [6] See *SHS* Ch. 11

The First Sorrow of the Blessed Virgin
Hail Mary, Mother of Christ, holy queen of heaven.
You are, O holy Virgin, the gentle comforter of sorrows on this path.
I beseech you, most merciful lady, by all your sorrows,
great and many, which you endured in this life,
that you might deign to come down to me, wretched in whatsoever tribulation,
and that you might not refuse to console me with your honey-sweet consolation.
However great and many your sadnesses and sorrows were,
nevertheless, there were seven especially chief and greater.
Most merciful mother, you had then the first sorrow
when you heard the prophesy of Simeon in the temple of the Lord.
You came with great joy and delight to the temple;
you withdrew from the temple with great sadness and sorrow.
In offering your son to so great a Father you had great joy,
but on the spot the joy was suddenly turned into great sadness.
For the ancient Symeon proclaimed sorrowful news to you
when he prophesied to you concerning the sword of your most beloved son,
which sword, he said, would run through your beloved soul
from which words you gave birth to no small grief in your heart.
You well understood the application of this prophecy
and concerning it, you were carrying sorrow in your heart thereafter.
By this your sorrow, Mother most clement, I beg you—
pray to your beloved son our Lord Jesus Christ for me
that for the sake of your most bitter passion
he will lead me after this exile to eternal consolation.
May our Lord Jesus Christ deign to grant this to us,
who with the Father and the Holy Spirit is forever blessed. Amen.

Second Sorrow
Hail Mary, Mother of Christ, merciful queen of heaven.
You are, O holy virgin of sorrows, the gentle comforter on this path.
At that time, sweetest mother, you had the second sorrow
when you were a fugitive in Egypt with your beloved son.
King Herod was intending to seek out and kill your son

Et hoc angelus domini in sompnis ioseph nunciabat.
Surge inquit et accipe puerum et matrem eius et fuge in egiptum
Futurum est enim ut herodes querat puerum ad perdendum ipsum.
Hec uerba[1] mitissima animam tuam ualde vvlnerauerunt
Et cordi tuo uirgineo magnam tristiciam intulerunt.
Tunc oportebat te cognatos et notos et patriam deserere.
Et nocturno tempore per desertum ad terras paganorum fugere.
Rex autem herodes querebat filium cum tanta inuidia
Quod occidit propter eum puerorum centum xl iiii[2] milia.
Tu clementissima domina ad terram alienam ueniebas
Vbi nec cognatos nec amicos nec notos habebas.
Magnam {t}ibi inediam et penuriam sustinuisti
Colo et acu filio tuo tibi uictum et uestitum conquesisti.
Hanc peregrinacionem et tristiciam vii annis tolerasti.
Et tunc defuncto herode cum filio tuo et ioseph repatriasti.
Per hanc tristiciam mater clementissima rogo te
Ora dilectum tuum filium dominum ihesum christum pro me.
Vt in hac peregrinacione ab omni malo nos custodiat
Et post hoc exilium ad celestem patriam nos perducat.
Quod nobis omnibus prestare dignetur dominus noster ihesus christus.
Qui cum patre et spiritu sancto est in perpetuum benedictus.

49rb[3] *tercia tristicia.*

*A*ve maria mater [\christi pia celestis][4] mediatrix
Tv es uirgo dya tristium in hac uia clemens consolatrix.
Terciam tristiciam mater dulcissima tunc habuisti
Quando filium tuum dilectum duodenem amisisti.[5]
Cum enim filius tuus dilectissimus esset annorum xii.
Ibat tecum de nazareth ad diem festum pasce in ierusalem.
Quando autem festiuitas illa peracta et completa erat
Tv rededibas et ipse te nesciente in ierusalem remanebat.
Sed hoc non peruenie bat pia mater ex tua negligencia
Sed ordinante et disponente diuina clemencia.[6]
Tv putabas puerum esse cum ioseph in turba uirorum
Joseph putabat eum tecum esse in turba mulierum.

[1] uerba] virga, L [2] Cf. Mt. 2.16 [3] Right Panel: Third Sorrow: Christ Among the Doctors. This event normally recalls Mary's anguish at discovering that Jesus was missing, and her frantic search for him back in Jerusalem, where she and Joseph found him three days later (Lk. 1.46—not twelve days, as the SHS text has it, before correcting it several lines later). The image here is tranquil, showing the youthful Jesus as a *magister* teaching Jewish elders but also, in the foreground, a fourteenth-century monk. [4] Corrected in heavy black ink by a later hand. The 'a' in mediatrix has also been touched up. [5] Cf. Lk. 2.41–52 [6] clemencia] sapiencia, L

and an angel of the Lord announced this to Joseph in a dream;
"Rise up," he said, "and take the boy and his mother and flee into Egypt,
for it will come to pass that Herod will search for the boy in order to destroy him."
These most gentle words greatly wounded your soul,
and they brought great sorrow to your virginal heart.
Then it was necessary for you to leave your family and aquaintances and homeland
and to flee at night through the wilderness to the lands of pagans.
King Herod, however, was searching for the son with such hatred
that, on account of him, he killed 144,000 boys.
You, most gentle lady, went to a foreign land
where you had neither family nor friends nor acquaintances.
There you endured great hunger and poverty
with distaff and needle you sought out food and clothing for your son and yourself.
You endured this pilgrimage and sorrow for seven years,
and then after the death of Herod, you and Joseph returned home with your son.
By this sorrow I ask you, most gentle mother,
pray to your beloved son, the Lord Jesus Christ for me
that in this pilgrimage he might protected us from all evil
and after this exile he might guide us to the heavenly homeland.
May our Lord Jesus Christ deign to grant this to us all,
who with the Father and the Holy Spirit is forever blessed. Amen.

Third Sorrow
Hail Mary, Mother of Christ, holy heavenly mediator,
you are, O holy Virgin of sorrows, the gentle comforter on this path.
At that time, sweetest mother, you had the third sorrow
when you lost your beloved twelve-year-old son.
For when your most beloved son was twelve years old,
he went with you from Nazareth into Jerusalem for the day of the Pascal Feast.
When, however, that festival was celebrated and completed,
you began to return and your son, without you knowing, remained in Jerusalem.
But this came to pass, merciful mother, not because of your negligence
but from the ordinance and arrangement of divine clemency.
You thought that the boy was with Joseph in the crowd of men;
Joseph thought he was with you in the crowd of women.

Viri enim ibant soli ad festum et mulieres sole
Pueri autem pro placito suo ire poterant utrobique.
Cum igitur de ierusalem per unam dietam recessisses
Et puerum cum patre suo ioseph putatiuo non inuenisses.
Qualis dolor et quam inmensa tristicia tunc inuasit te.
Difficile potest cor conperi difficilius os enarrare
Vsque in diem tercium cum magna tristicia eum quesiuisti
Donec eum in templo in medio doctorum sedentem inuenisti.
Per hanc tristiciam mater clementissima rogo te
Ora dilectum filium tuum dominum ihesum christum pro me.
Vt doceat me in hac uita tam diligenter querere se.
Vt ipsum in celesti templo feliciter merear inuenire
Quod nobis omnibus prestare dignetur dominus ihesus christus.
Qui cum patre et spiritu sancto est in perpetuum benedictus.

49va[1] *Quarta tristicia*

*A*ve maria mater christi pia celestis imperatrix
Tv es uirgo dya tristium in hac uia clemens consolatrix.
Quartam tristiciam mater dulcissima tunc habuisti
Quando dilectissimum filium tuum traditum et captum audiuisti.[2]
Judei quibus magna et multa beneficia sepius exibuerat
Et gentiles quibus numquam in aliquo molestus fuerat.
Pariter conglobati contra eum cum gladiis et fustibus exierunt
Et tamquam furem et latronem ipsum ceperunt et ligauerunt.
Discipulus ille quem procuratorem curie sue fecerat
Ipse infidelissime et fraudulenter per osculum tradebat.[3]
Discipuli omnes qui se uelle mori cum ipso dixerant
Ipsum solum reliquentes omnes ab eo fugiebant.[4]
Filius tuus autem solus ad iudices est productus
Et multis contumeliis verbis et verberibus est afflictus.
De platea in plateam de domo in domum ipsum trahebant
Alaparum et colaphorum et sputorum mensuram non tenebant.
O qualem et quantam tristiciam pia uirgo tunc habuisti
Quando tibi tanta et talia de filio tuo nunciari audiuisti
Puto quod nulla mens ipsam posset excogitare
Nec aliqua lingua sufficiat enarrare.

[1] Left Panel: Fourth Sorrow: The Betrayal and Arrest. The representation is conventional, except that one of the soldiers ominously carries three nails. [2] See *SHS* Ch. 17 [3] Mt. 26.47–50, Mk. 14.43–45 [4] Mt. 26.56, Mk. 14.50

For the men and women were going each by themselves to the festival.
The children, however, were able to go in either group, with the one that pleased them.
When, therefore, you had withdrawn a day's walk from Jerusalem
and you did not find the child with his supposed father Joseph,
what sort of sorrow and how great a sadness then took possession of you,
the heart can conceive with difficulty, and the mouth can tell with still more difficulty.
For three days, you sought him with great sorrow
until you found him in the temple sitting in the midst of the teachers.
By this sorrow I beg you, most gentle mother,
pray to your beloved son, the Lord Jesus Christ for me
that he might teach me in this life to seek him so diligently
that I might be worthy to happily find him in the heavenly temple.
May the Lord Jesus Christ deign to grant this to us all,
who with the Father and the Holy Spirit is forever blessed.

Fourth Sorrow
Hail Mary, Mother of Christ, holy empress of heaven.
You are, O holy Virgin, the gentle comforter of sorrows on this path.
At that time, sweetest mother, you had the fourth sorrow
when you heard that your most beloved son was betrayed and captured.
The Jews, to whom benefits many and great had often been shown,
and Gentiles to whom he had never in anything been troublesome,
joined together equally and marched forth against him with swords and clubs
and seized and bound him like a thief and a robber.
That disciple whom he had made the agent of his sorrow,
that one most unfaithfully and falsely handed him over through a kiss.
All the disciples who had said that they wanted to die with him,
left him alone and all fled from him.
Your son, moreover, was led forth alone to the judges
and was afflicted with many insults, words, and beatings.
From street to street, from home to home, they dragged him;
there was no limit of blows and buffets and spitting.
O how great and what sort of sorrow did you, O merciful Virgin, then have
when you heard things so great and so terrible announced to you about your son.
I think that no mind is able to imagine it
nor does any tongue suffice to tell it.

Per hanc tristiciam mater clementissima rogo te
Hora dilectum filium tuum dominum Ihesum christum pro me.
Quatenus propter captiuitatem suam et ligamina suorum vinculorum.
Me absoluat a vinculis omnium delictorum meorum.
Quod nobis omnibus prestare dignetur dominus ihesus christus.
Qui cum patre et spiritu sancto est in perpetuum benedictus.

49vb[1] *Quinta tristicia*
*A*ve maria mater christi pia celestis mediatrix[2]
Tv es uirgo dya tristium in hac uia clemens consolatrix.
Quintam tristiciam mater dulcissima tunc habuisti
Quando dulcissimum filium tuum in cruce pendentem conspexisti.[3]
Quando ipsum in tam multiplicibus penis videbas
Et tv ei nullum auxilium uel solamen prestare ualebas.
Tv uidebas eum pendere nudum omnino sine uelamine
Et non sinebaris nuditatem eius pallio tuo contegere.
Et tu audiebas eum sitim suam querulose recitare
Et non sinebaris vnicam guttam ei propinare.
Tv uidebas caput eius miserabiliter deorsum dependere
Et non sinebaris illud manibus tuis subleuare uel tenere.
Tv audiebas malificos diuersimode ipsum subsannare
Et non ualebas iniurias aliquatenus iudicare.
Tv audiebas quod commendabat patri suo ipsum[4]
Et non sinebaris vn[/um] ei dare finale amoris osculum.
Nec sinebant impii quod tam prope ad eum accessisses
Vt in obitu suo more matris oculos eius clausisses.
In nullo prorsus ei subuenire aliquatenus potuisti
Et tanto maiorem tristiciam in corde ⸤t⸥uo[5] sustinuisti.
Per hanc tristiciam mater dulcissima rogo te
Ora dilectum filium tuum iesum christum pro me.
Quatenus mihi in extrema hora mors sua subueniat
Et post hanc miseriam ad uitam eternam perducat.
Quod nobis omnibus prestare dignetur dominus iesus christus
Qui cum patre et spiritu sancto est in perpetuum benedictus.

---

[1] Right Panel: Fifth Sorrow: Crucifixion. Essentially a repeat of the image at 48R, Right Panel. [2] mediatrix] imperatrix, L [3] John 19.23–28 [4] Lk. 23.46 [5] tuo, L] suo, G

Through this sorrow I ask you, most gentle Mother
pray to your beloved son the Lord Jesus Christ for me,
so that for the sake of his captivity and the bounds of his chains.
he may release me from the chains of all my sins.
May the Lord Jesus Christ deign to grant this to us all,
who with the Father and the Holy Spirit is forever blessed.

Fifth Sorrow
Hail Mary, Mother of Christ, holy mediator of heaven,
you are, O holy Virgin of sorrows, the gentle comforter on this path.
At that time, sweetest mother, you had the fifth sorrow
when you saw your sweetest son hanging on the cross.
When you were watching him in so much pain
and you were able to supply him with no aid or solace,
you watched him hang naked without any covering
and you were not allowed to conceal his nakedness with your cloak.
And you were hearing him speak of his thirst pleadingly,
and you were not allowed to offer a single drop to him.
You were watching his head miserably hang downwards
and you were not allowed to support it or hold it with your hands.
You heard evildoers insult him in various ways,
and you were not able to condemn the wrongs for a long time.
You were hearing him commend himself to his father,
and you were not allowed to give him one last kiss of love.
Nor did the wicked ones allow you to approach near to him
so that you could close his eyes in death as is the custom for mothers.
In short, you were able in no way to then help him
and you endured a sorrow in your heart so much the greater.
By this sorrow, I ask you, sweetest mother,
pray to your beloved son Jesus Christ for me
that his death might help me in my final hour
and after this misery may lead me to the eternal life.
May Lord Jesus Christ deign to grant this to us all,
who with the Father and the Holy Spirit is forever blessed. Amen.

50ra[1] *Sexta tristicia.*

*A*ve maria mater pia celestis imperatrix
Tv es uirgo dya tristium in hac uia clemens consolatrix.
Sextam tristiciam mater dulcissima tunc habuisti
Quando dilectum filium tuum mortuum suscepisti.
Quando ipsum brachiis tuis dulcissima uirgo maria[2]
Mortuum et liuidum imposuit ioseph ab aramathia.[3]
Quem olim crebro dulciter et letanter viuum portaueras
Hunc hev mortuum cum magna tristicia portabas.[4]
Novvs luctus et nouus gemitus in corde tuo oriebatur
Et tristicia tua magis ac magis accumulabatur.
O quantus erat pia mater tuus luctus et ploratus
O qualis erat dulcis virgo tuus planctus et ululatus.
O quam modicam quietem et consolacionem maria habuisti
Antequam filium tuum dilectum resurrexisse conspexisti.
Tantam habuisti pia mater tristiciam et dolorem
Quod libenter pro filio tuo dilecto uel cum eo subiisses passionem.
Die noctuque luxisti planxisti doluisti et fleuisti
Quam div illa melliflua presencia filli tui caruisti.
O quam durum et quam lapideum cor habere uideretur
Qui tue tristicie tam inmense virgo pia non compateretur.
Rogo ergo te clementissima mater per hanc tristiciam
Ora pro me dilectum filium tuum omnium saluatorem.
Vt mihi in omnibus tribulacionibus meis pie subueniat
Et in hora mortis mee animam meam feliciter suscipiat.
Quod nobis omnibus prestare dignetur dominus iesus christus.
Qui cum patre et spiritu sancto est in perpetuum benedictus.

50rb[5] *Septima tristicia.*

*A*ve maria mater christi pia celestis imperatrix
Tv es uirgo dya tristium in hac uia clemens consolatrix.
Septimam tristiciam mater dulcissima tunc habuisti
Quando post ascensum filii tui tam div in hoc exilio remansisti.
Semper tristis eras semper merebas semper lugebas

[1] Left Panel: Sixth Sorrow: Entombment. Repeats the entombment image at 30V Left Panel, but with the addition of the ladder from 29V Left Panel. [2] Cf. Mt. 27.55–56, Mk. 15.46, Lk. 23.53, John 19.38; See also *SHS* Ch. 26 [3] Cf. Mt. 27.57–60, Mk. 15.42–46, Lk. 23.50–54, John 21.38–42 [4] Lk. 2.34–35 [5] Right Panel: Seventh Sorrow: The Virgin Revisits Holy Sites. With a rearrangement of the iconic signs of Christ's flagellation, crucifixion (chalice with nails) footprints left after his ascension, a sarcophagus (presumably), the cross, and a sign of the Sun of Righteousness, this is another version of fol. 38v, Left Panel.

Sixth Sorrow
Hail Mary, Mother of Christ, holy empress of heaven
you are, O holy Virgin of sorrows, the gentle comforter on this path.
At that time, sweetest mother, you had the sixth sorrow
when you took up your beloved son, dead.
When in your arms, O sweetest virgin Mary,
Joseph of Aramathia placed him, dead and bruised,
he whom long ago you had so often sweetly and joyfully carried alive,
now, alas! you were carrying him dead in great sorrow.
A new grief and a new groan rose up in your heart
and your sorrow accumulated more and more.
O how great was your mourning and wailing, merciful mother!
O how intense was your lamentation and wailing, sweet virgin!
O how small was the peace and comfort you had, O Mary!
Before you understood that your beloved son would rise,
you had such sorrow and sadness, holy Mother,
because you would have freely endured the Passion in place of your beloved son, orwith him.
Through day and night you lamented, you cried, you grieved, and you wept,
as long as you lacked that honey-sweet presence of your son.
O how hard and how stony the heart would he seem to have
who did not have compassion, O holy Virgin, on your sorrow so great.
I therefore beg you, most gentle Mother, by this sorrow,
pray for me to your beloved son, the savior of all,
that he might mercifully come to me in all my tribulations
and at the hour of my death happily take up my soul.
May the Lord Jesus Christ deign to grant this to us all
who with the Father and the Holy Spirit is forever blessed.

Seventh Sorrow
Hail Mary, Mother of Christ, holy empress of heaven,
you are, O holy Virgin of sorrows, the gentle comforter on this path.
At that time, sweetest mother, you had the seventh sorrow
when after the ascension of your Son you so remained for a long time in this exile.
Always you were sorrowful, always were you mourning, always were you lamenting,

Quam div illa mellifua prescencia filii tui carebas.
O quanto desiderio reditum eius ad te affectabas.
Cuius dulcissima presencia tam grauiter carere poteras.
O quanto tedio aduentum eius exspectabas.
Quem uirgo intacta conceperas et sine grauamine portaueras.
O quanto affectu prescenciam eius crebro recogitabas
Quem inuiolata pepereras et uirgineo lacte tu paueras
O quantis lacrimis omnia loca filii tui perambulabas
O qualibet et quantis osculis et amplexibus singula pertractabas.
Omnia enim loca deuotissime uisitare solebas
In quibus filium tuum conceptum natum et moratum sciebas.
Vbi fuerat traditus captus ligatus consputus et illusus
Flagellatus coronatus mortuus sepultus et assumptus.
Hec loca et alia plura cum magna tristicia perambulabas.
Ita ut dicit epyphanius xxiiii annis preseuerabas.
Per hanc tristiciam mater clementissima rogo te
Ora dilectum filium tuum dominum ihesum christum pro me.
Vt dignetur me clementer a presenti tristicia liberari
Et perducere ut eterna merear leticia perfrui.
Quod nobis omnibus prestare dignetur dominus ihesus christus.
Qui cum patre et spiritu sancto est in perpetuum benedictus.

50va[1] *capitulum xlv^m scilicet de vii gaudiis beate virginis.*

*I*n precedenti capitulo audimus de beate uirginis vii tristiciis
Consequenter audiamus de vii eius gaudiis.
Gaudia beate virginis debemus deuote honorare
Vt ipsa nos dignetur ⌊in⌋[2] nostris tribulacionibus letificare.
Quam acceptum sit hoc obsequium beate uirgini et quam gratum
In quodam sacerdote beate virgini deuoto est demonstratum.
Qui solitus erat gaudia beate virginis crebro recogitare
Et oracionibus et canticis prout potuit deuocius honorare
Hic quodam tempore egritudine correptus[3] cepit infirmari
Et peccata sua recogitans cepit anxius contristari.

[1] Left Panel: The Virgin and an Angel Appear to a Priest. In this legend, a priest who was a devotee of the Joys of Mary is visited in extremis to tell him that he need not fear for his sins, for he will be led directly to heaven. Originally five in number, this late medieval devotion grew to seven joys by the 15th century, with Franciscans substituting for the Visitation to Elizabeth the Finding in the Temple, Pentecost, and the Coronation of the Virgin in Heaven. [2] in, L] a, G [3] Other mss. read *conceptus*

for as long as you were lacking that honey-sweet presence of your son.
O with how much desire did you yearn for to his return to you,
whose sweet presence you missed so deeply!
O with what weariness were you waiting for his return,
whom you, untouched Virgin, conceived and bore without grief!
O with how much love did you remember constantly his presence,
to whom you had given birth, still inviolate, and whom you had fed with a maiden's milk!
O with how many tears were you going about all the shrines of your son!
O with how many kisses and embraces of what kind did you touch each one!
For you were accustomed to most devoutly visit all the places
in which you knew your son was conceived, born, and died;
where he was handed over, captured, bound, spit upon, and mocked;
scourged, crowned, killed, buried, and taken up.
You made a tour of these places and many others with great sorrow;
As Epiphanius said, you went on in this way for twenty-three years.
By this sorrow I beg you, most gentle Mother
pray to your beloved son the Lord Jesus Christ for me
that he may deign to mercifully to free me from present sorrow
and to guide me so that I might become worthy to enjoy eternal joy.
May the Lord Jesus Christ deign to grant this to us all,
who with the Father and the Holy Spirit is forever blessed.

The Forty-Fifth Chapter Concerning the Seven Joys of the Blessed Virgin.

In the last chapter we heard about the seven sorrows of the Blessed Virgin
now let us hear about her seven joys.
We should honor devoutly the joys of the Blessed Virgin
that she might deign to gladden us in our difficulties.
How welcome and how pleasing this deference is to the Blessed Virgin,
was shown by a certain priest devoted to the Blessed Virgin.
He was accustomed day after day to recall the joys of the blessed Virgin,
and, as he was able, to more fervantly honor her in prayer and song.
One time this man, wasted by sickness, became very ill
and recognizing his sins, he was anxiously despondent.

Hev inquit mihi misero quid dicam et quid respondebo
Cum ad districtum examen superni iudicis peruenero.
Vbi exigetur a me ratio omnium operacionum mearum
Omnium uerborum cogitacionum temporum et negligenciarum.
Et ecce ex inprouiso matrem misericordie aduenire conspiciebat
Que leto vvltu et hylari uoce eum consolans dicebat.
Gaude fili mi dilecte gaude et noli contristari
Quia ecce uenio ad te in extrema necessitate tua consolari.
Obsequium ualde gratum mihi sepius prestitisti
Eo quod gaudiis meis tantum honorem quam crebro exhibuisti.
Gaudium enim magnum mei est quod gaudia mea recitantur
Quod decantantur quod audiuntur et quod recogitantur.
Et quia tam deuote crebro honorasti mea gaudia
Ego honorabo te et perducam te ad eterna gaudia.
Qua propter debemus gaudia beate uirginis libenter honorare
Et sequentes oraciones legere feruenter et decantare.

50vb[1] *Primum gaudium*
*G*aude maria mater pia diues in deliciis
Tuis gaudiis non fuit in cunctis seculis leticia similis.
Quamuis tua gaudia nullus hominum sufficiat enarrare
Tamen super alia satago specialiter vii honorare.
Primum gaudium fuit inopinabiliter supra modum magnum
Quando nunciauit tibi dominus per gabrielem suum archangelum.
Quod ipse te super omnes mulieres huius mundi elegisset
Et de te humanam naturam assumere decreuisset.[2]
Confestim quando anima tua benedicta consensum nuncio prebebat
Tuus castissimus uterus filium dei uiui concipiebat.
Ergo tuus sanctissimus uterus per archam sethy prefiguratur
Et tua sanctissima anima per urnam auream defiguratur.
In archa illa et in vrna manna celi conseruabatur.
Et in te panis viuus id est christus deus et homo concludebatur.
⌊Te⌋[3] etiam prefigurauit illa uirga arida que floruit propter aaron
Te quoque prefigurauit illud uellus qu[od/em] repleri pecii⌊t⌋[4] gedeon.
Virga aaron floruit contra naturam de dono dei speciali

[1] Right Panel: The First Joy: The Annunciation. Gabriel kneels before an enthroned Mary to give her the news. The image here is, as is typical for the SHS, minimalist. Mary is not reading, but folds her arms in the *ecce ancilla* gesture, and there is no lily signifying her virginal purity. [2] See *SHS* ch. 7 [3] Te, L] Et, G [4] Line shows signs of erasures and appears to have originally read "quod repleri petiis"

He said "Oh, wretch that I am, what I will say and what I will answer
when I come to the stern examination of the highest judge,
where I will have to give an account all my deeds,
all of my words, thoughts, time, and omissions?"
And behold, he saw suddenly the mother of mercy appear.
Consoling him, she spoke with happy voice and countenance:
"Rejoice, my beloved son, rejoice, and do not be discouraged
because see, I come to you in your final need that you may be consoled.
You have often greatly evinced a welcome deference toward me,
in that you honored my joys, day after day.
For it is a great joy for me that my joys are recited,
that they are sung, that they are heard, and that they are meditated on.
And because you have honored my joys so devoutly day after day,
I will honor you and will lead you to eternal joy."
Therefore, we ought to gladly honor the joys of the Blessed Virgin
and to read and sing the following prayers eagerly:

First Joy
Rejoice, Mary, holy mother, rich in delights;
there has been no pleasure in the all the ages like your joys.
Although no one can describe your joys,
Nevertheless, I strive especially to honour these seven above the rest.
The first joy was unexpectedly beyond the highest measure,
when the Lord announced to you through Gabriel, his archangel,
that he had chosen you above all women on earth
and had decided to take on human nature from you.
At once, when your blessed soul gave consent to the ambassador,
your most chaste womb conceived the Son of the Living God.
Therefore, your most holy womb is prefigured through the chest of shittim
and your most holy soul is symbolized through the golden urn.
In that ark and in the urn the manna of heaven was protected.
And in you, the living bread, that is, Christ—God and man—was enclosed.
And that dry rod which flowered for Aaron's sake prefigured you.
Also, that fleece foreshadowed you, which Gideon asked to be soaked.
Aaron's staff flowered contrary to nature as a special gift of God;

Tu impregnata fuisti supra naturam de uirtute spiritus sancti.
Solum uellus repletum est rore tota terra sicca manente
Tv sola repleta es dei filio nulla alia in hoc digna existente.
Per hoc primum gaudium tuum mater clementissima rogo te
Ora dilectum filium tuum dominum ihesum christum pro me.
Vt in hora mortis mee dignetur animam meam letificare
Et a morte secunda siue perpetua intactam feliciter conseruare.
Quod nobis omnibus prestare dignetur dominus ihesus christus.
Qui cum patre et spritu sancto est in perpetuum benedictus.

51ra[1] *Secundum gaudium.*
*G*aude maria mater christi pia que ˋperˊ solem designaris.
Nam diuersis gaudiis et uariis deliiciis plena conprobaris.
Secundum gaudium mater dulcissima tunc habuisti
Quando cognatam tuam elyzabeth dulcibus amplexibus circumdedisti.[2]
Quando infans iohannes in utero matris pregaudio exultabat
Et anima tua sanctissimum dominum in iubilo magnificabat.[3]
Spiritus tuus o felicissima in domino salutari tuo exultauit
Os tuum benedictum canticum novvm domino in gaudio cantauit.
Vterus tuus castissimus vasi balsami similis erat
In quo dominus balsamum suum celestem reconditum tenebat.
Tu es rubus igne plenus sine uiriditatis combustione
Quia grauidata fuisti sine virginitatis amissione.
Tu omnium aromatum et deliciarum ortus es conclusus[4]
Cuius clauicularius erat deus verus trinus et unus.
Te abygail illa sunamitis virgo casta pretendebat
Que regem dauid gremio suo fouit et tamen intacta permanebat.[5]
Sic tu regem celi nouem mensibus et ingremio tuo fouisti
Et tamen uirgo immaculata et intacta perpetuo permansisti.
Pro tantis beneficiis domino deo gratias magnificas egisti
Et cum magno gaudio canticum magnificat sibi edidisti.
Per hoc secundum gaudium mater dulcissima rogo te
Ora dilectum filium tuum dominum ihesum christum pro me.
Qui ix mensibus requieuit in tuo castissimo utero
Vt me secum quiescere faciat in suo regno perpetuo.

[1] Left Panel: Third Joy: Nativity. Also a repeat image, from fol. 11v Left Panel, except that Joseph no longer leans on his staff, and his Jewish hat is falling off, suggesting perhaps his advancing age and changed racial identity—he will now be a guardian for Christ and Mary. [2] Cf. Lk. 1.39–42 [3] Lk. 1.46–55 [4] Ct. 4.12–15 [5] Cf. 1 Kings 25.1–42, 2 Kings 3.3

you were impregnated beyond nature by the power of the Holy Spirit.
The fleece alone was soaked with dew, the whole ground remaining dry;
you alone were filled with the Son of God, with no other woman existing worthy in this way
By this your first joy, I ask you, Mother most gentle,
pray to your beloved son the Lord Jesus Christ for me.
That in the hour of my death he might deign to gladden my soul
and to happily keep it safe from the second, endless death.
May the Lord Jesus Christ deign to grant this to us all,
who with the Father and the Holy Spirit is blessed forever.

Second Joy
Rejoice Mary, holy mother of Christ, who are signified by the sun,
for you are shown to be full of manifold joys and all sorts of delights.
You had then, sweetest mother, the second joy
when your kinswoman Elisabeth enveloped you in her sweet embrace,
when the infant John leapt with joy in the womb of the mother,
and your soul was magnifying the most holy Lord in jubilant song.
Your spirit, O most happy one, exulted in the Lord your salvation;
your blessed mouth sang a new song to the Lord in joy.
Your most pure womb was like a pot of balm
in which the Lord was holding his own heavenly balm, hidden.
You are the bush, full of flames, whose greenness is unconsumed,
because you have become heavy with child without loss of virginity.
You are a walled garden full of all scents and delights,
whose doorwarden was the true God, three and one.
Abigail the chaste Shunammite virgin anticipated you;
she embraced King David on her lap and nonetheless remained undefiled.
So, too, you held the king of heaven for nine months in your lap
but yet continued an immaculate and untouched virgin forever.
You gave marvelous thanks to the Lord God for to such deeds
and with great joy you uttered to him your canticle, the Magnificat.
By this second joy I ask you, sweetest mother,
pray for me to your beloved son the Lord Jesus Christ—
who for nine months rested in your most chaste womb—
that he might make me rest with him in his own never-ending kingdom.

Quod nobis omnibus prestare dignetur dominus ihesus christus.
Qui cum patre et spiritu sancto est in perpetuum benedictus.

51rb[1] *Tercium gaudium.*
Gaude maria mater christi ⌊florens virga jesse⌋[2]
Tv vere paradysus omnium deliciarum esse probaris.
Tercium gaudium mater dulcissima tunc habuisti
Quando dilectum filium tuum clausa et intacta peperisti.[3]
Quod figuratum erat in clausa porta demonstrata ezechieli[4]
Et in monte mirabili cuius mysterium reuelatum est danieli.[5]
Dominus solus portam clausam et infractam pertransiuit
Sic tuus uterus in ortu christi claustrum uirginitatis non amisit.
De morte predicto abscisus est lapis sine manibus
Et ex te natus est ihesus christus sine tactibus maritalibus.
Sicut radius solis pertransit uitrum sine vitri lesione
Ita ex te natus est christus sine uirginitatis corrupcione.
O quale et quantum gaudium mater dulcissima tunc habuisti
Quociens illam tam delectabilem faciem filii tui conspexisti.
O quam inmenso gaudio virgo delicatissima gaudebas
Quociens tam mellifluo puero vbera tua prebebas.
O quam dulcissimis amplexibus tam dilectum filium tuum constingebas.
Quem non aliquo homine sed a solo deo te concepisse[6] sciebas.
O quam suauissimis osculis et quam creberrime ipsum osculabaris
Qui fuit tibi tam dulcissimus tam vnicus quam peculiaris.
Per hoc tercium gaudium mater clementissia rogo te
Ora dilectum filium tuum dominum ihesum christum pro me.
Vt me perducat post hanc uitam ad supernam patriam
Vt suam dilectabilem faciem sine fine uideam.
Quod nobis omnibus prestare dignetur dominus ihesus christus.
Qui cum patre et spritu sancto est in perpetuum benedictus.

51va[7] *Quartum gaudium.*
Gaude maria mater christi pia fulgida stella maris
Que tota gaudiosa et tota radiosa esse comprobaris.
Quartum gaudium mater dulcissima tunc habuisti
Quando tam laudabile testimonium regum de filio tuo audiuisti.[8]

[1] Right Panel: Second Joy: Visitation. Out of temporal sequence, this image follows the Nativity. The scribe has written "b" over the Visitation and "a" over the Nativity to restore the proper sequence. [2] florens virga jesse, L] quae persolem designaris, G (a duplication from previous section) [3] See *SHS* Ch. 8 [4] Ez. 44.2 [5] Dn. 2.45 [6] concepisse, L] concupiscere, G [7] Left Panel: Fourth Joy: Visit of the Magi. This image repeats that at 12V Left Panel. [8] See *SHS* Ch. 9

May the Lord Jesus Christ deign to grant this to us all,
who with the Father and the Holy Spirit is blessed forever.

Third Joy
Rejoice, Mary, mother of Christ, flowering rod of Jesse,
you are truly declared to be the paradise of all delights.
For you, sweetest mother, had the third joy then
when you, sealed-up and untouched, gave birth to your beloved son.
This was symbolized in the closed gate shown to Ezechiel
and the miraculous mountain, whose mystery was revealed to Daniel.
The Lord alone passed through the closed and unbroken gate
so too your womb did not lose the lock of virginity in the birth of Christ.
Regarding the death mentioned before, the stone was moved without hands;
and from you Jesus Christ was born without a husband's touch.
Just as a ray of the sun passes through a piece of glass without stain of defect
so from you Christ was born without virginity being violated.
O how much and what great joy, sweetest mother, you had then!
How often did you gaze on your son's countenance, so delightful!
O how you were rejoicing with immense joy, delightful maiden!
How often were you offering your breasts to the baby boy, so honey-sweet!
O in what sweet embraces were you clasping your very beloved son,
whom you knew that you conceived only from the God, not any man!
O what exceedingly sweet kisses were you raining down on him—and how so very often—
who was so very sweet, so singular, so unparalleled!
By this third joy I ask you, most gentle mother,
pray to your beloved son, the Lord Jesus Christ, for me.
That he might lead me after this life to the heavenly homeland,
that I might see his beloved face without end.
May the Lord Jesus Christ deign to grant this to us all,
who with the Father and the Holy Spirit is blessed forever.

Fourth Joy
Rejoice, Mary, holy mother of Christ, shining star of the sea,
who is shown to be wholly joyful and wholly radiant.
You, sweetet mother, had then the fourth joy
when you heard the very praiseworthy testimony of the kings about your son.

Qui coram te procidentes deum et regem eum esse ostendebant
Et mistica munera aurum thus et mirram ei offerebant.
In eo quod coram ipso procidebant et eum adorabant
Deum verum et uiuum esse ipsum demonstrabant.
Oblacio thuris ad sacerdotes pertinere solebat
Et hec oblacio filium tuum sacerdotem futurum pretendebat.
Cum mirra solebant antiqui corpora mortuorum condire
Quo innuebatur quod filius tuus uenit mortem ⌊propter⌋[1] nos subire
Oblacio auri munus esse regale solebat
Et hec oblacio filium tuum regem ostendebat.[2]
Rex iste videlicet christus vsus fuit pro throno regali
Tuo sacratissimo et beatissimo utero uirginali.
Te ergo uirgo pia thronus ille eburneus pretendebat
Super quem salomon rex sapientissimus residere solebat.[3]
Tv es turtur sine felle et uere tota bona
Tv es angelorum et beatorum omnium gloria et corona.
Per quod quartum gaudium mater clementissima rogo te.
Ora dilectum filium tuum dominum ihesum christum pro me.
Vt mihi concedat in hoc seculo sibi taliter seruire
Vt in futuro ad suam mellifluam presenciam ualeam peruenire.
Quod nobis prestare dignetur dominus ihesus christus.
Qui cum patre et spritu sancto est in perpetuum benedictus.

51vb[4] *Quintum gaudium.*

*G*aude Maria mater christi pia sine spina rosa
Tv es ex regali progenie exorta et tota generosa.
Quintum gaudium mater dulcissima tunc habuisti
Quando dilectum filium tuum cum gaudio in templo obtulisti.[5]
Cum gaudio magno exiuisti de urbe natiuitatis id est de bethleem[6]
Cum gaudio peruenisti ad urbem oblacionis id est in ierusalem
Cum gaudio magno in templum domini introisti
Cum magno gaudio filium tuum domino obtulisti.
Obtulisti eum domino vero deo uiuo et deo summo
Quem patrem eius sciebas et nullum alium in mundo.
O quam ineffabile gaudium cordi tuo erat

[1] propter, L] post, G [2] Cf. Origen's *Contra Celsum* I.60 [3] 3 Kings 10.18–20 [4] Right Panel: Fifth Joy: Christ Offered in the Temple. The image repeats the one at 13V Left Panel, with the addition of another worshipper, kneeling on the left. [5] See *SHS* Ch. 10 [6] MS reverses the order of the lines 4 and 5. They have here been reordered in keeping with the ordering found L and biblical chronology.

Falling down before you, they showed that he was both God and King
and offered to him mystical gifts, gold, incense, and myrrh.
In that they were falling prostrate before him and adoring him,
they revealed that he was the true and living Lord.
Customarily, the offering of incense belongs to priests,
and this offering anticipated that your son would be a priest.
The ancients were accustomed to preserve the bodies of the dead with myrrh,
by which it was indicated that your son came to undergo death for us.
The offering of gold was usually a royal gift
and this offering revealed your son to be a king.
That king (that is, Christ) used for his royal throne
your most holy and blessed virginal womb.
Therefore that ivory throne anticipated you, O holy virgin,
upon which the wisest king Solomon was accustomed to sit.
You are a turtle-dove, without guile, and wholly good indeed,
you are the glory and crown of the angels and all of the blessed.
By that fourth joy, I ask you, most gentle mother:
pray to your beloved son the Lord Jesus Christ for me,
that he might allow me so to serve him in this current age in such a way
that in the future I might be able to arrive at his own honey-sweet presence.
May the Lord Jesus Christ deign to grant this to us all,
who with the Father and the Holy Spirit is blessed forever.

Fifth Joy
Rejoice, Mary, holy mother of Christ, a rose without a thorn,
you are born from a royal race and entirely noble.
At that time, sweetest mother, you had the fifth joy,
when you offered your beloved son with joy in the temple.
With great joy you departed from the city of his birth, that is, from the city of Bethlehem;
with joy you came to the city of his offering, that is, into Jerusalem;
with great joy you entered into the temple of the Lord;
with great joy you offered your son to the Lord.
You offered him to the true lord, the living God and highest God,
whom you knew to be his Father and that there was no other father on earth.
O how indescribable was the joy in your heart,

Quod filius tuus tam nobilem et tam potentem patrem habebat.
Senex ille Symeon qui eum cum magno desiderio exspectauerat
Eo uiso pre gaudio ultra uiuere non affectabat.
Anna prophetissa etiam ad hoc gaudium ueniebat
Et cum magno gaudio filium tuum laudabat et benedicebat.[1]
Omnes qui aderant eum laudabant et magnificabant.
Et eo uiso cum magno gaudio et iubilo exultabant.
O quale et quantum gaudium mater dulcissima habuisti
Quando talem et tantum filium tali et tanto patri obtulisti.
Per hoc quintum gaudium mater clementissima rogo te
Ora dilectum filium tuum ihesum christum pro me.
Quatenus me in omnibus angustiis meis dignetur consolari
Et a te numquam faciat in eternum separari.
Quod nobis omnibus prestare dignetur dominus ihesus christus.
Qui cum patre et spritu sancto est in perpetuum benedictus.

52ra[2] *Sextum gaudium.*

*G*aude Maria mater christi pia aurora delectabilis
Tv pulcherrima es et amena et tota desiderabilis.
Sextum gaudium mater dulcissima tunc habuisti
Quando filium tuum quem amiseras et quesieras in templo inuenisti.[3]
Quem cum inuenisses humiliter tibi subditus erat
Et summus deus tibi mater dulcissima obedire non respuebat.
Tv uirgo purissima tanta caritate pollebas
Quod per eam unicornem quem nemo capere potest capiebas.
Tv de leone ferocissimo agnum mansuetissimum fecisti
Tv aquilam quam nemo domare potuit virgo domuisti.
Tv uinxisti et ligasti fortissimum sampsonem[4]
Tv uicisti et superasti sapientissimum salamonem.
Tv ⌊p⌋ellicanum[5] sol[lic]itudinis uirgo solitaria cepisti
Tv salamandram igne tue caritatis ad allexisti.
Tv pantheram atrocissimam uirgo mitissima mitigasti.
Tv elephantem maximum virgo humillima tibi subiugasti.
Tv fecisti unuenem fenicem vnicum et antiquissimum
Ad te fecit yditum saltum de celo altissimum.
Quando de te filius altissimi uoluit incarnari

---

[1] Lk. 2.22–38 [2] Left Panel: Sixth Joy: The Finding in the Temple. Here the image is of Jesus teaching the elders; Mary and Joseph are not shown. Cf. fol. 49r Right Panel. [3] Lk. 2.45–46 [4] Jdg. 16.19 [5] L] bellicanum, G

that your son had a father so noble and so powerful.
That old man Symeon, who had waited for him with great longing,
once having seen this joy, did not desire to live any longer.
And Anna the prophetess took part in this joy
and with great joy she praised and blessed your son.
All who were there praised and magnified him,
and having seen him, they were exulting with joy and jubilation.
O how unique and great a joy did you have, sweetest mother,
when you offered so excellent and so great a son to so excellent and so great a father.
By this fifth joy I ask you, most merciful mother,
pray to your beloved son Jesus Christ for me,
that he may deign to console me in all my difficulties
and never let me become separated eternally from you.
May the Lord Jesus Christ deign to grant this to us all,
who with the Father and the Holy Spirit is blessed forever.

Sixth Joy
Rejoice, Mary, holy mother of Christ, dawn of delight,
you are beautiful and charming and wholly lovable.
You, sweetest mother, had then the sixth joy,
when you found your son whom you had lost and sought in the temple,
and when you had arrived, he humbly submitted himself to your authority
and the highest God did not scorn to obey you, sweetest mother.
You, purest Virgin, abounded with so mighty a charity
that through it you captured the unicorn which no one is able to catch.
You turned the fiercest lion into the meekest lamb;
you, a maiden, tamed the eagle that no man was able to tame.
You fettered and bound the very strong Sampson;
you conquered and overpowered the very wise Solomon.
You, solitary maiden, caught the wild pelican,
you coaxed forth the salamander with your fire of charity,
you, mildest Virgin, gentled the fiercest panther,
you, most humble Virgin, yoked the largest elephant for yourself.
You made young the one and only most ancient phoenix,
for you he made the highest leap down from heaven,
when the Son of the Most High wished to be incarnate from you,

Et tibi tamquam puer matri sue humiliter subuigari.
Per hoc sextum gaudium mater dulcissima rogo te.
Ora dilectum filium tuum dominum ihesum christum pro me.
Vt concedat mei in hoc seculo ita sibi subiugari
Vt ab eo in futuro seculo numquam merear seperari.
Quod nobis omnibus prestare dignetur dominus ihesus christus.
Qui cum patre et spritu sancto est in perpetuum benedictus.

52rb[1] *Septimum gaudium.*
*G*aude maria pia mater christi. regina celorum
Septimum tuum gaudium excedit corda et sensus hominum.
Quod tu regina potentissima in extremo habuisti
Quando cum corpore et anima in celum assumpta fuisti.
Quando te filius tuus in throno suo secum collocauit
Et corona regni sui perpetua feliciter te coronauit.
Tv ergo olim prefigurata eras per fontem illum paruulum
Qui creuit et emanauit et factus est in flumen maximum
Sicut enim rex assuersus humilem hester exaltauit
Ita te humillimam rex celestis exaltauit et coronauit.[2]
Te [\etiam] illa abygail prudens olim pretendebat
Quam propter suam prudenciam rex dauid sibi sponsam sumebat.[3]
Ita rex celestis elegit te et assumpsit te ⌞in⌟ sponsam et amicam
In matrem et in sociam in sororem et in reginam.
Te etiam mater salomonis conuenienter presignauit
Cui ille salomon thronum ad dextram suam collocauit.[4]
Ita rex celorum te matrem suam honorauit
Et ad dextram suam in throno suo te locauit.
O domina felicissima quam ineffabile gaudium habuisti
Quando corpore et anima in gaudium perpetuum introisti.
Per hoc ineffabile gaudium regina celi rogo te
Ora dilectum filium tuum regem celestem pro me.
Vt post exilium perducat me ad thronum regni sui
V⌞t⌟[5] sine fine merear gaudio sempiterno frui.
Quod nobis omnibus prestare dignetur dominus ihesus christus
Qui cum patre et spritu sancto est in perpetuum benedictus. amen.

[1] Right Panel: Seventh Joy: Coronation of the Virgin. See 39V Left Panel. [2] Apc. 12.1 [3] 1Kings 25.1–42
[4] 3Kings 2.19 [5] Ut, L] ubi, G

and to you as a boy to his mother, he subjugated himself humbly.
By this sixth joy, most sweet mother, I ask you,
pray for me to your beloved son the Lord Jesus Christ
that he grant unto me so to be obedient to him in this world
that I might never deserve to be separated from him in the world to come.
May the Lord Jesus Christ deign to grant this us all,
who with the Father and the Holy Spirit is blessed forever.

Seventh Joy
Rejoice, Mary, holy mother of Christ, Queen of Heaven.
Your seventh joy exceeds the heart and understanding of man.
You, most powerful Queen, enjoyed it at the end of life
when you were taken up, body and soul, into heaven,
when your son established you on his throne with him
and he happily crowned you with the eternal crown of his kingdom.
Therefore, you were prefigured long ago through that little fountain,
which sprang up and flowed out and became a great river.
For as the King Ahasuerus exalted humble Ester,
so the king of heaven exalted and crowned you.
Wise Abigail formerly anticipated you,
whom King David took for his wife on account of her wisdom.
So too the king of heaven chose you and took you as wife and beloved,
as mother and companion, as sister and queen.
Also the mother of Solomon aptly foreshadowed you,
she for whom Solomon set up a throne at his right hand.
So, too, the king of heaven honored you, his mother,
and placed you on his throne on the right hand.
O most happy lady, what indescribable joy you had
when you entered into perpetual joy with body and soul.
By this indescribable joy, I ask you, Queen of Heaven,
pray for me to your beloved son, the heavenly king
that he may lead me after my exile to the throne of his kingdom,
so that I might worthily enjoy joy without end.
May the Lord Jesus Christ deign to grant this to us all,
who with the Father and the Holy Spirit is blessed forever. Amen.

#Va *Qualis fuerit vita et conuersacio sancte maria virginis*[1]
Incipit prologus operis sequenti
*H*ec est vita virginis maria gloriose.
Summi dei filii matris generose.
Qua vixit in hoc seculo in custodia iohannis.
Post ascensum filii plusquam nouem annis.
*M*aria sibi regulam statuit viuendi.
et sub quodam ordine deo seruiendi.
A noctis enim tempore hore matutine.
Oracioni iugiter vacabat hec diuine.
Usque dum inciperet dies et hec hora.
A nobis que vvlgariter dicitur aurora.
Ab hac enim se contulit meditacioni.
Verborum evvangelii ac recordacioni.
Dulcis sui filii cuncta recolendo.
Ipse que sustinuit pro mundo paciendo.
Quod ab eius utero fuit incarnatus.
Et sine doloribus ab ipsa baiulatus.
Quod ab ea virgine permanente natus.
Et suis uberibus virgineis lactatus.
Qualiter annis plurimis secum morabatur.
Et illius dulcedine semper fruebatur.
Qualiter ab impiis et falsis est iudeis.
Captus uinctus uinculis. cesusque ab eis.
Qualiter ad statuam fuerat ligatus.
Et a satellitibus dire [] flagellatus.
Coronaque spinea dure coronatus.
A pylato preside morte condempnatus.
Crucifixus et mortuus. eratque sepultus.
Quod erat ei gemitus atque dolor multus.
Et quod die tercia de morte resurrexit.
Ipsumque cum gaudio viuentem respexit.
Et qualiter ascenderit celorum in sublime.
Istam consuetudinem compleuit hora prime.
Abhinc usque terciam contemplacioni.
Vacabat et celestium delectacioni.
Usque nonam operi postea vacabat.
Atque suis manibus intente laborabat.

[1] Rubricated subsequently in different hand.

What was the life and habit of St. Mary the Virgin.
Here begins the prologue of the following work.
this is the life of the glorious Virgin Mary,
the noble mother of the highest, the Son of God
who lived in the custody of John in that age
for more than nine years after the ascension of her son.
Mary established a rule of living for herself,
for serving God under some order.
From nighttime to the hour of matins,
she was free for divine prayer,
until the day and this hour began,
which we commonly call the daybreak.
From then on she lifted herself in meditation
and recollection of the words of the Evangelist,
by considering everything about her sweet son.
what things he sustained for the world by suffering:
that from her womb he was made flesh,
And she carried him without sorrows;
that he was born while she remained a virgin,
and he was nursed by her own virginal breasts;
how for many years he resided with her,
and she always enjoyed that child's sweetness;
how by the impious and false Jews
he was captured and bound with chains and slaughtered by them;
how he had been bound to the pillar,
horribly scourged by the attendants,
and crowned harshly with a thorny crown;
How he was condemned to death by Pilate the governor,
crucified and dead and buried;
that his groan and sorrow were great,
and that he resurrected from death on the third day,
and how she with joy saw him living;
and how he had ascended into heights of heaven.
The hour of Prime ended this custom.
Henceforth, she was free for the contemplation and delight
and delight of heaven until the third hour.
Until the ninth hour she was free for work
and she labored intently with her own hands.

Hec vel pannos purpureos de serico texebat.
Vel ut solent femine cum acu consuebat.
Nam artem feminarum per optime sciebat.
De lino lana serico. sicut hanc decebat
Hanc loqui si oportuit. vel cuique respondere.
In hac hora debite studuit implere.
Ad templum ibat vt decuit. si volebat ire.
Ut ibi laudes domini posset expedire.
A domo tamen rarius hec egrediebatur.

#V[a] Et perplateas minime vel domos vagabatur.
Sed cum oportuit ire ad templum salomonis.
Causa legis domini uel oracionis.
Per viam ibat capite decenter ornato.
Atque cum velamine mundissime velato.
Ad terram vvltum oculos modicum reflexit.
Transeuntes homines rarissime inspexit.
Ipsam tamen aliquis si forte salutauit.
Caput huic humiliter statim inclinauit.
Dicens deo gracias. tibi pax. habebat
Semper illum familiaritatis modum dum viuebat.
In templo nichil aliud exercuit maria.
Nisi oracionibus uacans cum psalmodia.
Vacabat et celestium contemplacioni.
Et mandatorum domini meditacioni.
Non in turba populi solebat apparere.
Sed in loco anguli consueuit residere.
Nec enim cum aliquo colloquiis vacabat.
Sed pactis omnibus domum remeabat.
Postque autem aduenerat hora diei nona.
Suis in oracionibus manens virgo bona.
Donec venit angelus ipsam confortans.
Panem quoque celitus missum sibi portans.
Maria cibo alio tunc non vtebatur.
Nisi pane qui diuinitus sibi mittebatur.
Quicquid autem laboribus manu lucrari
Valuit. hoc ordinauit egenis erogari.
Hec refecta celitus manens in labore.
Donec uenit spacium vespertine hore.
A cunctis tunc laboribus manuum cessauit.
Atque oracionibus et psalmis tunc vacauit.

This woman was either weaving purple garments from silk
or sewing with a needle as women are accustomed.
For she knew women's art very well,
with linen, wool, and silk, as was fitting for her.
If it was proper for her to speak or to respond to anyone,
she was eager to complete it at this hour.
She went to the temple as was fitting if she wished to go
so that she be able there to have nearby praises of the Lord.
Rarely, however, did she go out from the house

and she did not wander through streets or the houses at all.
But when it was proper to go to the temple of Solomon
for the cause of prayer or of the law of the Lord,
she went through the path with her head appropriately adorned
and covered with a very neat veil.
She turned her face and eyes modestly to the ground.
She very rarely observed the men passing before her.
If by chance anyone happened to greet her,
she inclined at once her head humbly to them,
saying thanks to God she said, "peace to you"
as she always lived that sort of friendship.
Mary practiced nothing else in the temple
except being free for prayers with psalmody.
She was free also for the contemplation of heavenly things,
and meditation on the commandments of the Lord.
She was not accustomed to appear in a crowd of people,
but it was her custom to settle in a corner.
For neither was she free for conversations with anyone,
but she returned to the house when all things were settled.
After this, the ninth hour of the day had arrived.
The good Virgin remained in her own prayers
until a comforting angel came to her
carrying bread sent from heaven.
Mary then did not consume any other bread
except bread sent from heaven to her.
Whatever she was able to gain from labors by hand
she arranged for distribution to the destitute.
Nourished from heaven, she remained at her labor
until there came the hour of Vespers.
Then she ceased from all the labors of her hands
and was free then for prayers and psalms.

Sic hora completorii diem consumauit.
Sic indie sepcies laudes decantauit.
Postea dulciflue se deuocioni.
Dedit et celestium contemplacioni.
Secretaque celestia corde meditando.
Ac eleuato spiritu iocunde iubilando.
In virginis consorcio femine fuerunt.
Quiaque caste virginis existis extiterunt.
Tres et due vidue marie commemorantes.
Sibi cum obsequio solamen exhibentes.
Vestes quoque uirginis non erant preciose.
Nec tincte coloribus nec multum curiose.
Semper autem uestibus hiis induebatur.
Tunica cum camisia supraque tegebatur.
Religioso pallio proprii coloris.
Sicut erat feminis diebus illis moris.

#V[a] Erantque mundissime vestes et decentes.
Sicut eam decuit scissuras non habentes.
Nemo tamen impius aut detrahens causetur.
De marie vestibus vel scandalizetur.
Quia hanc mundissimam virginem decebat.
Uti mundis vestibus quia non habebat.
Causam cur cilicium uel sagulum portaret.
Vel uestem penitencie. nam quod emendaret.
Per luctum tristicie numquam hec peccatum
Fecit innocencie sancte seruans statum.
Vestimenta uirginis numquam sunt attrita.
Post ascensionem filii sed mansuerunt ita.
Sicut ea induit in prima nouitate.
Nec scissa sunt nec aliqua consumpta vetustate.
Peploque mundissimo, semper utebatur.
Super caput desuper quoque tamen tegebatur.
Velo candidissimo hoc modicum dependit.
Nuda colli protegens ad scapulas descendit.
Et a fronte medio. Se modicum reflexit.
Non gene aut auricule vel mentum arcebantur.
Sed cum peplo composite subtus stringebantur.
Sic que tota facies libera manebat.
Sic se nostra domina honeste componebat.
Crines sui capitis semper dependebant.

She thus finished the day at the hour of Compline
and chanted praises seven times a day.
She gave herself afterwards to sweetly-flowing devotion
and heavenly contemplation
and to meditating in her heart the secret and heavenly things
and to joyfully rejoicing with an uplifted spirit.
There were women in a fellowship of the virgin,
and because she arose, the chaste virgins arose.
Three and two widows recollected with Mary,
producing comfort for themselves with deference to her,
The clothing of the Virgin was not precious,
neither dyed with colors nor very attentively.
She always wore these clothes:
A tunic was covered by a gown, along with
A religious pallium of her own color,
As was the custom for women in those days.

And the clothing was very clean and seemly,
as it was befitting her that they not have splits.
No one impious or detracting would argue about
or be scandalized by Mary's clothing,
because it was fitting for this finest virgin
that she not have fine clothes.
Therefore, she carried a cilice or hair-shirt
or some clothing for penance. What was she correcting?
She acted through sorrow for sin: never had she committed
A sin, guarding her state of holy innocence.
The Virgin's garments were never worn down
but remained as they were after her son's ascension,
just as she put on in her first novitiate.
Neither were they cut nor used up by the ravages of time.
She always used the finest robe
and she covered herself over her head
with a very bright veil she hung this modestly.
It descended to her shoulders, covering the naked parts of her neck
and it turned back on itself a little from the middle of her forehead.
She exposed neither her cheeks or ears or chin,
But they were tightly covered when the robe was drawn together.
Thus her whole face remained free.
In this was our mistress composed herself modestly.
The hair of her head was always undressed

Tecti tamen pallio vel tunica manebant.
Tulit quoque cingulum de retorta zona.
Aut cordam vt feminis mos est. hec uirgo bona
Vtebatur calceis. sed tunc se calciauit.
Ire dum oportuit quoquam. quia cauit.
Ne nudi appareant sui pedes vlla vice.
Tenens se humiliter nimis et pudice
Lectus quoque virginis non habuit ornatum.
Vilem. sed mundissimum erat suum stratum.
De sago super stramina pannum habebat.
Et ceruical modicum inquo quiescebat.
Ad lectum locus fuerat. Orare quo solebat.
Aut contemplabatur suauiter. scripturas vel legebat.
Ad partem vero alteram fuerat locata.
Sedes inqua residebat ad opus hec beata.
Numque vacans ocio. intente laborauit.
Orans mente ˊetˋ spiritu. psalmos ruminauit.
Aut psallebat domino. aut contemplabatur.
Aut in mentis iubilo deo fruebatur.
Sic per dies singulos maria faciebat.
Quibus inhoc seculo viuens permanebat.
Oracio ad beatam virginem mariam.
O regina virginum fac tecum gratulari.

#V[a] Quos hic in exilio vides tribulari.
Iube tuum filium. roga tuum patrem.
Pro nobis peccatoribus te ostendens misericordem.
Vt nos velis protegere. dareque iuuamen.
Gaudentesque perducere ad celi regna AMEN.

And remained covered by a pallium or tunic.
Also she bore a belt or a twisted girdle
Or a cord, as the custom is for women. This good Virgin
wore slippers but put her shoes on herself
when it was right to go anywhere, but she was careful
Lest at any turn her feet be seen uncovered,
holding herself exceedingly humbly and chastely.
Also, the Virgin's bed had no common ornament
aside from her very neat coverlet.
She had a cloth above the straw but under the covers
and a little pillow on which she slept.
At the bed there was a place where she was accustomed to pray,
Or to consider things sweetly or to read the scriptures.
In another part there was placed
a seat in which this blessed woman she settled into her work.
She labored intently, never free for rest,
praying in mind and spirit, while she meditated on the psalms,
or sang psalms to the Lord, or considered,
or enjoyed God in the joy of her mind.
Mary thus acted each day,
by which, living in this age, she endured.
The Prayer to the Blessed Virgin Mary
O Queen of Virgins, make us to rejoice with you,

we whom here in exile you see are troubled.
Command your son, beseech your Father,
for us sinners, showing yourself merciful,
that you wish to cover us and give us aid,
while we rejoice to come to the kingdoms of heaven AMEN.

Facsimile

∵

Istū libr̄ dedit monastīo scī Johis
in Stams · mgr̄ chunradꝰ pictor
ducis Leupoldi · p̄ signo spāl' amicicie

Comitis Francisci Koháry
de Csábrag et Szitna, perpetui
Comitis Hontensis et in Murány
1789.

Speculū humanæ Sal=
vationis
Cum Rythmis et
Figuris

donum Excellentissimi Domini Comitis
Nicolai Pálffy ab Erdöd, Aurei Velleris
Equitis, et per Regnum Hungariæ Judicis
Curiæ regiæ. 1774.

Fig-4b

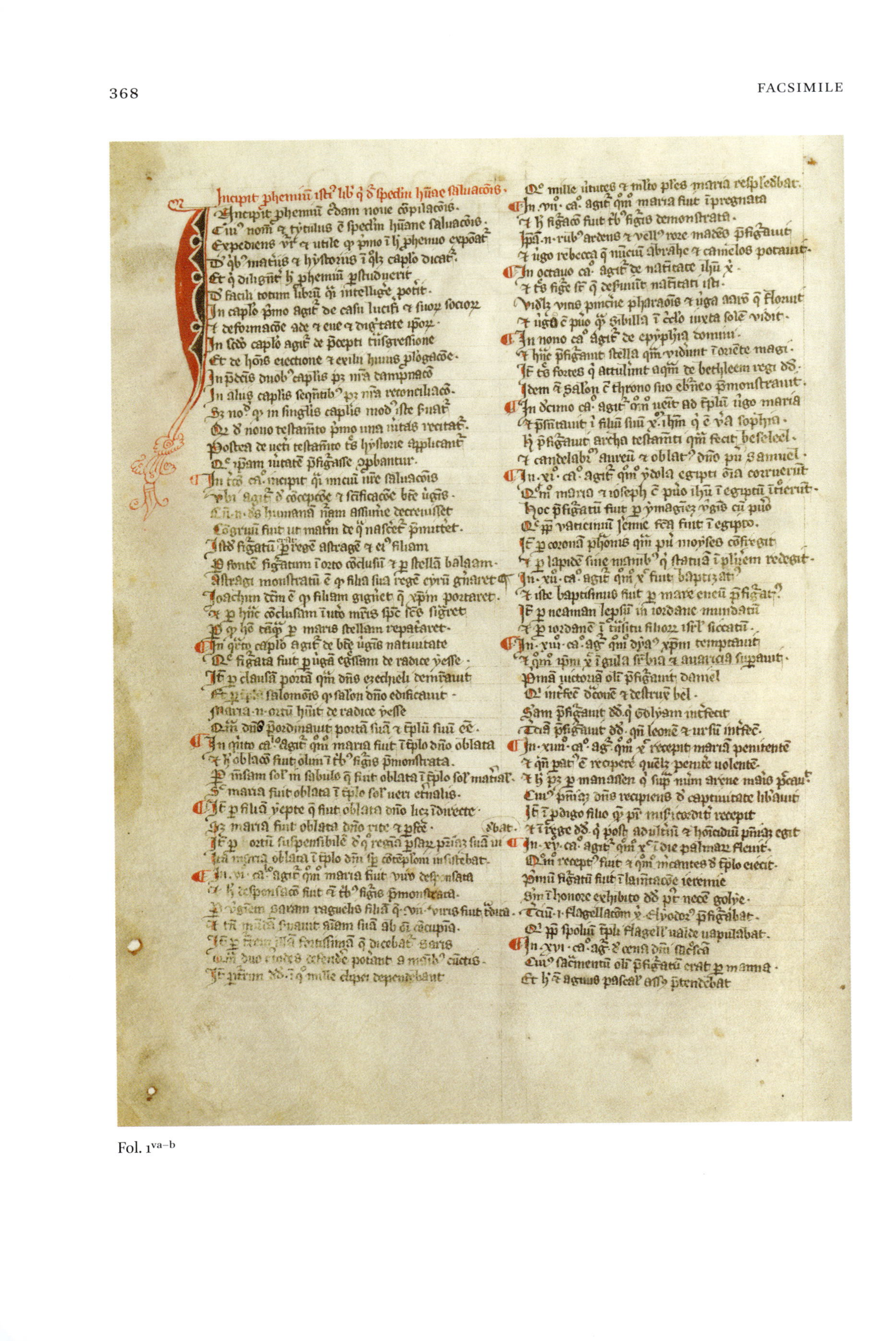

Fol. 1va–b

Fol. 2ra–b

Fol. 2^{va-b}

Fol. 3ra–b

Fol. 3va–b

Fol. 4ra–b

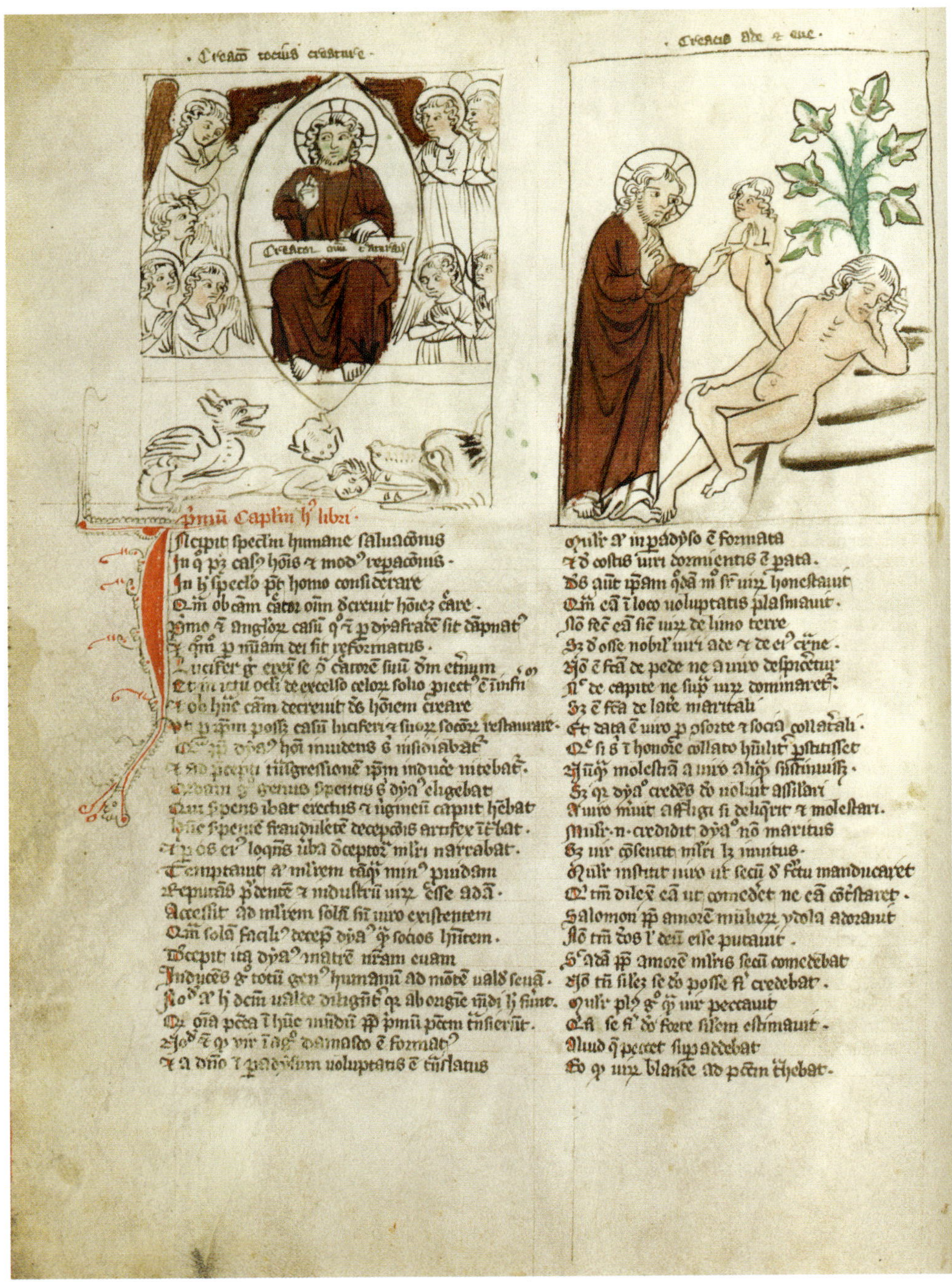

Fol. 4va–b. Image Captions (a): *Creator tocius creature; Creator omnium creaturarum* / Image Caption (b): *Creatio ade et eue*

Fol. 5^{ra-b}

Fol. 5va–b

Fol. 6^{ra-b}. Image Caption (a): *Adam cui dixit deus in sudore uultus tui vesceris pane tua* / Image Captions (b): *archa noe; columba; coruus*

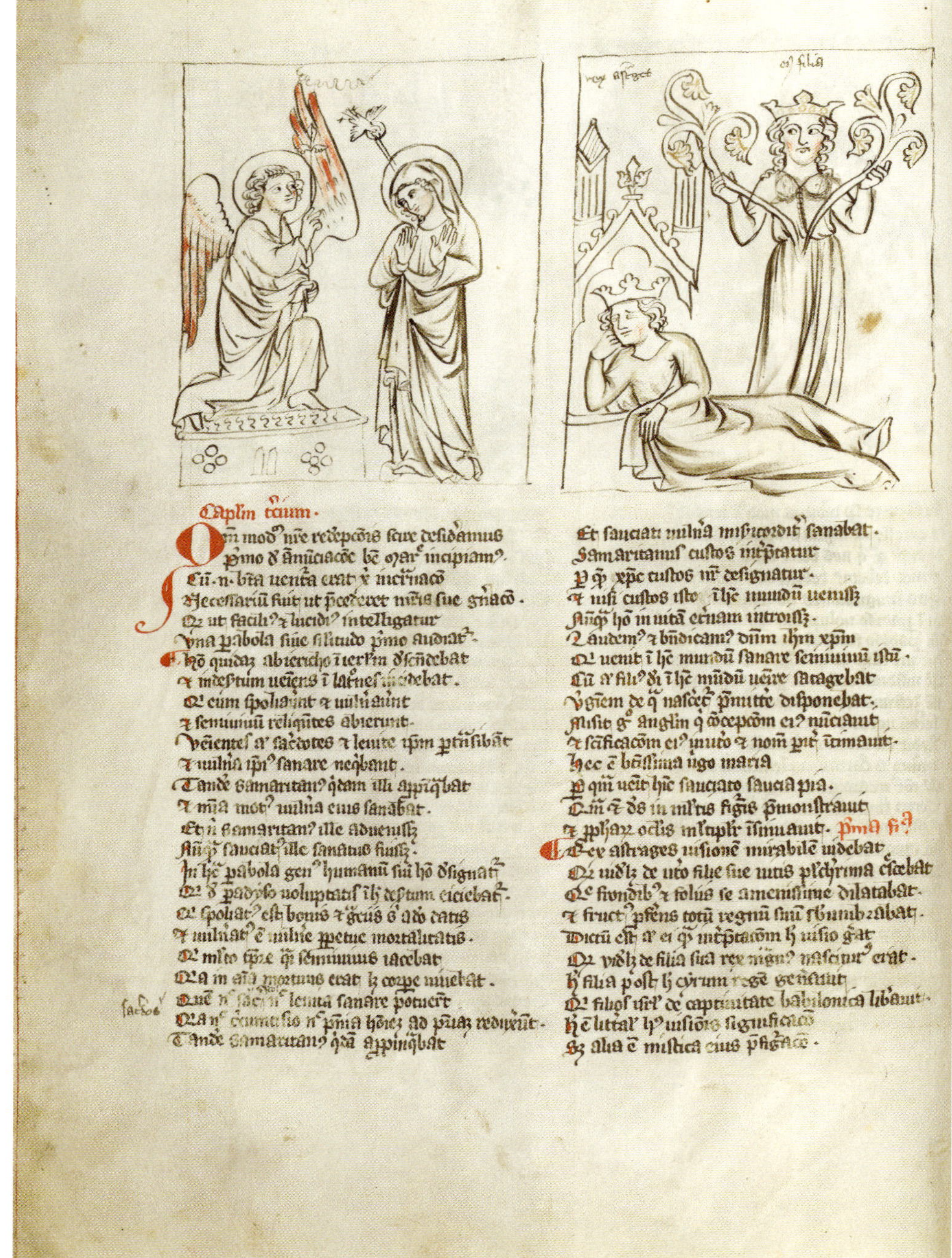

Fol. 6$^{va–b}$. Image Captions (b): *rex astrages; eius filia*

Fol. 7[ra–b]. Image Caption (a): *hortus conclusus est sigillatus* / Image Captions (b): *balaam . ariolus*; second caption illegible

Fol. 7$^{va–b}$. Image Captions (b): *uirga; yesse*

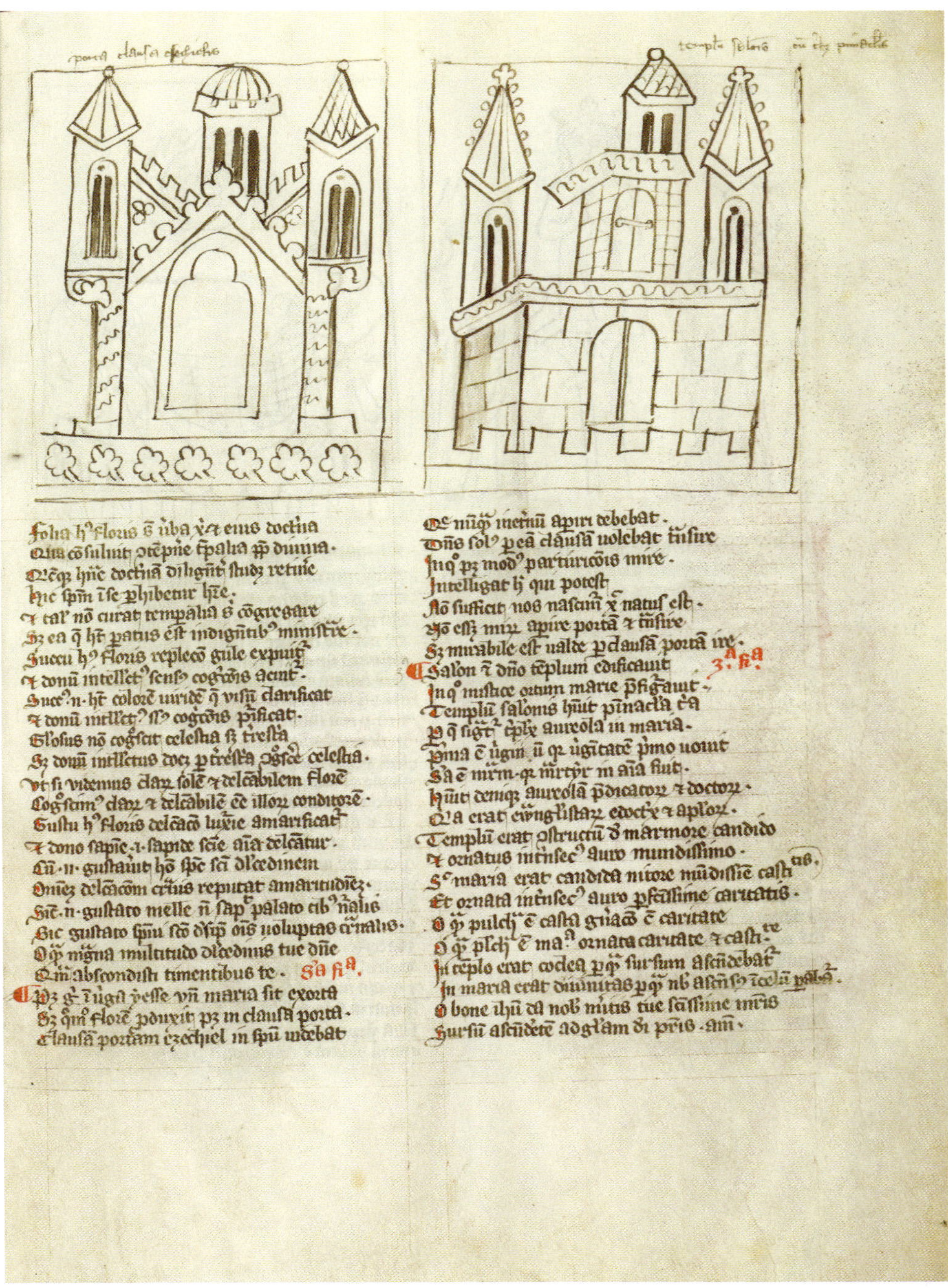

Fol. 8ra–b. Image Caption (a): *porta clausa ezechielis* / Image Caption (b): *templum salomonis cum tribus pinnaculis*

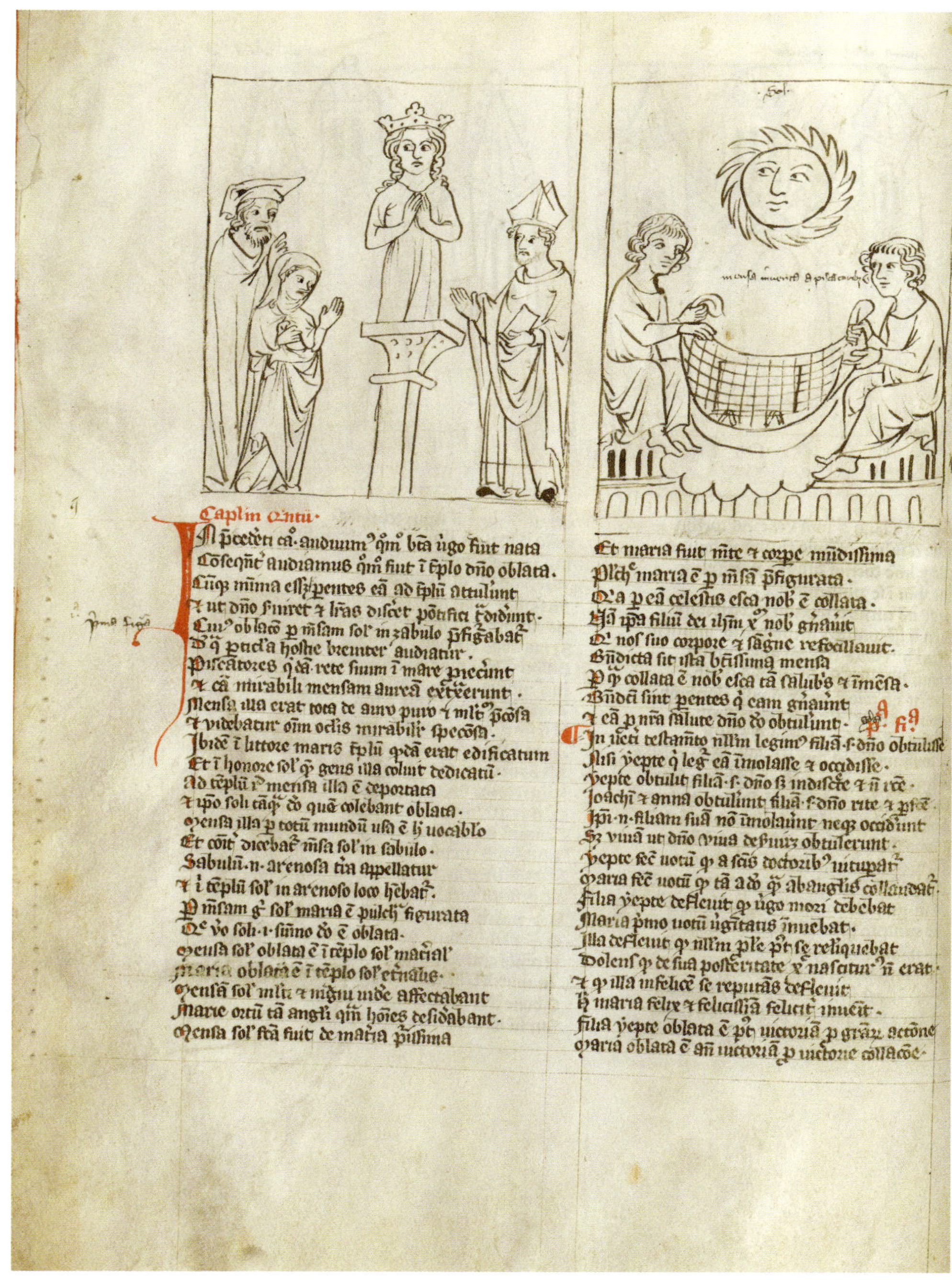

Fol. 8va–b. Image Captions (b): *sol; mensa inuenta a piscatoribus*

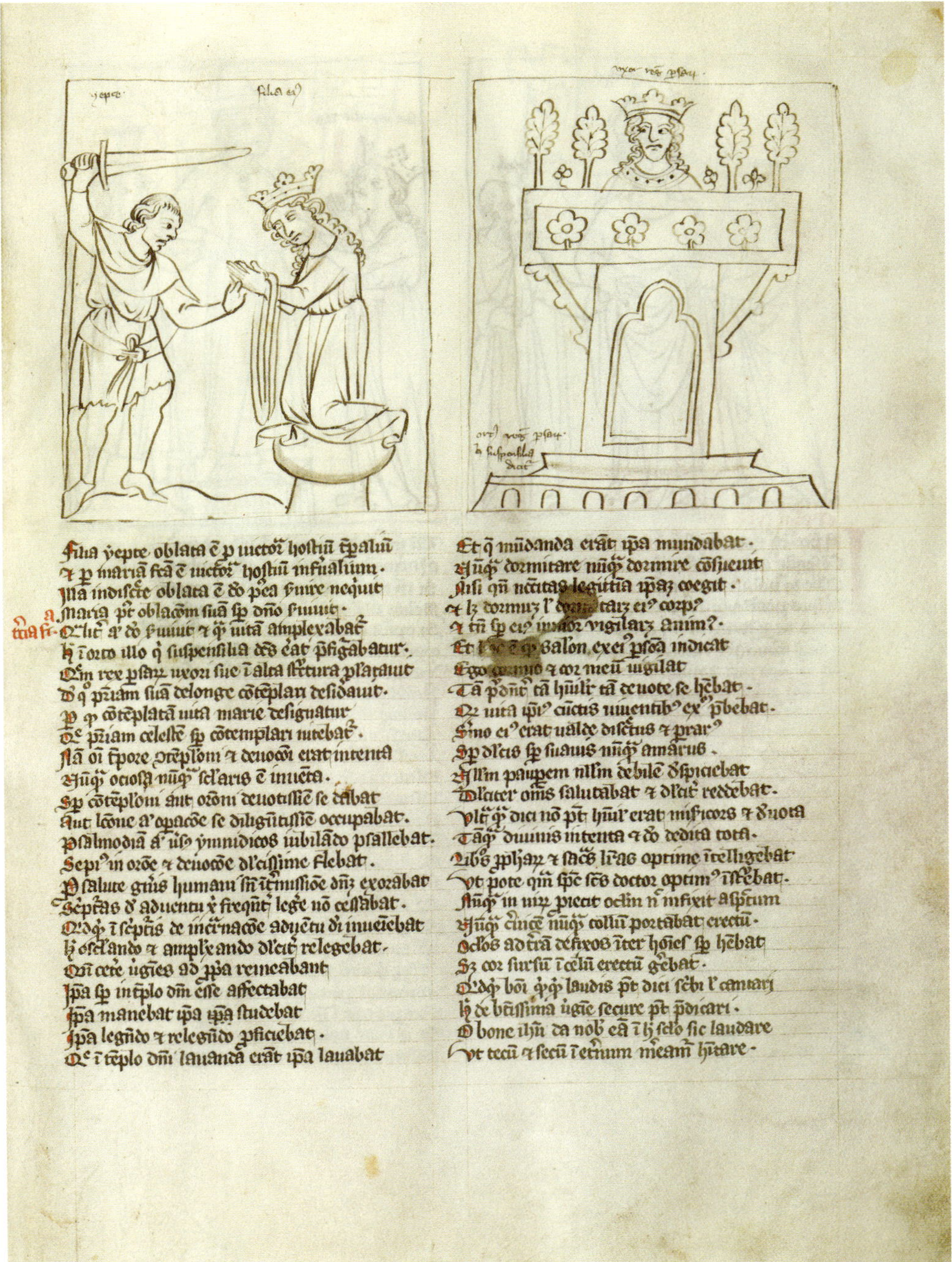

Fol. 9ra-b. Image Captions (a): *yepte; filia eius* / Image Caption (b): *uxor regis persarum; ortus regis persarum que suspensilia dicitur*

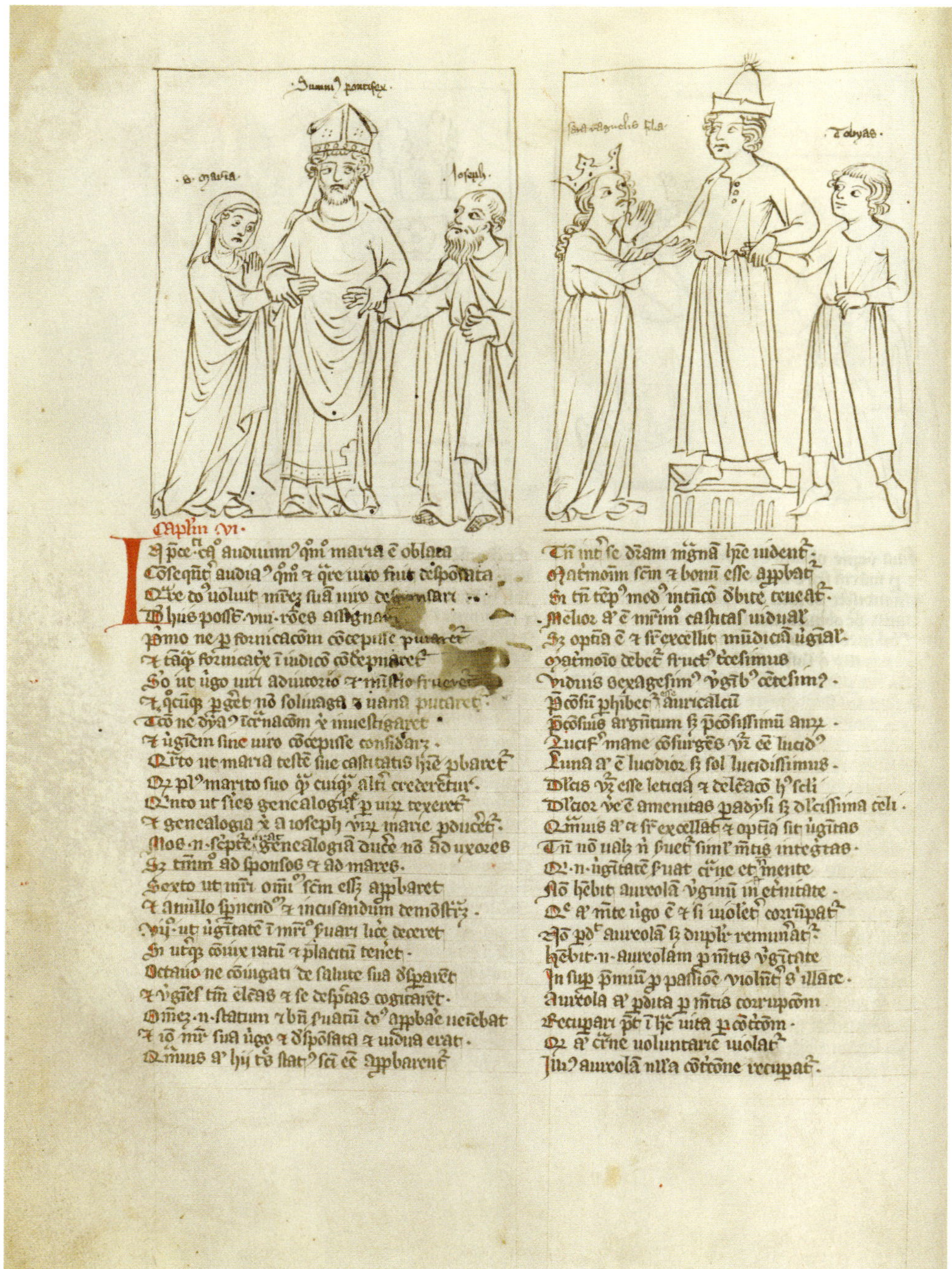

Fol. 9[va-b]. Image Caption (a): *summus pontifex; sancta maria; Ioseph* / Image Caption (b): *Sara raguelis filia.; Tobyas.*

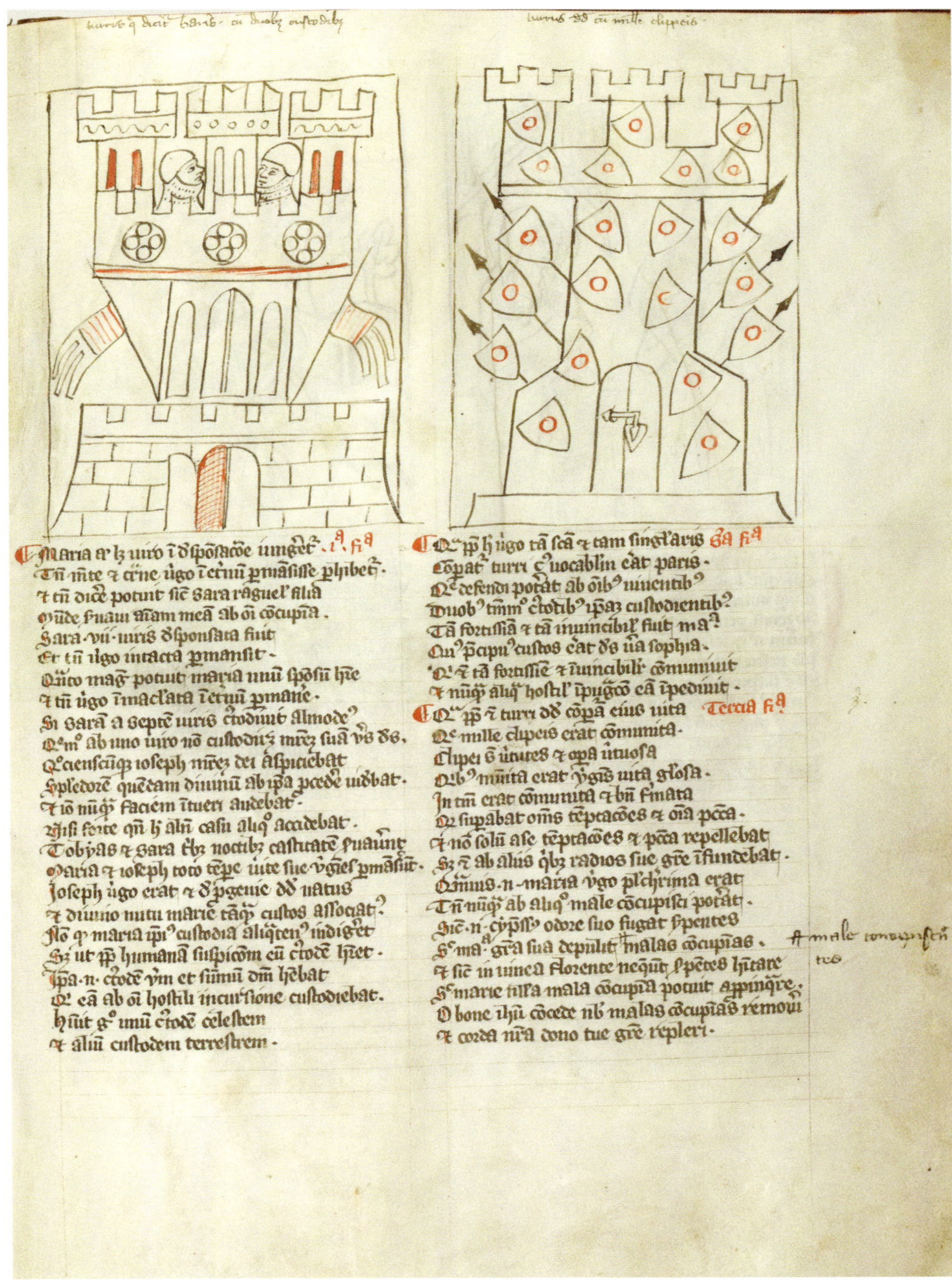

Fol. 10[ra-b]. Image Caption (a): *turris que dicitur baris cum duobus custodibus* / Image Caption (b): *turris dauid cum mille clippeis*

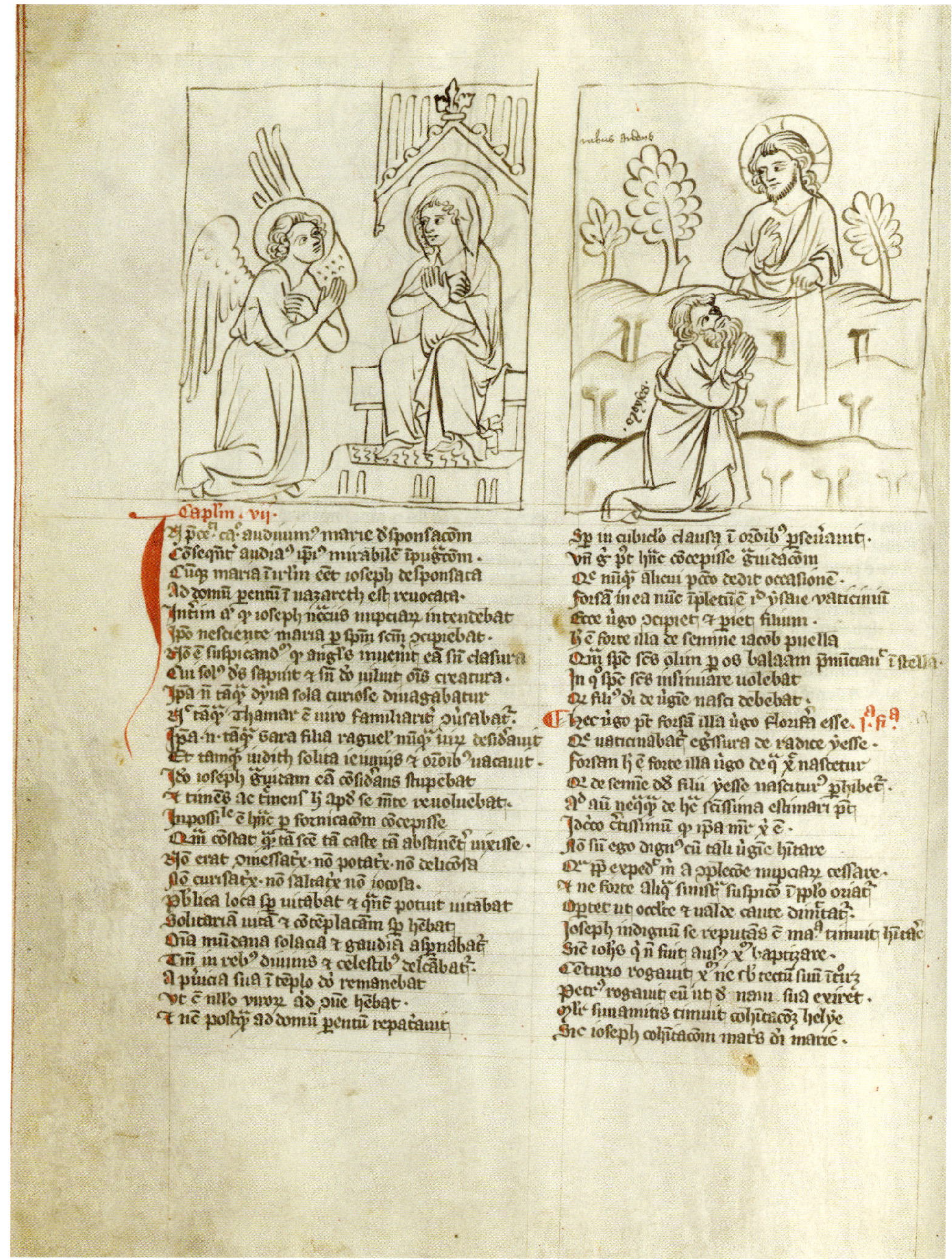

Fol. 10[va-b]. Image Captions (b): *rubus ardens; moyses*

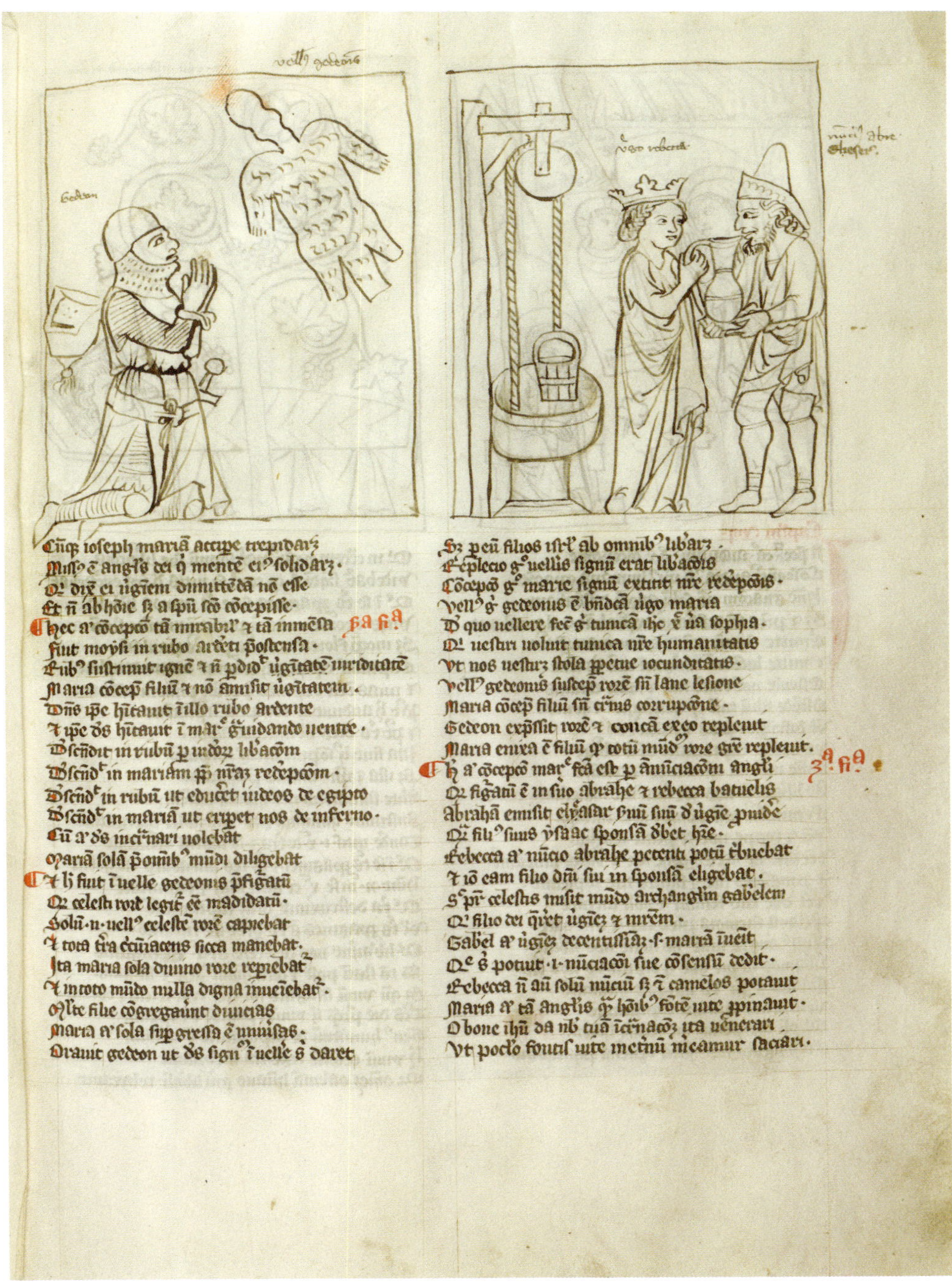

Fol. 11ra-b. Image Captions (a): *vellus gedeonis; Gedeon* / Image Captions (b): *nuncius Abre eliesar; uirgo Rebecca*

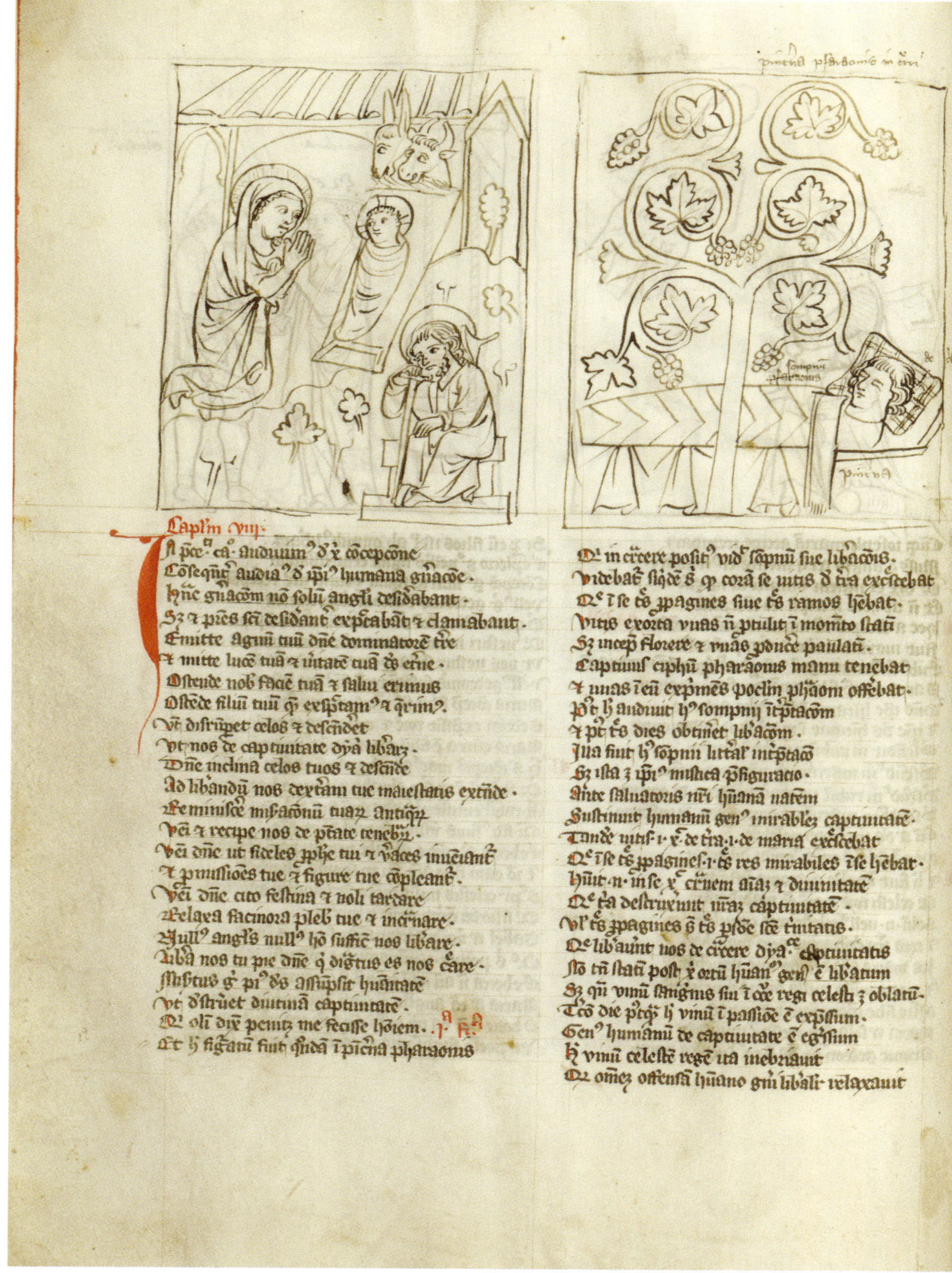

Fol. 11va-b. Image Captions (b): *pincerna pharaonic in terra; sompnium pharaonis; pincerna; de Abraham*

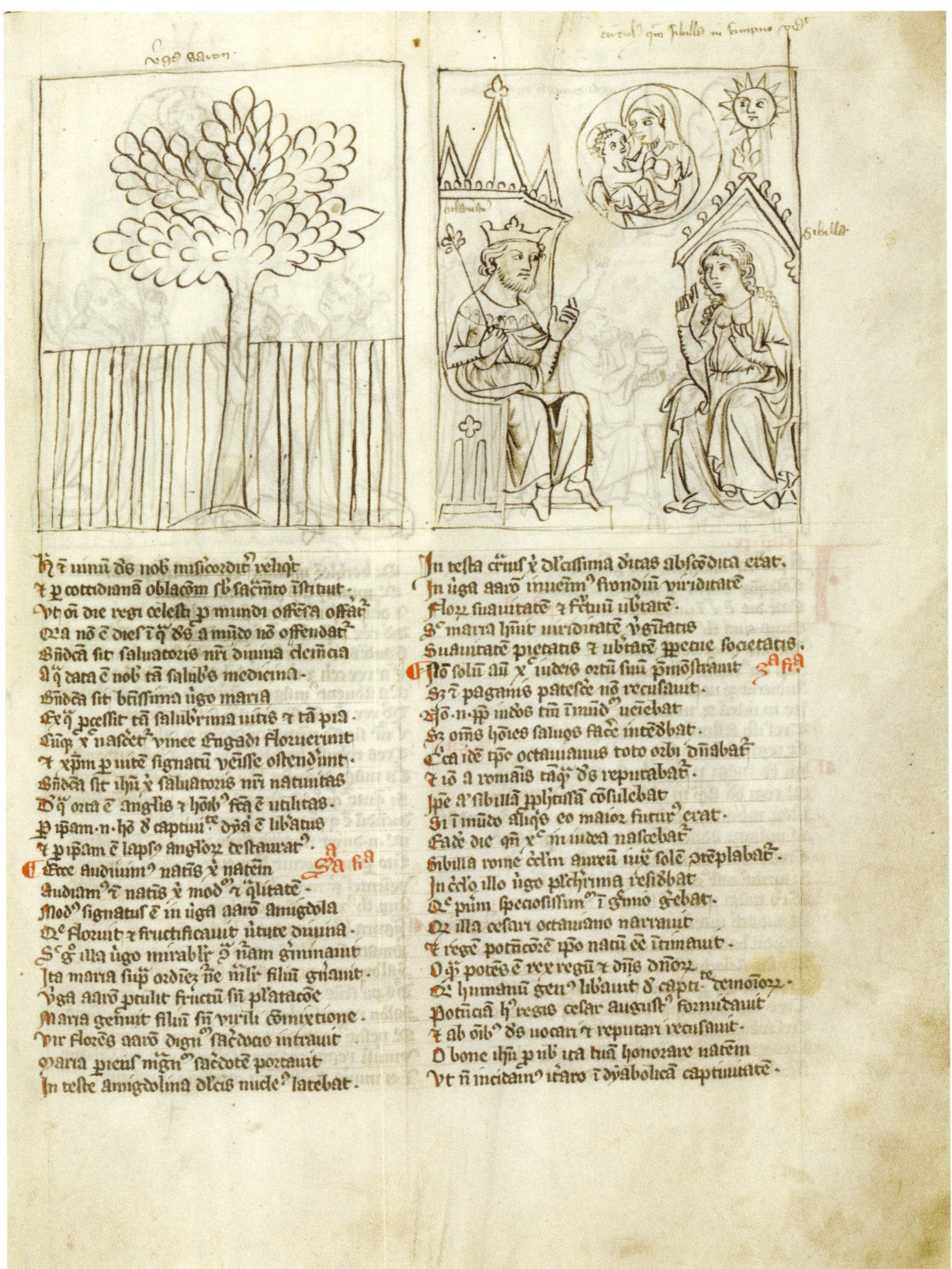

Fol. 12[ra-b]. Image Caption (a): *virga aaron* / Image Captions (b): *circulus quem sibilla in sompno vidit; octauianus; sibilla*

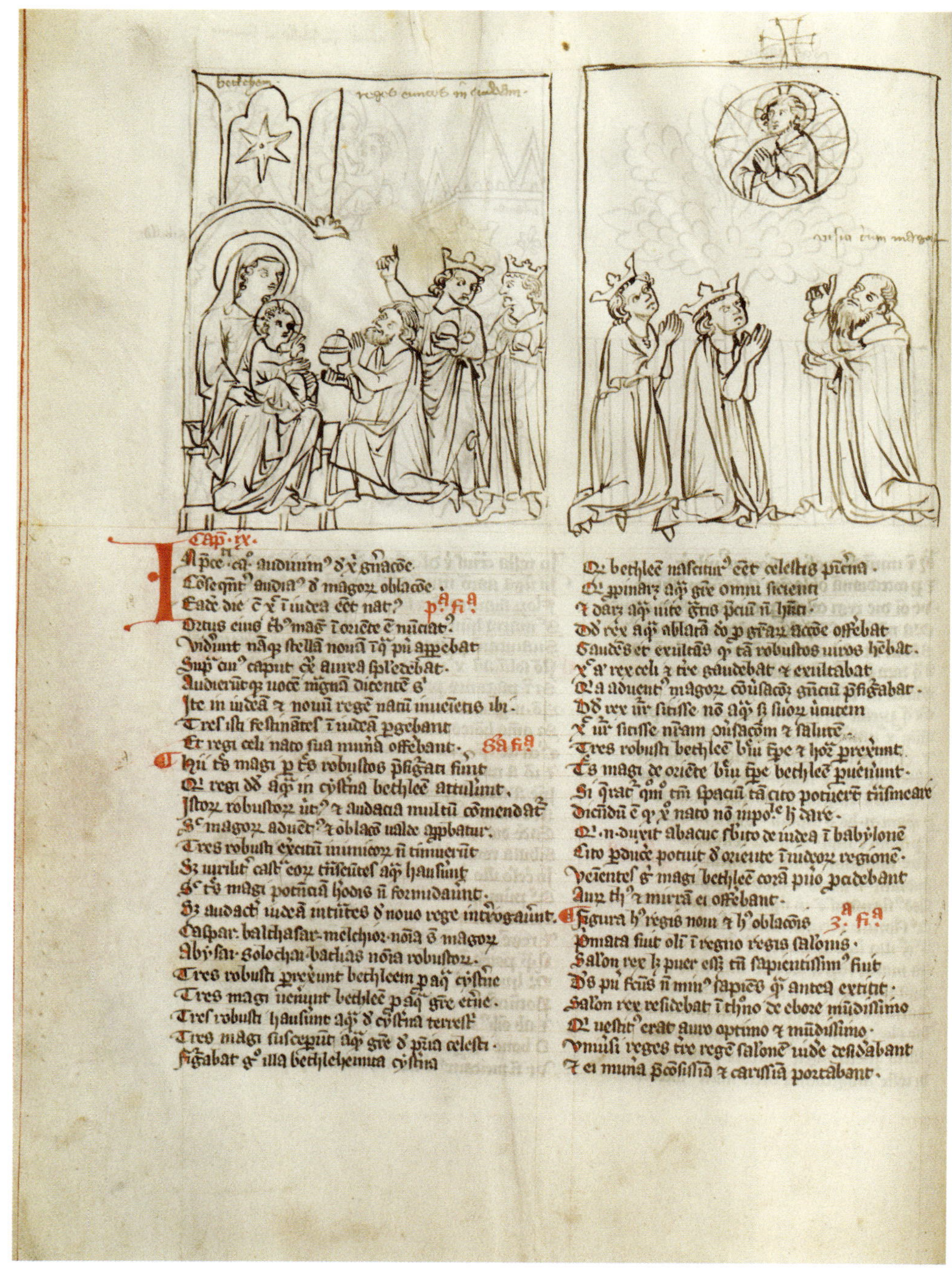

Fol. 12[va-b]. Image Captions (a): *bethelem.; reges euntes in stellam* / Image Caption (b): *uisio trium magorum*

Fol. 13[ra-b]. Image Captions (a): *dauid; tres uiri portantes aquam; nomina trium robustorum; bathais; abisay; solothay* / Image Caption (b): *saolmonis thronus*

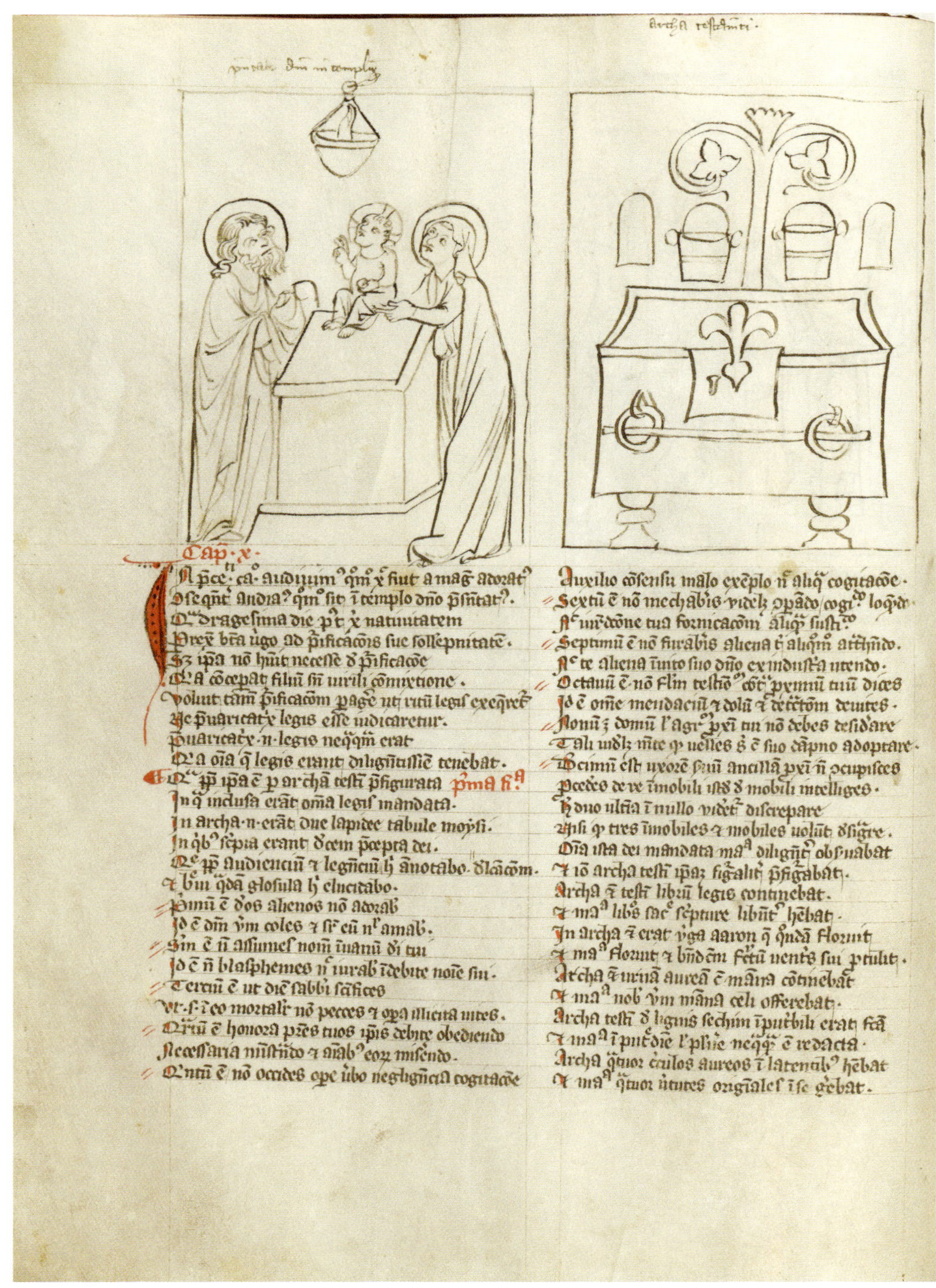

Fol. 13^{va-b}. Image Caption (a): *presentatio domini in templo* / Image Caption (b): *archa testamenti.*

Fol. 14[ra-b]. Image Caption (a): *aureum candelabrum* / Image Captions (b): *hely sacerdos.; samuel; anna mater eius uxor elkane.*

Fol. 14[va-b]. Image Captions (a): *hic est egiptus; et statue ydolorum corrupte* / Image Caption (b): *ymago uirginis cum puero*

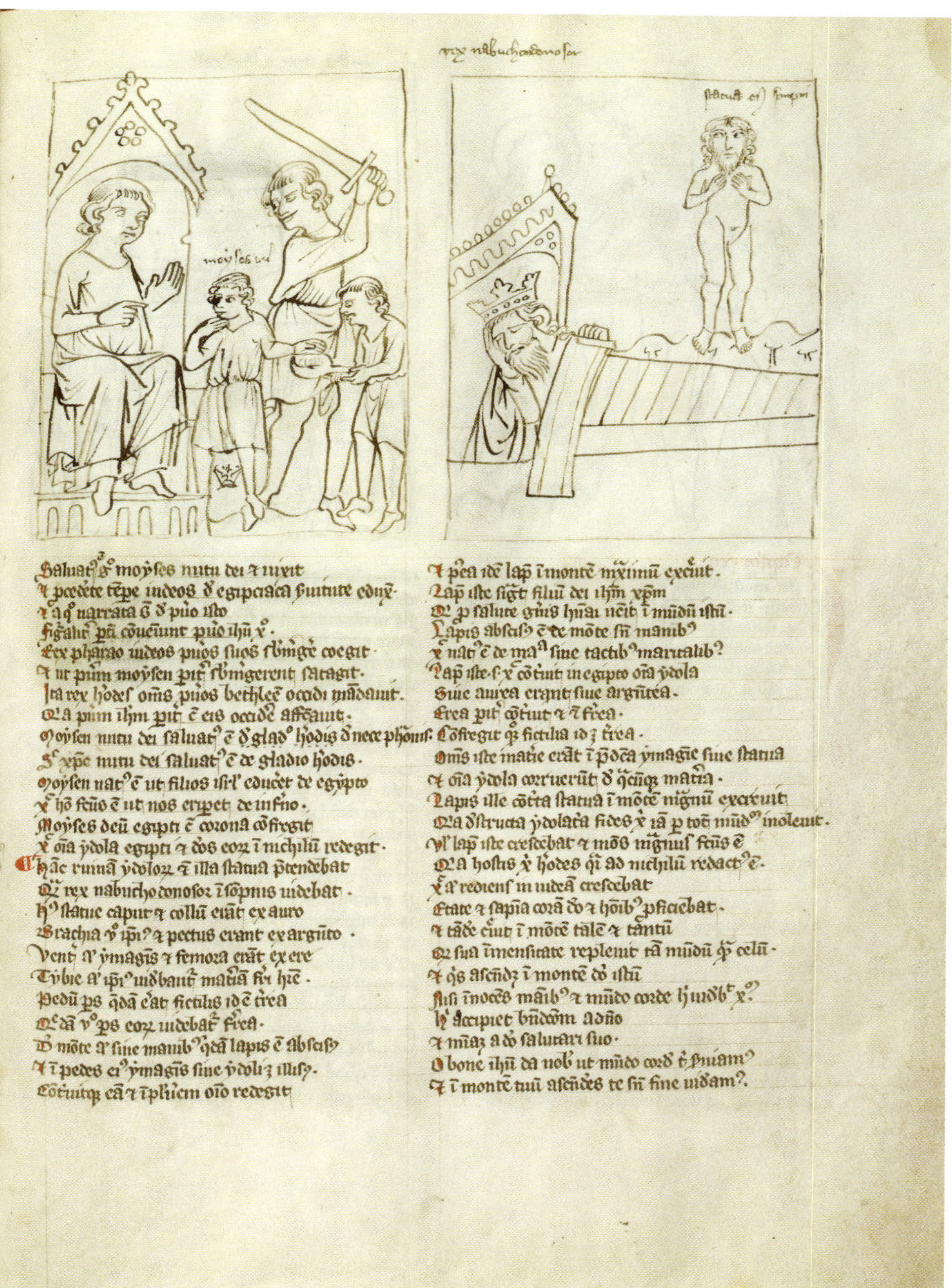

Fol. 15[ra-b]. Image Caption (a): *moyses puer* / Image Captions (b): *rex nabuchondonosor; statua eius sompni*

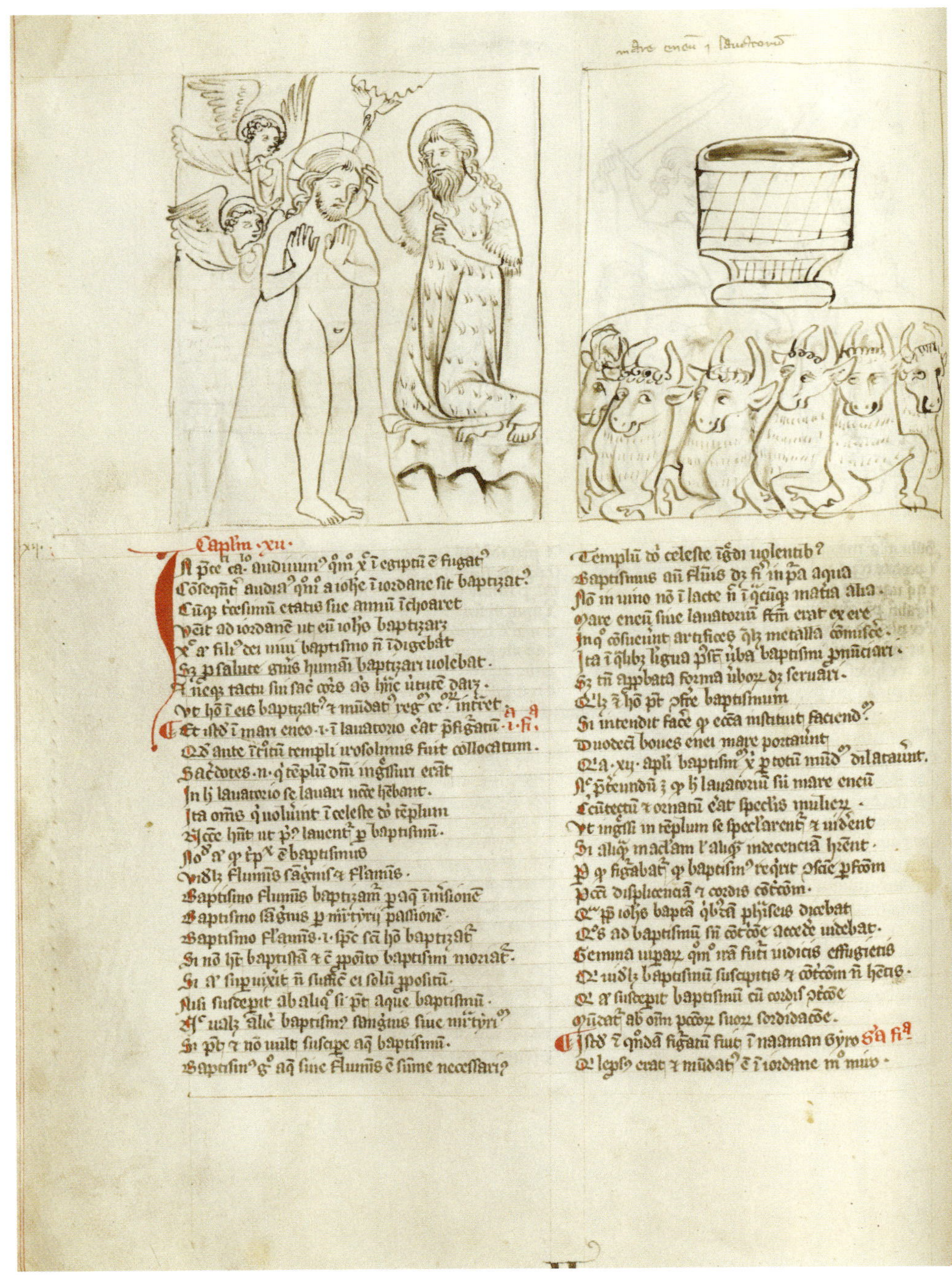

Fol. 15va-b. Image Caption (b): *mare eneum in lauatorio*

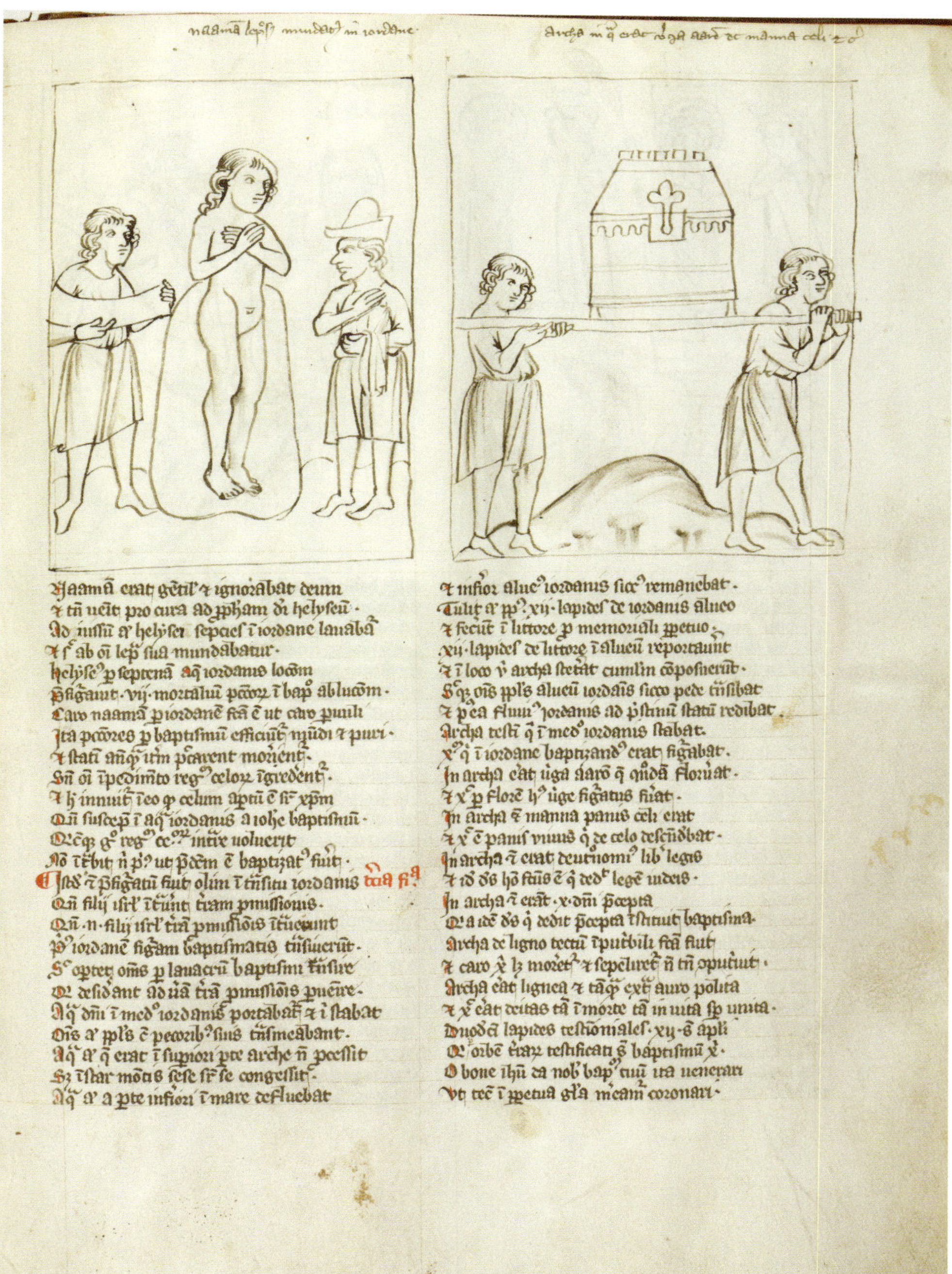

Fol. 16[ra-b]. Image Caption (a): *Naaman leprosus mundatur in iordane.* / Image Caption (b): *archa in qua erat uirga aaron et manna celi et testamenta*

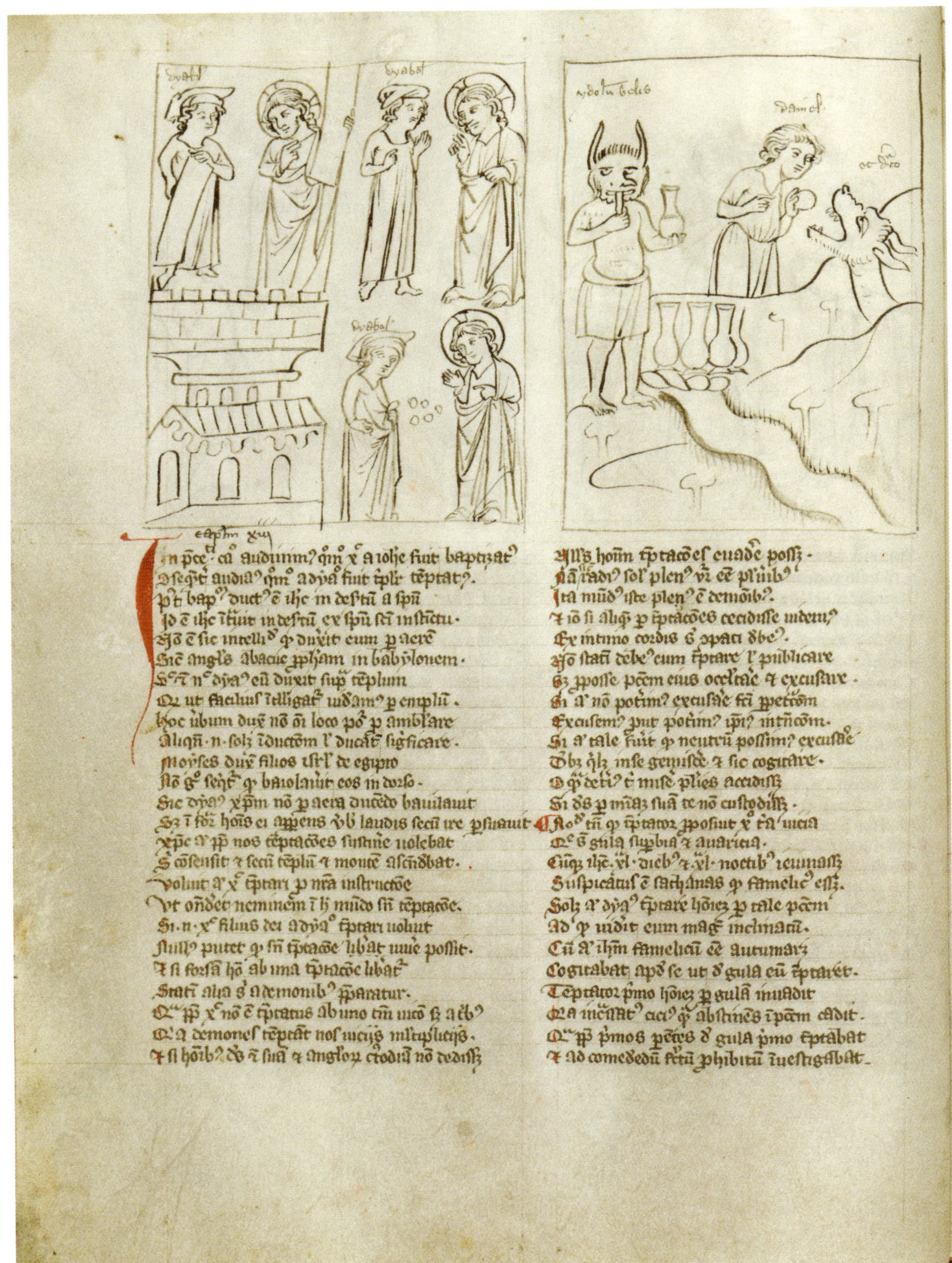

Fol. 16va-b. Image Captions (a): *dyabolus; dyabolus; dyabolus* / Image Captions (b): *yodolum belis; daniel; et draco*

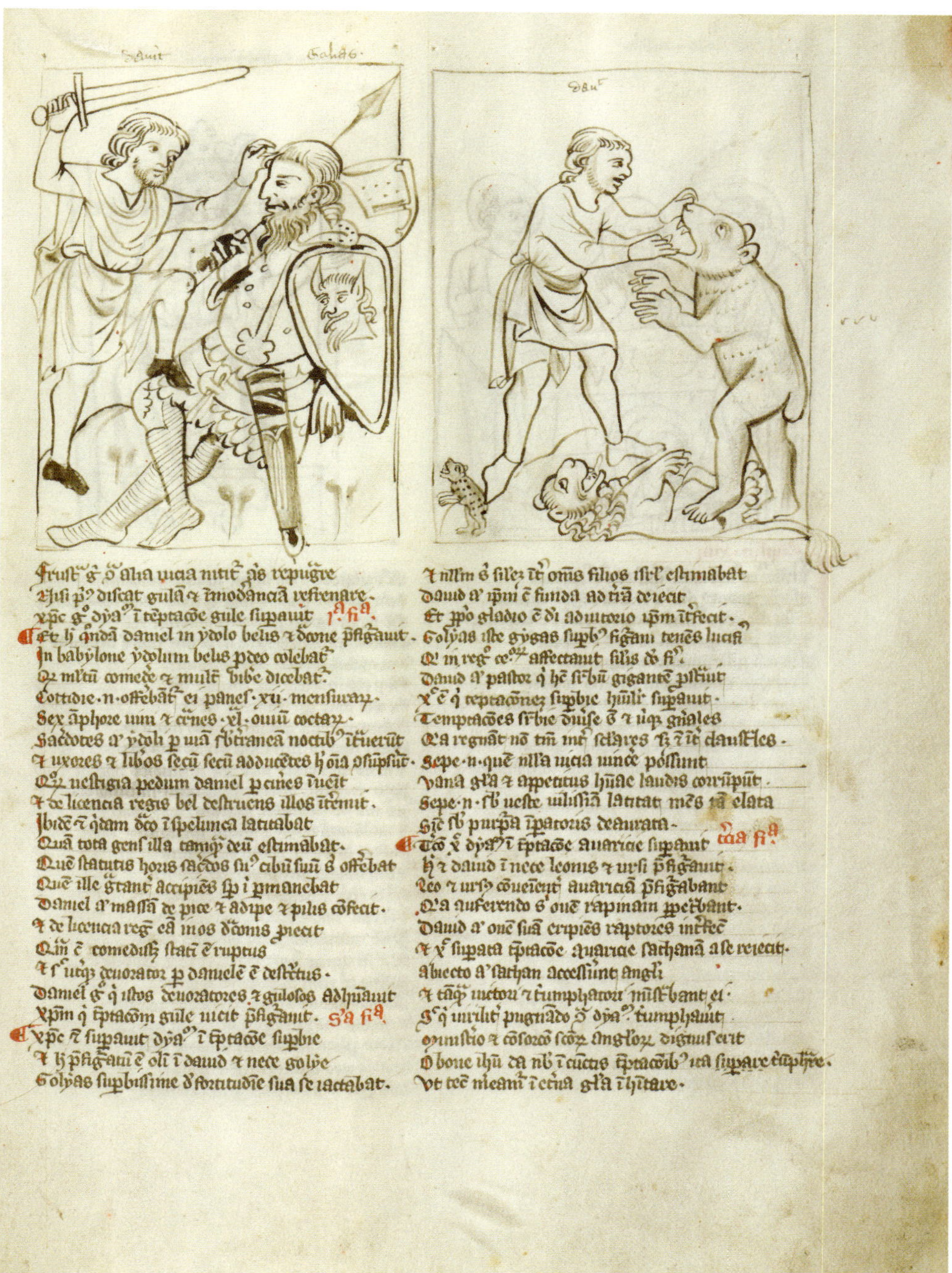

Fol. 17[ra-b]. Image Captions (a): *dauid; Golias.* / Image Captions (b): *dauid*; (illegible)

Fol. 17[va-b]. Image Caption (a): *quomodo Christus curauit mariam magdalenam; magdala* / Image Caption (b): *rex mannasen poenitentie eius depictus*

Fol. 18ra-b. Image Caption (a): *prodigus filius reuersus ad patrem* / Image Captions (b): *natan qui dauid redarguit; dauid trystis; penituit peccatum in uria*

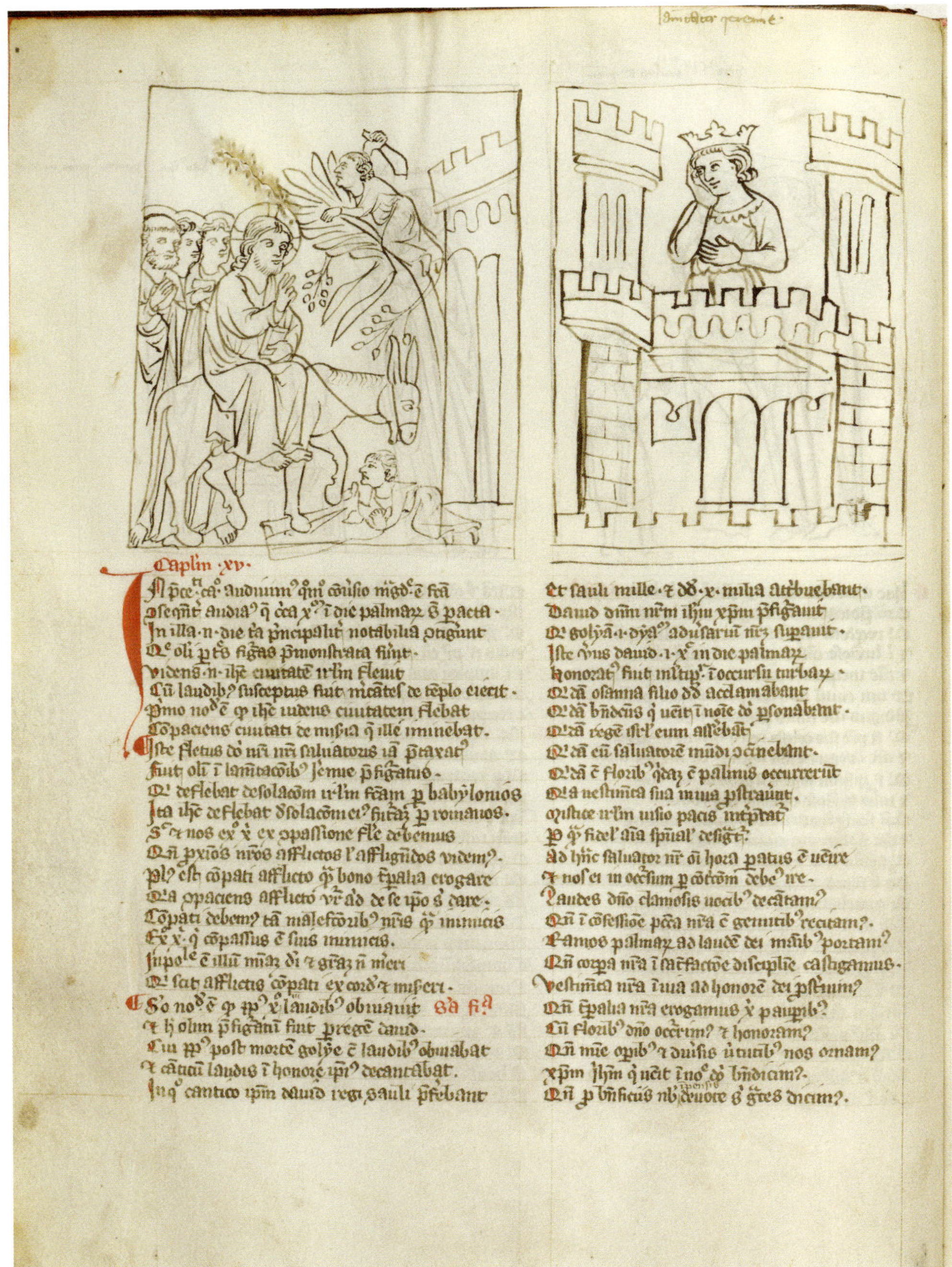

Fol. 18va-b. Image Caption (b): *lamentationes jeremie*

Fol. 19[ra-b]. Image Caption (a): *exhibitio honores dauid post necem goliae.* / Image Captions (b): *elyodorus; vapulsus est propter spolium templi*

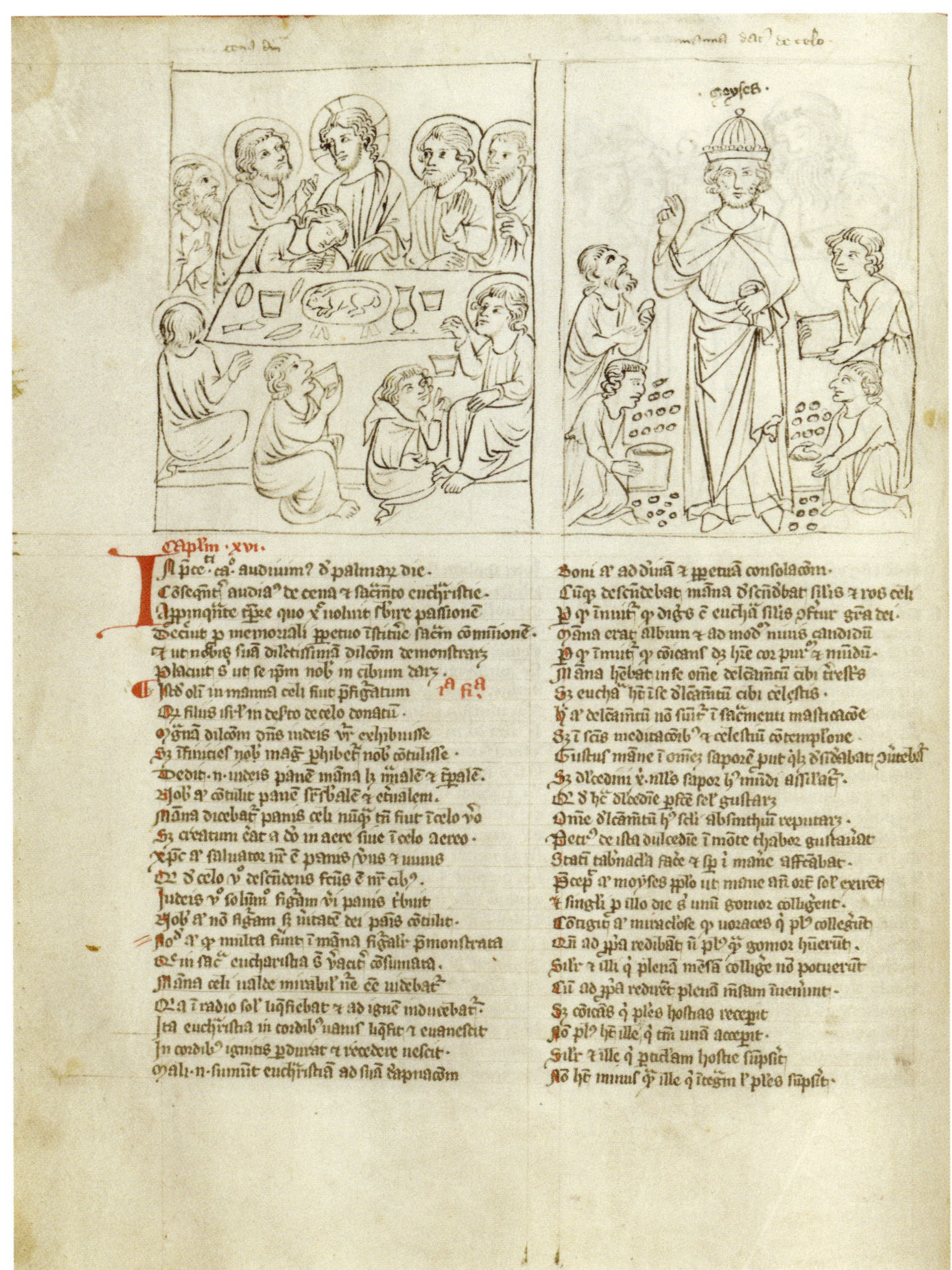

Fol. 19va-b. Image Caption (a): *cena domini* / Image Captions (b): *manna data de celo.; moyses* (different hand)

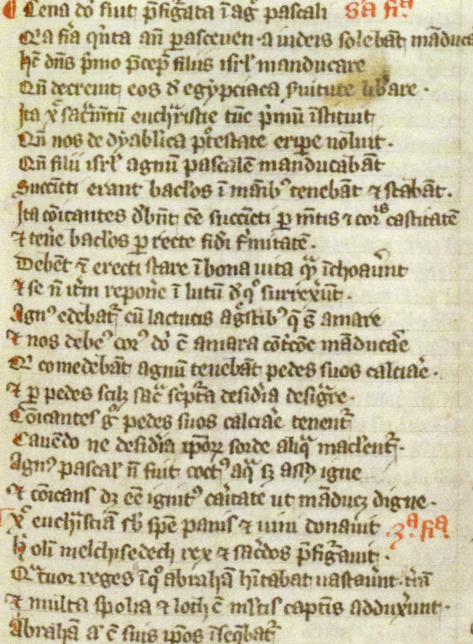

Fol. 20ra-b^. Image Caption (a): *agnus pascalis* / Image Caption (b): *melchisedech rex salem.; Abraham.*

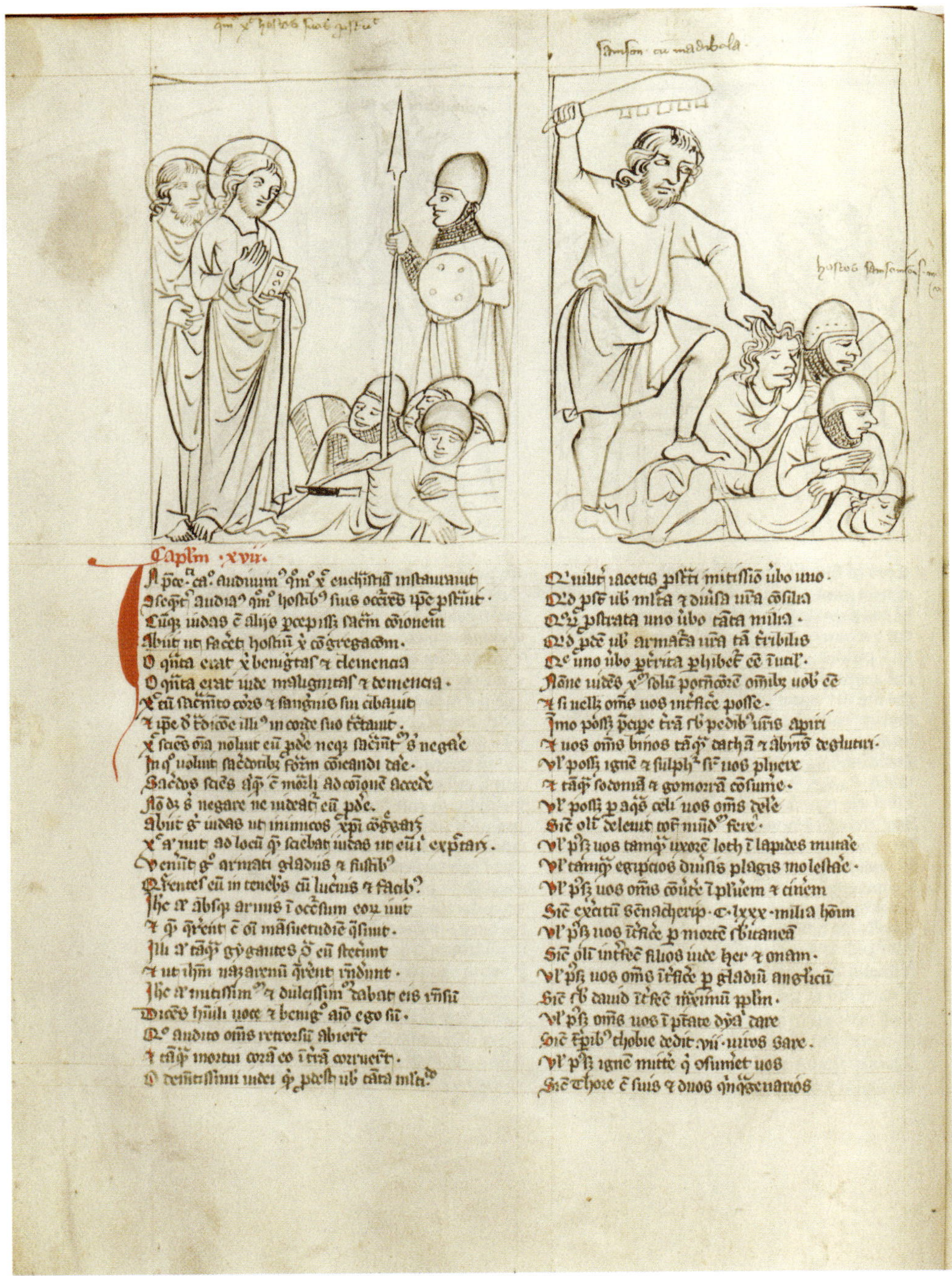

Fol. 20va-b. Image Caption (a): *quomodo Christus hostes suos prostauit* / Image Captions (b): *samson cum madibula; hostes samsonis mortui*

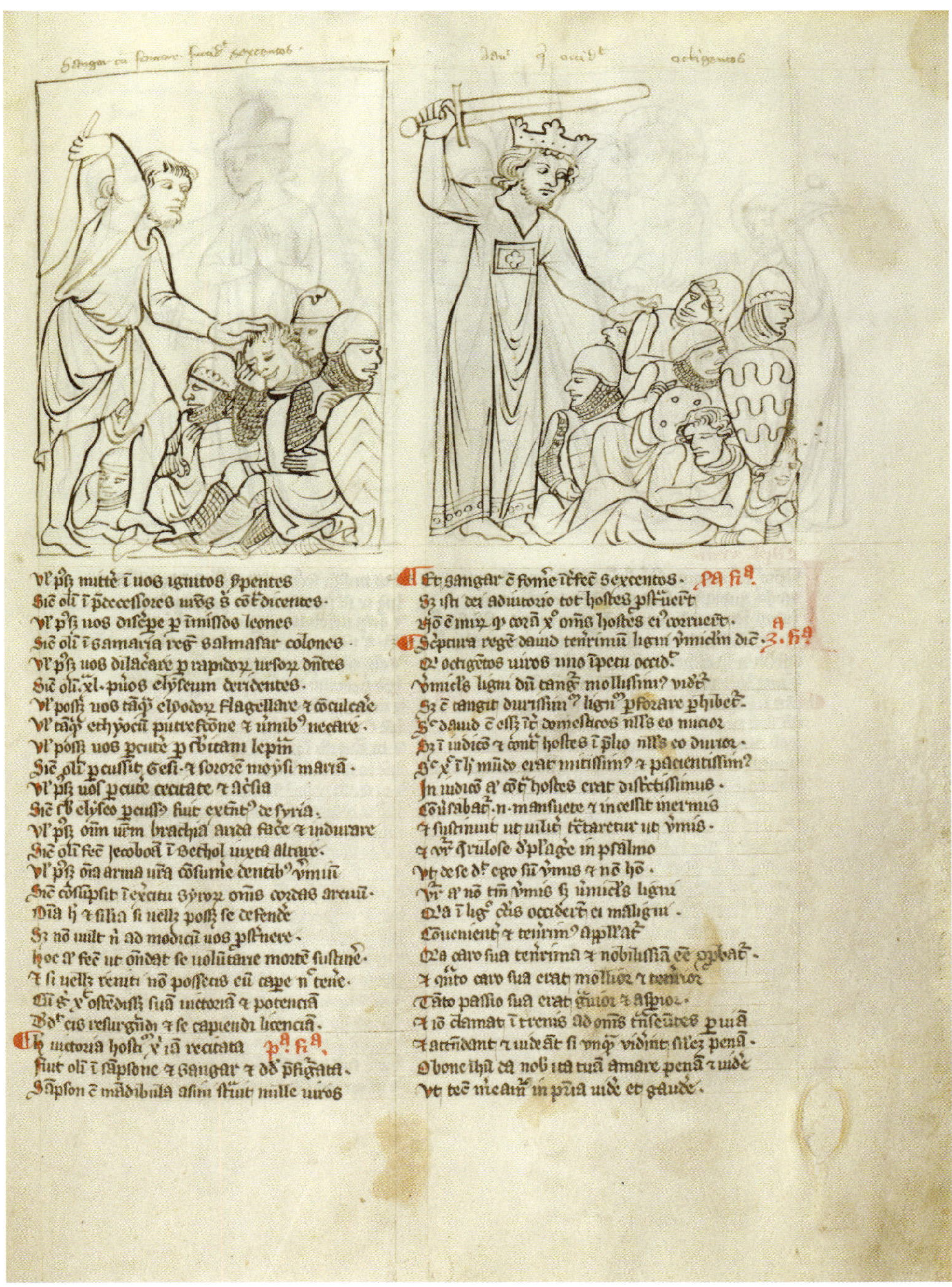

Fol. 21ra-b. Image Caption (a): *Samgar cum fomore succidit sexcentos.* / Image Caption (b): *dauid qui occidit octigentos*

Fol. 21va-b. Image Captions (a): *petrus; Iudas* / Image Captions (b): *amasam; joab*

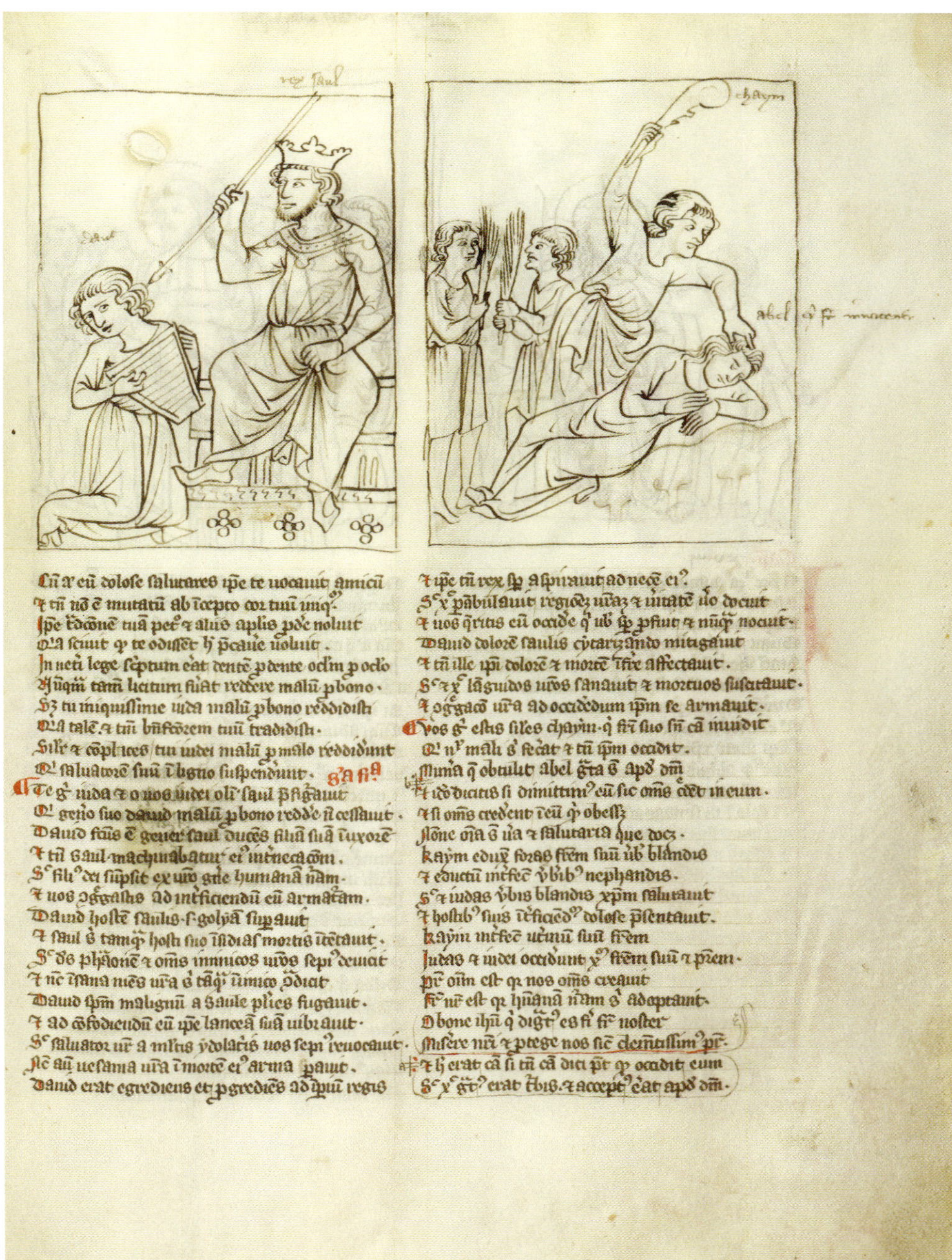

Fol. 22ra-b. Image Captions (a): *rex Saul; dauid* / Image Captions (b): *abel qui fuit innocens; chaym*

Fol. 22[va-b]. Image Caption (b): *iesus conspusus et velatus conlaphisatus*

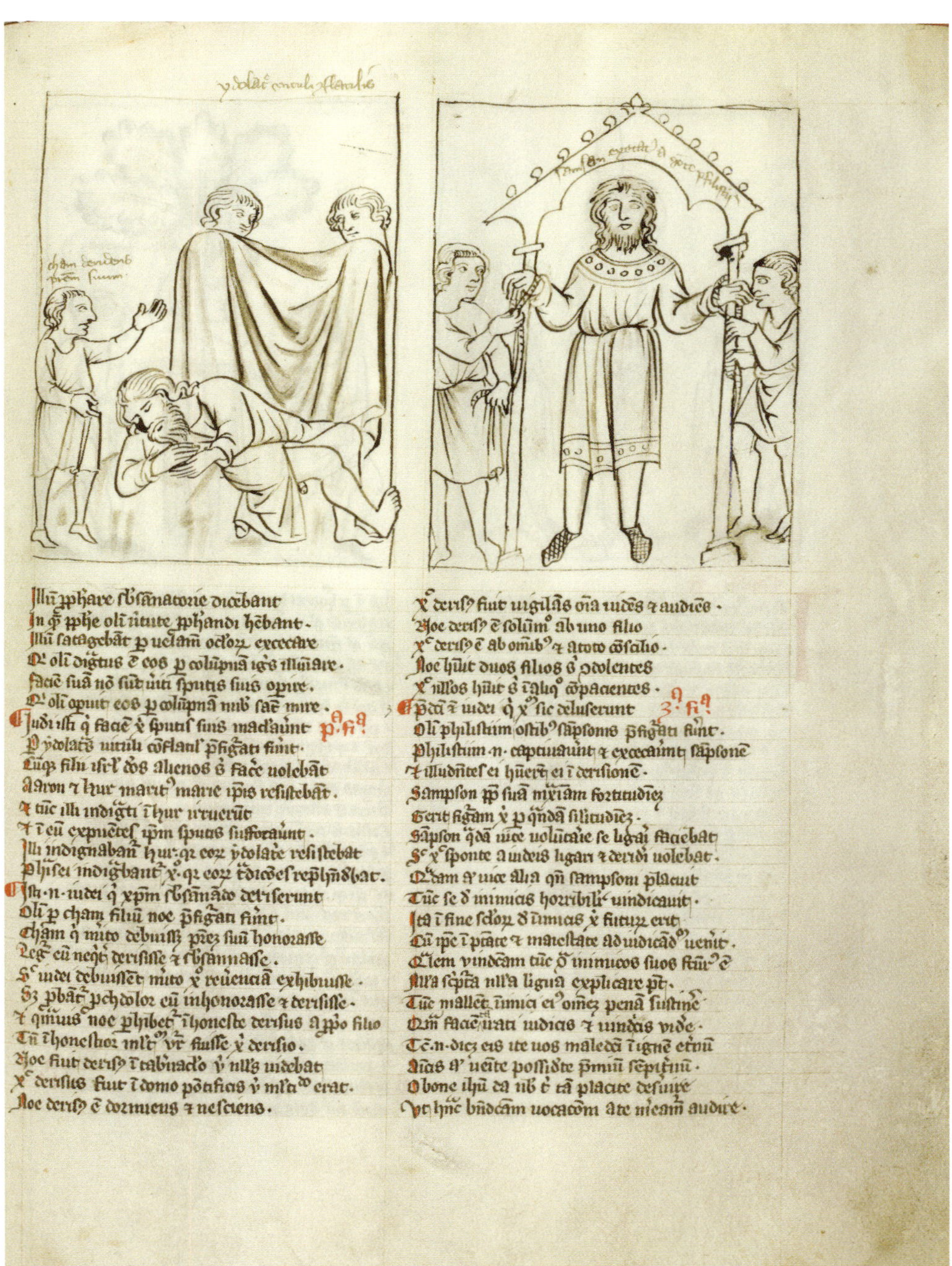

Fol. 23[ra-b]. Image Captions (a): *ydolater uituli conflatilis; cham deridens patrem suum.* / Image Caption (b): *samson excecatus a gente philistinorum*

Fol. 23[va-b]. Image Caption (b): *Achior princeps.*

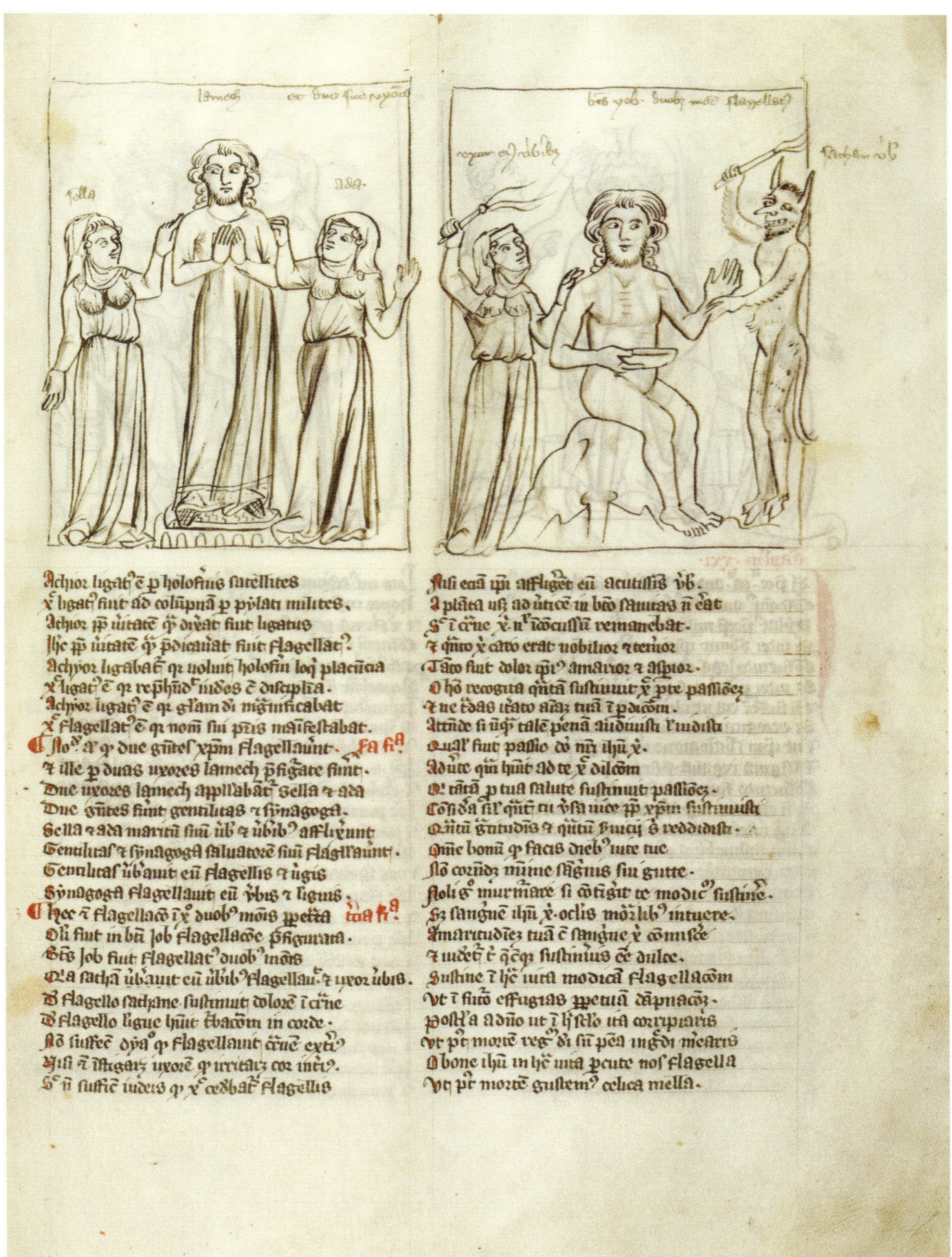

Fol. 24[ra-b]. Image Captions (a): *Lamech; et duo sue uxores; Sella; Ada.* / Image Captions (b): *sathan uerbis* (*error*); *beatus yob. Duobus modis flagellatus* (error); *uxor eius uerberibus*

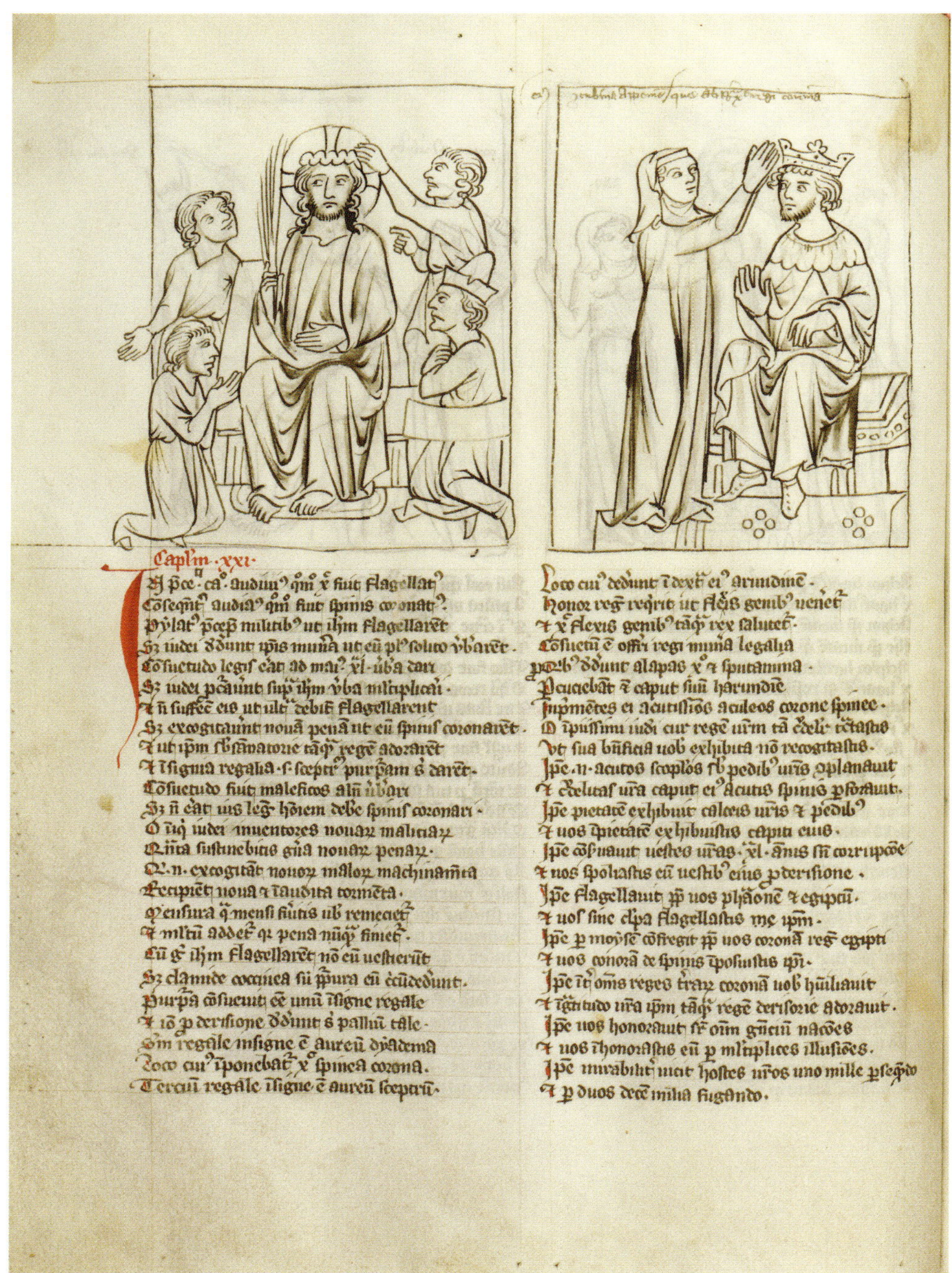

Fol. 24va-b. Image Captions (b): *concubine appemen; quis ab rex et regi coronam* (error)

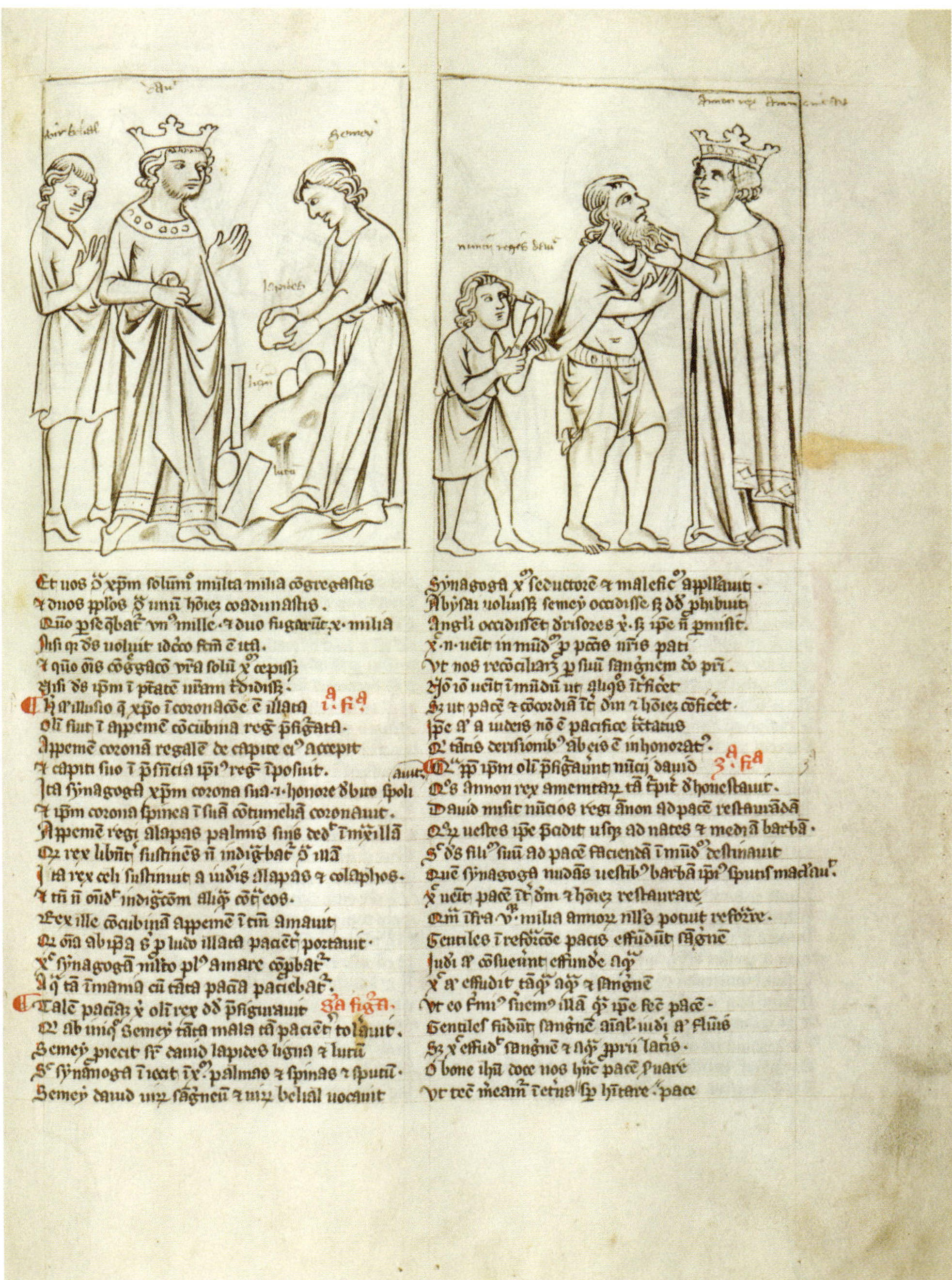

Fol. 25[ra-b]. Image Captions (a): *dauid; semei; turbatus; lapides; lignea; lutum* / Image Captions (b): *nuntius regis dauid; Amon rex amonitarum*

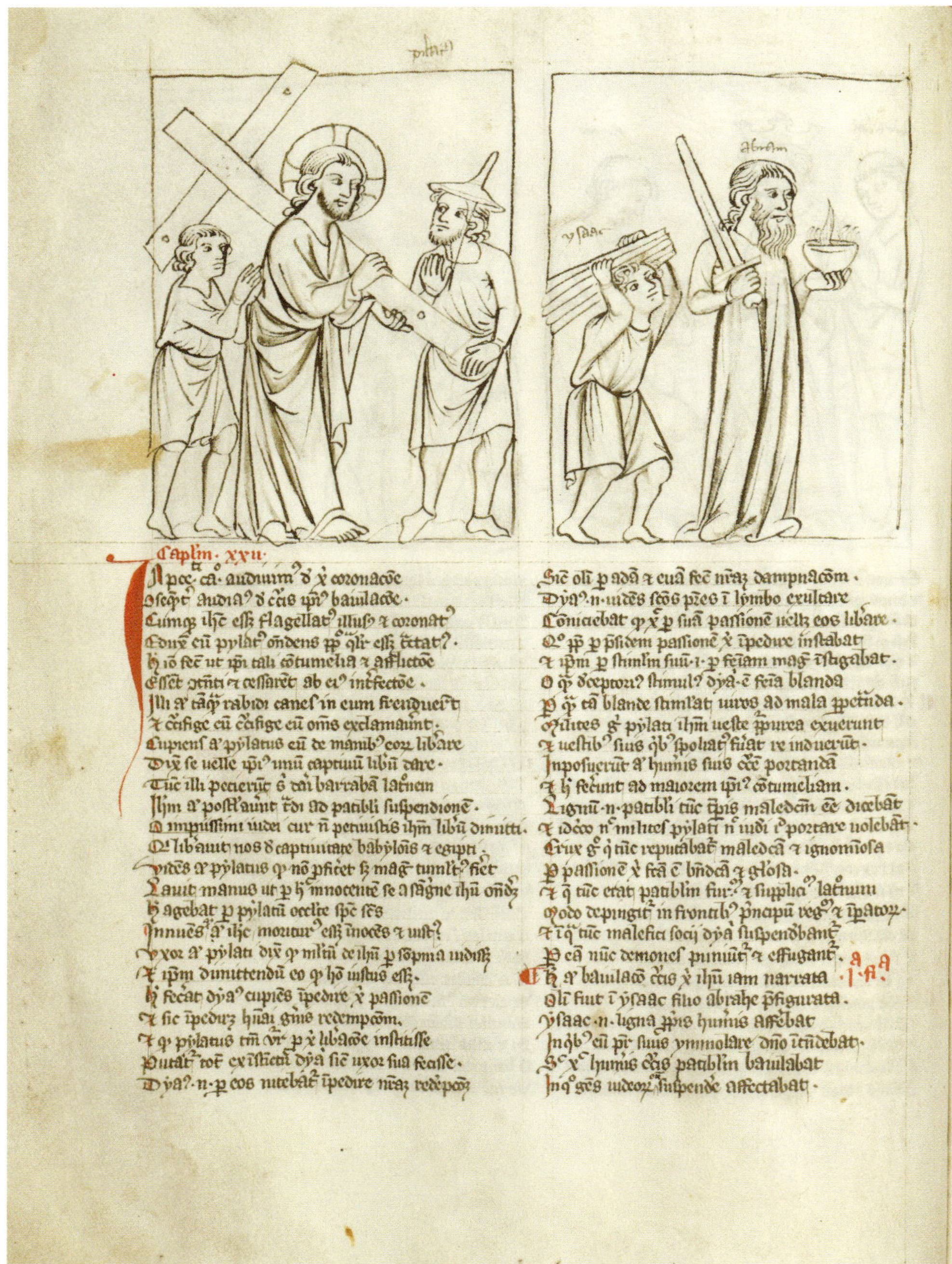

Fol. 25^{va-b}. Image Caption (a): *Pilatus* / Image Caption (b): *Abram; ysaac*

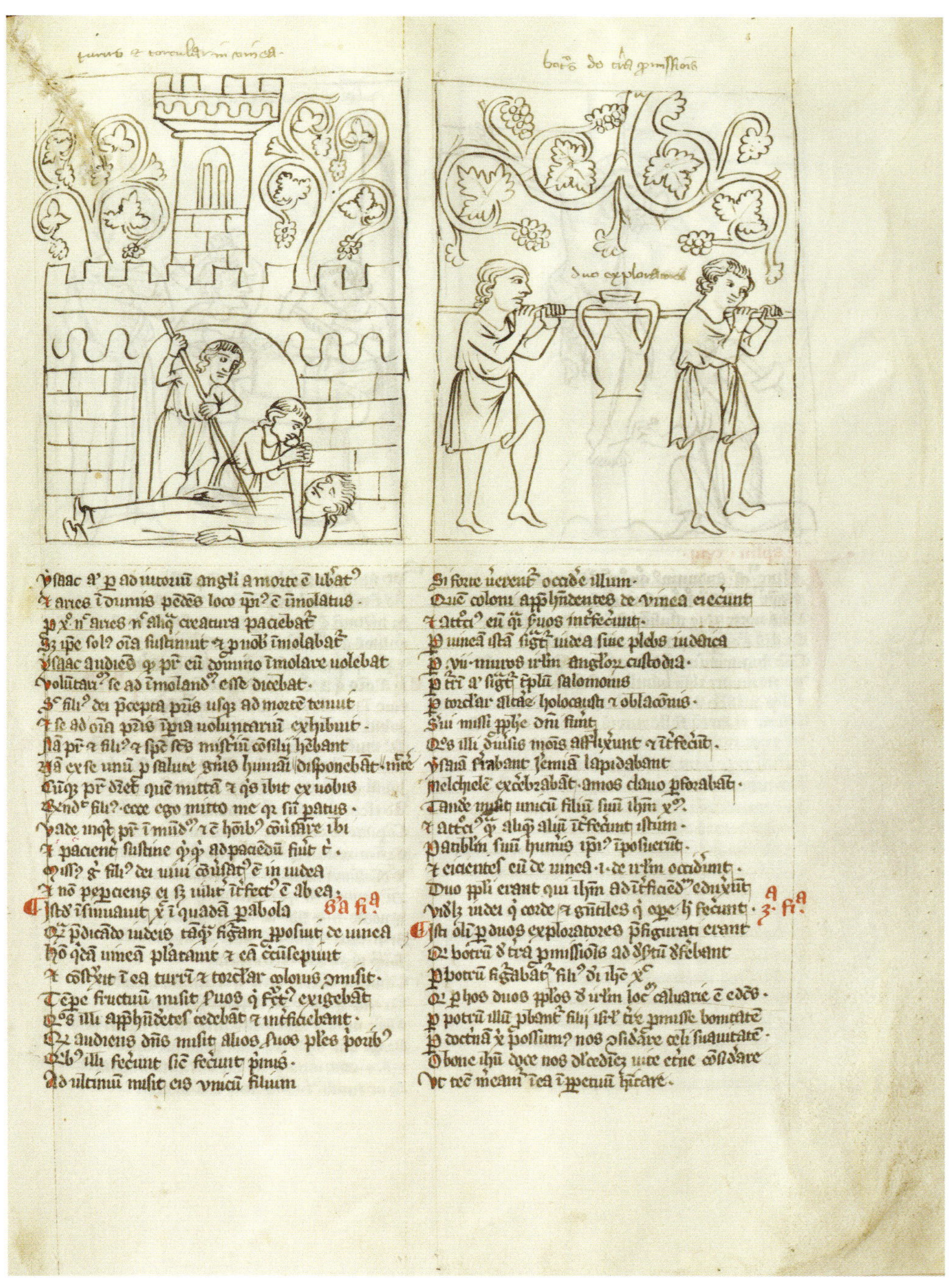

Fol. 26[ra-b]. Image Caption (a): *turris et torcular in uinea.* / Image Captions (b): *botrum de terra promissionis; duo exploratores*

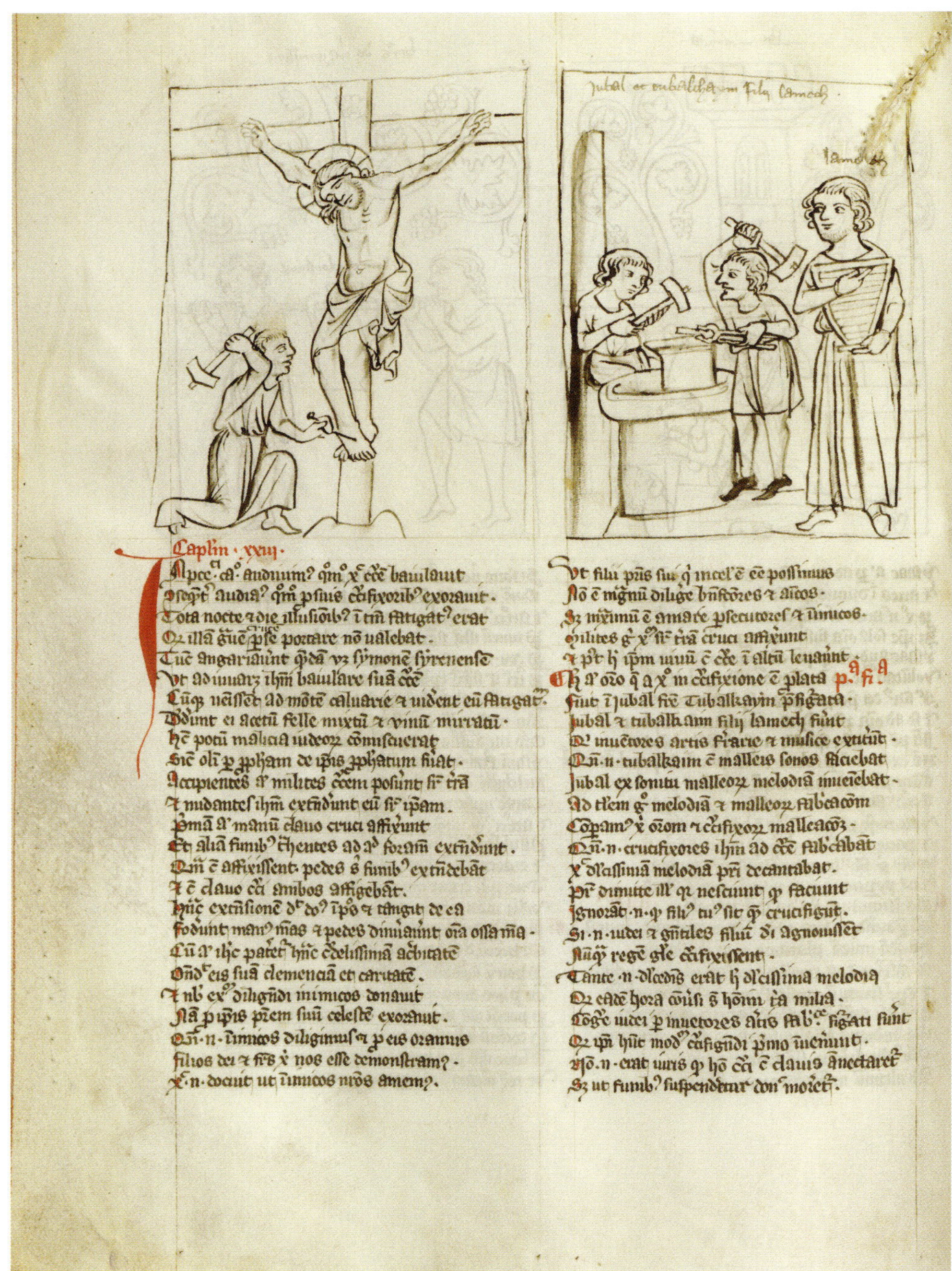

Fol. 26va-b. Image Captions (b): *Tubal et tubalchaym filius Lamech.; Lamech*

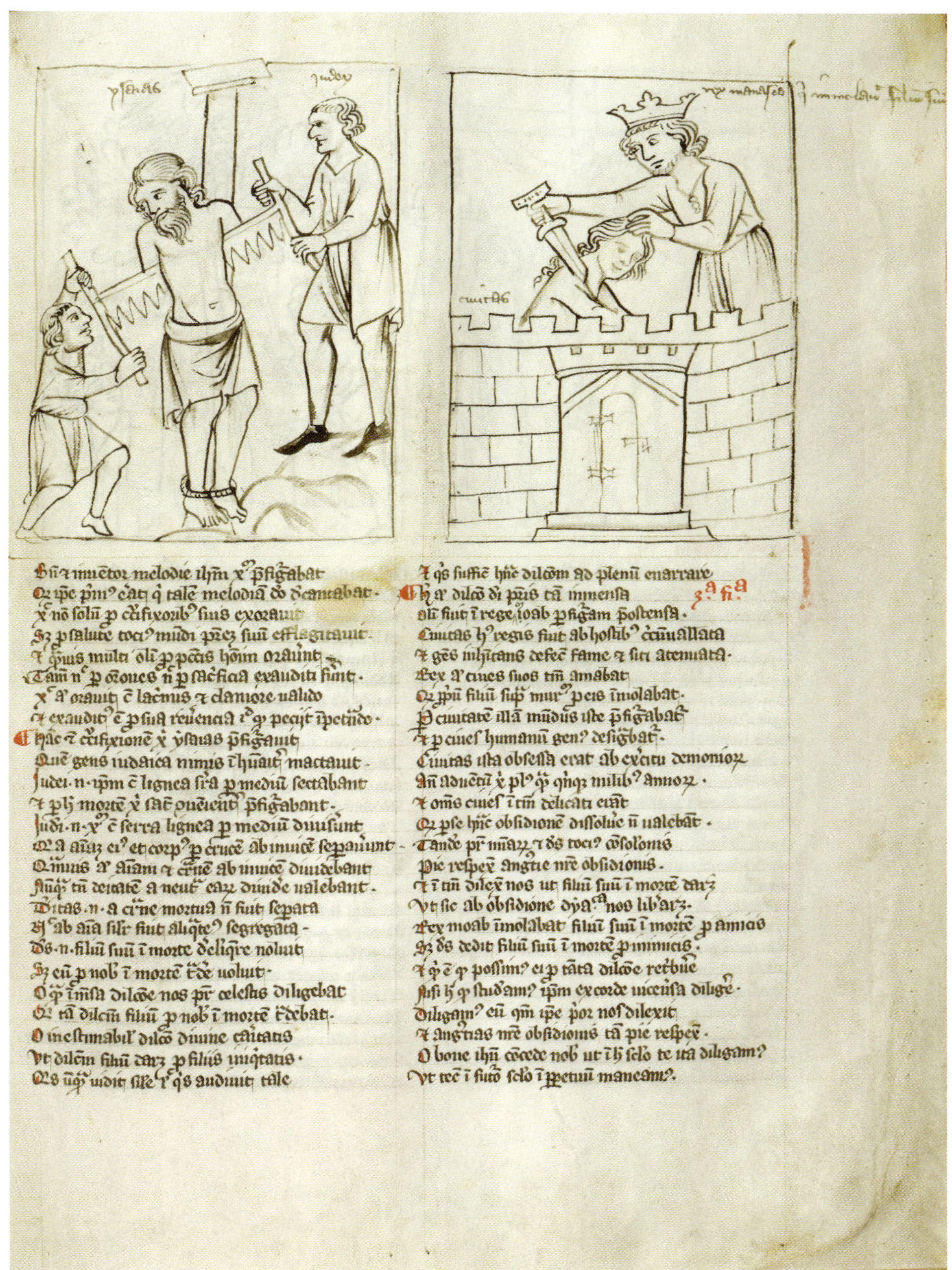

Fol. 27[ra-b]. Image Captions (a): *ysaias; judeorum* / Image Captions (b): *rex manases qui immolauit filium suum; ciuitas*

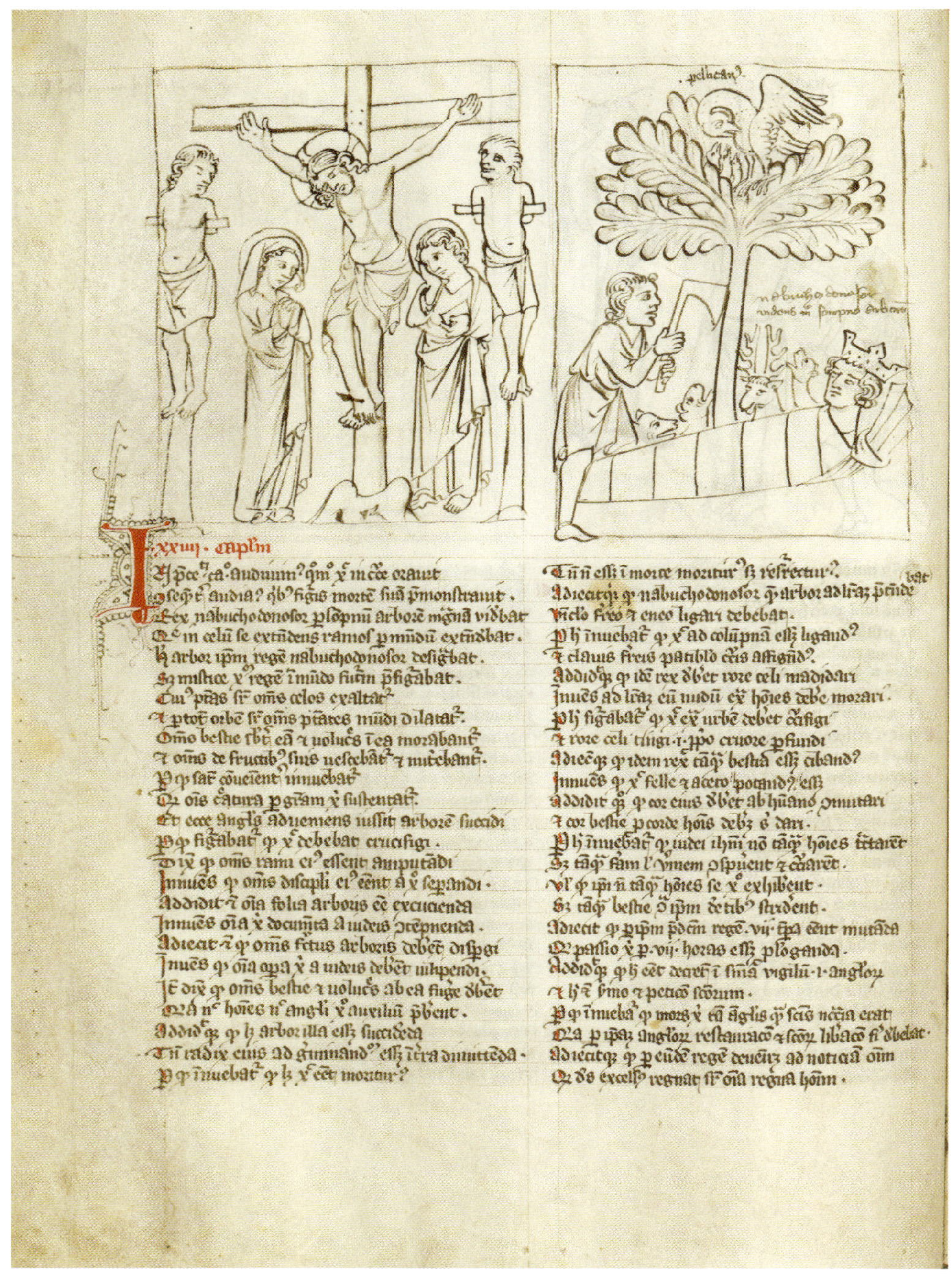

Fol. 27[va-b]. Image Captions (b): *pellicanus.; nabuchodonosor uidens in sompno arborem*

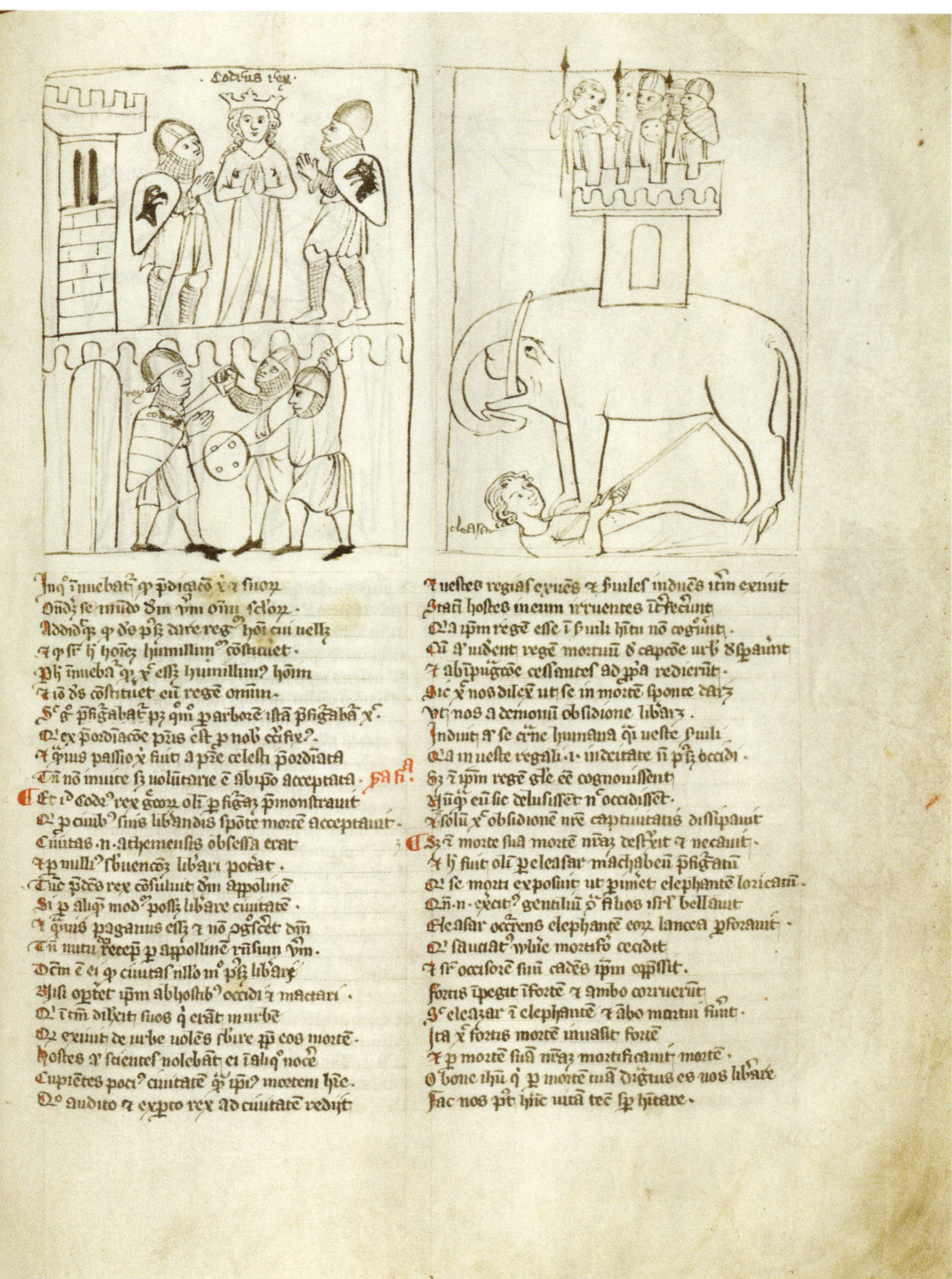

Fol. 28[ra-b]. Image Captions (a): *Codrus rex.; rex; codrus* / Image Caption (b): *eleasar*

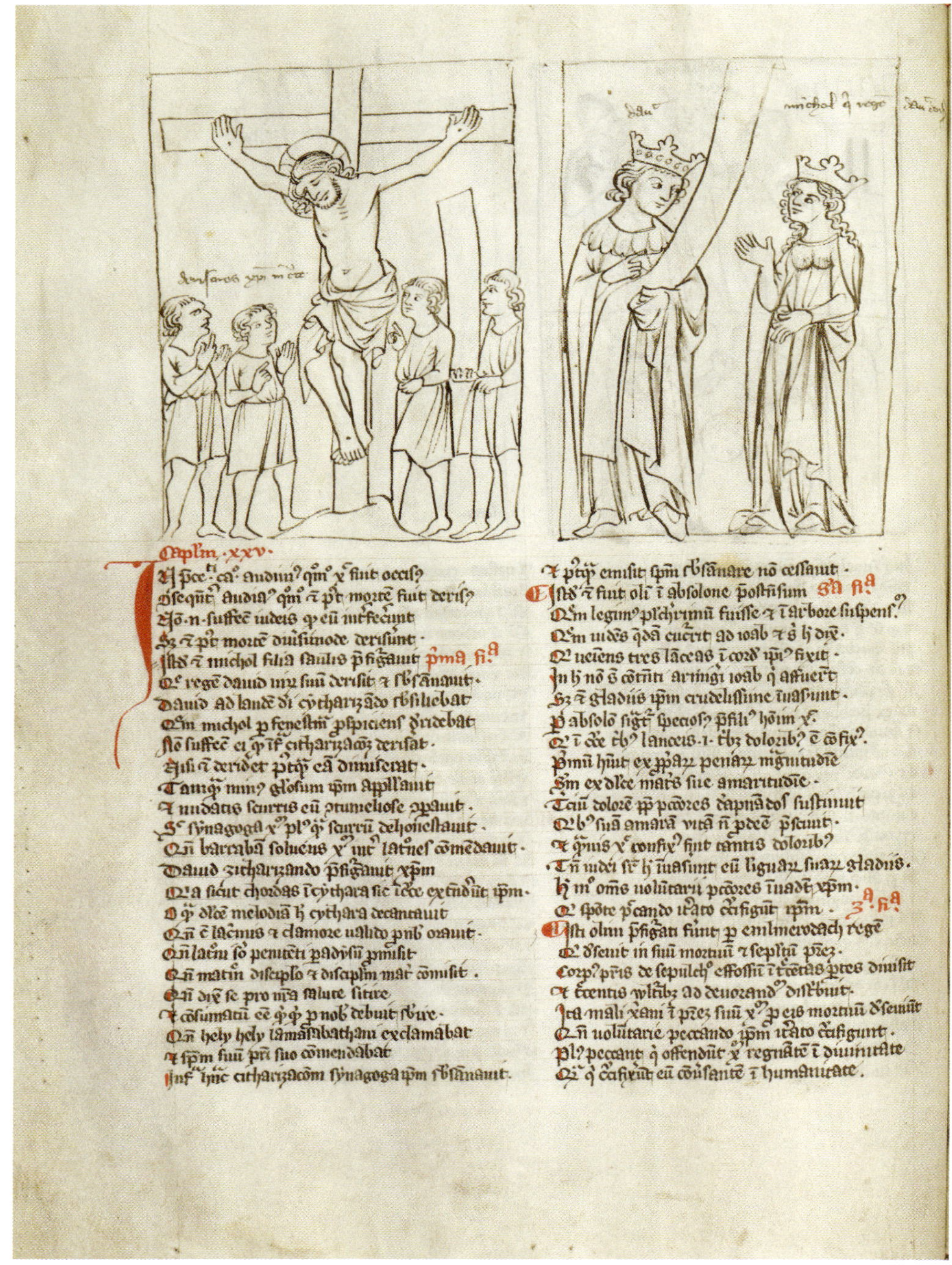

Fol. 28[va-b]. Image Caption (a): *derisores Christi in cruce* / Image Captions (b): *dauid; michol que regem dauid derisit*

Fol. 29[ra-b]. Image Caption (a): *Absolon tribus lanceis perfixus* / Image Caption (b): *euilmerodach qui patrem suum sepultum exhumauit*

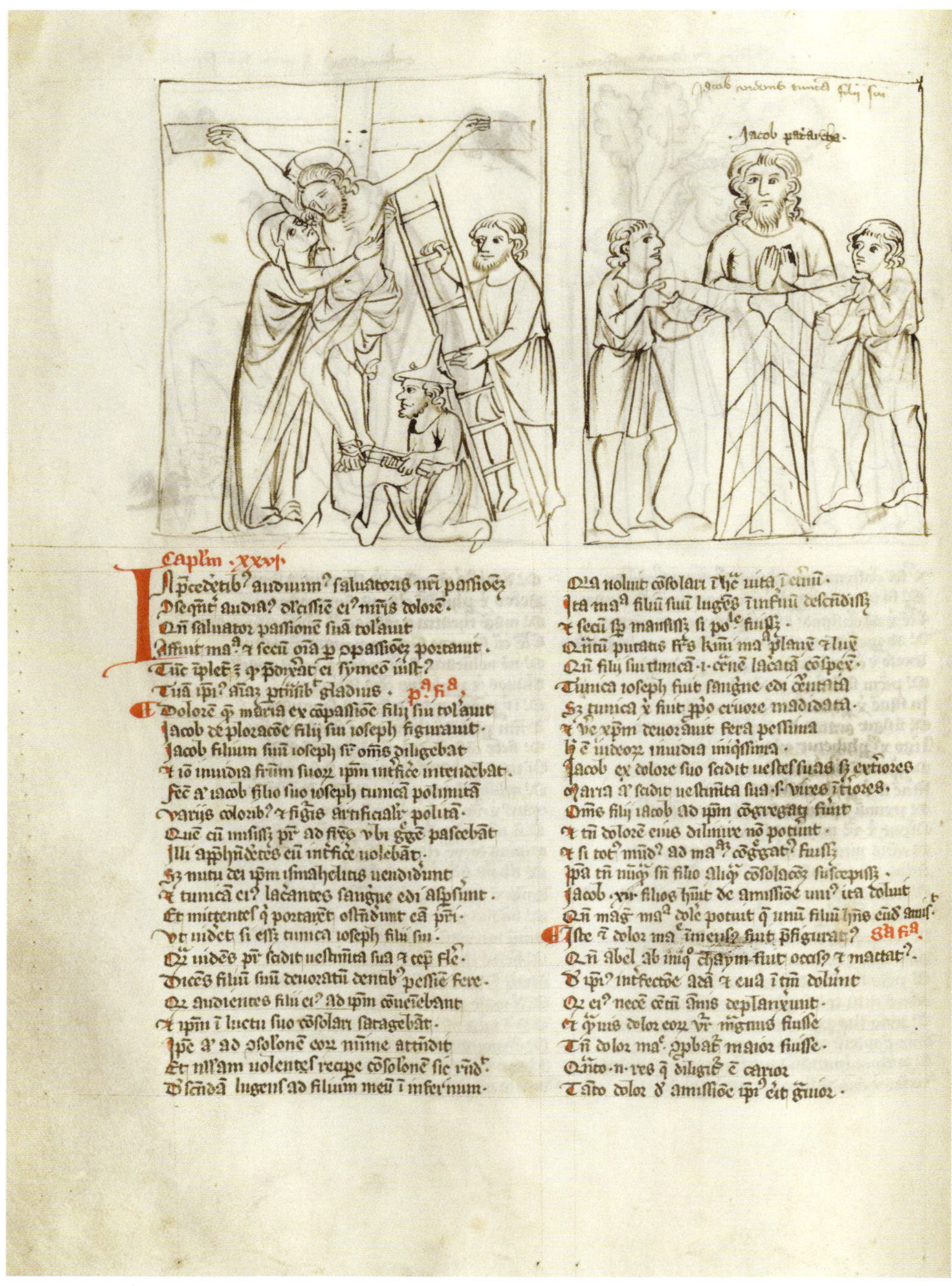

Fol. 29va-b. Image Captions (b): *Jacob uidens tunicam filii sui; Jacob patriarcha.*

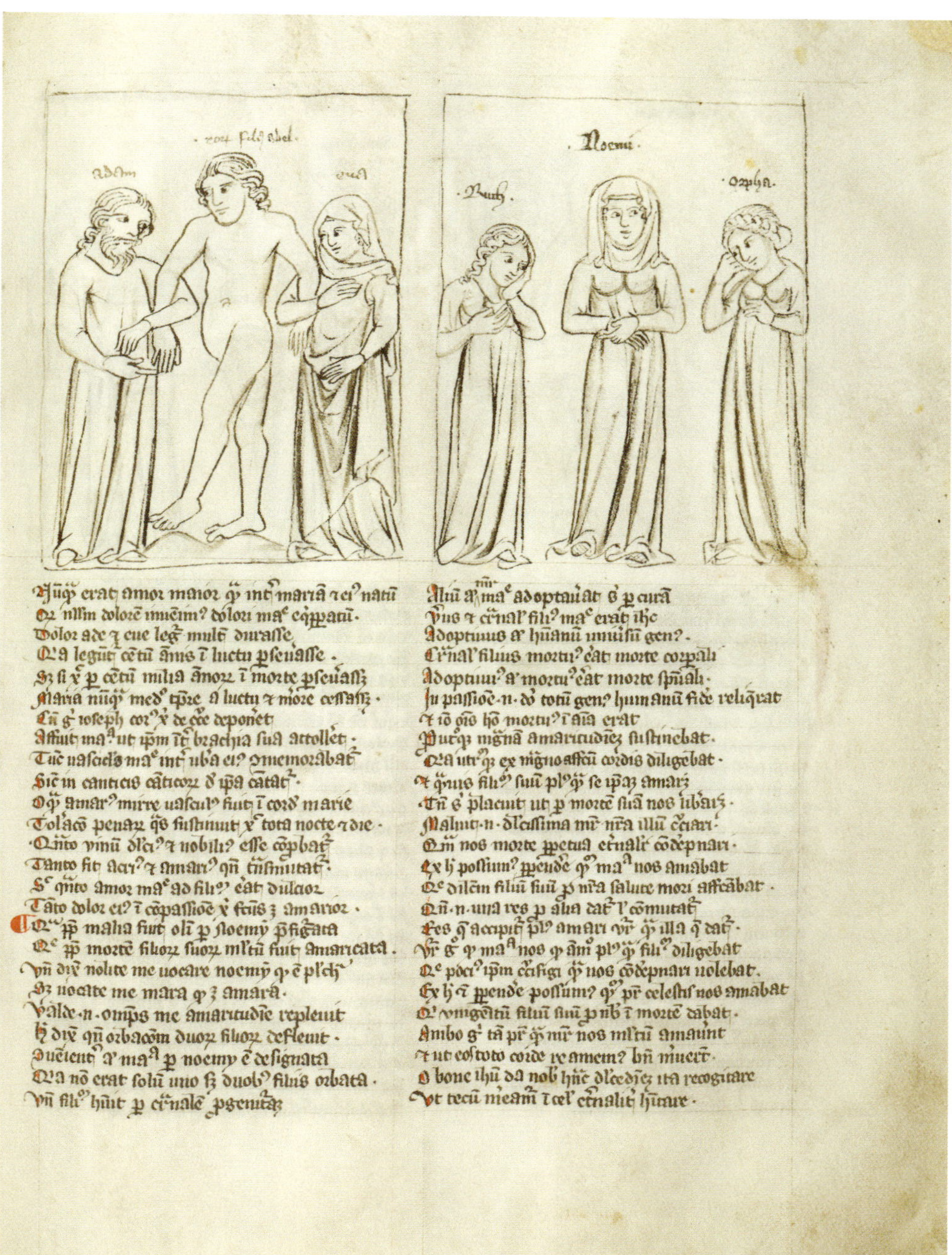

Fol. 30[ra-b]. Image Captions (a): *adam; eorum filius abel; eua* / Image Captions (b): *Ruth.; Noemi.; Orpha.*

Fol. 30va-b^. Image Caption (a): *Sepultura christi.* / Image Captions (b): *dauid qui fleuit quod abner fraudulenter interfectus erat a yoab.; dauid rex.; abner mortuus.*

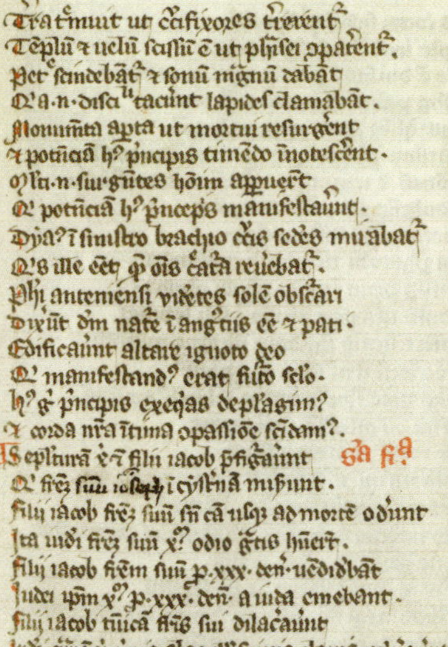

Fol. 31^{ra-b}. Image Captions (a): *frater eius; josep.; cysterna; frater eius.* / Image Captions (b): *jonas; cetus*

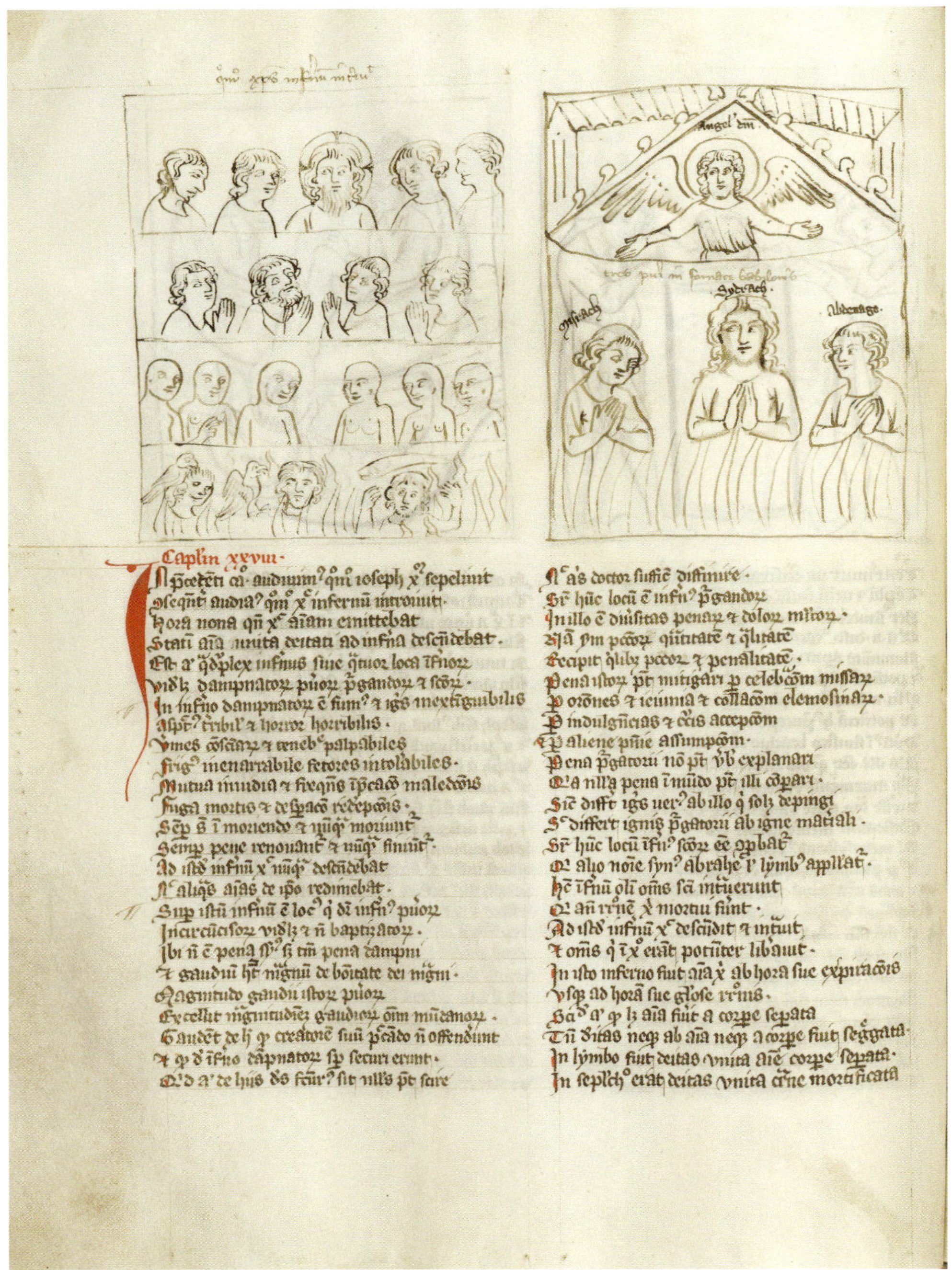

Fol. 31va-b. Image Caption (a): *quomodo christus intrauit* / Image Captions (b): *Angelus domini.; tres pueri in furnace babylonis; Misrach; Sydrach.; abdenage.*

Fol. 32[ra-b]. Image Caption (a): *daniel in lacu leonum quem angelus cibauit* / Image Captions (b): *vitreum uas puero strutio* (*error*); *strutio salomonis*

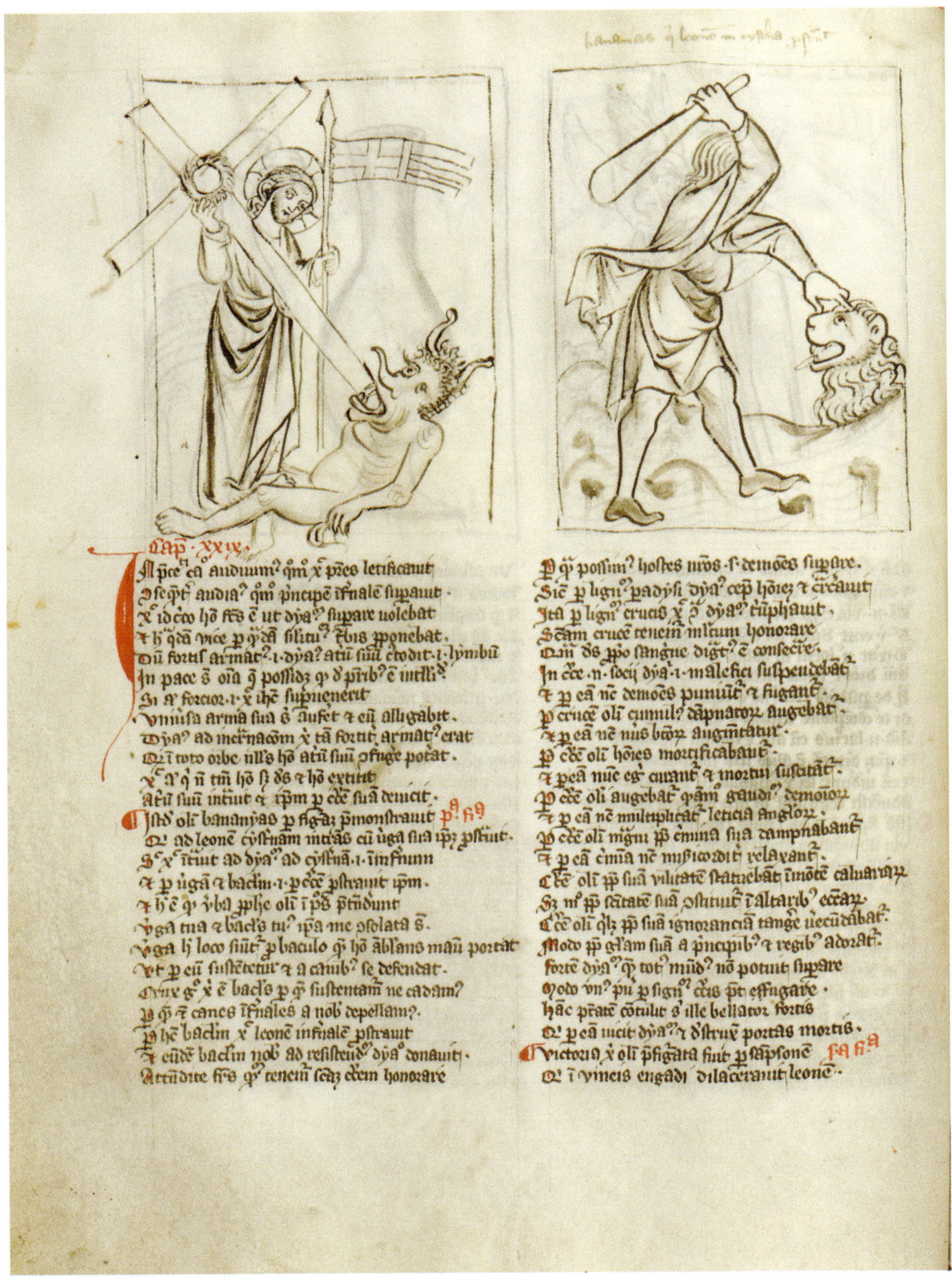

Fol. 32[va-b]. Image Caption (b): *bananias qui leonem in cysterna prosternuit*

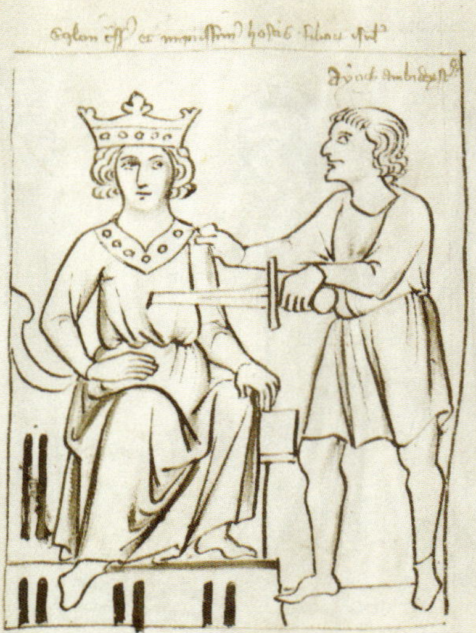

Fol. 33[ra-b]. Image Caption (a): *samson qui in uineis engadi leonem delacerauit* / Image Captions (b): *Eglon esset et pinguissimus hostibus filiorum Israel; Ayoch ambidexstrus*

Fol. 33^{va-b}. Image Caption (a): *compassio marie quomodo ipsa uicit dyabolum* / Image Captions (b): *Judith 13°* (in a later hand); *Judith quam restitit; Holofernes*

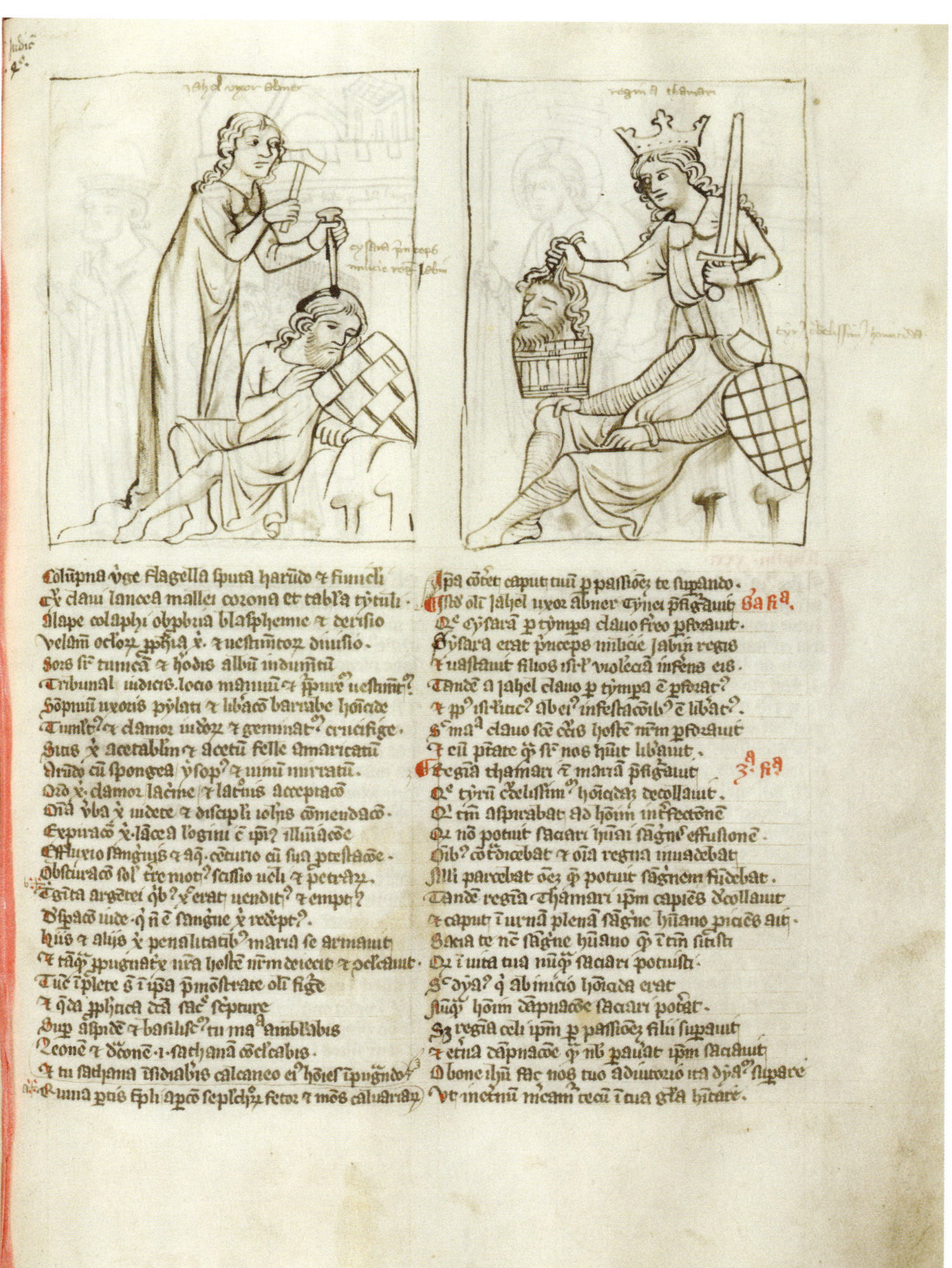

Fol. 34[ra-b]. Image Captions (a): *jahel uxor abner; sysara princeps militia regis Jabim* / Image Captions (b): *regina thamari; cyrus crudelissimus homicida*

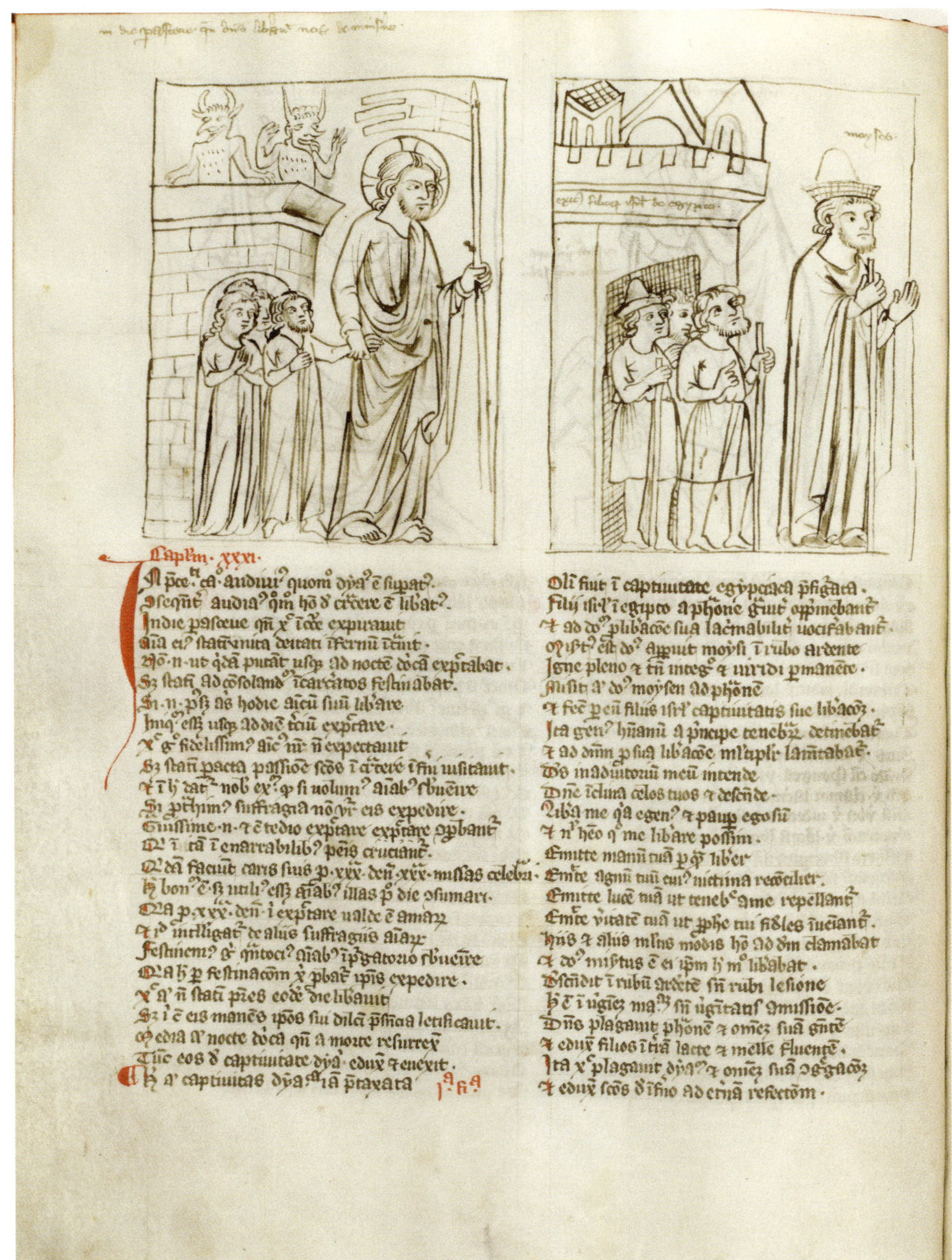

Fol. 34[va-b]. Image Caption (a): *in die parasceue quando dominus liberauit nos de inferno.* / Image Captions (b): *moyses; exitus filiorum Israel de egypto.*

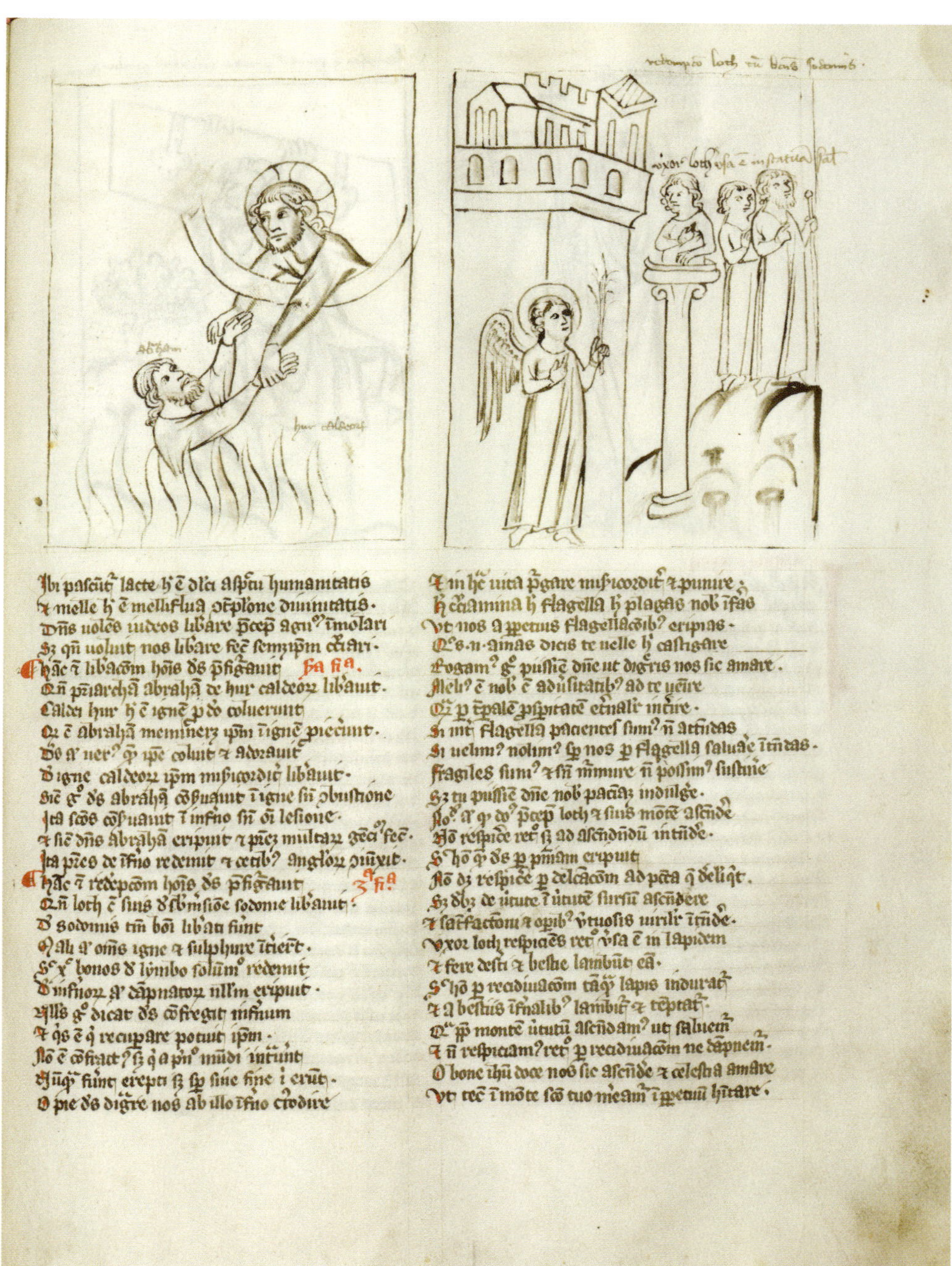

Fol. 35[ra-b]. Image Captions (a): *abraham; hur caldeorum* / Image Captions (b): *redempcio loth cum bonis sodomis; uxor loth uersa est in statuam statim*

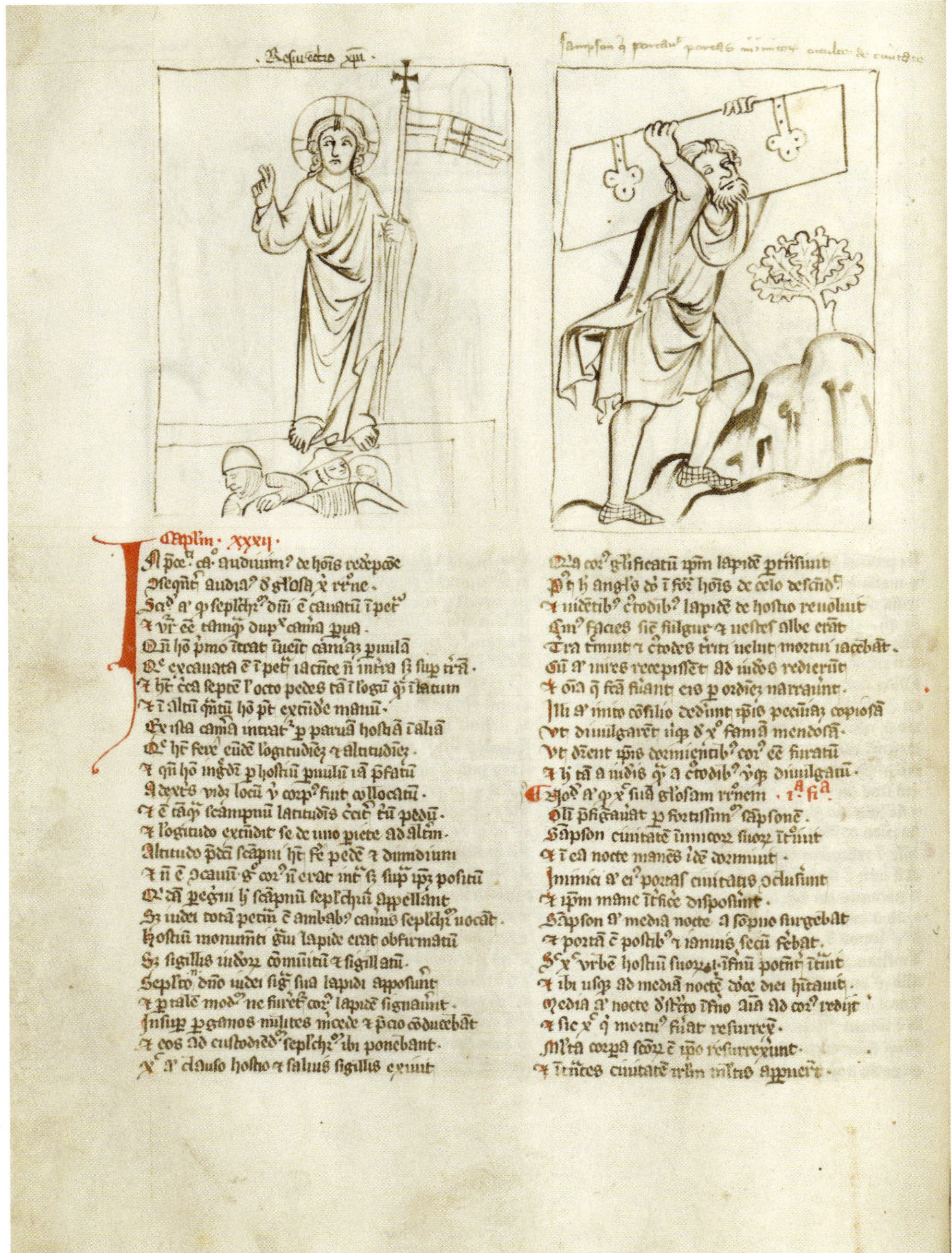

Fol. 35^{va-b}. Image Caption (a): *Resurrectio christi.* / Image Caption (b): *Sampson qui portauit portas inimicorum occulte de ciuitate*

Fol. 36[ra-b]. Image Caption (a): *jonas in uentro ceti* / Image Caption (b): *lapis respuebatur factus est caput anguli*

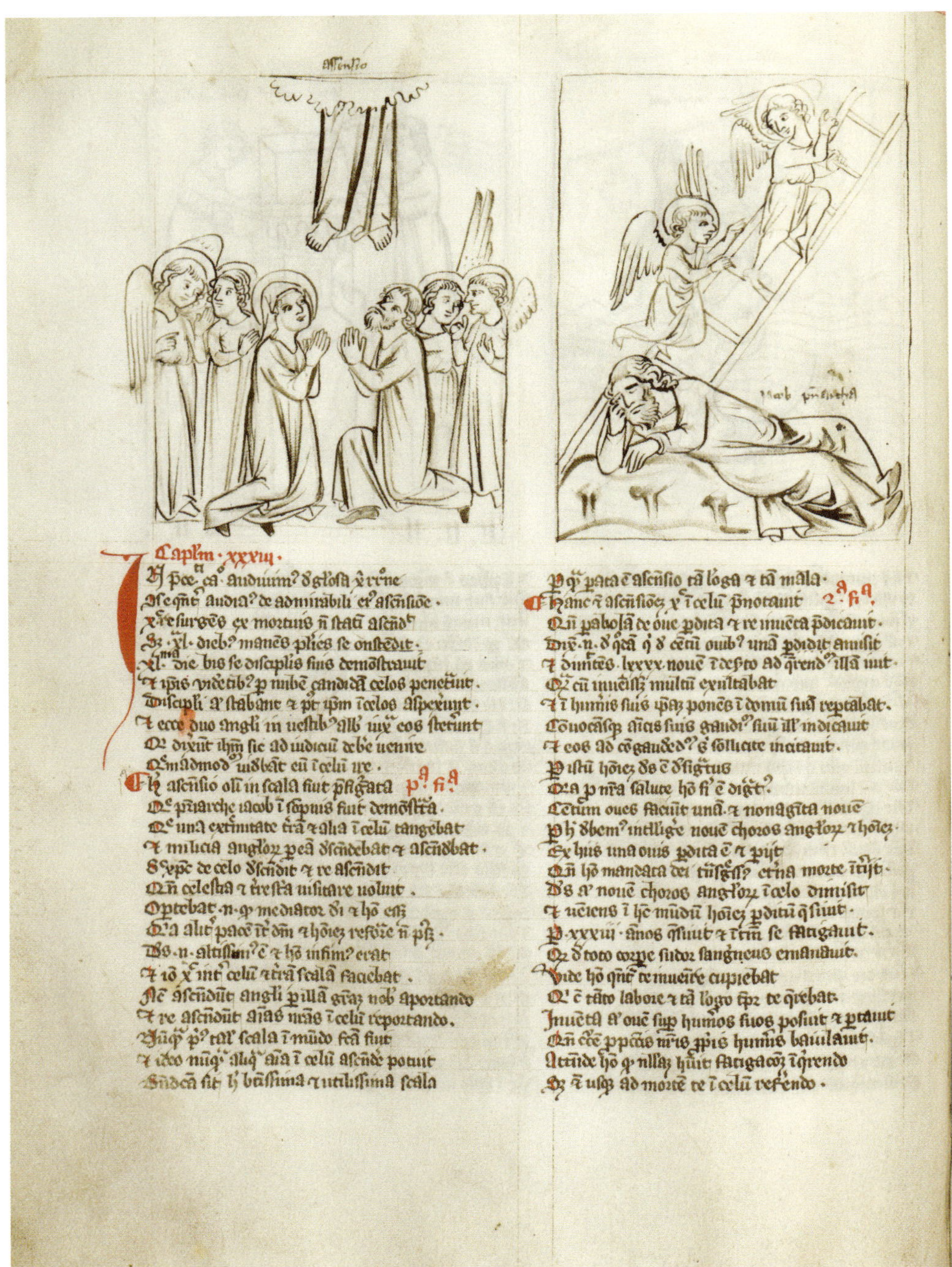

Fol. 36^{va-b}. Image Caption (a): *assensio* / Image Caption (b): *jacob patriarcha*

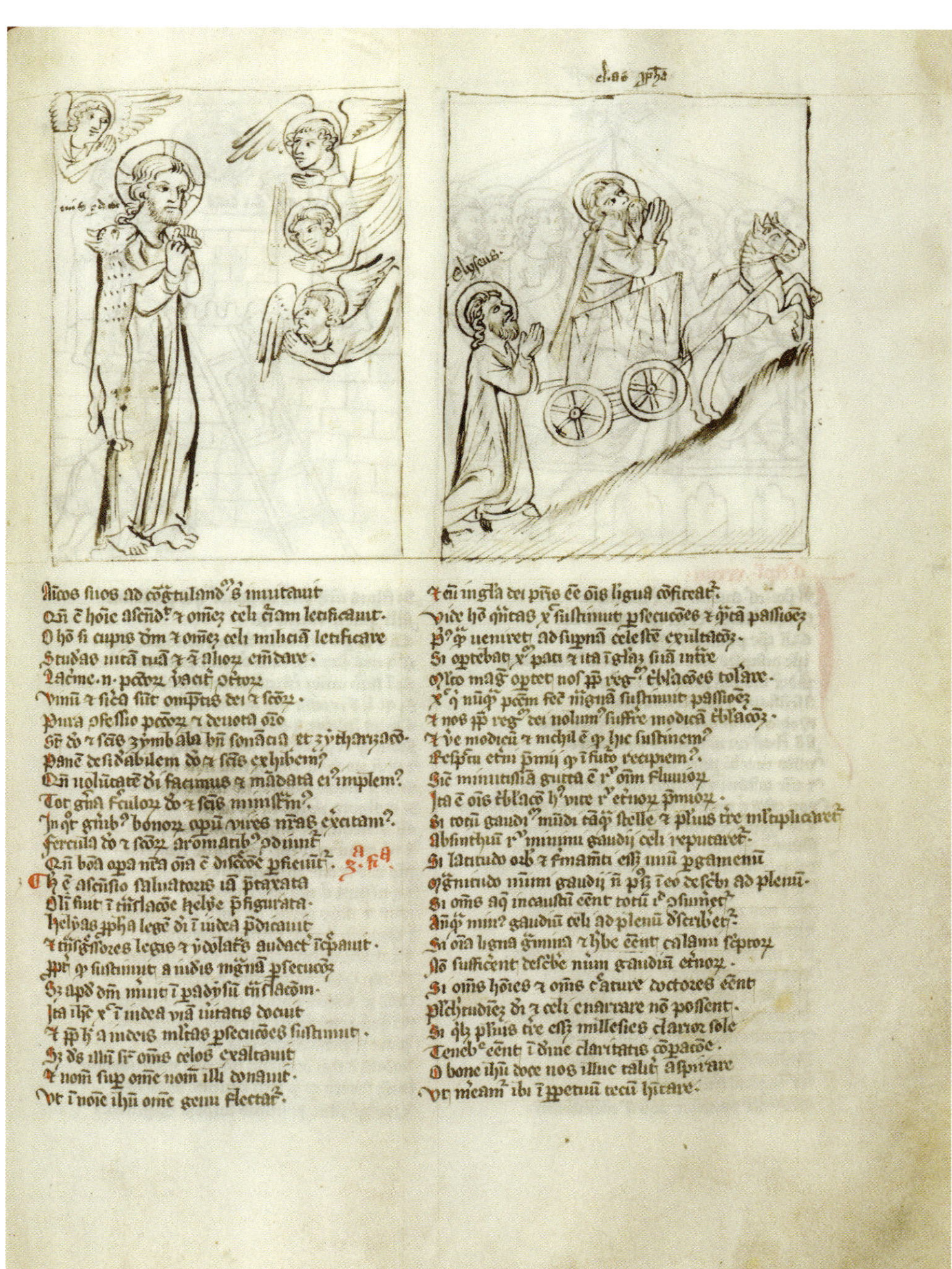

Fol. 37[ra-b]. Image Caption (a): *ouis perdita* / Image Captions (b): *elias propheta; elyseus.*

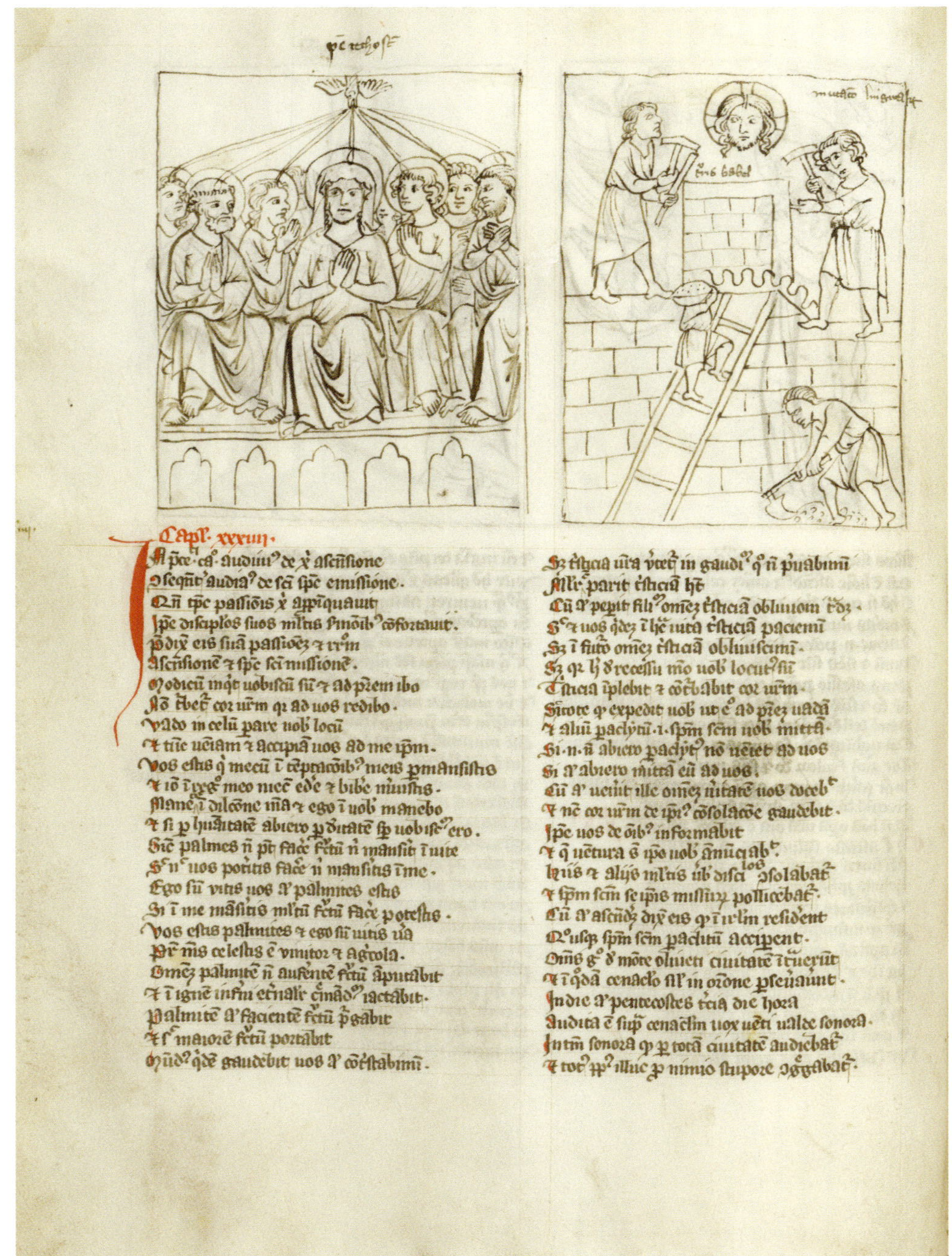

Fol. 37va-b. Image Caption (a): *pentechosten* / Image Captions (b): *mutacio linguarum; turris babel*

Fol. 38[ra-b]. Image Captions (a): *moyses.; decem precepta ipsis data; mons Syna* / Image Captions (b): *eliseus; pauper uidus* (error)

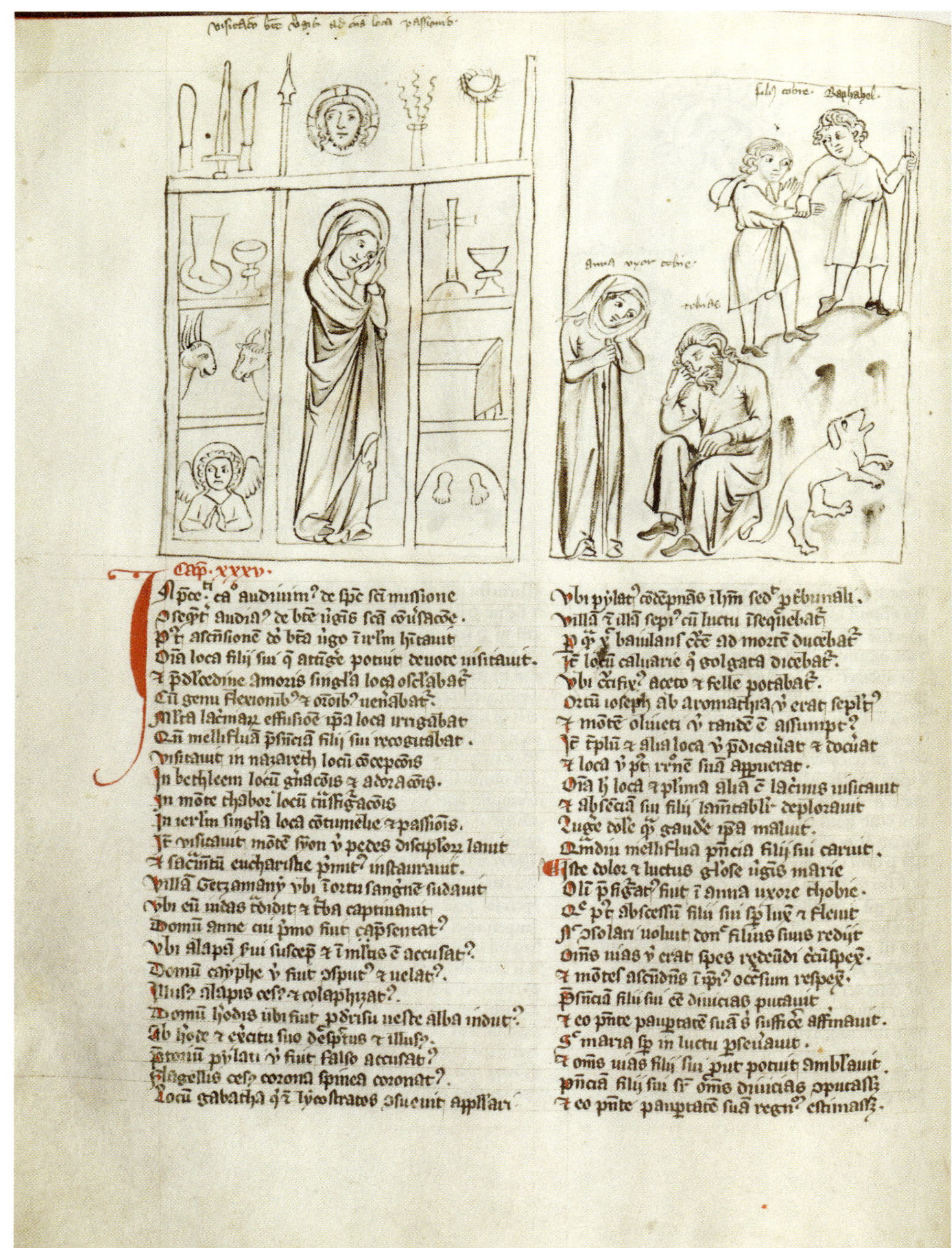

Fol. 38va-b. Image Caption (a): *uisitacio beate virginis ad sancta loca passionis.* / Image Captions (b): *filius tobie. Raphahel.; anna uxor tobie; tobias*

Fol. 39[ra-b]. Image Captions (a): *ix dragme; Lucerna* / Image Captions (b): *phaltyel uir iustus; saul.; mychol sponsa dauid*

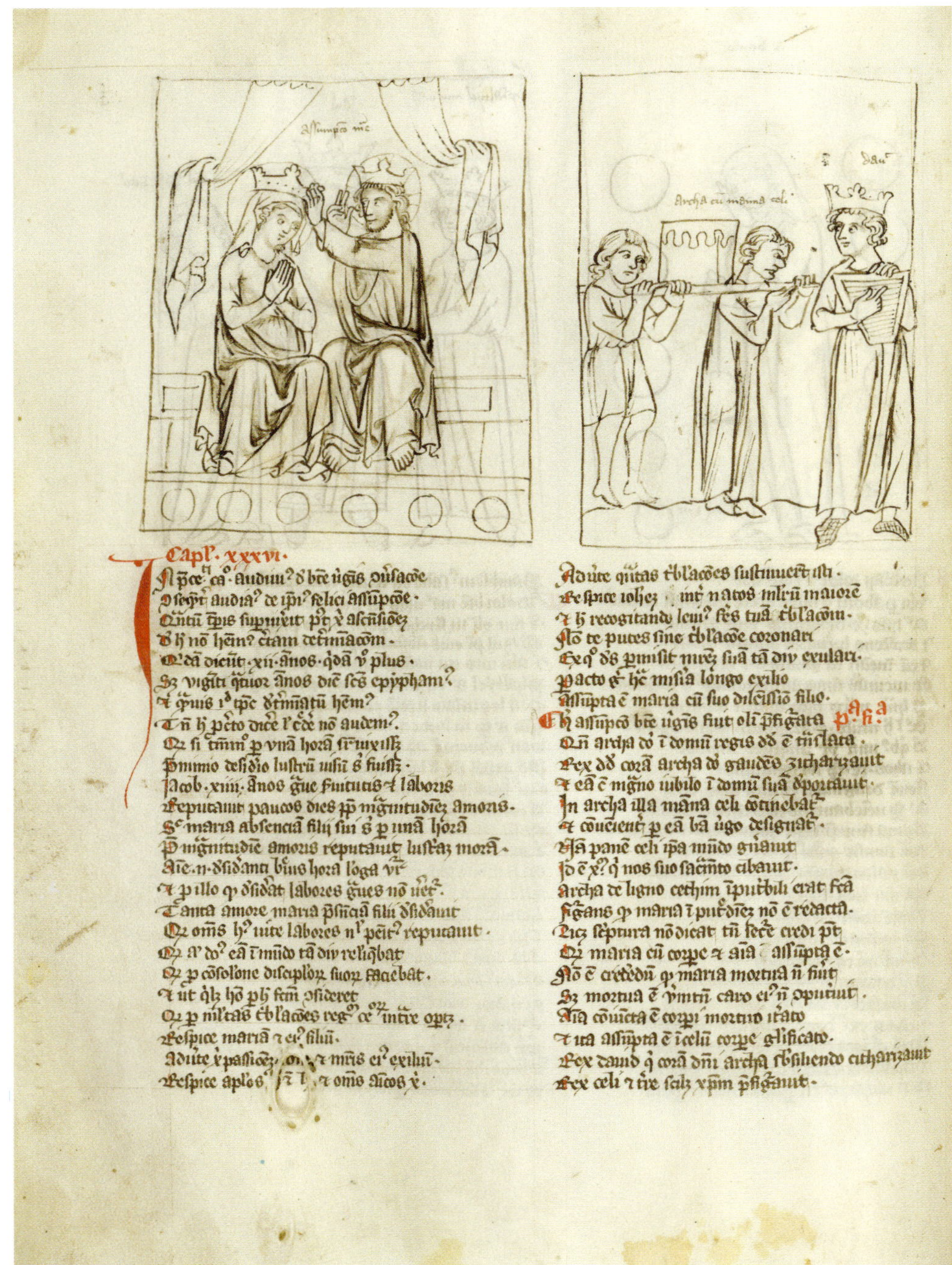

Fol. 39va-b. Image Caption (a): *assumpcio marie* / Image Captions (b): *archa cum manna celi; dauid*

Fol. 40ra-b. Image Caption (a): *signum iohannis in pathmos insula.* / Image Captions (b): *mater eius; rex salomonis*

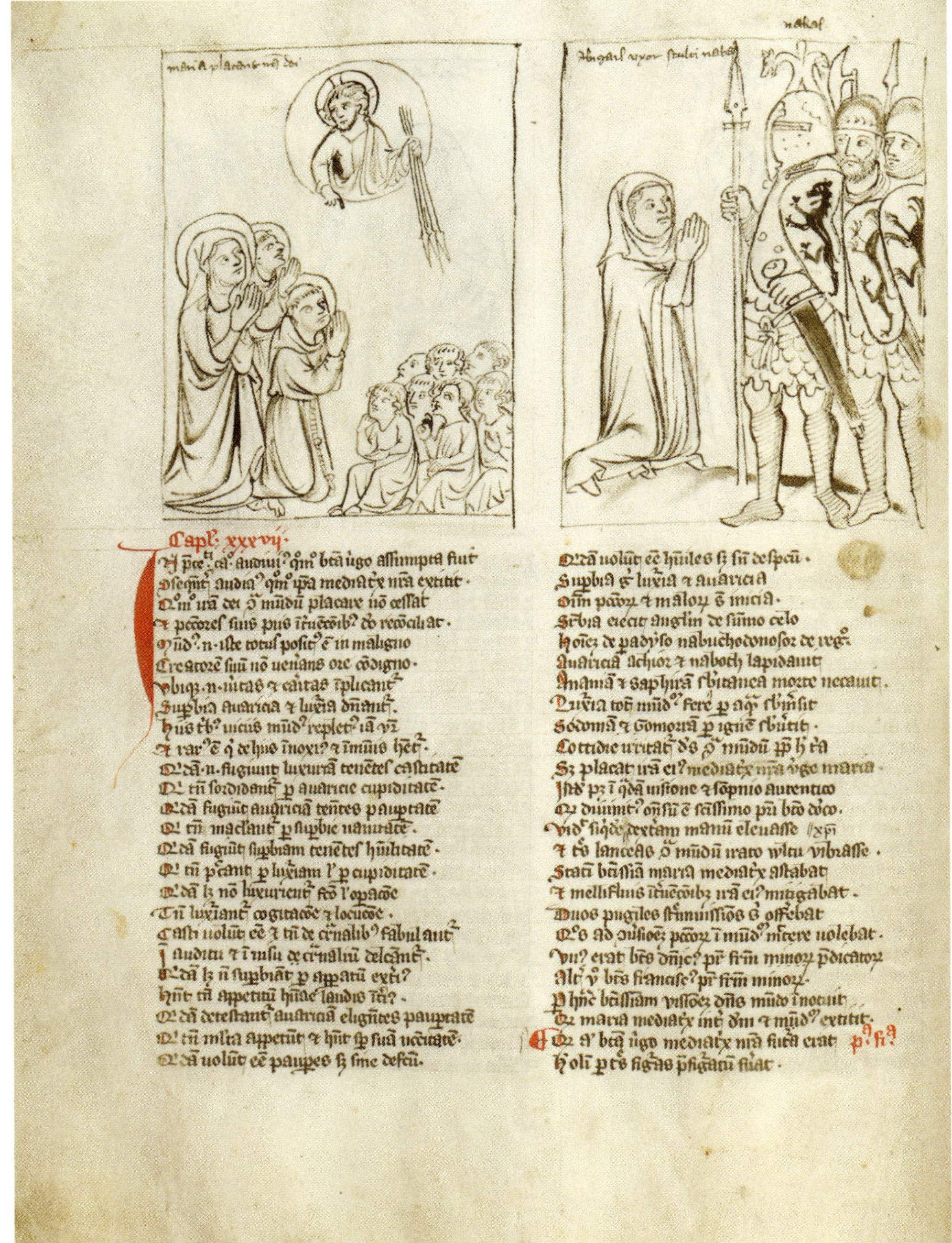

Fol. 40[va-b]. Image Caption (a): *maria placans iram dei* / Image Caption (b): *nabal; Abigail uxor stulti nabal*

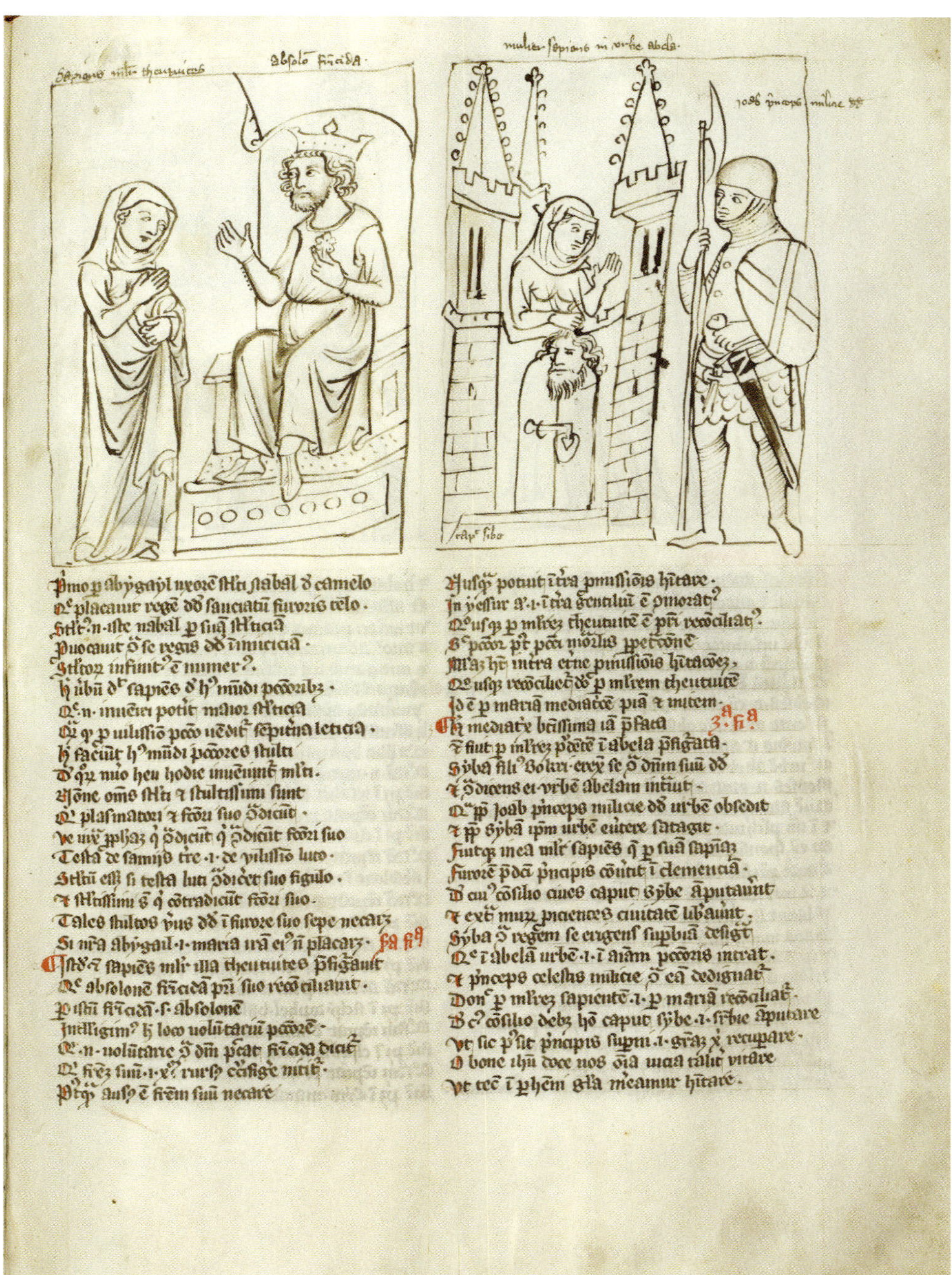

Fol. 41[ra-b]. Image Caption (a): *sapiens mulier theutuites; absolon fratricida.* / Image Caption (b): *mulier sapiens in urbe abela.; joab princeps milicie dauid; caput sibe*

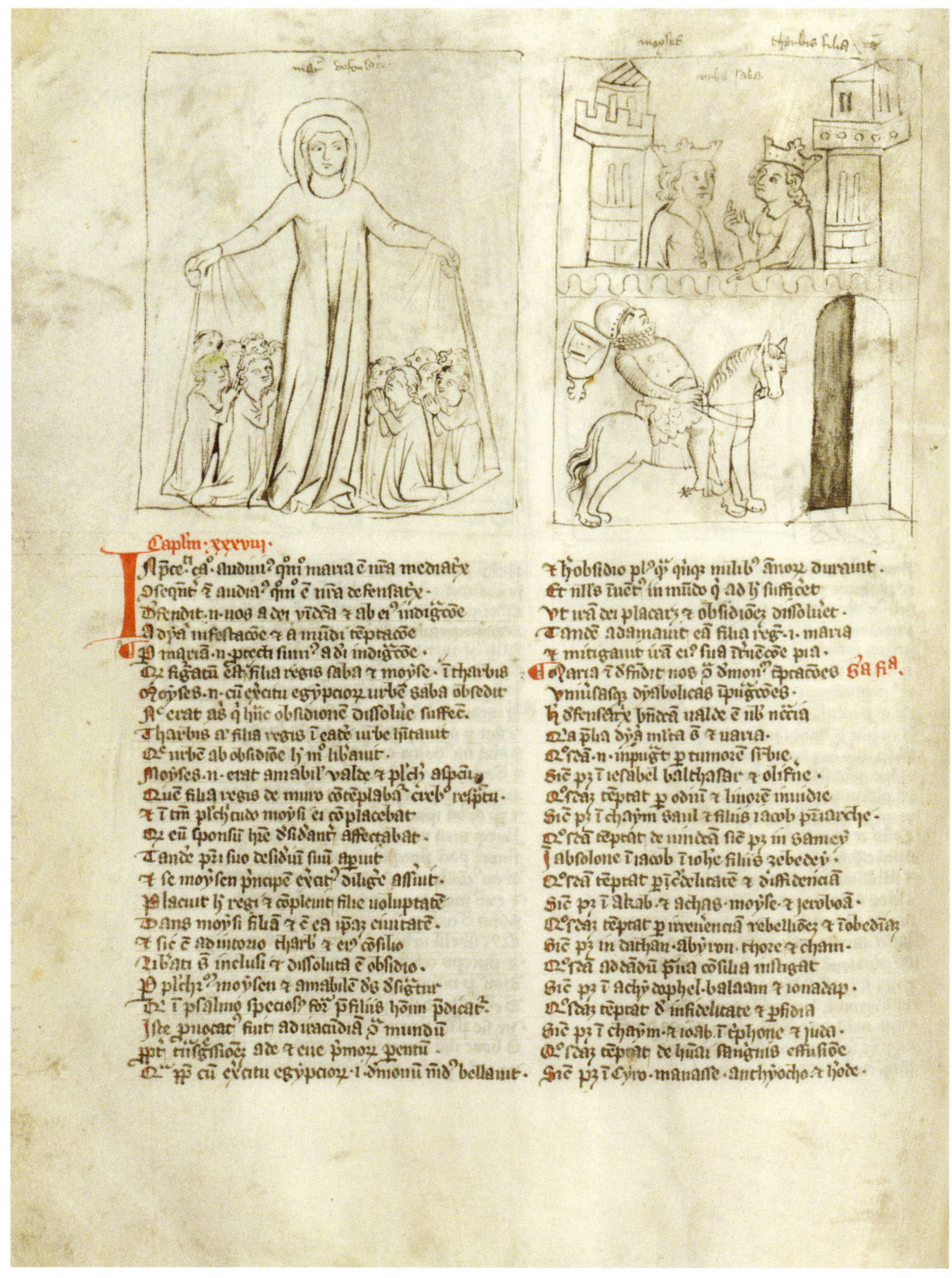

Fol. 41va-b. Image Caption (a): *maria defensatrix.* / Image Captions (b): *moyses; tharbis filia regis; urbs*

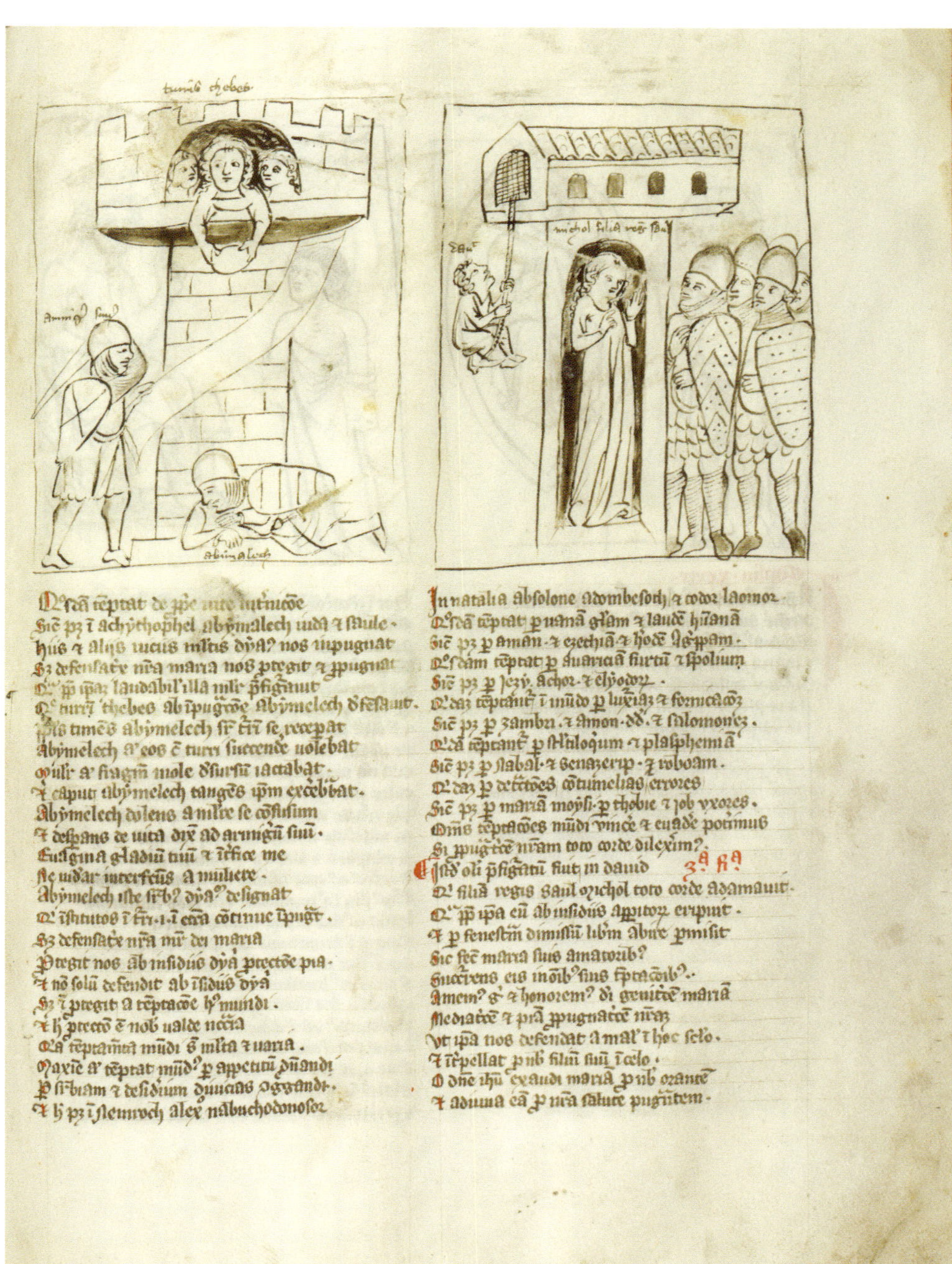

Fol. 42[ra-b]. Image Captions (a): *turris thebes.; armiger suus; abimalech* / Image Captions (b): *dauid; michol filia regis saul*

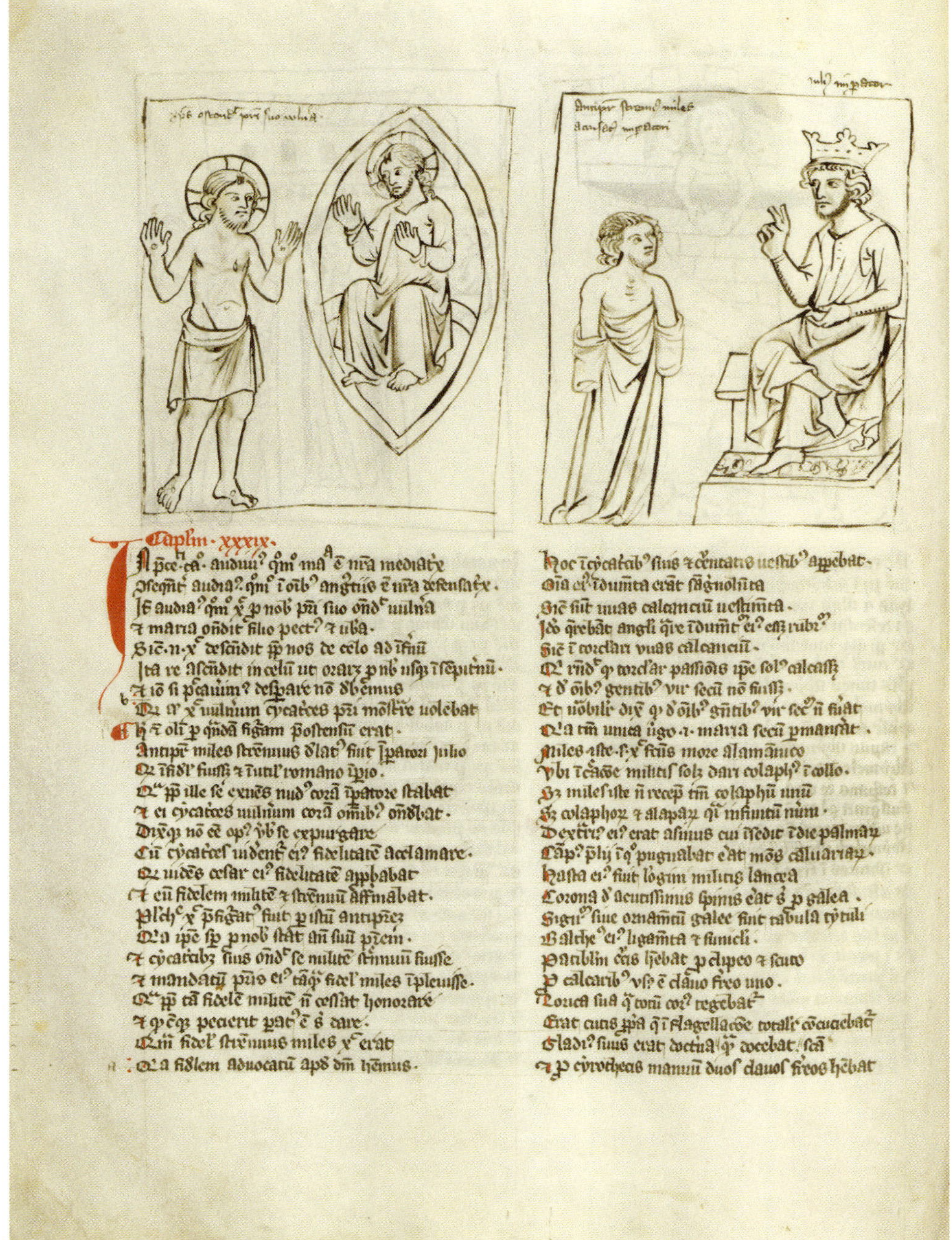

Fol. 42[va-b]. Image Caption (a): *Christus ostendit patri suo vulnera.* / Image Captions (b): *julius imperator; antipater strenuous miles auersatus imperatori*

Fol. 43ra-b. Image Caption (a): *maria armigera christi* / Image Captions (b): *regina hester.; rex ahuerus.* (error)

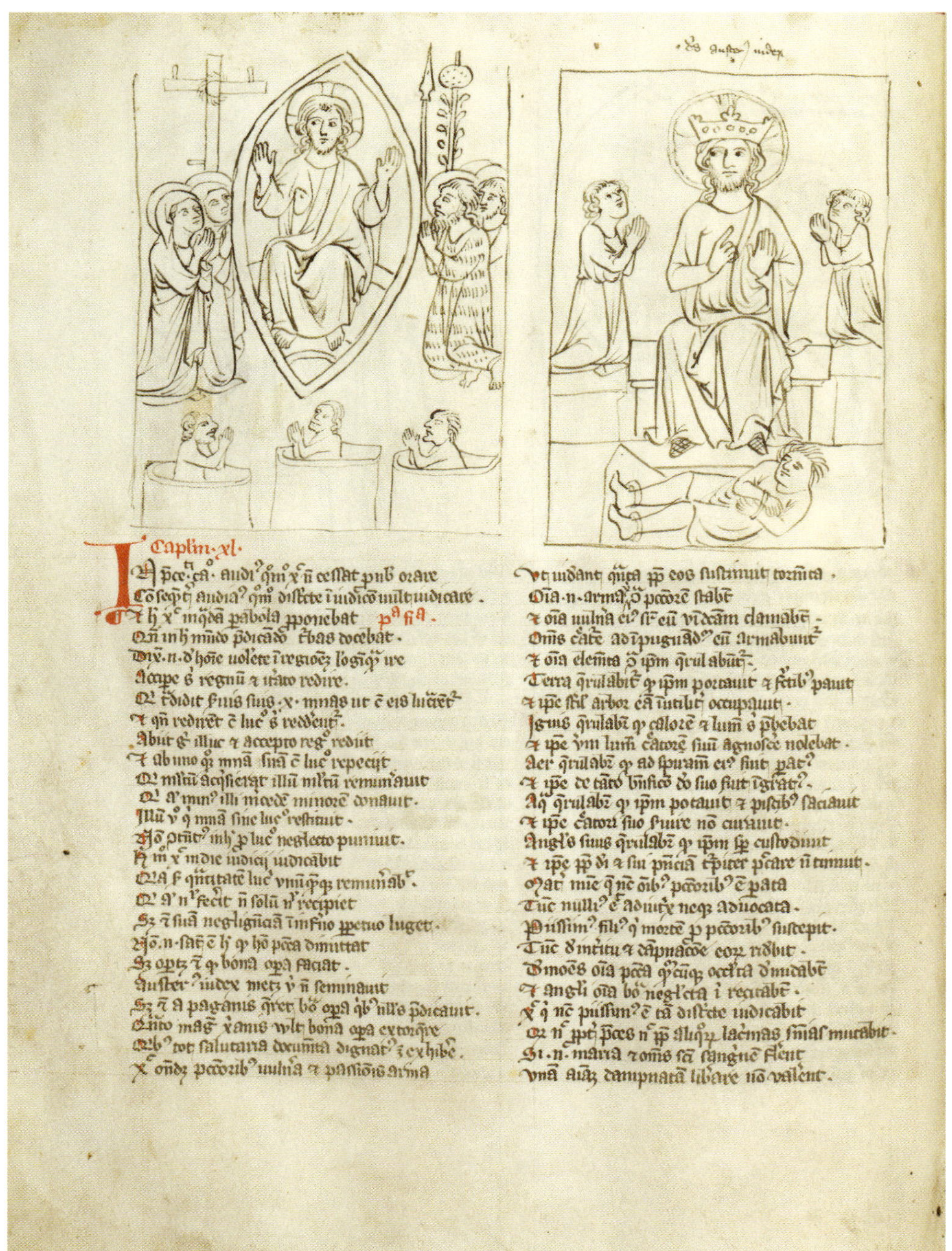

Fol. 43^{va-b}. Image Caption (a): *iudicium districtum* / Image Caption (b): *deus austerus iudex*

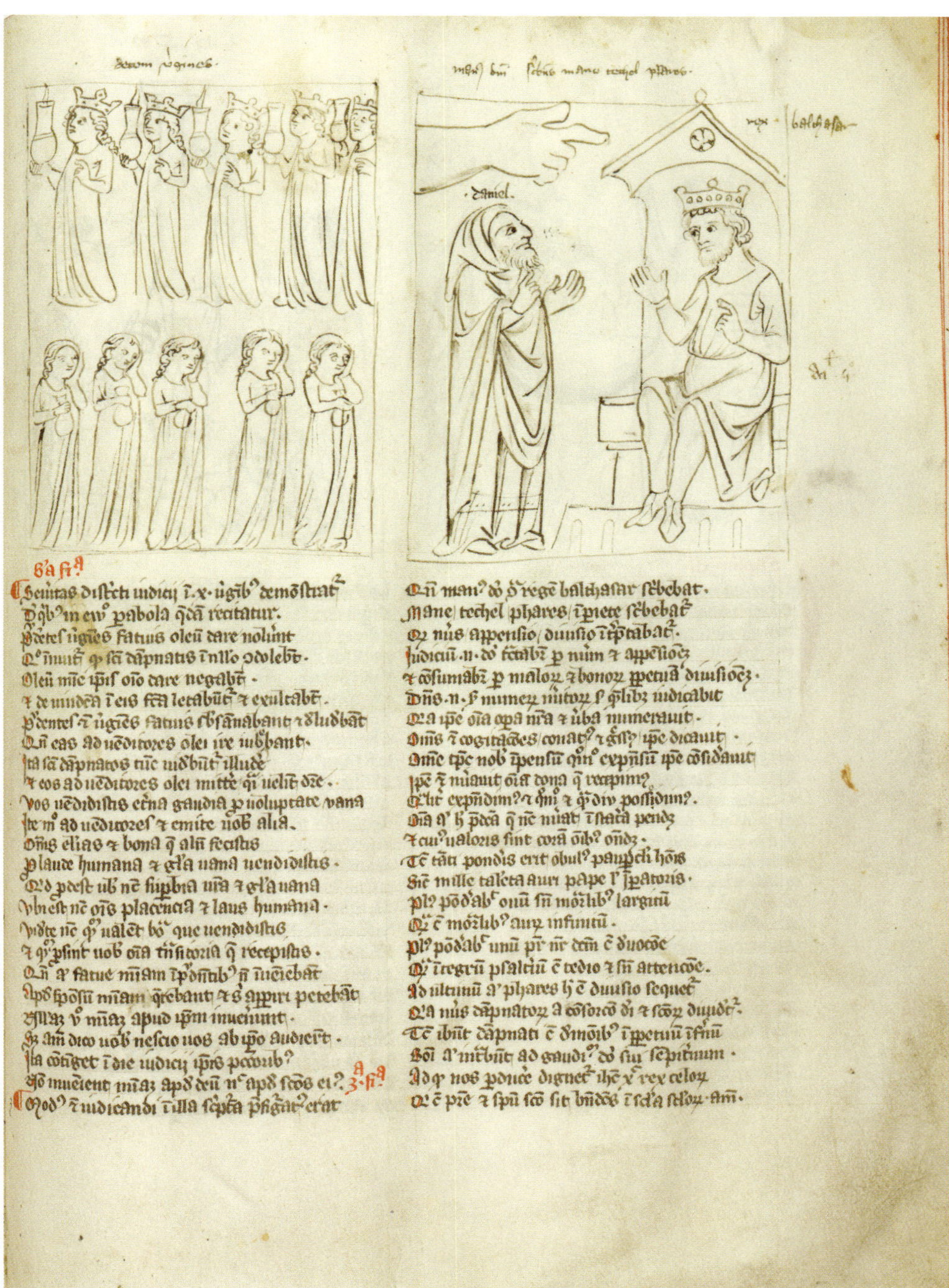

Fol. 44ra-b. Image Caption (a): *decem uirgines.* / Image Captions (b): *manus domini scribens mane techel phares.; rex balthasar; daniel.*

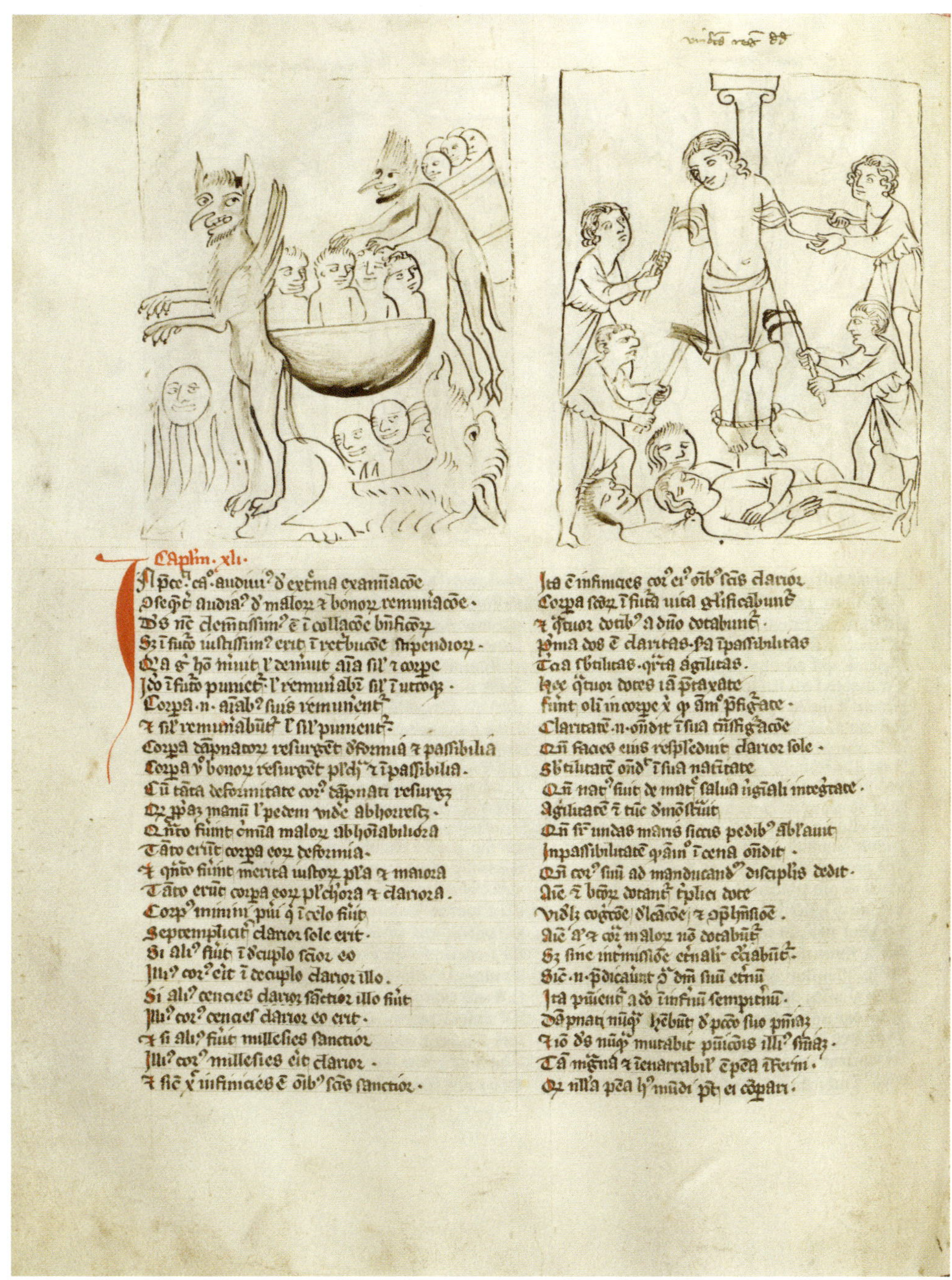

Fol. 44^{va-b}. Image Caption (b): *vindicens regem dauid*

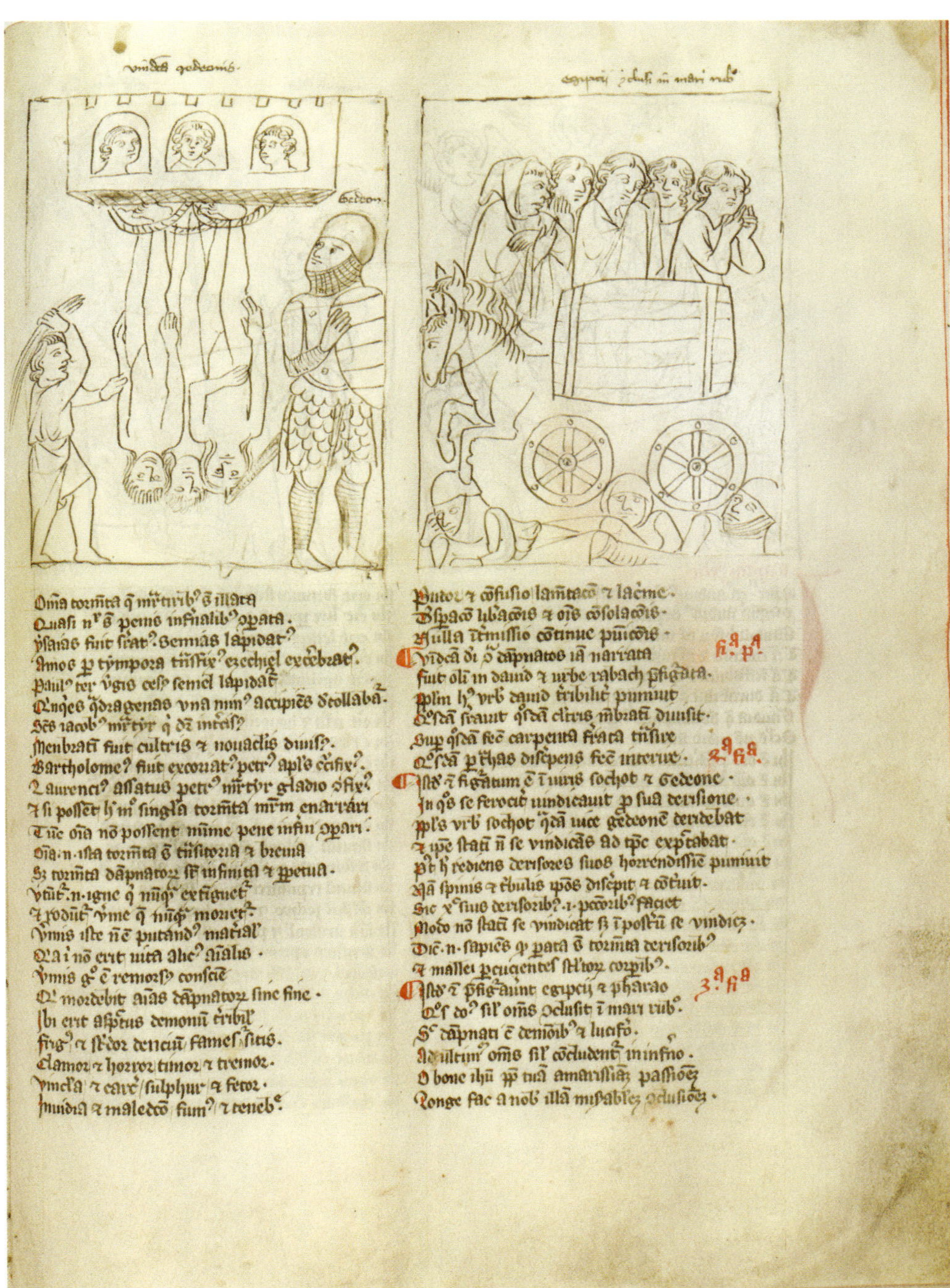

Fol. 45[ra-b]. Image Captions (a): *vindicacio gedeonis; Gedeon* / Image Caption (b): *egipcii conclusi in mari rubro*

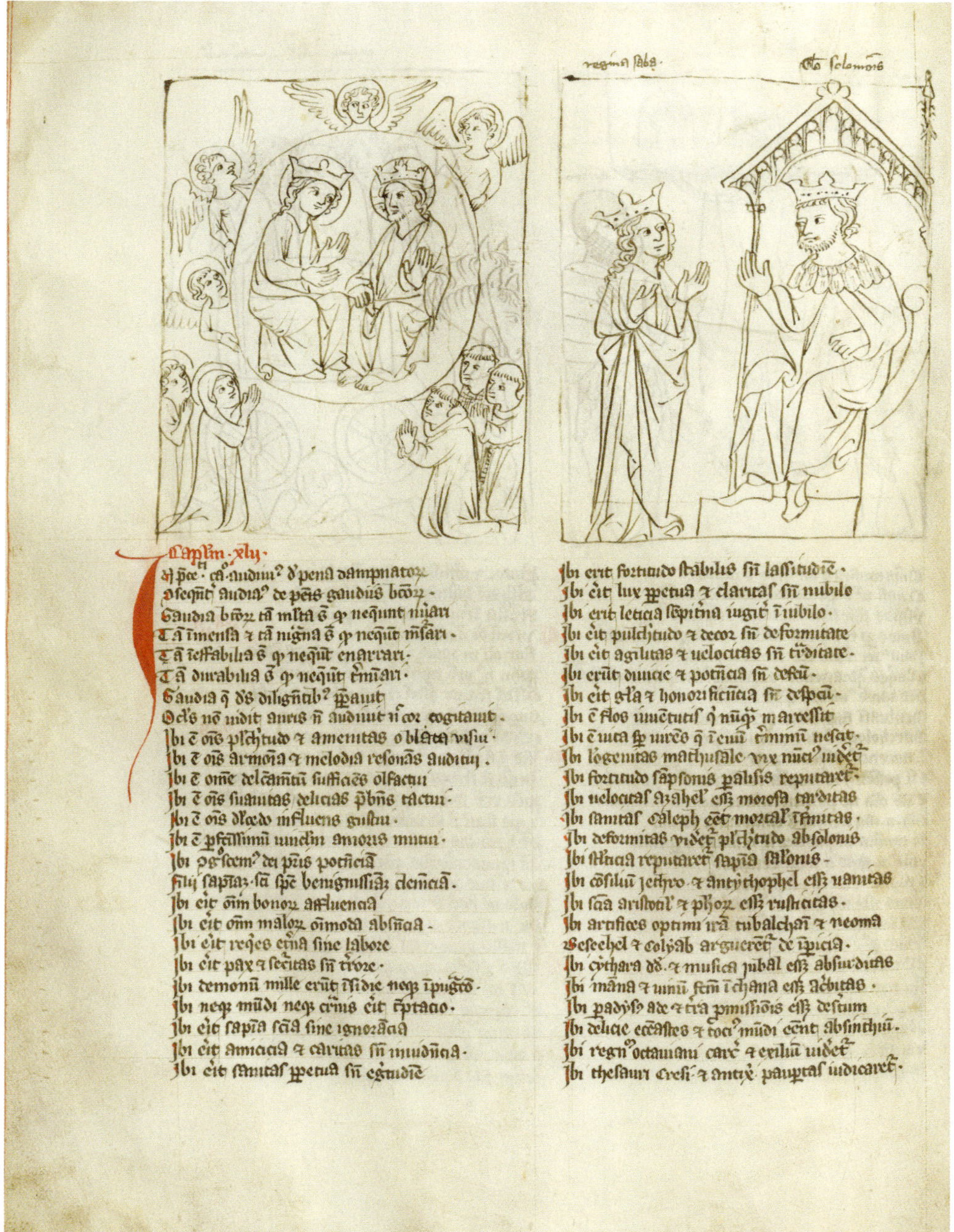

Fol. 45[va-b]. Image Caption (b): *regina saba.; thronus solomonis*

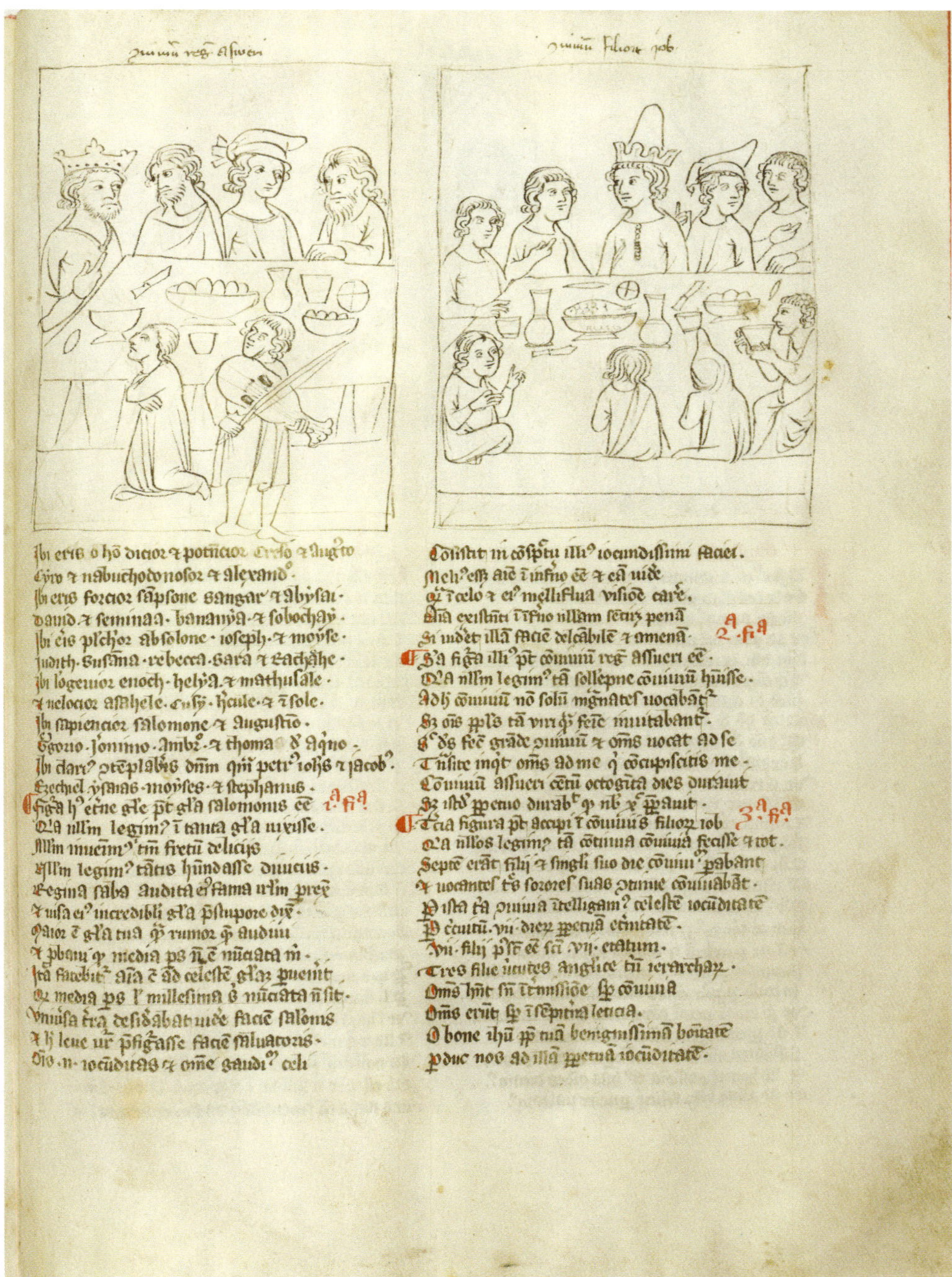

Fol. 46[ra-b]. Image Caption (a): *conuiuium regis asuersi* / Image Caption (b): *conuiuium filiorum job.*

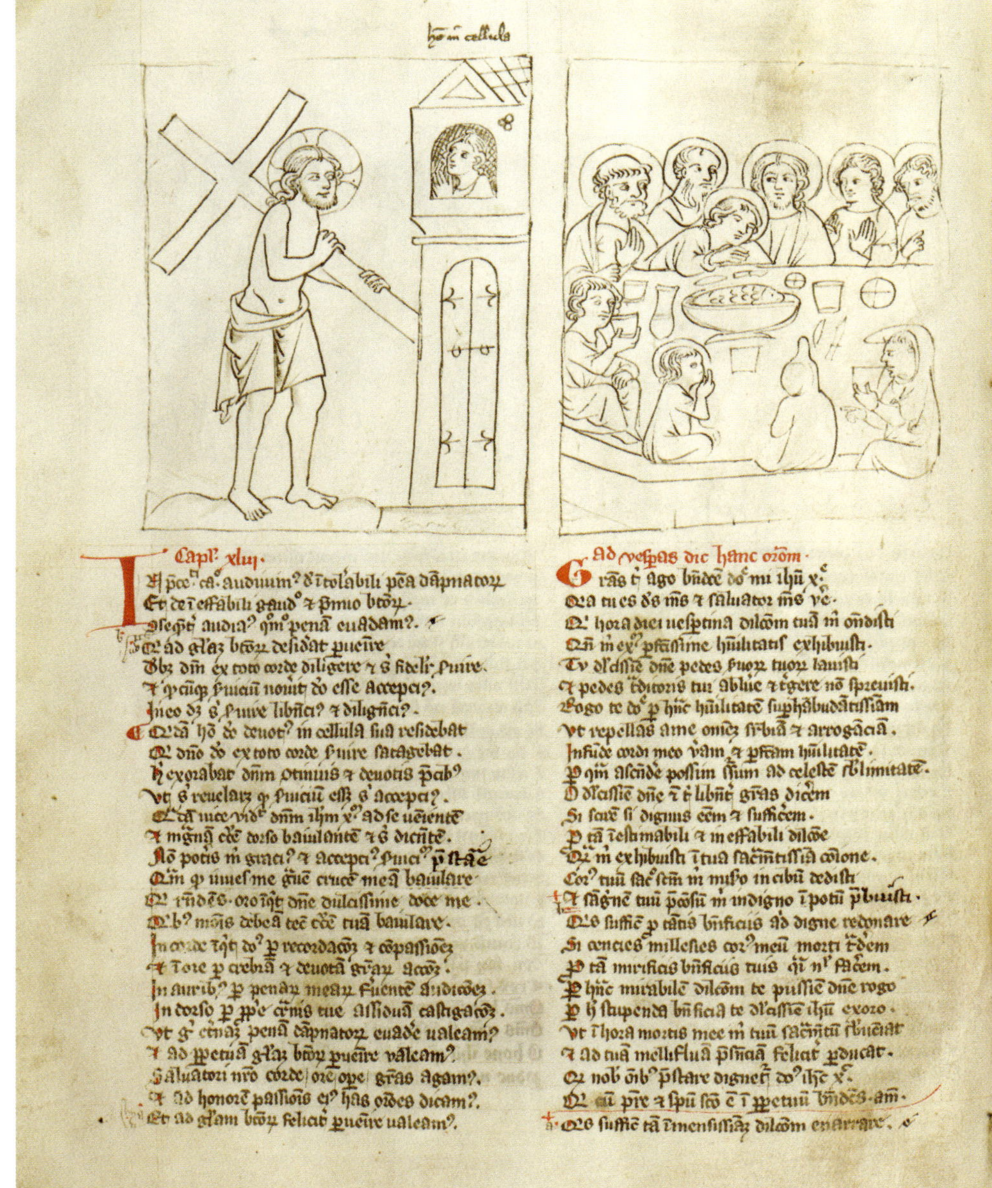

Fol. 46[va-b]. Image Caption (a): *heremite cellula*

Fol. 47[ra-b]

Fol. 47[va-b]

Fol. 48[ra-b]

Ad Sextam.
Gras t ago bndce dne ihu x̄.
Qa tu es ds m̄s t saluator m̄s ve.
Q hora diei sexta dilcōm m̄ ōstdisti
Qn p̄ me morti Adiudicat̄ z cafigi uoluisti.
P mitas accusaco̅es pilat̄ mā sua̅ lauit
z te i paublin eī suspendeō sentēciauit.
Cce cruc tuā hıu̅s bauladā t poneb̄at
t hı ad maiore tuā cōtumeliā faceb̄at.
Sup cce te extendentes finib9 tverūt
z manu9 et pedes tuos clauis fireis Affiuūt.
Post h in altum cū cruce te ereuūt.
t diuisis s᷑ uaco̅ib9 z chachinis te deriserūt.
Iuxt pie dn̄e dilcōm tuā nixima d͞msti
Qn p ip̄is p̄tez tuū supplicit᷑ exorasti.
Pt hoc dilassie ihu alia cōtumelia sustinuisti
Qn mr̄ez tuā uir͡ cce amarissie respexisti.
Ad ā plianda̅ tuā p̄tumeliā duos latrnes adducebāt
t te i medio ı͞por: tā˛ ōsrōc suspendebat.
Q vm ı͞mensissima̅ miā z tuā ōstdisti
Cū textius p̄ēdo̅ t̅mu͞isti t padysū p̅mis͡isti.
O dlassie dn̄e rogo te p̄ psinam sup̄ dicta
t exoro te p omez pena̅ t̅ ı͞nocit᷑ illata.
Vt me ab horribili sit͡ a sinistr᷑ eripias
Vt cū collegio dextro˛ t regnui tuu̅ trnmittas.
Q nob oib9 p̄fare dignet᷑ dn̄s nr̅ ı͞he x̅.
Q c p̄re t spu sc̄o c i p̄petuū bn̅dcs. am

Ad Nonam.
Gras ugo c̄ bndce mı dn̄e ihu x̄.
Qa tu es ds m̄s t saluator m̄s ve.
Q hora diei nona dilcōm tuā m̄ ostdidisti
Qn p̄ me īccis patib̄lō mortu9 fuisti.
Lamtaco̅em nimis magnā m̄ sādis plecisti.
Qn hely help lamasabatham dixisti.
Ds m̄s ds m̄s ut qd deliquisti me.
Cū tū ds tu9 nūq̄ fuit separ̅ a te.
Dinde dlcissime dn̄e mi dixisti sicio
t dabāt t̅ uinū mirratū t̅ aceto felle mixto.
Dulsi modis derisio̅ib9 t̅ te plasmaūt
Oms q̄ potuerūt cōtumelias t̅ intulerūt.
Pt h amantissie ihu cōsumatū e dixisti
t spm tuū p̄ri ōmdans mortu9 fuisti.
Tūc lat᷑ tuū lancea p̄forauit
D q̄ sāgs t aq̄ ı̅ medicamtū meū effluxerūt.
Oms caure t c̄opati t c̄dole udebāt
Sol obsurat9 e t̅ a petre sindebant.
Tre mot9 k᷑us e t̅ monum̄ta aperta sunt
t mlti sc̄or: pt irrēc tua̅ resinrexerūt.
O pie dn̄e rogo te p morte tua̅ amarissimā.
Q fō infundas m̄ tuā grā; beneficiā;
Vt ita ualea te diligē t talit᷑ suire
Q pt h exitu̅ Ad bdo˛ gl̅am mea̅ p̄vē˛.
Q oib9 p̄stare dignet᷑ dn̄s nr̅ ı͞he x̅.
Q c p̄re t spu sc̄o c i p̄petuū bn̅dcs. am

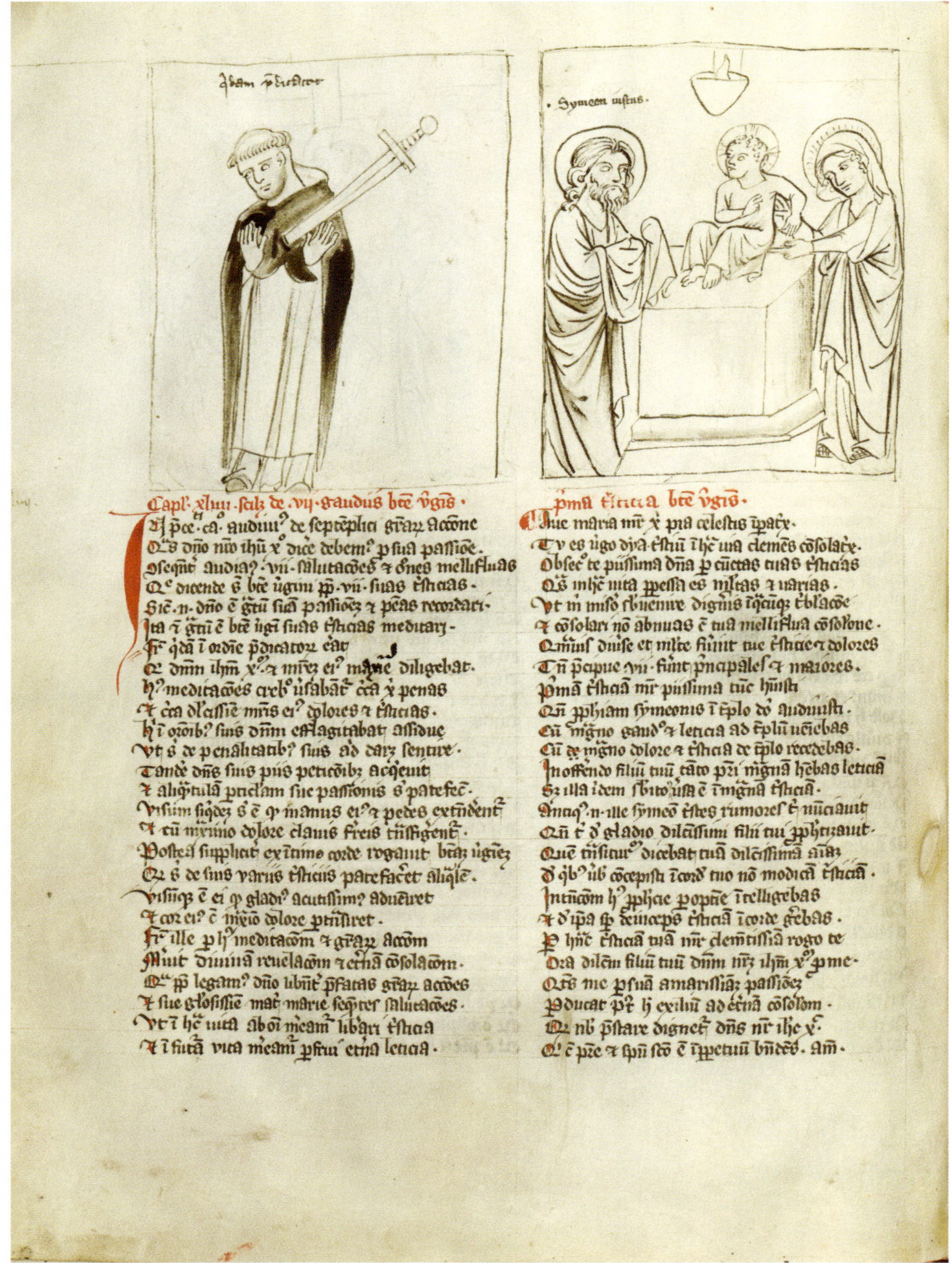

Fol. 48va-b. Image Caption (a): *quidam predicator* / Image Caption (b): Symeon iustus.

Fol. 49[ra-b]

Fol. 49[va-b]

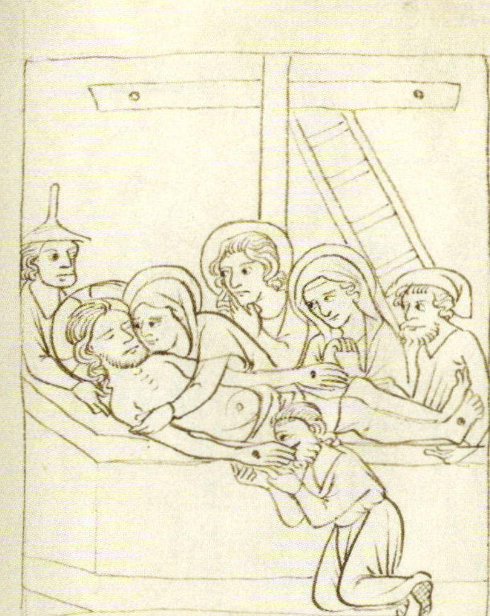

Fol. 50^{ra-b}

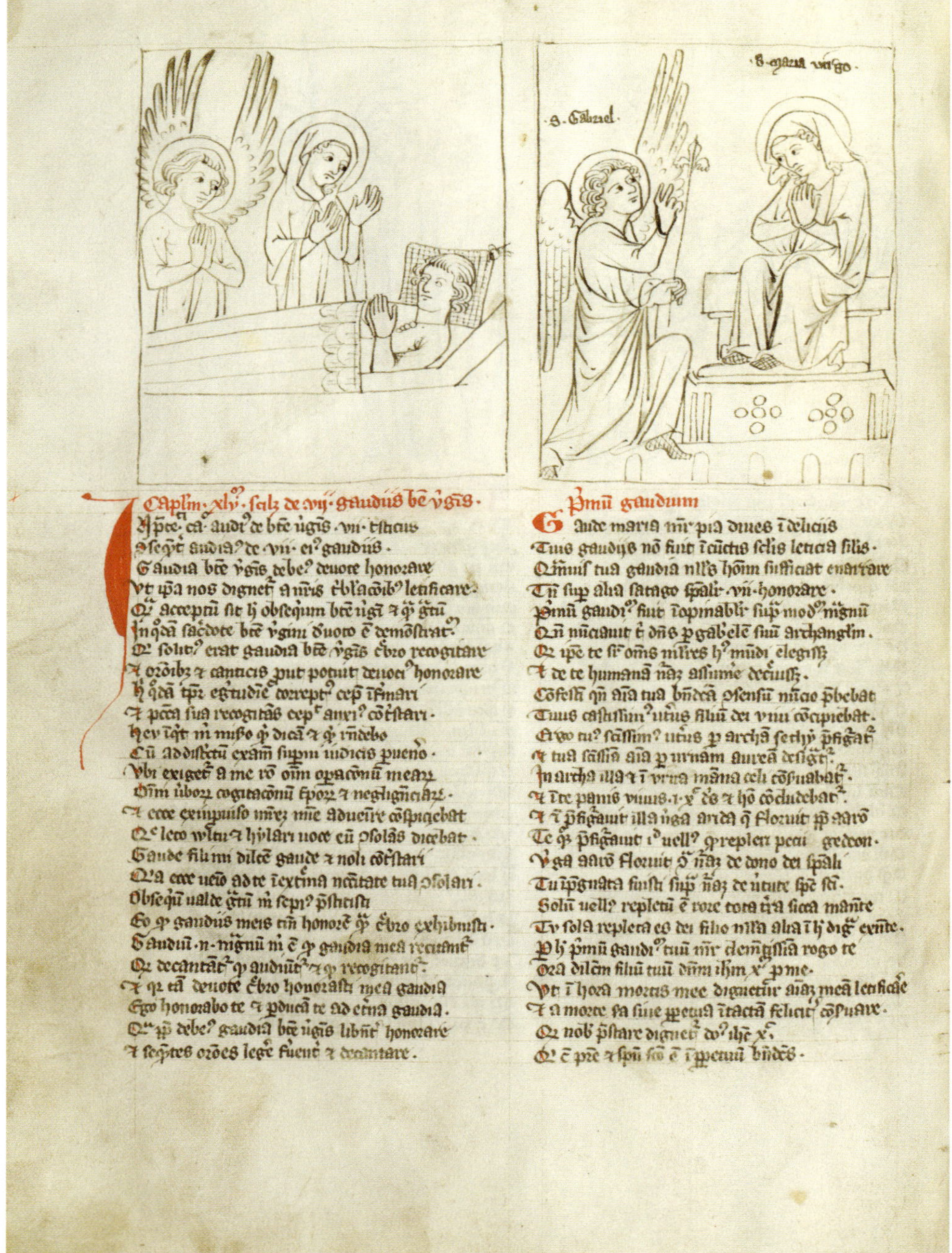

Fol. 50[va-b]. Image Caption (b): *sancta Gabriel.; sancta maria uirgo.*

Fol. 51ra-b. Image Caption (a): *.b.* / Image Caption (b): *.a.; .sancta maria virgo.; .Elysabeth.*

Fol. 51^{va-b}

Fol. 52ra-b

Sextū gaudiū·

Gaude maria uirx̄ pia aurora delectabilis
Tu pulchrima es τ amena τ tota desidabilis.
Sextū gaudiū mr dlcissima tue huisti
Cū filiū tuū q̄ amisās τ q̄sierās t tp̄lo inuēisti
Qui cū fuisses huīliū ē sbdit̄ erat
τ suū dn̄ū ē mr dlcissiā obedire nō respuebat
Tu ūgo pulima tāta castitate pollebas
Q̄r p̄ eā unicorne q̄ nēo cape pt capiebas
Tu de leone fortissimo agnū mansuetissimū fecisti
Tu aq̄lā q̄ nēo domare potuit ūgo domuisti
Tu unxisti τ ligasti fortissim̄ Sāpsone
Tu uixisti τ supasti sapientissimū Salone
Tu bellicam sollicitudis ūgo solitaria cepisti
Tu salamandrā igne tue caritatis ad ālle uisti
Tu panth̄ā artissimū ūgo nutristi mu̧gasti
Tu elephante māuinū ūgo huīliā ē sbiugasti
Tu fecisti uiuēce fenice uincl̄ τ antiquissimū
Ad te sēd ȳdiui saltū de celo altissimū
Cū de te fil̄s altissimū uoluit tc̄ nari
τ ē māq̄r pri matr sue huīlit sbiugari·
P hi sextū gaudiū mr dlcissima rogo te
Ōra dilc̄m filiū tuū dn̄m ih̄m xp̄m p me.
Vt pcedat m̄ ih̄ s ̄co ita sbiugari
Qr ab eo istud s̄clo nūq̄ mear separi
Q̄r ub oīb ̄s p̄stare dignetr dn̄s ih̄c x̄
Q̄r ē p̄re τ sp̄u sc̄o ī ī peptuū bn̄dc̄s.

Septimū gaudium·

Gaude maria pia uirx̄ regina celoȝ
Septimū tuū gaudiū excedit corda τ sp̄m hōim·
Qr tu regia potētissiā sextino huīsti·
Cū ē corpe τ āia īcelū assūpta fuīsti·
Cū fil̄s tu9 inthōno suo sed collocauit
τ corona regni sui ṗetuā felicit̄ te coronauit·
Tu q̄ oli p̄figata eras p̄ sonte illi p̄uili·
Q̄r eiuit τ emanauit τ sed ē ī flum nīxm·
Sic n· rex Assuer huīle hester exaltauit
Ita te huīliā rex celestis exaltauit τ coronauit·
Talia abigael p̄ens oli p̄nidebat
Q̄r xp̄s suū p̄denciā rex dn̄ s q̄ sp̄ōsā sumebat·
Ita rex celestis elegit te τ assūpsit te ī sp̄ōsā τ ancillā
In matrē τ sociā ī sororē τ in reginam·
Te τ mr Salomonis oubient p̄ignamt
Cum ille Salom thr̄nū ad dextrā suā collocauit·
Ita rex celoȝ te m̄rem suā honorauit
τ a dexteriū suā ī thr̄no suo te locauit·
O dn̄a feliciss̄a q̄ tēsstabile gaudī huīsti
Cū corpe τ āia ī gaudiū ṗpetuā inuēisti·
P hi tēsstabile gaudiū regīa celi rogo te
Oꝛa dilc̄m filiū tuū rege celeste p me·
Vt p̄ exiliū p̄ducat me Ad thr̄nū regni sui
Vt sine fine micar gaudio septimo fruī·
Q̄r ub oīb ̄s p̄stare dignetr dn̄s ih̄c x̄
Q̄r ē p̄re τ sp̄u sc̄o ī ī peptuū bn̄dc̄s. Am̄.

Fol. 52va-b

Feratque mundissime vestes et decentes.
Sicut eam decuit sollicitas nō habentes.
Nemo tamen impius aut detrahens causetur
De marie vestibus vel scandalizetur.
Quia hanc mundissimā virginē decebat.
Vt mundis vestibus quia non habebat.
Causam cur ciliciū vel sagulū portaret.
Vel uestem penitencie. nam quod emendaret.
Per luctum tristicie nūquam hec peccatū
Fecit innocencie sancte seruans statū.
Vestimenta virginis numquam sunt attrita
Post ascensionem filij sed manserunt ita.
Sicut ea induit in prima nouitate.
Nec scissa sūt nec aliqua cōsumpta vetustate.
Peploque mūdissimo. semper vtebatur.
Super caput desuperque tamen tegebatur.
Velo candidissimo hoc modicū dependit.
Nuda colli protegens ad scapulas descendit.
Et a fronte medio. se modicū reflexit.
Non gene aut auricule vel mentū arcebatur.
Sed cum peplo composite subtus stringebantur.
Sicque tota facies libera manebat.
Sic se nr̄a dn̄a honeste componebat.
Crines sui capitis semper dependebant.
Tecti tamen pallio vel tunica manebant.
Tulit quoque cingulū de retorta zona.
Aut cordam vt feminis mos ē. hec v̄go bona
Vtebatur calceis. sed tunc se calciauit.
Ire dum oportuit quoquam. quia cauit.
Ne nudi appareant sui pedes vlla vice.
Tenens se humiliter nimis et pudice
Lectus quoque virginis non habuit ornatū.
Vilem. sed mūdissimū erat suū stratum.
De sago super stramina pannū habebat
Et ceruical modicū in quo quiescebat.
Ad lectū locus fuerat orare quo solebat.
Aut contemplabatur suauiter scripturas vel legebat.
Ad partem vero alteram fuerat locata.
Sedes in qua residebat ad opus hec beata.
Numquam vacans ocio. intente laborauit.
Orans mente et spiritu. psalmos ruminauit.
Aut psallebat dn̄o. aut contemplabatur.
Aut in mentis iubilo deo fruebatur.
Sic per dies singulos maria faciebat.
Quibus in hoc seculo viuens permanebat.
Oracio ad beatam v̄ginē mariam.
O regina virginū fac teū gratulari.
Quos hic in exilio vides tribulari.
Iube tuū filium. roga tuum patrem.
Pro nobis peccatoribus te ostendens matrem.
Vt nos velis protegere. daque iuuamē.
Gaudentesque perducas ad celi regna Amen.

Fol. 53ra-b

Fol. 53^{va-b}

Index of Biblical Names and Figures

Index of Biblical Passages